PHILIP'S

ROAD ATLAS

COMPACT BRITAIN

CONTENTS

II **Route planning maps** with key to map pages

VIII **Key to road map symbols**

2 **Road maps of Great Britain**

289 **Index** to road maps of Great Britain

www.philips-maps.co.uk

First published in 2006 by Philip's
a division of Octopus Publishing Group Ltd
Carmelite House, 50 Victoria Embankment
London EC4Y 0DZ
An Hachette UK Company
www.hachette.co.uk

Ninth edition 2022
First impression 2022

ISBN 978-1-84907-578-7

Cartography by Philip's
Copyright © 2022 Philip's

While every reasonable effort has been made to ensure that the information compiled in this atlas is accurate, complete and up-to-date at the time of publication, some of this information is subject to change and the Publisher cannot guarantee its correctness or completeness.

The information in this atlas is provided without any representation or warranty, express or implied and the Publisher cannot be held liable for any loss or damage due to any use or reliance on the information in this atlas, nor for any errors, omissions or subsequent changes in such information.

The representation in this atlas of any road, drive or track is no evidence of the existence of a right of way.

Information for National Parks, Areas of Outstanding Natural Beauty, National Trails and Country Parks in Wales supplied by the Countryside Council for Wales.

Information for National Parks, Areas of Outstanding Natural Beauty, National Trails and Country Parks in England supplied by Natural England.

Data for Regional Parks, Long Distance Footpaths and Country Parks in Scotland provided by Scottish Natural Heritage.

Gaelic name forms used in the Western Isles provided by Comhairle nan Eilean.

Data for the National Nature Reserves in England provided by Natural England.

Data for the National Nature Reserves in Wales provided by Countryside Council for Wales. Darparwyd data'n ymwneud â Gwarchodfeydd Natur Cenedlaethol Cymru gan Gyngor Cefn Gwlad Cymru.

Information on the location of National Nature Reserves in Scotland was provided by Scottish Natural Heritage.

Data for National Scenic Areas in Scotland provided by the Scottish Executive Office. Crown copyright material is reproduced with the permission of the Controller of HMSO and the Queen's Printer for Scotland. Licence number C02W0003960.

Printed in China

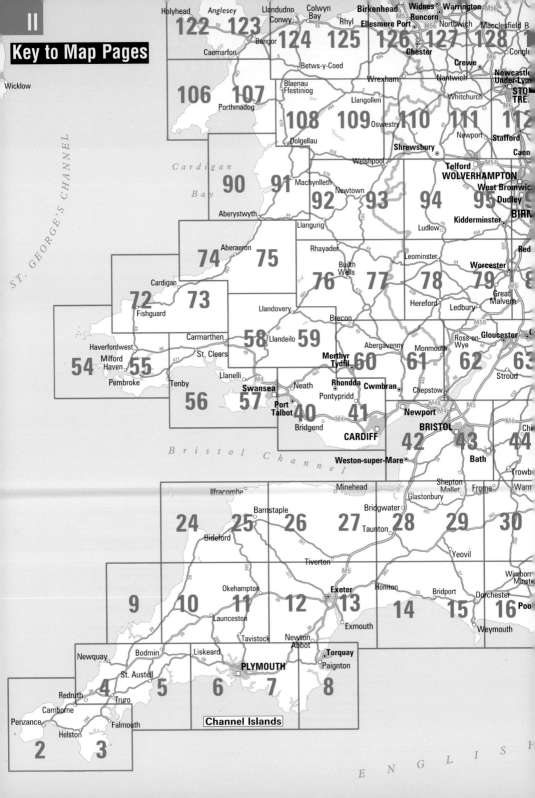

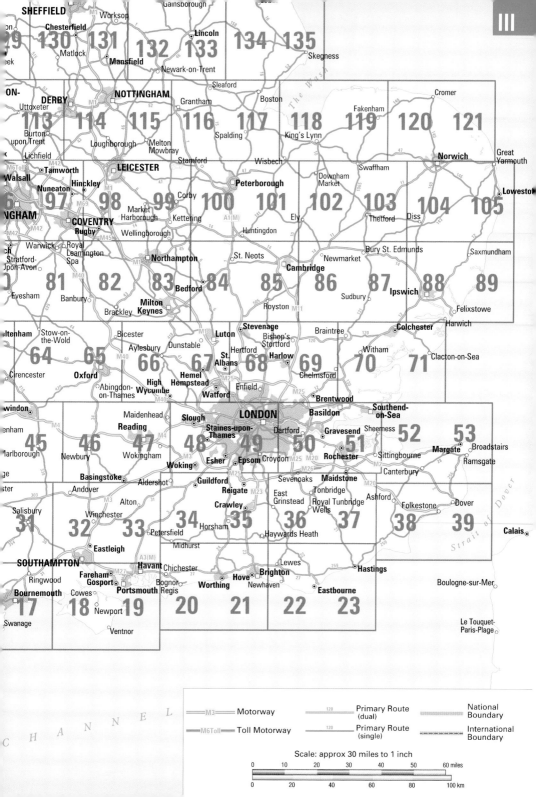

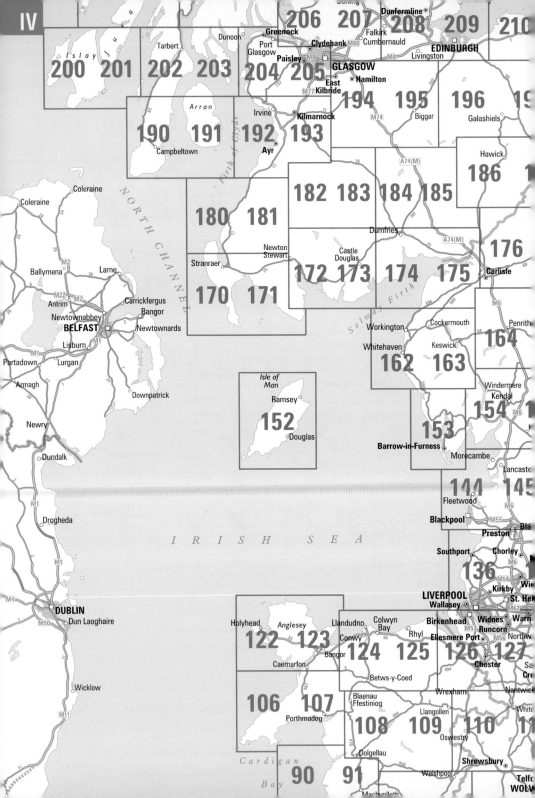

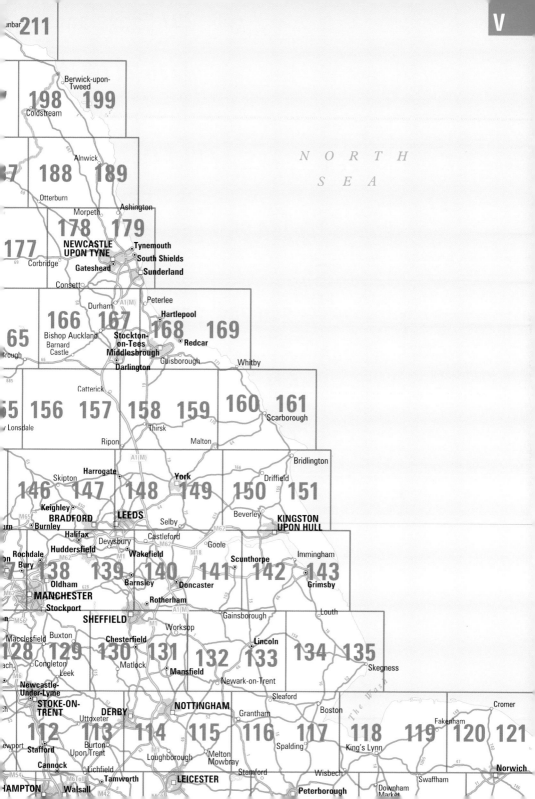

nbar **211**

Berwick-upon-Tweed
198 **199**
Coldstream

7 **188** **189**
Alnwick
Otterburn

177 **178** **179**
Morpeth
Ashington
NEWCASTLE UPON TYNE **Tynemouth**
Corbridge **South Shields**
Gateshead **Sunderland**
Consett

Peterlee
Durham A1(M)
166 **167** Hartlepool **168** **169**
Bishop Auckland **Stockton-on-Tees** Redcar
65 Barnard **Middlesbrough**
rough Castle **Darlington** Guisborough Whitby

Catterick
55 **156** **157** **158** **159** **160** **161**
Scarborough
Lonsdale Thirsk
Ripon Malton

Bridlington
A1(M)
Harrogate Driffield
146 **147** **148** York **149** **150** **151**
Skipton
Keighley **KINGSTON**
BRADFORD **LEEDS** Selby Beverley **UPON HULL**
rn Burnley Halifax Dewsbury Castleford
Rochdale Huddersfield **Wakefield** Goole
n Bury M62 M18 Scunthorpe Immingham
7 **38** **139** **140** **141** **142** **143**
Oldham **Barnsley** **Doncaster** **Grimsby**
MANCHESTER Rotherham
Stockport **SHEFFIELD** Gainsborough Louth

Worksop
128 **129** **130** **131** **132** **133** **134** **135**
Macclesfield Buxton **Chesterfield** **Lincoln**
ch Congleton Matlock Skegness
Leek **Mansfield**
Newcastle- Newark-on-Trent
Under-Lyme Sleaford
STOKE-ON- **NOTTINGHAM** Boston Cromer
TRENT **DERBY** Grantham Fakenham
Uttoxeter
112 **113** **114** **115** **116** **117** **118** **119** **120** **121**
ewport Burton Spalding King's Lynn
Stafford Upon Trent Loughborough Melton
Mowbray
Cannock Lichfield Stamford Wisbech **Norwich**
Tamworth **LEICESTER** Swaffham
AMPTON **Walsall** M42 **Peterborough** Downham
Market

NORTH SEA

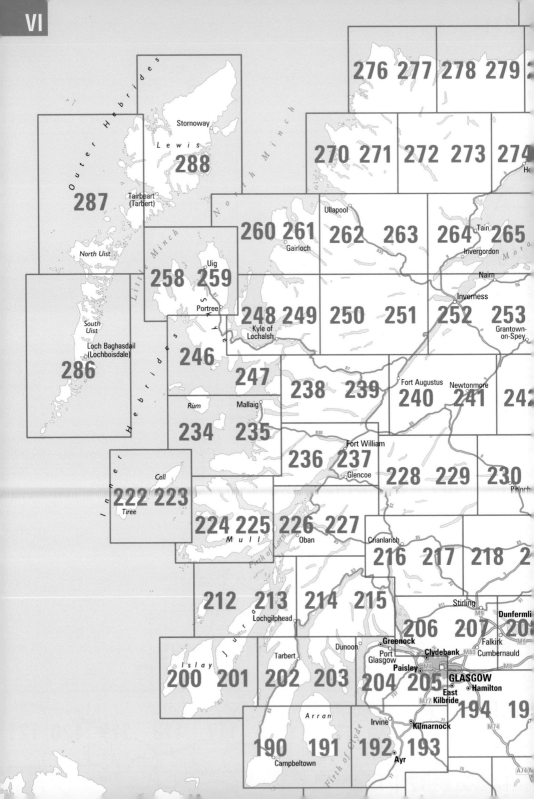

Shetland

284

Mainland

Lerwick

285

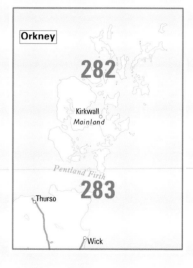

Orkney

282

Kirkwall
Mainland

Pentland Firth

283

Thurso

Wick

N O R T H

S E A

Road map symbols

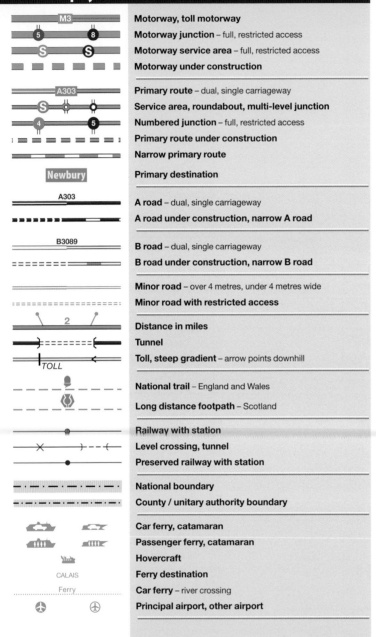

	Motorway, toll motorway
	Motorway junction – full, restricted access
	Motorway service area – full, restricted access
	Motorway under construction
	Primary route – dual, single carriageway
	Service area, roundabout, multi-level junction
	Numbered junction – full, restricted access
	Primary route under construction
	Narrow primary route
	Primary destination
	A road – dual, single carriageway
	A road under construction, narrow A road
	B road – dual, single carriageway
	B road under construction, narrow B road
	Minor road – over 4 metres, under 4 metres wide
	Minor road with restricted access
	Distance in miles
	Tunnel
	Toll, steep gradient – arrow points downhill
	National trail – England and Wales
	Long distance footpath – Scotland
	Railway with station
	Level crossing, tunnel
	Preserved railway with station
	National boundary
	County / unitary authority boundary
	Car ferry, catamaran
	Passenger ferry, catamaran
	Hovercraft
	Ferry destination
	Car ferry – river crossing
	Principal airport, other airport

Road map symbols

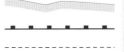

MENDIP HILLS

National park or
Area of Outstanding Natural Beauty (England and Wales)
or **National Scenic Area** (Scotland)
or **forest park / regional park / national forest**

Beach

Linear antiquity

Roman road

Hillfort, battlefield – with date

Viewpoint, nature reserve, spot height – in metres

Golf course, youth hostel, sporting venue

Camp site, caravan site, camping and caravan site

Shopping village, park and ride

Adjoining page number – road maps

Road map scales

1:212 750 • 1cm = 2.13 km • 1 inch = 3·36 miles

0 1 2 3 4 5 6 7 8 9 10 11km

0 1 2 3 4 5 6 7 miles

Outer Hebrides, Orkney and Shetland

1:425 700 • 1 cm = 4.25 km • 1 inch = 6.72 miles

0 2 4 6 8 10 12 14 16 18 20 22 km

0 1 2 3 4 5 6 7 8 9 10 11 12 13 14 miles

Tourist information

✝ **Abbey, cathedral or priory**

🏛 **Ancient monument**

🐟 **Aquarium**

🖼 **Art gallery**

🦅 **Bird collection or aviary**

🏰 **Castle**

⛪ **Church**

Country park
🎎 England and Wales
🎎 Scotland

🐕 **Farm park**

❀ **Garden**

⚓ **Historic ship**

🏠 **House**

🏡 **House and garden**

▦ **Motor racing circuit**

🏛 **Museum**

🅿 **Picnic area**

🚂 **Preserved railway**

🏇 **Race course**

🏛 **Roman antiquity**

🦁 **Safari park**

🎡 **Theme park**

ℹ **Tourist information**

🐘 **Zoo**

✦ **Other place of interest**

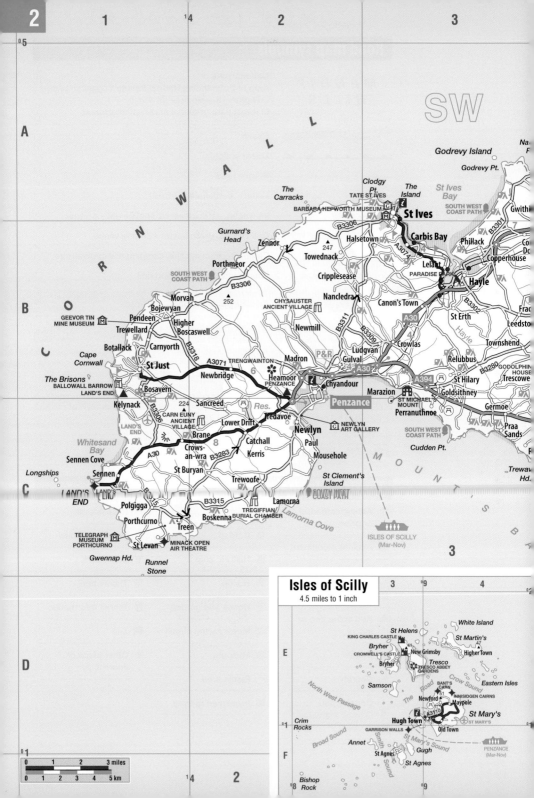

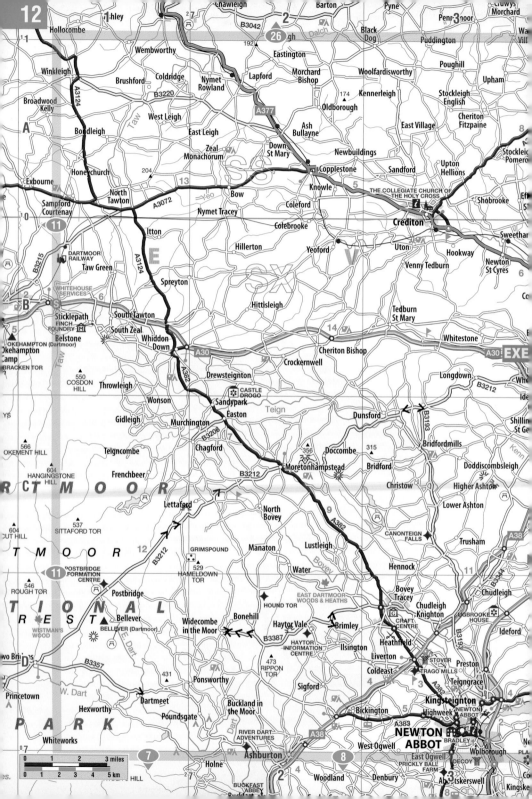

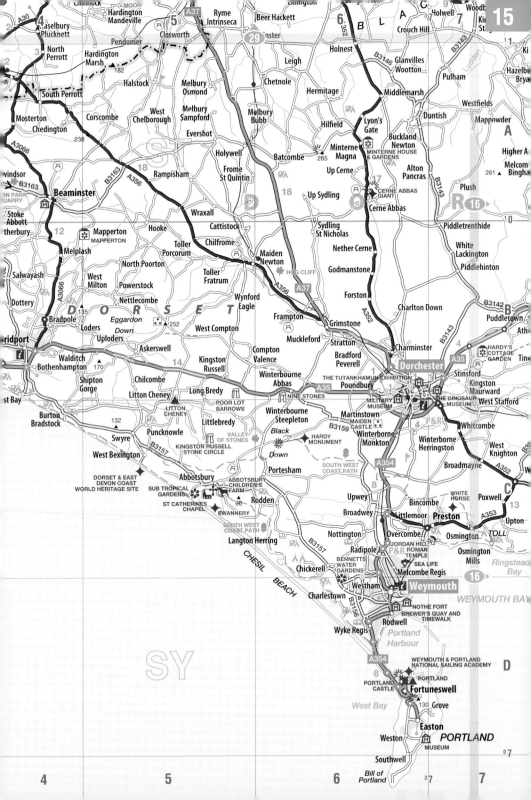

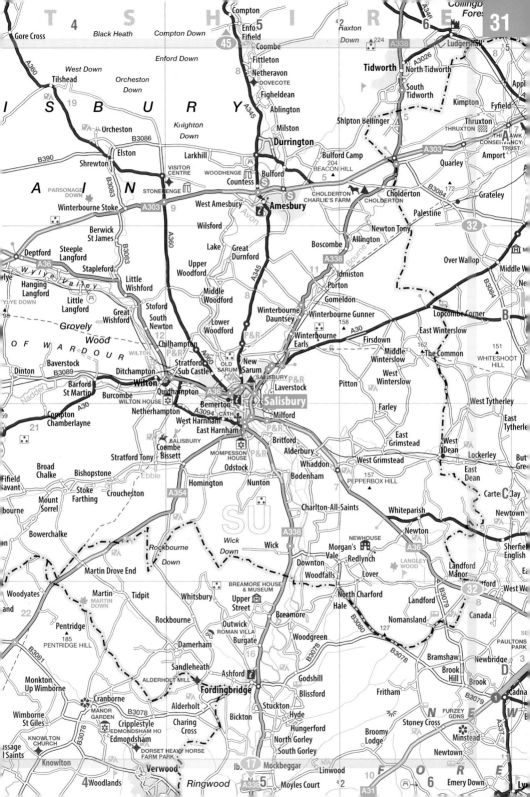

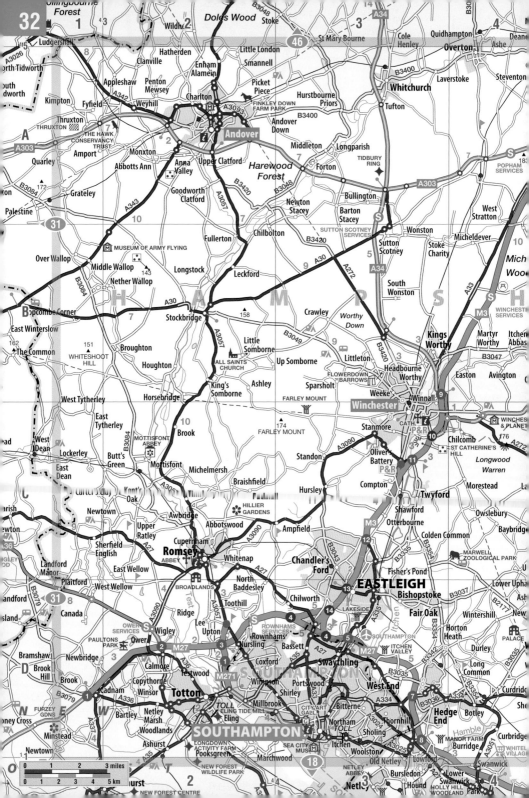

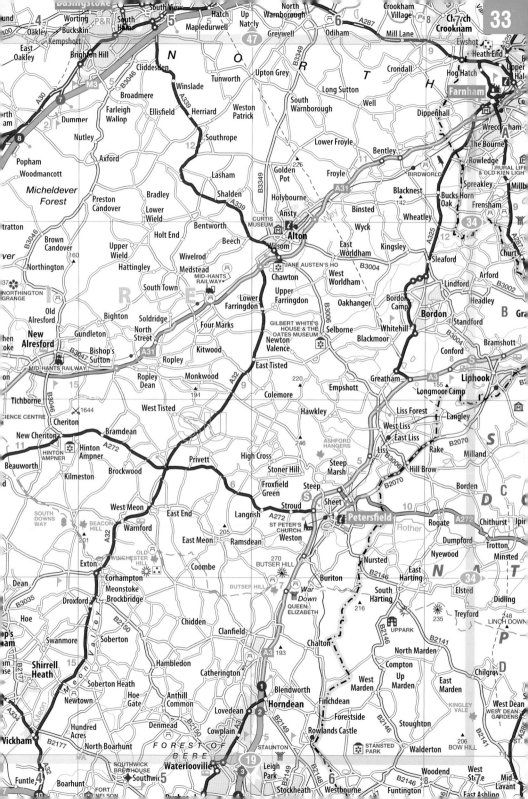

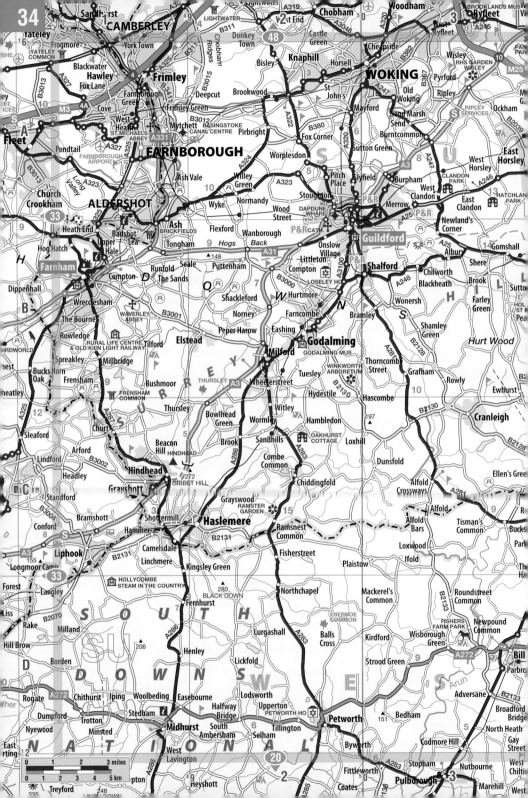

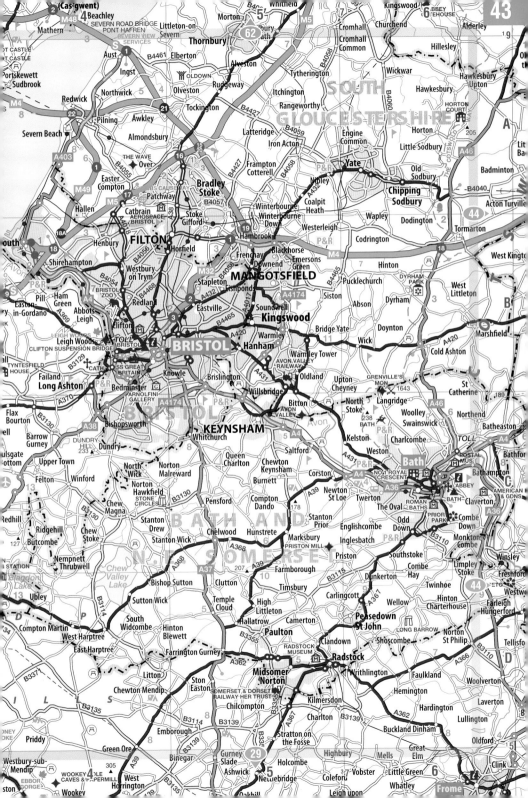

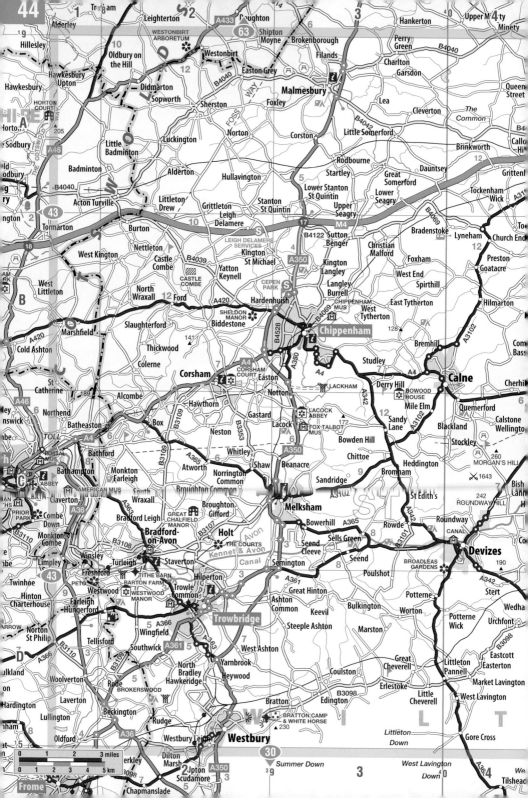

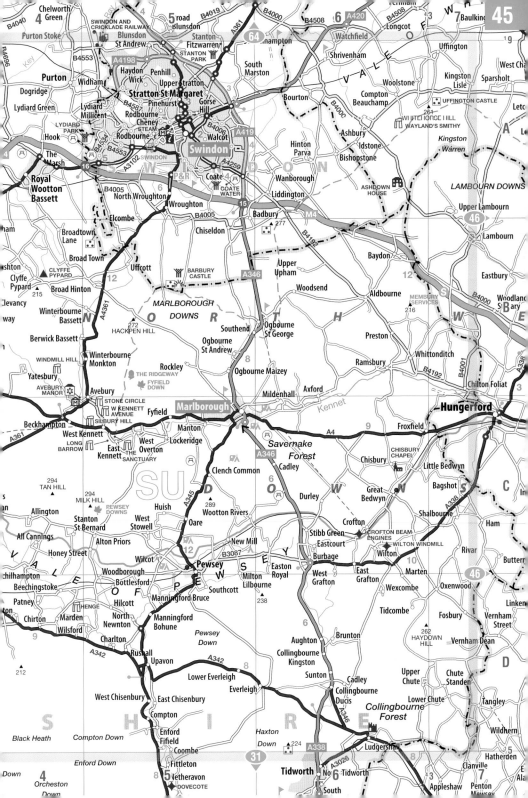

1 ¹6 2 3 4

A

²3

**ST. DAVID'S
HEAD
PENMAEN DEWI**

Ynysduellyn

Penclegyr · Porthgain · Tr

Abereiddy
Croes-goch · Llanrhian

181 · Treleddyd-fawr · Tretio
ST DAVID'S · Carnhedryn · Treffynn
Rhodiad · Treglemais

*Whitesand Bay
Porth-mawr*

B4583
BISHOP'S PALACE

Caerfarchell

Rhosson

Ramsey Sound

CATHEDRAL

Whitchurch · Middle Mill

**St David's
(Tyddewi)**

B

**Ramsey
Island
Ynys Dewi**

RAMSEY
ISLAND

Nine
Wells

Solva

ST. BRIDES

BAY

PEMBROKE
COAST
LLWYBR ARF
P

BAE SAIN FFRAID

BRO

Bro

Little

Talbenny

C

SM

Tower Point
Trwyn Tŵr

**NATIONAL
NATURE RESERVE**

79

*Wooltack Point
Trwyn Wooltack*

St Bi

GRASSHOLM
ISLAND

**Skomer
Island
Ynys Skomer**

SKOMER
ISLAND

Marloes

B4327

Hasg

MARLOES
SANDS

Sa
Ha

Broad Sound

St
Ishmael's

**Gateholm
Island
Ynys Gateholm**

Dale

MILFOR
ABERDAU

D

**Skokholm
Island
Ynys Skokholm**

71

P

St Ann's Hd.
Pentir St. Ann

ROSSLARE

Sheep
Island
Ynys y Defaid

E

²0

M
B
R
O
K
E
S
H
I
R
E
P

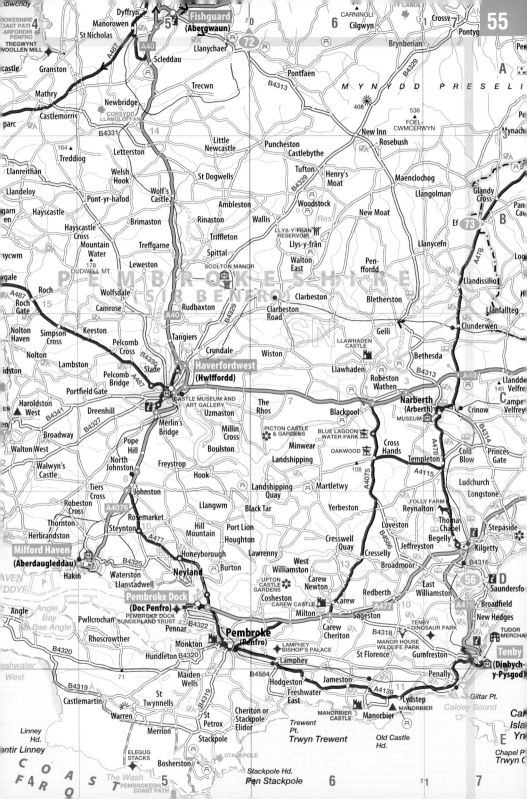

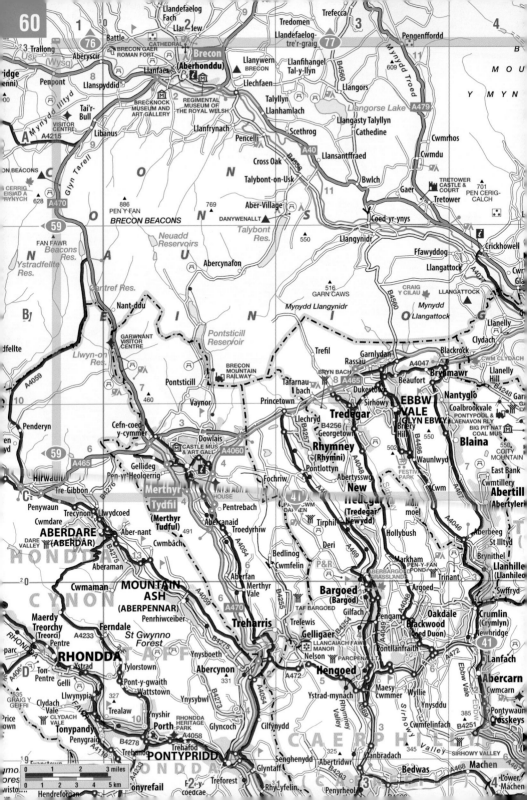

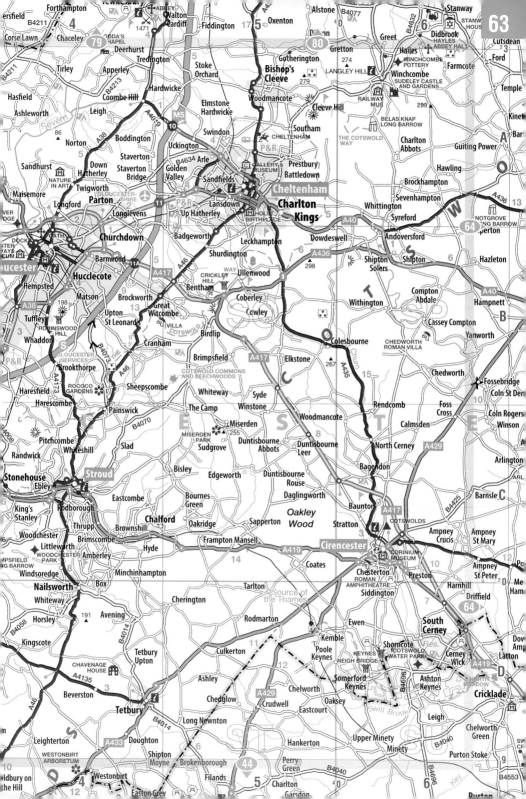

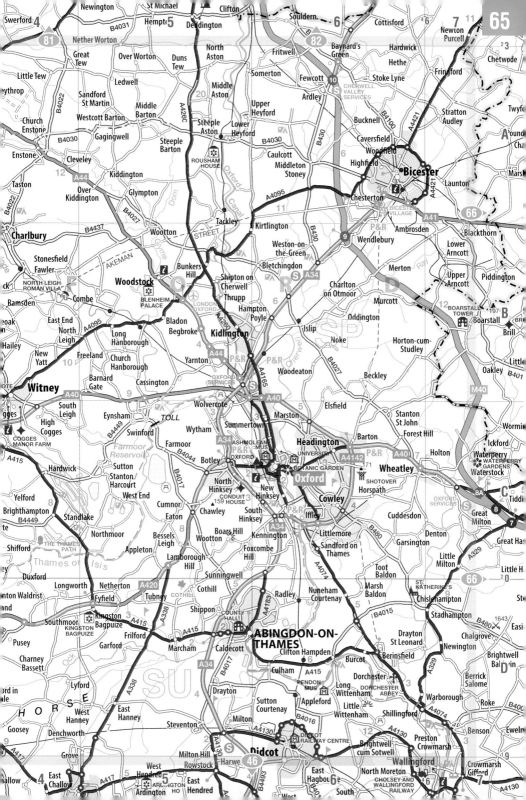

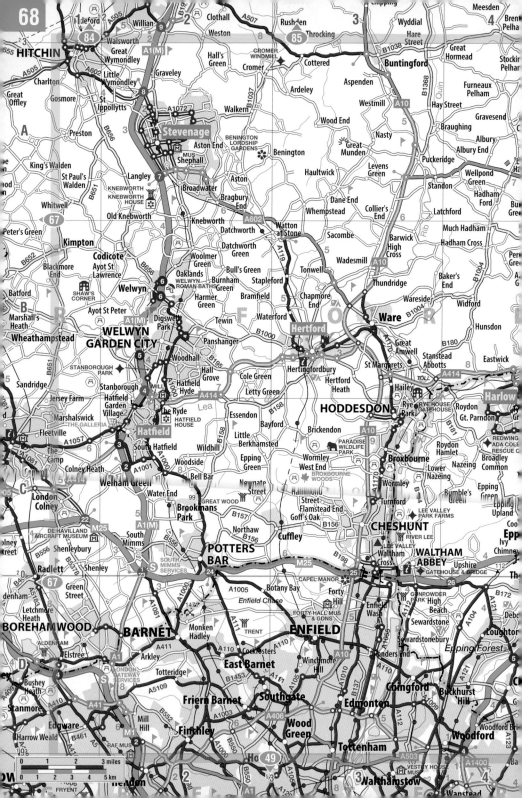

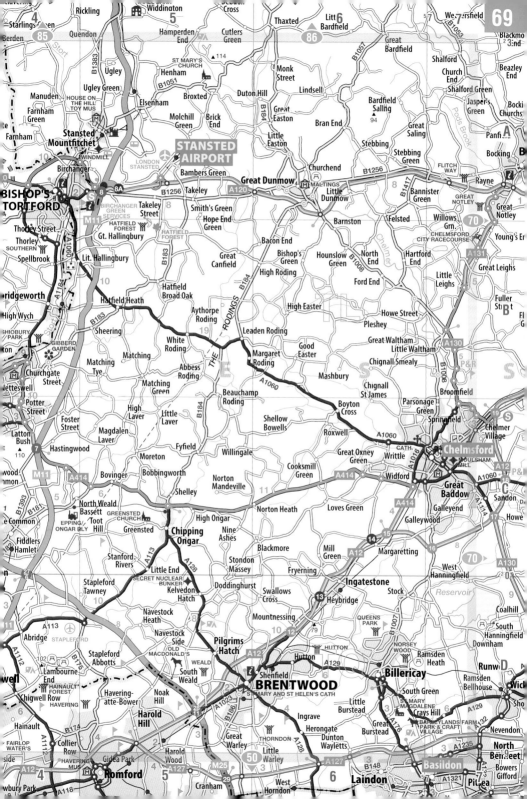

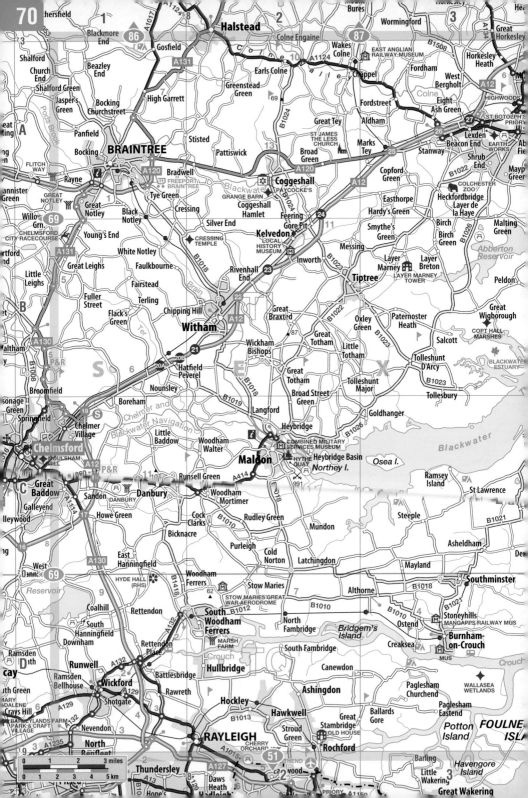

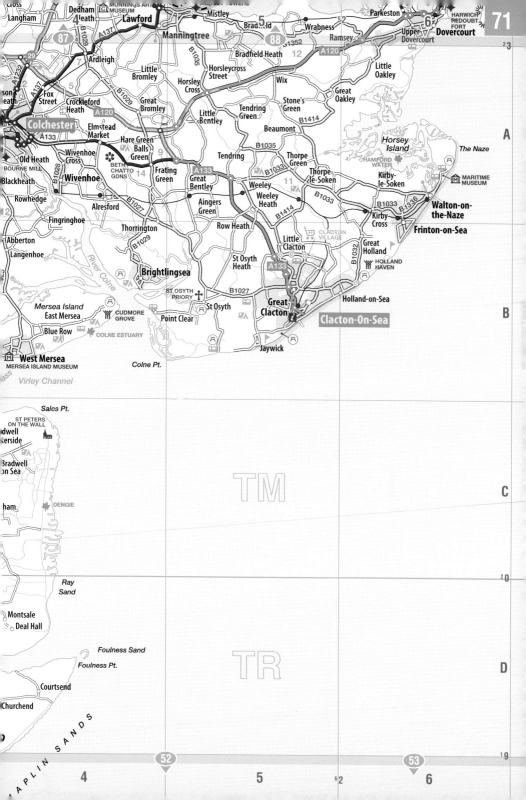

SM

Cardig

Cemaes Head
Pen Cemaes   Abe

POPPIT SAN
Cippyn

PEMBROKESHIRE COAST
ARFORDIR PENFRO

St D

PEMBROKESHIRE
COAST PATH
LLWYBR ARFORDIR PENFRO

Moylgrove

Monington

ROSSLARE

Strumble Head
Pen Caer

Newport
Bay

Glanrhyd

197

Pontgareg

COAST

Tresinwen

Dinas Head

Bae
Trefdraeth

Berry
Hill

Nevern   B4582

Felindre
Farchog

PENG
FORES

Fishguard
Bay

Brynhenllan

NEWPORT
PEMBROKESHIRE

19

FRO

PWLL
DERI

Llanwnda

213

Goodwick
(Wdig)

Bae
Abergwaun

Parrog

A487

CASTELL
HENLLYS
FORT

Newport
(Trefdraeth)

Crosswell

DYF
HOR

Penbwchdy

Trefasser

191

Lower
Town

Dyffryn

Dinas
Cross

Afon Ne

PEMBROKESHIRE
COAST PATH
LLWYBR ARFORDIR
PENFRO

Fishguard
(Abergwaun)

347

CARNINGLI

TY CANOL

Manorowen

St Nicholas

Cilgwyn

Crosswell

TREGWYNT
WOOLLEN MILL

Llanychaer

55

Brynberian

Pontyglasier

Abercastle

Granston

Scleddau

A40

Pontfaen

MYNYDD   PRESE

Trecwn

B4313

468

536

B4329

Penparc

16

Mathry

Newbridge

CORSYDD
LLANGLOFFAN

FOEL-
CWMCERWYN

55

B4331

14

164

New Inn

Rosebush

Treddiog

Llanreithan

Little
Newcastle

Puncheston
Castlebythe

Llandeloy

Welsh
Hook

St Dogwells

Tufton

Maenclochog

Llangolman

Glandy
Cross

Wolf's
Castle

Henry's
Moat

B4329

Trefgarn
Owen

Hayscastle

Pont-yr-hafod

Ambleston

Woodstock

New Moat

Llanycefn

Efailwen

Brimaston

Rinaston

Wallis

A478

Penycwm

Hayscastle
Cross

Treffgarne

Triffleton

178

Mountain
Water

DUDWELL MT.

Spittal

LLYS-Y-FRAN
RESERVOIR

Llys-y-frân

Walton
East

Pen-
ffordd

Llandissilio

Llanll

Newgale

Roch

A487

Leweston

SCOLTON MANOR

Res

Efin

Roch
Gate

15

Wolfsdale

Camrose

PEMBROKESHIRE
(SIR BENFRO)

Clarbeston

Bletherston

Clun

Pelcomb
Cross

2

Tangiers

Rudbaxton

A40

Clarbeston
Road

B4329

Gelli

Clunderwen

Llant

Nolton

Crundale

Wiston

3

AWHADEN
CASTLE

4

Rathe

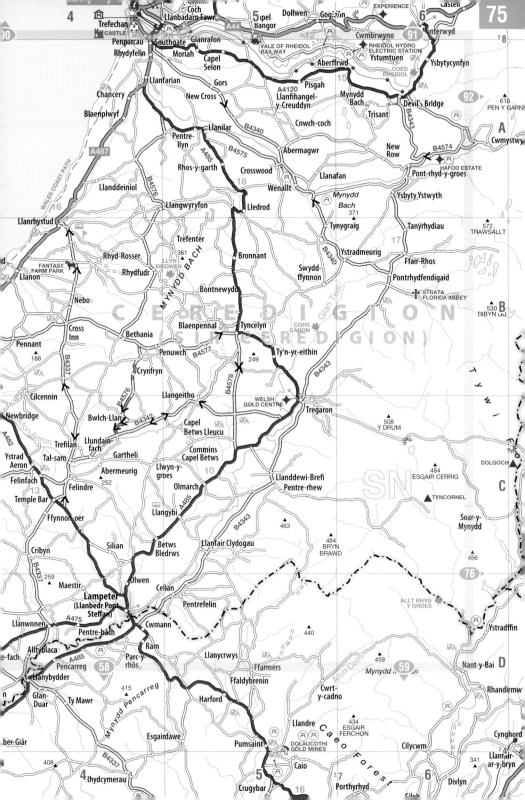

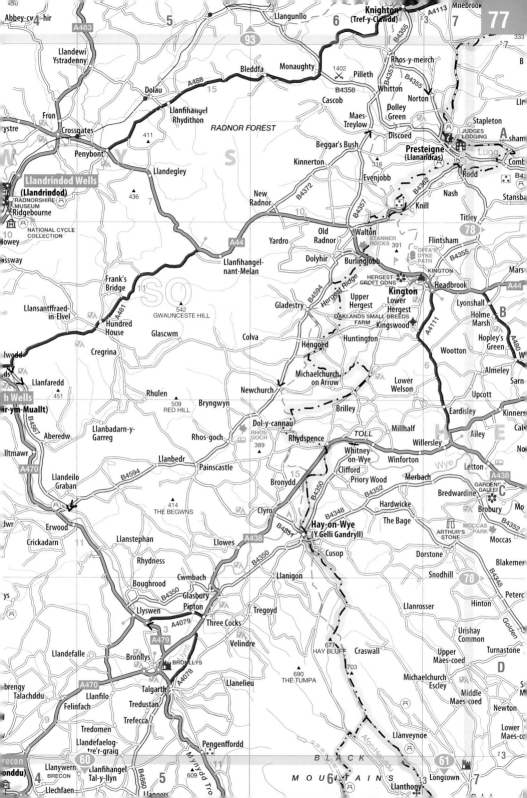

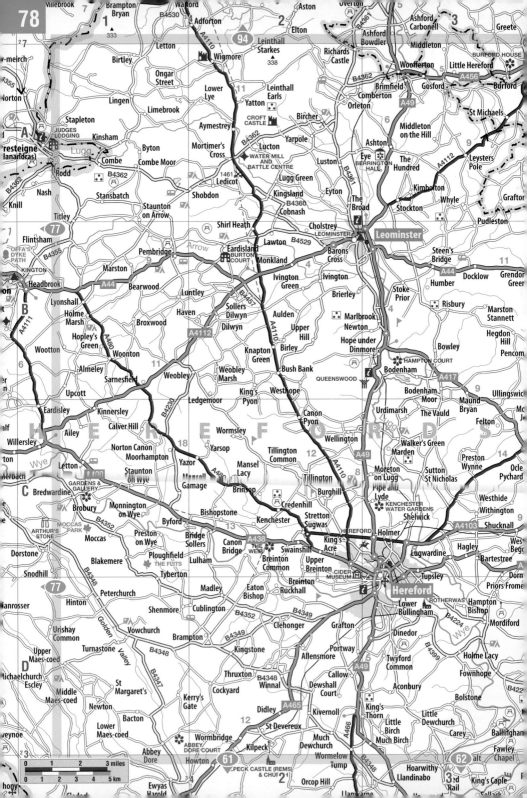

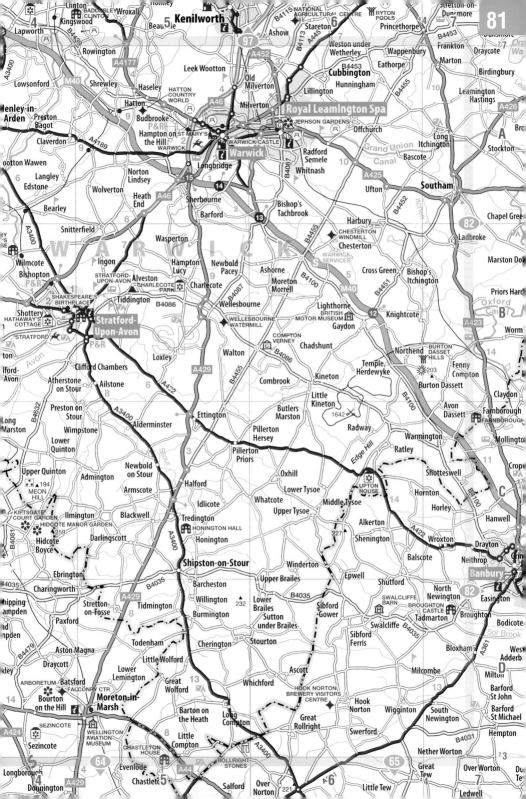

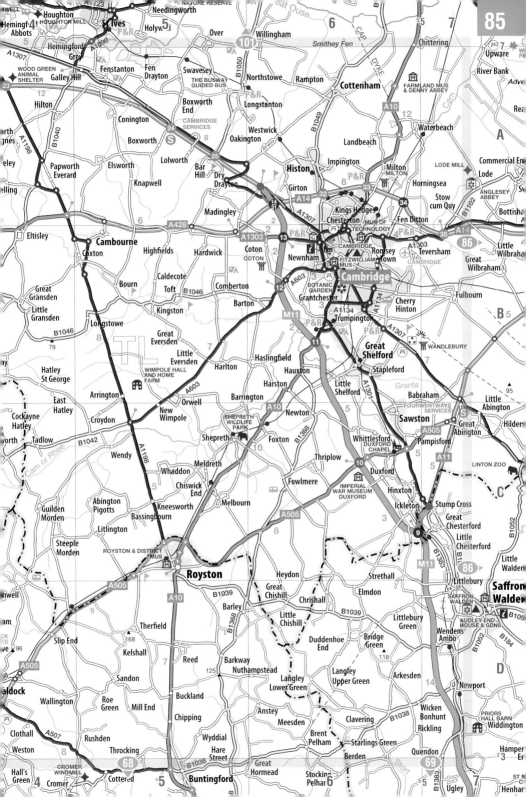

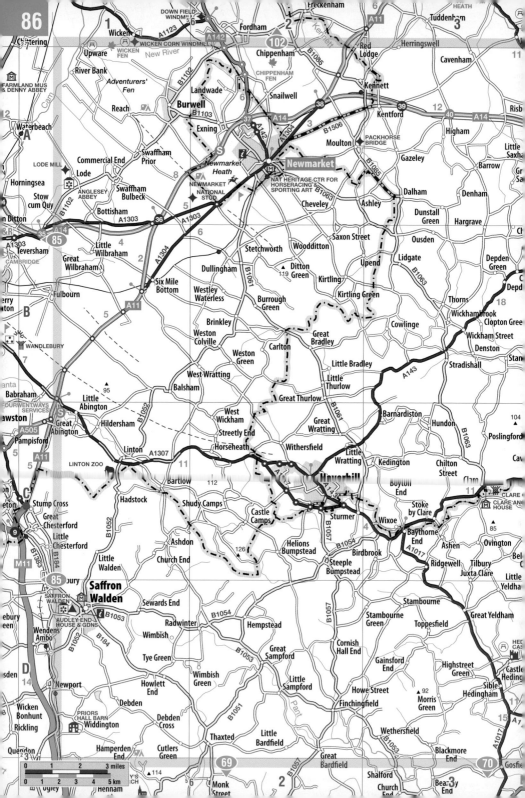

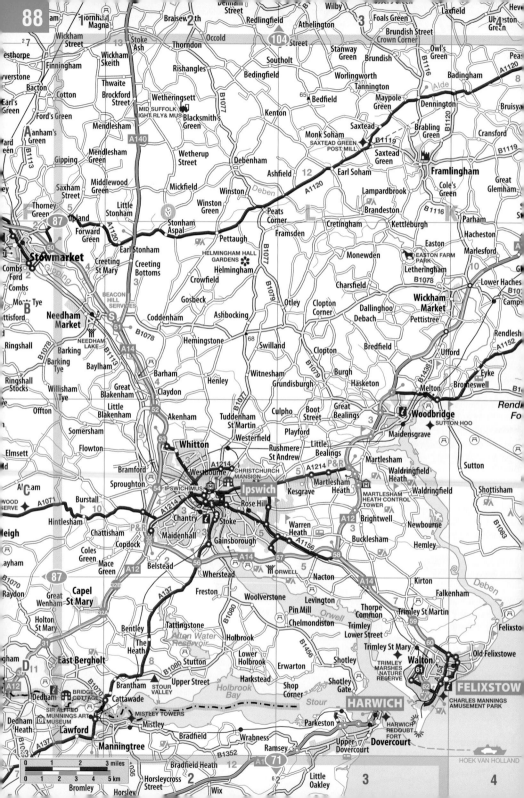

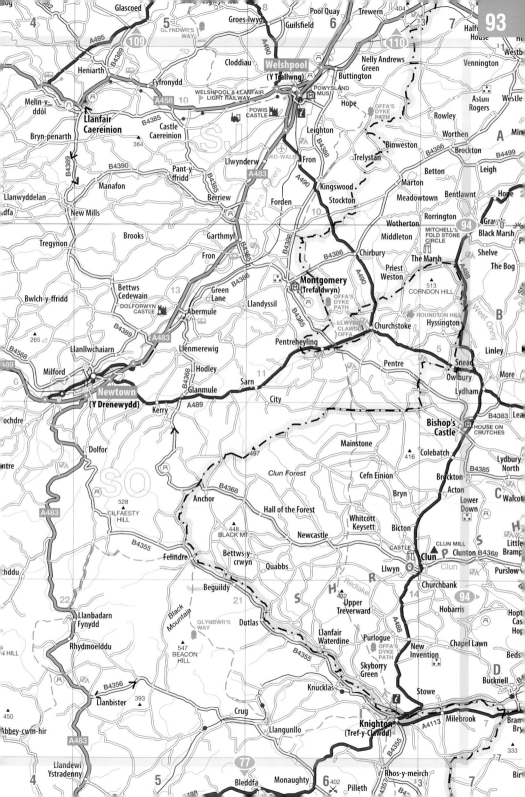

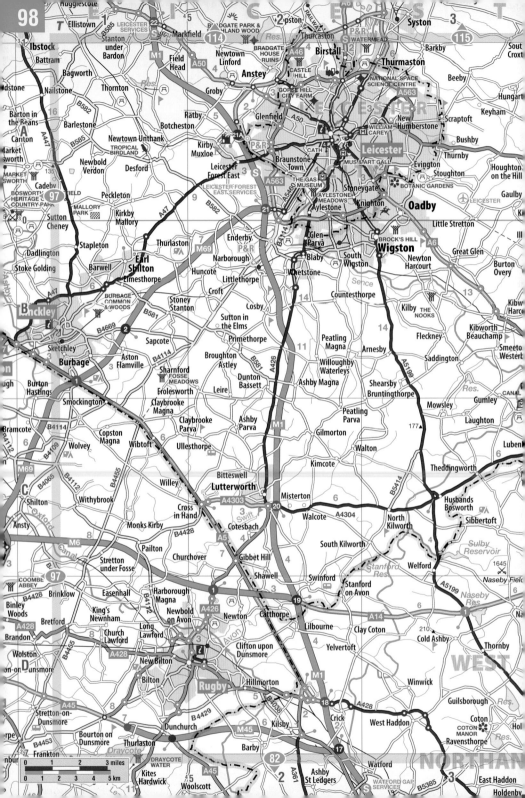

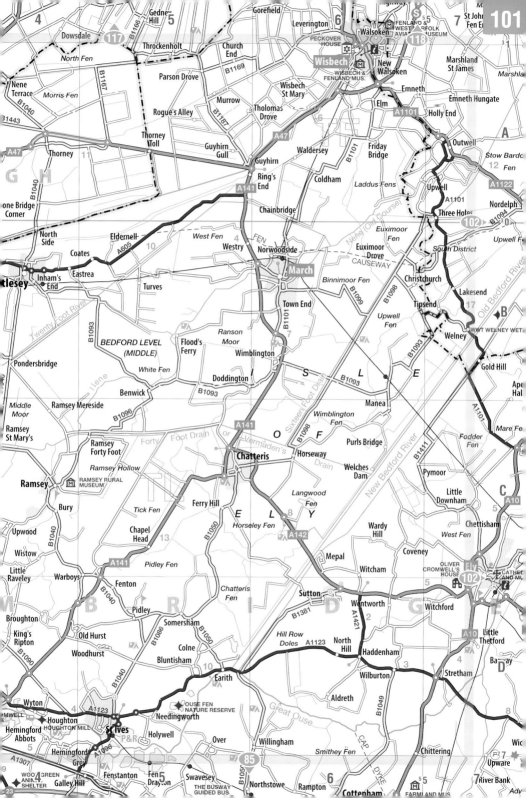

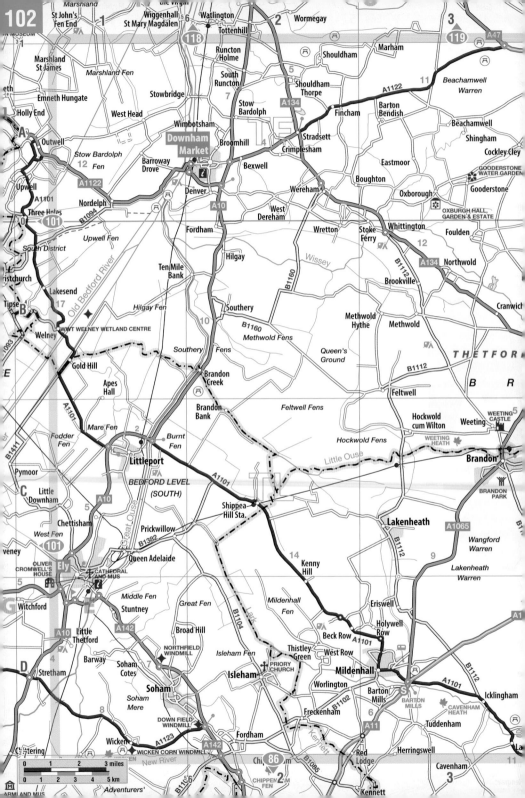

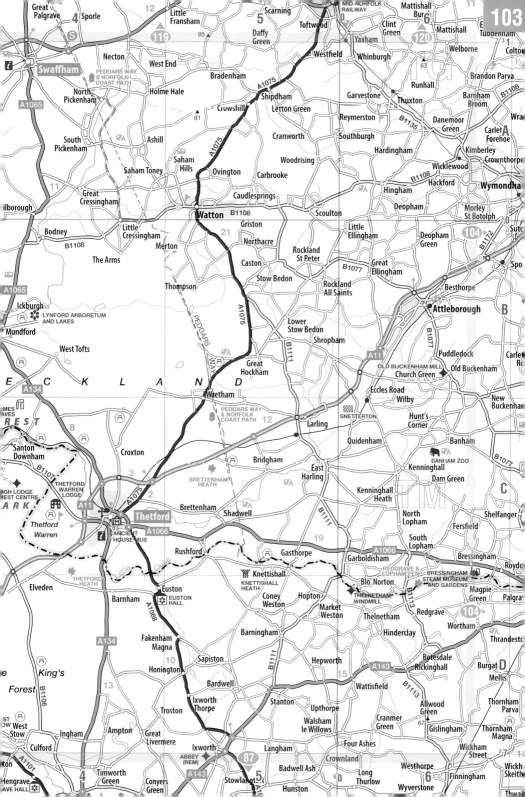

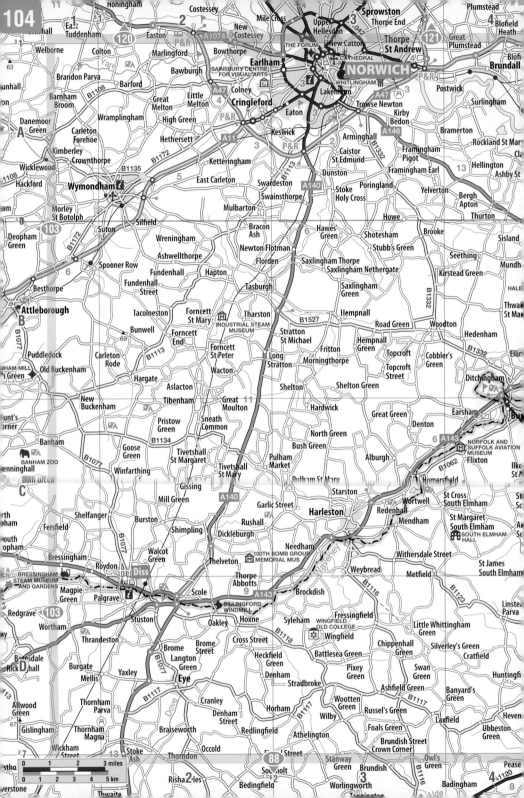

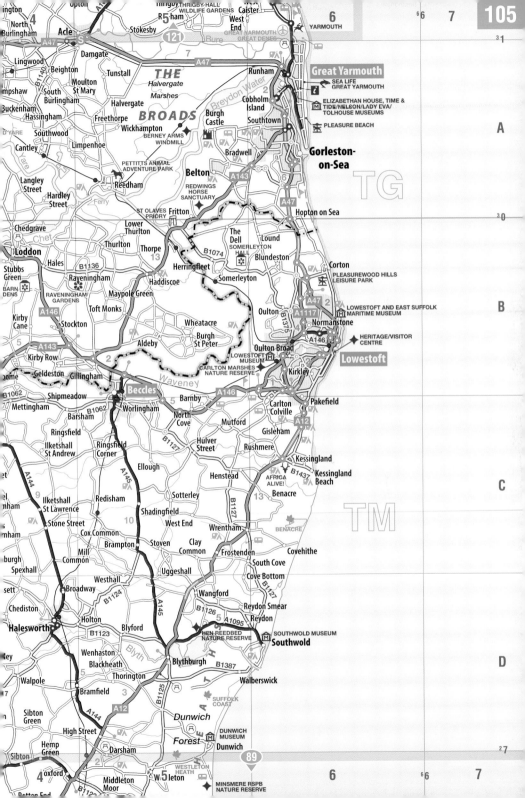

1 2 2 2 122 3 36

A

CAERNARFO

BAY

BAE

CAERNARFON

B

SH

LLEYN

Ynys Llanddwyn

Gyrn-

Bryn-yr-eryr

Trefor

564
YR EIFL

Lla

B4417 6

Llithfaen

Llwyndyrys

Carreg Ddu

Porth
Dinllaen

WALES COAST PATH

Pistyll

B4354

Morfa Nefyn

Nefyn

Fron

Rhos-fawr

A499

Edern

LLEYN MARITIME
MUSEUM

Tan-y-
graig

A497

Porth Ysgadan

L

Glanrhyd

B4417

Boduan

Llannor

Rhos-y-llan

CORS
GEIRCH

7

Efailnewydd

Tudweiliog

Dinas

Rhyd-y-
clafdy

Denio

Pwllhe

C

Porth Golmon

14

Garnfadryn

Penrhos

South Beach

Ca

Bryn-mawr

Llaniestyn

B4415

Pen-y-graig

PENRHYN

Rhedyn

7

Penrhyn Mawr

Llangwnnadl

Sarn
Meyllteyrn

B4413

Llanbedrog

Pen-y-
groeslon

Botwnnog

Nanhoron

Ty-hen

Bryncroes

Mynytho

Trwyn Llanbedrog

Methlem

Llandegwning

Rhydlios

St Tudwal's
Road

Angorfa St Tudwal

Capel Carmel

Rhoshirwaun

304
MYNYDD
RHIW

PLAS-YN-
RHIW

Llawdref
Bellaf

Llangian

A499

Abersoch

191

Rhiw.

B4413

Porth Neigwl or
Hell's Mouth

Llanengan

St Tudwal's Island East
Ynys St Tudwal Dwyrair

Uwchmynydd

Aberdaron

Llanfaelrhys

Sarn Bach

Bwlchtocyn

Marchroes

St Tudwal's Island West
Ynys St Tudwal Gorllewin

Bodermid

D

Bardsey Sound
Swnt Enlli

Pen-y-cil

Cilan Uchaf

Trwyn Cilan

N

YNYS ENLLI

167

Bardsey
Island
Ynys Enlli

32

L L E Y N

0 1 2 3 miles
0 1 2 3 4 5 km

2 2 3

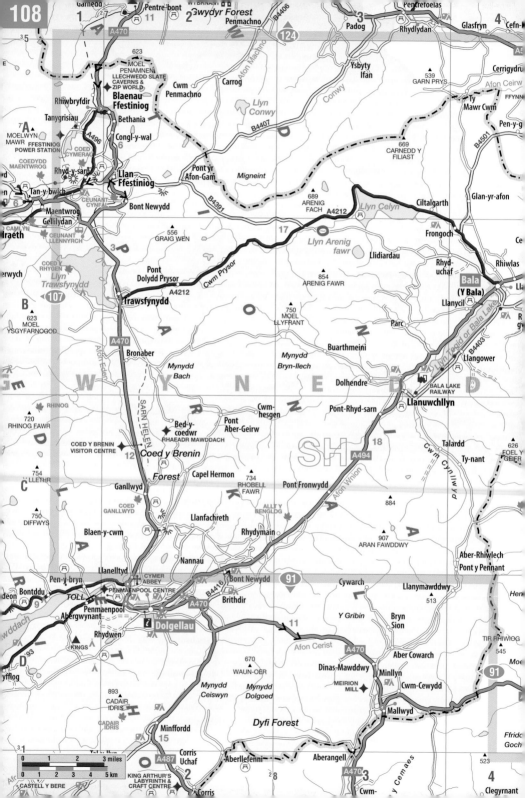

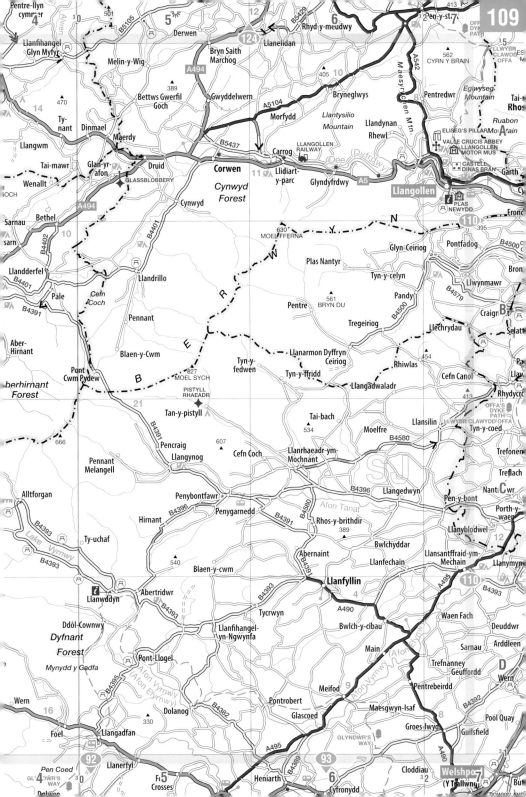

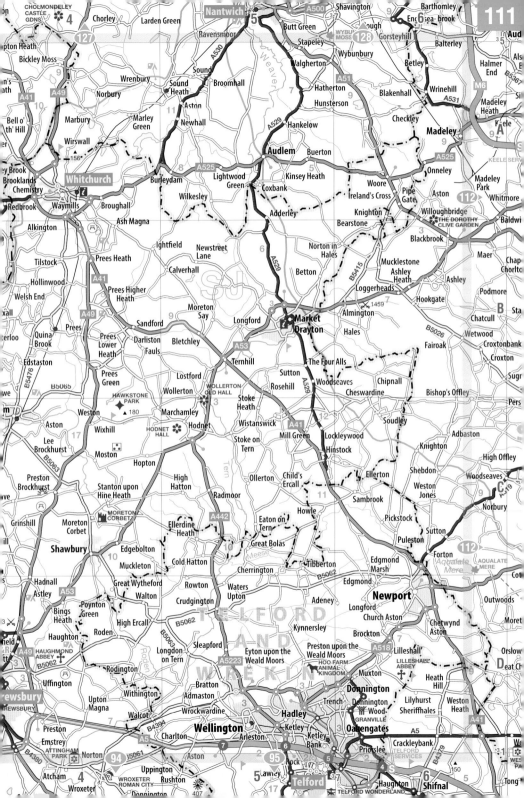

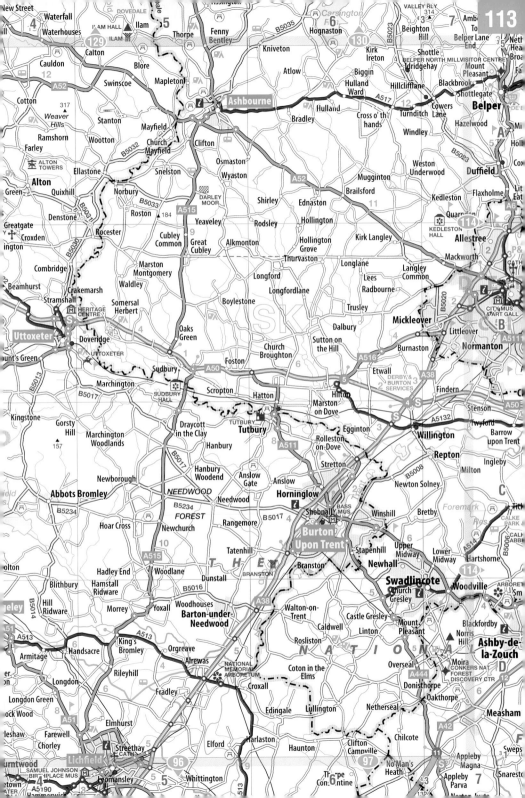

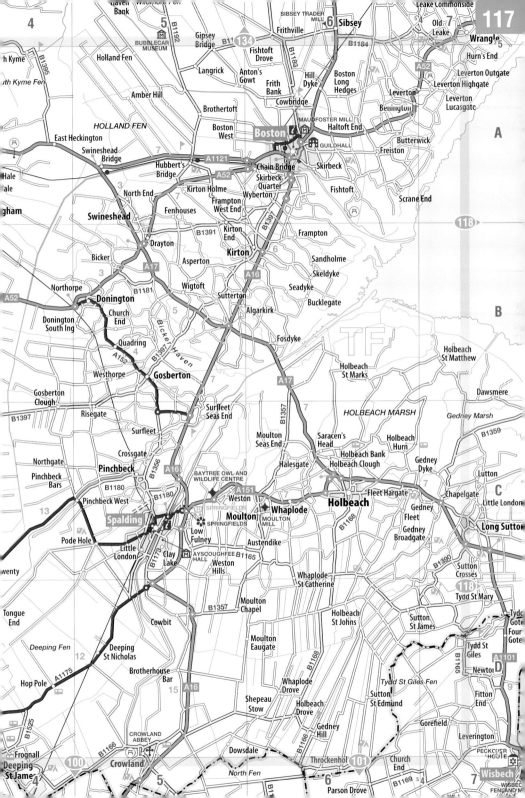

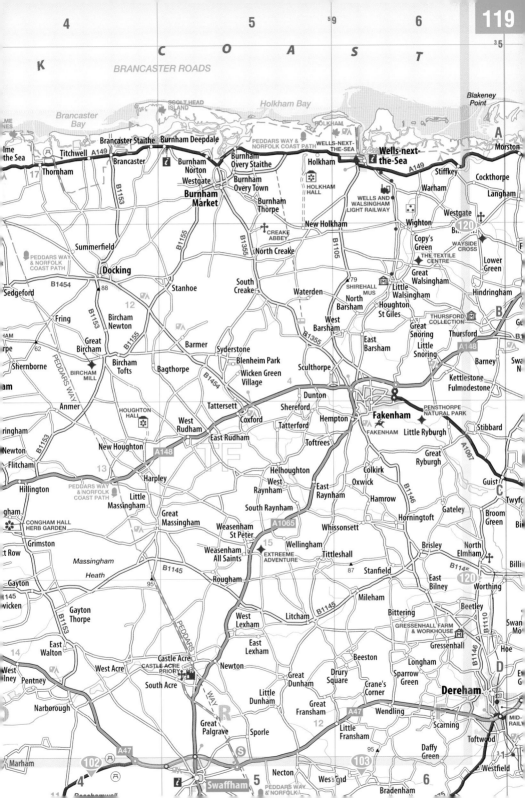

1   2   2   3

The Skerries
Ynysoedd y
Moelrhoniaid

Carmel Head
Pen Carmel

A N G L E S E Y   M Ô N

Wilfa
Head
Pen Wilfa

Cemaes
Bay
Bae
Cemaes

Cemlyn Bay
Bae Cemlyn

Llanbadr

Cemaes

Tregele

17

Llanfairynghornwy

Llanfechell

Llanfflewyn

I S L E

Church Bay
Porth Swtan

Rhydwyn

Llanrhyddlad

Carre

A5025

Llanfaethlu

Llanbabo

LLYNON
WINDMILL

Llanddeusant

Elim

HOLYHEAD BAY
BAE
CAERGYBI

Llanfwrog

A N G L

Llan

BREAKWATER

North Stack

HOLYHEAD MOUNTAIN   220

Llaingoch

**Holyhead
(Caergybi)**

Llanfachraeth

Llantrisant

Carmel

Pen-llyn
Res.

Llech

South Stack

ELLINS TOWER RSPB RESERVE

PENRHOS FEILW
STANDING STONES

Goferydd

Kingsland

A5

Newlands
Park

Llanynghenedl

Bodedern

(S I R Y N

Trefor

Penrhosfeilw

ANGLESEY

6

Valley

Penrhyn Mawr

Trearddur

Glan-traeth

B4545

Four Mile
Bridge

Caergeiliog

A55

3

4

A5

Bryngwran

5

Gwalchm

**Holy Island
Ynys Gybi**

Llanfihangel
yn Nhowyn

Llanfairyneubwll

Capel-
gwyn

Rhoscolyn

Cymyran
Bay
Bae Cymyran

Llanfaelog

Pencarnisiog

Bryn Du

Ddrydwy

Beth

Rhosneigr

WALES COAST
PATH

Llangwyfan-isaf

Aberffraw

Llangadwaladr

Hermon

Bodorgan

A N G L E S E Y   M Ô N

NEWBOROUGH WARREN
AND YNYS LLANDDWYN

Malltraeth Bay
Bae Malltraeth

Llanddwyn I.
Ynys Llanddwyn

DUBLIN

DUBLIN

A

B

C

D

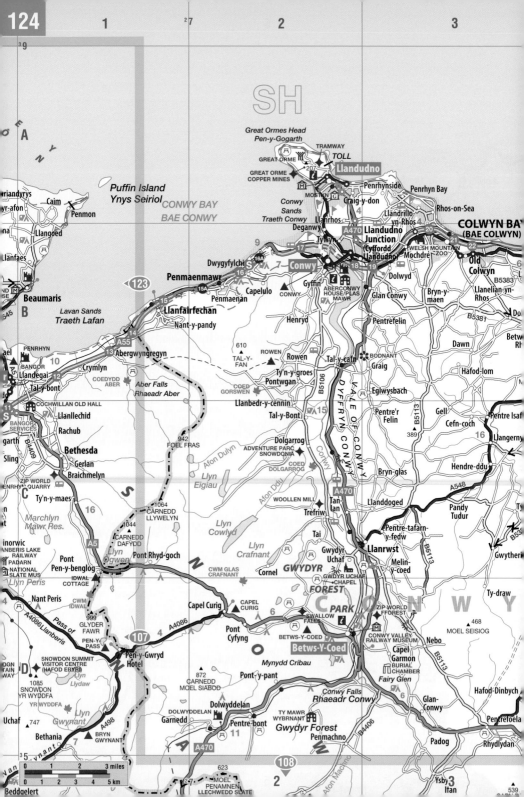

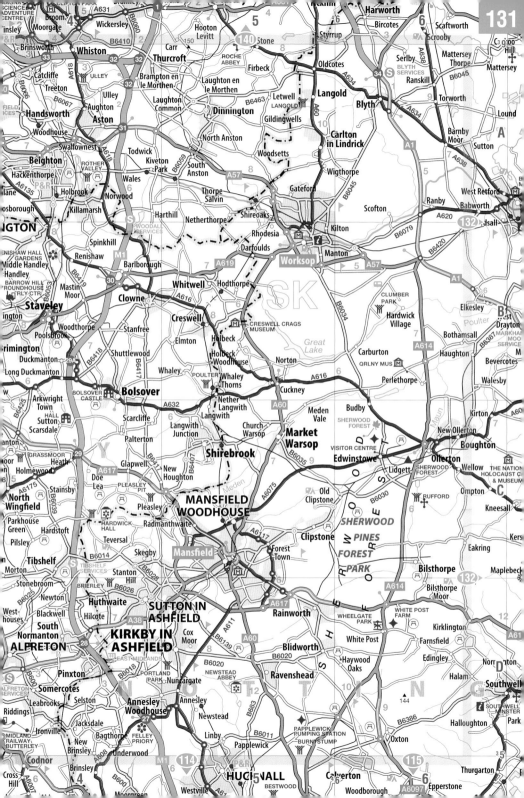

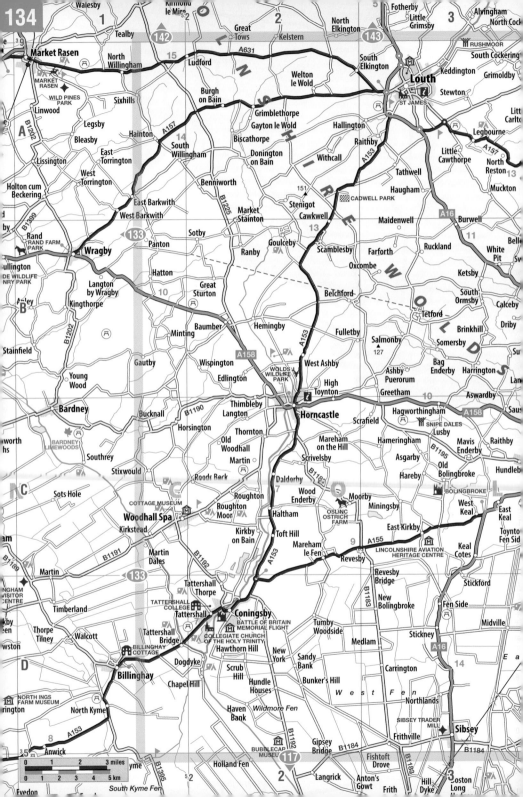

A

B

TF

C

D

Saltfleetby
St Clements
4
143
Saltfleetby
All Saints
Saltfleetby
St Peter
Theddlethorpe
St Helen
Theddlethorpe
All Saints

SALTFLEETBY
THEDDLETHORPE

5

5 6

6

3 9

Great
Carlton
uth
eston
Gayton
le Marsh
Withern
A157
Strubby
Maltby
le Marsh
Beesby
Thorpe

Meers
Bridge

SEAL SANCTUARY
& NATURE CENTRE

Mablethorpe

Trusthorpe

Sutton
on Sea

A1104

1

2

Sandilands

Tothill
thorpe
Woodthorpe
4
Saleby
CLAYTHORPE WATER MILL
AND WILDFOWL GARDENS
Aby

8
Markby
Hannah
Asserby

A52

A1111

uth
oresby
Haugh
ALFORD
WINDMILL
ALFORD
MANOR HOUSE
Rigsby
Alford
B1449
Bilsby
Huttoft

Farlesthorpe

Anderby
ON YOUR MARQUES

3
A1104
Well
Ulceby
Claxby
Bonthorpe

Cumberworth
Mumby

17

Authorpe
Row

Chapel
St Leonards

Helsey

Hogsthorpe

Willoughby
Sloothby
A52

4
16
5
B1196

Skendleby
A1028
Partney
Scremby
4

Welton
le Marsh
Orby

Candlesby
GUNBY HALL
Burgh
le Marsh
A158

Orby Marsh
Addlethorpe

Winthorpe

HARDY'S ANIMAL FARM

Ingoldmells
FANTASY ISLAND

BUTLINS SKEGNESS

Seathorne

oilsby
Ashby by
Partney
NORTHCOTE HEAVY
HORSE CENTRE
Great
Steeping
Halton
Holegate
B1195
Toynton
St Peter
Bratoft
N
Irby in
the Marsh
Little
Steeping
Firsby
Thorpe
Culvert
Thorpe
St Peter
BURGH LE
MARSH WINDMILL

7

THE VILLAGE
CHURCH
FARM

NATURELAND SEAL
SANCTUARY

Skegness
THE LIFEBOAT
STATION
AQUARIUM

C

Thorpe
Fendykes
Wainfleet
All Saints
Wainfleet Bank
New
eake
astville
LINCOLNSHIRE
WILDLIFE PARK
F e n
Friskney
Bank
20
Wrangle
Bank
Friskney
Eaudike
Friskney
Tofts

Croft
A52
Croft Marsh

Seacroft

MAGDALEN
MUSEUM
Wainfleet Tofts
Wainfleet St Mary

Wainfleet
Sand

GIBRALTAR POINT

Old
Leake
Wrangle Lowgate
Wrangle

Friskney Flats

3 5

Hurn's End
4
Leverton Outgate
Leverton Highgate

118

5

5 6

6

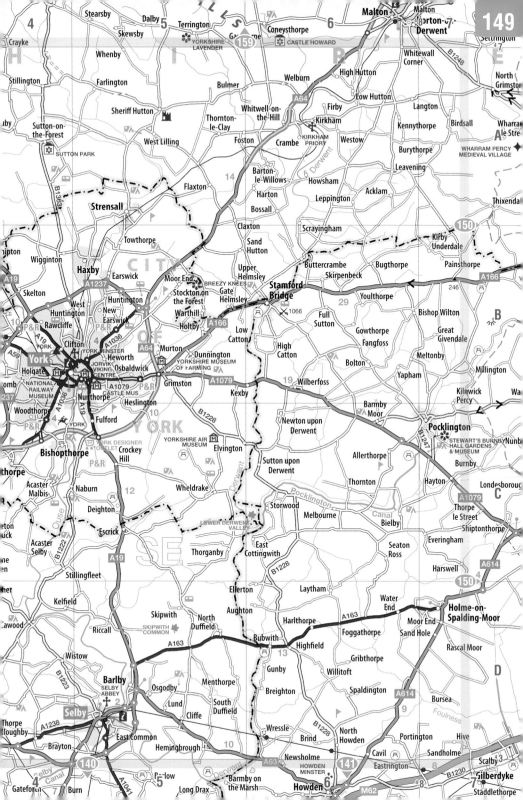

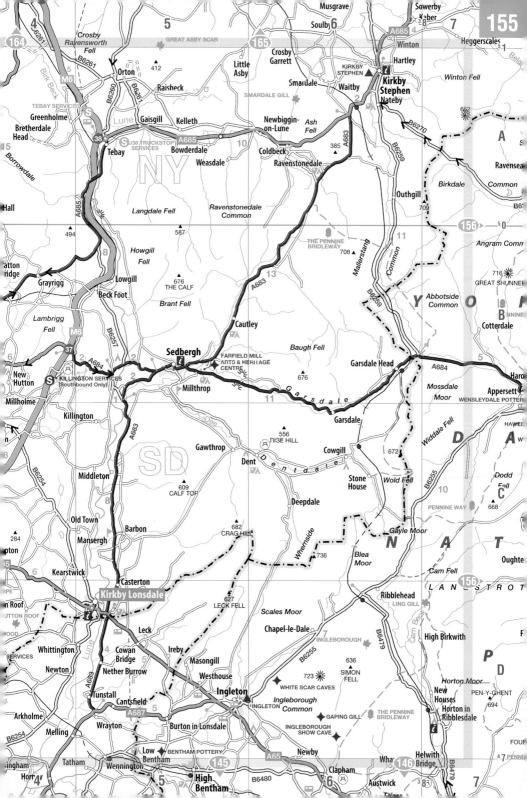

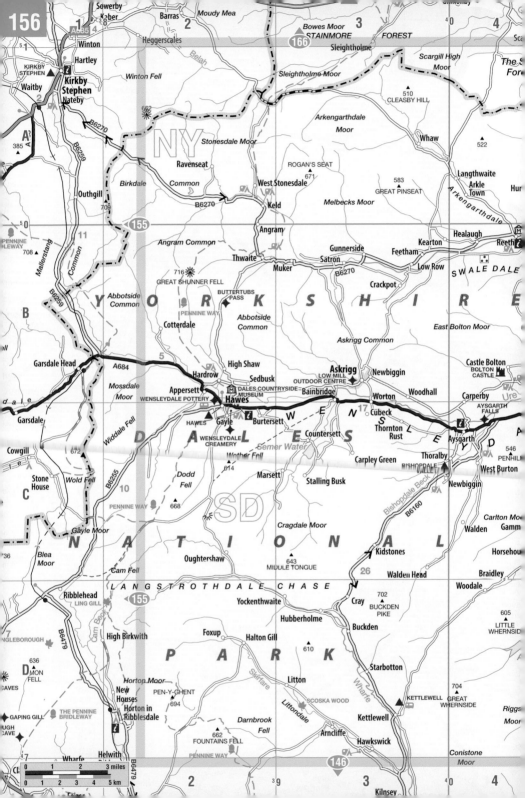

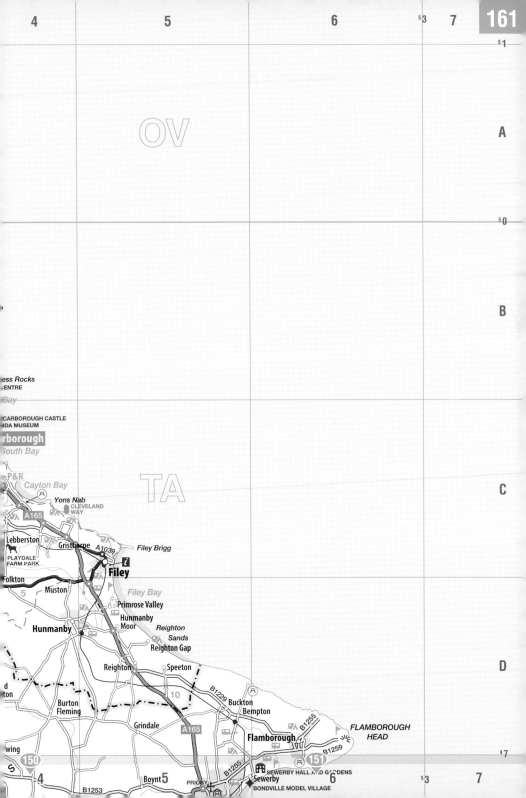

4 5 6 7

A

B

OV

C

ess Rocks
ENTRE

Bay

CARBOROUGH CASTLE
DA MUSEUM

rborough
South Bay

P&R
Cayton Bay

TA

Yons Nab
CLEVELAND WAY

A165

Lebberston
Gristhorpe A1039 Filey Brigg

PLAYDALE
FARM PARK

Folkton Filey

Muston
5 Filey Bay

Primrose Valley

Hunmanby
Moor Reighton
Sands

Hunmanby Reighton Gap

D

Reighton Speeton

10 B1229 Buckton

Burton Bempton
Fleming

Grindale A165 B1255

FLAMBOROUGH
HEAD

Flamborough

B1259

wing
150 151

4 5 SEWERBY HALL AND GARDENS 6 7

Boynt Sewerby
PRIORY

B1253 BONDVILLE MODEL VILLAGE

NX

Allonby Bay

A 173

A 174

B5300

Crosscanonby
Allerby
Crosby

MARYPORT
MARITIME
MUSEUM
Maryport
Dearham

Flimby
Dovenby
Standingstone
Broughton
Moor
Great
Broughton
Little
Brough

A 596
Siddick
Camerton

Derwent

Seaton
Great
Clifton
Bridgefoot
Br

North Side
Bridgefoot
Greysouthe

Workington
Stainburn
HELENA
THOMPSON MUS
Little Clifton
Eaglesfie

Westfield
A 595
Deanscales

Mossbay
A 596
Winscales
Dean

Harrington
High
Harrington
Branthwaite
Ullock

Distington
Pica

Lowca
Keekle
247
Asby
L

Moresby
Arlecdon
A5086
15

Parton
Moresby
Parks
Rowrah
Kirkland

Bransty
WALK MILL
HIGH LEYS

THE RUM STORY
Frizington

Whitehaven
Hensingham
B5294
Ehen

Saltom Bay
Mirehouse
Moor
Row
**Cleator
Moor**
Ennerdale
Bridge

C
ST
BEES HEAD
Sandwith
A595
B5295
Wath Brow

Rottington
Cleator
LONGLANDS LAKE

St Bees
Wilton

Egremont

B5345
Coulderton
Thornhill
Haile

Middletown
Calder

Nethertown
Beckermet
322

Braystones
A595
Welling

D
High
Sellafield
Calder Hall
Gosforth

B5344
Calder Bridge

Seascale
HALLSENNA
MOOR

A 153
Holmrook
Irt

0   1   2   3 miles
0 1 2 3 4 5 km

Drigg

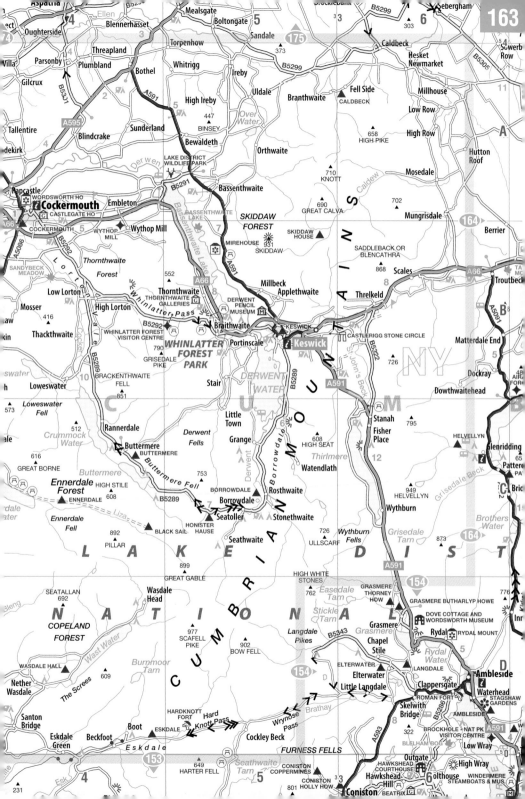

A

B

NZ

C

MINIATURE
RAILWAY
◆ **Saltburn-
by-the-Sea**
CHRIS BIRKBECK
INTERNATIONAL RALLY
SCHOOL
166 ▲
🅙
Brotton
Skinningrove
ENGLAND COAST PATH
Boulby
Carlin
How
5
Loftus
A174
Staithes
North
Skelton
Kilton
Thorpe
Easington
Port Mulgrave
Lingdale
Hinderwell
Runswick Bay
Margrove
Park
Stanghow
Roxby
Runswick
Bay
Kettleness
Liverton
Newton
Mulgrave
Goldsborough
9
Moorsholm
B1366
Ellerby
14
D
Scaling
A174
Lythe
B1266
Sandsend
Mickleby
East
Barnby
Sandsend Wyke
Scaling Dam
Res.
West
Barnby
East Row
Dunsley
SUTCLIFFE GALLERY
Whitby
*Saltwick
Bay*
Danby Low Moor
Ugthorpe
Newholm
P&R
WHITBY ABBEY
WHITBY
Commondale
Moor
299
🅜
CAPTAIN COOK
MEMORIAL MUSEUM
5·1
159
MOORS
CENTRE
Stonegate
A171
13
160
Ruswarp
B1410
Sn..sacre
Danby
Houlsyke
Lealholm
Aislaby
Briggswath
High Hawsker
4   5   6   7

LAGGANGAIRN STANDING STONES

Knowe

PENNINGHAME FOREST

Challoch

Minnigaff
Creebridge
MINNIGAFF
Newton Stewart

WILD GOAT PARK

KIRROUGHTREE VISITOR CENTRE

CAINSMORE OF FLEET

Palnure

A712

Carseriggan

Artfield Fell

244

Black Loch

Loch Heron

Loch Ronald

Drumphail

205

Shennanton

Benfield

Baltersan

Causeway End

Carsegowan

Cree

GEM ROCK MUSEUM

Creetown

Tarf Water

Carscreugh

Kirkcowan

Craighlaw Mains

A75

B733

B726

High Mindork

Dernaglar Loch

Knock Moss

Whitefield Loch

Castle Loch

luce

ton

Auchenmalg

B7027

A714

123

213

Spittal

131

Fell Loch

Torhousemuir

TORHOUSE STONE CIRCLE

B7052

Culmazie

Mochrum Loch

B7005

Wigtown Sands

Wigtown

SCOTLAND'S BOOK TOWN

Bladnoch

VISITOR CENTRE

Braehead
Kirkinner

Baldoon Sands

Carsluith

CARS CAST

Ravens

chenmalg Bay

Culshabbin

Alticry

B7005

197

Loch Head

CHAPEL FINIAN

Elrig

Mochrum

Milton Pt.

A747

6

Barrachan

MOTE OF DRUCHTAG

75

Whauphill

Sorbie

B7052

Garlieston

Eggerne

B7005

B7052

11

Airyhassen

Drumtroddan

Drummoddie

DRUMTRODDAN STONES

Port William

B7085

Monreith Mains

Moor of Ravenstone

Cults

GALLOWAY HOUSE GARDENS

B7063

CRUGGLETON

Port Allen

Barsalloch Pt.
MONREITH ANIMAL WORLD, SHORE CENTRE AND MUSEUM

BARSALLOCH FORT

Monreith

Bishopton

Whithorn

172

Portyerrock

Monreith Bay

9

PRIORY AND MUSEUM

WHITHORN TRUST DISCOVERY CENTRE

Cairn Hd.

Glasserton

146

FELL OF CARLETON

A746

B7004

ST NINIAN'S

A747

ST NINIAN'S CAVE

Isle of Whithorn

Port Castle Bay

BURROW HEAD

Cutcloy

CE BAY

Port William

Barsalloch Fort

NX

THE MACHARS

A75

A712

A714

A746

A747

Bladnoch

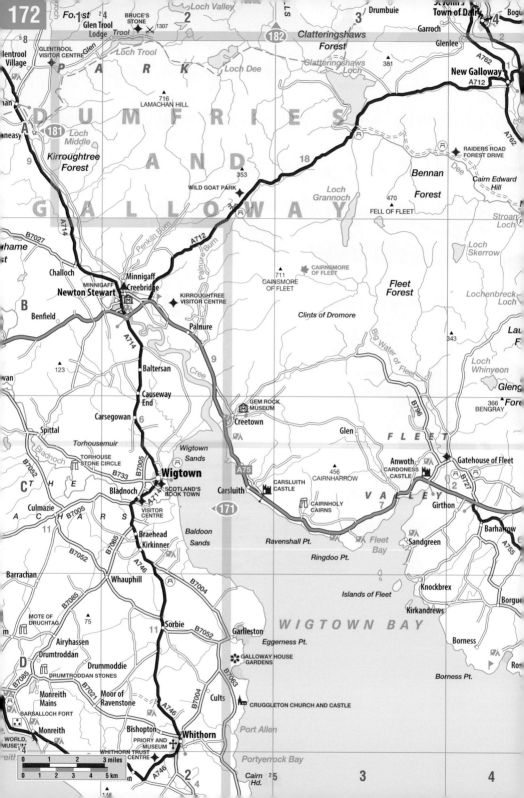

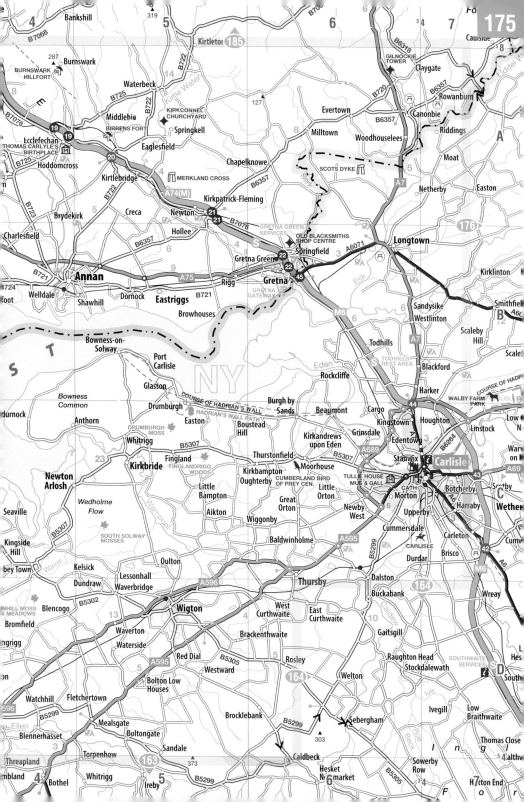

Map places (north to south, west to east):

Bankshill
Burnswark
BURNSWARK HILLFORT
Waterbeck
Kirtleton
Caulside
GILNOCKIE TOWER
Claygate
Middlebie
KIRKCONNEL CHURCHYARD
Springkell
Rowanburn
BIRRENS FORT
Eagelsfield
Evertown
Canonbie
Ecclefechan
THOMAS CARLYLE'S BIRTHPLACE
Milltown
Woodhouselees
Riddings
Hoddomcross
Kirtlebridge
Chapelknowe
SCOTS DYKE
Moat
Creca
MERKLAND CROSS
Kirkpatrick-Fleming
Netherby
Easton
Newton
Brydekirk
Hollee
GRETNA GREEN SERVICES
OLD BLACKSMITHS SHOP CENTRE
Longtown
Charlesfield
Annan
Gretna Green
Springfield
Kirklinton
Welldale
Gretna
GRETNA GATEWAY
Smithfield
Shawhill
Dornock
Rigg
Sandysike
Westlinton
Eastriggs
Browhouses
Scaleby Hill
foot
Bowness-on-Solway
Todhills
Blackford
Port Carlisle
TODHILLS REST AREA
Harker
Glasson
COURSE OF HADRIAN'S WALL
Rockcliffe
WALBY FARM PARK
Bowness Common
Drumburgh
HADRIAN'S WALL PATH
Burgh by Sands
Beaumont
Cargo
Kingstown
Houghton
Linstock
Anthorn
Easton
Boustead Hill
Grinsdale
Edentown
DRUMBURGH MOSS
Whitrigg
Kirkandrews upon Eden
Moorhouse
Stanwix
Carlisle
Newton Arlosh
Kirkbride
Fingland
FINGLANDRIGG WOODS
Thurstonfield
Kirkbampton
Oughterby
CUMBERLAND BIRD OF PREY CEN.
Little Orton
TULLIE HOUSE MUS & GALL
Botcherby
Seaville
Wedholme Flow
Little Bampton
Great Orton
Newby West
Morton
Upperby
Harraby
Kingside Hill
SOUTH SOLWAY MOSSES
Aikton
Wiggonby
Cummersdale
Carleton
bey Town
Baldwinholme
CARLISLE
Durdar
Brisco
Kelsick
Lessonhall
Waverbridge
Oulton
Thursby
Dalston
Buckabank
Wreay
Dundraw
NHILL MOSS & MEADOWS
Blencogo
Wigton
West Curthwaite
East Curthwaite
Gaitsgill
Bromfield
Waverton
Waterside
Brackenthwaite
Rosley
Raughton Head
Stockdalewath
SOUTHWAITE SERVICES
nrigg
Red Dial
Westward
Welton
Watchhill
Fletchertown
Bolton Low Houses
Low Braithwaite
Blennerhasset
Mealsgate
Boltongate
Brocklebank
Sebergham
Ivegill
Threapland
Torpenhow
Sandale
Caldbeck
Hesket Newmarket
Sowerby Row
Thomas Close
Bothel
Whitrigg
Ireby

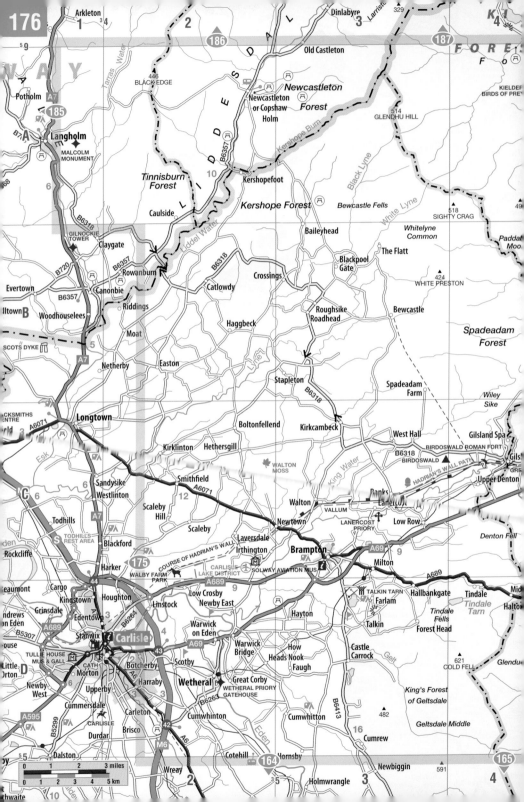

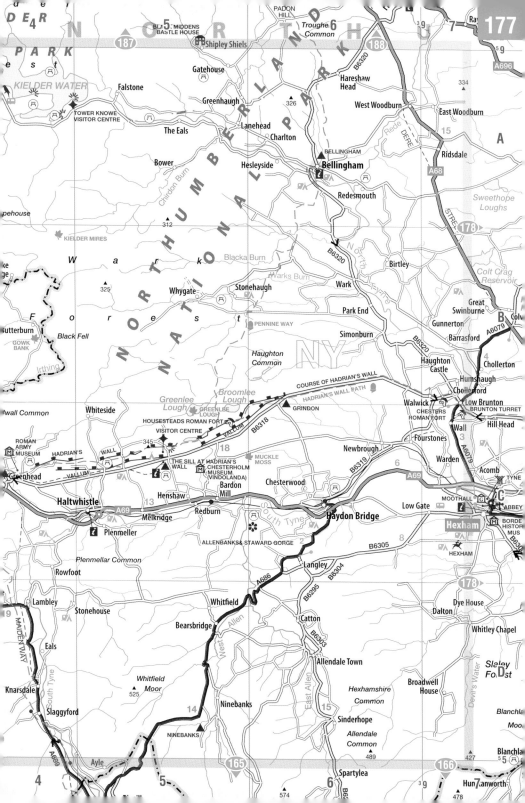

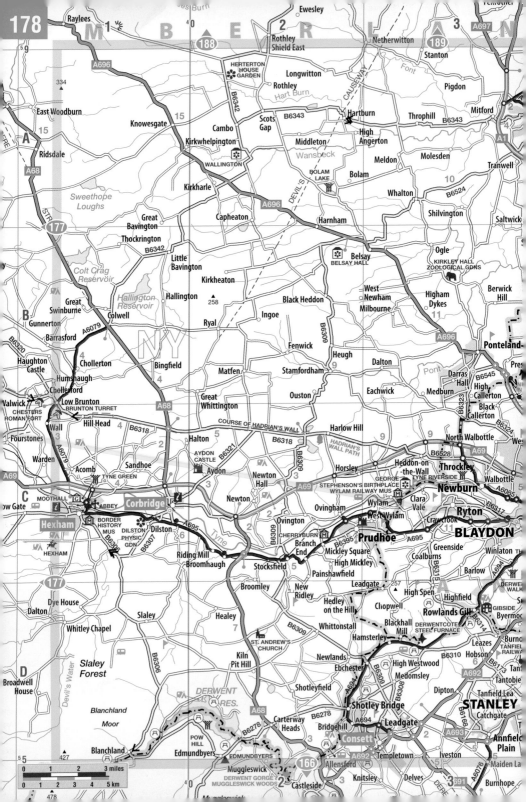

Longhirst

Pegswood

B1337

Morpeth

lifton

NORTHUMBRIA
FT CENTRE
Bothal

A197

A196

Hepscott

Nedderton

Bedlington

B1331

Choppington

Guide Post

Scotland
Gate

Bedlington
Station

Stakeford

A189

A1068

A1068

QUEEN ELIZABETH II
WOODHORN
MUSEUM

189

Woodhorn

Beacon Pt.

Ashington

Hirst

WANSBECK

North
Seaton

West Sleekburn

Cambois

East
Sleekburn

Cowpen

BLYTH

Newbiggin-by-the-Sea

A

East
Hartford

A192

B1505

Bebside

Newsham

B1329

East
Cramlington

Nelson Village

A1068

SEATON BURN
SERVICES

Seaton
Burn

Southfield

New
Delaval

A189

Shankhouse

PLESSEY
WOODS

New
Hartley

A1061

ENGLAND COAST PATH

Cramlington

A1172

Dudley

Burradon

Seghill

Seaton

Seaton Sluice

Hartley

SEATON DELAVAL HALL

ST MARY'S LIGHTHOUSE
St Mary's or Bait I.

B

Seaton
Delaval

Holywell

A193

B1325

A1056

A1058

Wide
Open

Annitsford

Backworth

Larsdon

Camperdown

WHITLEY BAY

NZ

Brunswick
Village

Dinnington

Hazlerigg

Killingworth

Monkseaton

Shiremoor

Marden

Cullercoats

BLUE REEF AQUARIUM
TYNEMOUTH

AMSTERDAM

NEWCASTLE
P&R

A1

A189

A188

Longbenton

A191

STEPHENSON
RAILWAY MUSEUM

THE
RISING SUN

A19

North
Shields

Tynemouth

TYNEMOUTH
CASTLE & PRIORY

fenton

kfoot

Gosforth

Kenton

Jesmond

A186

A191

A1058

Willington

ARBEIA ROMAN FORT AND MUSEUM

**NEWCASTLE
ON TYNE**

wood

95 NEWCASTLE
DISCOVERY

Gateshead

Heaton

Byker

CASTLE KEEP

Walker

SEGEDUNUM
FORT

WALLSEND

TOLL

Jarrow

Royal Quays

Tyne Tunnel

JARROW HALL
ST PAUL'S
MONASTERY

Harton

Westoe

South Shields

SOUTH SHIELDS MUSEUM

THE LEAS AND
MARSDEN ROCK

Marsden Bay

Marsden

SOUTER
LIGHTHOUSE

C

Dunston

Bensham

A187

INTERNATIONAL
STADIUM

Hebburn

Hedworth

A194

A1300

A1300

84

Whitburn Colliery

kham

SHIPLEY
ART GALL

B1426

Pelaw

Boldon
Colliery

Whiteleas

Cleadon

Whitburn

Felling

Carr Hill

B1288

B1296

Low Fell

A194

A194

Boldon

A184

A1018

A184

A692

Chowdene

A194(M)

Wrekenton

BOWES
RLY

Usworth

Downhill

Hylton
Castle

A183

Southwick

FULWELL WINDMILL

Fulwell

Roker

Street
Gate

Lamesley

Marley
Hill

ANGEL OF
THE NORTH

A6076

Springwell

Blackfell

A1290

Castletown

A1231

South
Hylton

Pallion

High
Barnes

STATION
MUS

MONKWEARMOUTH
ST PETER'S CHURCH

NATIONAL GLASS CENTRE

Sunderland

SUNDERLAND MINSTER

Kibblesworth

Birtley

Ouston

WASHINGTON

WASHINGTON
SERVICES

65

Lambton

THE WILDFOWL &
WETLANDS TRUST
PENSHAW MON

Pennywell

South

Hendon

A1018

D

BEAMISH

Urpeth

Perkinsville

64

Barley
Mow

Rickleton

Fatfield

Penshaw

East
Herrington

New
Silksworth

Beamish

A6127

Pelton

A693

A183

New
Herrington

A690

Tunstall

Ryhope

RYHOPE ENGINES MUS

A19

B1286

B1287

West Pelton

Grange
Villa

B6313

**Shiney
Row**

A182

Newbottle

Doxford
Park

Burdon

Northlea

B1285

leghead

**CHESTER-
LE-STREET**

B6532

Waldridge

Chester
Moor

A167

THE ANKERS
HOUSE

B1284

A1(M)

A183

Broomroor

Great
Lumley

Colliery
Row

167

**HOUGHTON-LE-
SPRING**

Fence
Houses

DOWN AT
THE FARM

B1404

Seaton

SEAHAM

5 5

A167

Edmondsley

WALDRI

Nettlesworth

Plawsworth

4

A167

East
Rainton

A182

West
Lea

B1287

Dalton-le-

6

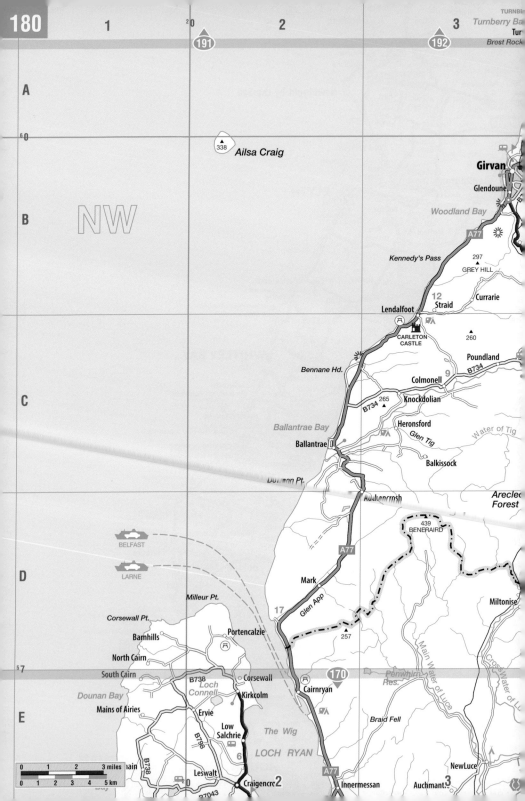

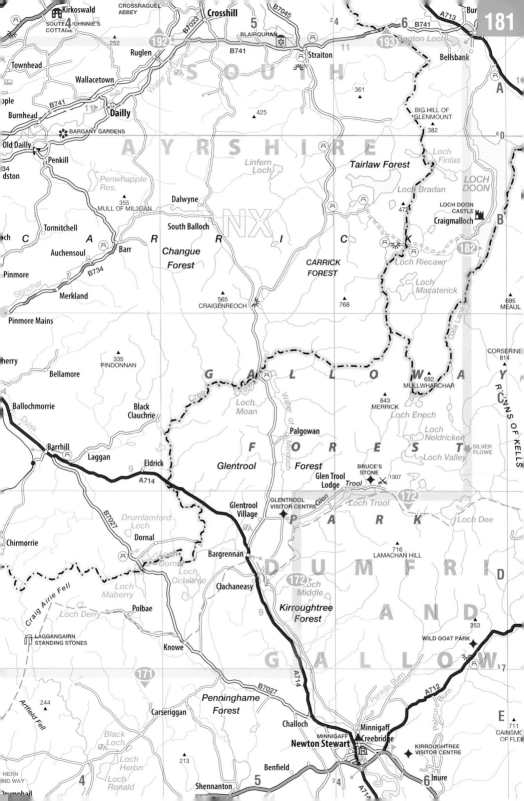

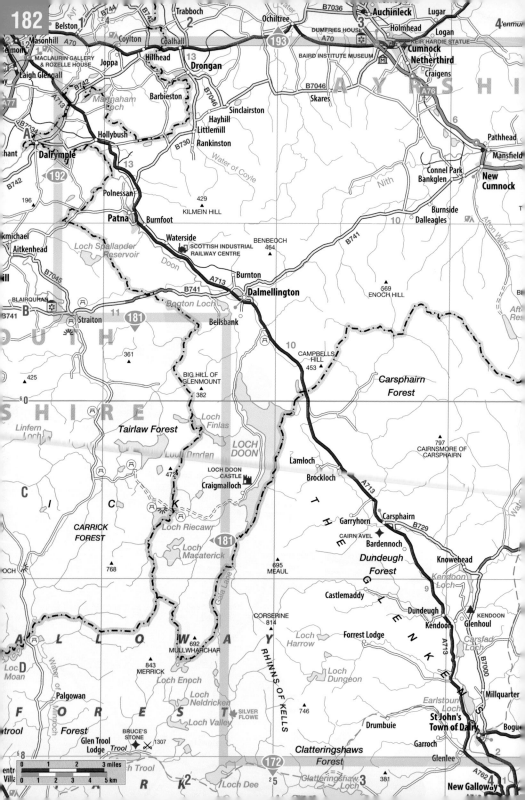

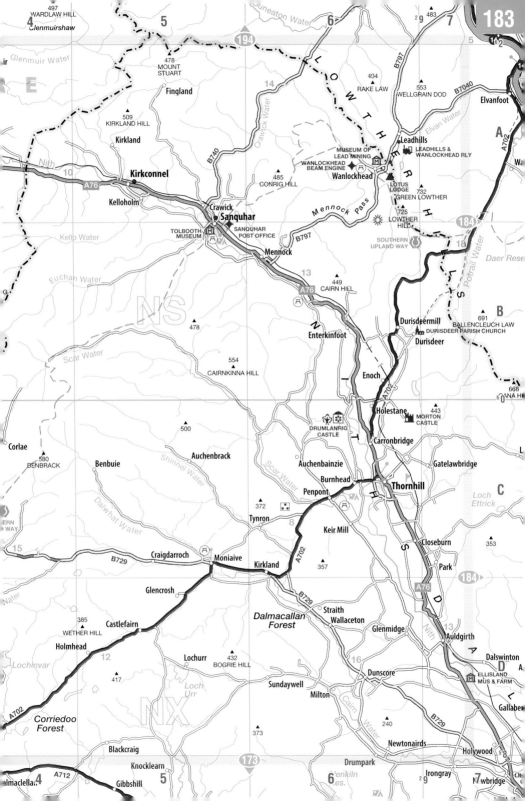

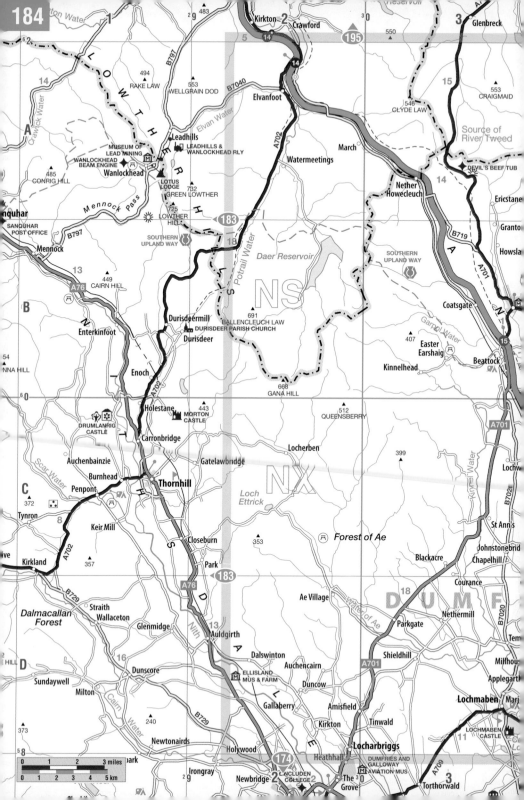

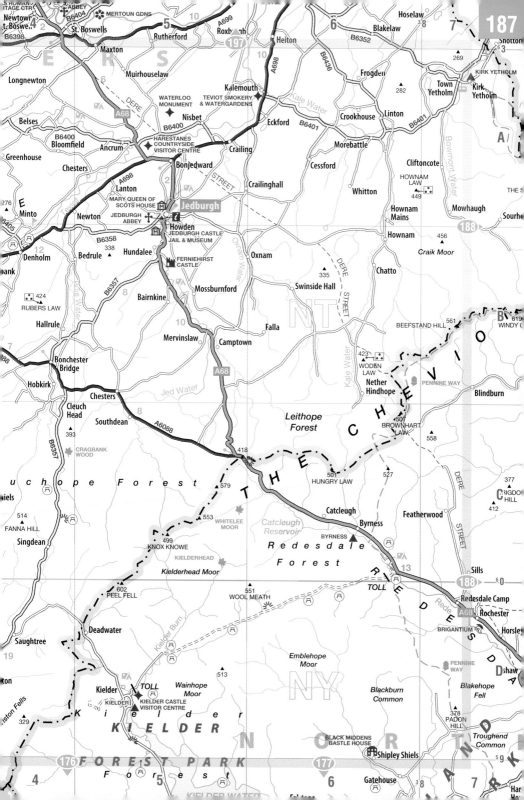

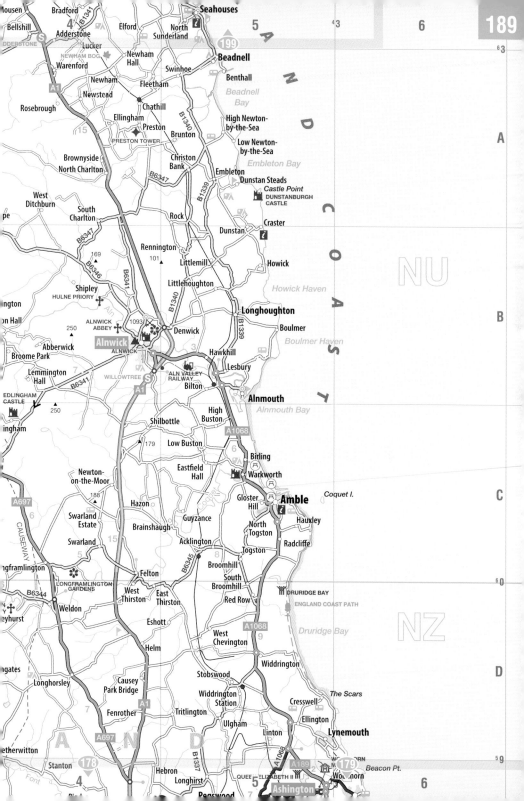

MULL
OF
KINTYRE

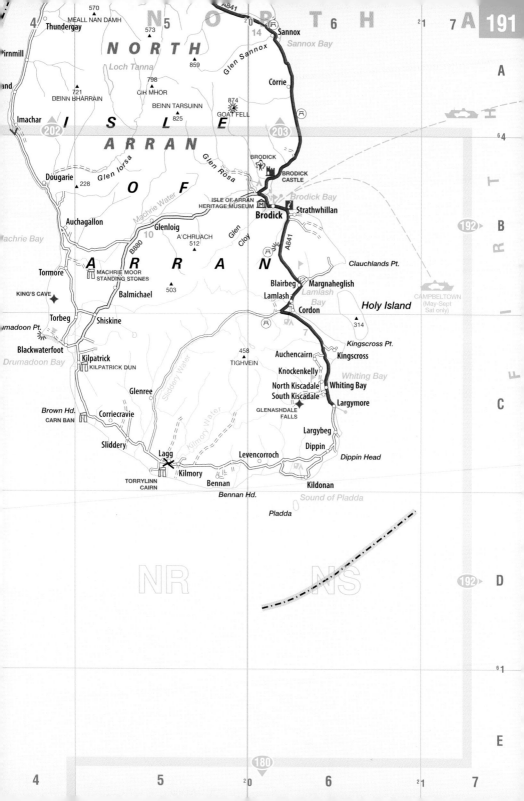

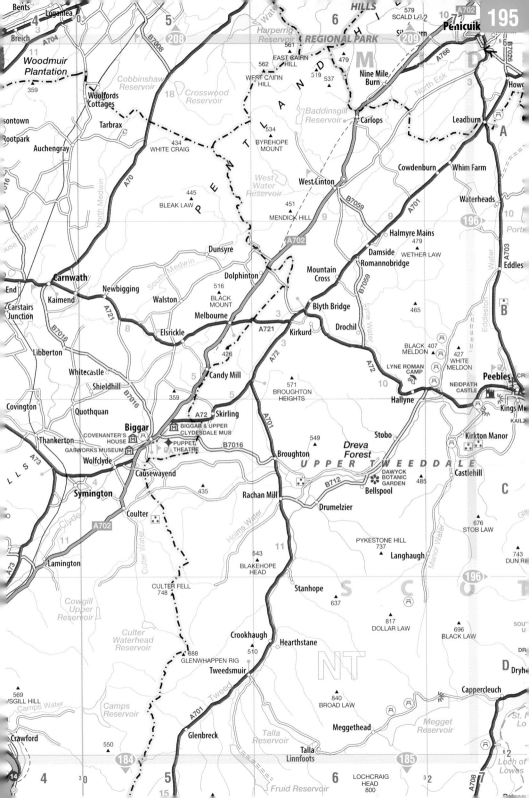

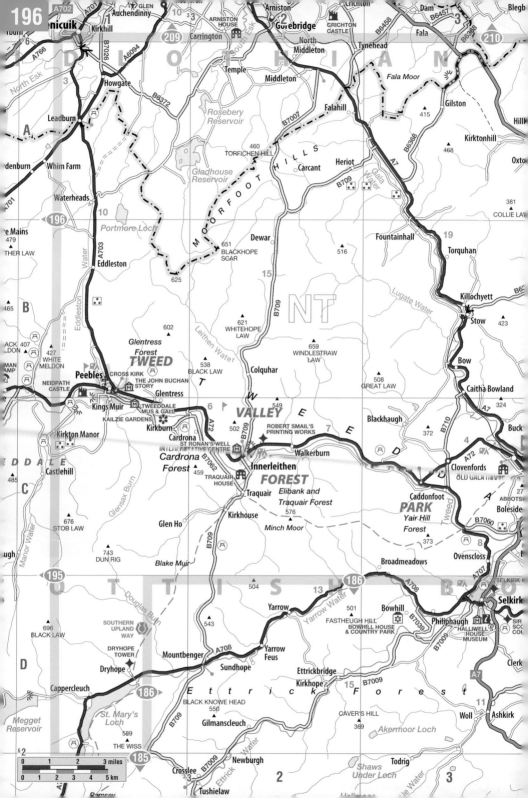

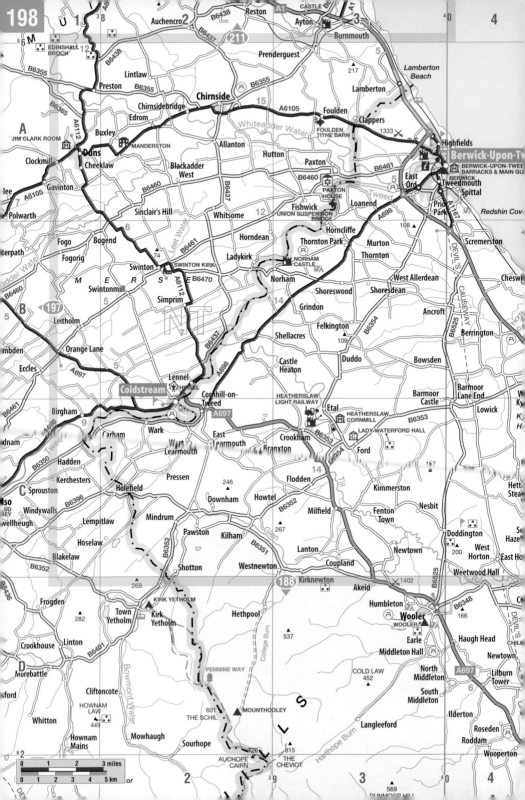

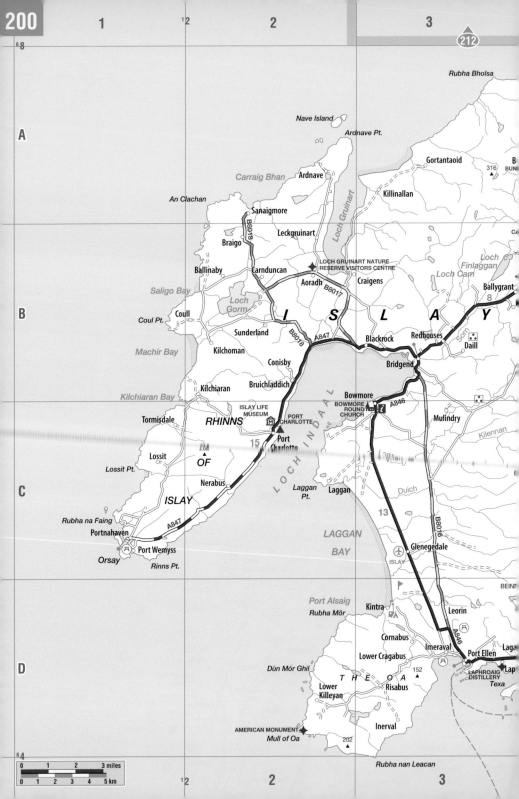

212

Rubha Bholsa

A

Nave Island

Ardnave Pt.

Carraig Bhan

Gortantaoid

316
BUNN
B

An Clachan

Ardnave

Killinallan

Sanaigmore

Loch Gruinart

Leckgruinart

Killinallan

B8018

Braigo

LOCH GRUINART NATURE
RESERVE VISITORS CENTRE

Loch
Finlaggan

Ballinaby

Carnduncan

Aoradh

B8017

Craigens

Loch Cam

Ballygrant

Saligo Bay

Loch
Gorm

ISLAY

8

B

Coul Pt.

Coull

Sunderland

B8018

A847

Blackrock

Redhouses

Daill

Son

Machir Bay

Kilchoman

Conisby

Bridgend

Kilchiaran Bay

Kilchiaran

Bruichladdich

Kilennan

Tormisdale

ISLAY LIFE
MUSEUM

PORT
CHARLOTTE

Bowmore

BOWMORE
ROUND
CHURCH

A846

Mulindry

RHINNS

Port
Charlotte

15

Lossit

OF

Nerabus

LOCH INDAAL

Laggan
Pt.

Laggan

Duich

13

B8016

Lossit Pt.

ISLAY

Rubha na Faing

A847

C

Portnahaven

Port Wemyss

Orsay

Rinns Pt.

ISLAY

**LAGGAN
BAY**

Glenegedale

Port Alsaig

Rubha Mòr

Kintra

Leorin

BEINN

Cornabus

Imeraval

A846

Laga

Lower Cragabus

Port Ellen

Lap

D

Dùn Mòr Ghil

Lower
Killeyan

TH E O A

Risabus

152

LAPHROAIG
DISTILLERY

Texa

Inerval

AMERICAN MONUMENT
Mull of Oa

202

Rubha nan Leacan

0   1   2   3 miles
0 1 2 3 4 5 km

1   2   3

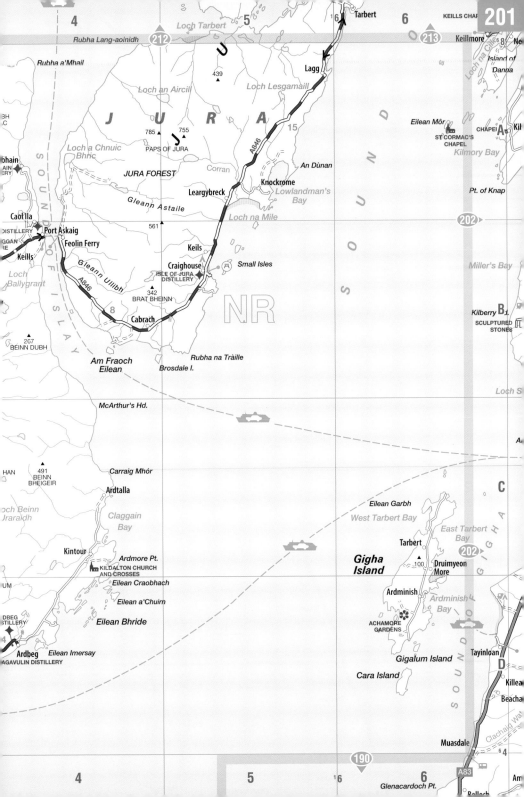

4

5

6

Tarbert

212 Rubha Lang-aoinidh

213 Keillmore 26 Ne

Loch Tarbert

Lagg

Island of Danna

Rubha a'Mhail

Loch an Aircil

439

Loch Lesgamaill

CHAPEL A Kil

Eilean Môr
ST CORMAC'S
CHAPEL

Kilmory Bay

U

J U R A

785 755
PAPS OF JURA

Loch a Chnuic Bhric

A846

15

Pt. of Knap

Corran

An Dùnan

JURA FOREST

Knockrome

Lowlandman's Bay

Gleann Astaile

Leargybreck

202

Caol Ila
DISTILLERY

561

Loch na Mile

Miller's Bay

Port Askaig

Feolin Ferry

Keils

Keills

Small Isles

Loch Ballygrant

Gleann Ullibh

Craighouse
ISLE OF JURA
DISTILLERY

Kilberry B
SCULPTURED STONES

A846

342
BRAT BHEINN

8

Cabrach

NR

267
BEINN DUBH

Am Fraoch Eilean

Rubha na Tràille

Loch S

Brosdale I.

McArthur's Hd.

A

HAN

491
BEINN BHEIGEIR

Carraig Mhór

Eilean Garbh

C

Ardtalla

West Tarbert Bay

och Beinn Uraraidh

Claggain Bay

East Tarbert Bay

202

Tarbert

Kintour

Ardmore Pt.

KILDALTON CHURCH
AND CROSSES

Gigha Island

100

Druimyeon More

UM

Eilean Craobhach

Eilean a'Chuirn

Ardminish

Ardminish Bay

DBEG
STILLERY

Eilean Bhride

ACHAMORE
GARDENS

Ardbeg

Eilean Imersay

GAVULIN DISTILLERY

Gigalum Island

Tayinloan

D

Cara Island

Killea

Beacha

190

Muasdale

A83

Am

4

5

6

Glenacardoch Pt.

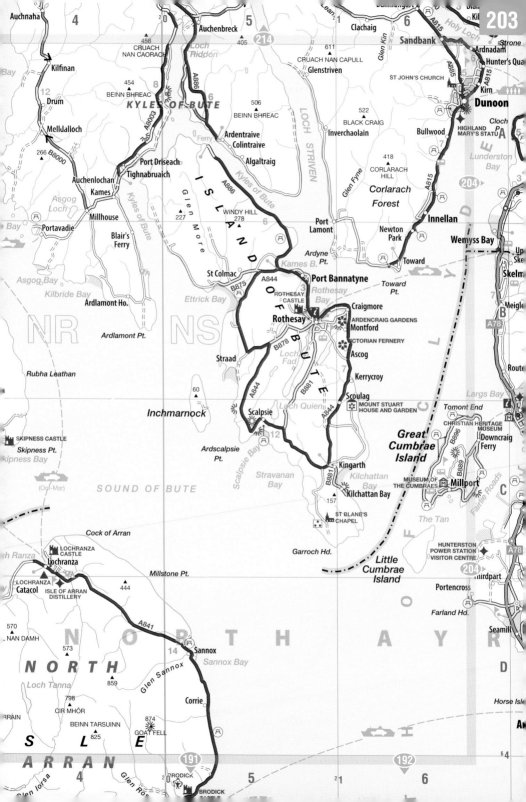

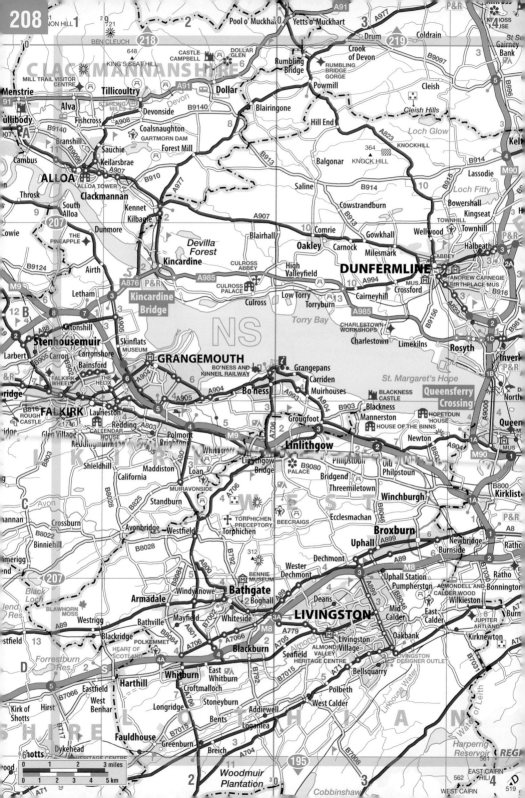

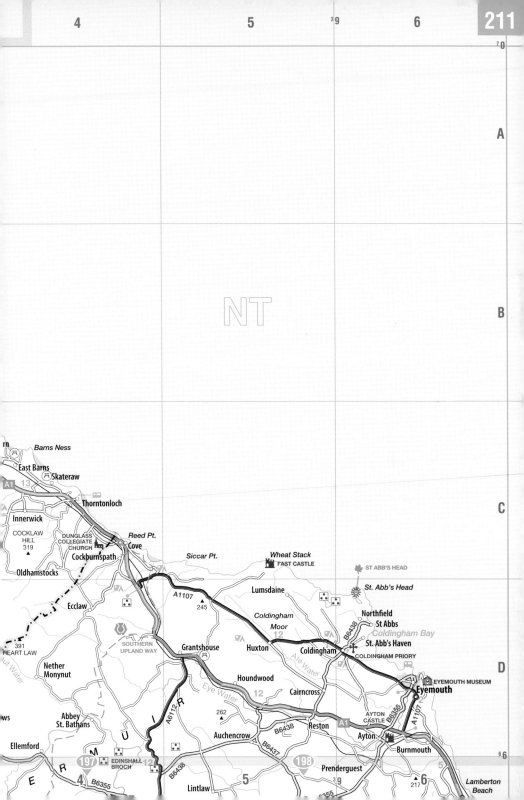

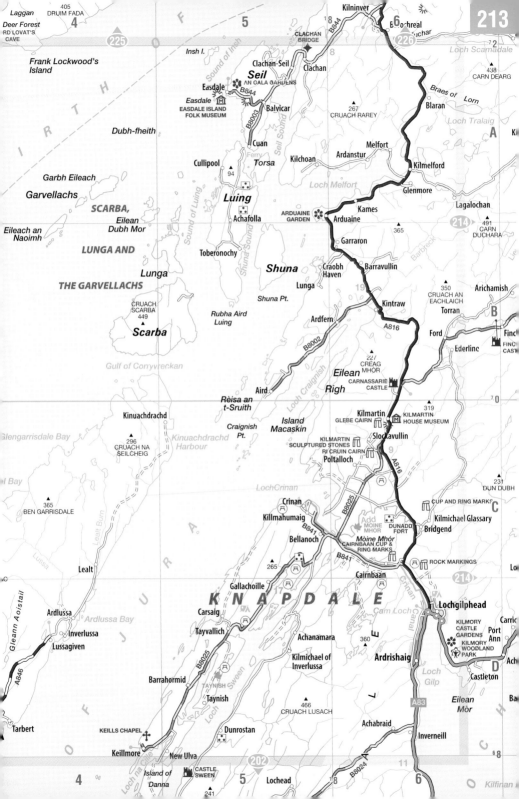

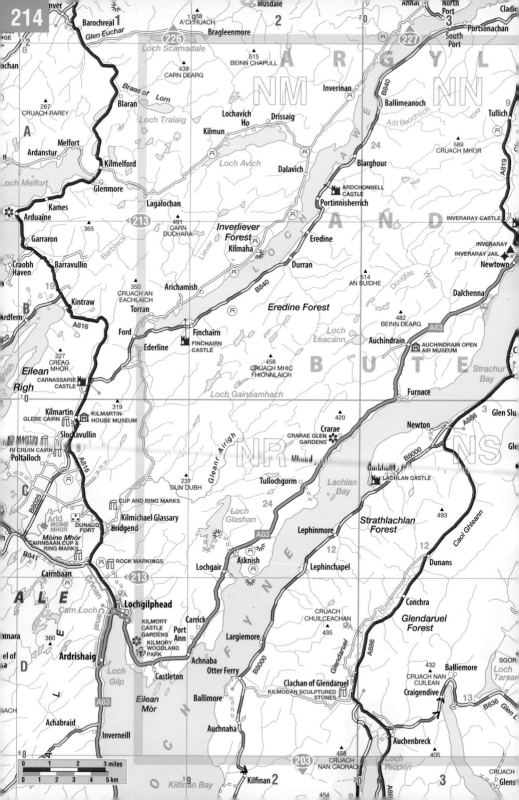

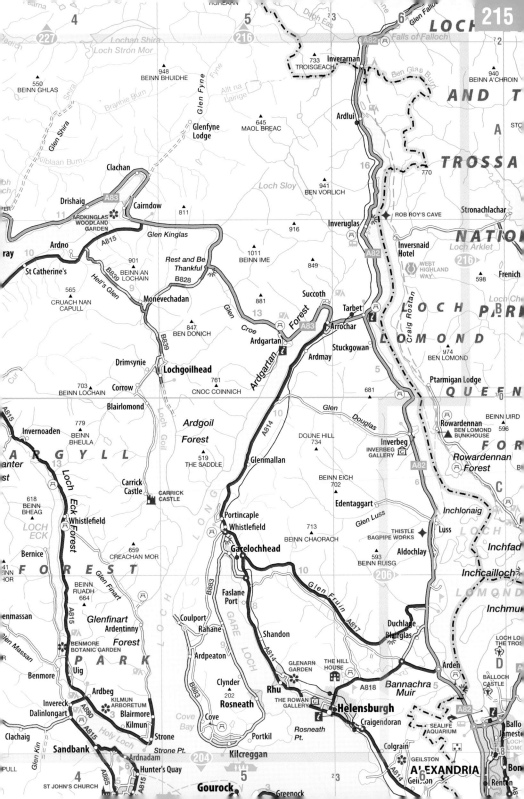

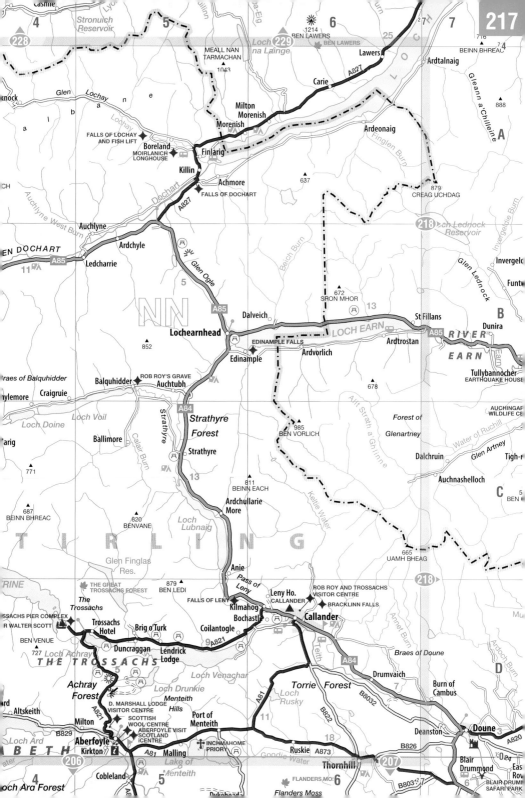

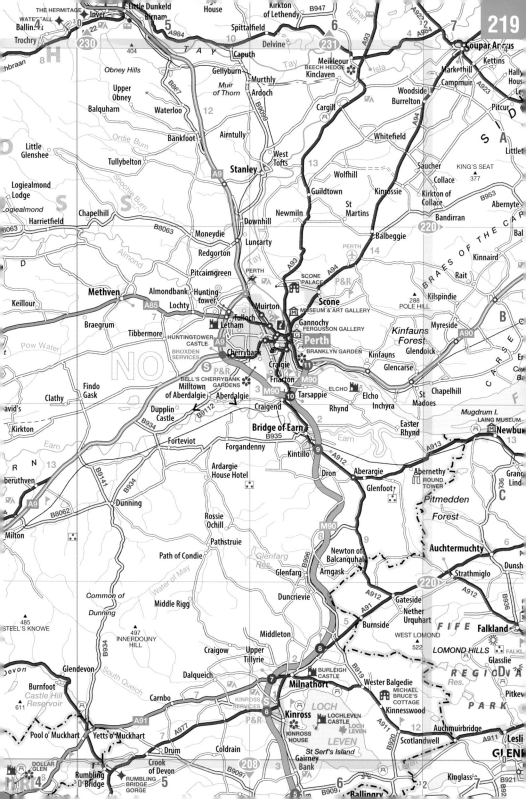

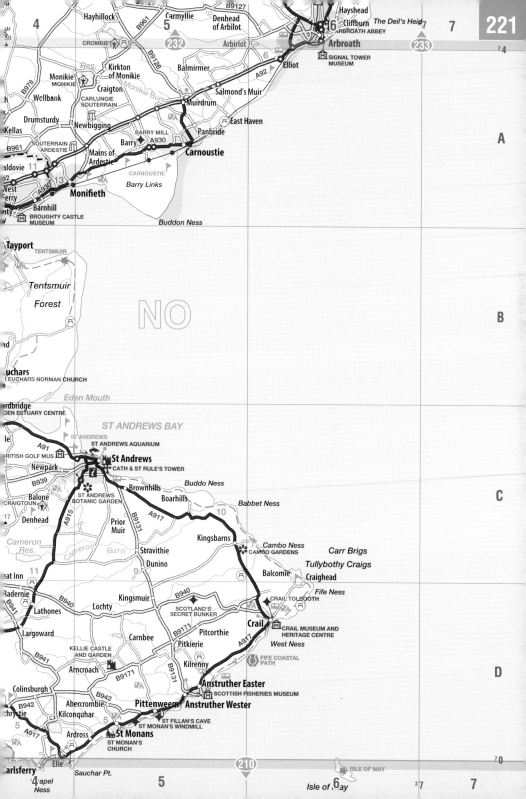

286

A

NL

B

CASTLEBAY
(Apr - Oct, Wed only)

Feall Bay

Calgary Pt.

Crossa Bay

Gunna

T I R E E

Vaul Bay

Salum   Caolas

Rubha Dubh

Vaul

Balephetrish Bay

B8069

Hough Skerries

Ruaig

Balevullin

Gott Bay

R. Chraiginis

Kenovay

B8068

Soa

C

Kilkenneth

TIREE

Scarinish

B8068

B8065

Moss

Middleton   Heylipol

Heanish

Port Mor

Crossapol

Rubha Traigh an Duin

B8065

Loch a' Phuill

Barrapol

Hynish Bay

B8067

Balemartine

Rinn Thorbhais

Balephuil

B8066

Mannal

141 ▲

Balephuil Bay

Hynish

Port Snoig

D

0   1   2   3 miles
0 1 2 3 4 5 km

CASTLEBAY
LOCHBOISDALE
(Oct - Mar)

Sanna Point

Sanna Bay

Sanna

Portuairk

Point of
Ardnamurchan
ARDNAMURCHAN LIGHTHOUSE

Achosni

A

Cairns of Coll

234

Orm

Ormsai

Rubha Mor

Eilean Mor

An Acairseid

Sorisdale

Bousd

Gallanach

B8072

COLL

73

Ardmore B

Cliad Bay

Arnabost

Grishipoll

B8071

Loch
Cliad

104

Quinish Pt.

Glengorm
Castle

lyhaugh

B8071

Rubha
an Aird

Q
u
i
n
i
s
h

M sh

B

Bay

B8070

Arinagour

Sunipol

MULL
THEATRE

Totronald

Loch Eatharna

Caliach Pt.

M o r n i s h

Penmore
Mill

Acha

Eilean
Ornsay

Dervaig

Ach

Breachacha
Castle

Friesland

Calgary

THE OLD BYRE
HERITAGE CEN

Loch Breachacha

Calgary Bay

Soa

342
CARN MOR

Bellart

Ensay

Treshnish Pt.

Achna

Haunn

B8073

Kilninian

Rubh a'Chaoil

224

Burg

Achleck

23

Fanmore

390

C

Treshnish Isles

Fladda

Ballygown

L O C H   T U A T H

EAS FORS
WATERFALL

Eilean Dioghlum

Gometra

Laggan
Bay

Lunga

Bearnus

313

U l v a

Ulva House

Bac Mor

L O C H   N A

Little
Colonsay

INCH KENNETH
CHAPEL

I S L

D

Staffa

STAFFA

*Inch
Kenneth*

Ba

FINGAL'S CAVE

MACKINNON'S CAVE

Erisgeir

519

73 BEIN NA SF

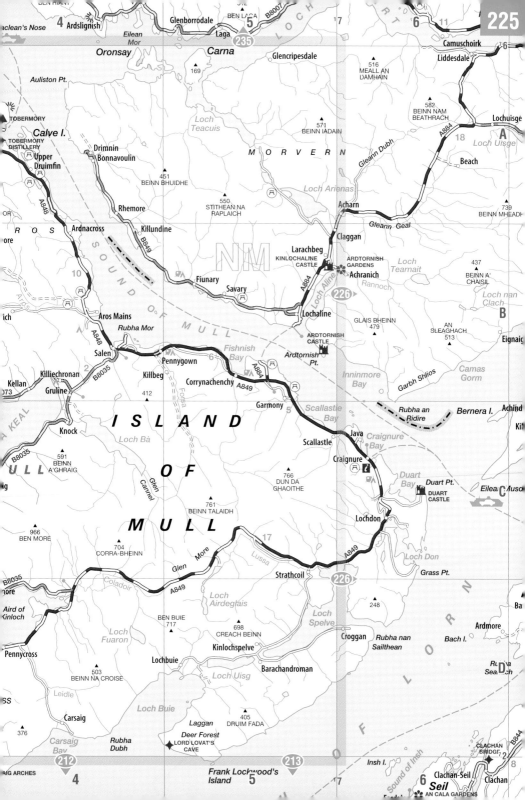

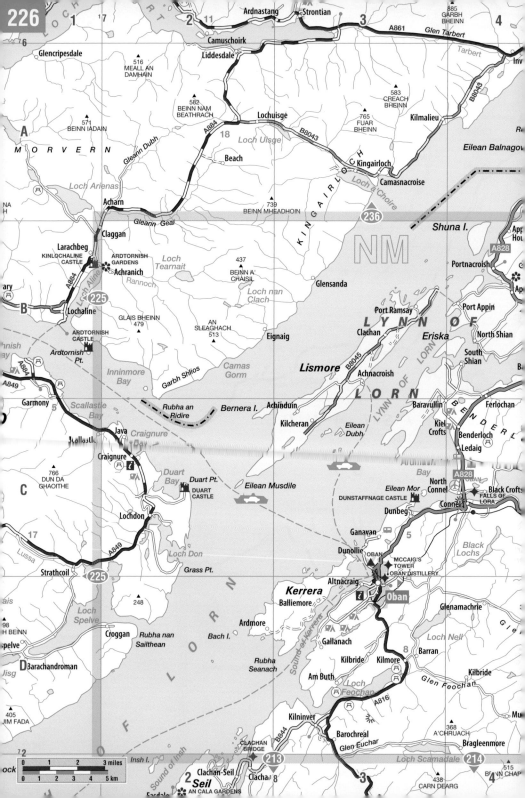

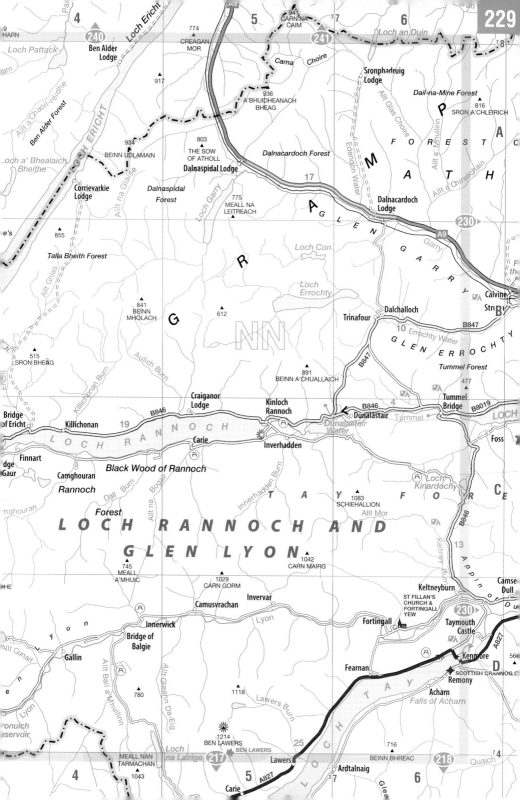

THE SMALL ISLES

1 **2** **3**

246 Kinloch Glen

Souç Gui̇ll
Bay

ilmory Glen

388

A'Bhrideanach

R Ù M

Kinloch

Rubha na Roinne

Loch Scresort

571
ORVAL

RÙM

KINLOCH
CASTLE

Rubha Port
na Caranean

Schooner Pt.

A

Harris

Glen Harris

812
ASKIVAL

Rubha Sgorr an t-Snidhe

781
AINSHVAL

SOUND

OF

RÙM

Rubha nam
Meirleach

Bay of Laig

Cleadale

Rubha an
Fhasaidh

Eigg

Kil

B

393
AN SGURR

Galmis

Ei

SOUND

OF

EIGG

Eilean nan Each

Muck

137

Port Mor

C

CASTLEBAY
LOCHBOISDALE
(Oct - Mar)

Sanna Point

223

Sanna Bay

Sanna

Achnaha

Portuairk

Point of
Ardnamurchan
ARDNAMURCHAN LIGHTHOUSE

Achosnich

Cairns of Coll

223

D

Rubha Mor

Eilean Mor

An Acairseid

B8007

Ormsaigmore

Kilch

Sorisdale

Ormsaigbeg

Bousd

Kilchoan
Bay

B8072

Gallanach

0   1   2   3 miles
0   1   2   3   4   5 km

L L

224

Ardmore Bay

Ardmore Pt.

Bloody

LOCH ARKAIG
4
5
2 2
6
9

Ardechvie
636
Letterfinlay
Glen Gloy
PARALLEL ROADS

Achnasaul
B8005
Clunes Forest
Altrua

727
Locheil Forest
Inver Mallie
Clunes
Upper Glenfintaig
684

Glen Mallie
Achnacarry
Bunarkaig
A82

Mallie
796
BEINN BHAN
CLAN CAMERON MUSEUM
Stronaba
654 COIRE CEIRSLE HILL
Bohuntine

A

Glen
Loy
Gairlochy
Kilmonivaig
COMMANDO MEMORIAL
Bohenie

Druim Fada
Glen Loy Forest
GREAT GLEN WAY
Brackletter
Highbridge
Spean Bridge
Inverroy
Roybridge
Achluachrac

Muirshearlich
Strone
Killiechonate
MONESSIE FALLS Braes
A8

239
Spean

Fassfern
NEPTUNE'S STAIRCASE LOCKS
TOR CASTLE
Leanachan Forest
724 BEINN CHLIANAIG

A830
11
TREASURES OF THE EARTH
B8004
A82
7

EIL
Corpach
Banavie
Torlundy
NEVIS RANGE MOUNTAIN EXPERIENCE
228

A861
Blaich
20
NN
B

Duisky
Caol
Lochside

Achaphubuil
INVERLOCHY CASTLE
Inverlochy
BEN NEVIS DISTILLERY VISITOR CENTRE
1177 STOB CHOIRE CLAURIGH

770 STOB COIRE A'CHEARCAILL
Camusnagaul
Claggan
1106

Trislaig
Fort William
Achintee
GLEN NEVIS VISITOR CENTRE
1345 BEN NEVIS
1234 AONACH BEAG
1094

Stronchreggan
WEST HIGHLAND MUSEUM
Ach an Todhair
GLEN NEVIS

Conaglen House
Glen Nevis House
11 ST

Druimarbin
Amhainn Rath
Creaguaineach Lodge

Inverscaddle Bay
14
Blarmachfoldach
Achriabhach
Nevis

Coruanan Lodge
Klachnish
1099 SGURR A' MHAIM
1130 BINNEIN MOR
Loch Eilde Beag
630

616
Blar a'Chaorainn
MAMORE FOREST
789

BEINN NA GUCAIG
WEST HIGHLAND WAY
Loch Eilde Mor
C

Glenrigh Forest
Inchree
796 MAM NA GUALAINN
Kinlochmore
Kinlochleven
BLACKWATER RESE

Keppanach
Onich
615
9
ALUMINIUM STORY VISITOR CENTRE
Leven

A82
North Ballachulish
B863
6 B863
867

HE
South Ballachulish
Loch
Leven
GLENCOE AND NORTH LORN FOLK MUSEUM
AONACH 967
953

A828
Ballachulish
Glencoe
GLENCOE
11
Coe
Altnafeadh
857 BEINN A' CHRULAISTE
228 Blac Lod

Glenduror Forest
947
GLENCOE VISITOR CENTRE
A82
BEN NEVIS AND
925
Kingshouse Hotel

Beinn a'Bheithir
1150 BIDEAN NAM BIAN
Coupall
GLENCOE SKI CENTRE
A82

Duror
994 SGOR NA H-ULAIDH
Dalness
Royal Forest
GLEN COE
Etive

879 FRAOCHAIDH
959 BEINN FHIONNLAIDH
Glen Etive
Alltchaorunn
1188

Elleric
227
4
5
883 STOB DUBH
2 2
1099 CLACH LEATHAD
6
Bà
228
5

Inverchornan
Loch h-Achlaise

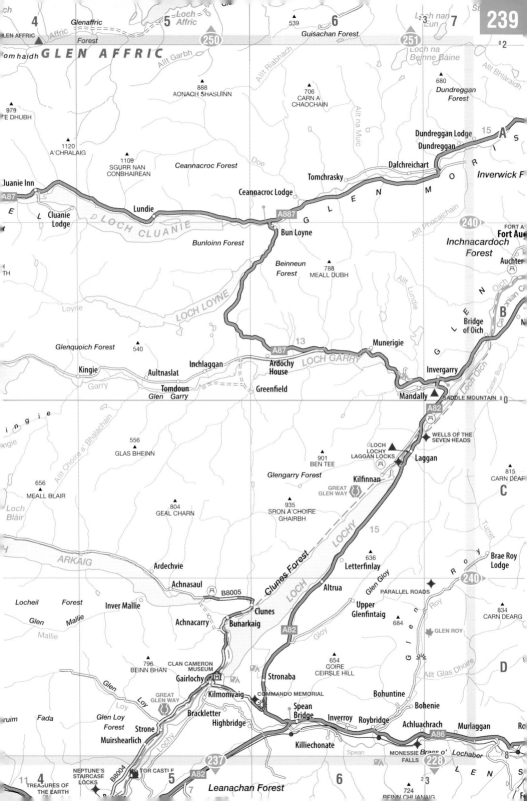

GLEN AFFRIC

Glenaffric
Loch Affric
GLEN AFFRIC Forest
250
251
539
Guisachan Forest
Loch nan Eun
Loch na Beinne Bàine
888
AONACH SHASUINN
706
CARN A CHAOCHAIN
680
Dundreggan Forest
979
E DHUBH
Dundreggan Lodge
Dundreggan
Inverwick F
1120
A'CHRALAIG
1109
SGURR NAN CONBHAIREAN
Ceannacroc Forest
Doe
Dalchreichart
Tomchrasky
GLEN
M
A
15
luanie Inn
A87
Ceannacroc Lodge
Lundie
Cluanie Lodge
LOCH CLUANIE
A887
Bun Loyne
Bunloinn Forest
G
Allt na Muic
Allt Phocaichain
Inchnacardoch Forest
Fort A
Fort Au
240
Auchter
Beinneun Forest
788
MEALL DUBH
Loch Loyne
LOCH LOYNE
Allt Lundie
E
Bridge of Oich
B
N
Loyne
Glenquoich Forest
540
Munerigie
13
A87
LOCH GARRY
G
Invergarry
LOCH OICH
Kingie
Aultnaslat
Inchlaggan
Ardochy House
Greenfield
Tomdoun
Glen Garry
Mandally
SADDLE MOUNTAIN
A82
WELLS OF THE SEVEN HEADS
ingie
556
GLAS BHEINN
901
BEN TEE
LOCH LOCHY LAGGAN LOCKS
Laggan
815
CARN DEAR
656
MEALL BLAIR
Loch Blàir
Glengarry Forest
Kilfinnan
804
GEAL CHARN
935
SRON A'CHOIRE GHAIRBH
GREAT GLEN WAY
C
ARKAIG
Ardechvie
Achnasaul
B8005
Clunes Forest
LOCH LOCHY
15
636
Letterfinlay
Glen Gloy
Brae Roy Lodge
240
Locheil Forest
Inver Mallie
Glen Mallie
Achnacarry
Bunarkaig
Clunes
A82
Altrua
PARALLEL ROADS
834
CARN DEARG
Mallie
Upper Glenfintaig
684
GLEN ROY
796
BEINN BHAN
CLAN CAMERON MUSEUM
Gairlochy
Stronaba
654
COIRE CEIRSLE HILL
Bohuntine
D
Glen
Loy
Kilmonivaig
GREAT GLEN WAY
COMMANDO MEMORIAL
Bohenie
Glen Loy Forest
Strone
Muirshearlich
Brackletter
Highbridge
Spean Bridge
Inverroy
Roybridge
Achluachrach
Murlaggan
A86
ruim
Fada
Killiechonate
Spean
MONESSIE FALLS
Brae o' Lochaber
8
GLEN
11
4
TREASURES OF THE EARTH
NEPTUNE'S STAIRCASE LOCKS
B8004
TOR CASTLE
237
A82
Leanachan Forest
6
228
724
BEINN CHLIANAIG
3
5
7

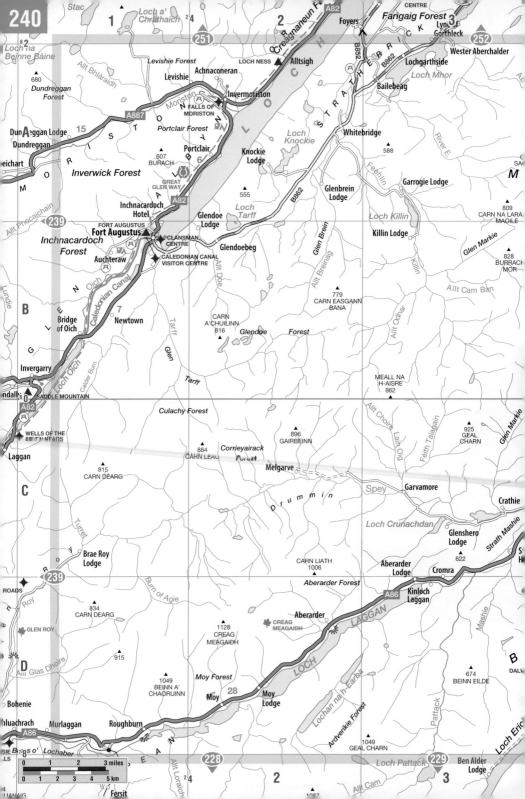

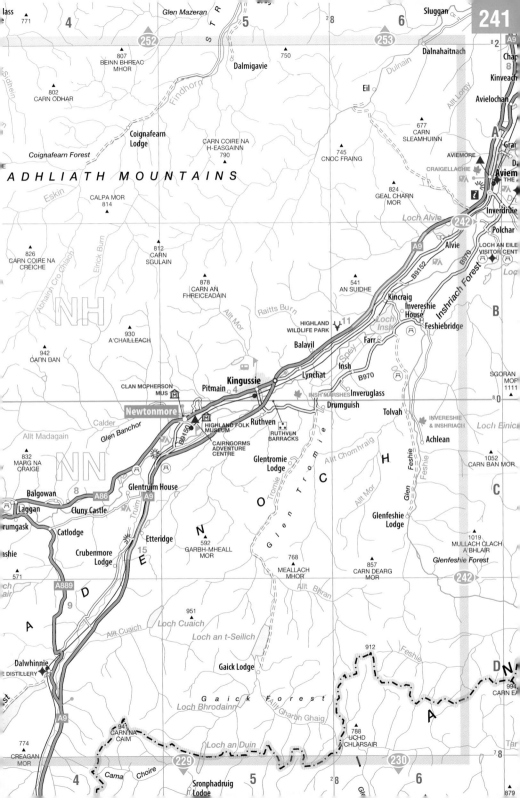

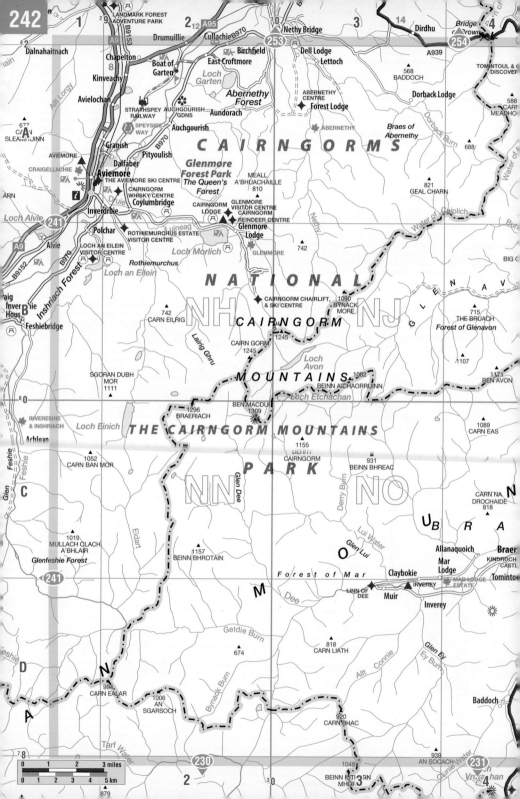

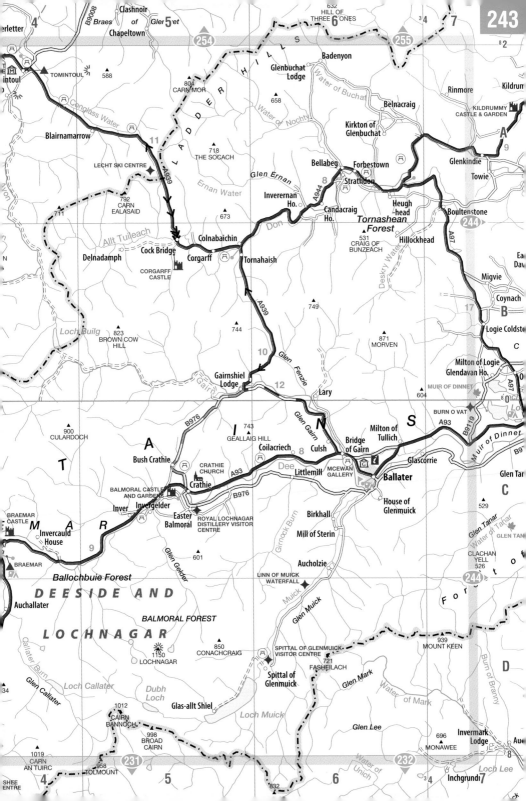

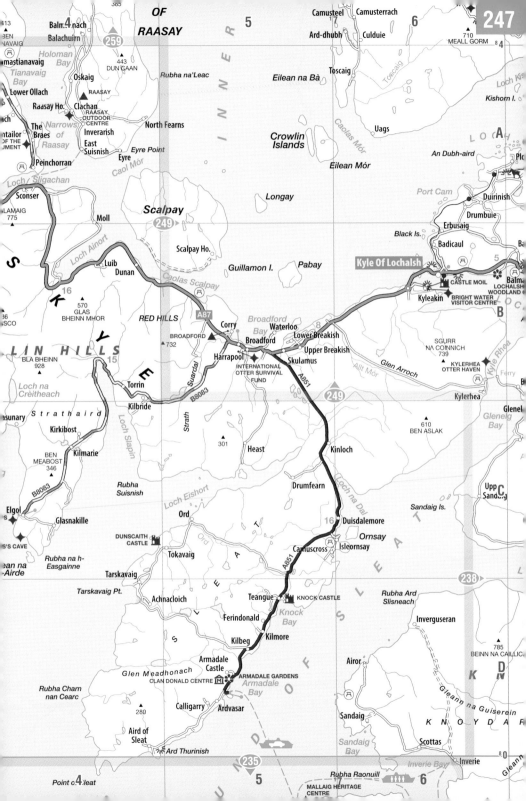

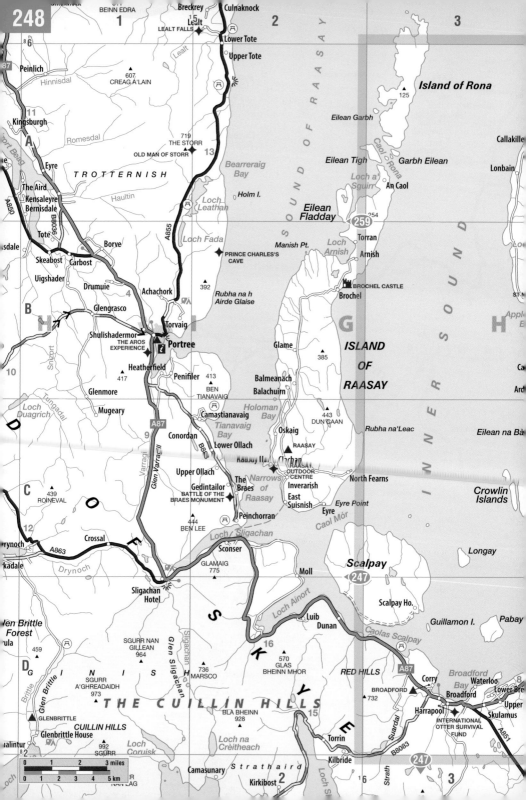

1   **2**   **3**

BEINN EDRA

Breckrey   Culnaknock

Lealt   Lealt FALLS

Lower Tote

Upper Tote

Peinlich

Hinnisdal

Kingsburgh

Romesdal

607
CREAG A'LAIN

THE STORR

OLD MAN OF STORR   719
THE STORR   13

Island of Rona   125

Eilean Garbh

Eilean Tigh   Garbh Eilean

Callakille

Lonbain

TROTTERNISH

Haultin

Bearreraig
Bay

SOUND OF RAASAY

Loch a'
Sguirr

Caol Rona

An Caol

ST.

Eyre

The Aird

Kensaleyre

Bernisdale

Tote

B8036

Loch
Leathan

Holm I.

Eilean
Fladday

Loch
Arnish

Torran

Arnish

259

Skeabost   Carbost

Uigshader

Loch Fada

Loch
Duagrich

Drumuie

Achachork

392

Rubha na h
Airde Glaise

PRINCE CHARLES'S
CAVE

Manish Pt.

BROCHEL CASTLE

Brochel

Glengrasco

Shulishadermor
THE AROS
EXPERIENCE
Portree

Torvaig

Glame

385

ISLAND
OF

RAASAY

Apple
B

Heatherfield

Penifiler

417

413

BEN
TIANAVAIG

Balmeanach
Balachuirn

443
DUN CAAN

Rubha na'Leac

Eilean na Bà

Glenmore

Mugeary

A87

Camastianavaig

Tianavaig
Bay

Holoman
Bay

Oskaig

Conordan

Glen Varragill

Lower Ollach

RAASAY

Clachan

RAASAY
OUTDOOR
CENTRE

Crowlin
Islands

439
ROINEVAL

Upper Ollach

Gedintailor
BATTLE OF THE
BRAES MONUMENT

The
Braes

Narrows
of
Raasay

Inverarish

East
Suisnish

North Fearns

Eyre Point

Eyre

INNER SOUND

Crossal

444
BEN LEE

Peinchorran

Loch Sligachan

Caol Mòr

Longay

Drynoch

A863

Sconser

Moll

Scalpay

Scalpay Ho.

247

Pabay

Sligachan
Hotel

GLAMAIG
775

Loch Ainort

Luib
Dunan

Caolas Scalpay

Guillamon I.

Glen Brittle
Forest

459

SGURR NAN
GILLEAN
964

736
MARSCO

570
GLAS
BHEINN MHOR

RED HILLS

A87

Broadford
Bay

Waterloo

Lower Bre

Corry

SGURR
A'GHREADAIDH
973

THE   CUILLIN   HILLS

BROADFORD

732

Broadford

Upper
Skulamus

Glenbrittle

CUILLIN HILLS

992
SGURR

BLA BHEINN
928

Harrapool
INTERNATIONAL
OTTER SURVIVAL
FUND

A851

Glenbrittle House

Loch
Coruisk

Loch na
Crèitheach

Torrin

247

Strath

B8083

Camasunary   Strathaird

Kirkibost

Kilbride

0   1   2   3 miles
0   1   2   3   4   5 km

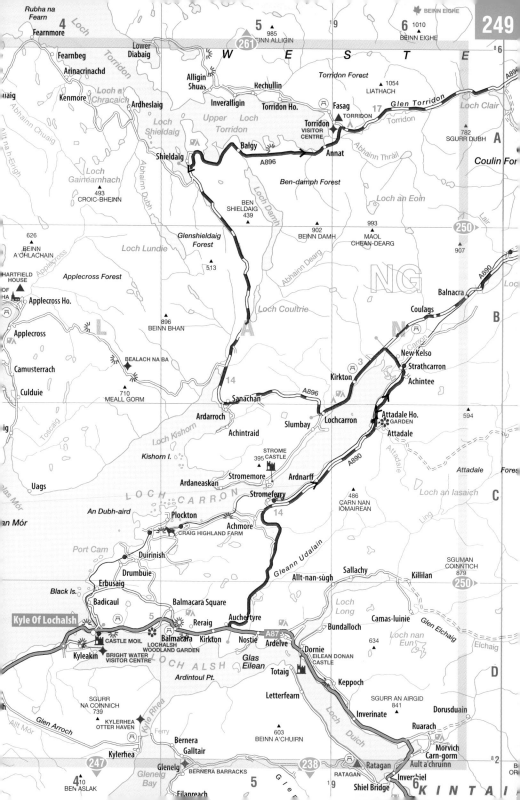

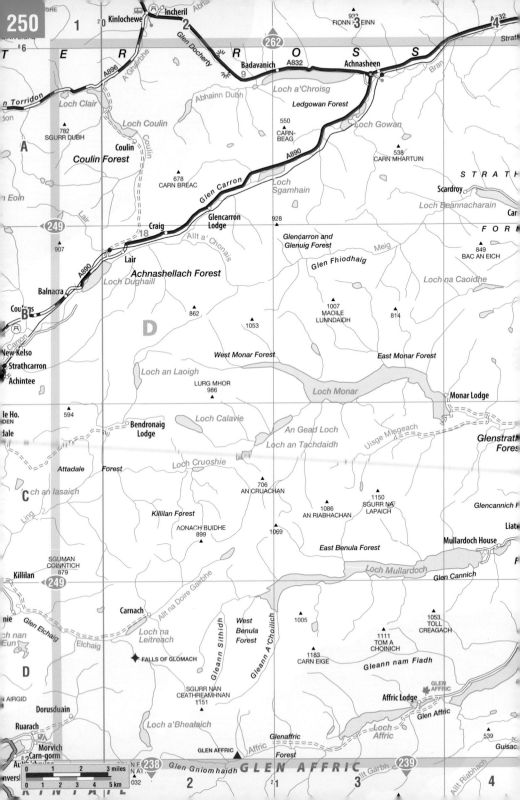

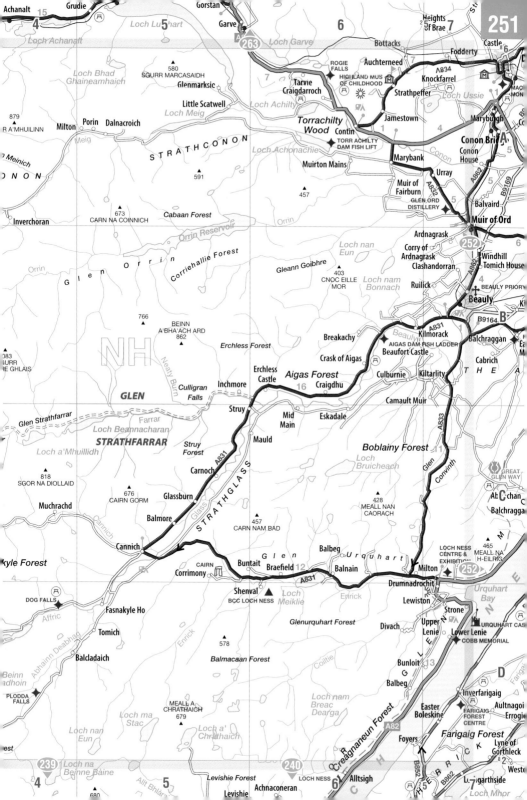

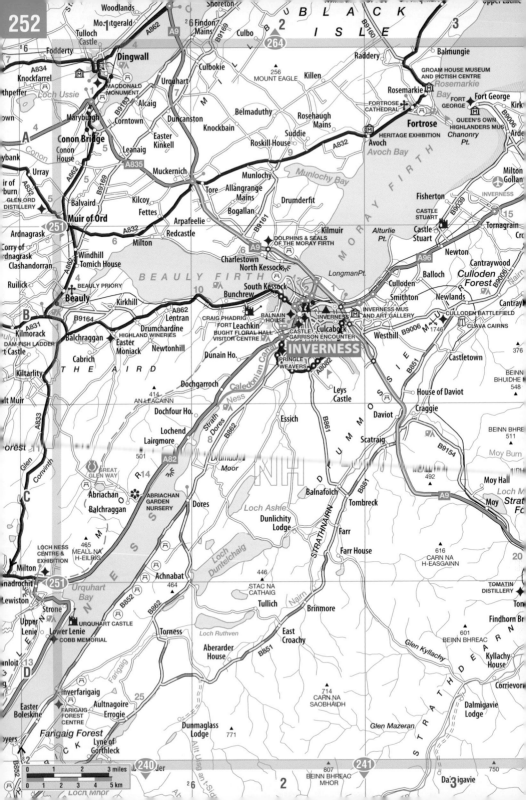

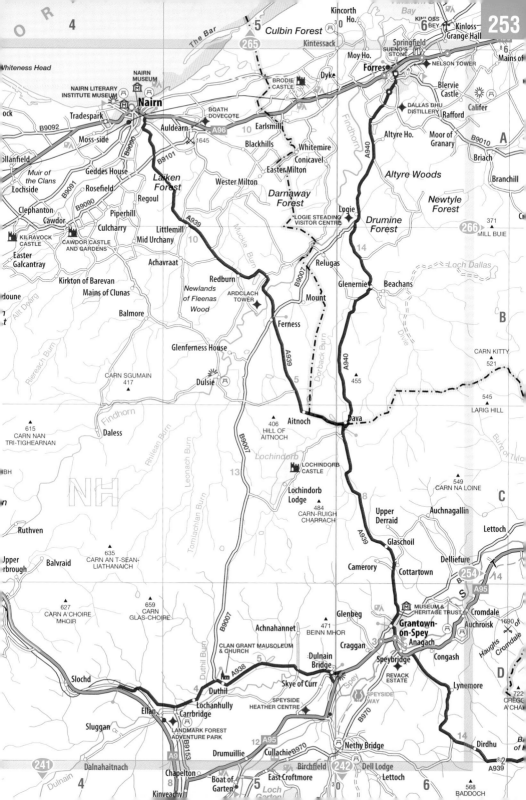

1 2 2 3

Fladda-chùain

A

TARBERT

LOCHMADDY

287

Rubha

Lub Score

Hungladder
Bornesketaig
Kilmuir
FLORA MACDONALD'S
MEMORIAL
Ki
Ba
L
Totscore

Idrigill

Waternish Point

B

Ascrib Islands

Kilbride Point

Uig Bay

BEN
GEARY
284

Ard Beag TRUMPAN CHURCH
Trumpan

Geary
Knockbreck
Gillen

Ru Chorachan

L O C H

Ardmore Pt.

Lower
Halistra
Upper Halistra
Hallin

S N I Z O R T

A87

Dunvegan Head

Mingay

Isay

Stein

Lusta

Greshornish Pt.

Lyndale Pt.

C

Galtrigill

Borreraig Uig

Husabost

Feriniquarrie

An Ceannaich

Lower Milovaig

Glasphein

Totaig

Upper
Milovaig

Lephin

B884

Oisgill Bay

Holmisdale

LIGHTHOUSE

Neist
Point

Skinidin

Ramasaig

Moonen Bay

Hoe Rape

Hoe Point

Loch
Bay

Claigan

327
BEINN
BHREAC

COLBOST FOLK
MUSEUM
Colbost

DUNVEGAN
CASTLE

Dunvegan

GIANT ANGUS
MACASKILL MUSEUM

Kilmuir
Lonmore

HEALABHAL
MHOR
468

Roag

Orbost

Macleod's
Tables

488
HEALABHAL BHEAG

Loch
Varkasaig

Greshornish

Lyndale Ho.

Treaslane

18
Flashader

Suladale

Edinbane

Blackhill

Glen Bernisda

CRUACHAN BEINN
A'CHEARCAILL
266

S
L
A

Roskhill

Vatten

Harlosh

Balmore

Loch Connan

10

Ose

Z

B885

246

Bracadale

D

8 4

0   1   2   3 miles
0 1 2 3 4 5 km

Geodha Mor

2

Harlosh I.

Tarner I. Ullinish

3

260

261

Eilean Trodday

Rubha na h-Aiseig

Long

20
Balmacqueen
Kilmaluag

A

MUSEUM OF
ISLAND LIFE

Eilean
Flodigarry
Flodigarry

MEALL NA
SUIRAMACH
543
Digg
Glashvin
THE QUIRAING
Stenscholl
Brogaig
Staffin
Staffin I.

Staffin
Bay

NG

B

TROTTERNISH

466
BIOD BUIDHE
Maligar
Elishader

Marishader
Loch Mealt
Valtos

Garros
Rubha nam
Brathairean

Balnaknock
611
BEINN EDRA
Breckrey
Culnaknock

Lealt
LEALT FALLS
Lower Tote

A855

Kilt Rock
KILT ROCK & MEALT FALLS

Upper Tote

Island of Rona

125

607
CREAG A'LAIN
Hinnisdal

Eilean Garbh

S
O
U
N
D

O
F

R
A
A
S
A
Y

burgh
Romesdal
719
THE STORR
OLD MAN OF STORR
13

Eilean Tigh
Garbh Eilean

Callakille

Lonbain

C

Eyre
TROTTERNISH
Haultin

Bearreraig
Bay
Holm I.

An Caol

Caol Rona

e Aird
ensaleyre
ernisdale
Tote
B8036
Borve
Carbost

Loch
Leathan

Eilean
Fladday
Loch a
Sguirr

249

Torran
Arnish

Manish Pt.
Loch
Arnish

Loch nan
Eun

CHAPEL O
ST MAELRUBH

D

Skeabost
Uigshader
Drumuie

Loch Fada

A855

4
Achachork

392
Rubha na h
Airde Glaise

BROCHEL CASTLE
Brochel

Applecross
Bay

Glengrasco

Torvaig

Glame

ISLAND

Camusteel

H
Shulishadermor
THE AROS
EXPERIENCE
Portree

Heatherfield
417
Penifiler
413
BEN
TIANAVAIG
Balmeanach
Balachuirn

OF
RAASAY
385
Ard-dhubh
8 4

H

Glenmore

Mugeary
A87
4
Camastianavaig
Tianavaig
Bay
Conordan
9
Holoman
Bay
Oskaig
5
248
443
DUN CAAN
Rubha na'Leac
6
Eilean na Bà
Tosca

G

EAN

1   ¹⁵   2   3

Garbh
Eilean
⁹0

Eilean Mhuire

Eilean an Tighe

Na h-Eileanan Mòra
(Shiant Islands)

◄288

A

B

NG

288

◄259

Eilean Trodday

Hunish

Rubha na h-Aiseig

C

DUNTULM
CASTLE
20
Balmacqueen

Duntulm   **Kilmaluag**

MUSEUM OF
ISLAND LIFE

Eilean
Flodigarry

Flodigarry

MEALL NA
SUIRAMACH
543 ▲

Staffin I.

◄259

Digg

ilvaxter
algown

Glashvin

Staffin
Bay

THE QUIRAING ◆   **Brogaig**

inicro

Stenscholl   **Staffin**

TROTTERNISH

Kilt Rock

466 ▲
BIOD BUIDHE

KILT ROCK & MEALT FALLS

Maligar   **Elishader**

D

Uig   *Loch Mealt*

Marishader   **Valtos**

▲ UIG

Garros

Rubha nam
Brathairean

Balnaknock   611 ▲
BEINN EDRA

Breckrey   **Culnaknock**

Earlish

Lealt

LEALT FALLS ◆

⁸6

Lower Tote

ASAY

0   1   2   3 miles

0   1   2   3   4   5 km

Upper Tote

¹5   2   3

607
CREAG A'LAIN

Hinnisdal

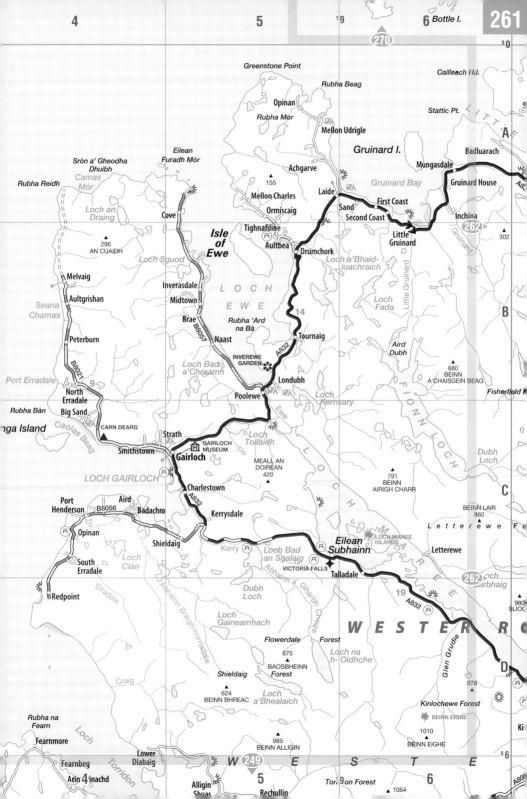

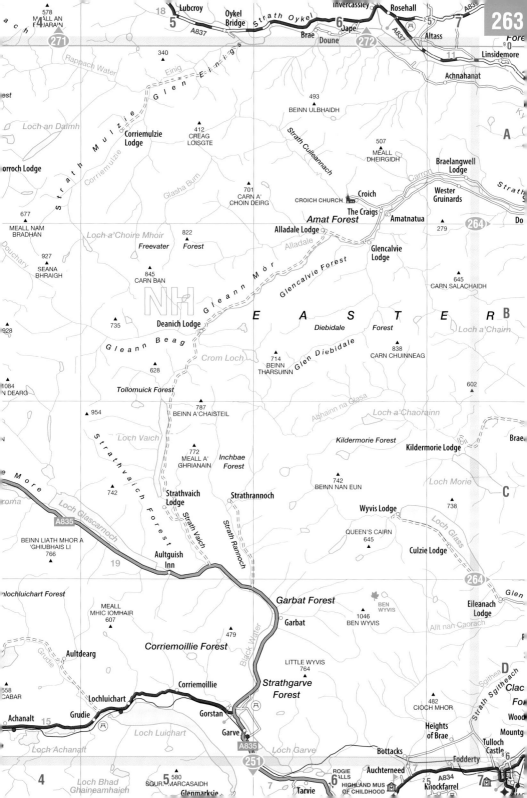

5 3⁰ **6** 9⁰

A274

NH   NJ   **A**

Backies

4 DUNROBIN CASTLE MUSEUM & GARDENS

Golspie

ton

LOCH FLEET

Littleferry

ourpenny

Embo

Embo Street

dy

WITCHES STONE
CARNEGIE
COURTHOUSE
VISITOR CENTRE

noch

OCH FIRTH

Tarbat Ness
TARBAT NESS LIGHTHOUSE

Wilkhaven

Whiteness Sands

B

TARBAT DISCOVERY
CENTRE

Bindal
Portmahomack

US'S

Inver

Rockfield

Balnagall

Arboll

Tarrel

Lochslin

Loch Eye
n

B9165

Geanies House

Rhynie

Fearn Station

165

Hill of Fearn   Fearn

FEARN
ABBEY   B9166

Hilton of Cadboll

Loans of Tullich

Balintore

B9175

SHANDWICK STONE
Shandwick

Ankerville

C

Chapelhill

Pitcalnie

Port an Righ

Nigg

203

King's Cave

nt Canisp

abruaich

A266   Burghea

Castlecraig

Ferry

RTY
HOUSE

Sutors of Cromarty

R'S BIRTHPLACE
& MUSEUM

BURGHEAD BAY

D

Lower
Hempriggs

Findhorn

Miltonhill

Findhorn Bay

ORAY FIRTH

Kincorth
Ho.

KINLOSS
ABBEY

B9011

Kinloss

Springfield   Grange Hall

A96

The Bar

Culbin Forest

Kintessack

Moy Ho.

SUENO'S
STONE

Mains o

NELSON TOWER

8 6 ₁

Whiteness Head

4

NAIRN
MUSEUM

253

5

BRODIE
CASTLE

Dyke 3⁰

Forres

6

Blervie

NAIRN LITERARY

A

B ◄ 265

C

D

E

1 **2** **3** **4**

8

Halliman
Skerries

Covesea
Skerries

LOSSIEMOUTH FISHERIES
& COMMUNITY MUSEUM

Stotfield

Branderburgh

Lossiemouth

Covesea

BURGHEAD
VISITOR
CENTRE

Burghead

Hopeman

Cummingston

Roseisle

B9040

Duffus

Gordonstoun

B9135

A941

Loch
Spynie

Lossie Forest

SPE

DUFFUS CASTLE

6

Lossie

Kingston

*Roseisle
Forest*

B9069

B9013

B9012

Quarrywood

PALACE OF
SPYNIE

Spynie

B9103

Leuchars Ho.

Lochhill

SCOTTISH
DOLPHIN
CENTRE

BURGHEAD BAY

Lower
Hempriggs

Newton

Coltfield

Miltonhill

Alves

Bishopmill

Elgin

ELGIN MUSEUM
CATHEDRAL
CASHMERE VISITOR
CENTRE

Garmouth

Urquhart

Lochs
Crofts

B9015

KINLOSS
ABBEY

Kinloss

Grange Hall

A96

OLD MILLS

Pittendreich

MORAY
MOTOR
MUSEUM

New
Elgin

A96

Lhanbryde

Moss of
Barmuckity

COXTON TOWER

9

BAXTERS
HIGHLAN
VILLAGE

Mosstodloch

12

Mains of Burgie

NELSON TOWER

Miltonduff

Paddockhaugh

Longmorn

Blackhills

B9103

Orbliston

Dipple

Orc

Monaughty Forest

PLUSCARDEN ABBEY

Auchtertyre

BIRNIE
CHURCH

Inchberry

Blervie
Castle

Califer

Barnhill

Foresterseat

Thomshill

MILLBUIES

*Teindland
Forest*

DALLAS DHU
DISTILLERY

Rafford

Door of
Granary

Woods

B9010

Briach

Branchill

*Dallas
Forest*

319

Kellas

B9010

Glenlatterach

338

13

Auchinroath

Newlands

B90

Spey

Newtyle
Forest

253

Dallas

Craigroy

365
CAIRN UISH

Glen of Rothes

A941

M O R A Y

371

MILL BUIE

5

Loch Dallas

Lossie

Rothes

GLEN GRANT
DISTILLERY

Burn of Rothes

SPEYSIDE
WAY

12

Ros

404
CARN NA
CAILLICHE

Elchies Forest

369

Whiteacen

471
BEN AIGAN

B90

Dandaleith

MACALLAN
DISTILLERY

Maggieknockate

0   1   2   3 miles

0 1 2 3 4 5 km

254

CARN KITTY

Upper
Knockando

CARDHU
DISTILLERY

Cardo

Archiestown

Knockando Ho.

B9102

Ringorm

SPEYSIDE WAY VISITOR CENTRE

Craigellachie

SPEYSIDE
COOPERAGE
VISITOR CENTRE

A941

Kininvie Ho.

Midtown of
Burnbroom

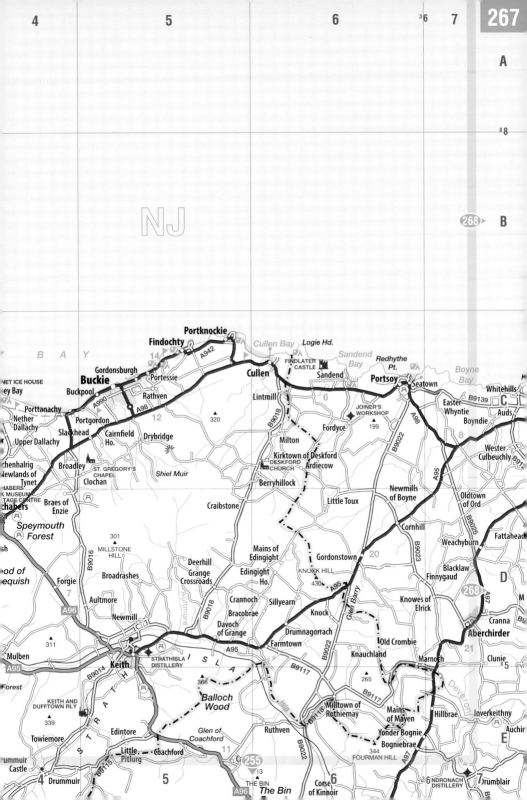

NJ

A

⁸8

268▶ B

C

Portknockie
Findochty
Buckie
Gordonsburgh
Portessie
Buckpool
Rathven
Porttanachy
Portgordon
Nether Dallachy
Upper Dallachy
Slackhead
Cairnfield Ho.
Drybridge
Broadley
ST. GREGORY'S CHAPEL
Clochan
Shiel Muir
Braes of Enzie
Speymouth Forest
Forgie
Aultmore
Newmill
Broadrashes
MILLSTONE HILL
Deerhill
Grange Crossroads
Crannoch
Bracobrae
Davoch of Grange
Keith
STRATHISLA DISTILLERY
KEITH AND DUFFTOWN RLY
Edintore
Towiemore
Little Pitlurg
Coachford
Glen of Coachford
Drummuir

Cullen Bay
Logie Hd.
Sandend Bay
Redhythe Pt.
Boyne Bay
Cullen
FINDLATER CASTLE
Sandend
Portsoy
Seatown
Whitehills
Lintmill
Easter Whyntie
Auds
Boyndie
JOINER'S WORKSHOP
Fordyce
Milton
Wester Culbeuchly
Kirktown of Deskford
DESKFORD CHURCH
Ardiecow
Newmills of Boyne
Oldtown of Ord
Berryhillock
Little Toux
Craibstone
Cornhill
Weachyburn
Fattahead
Mains of Edingight
Gordonstown
KNOCK HILL
Blacklaw
Finnygaud
Edingight Ho.
Sillyearn
Glen Barry
Knowes of Elrick
268
Cranna
Knock
Aberchirder
Drumnagorrach
Farmtown
Old Crombie
Knauchland
Marnoch
Clunie
A95
Balloch Wood
B9117
Milltown of Rothiemay
Mains of Mayen
Hillbrae
Inverkeithny
Auchir
Glen of Coachford
Ruthven
Yonder Bognie
Bogniebrae
FOURMAN HILL
255
THE BIN
The Bin
Corse of Kinnoir
NDRONACH DISTILLERY
rumblair

BAY

D

⁸8

21

E

A942
A990
A98
A95
A96
B9016
B9018
B9014
B9117
B9022
B9118
B9023
B9025
B9139
B9117

14
12
320
6
199
8
301
20
430
7
311
265
366
339
344
13
11

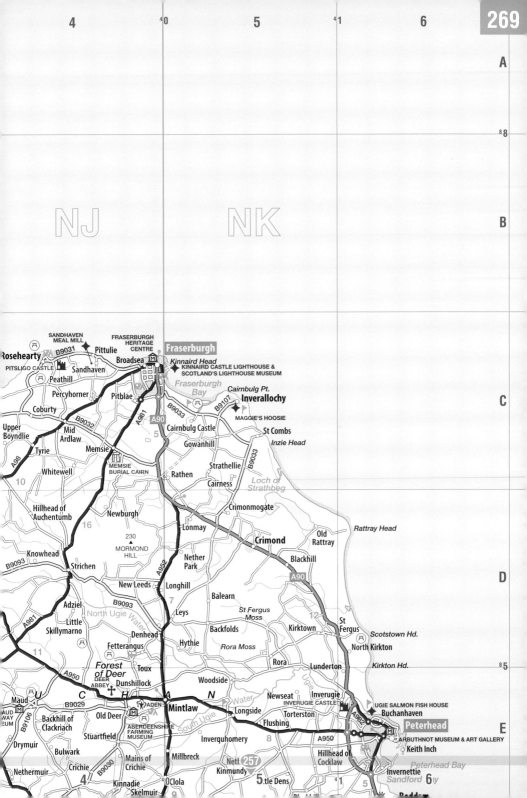

NJ NK

SANDHAVEN
MEAL MILL
Rosehearty
PITSLIGO CASTLE
B9031
Pittulie
Sandhaven
Peathill
Percyhorner
Coburty
Upper
Boyndlie
A98
Tyrie
Mid
Ardlaw
Memsie
Whitewell
MEMSIE
BURIAL CAIRN
Hillhead of
Auchentumb
Newburgh
Knowhead
230
MORMOND
HILL
B9093
Strichen
New Leeds
B9093
Adziel
Little
Skillymarno
A981
Denhead
Fetterangus
Forest
of Deer
DEER
ABBEY
Toux
Dunshillock
Maud
U
C
H
A
N
B9029
Old Deer
Mintlaw
AUD
WAY
EUM
B9106
Backhill of
Clackriach
ABERDEENSHIRE
FARMING MUSEUM
Drymuir
Stuartfield
Bulwark
Mains of
Crichie
Nethermuir
Crichie
B9030
Kinnadie
Skelmuir
Clola

FRASERBURGH
HERITAGE
CENTRE
Fraserburgh
Broadsea
Kinnaird Head
KINNAIRD CASTLE LIGHTHOUSE &
SCOTLAND'S LIGHTHOUSE MUSEUM
Fraserburgh
Bay
Pitblae
A981
A90
B9033
Cairnbulg Pt.
Inverallochy
B9107
MAGGIE'S HOOSIE
Cairnbulg Castle
St Combs
Gowanhill
Inzie Head
Rathen
Strathellie
B9033
Cairness
Loch of
Strathbeg
Crimonmogate
Lonmay
Crimond
Old
Rattray
Rattray Head
Nether
Park
Blackhill
A90
A952
Longhill
Balearn
Leys
St Fergus
Moss
Kirktown
St
Fergus
Scotstown Hd.
North Kirkton
Backfolds
Rora Moss
Kirkton Hd.
Hythie
Rora
Lunderton
Woodside
Newseat
Inverugie
INVERUGIE CASTLE
UGIE SALMON FISH HOUSE
Buchanhaven
Torterston
Longside
Peterhead
Flushing
A952
ARBUTHNOT MUSEUM & ART GALLERY
A950
Keith Inch
Inverquhomery
Millbreck
Hillhead of
Cocklaw
Invernettie
Peterhead Bay
Sandford
Nett
257
Kinmundy
tle Dens

1 ¹9 2 ²0 3 4

276

⁹4

Eil. a'Bhreitheimh

Rubha a

Meall Mór

Eddrachillis Bay Ca E

A

Point of Stoer

Oldany Island

Cirean Geardail

R. nan Còsan

Eilean Chrona

Culkein Drumbeg

▲ 161

Culkein

Oldany

Loch Nedd

Cluas Deas

Clashnessie Bay

Drumbeg

Nedd

Achnacarnin

Clashmore

Clashnessie

Loch Poll

Balchladich

Rienachait

13

Stoer

Loch Bear

B

Rubh'a' Mhill Dheirg

Clachtoll

Loch Cròcach

Bay of Stoer

B869

R. Leumair

Achmelvich Bay

Rhicarn

NB

Achmelvich

A837

Inver

ACHMELVICH BEACH

ASSYNT VISITOR CENTRE

Brackloch

Rubha Rodha

Baddidarach

Lochinver

Glencanisp Lodge

Soyea I.

Loch Inver

Kirkaig Pt.

Badnaban

ASS

A'Chleit

Strathan

Loch Kirkaig

Inverkirkaig

Kirkaig

Rubha na Breige

Fion

Rubha Coigeach

Eilean Mór

Falls

C

E N A R D   B A Y

COI

Camas Eilean Ghlais

Rubha Mor

Rubh'a' Choin

Reiff

Inverpolly Lodge

Loch Sionasc

Brae of Achnahaird

Altandhu

SUMMER ISLES SMOKEHOUSE

Polly

Eilean Mullagrach

Loch Vatachan

Loch Osgaig

Aird of Coigach

Inverpolly Forest

Isle Ristol

Polbain

613 ▲ STAC POLLAIDH

Glas-leac Mór

Loch Bad a'Ghaill

Loch Lurgainn

769 CUL BE

Achiltibuie

ACHILTIBUIE GARDENS

Badentarbat Bay

Polglass

Tanera Beg

Summer Isles

Tanera Mór

Horse I.

Achininver

C O I G A C

D

Horse Sound

Glas-leac Beag

Culnacraig

743 BEINN MOR COIGACH

Priest I.

Eilean Dubh

Achduart

Runie

Bottle I.

Carn nan Sgeir

Camas Mór

Strath

⁹0

Loch Kanaird

3 miles

0 1 2 3 4 5 km

261

262

Isle Martin

Gr

2 Cailleach Hd. ²0

STORNOWAY

3

4 ⁴5

Ardmair

Rubha Beag

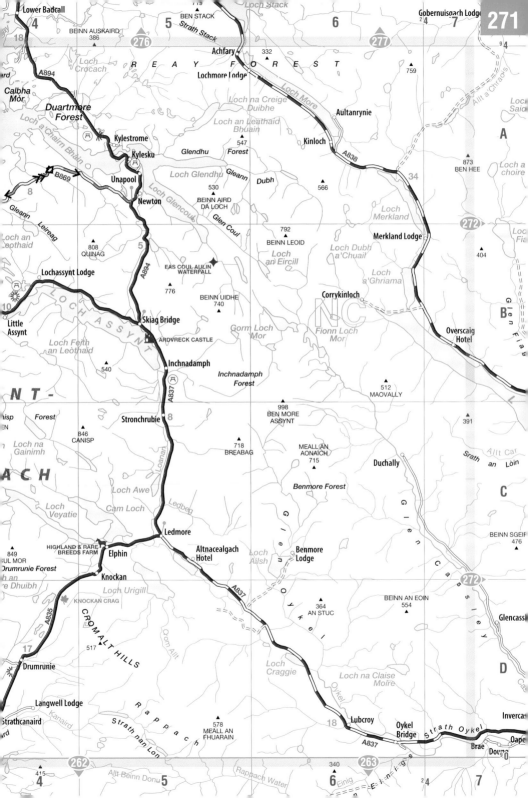

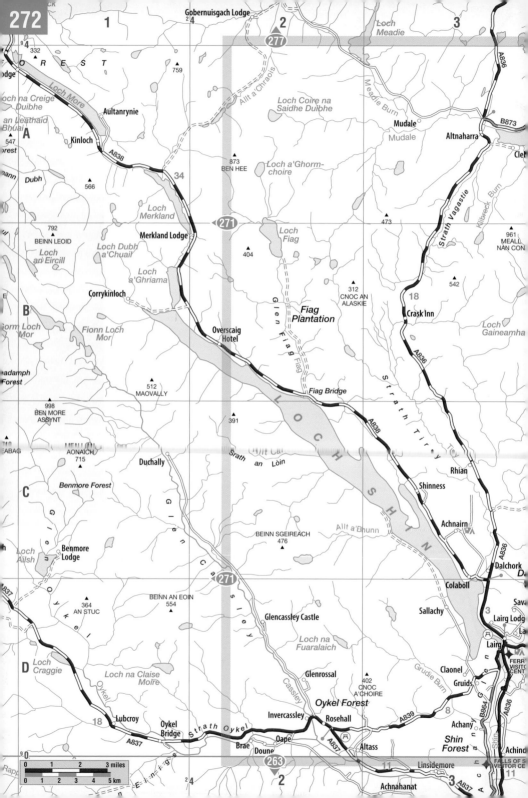

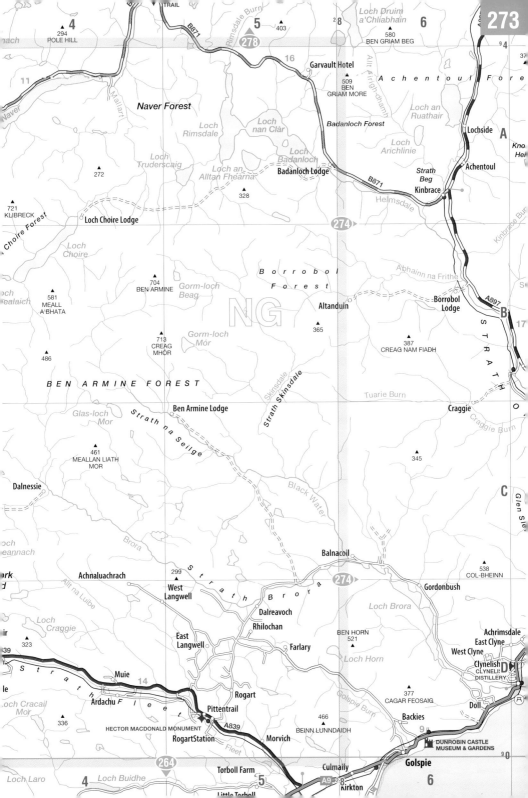

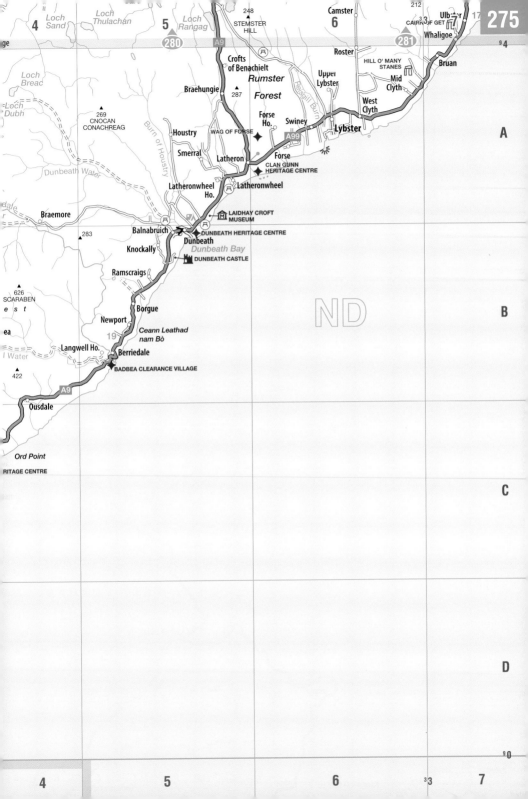

4 Loch Sand Loch Thulachan **5** Loch Rangag **6** Camster 212 Ulb... 17

280 A9 248 STEMSTER HILL CAIRN OF GET 281 Whaligoe 9 4

Loch Breac Crofts of Benachielt Roster HILL O' MANY STANES Bruan

Braehungie *Rumster* 287 Upper Lybster Mid Clyth

269 CNOCAN CONACHREAG *Forest* West Clyth

Loch Dubh Houstry Forse Ho. Swiney **A**

WAG OF FORSE Lybster

Smerral Latheron Forse **A99**

Dunbeath Water CLAN GUNN HERITAGE CENTRE

Latheronwheel Ho. Latheronwheel

Braemore LAIDHAY CROFT MUSEUM

283 Balnabruich Dunbeath DUNBEATH HERITAGE CENTRE

Knockally *Dunbeath Bay* **B**

Ramscraigs DUNBEATH CASTLE

626 SCARABEN Borgue **ND**

Newport *Ceann Leathad nam Bò*

422 19 Langwell Ho. Berriedale

A9 BADBEA CLEARANCE VILLAGE **C**

Ousdale

Ord Point

RITAGE CENTRE **D**

9 0

4 **5** **6** 3 3 **7**

CAPE WRATH

Kearvaig

371
SGRIBHIS-
BHEINN

Inshore

Geodha Ruadh na Fola

Bay of Keisgaig

Loch
Keisgaig

Geodha Ruadh

457
FASHVEN

Ac

Loch A
na Be

Am Balg

Sandwood
Loch

423
BEINN DEARG

Rubh'an Fhir Léithe

485
CREAG
RIABHACH

Gruc

Loch na
Gáinimh

S t r a t h   S h i n a r y

332
GHLAS
BHEINN

Sheigra

Balchrick

A838

Droman

Oldshore Beg

521
FARRMHEALL

Eilean Roin Mor

Oldshoremore

19

Kinlochbervie

Gualin Ho.

Loch Clash

B801

Badcall

Bagh Loch an Roin

Achriesgill

9

CRA

Strath Diona
Dionard

L. na Claise
Carnaich

Achlyness

Loch Dughaill

Ceathramh Garbh

Rhiconich

Ardmore Pt.

GANU MOR
908

Rubha Ruadh

Ardmore

A838

Foinaven

Fanagmore

N O R T H - W E S T   S U T H E R L A N D

Loch Dior

Tarbet

Loch a'Garbh-
bhaid Mór

Handa Island

Foindle

Loch an Eas
Uaine

Loch nam
Brac

A894

Laxford Bridge

Scourie Bay

787
ARKLE

Scourie More

Scourie

Lochstack Lodge

Rubh'Aird an t-Sionnaich

A838

Gorm Loch

Loch Stack

Upper Badcall

Lower Badcall

719
BEN STACK

Badcall Bay

18

BEINN AUSKAIRD
386

Strath Stack

Lochmore Lodge

270

271

Achfary

332

Rubha a'Mhuileard

A894

Loch
Crocach

R   E   A   Y   F   O   R   E

Lochmore Lodge

Meall Mór

0   1   2   3 miles

0   1   2   3   4   5 km

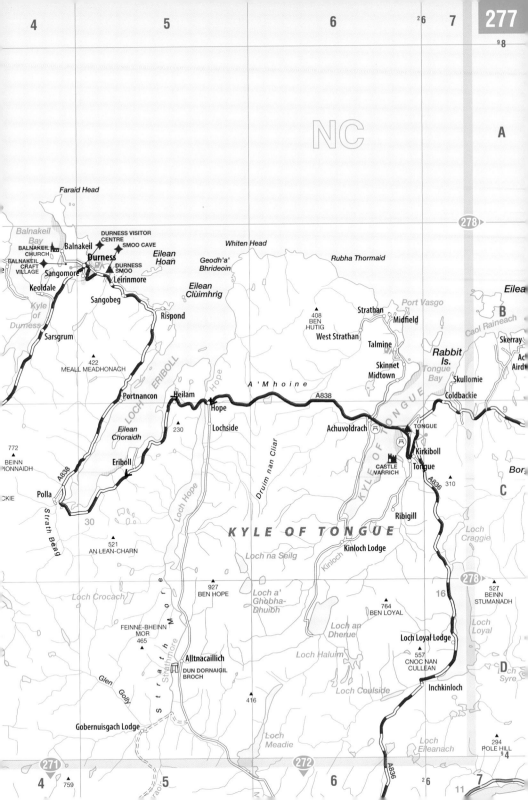

4 5 6 ²6 7

⁹8

NC

A

Faraid Head

〈278〉

Whiten Head

Rubha Thormaid

Eilea

Balnakeil
Bay
BALNAKEIL
CHURCH
BALNAKEIL
CRAFT
VILLAGE
Balnakeil
DURNESS VISITOR
CENTRE
SMOO CAVE
Durness
DURNESS
SMOO
Sangomore
Leirinmore
Keoldale
Sangobeg
Kyle
of
Durness
Sarsgrum
Eilean
Hoan
Eilean
Clùimhrig
Geodh'a'
Bhrideoin

Port Vasgo

Strathan

Midfield

Eilea

Caol Raineach

B

West Strathan

408
BEN
HUTIG

Talmine

Skerray

Ac
Airdt

Rabbit
Is.

422
MEALL MEADHONACH

Skinnet
Midtown

Skullomie

Rispond

Tongue
Bay

Coldbackie

LOCH ERIBOLL

Portnancon

Heilam

Hope

A'Mhoine

A838

Achuvoldrach

Tongue

772
BEINN
PIONNAIDH

Eilean
Choraidh

230

Lochside

Loch Hope

Druim nan Cliar

Kirkiboll

Tongue

Bor

A838

Eriboll

Polla

KIE

Strath Beag

30

521
AN LEAN-CHARN

CASTLE
VARRICH

KYLE OF TONGUE

Ribigill

C

310

Loch
Craggie

〈278〉

KYLE OF TONGUE

Loch na Seilg

Kinloch Lodge

16

527
BEINN
STUMANADH

927
BEN HOPE

Loch a'
Ghobha-
Dhuibh

Loch Crocach

FEINNE-BHEINN
MOR
465

Strathmore

Kinloch

764
BEN LOYAL

Loch an
Dherue

Loch
Loyal

Alltnacaillich
DUN DORNAIGIL
BROCH

Loch Halium

Loch Loyal Lodge

557
CNOC NAN
CULLEAN

D

ch
Syre

416

Loch Coulside

Inchkinloch

Glen Golly

Gobernuisgach Lodge

294
POLE HILL
⁹4

Loch
Meadie

Loch
Eileanach

Loch

A836

〈271〉

759

〈272〉

4 5 6 ²6 7

11

1 ²6 2 3

⁹8

A

277

Whiten Head

Rubha Thormaid

Port Vasgo

Eilean nan Ron

Ardmore Pt.

B 408
BEN
HUTIG

Strathan

Midfield

West Strathan

Talmine

Skinnet
Midtown

A'Mhoine

A838

Achuvoldrach

Rabbit
Is.

Tongue
Bay

Skullomie

Coldbackie

Caol Raineach

Skerray

Achtoty
Airdtorrisdale

Torrisdale

Neave I. or
Coombe I.

Torrisdale
Bay

Borgie

9

Farr Pt.

Kirtomy Pt.

STRATHNAVER
MUSEUM

Bettyhill

Invernaver

Leckfurin

Farr

Swordly

Achina

Kirtomy

Armadale
Bay

Armadale

A836

17

Loch Meadie

KYLE OF TONGUE

Tongue

Kirkiboll

CASTLE
VARRICH

Tongue

310

Borgie Forest

Borge

B871

Buidhe Mor

ACHANLOCHY
CLEARANCE VILLAGE

Skelpick

Skelpick Burn

Clachan Burn

Loch Mor na
Caorach

Loch nan
Clach

C Uim nan C ar

Ribigill

YLE OF TONGUE

Loch na Seilg

Kinloch Lodge

Kinloch

A836

Loch
Craggie

Achagary

Carnachy

Rhifail

9

STRATHNAVER

293
BEINN
RIFA-GIL

Loch
Strathy

Loch a'
Ghobha-
Dhuibh

277

16

764
BEN LOYAL

527
BEINN
STUMANADH

Loch an
Dherue

557
CNOC NAN
CULLEAN

Loch Loyal Lodge

Loch
Loyal

Skail

D 416

Loch Halium

Inchkinloch

Loch Coulside

Loch
Syre

Langdale

Syre

Dalvina Lo.

Naver

ROSAL CLEARANCE
TRAIL

B873

Rimsdale Burn

403

Loch
Meadie

Loch
Eileanach

294
POLE HILL

273

Garvar

A836

0 1 2 3 miles
0 1 2 3 4 5 km

⁹4

²6

11

2

3

16

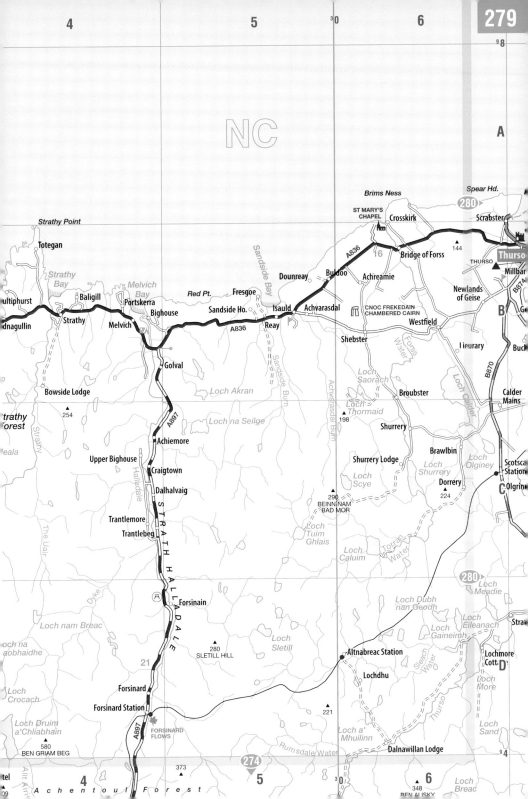

PENTLAND FIRTH

Brough Ness

4 · 5 · 6 · ³5 · 7

⁹8

Langaton Point

Muckle
Skerry

Nethertown

**Island of
Stroma**

53 ▲

Red Head

Pentland
Skerries

Mell Head

Uppertown

(May–Sept)

A

Men of Mey

St John's Pt.

Boars of Duncansby

East Mey

Gills Bay

Huna

DUNCANSBY HEAD

CASTLE
OF MEY

Gills

Kirkstyle

Mey

A836

John o'
Groats

Barrock

Canisbay

A99

Stacks of Duncansby

Inkstack

19

283

124 ▲

Brabster

Skirza

Lochend

Tofts

Gill Burn

Skirza Head

Freswick

Freswick Bay

Slickly

A99

Ness Head

ND

Reaster

BUCHOLLY CASTLE

madden

Alterwall

CAITHNESS
BROCH CENTRE

Lyth

LYTH ARTS CENTRE

Auckengill

B

Barrock Ho.

Sortat

Nybster

Howe

16

Brough Head

Keiss

Burn of Lyth

Mireland

KEISS CASTLE

Kirk

*Loch of
Wester*

Myrelandhorn

B870

SINCLAIR'S

Killimster

BAY

B876

ains of Watten

CASTLE
GIRNIGOE

Reiss

CASTLE
SINCLAIR

Winless

Noss Head

Wick

60

A99

B874

Ackergill

Sealky Head

C

Bilbster

WICK

Staxigoe

Strath

Reiss

A882

WICK
HERITAGE
MUS

Papigoe

Stirkoke Ho.

Milton

Broadhaven

Wick Bay

Newton

Old Wick

Whiterow

CASTLE OF OLD WICK

South Hd.

pster

Tannach

Hempriggs House

Gote O'Tram

141 ▲
HILL OF
OLICLETT

*Loch
Hempriggs*

Helman Hd.

A99

D

Gansclet

Thrumster

*Loch of
Yarrows*

Sarclet

212 ▲

Sarclet Hd.

Ulbster

17

CAIRN OF GET

Whaligoe

⁹4

275

HILL O' MANY
STANES

4

Bruan

Mid

5 · 6 · ³5 · 7

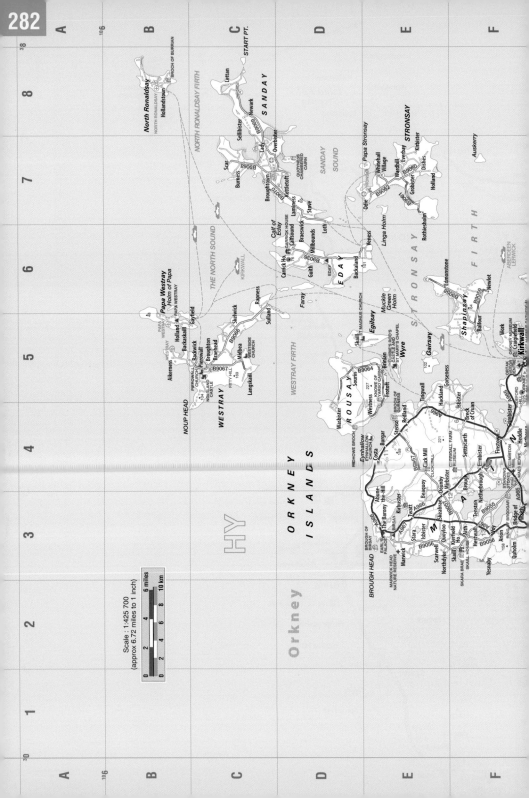

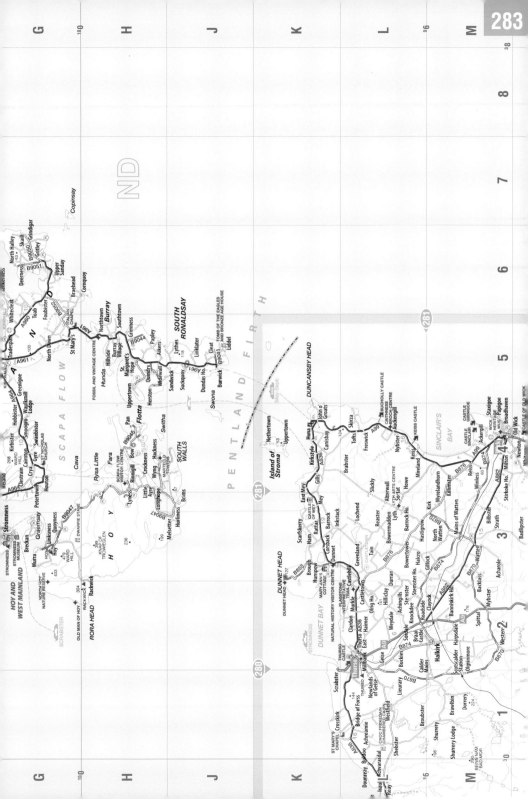

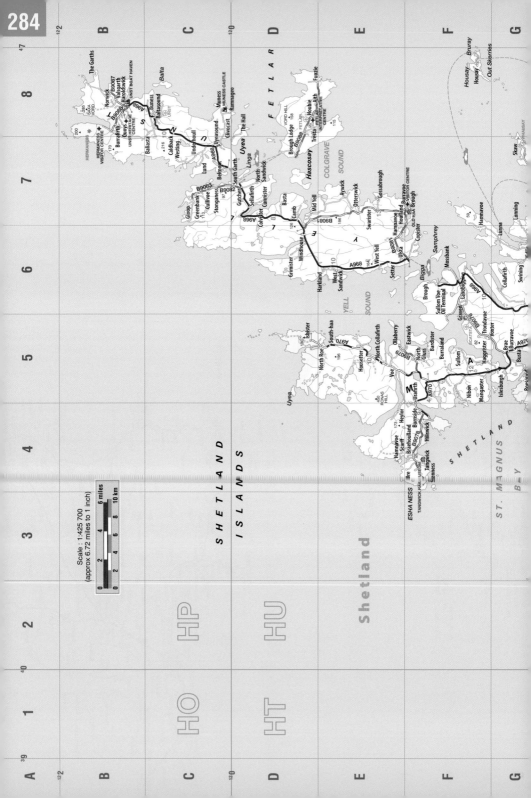

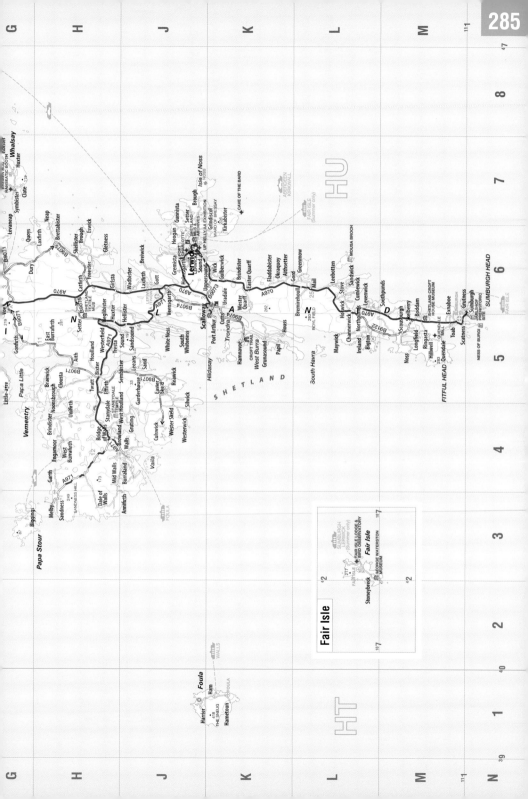

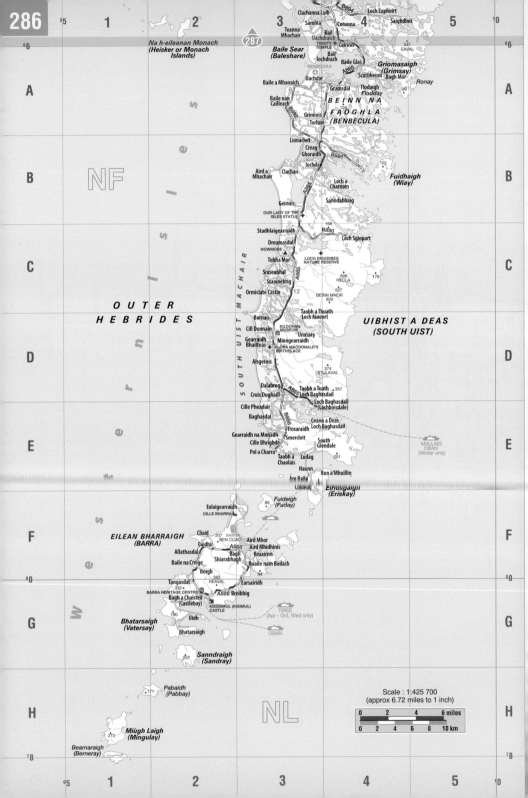

Scale : 1:425 700
(approx 6.72 miles to 1 inch)

| 0 | 2 | 4 | 6 miles |

| 0 | 2 | 4 | 6 | 8 | 10 km |

St. Kilda

NA

NF

Boreray
384

CNOC
GLAS *Soay*
376   *ST KILDA*

CONACHAIR
376

MULLACH BI
358 ST KILDA
*St Kilda or Hirta
(Hiort)*

AN CAOLAS
IRON AGE HOUSE
Croft
*Pabay
Mor*
Tobson
NORSE
Aird Uig
MILL
Bhaltos
Cliobh
Breacleit
Timsgearraidh
Miabhig
BERNERA
Cradhlastadh
Riof
Uigen
A
Càrnais
Crulabh
Mangurstadh
Eadar Dha
Geisiadar
Fhadhail
SUAINAVAL
429
288
Einacleite
Islibhig
Breanais
574
B901
MEALISVAL
Giosla
B
719
Mealasta Island
BEINN MHEADHONACH

NB

Scarp
308
STULAVAL
579
C
Huisinis SOUTH LEWIS
489 TIRGA MOR 659 Aird a' Mh
679 ULLAVAL
Abhainn Suidhe UISGNAVAL
MORE CLISHAM
Gobhaig 729 799
HARRIS AND
Cliasmol B887 CEANN A TUATH
Miabhag HEARADH A85
Bun Al
NORTH UIST Ead
OLD WHALING
STATION
Tarasaigh Aird Asaig
(Taransay) 436
BEN LUSKENTYRE
99 Paible Losgaintir Tairbeart
LUSKENTYRE 467 (Tarbert)
BEACH 288 Mia
Seilebost
D
E
OUTER Seilebost
A859
HEBRIDES Borve Lodge 23 A859 Na Hearadh
Buirgh (HARRIS)
SCARISTA
STANDING STONE
CHAIPAVAL Aird Mhighe
365 Sgarasta Mhor 386 Liceasto Greosabhagh
398 Geocrab Leac a' Li
BLEAVAL Beacrabhaic Cliuthar
Taobh Tuath Caolas
SEALLAM Fleoideabhagh Stocinis
Pabaidh Aird
(Pabbay) Manais
Mhighe
Fionnsbhagh Cuidhtinis
An t-Ob 459
(Leverburgh) ROINEABHAL Boirseam
Ensay Cairminis Sraanda Lingreabhagh
Killegray Roghadal
Eilean Ruisigearraidh
Bhearnaraigh BERNERAY ST CLEMENT'S
(Berneray) Borgh CHURCH
Baile
Boreray

NF

Port nan Long
Valley Baile Mhic Phail
Oronsay 190
Scolpaig Greinetobht Trumaisgearraidh
SCOLPAIG TOWER 20 A865 Solas
Baile Mhartainn Maladeit *Hermetray*
Hosta 180 A865
Taigh a Ghearraidh 133 Lochportain
Hoga Baile
Gearraidh Raghaill Loch nam Madadh
230 (Lochmaddy)
Ceann a Bhaigh MARRIVAL TAIGH
Claddach-knockline CHEARSABHAGH
Paibeil MUSEUM UIG
Baile Mor Cladach
CLACH MHOR A CHE Chirebost 250
STANDING STONES UIBHIST A TUATH
NG
Kirkibost Island (NORTH UIST)
Clachan na Luib 281
Na h-eileanan Monach BARPA LANGASS CAIRN SOUTH LEE
(Heisker or Monach Samhla
Islands) Loch Euphoirt Saighdinis
Teanna Mhachair Corunna
Bail
Uachdraich
Baile Sear Cairinis
(Baleshare) TRINITY 286 457
TEMPLE EAVAL
Bail *Griomasaigh*
Iochdrach *(Grimsay)*
Baile Glas Scotbheinn Bagh Mor
Bonay
Uachdar
BENBECULA

Index to road maps

How to use the index

Example

Thistleton Rutland **116 D2**

└ grid square

└ page number

└ county or unitary authority
(only shown for duplicate
names)

Guern	**Guernsey**	Reading	**Reading**
Gwyn	**Gwynedd**	Redcar	**Redcar and**
Halton	**Halton**		**Cleveland**
Hants	**Hampshire**	Renfs	**Renfrewshire**
Hereford	**Herefordshire**	Rhondda	**Rhondda Cynon Taff**
Herts	**Hertfordshire**	Rutland	**Rutland**
Highld	**Highland**	S Ayrs	**South Ayrshire**
Hrtlpl	**Hartlepool**	Scilly	**Scilly**
Hull	**Hull**	S Glos	**South**
Invclyd	**Inverclyde**		**Gloucestershire**
IoM	**Isle of Man**	Shetland	**Shetland**
IoW	**Isle of Wight**	Shrops	**Shropshire**
Jersey	**Jersey**	S Lanark	**South Lanarkshire**
Kent	**Kent**	Slough	**Slough**
Lancs	**Lancashire**	Som	**Somerset**
Leicester	**City of Leicester**	Soton	**Southampton**
Leics	**Leicestershire**	Southend	**Southend-on-Sea**
Lincs	**Lincolnshire**	Staffs	**Staffordshire**
London	**Greater London**	Stirling	**Stirling**
Luton	**Luton**	Stockton	**Stockton-on-Tees**
Mbro	**Middlesbrough**	Stoke	**Stoke-on-Trent**
Medway	**Medway**	Suff	**Suffolk**
Mers	**Merseyside**	Sur	**Surrey**
Midloth	**Midlothian**	Swansea	**Swansea**
M Keynes	**Milton Keynes**	Swindon	**Swindon**
Mon	**Monmouthshire**	S Yorks	**South Yorkshire**
Moray	**Moray**	T&W	**Tyne and Wear**
M Tydf	**Merthyr Tydfil**	Telford	**Telford and Wrekin**
N Ayrs	**North Ayrshire**	Thurrock	**Thurrock**
Neath	**Neath Port Talbot**	Torbay	**Torbay**
NE Lincs	**North East**	Torf	**Torfaen**
	Lincolnshire	V Glam	**The Vale of**
Newport	**City and County of**		**Glamorgan**
	Newport	Warks	**Warwickshire**
N Lanark	**North Lanarkshire**	Warr	**Warrington**
N Lincs	**North Lincolnshire**	W Berks	**West Berkshire**
N Nhants	**North**	W Dunb	**West**
	Northamptonshire		**Dunbartonshire**
Norf	**Norfolk**	Wilts	**Wiltshire**
Northumb	**Northumberland**	Windsor	**Windsor and**
Nottingham	**City of Nottingham**		**Maidenhead**
Notts	**Nottinghamshire**	W Isles	**Western Isles**
N Som	**North Somerset**	W Loth	**West Lothian**
N Yorks	**North Yorkshire**	W Mid	**West Midlands**
Orkney	**Orkney**	W Nhants	**West**
Oxon	**Oxfordshire**		**Northamptonshire**
Pboro	**Peterborough**	Wokingham	**Wokingham**
Pembs	**Pembrokeshire**	Worcs	**Worcestershire**
Perth	**Perth and Kinross**	Wrex	**Wrexham**
Plym	**Plymouth**	W Sus	**West Sussex**
Powys	**Powys**	W Yorks	**West Yorkshire**
Ptsmth	**Portsmouth**	York	**City of York**

Abbreviations used in the index

Aberdeen	**Aberdeen City**	Ches W	**Cheshire West**
Aberds	**Aberdeenshire**		**and Chester**
Ald	**Alderney**	Clack	**Clackmannanshire**
Anglesey	**Isle of Anglesey**	Conwy	**Conwy**
Angus	**Angus**	Corn	**Cornwall**
Argyll	**Argyll and Bute**	Cumb	**Cumbria**
Bath	**Bath and**	Darl	**Darlington**
	North East Somerset	Denb	**Denbighshire**
BCP	**Bournemouth,**	Derby	**City of Derby**
	Christchurch and	Derbys	**Derbyshire**
	Poole	Devon	**Devon**
Bedford	**Bedford**	Dorset	**Dorset**
Blackburn	**Blackburn with**	Dumfries	**Dumfries and**
	Darwen		**Galloway**
Blackpool	**Blackpool**	Dundee	**Dundee City**
Bl Gwent	**Blaenau Gwent**	Durham	**Durham**
Borders	**Scottish Borders**	E Ayrs	**East Ayrshire**
Brack	**Bracknell**	Edin	**City of Edinburgh**
Bridgend	**Bridgend**	E Dunb	**East Dunbartonshire**
Brighton	**City of Brighton**	E Loth	**East Lothian**
	and Hove	E Renf	**East Renfrewshire**
Bristol	**City and County of**	Essex	**Essex**
	Bristol	E Sus	**East Sussex**
Bucks	**Buckinghamshire**	E Yorks	**East Riding of**
Caerph	**Caerphilly**		**Yorkshire**
Cambs	**Cambridgeshire**	Falk	**Falkirk**
Cardiff	**Cardiff**	Fife	**Fife**
Carms	**Carmarthenshire**	Flint	**Flintshire**
C Beds	**Central Bedfordshire**	Glasgow	**City of Glasgow**
Ceredig	**Ceredigion**	Glos	**Gloucestershire**
Ches E	**Cheshire East**	Gtr Man	**Greater Manchester**

A

Abbas Combe......29 C7
Abberley.........79 A5
Abberton Essex...71 B4
Worcs............80 B2
Abberwick......189 B4
Abbess Roding...69 B5
Abbey...........27 D6
Abbey-cwm-hir...93 D4
Abbeydale......130 A3
Abbey Dore......78 D1
Abbey Field......70 A3
Abbey Hulton...112 A3
Abbey
St Bathans....211 D4
Abbeystead.....145 B5
Abbey Town....175 C4
Abbey Village...137 A5
Abbey Wood......50 B1
Abbots
Bickington....25 D4
Abbots
Bromley......113 C4
Abbotsbury......15 C5
Abbotsham......25 C5
Abbotskerswell...8 A2
Abbots Langley...67 C5
Abbots Leigh....43 B4
Abbotsley.......84 B4
Abbots Morton...80 B3
Abbots Ripton...100 D4
Abbots Salford...80 B3
Abbotswood......32 C2
Abbotts Ann.....32 A2
Abcott...........94 D1
Abdon...........94 C3
Aber.............74 D3
Aberaeron......74 B3
Aberaman........41 A5
Aberangell......91 A6
Aber-Arad.......73 C6
Aberarder......240 D2
Aberarder
House..........252 D2
Aberarder
Lodge.........240 D2
Aberargie......219 C6
Aberarth........74 B3
Aberavon........40 B2
Aber-banc.......73 B6
Aberbeeg.........41 A7
Abercanaid......41 A5
Abercarn........41 B7
Abercastle......55 A4
Abercegir........91 B6
Aberchirder...268 D1
Aber Cowarth...91 A6
Abercraf........59 D5
Abercrombie....221 D5
Abercych........73 B5
Abercynafon....60 B2
Abercynon........90 C3
Aberdalgie.....219 B5
Aberdâr
=Aberdare....41 A4
Aberdare
=Aberdâr....41 A4
Aberdaron......106 D1
Aberdaugleddau =
Milford Haven...55 D5
Aberdeen.......245 B6
Aberdesach....107 A4
Aberdour......209 B4
Aberdovey.......90 C4
Aberdulais......40 A2
Aberedw.........77 C4
Abereiddy........54 A3
Abererch.......106 C3
Aberfan.........41 A5
Aberfeldy......230 D2
Aberffraw......122 D3
Aberffrwd.......75 A5
Aberford.......148 D3
Aberfoyle......217 D5
Abergavenny =
Y Fenni........61 B4

Abergele.......125 B4
Aber-Giâr.......58 A2
Abergorlech.....58 B2
Abergwaun
=Fishguard....72 C2
Abergwesyn......76 B2
Abergwili........58 C1
Abergwynant....91 A4
Aber-gwynfi.....40 B3
Abergwyngregyn
...............123 C6
Abergynolwyn...91 B4
Aber-Hirnant...109 B4
Aberhonddu
=Brecon.......60 A2
Aberhosan.......91 C6
Aberkenfig......40 C3
Aberlady.......210 B1
Aberlemno......232 C3
Aberllefenni....91 B5
Abermagwr......75 A5
Abermaw
=Barmouth....90 A4
Abermeurig......75 C4
Abermule.........93 B5
Abernaint......109 C6
Abernant........73 D6
Aber-nant........41 A5
Abernethy......219 C6
Abernyte........220 A2
Aberpennar
=Mountain Ash..41 B5
Aberporth.......73 A5
Aber-Rhiwlech..108 C4
Abersychan......61 C4
Abertawe
=Swansea.....57 C6
Aberteifi
=Cardigan....73 B4
Aberthin........41 D5
Abertillery
=Abertyleri....41 A7
Abertridwr Caerph 41 C6
Powys........109 D5
Abertyleri
=Abertillery....41 A7
Abertysswg......60 C3
Aberuthven.....219 C4
Aber-Village....60 A3
Aberyscir.......60 A1
Aberystwyth.....90 D3
Abhainn Suidhe.287 D2
Abingdon-on-
Thames........65 D5
Abinger Common.35 B4
Abinger Hammer..34 B3
Abington......194 D4
Abington Pigotts.85 C5
Ab Kettleby....115 C5
Ab Lench........80 B3
Ablington Glos...64 C2
Wilts...........31 A5
Abney..........130 B1
Aboyne........244 C2
Abram..........137 C5
Abriachan......252 C1
Abridge.........69 D4
Abronhill......207 C5
Abson...........43 B6
Abthorpe........82 C3
Abune-the-Hill.282 E3
Aby.............135 B4
Acaster Malbis.149 C4
Acaster Selby..149 C4
Accrington.....137 A6
Acha...........223 B4
Achabraid......213 D6
Achachork......259 D4
Achafolla......213 A5
Achagary......278 C3
Achahoish......202 A2
Achalader......231 D5
Acha Mor.......288 E4
Achanalt.......263 D4
Achanamara....213 D5
Achandunie....264 C2
Ach'an Todhair.237 B4
Achany.........272 D3
Achaphubuil...237 B4
Acharacle......235 D5

Acharn Highld..236 D1
Perth..........229 D6
Acharole.......280 C4
Achath.........245 A4
Achavanich.....280 D3
Achavraat......253 B5
Achddu..........57 B4
Achduart.......270 D3
Achentoul......274 A2
Achfary........271 A5
Achgarve......261 A5
A'Chill........246 D1
Achiltibuie....270 D3
Achina.........278 B3
Achinduich.....272 D3
Achinduin......226 C3
Achingills.....280 B3
Achintee Highld.237 B5
Highld.........249 B6
Achintraid.....249 C5
Achlean........241 C6
Achleck........224 B3
Achluachrach...239 D6
Achlyness......276 C3
Achmelvich.....270 B3
Achmore Highld..249 C5
Stirling.......217 A5
Achnaba Argyll..214 D2
Argyll.........226 C4
Achnabat.......252 C1
Achnacarnin...270 A3
Achnacarry.....239 D5
Achnacloich
Argyll.........227 C4
Highld.........247 D4
Achnaconeran...240 A2
Achnacraig.....224 B3
Achnacroish....226 B3
Achnadrish.....224 A3
Achnafalnich...227 D7
Achnagarron...264 D2
Achnaha........234 D3
Achnahanat.....263 A7
Achnahannet...253 D5
Achnairn.......272 C3
Achnaluachrach 273 D4
Achnasaul......239 D5
Achnasheen....250 A3
Achosnich......234 D3
Achranich......226 B2
Achreamie......279 B6
Achriabhach....237 C5
Achriesgill....276 C3
Achrimsdale....274 D3
Achtoty........278 B2
Achurch........100 C2
Achuvoldrach..277 C6
Achvaich.......264 A3
Achvarasdal....279 B5
Ackergill......281 C5
Acklam Mbro...168 D2
N Yorks.......149 A6
Ackleton........95 B5
Acklington....189 C5
Ackton.........140 A2
Ackworth Moor
Top...........140 B2
Acle...........121 D6
Acock's Green...96 C4
Acol............53 C5
Acomb Northumb.178 C1
York...........149 B4
Aconbury........78 D3
Acre...........137 A6
Acrefair.......110 A1
Acre Street.....19 B6
Acton Ches E...127 D6
Dorset.........16 D3
London.........49 A5
Shrops.........93 C7
Suff............87 C4
Wrex..........126 D3
Acton
Beauchamp.....79 B4
Acton Bridge...127 B5
Acton Burnell...94 A3
Acton Green.....79 B4
Acton Pigott....94 A3
Acton Round.....95 B4

Acton Scott......94 C2
Acton Trussell..112 D3
Acton Turville..44 A2
Adbaston.......111 C6
Adber...........29 C5
Adderley.......111 A5
Adderstone....199 C5
Addiewell......208 D2
Addingham.....147 C4
Addington Bucks.66 A2
Kent............37 A4
London.........49 C6
Addinston......197 A4
Addiscombe......49 C6
Addlestone......48 C3
Addlethorpe...135 C5
Adel...........148 D1
Adeney.........111 D6
Adfa............93 A4
Adforton........94 D2
Adisham.........53 D4
Adlestrop.......64 A3
Adlingfleet....141 A6
Adlington.......137 B5
Admaston Staffs.112 C4
Telford........111 D5
Admington.......81 C5
Adstock.........83 D4
Adstone.........82 B2
Advie..........254 C2
Adwalton......139 A5
Adwell.........66 D1
Adwick le Street 140 C3
Adwick upon
Dearne........140 C2
Adziel.........269 D4
Ae Village.....184 D2
Affeck.........256 D3
Affpuddle.......16 B2
Affric Lodge...250 D3
Afon-wen......125 B6
Afton...........18 C2
Agglethorpe...157 C4
Agneash........152 C4
Aigburth.......126 A3
Aiginis........288 D5
Aike...........150 C3
Aikerness.....282 B5
Aikers.........283 H5
Aiketgate......164 A2
Aikton.........175 C5
Ailey...........78 C1
Ailstone........81 B5
Ailsworth......100 B3
Ainderby
Quernhow....158 C2
Ainderby
Steeple.......158 B2
Aingers Green...71 A5
Ainsdale.......136 B2
Ainsdale-on-
Sea...........136 B2
Ainstable......164 A3
Ainsworth.....137 B6
Ainthorpe.....159 A6
Aintree........136 D2
Aird Argyll....213 B5
Dumfries......170 A2
Highld.........261 C4
W Isles.......288 D6
Aird a Mhachair 286 B3
Aird a' Mhulaidh 288 F2
Aird Asaig.....288 G2
Aird Dhail.....288 A5
Airdens........288 D3
Aird Mhidhinis 286 F3
Aird Mhighe
W Isles.......287 F5
W Isles.......288 H2
Aird Mhor.....286 F3
Aird of Sleat..247 D4
Airdrie........207 D5
Aird Thunga...288 D5
Airdtorrisdale 278 B2
Aird Uig.......287 A5
Airidh a
Bhruaich.....288 F3
Airieland......173 C5
Airmyn........141 A5
Airntully......219 A5
Airor..........247 D6

Airth..........208 B1
Airton.........146 B3
Airyhassen....171 C5
Aisby Lincs....116 B3
Lincs..........141 D6
Aisgernis......286 D3
Aiskew.........157 C6
Aislaby N Yorks.159 C6
N Yorks.......160 A2
Stockton......168 D2
Aisthorpe......133 A4
Aith Orkney....282 F3
Shetland......284 D8
Shetland......285 H5
Aithsetter....285 K6
Aitkenhead....192 E3
Aitnoch........253 C5
Akeld..........188 A2
Akeley..........83 D4
Akenham.........88 C2
Albaston........11 D5
Alberbury......110 D2
Albourne........21 A5
Albrighton Shrops 95 A6
Shrops........110 D3
Alburgh........104 C3
Albury Herts....68 A4
Sur.............34 B3
Albury End......68 A4
Alby Hill......120 B3
Alcaig.........252 A1
Alcaston........94 C2
Alcester........80 B3
Alciston........22 B3
Alcombe Som....27 A4
Wilts..........44 C2
Alconbury.....100 D3
Alconbury
Weston........100 D3
Aldbar Castle..232 C3
Aldborough Norf 120 B3
N Yorks.......148 A3
Aldbourne......45 B6
Aldbrough.....151 D5
Aldbrough
St John.......167 D5
Aldbury........67 B4
Aldcliffe......145 A4
Aldclune......230 B3
Aldeburgh......89 B5
Aldeby.........105 B5
Aldenham.......67 D6
Alderbury......31 C5
Aldercar......114 A2
Alderford.....120 D3
Alderholt.......31 D5
Alderley........61 B5
Alderley Edge.128 B3
Aldermaston....46 C3
Aldermaston
Wharf..........47 C4
Alderminster....81 C5
Alder's End.....79 C4
Aldersey Green.127 D4
Aldershot.......34 A1
Alderton Glos...80 D3
Shrops........110 C3
Suff............88 C4
Wilts..........44 A2
W Nhants.......83 C4
Alderwasley...130 D3
Aldfield......147 A6
Aldford.......127 D4
Aldham Essex...70 A3
Suff............87 C6
Aldie..........264 B3
Aldingbourne...20 B2
Aldingham.....154 D1
Aldington Kent..38 B2
Worcs..........80 C3
Aldington Frith.38 B2
Aldochlay.....206 A1
Aldreth.......101 D6
Aldridge.......96 A3
Aldringham.....89 A5
Aldsworth......64 B2
Aldunie.......255 D4
Aldwark Derbys.130 D2
N Yorks.......148 A3
Aldwick.........20 C2
Aldwincle.....100 C2
Aldworth........46 B3

Alexandria....206 C1
Alfardisworthy...24 D3
Alfington.......13 B6
Alfold..........34 C3
Lincs..........141 D6
Alfold Bars.....34 C3
Alfold Crossways 34 C3
Alford Aberds..244 A2
Lincs..........135 B4
Som............29 B6
Alfreton.......131 D4
Alfrick.........79 B5
Alfrick Pound...79 B5
Algaltraig....203 A5
Algarkirk......117 B5
Alhampton......29 B6
Aline Lodge...288 F2
Alisary........235 C6
Alkborough....141 A6
Alkerton........81 C6
Alkham..........39 A4
Alkington.....111 B4
Alkmonton.....113 B5
Alladale Lodge.263 B6
Allaleigh........8 B2
Allanaquoich...242 C4
Allangrange
Mains.........252 A2
Allanton Borders 198 A2
N Lanark......194 A3
Allathasdal...286 F2
All Cannings....45 C4
Allendale Town 177 D6
Allenheads....165 A6
Allensford....178 D2
Allens Green....69 B4
Allensmore......78 D2
Allenton.......114 B1
Aller...........28 C4
Allerby........162 A3
Allerford.......27 A4
Allerston.....160 C2
Allerthorpe...149 C6
Allerton Mers..127 A4
W Yorks.......147 D5
Allerton
Bywater.......140 A2
Allerton
Mauleverer....148 B3
Allesley........97 C6
Allestree......114 B1
Allet.............4 C2
Allexton........99 A5
Allgreave......129 C4
Allhallows......51 B5
Allhallows-on-
Sea............51 B5
Alligin Shuas..249 A5
Allimore Green.112 D2
Allington Lincs.115 A6
Wilts..........31 B6
Wilts..........45 C4
Allithwaite....154 D2
Alloa..........208 A1
Allonby.......174 D3
Alloway.......192 D3
All Saints South
Elmham.......104 C4
All Stretton....94 B2
Allt............57 B5
Alltchaorunn..237 D5
Alltforgan....109 C4
Alltmawr........77 C4
Alltnacaillich.277 D5
Allt na h-Airbhe 262 A3
Alltsigh.......240 A2
Alltwalis.......58 B1
Alltwen.........40 A2
Alltyblaca......75 D4
Allwood Green.103 D6
Almeley.........78 B1
Almer...........16 B3
Almholme......140 C3
Almington.....111 B6
Alminstone Cross 24 C4
Almondbank....219 B5
Almondbury....139 B4
Almondsbury....43 A5
Alne...........148 A3
Alness.........264 D2
Alnham.........188 B2

Alnmouth 189 B5
Alnwick. 189 B4
Alperton. 49 A4
Alphamstone. . . .87 D4
Alpheton 87 B4
Alphington 13 B4
Alport 130 C2
Alpraham 127 D5
Alresford 71 A4
Alrewas 113 D5
Alsager 128 D2
Alsagers Bank. . .112 A2
Alsop en le Dale 129 D6
Alston Cumb . . .165 A5
  Devon. 14 A3
Alstone. 80 D2
Alstonefield. 129 D6
Alswear 26 C2
Altandhu. 270 C2
Altanduin 274 B2
Altarnun. 10 C3
Altass 272 D2
Alterwall. 281 B4
Altham 146 D1
Althorne. 70 D3
Althorpe. 141 C6
Alticry 171 B4
Altnabreac
  Station 279 D6
Altnacealgach
  Hotel. 271 C5
Altnacraig 226 D3
Altnafeadh. 237 D6
Altnaharra 272 A3
Altofts 139 A6
Alton Derbys. . . .130 C3
  Hants. 33 B6
  Staffs. 113 A4
Alton Pancras. . . .15 A7
Alton Priors. 45 C5
Altrincham. 128 A2
Altrua 239 D6
Altskeith. 217 D4
Altyre House 253 A6
Alva 208 A1
Alvanley 127 B4
Alvaston. 114 B1
Alvechurch 96 D3
Alvecote 97 A5
Alvediston 30 C3
Alveley 95 C5
Alverdiscott. 25 C6
Alverstoke 19 B5
Alverstone 19 C4
Alverton 115 A5
Alves 266 C2
Alvescot 64 C3
Alveston S Glos. . .43 A5
  Warks. 81 B5
Alvie 241 B6
Alvingham 143 D5
Alvington 62 C2
Alwalton 100 B3
Alweston 29 D6
Alwinton 188 C2
Alwoodley 148 C1
Alyth 231 D6
Amatnatua 263 A6
Am Baile. 286 E3
Ambergate. 130 D3
Amber Hill 117 A5
Amberley Glos . . .63 C4
  W Sus. 20 A3
Amble 189 C5
Amblecote 96 C1
Ambler Thorn . . .138 A3
Ambleside 154 A2
Ambleston 55 B6
Ambrosden 65 B7
Am Buth 226 D3
Amcotts 141 B6
Amersham 67 D4
Amesbury. 31 A5
Amington 97 A5
Amisfield 184 D2
Amlwch 123 A4
Amlwch Port . . .123 A4
Ammanford
  =Rhydaman. 57 A6
Amod. 190 B3
Amotherby. 159 D6
Ampfield 32 C3

Ampleforth 159 D4
Ampney Crucis. . .63 C6
Ampney St Mary. .64 C1
Ampney St Peter .64 C1
Amport 32 A1
Ampthill 84 D2
Ampton. 103 D4
Amroth 56 B1
Amulree 218 A3
Anagach 253 D6
Anaheilt 236 C2
Anancaun. 262 D2
An Caol. 248 A3
Ancaster. 116 A2
Anchor 93 C5
Anchorsholme . . .144 C3
An Cnoc 288 D5
Ancroft 198 B3
Ancrum. 187 A5
Anderby 135 B5
Anderson 16 B2
Anderton 127 B6
Andover 32 A2
Andover Down . . .32 A2
Andoversford 63 B6
Andreas 152 B4
Anfield 136 D2
Angersleigh. 28 D1
Angle. 55 D4
Angmering. 20 B3
Angram N Yorks . .148 C5
  N Yorks 156 B3
Anie. 217 C5
Ankerville. 265 C4
Anlaby 142 A2
Anmer 119 C4
Annan 175 B4
Annat Argyll . . .227 D5
  Highld. 249 A5
Anna Valley 32 A2
Annbank 193 C4
Annesley 131 D5
Annesley
  Woodhouse . .131 D4
Annfield Plain . . .178 D3
Annifirth. 285 J3
Annitsford 179 B4
Annscroft. 94 A2
Ansdell 136 A2
Ansford. 29 B6
Ansley 97 B5
Anslow 113 C6
Anslow Gate 113 C5
Anstey Herts. 85 D6
  Leics. 98 A2
Anstruther
  Easter. 221 D5
Anstruther
  Wester. 221 D5
Ansty Hants. 33 A6
  Warks. 97 C6
  Wilts. 30 C3
  W Sus. 35 D5
Anthill Common. .33 D5
Anthorn 175 C4
Antingham 121 B4
An t-Ob
  =Leverburgh . . .287 F5
Anton's Gowt . . .117 A5
Antonshill 208 B1
Antony 6 B3
Anwick 133 D6
Anwoth 172 C5
Aoradh 200 B2
Apes Hall 102 B1
Apethorpe 100 B2
Apeton 112 D2
Apley 133 B6
Apperknowle. . . .130 B3
Apperley
  Bridge 147 D5
Appersett. 156 B2
Appin. 226 B4
Appin House . . .226 B4
Appleby-in-
  Westmorland . 165 C4
Appleby Magna . .97 A6
Appleby Parva . . .97 A6
Applecross. 249 B4

Applecross
  House. 249 B4
Appledore Devon. .25 B5
  Devon. 27 D5
  Kent 38 C1
Appledore Heath .38 B1
Appleford. 65 D6
Applegarthtown 185 D4
Appleshaw 32 A2
Applethwaite. . . .163 B5
Appleton Halton 127 A5
  Oxon. 65 C5
Appleton-le-
  Moors. 159 C6
Appleton-le-
  Street. 159 D6
Appleton
  Roebuck 149 C4
Appleton Thorn .127 A6
Appleton Wiske .158 A2
Appletreehall . . .186 B4
Appletreewick . . .147 A4
Appley. 27 C5
Appley Bridge . .136 C4
Apse Heath 19 C4
Apsley End. 84 D3
Apuldram. 20 B1
Aquhythie 245 A4
Arabella. 265 C4
Arbeadie. 244 C3
Arberth
  =Narberth. 55 C7
Arbirlot. 233 D4
Arboll 265 B4
Arborfield 47 C5
Arborfield Cross. .47 C5
Arborfield
  Garrison 47 C5
Arbourthorne . . .130 A3
Arbroath. 233 D4
Arbuthnott. 233 A5
Archiestown 254 B3
Arclid 128 C2
Ardachu 273 D4
Ardalanish. 224 F7
Ardanaiseig. 227 D5
Ardaneaskan. . . .249 C5
Ardanstur. 213 A6
Ardargie House
  Hotel. 219 C5
Ardarroch 249 C5
Ardbeg Argyll . . .201 D4
  Argyll 215 D4
Ardcharnich 262 B3
Ardchiavaig 224 E2
Ardchullarie
  More. 217 C5
Ardchyle. 217 B5
Ard-dhubh. 249 B4
Arddleen 110 D1
Ardechvie. 239 C5
Ardeley 68 A3
Ardelve 249 D5
Arden 206 B1
Ardens Grafton. . .80 B4
Ardentinny 215 D4
Ardentraive 203 A5
Ardeonaig 217 A6
Ardersier 252 A3
Ardessie 262 B2
Ardfern 213 B6
Ardgartan. 215 B5
Ardgay 264 A1
Ardgour 237 C4
Ardheslaig. 249 A4
Ardiecow 267 C6
Ardindrean 262 B3
Ardingly 35 D6
Ardington. 46 A2
Ardlair. 255 D6
Ardleigh 71 A4
Ardler 231 D6
Ardley 65 A6
Ardlui 215 A6
Ardlussa 213 D4
Ardmair 262 A3
Ardmay 215 B5
Ardminish 202 D1
Ardmolich 235 C6
Ardmore Argyll. .226 D2

Ardmore continued
  Highld. 264 B3
  Highld. 276 C3
Ardnacross 225 B4
Ardnadam 203 A6
Ardnagrask 251 B7
Ardnarff 249 C5
Ardnastang 236 C2
Ardnave 200 A2
Ardno 215 B4
Ardo 256 C3
Ardoch 219 A5
Ardochy House. .239 B6
Ardoyne 256 D1
Ardpatrick 202 B2
Ardpatrick
  House. 202 C2
Ardpeaton 215 D5
Ardrishaig 213 D6
Ardross Fife 221 D5
  Highld. 264 C2
Ardrossan 204 D2
Ardross Castle . .264 C2
Ardshealach 235 D5
Ardsley 140 C1
Ardslignish 235 D4
Ardtalla. 201 C4
Ardtalnaig 218 A2
Ardtoe. 235 C5
Ardtrostan 217 B6
Arduaine 213 A5
Ardullie 264 D1
Ardvasar 247 D5
Ardvorlich 217 B6
Ardwell. 170 C3
Ardwell Mains. . .170 C3
Ardwick 138 D1
Areley Kings 95 D6
Arford 34 C1
Argoed Caerph . . .41 B6
  Powys 76 A3
Arichamish 214 B2
Arichastlich. 216 A2
Aridhglas 224 D2
Arileod 223 B4
Arinacrinachd. . .249 A4
Arinagour. 223 B5
Arion 282 F3
Arisaig 235 B5
Ariundle 236 C2
Arkendale 148 A2
Arkesden 85 D6
Arkholme 155 D4
Arkleton 186 D2
Arkle Town 156 A4
Arkley 68 D2
Arksey 140 C3
Arkwright Town 131 B4
Arle 63 A5
Arlecdon 162 C3
Arlesey 84 D3
Arleston 111 D5
Arley 128 A1
Arlingham 62 B3
Arlington Devon. .25 A7
  E Sus 22 B3
  Glos 64 C2
Armadale Highld .278 B3
  W Loth 208 D2
Armadale Castle 247 D5
Armathwaite . . .164 A3
Arminghall. 104 A3
Armitage 113 D4
Armley 148 D1
Armscote 81 C5
Armthorpe 140 C4
Arnabost 223 B5
Arncliffe 156 D3
Arncroach 221 D5
Arne. 16 C3
Arnesby 98 B3
Arngask 219 C6
Arnisdale 238 A2
Arnish 248 C2
Ariston Engine 209 D6
Arnol 288 C4
Arnold E Yorks . .151 C4
  Notts 114 A3
Arnprior 207 A5
Arnside 154 D3
Aros Mains 225 B4

Arowry 110 B3
Arpafeelie 252 A2
Arrad Foot 154 C2
Arram 150 C3
Arrathorne. 157 B6
Arreton 18 C4
Arrington 85 B5
Arrivain. 216 A2
Arrochar. 215 B5
Arrow 80 B3
Arthington 147 C6
Arthingworth . . .99 C4
Arthog. 90 A4
Arthrath 257 C4
Arthurstone 231 D6
Artrochie 257 C5
Arundel. 20 B3
Aryhoulan 237 C4
Asby. 162 B3
Ascog 203 B6
Ascot 48 C2
Ascott 81 D6
Ascott-under-
  Wychwood 64 B4
Asenby 158 D2
Asfordby. 115 D5
Asfordby Hill . . .115 D5
Asgarby Lincs. . .116 A4
  Lincs. 134 C3
Ash Kent 50 C2
  Kent 53 D4
  Som 29 C4
  Sur. 34 A1
Ashampstead 46 B3
Ashbocking 88 B2
Ashbourne. 113 A5
Ashbrittle. 27 C5
Ash Bullayne 12 A2
Ashburton 7 A6
Ashbury Devon. . .11 B6
  Oxon. 45 A6
Ashby 141 C7
Ashby by
  Partney 135 C4
Ashby cum
  Fenby 143 C4
Ashby de la
  Launde. 133 D5
Ashby-de-la-
  Zouch 114 D1
Ashby Folville . .115 D5
Ashby Magna . . .98 B2
Ashby Parva 98 C2
Ashby Puerorum 134 B3
Ashby St Ledgers 82 A2
Ashby St Mary. .104 A3
Ashchurch 80 D2
Ashcombe 13 D4
Ashcott. 28 B4
Ashdon 86 C1
Ashe 32 A4
Asheldham. 70 C3
Ashen 86 C3
Ashendon. 66 B2
Ashfield Carms.. .58 C3
  Stirling 218 D2
  Suff 88 A3
Ashfield Green . .104 D3
Ashfold
  Crossways. 35 D5
Ashford Devon. . .25 B6
  Hants. 31 D5
  Kent 38 A2
  Sur. 48 B3
Ashford Bowdler .94 D3
Ashford
  Carbonell 94 D3
Ashford Hill. 46 C3
Ashford in the
  Water. 130 C1
Ashgill. 194 B2
Ash Green 97 C6
Ashill Devon 27 D7
  Norf 103 A4
  Som 28 D3
Ashingdon 70 D2
Ashington
  Northumb. . . .179 A4
  Som 29 C5
  W Sus. 21 A4
Ashintully Castle 231 B5
Ashkirk 186 A3

Aln–Ast 291

Ashlett 18 A3
Ashleworth 63 A4
Ashley Cambs. . . .86 A2
  Ches E 128 A2
  Devon. 26 D1
  Dorset 17 A5
  Glos 63 D5
  Hants. 17 B6
  Hants. 32 B2
  N Nhants 99 B4
  Staffs 111 B6
Ashley Green. . . .67 C4
Ashley Heath
  Dorset 17 A5
  Staffs 111 B6
Ash Magna 111 B4
Ashmanhaugh. . .121 C5
Ashmansworth . .46 D2
Ashmansworthy. .24 D4
Ash Mill 26 C2
Ashmore. 30 D3
Ashorne 81 B6
Ashover 130 C3
Ashow 97 D6
Ashprington 8 B2
Ash Priors 27 C6
Ashreigney 26 D1
Ash Street 87 C6
Ashtead 35 A4
Ash Thomas. 27 D5
Ashton Ches W . .127 C5
  Corn 3 C4
  Hants 33 D4
  Hereford 78 A3
  Invclyd 204 A2
  N Nhants 100 C2
  W Nhants. 83 C4
Ashton Common .44 D2
Ashton-In-
  Makerfield . . .137 D4
Ashton Keynes . .63 D6
Ashton under Hill 80 D2
Ashton-under-
  Lyne 138 D2
Ashton upon
  Mersey. 137 D6
Ashurst Hants. . . .32 D2
  Kent 36 C3
  W Sus. 21 A4
Ashurstwood. . . .36 C2
Ash Vale 34 A1
Ashwater 11 B4
Ashwell Herts. . . .85 D4
  Rutland. 115 D6
  Som 28 D3
Ashwellthorpe . .104 B2
Ashwick 29 A6
Ashwicken 119 D4
Ashybank 186 B4
Askam in
  Furness 153 C2
Askern 140 B3
Askerswell 15 B5
Askett 66 C3
Askham Cumb. . .164 C3
  Notts 132 B2
Askham Bryan . .149 C4
Askham Richard 148 C4
Asknish 214 C2
Askrigg. 156 B3
Askwith. 147 C5
Aslackby 116 B3
Aslacton 104 B2
Aslockton 115 B5
Asloun. 244 A2
Aspatria 174 D4
Aspenden. 68 A3
Asperton 117 B5
Aspley Guise 83 D6
Aspley Heath. . . .83 D6
Aspull 137 C5
Asserby 135 B4
Asserby Town . . .135 B4
Assington. 87 D5
Assynt House . . .264 D1
Astbury 128 C3
Astcote 82 B3
Asterley 94 A1
Asterton 94 B1

Asthall....64 B3
Asthall Leigh....64 B4
Astley Shrops....111 D4
  Warks....97 C6
  Worcs....79 A5
Astley Abbotts....95 B5
Astley Bridge....137 B6
Astley Cross....79 A6
Astley Green....137 D6
Aston Ches E....111 A5
  Ches W....127 B5
  Derbys....130 A1
  Hereford....94 D2
  Herts....68 A2
  Oxon....64 C4
  Shrops....111 C4
  Staffs....111 A6
  S Yorks....131 A4
  Telford....95 A4
  W Mid....96 C3
  Wokingham....47 A5
Aston Abbotts....66 A3
Aston Botterell....95 C4
Aston-By-Stone 112 B3
Aston Cantlow....80 B4
Aston Clinton....66 B3
Aston Crews....62 A2
Aston Cross....80 D2
Aston End....68 A2
Aston Eyre....95 B4
Aston Fields....80 A2
Aston Flamville....98 B1
Aston Ingham....62 A2
Aston juxta
  Mondrum....127 D6
Aston le Walls....82 B1
Aston Magna....81 D4
Aston Munslow....94 C3
Aston on Clun....94 C1
Aston-on-Trent 114 C2
Aston Rogers....94 A1
Aston Rowant....66 D2
Aston Sandford....66 C2
Aston Somerville....80 D3
Aston Subedge....80 C4
Aston Tirrold....46 A3
Aston Upthorpe....46 A3
Astrop....82 D2
Astwick....84 D4
Astwood
  M Keynes....83 C4
  Worcs....79 B6
Astwood Bank....80 A3
Aswarby....116 B3
Aswardby....134 B3
Atcham....94 A3
Atch Lench....80 B3
Athelhampton....16 B1
Athelington....104 D3
Athelney....28 C3
Athelstaneford....210 C2
Atherington....25 C6
Atherstone....97 B6
Atherstone on
  Stour....81 B5
Atherton....137 C5
Atley Hill....157 A6
Atlow....113 A6
Attadale....249 C6
Attadale House..249 C6
Attenborough....114 B3
Atterby....142 D1
Attercliffe....130 A3
Attleborough
  Norf....103 B6
  Warks....97 B6
Attlebridge....120 D3
Atwick....151 B4
Atworth....44 C2
Aubourn....133 C4
Auchagallon....191 B4
Auchallater....243 D4
Aucharnie....256 B1
Auchattie....244 C3
Auchavan....231 B5
Auchbreck....254 D3
Auchenback....205 C5
Auchenbainzie..183 C6
Auchenblae....233 A5

Auchenbrack....183 C5
Auchenbreck....214 D3
Auchencairn
  Dumfries....173 C5
  Dumfries....184 D2
  N Ayrs....191 C6
Auchencrosh....180 D3
Auchencrow....211 D5
Auchendinny....209 D5
Auchengray....195 A4
Auchenhalrig....267 C4
Auchenheath....194 B3
Auchenlochan....203 A4
Auchenmalg....171 B4
Auchensoul....181 B4
Auchentiber....204 D3
Auchertyre....249 D5
Auchgourish....242 A2
Auchincarroch..206 B2
Auchindrain....214 B3
Auchindrean....262 B3
Auchininna....256 B1
Auchinleck....193 C5
Auchinloch....205 A6
Auchinroath....266 D3
Auchintoul....244 A2
Auchiries....257 C5
Auchlee....245 C5
Auchleven....256 D1
Auchlochan....194 C3
Auchlossan....244 B2
Auchlunies....245 C5
Auchlyne....217 B5
Auchmacoy....257 C4
Auchmair....255 D4
Auchmantle....170 A3
Auchmillan....193 C5
Auchmithie....233 D4
Auchmuirbridge 220 D2
Auchmull....232 A3
Auchnacree....232 B2
Auchnagallin...253 C6
Auchnagatt....257 B4
Auchnaha....214 D2
Auchnashelloch 218 C2
Aucholzie....243 C6
Auchrannie....231 C6
Auchroisk....253 D6
Auchronie....244 D1
Auchterarder....218 C4
Auchteraw....240 B1
Auchterderran....209 A5
Auchterhouse....220 A3
Auchtermuchty..220 C2
Auchterneed....251 A6
Auchtertool....209 A5
Auchtertyre....266 D2
Auchtubh....217 B5
Auckengill....281 B5
Auckley....140 C4
Audenshaw....138 D2
Audlem....111 A5
Audley....128 D2
Audley End....87 D4
Auds....268 C1
Aughton E Yorks..149 D6
  Lancs....136 C2
  Lancs....145 A5
  S Yorks....131 A4
  Wilts....45 D6
Aughton Park..136 C3
Auldearn....253 A5
Aulden....78 B2
Auldgirth....183 D7
Auldhame....210 B2
Auldhouse....205 C6
Ault a'chruinn..249 D6
Aultanrynie....271 A6
Aultbea....261 B5
Aultdearg....263 D4
Aultgrishan....261 B4
Aultguish Inn....263 C5
Aultibea....274 B4
Aultiphurst....279 B4
Aultmore....267 D5
Aultnagoire....252 D1
Aultnamain Inn..264 B2
Aultnaslat....239 B5
Aulton....255 D7
Aundorach....242 A2
Aunsby....116 B3
Auquhorthies...256 D3

Aust....43 A4
Austendike....117 C5
Austerfield....141 D4
Austrey....97 A5
Austwick....146 A1
Authorpe....135 A4
Authorpe Row....135 B5
Avebury....45 C5
Aveley....50 A2
Avening....63 D4
Averham....132 D2
Aveton Gifford....7 C5
Avielochan....242 A2
Aviemore....242 A1
Avington Hants....32 B4
  W Berks....46 C1
Avoch....252 A3
Avon....17 B5
Avonbridge....208 C2
Avon Dassett....81 C7
Avonmouth....43 B4
Avonwick....7 B6
Awbridge....32 C2
Awhirk....170 B2
Awkley....43 A4
Awliscombe....13 A6
Awre....62 C3
Awsworth....114 A2
Axbridge....42 D3
Axford Hants....33 A5
  Wilts....45 C6
Axminster....14 B2
Axmouth....14 B2
Axton....125 A6
Aycliff....39 A5
Aycliffe....167 C5
Aydon....178 C2
Aylburton....62 C2
Ayle....165 A5
Aylesbeare....13 B5
Aylesbury....66 B3
Aylesby....143 C4
Aylesford....37 A5
Aylesham....53 D4
Aylestone....98 A2
Aylmerton....120 B3
Aylsham....120 C3
Aylton....79 D4
Aymestrey....78 A2
Aynho....82 D2
Ayot St Lawrence. 68 B1
Ayot St Peter....68 B2
Ayr....192 C3
Aysgarth....156 C4
Ayside....154 C2
Ayston....99 A5
Aythorpe Roding .69 B5
Ayton....211 D6
Aywick....284 E7
Azerley....157 D6

B

Babbacombe....8 A3
Babbinswood....110 B2
Babcary....29 C5
Babel....59 B5
Babell....125 B6
Babraham....85 B7
Babworth....132 A1
Bac....288 C5
Bachau....123 B4
Backaland....282 D6
Backaskaill....282 B5
Backbarrow....154 C2
Backe....56 A2
Backfolds....269 D5
Backford....127 B4
Backford Cross..126 B3
Backhill Aberds..256 C2
  Aberds....257 C5
Backhill of
  Clackriach...257 B4
Backhill of
  Fortree....257 B4
Backhill of
  Trustach....244 C3
Backies....274 D2
Backlass....280 C4
Back of
  Keppoch....235 B5

Back Rogerton..193 C5
Backwell....42 C3
Backworth....179 B5
Bacon End....69 B6
Baconsthorpe....120 B3
Bacton Hereford...78 D1
  Norf....121 B5
  Suff....87 A6
Bacton Green....87 A6
Bacup....138 A1
Badachro....261 C4
Badanloch
  Lodge....273 A5
Badavanich....250 A3
Badbury....45 A5
Badby....82 B2
Badcall....276 C3
Badcaul....262 A2
Baddeley Green.129 D4
Baddesley
  Clinton....97 D5
Baddesley Ensor. 97 B5
Baddidarach....270 B3
Baddoch....242 D4
Baddock....252 A3
Badenscoth....256 C2
Badenyon....243 A6
Badger....95 B5
Badger's Mount..50 C1
Badgeworth....63 B5
Badgworth....42 D2
Badicaul....249 D4
Badingham....88 A4
Badlesmere....52 D2
Badlipster....280 D4
Badluarach....262 A1
Badminton....44 A2
Badnaban....270 B3
Badninish....264 A3
Badrallach....262 A2
Badsey....80 C3
Badshot Lea....34 B1
Badsworth....140 B2
Badwell Ash....87 A5
Bae Colwyn
  =Colwyn Bay...124 B3
Bag Enderby....134 B3
Bagendon....63 C6
Bagh a Chaisteil
  =Castlebay....286 G2
Baghasdal....286 E3
Bagh Mor....286 A4
Bagh
  Shiarabhagh..286 F3
Bagillt....126 B2
Baginton....97 D6
Baglan....40 B2
Bagley....110 C3
Bagnall....129 D4
Bagnor....46 C2
Bagshot Sur....48 C2
  Wilts....45 C7
Bagthorpe Norf..119 B4
  Notts....131 D4
Bagworth....98 A1
Bagwy Llydiart..61 A6
Bail Àrd Bhuirgh 288 B5
Baildon....147 D5
Baile....287 F4
Baile Ailein....288 E3
Baile a
  Mhanaich....286 A3
Baile an Truiseil 288 B4
Bailebeag....240 A3
Baile Boidheach 202 A2
Baile Glas....286 A4
Baile Mhartainn 287 G2
Baile Mhic Phail 287 G3
Baile Mor Argyll..224 D1
  W Isles....287 H2
Baile na Creige..286 F2
Baile nan
  Cailleach....286 A3
Baile Raghaill...287 G2
Baileyhead....176 B3
Bailiesward....255 C5
Baillieston....205 B6
Bail' lochdrach..286 A4
Bail Uachdraich.287 H3
Bail' Ur
  Tholastaidh...288 C6

Bainbridge....156 B3
Bainsford....208 B1
Bainshole....255 C7
Bainton E Yorks..150 B2
  Pboro....100 A2
Bairnkine....187 B5
Baker's End....68 B3
Baker Street....50 A3
Bakewell....130 C2
Bala = Y Bala....108 B4
Balachuirn....248 B2
Balavil....241 B5
Balbeg Highld....251 C6
  Highld....251 D6
Balbeggie....219 B6
Balbithan....245 A4
Balbithan House 245 A5
Balblair Highld....264 A1
  Highld....264 D3
Balby....140 C3
Balchladich....270 A3
Balchraggan
  Highld....252 B1
  Highld....252 C1
Balchrick....276 C2
Balchrystie....221 D4
Balcladaich....251 D4
Balcombe....35 C6
Balcombe Lane...35 C6
Balcomie....221 C6
Balcurvie....220 D3
Baldersby....158 D2
Baldersby
  St James....158 D2
Balderstone....145 D6
Balderton
  Ches W....126 C3
  Notts....132 D3
Baldhu....4 C2
Baldinnie....220 C4
Baldock....84 D4
Baldovie....221 A4
Baldrine....152 C4
Baldslow....23 A5
Baldwin....152 C3
Baldwinholme..175 C6
Baldwin's Gate..112 A1
Bale....120 B2
Balearn....269 D5
Balemartine....222 C2
Balephuil....222 C2
Balerno....209 D4
Balevullin....222 C2
Balfield....232 B3
Balfour....282 F5
Balfron....206 B3
Balfron Station..206 B3
Balgaveny....256 B1
Balgavies....232 C3
Balgonar....208 A3
Balgove....256 C3
Balgowan....241 C4
Balgown....258 B3
Balgrochan....205 A6
Balgy....249 A5
Balhaldie....218 D3
Balhalgardy....256 D2
Balham....49 B5
Balhary....231 D6
Baliasta....284 C8
Baligill....279 B4
Balintore Angus..231 C6
  Highld....265 C4
Balintraid....264 C3
Balk....158 C3
Balkeerie....232 D1
Balkemback....220 A3
Balkholme....141 A5
Balkissock....180 C3
Ball....110 C2
Ballabeg....152 D2
Ballacannel....152 C4
Ballachulish....237 D4
Ballajora....152 B4
Ballaleigh....152 C3
Ballamodha....152 D2
Ballantrae....180 C2
Ballaquine....152 C4
Ballards Gore....70 D3
Ballasalla IoM....152 B3

Ballaugh....152 B3
Ballaveare....152 D3
Ballcorach....254 D2
Ballechin....230 C3
Balleigh....264 B3
Ballencrieff....210 C1
Ballentoul....230 B2
Ball Haye Green 129 D4
Ball Hill....46 C2
Ballidon....130 D2
Balliemore Argyll 214 C3
  Argyll....226 D3
Ballikinrain....206 B3
Ballimeanoch....214 A3
Ballimore Argyll..214 D2
  Stirling....217 C5
Ballinaby....200 B2
Ballindean....220 B2
Ballingdon....87 C4
Ballinger
  Common....67 C4
Ballingham....78 D3
Ballingry....209 A4
Ballinlick....230 D3
Ballinluig....230 C3
Ballintuim....231 C5
Balloch Angus..232 C1
  Highld....252 B3
  N Lanark....207 C5
  W Dunb....206 B1
Ballochan....244 C2
Ballochford....255 C4
Ballochmorrie..181 C4
Balls Cross....34 D2
Balls Green....71 A4
Ballygown....224 B3
Ballygrant....200 B3
Ballyhaugh....223 B4
Balmacara....249 D5
Balmacara
  Square....249 D5
Balmaclellan....173 A4
Balmacneil....230 C3
Balmacqueen....259 A4
Balmae....173 D4
Balmaha....206 A2
Balmalcolm....220 D3
Balmeanach....248 B2
Balmedie....245 A6
Balmer Heath....110 B3
Balmerino....220 B3
Balmerlawn....18 A2
Balmichael....191 B5
Balmirmer....221 A5
Balmore Highld..251 C5
  Highld....253 B4
  Highld....258 D2
  Perth....230 C3
Balmule....209 B5
Balmullo....220 B4
Balmungie....252 A3
Balnaboth....231 B7
Balnabruaich..264 D3
Balnabruich....275 B5
Balnacoil....274 C2
Balnacra....250 B1
Balnafoich....252 C2
Balnagall....265 B4
Balnaguard....230 C3
Balnahard Argyll..212 C2
  Argyll....224 C3
Balnain....251 C6
Balnakeil....277 B4
Balnaknock....259 B4
Balnapaling....264 D3
Balne....140 B3
Balochroy....202 C2
Balone....221 C4
Balornock....205 B6
Balquharn....219 A5
Balquhidder....217 B5
Balsall....97 D5
Balsall Common..97 D5
Balsall Heath....96 C3
Balscott....81 C6
Balsham....86 B1
Baltasound....284 C8
Balterley....128 D2
Baltersan....171 A6
Balthangie....268 D3
Baltonsborough. 29 B5
Balvaird....252 A1

Balvicar 213 A5
Balvraid Highld. . . 238 A2
Highld. 253 C4
Bamber Bridge . .137 A4
Bambers Green . . 69 A5
Bamburgh 199 C5
Bamff 231 C6
Bamford Derbys. .130 A2
Gtr Man 138 B1
Bampton Cumb . .164 D3
Devon. 27 C4
Oxon. 64 C4
Bampton
Grange. 164 D3
Banavie. 237 B5
Banbury 82 C1
Bancffosfelen . . . 57 A4
Banchory 244 C3
Banchory-
Devenick 245 B6
Bancycapel 57 A4
Bancyfelin 56 A3
Bancyffordd 73 C7
Bandirran. 220 A2
Banff 268 C1
Bangor 123 C5
Bangor-is-y-coed =
Bangor-on-Dee . .110 A2
Bangor-on-Dee =
Bangor-is-y-coed .110 A2
Banham 103 C6
Bank 18 A1
Bankend. 174 B3
Bankfoot 219 A5
Bankglen 182 A4
Bankhead
Aberdeen. 245 A4
Aberds 244 B3
Bank Newton . . .146 B3
Banknock. 207 C5
Banks Cumb 176 C3
Lancs. 136 A2
Bankshill 185 D4
Bank Street 79 A4
Banningham 120 C4
Banniskirk
House. 280 C3
Bannister Green. . 69 A6
Bannockburn . . . 207 A6
Banstead 35 A5
Bantham 7 C5
Banton 207 C5
Banwell 42 D2
Banyard's
Green. 104 D3
Bapchild. 51 C6
Barabhas 288 C4
Barabhas
Iarach 288 C4
Barabhas
Uarach 288 B4
Barachandroman
. . . . .225 D5
Barassie 192 B3
Baravullin 226 C3
Barbaraville. 264 C3
Barber Booth . . .129 A6
Barbieston. 182 A2
Barbon 155 C5
Barbridge. 127 D6
Barbrook 26 A2
Barby 98 D2
Barcaldine. 227 B4
Barcheston 81 D5
Barcombe 22 A2
Barcombe Cross. . 22 A2
Barden 157 B5
Bardennoch. 182 C3
Barden Scale. . . .147 B4
Bardfield Saling. . . 69 A6
Bardney 133 C6
Bardon 114 D2
Bardon Mill 177 C5
Bardowie. 205 A5
Bardrainney. 204 A3
Bardsea 154 D2
Bardsey 148 C2
Bardwell. 103 D5
Bare. 145 A4
Barfad. 202 B3
Barford Norf. 104 A2

Barford continued
Warks. 81 A5
Barford St John . . 82 D1
Barford St Martin. 31 B4
Barford
St Michael. 82 D1
Barfrestone 53 D4
Barnwell
St Andrew 100 C2
Barnwood 63 B4
Barochreal. 226 D3
Barons Cross. . . . 78 B2
Barr 181 B4
Barra Castle 256 D2
Barrachan 171 C5
Barrack. 256 B3
Barraglom 288 D2
Barrahormid 213 D5
Barran. 226 D3
Barrapol. 222 C2
Barras Aberds. . . 245 D5
Cumb 165 D6
Barrasford 177 B7
Barravullin 213 B6
Barregarrow 152 C3
Barrhead 205 C4
Barrhill 181 C4
Barrington Cambs 85 C5
Som 28 D3
Barripper 3 B4
Barmill 204 C3
Barrock. 281 A4
Barrock House . . 281 B4
Barrow Lancs . . .146 D1
Rutland. 116 D1
Suff. 86 A3
Barroway Drove 102 A1
Barrowburn. 188 B1
Barrowby. 116 B1
Barrowcliff 160 C4
Barrowden. 99 A6
Barrowford 146 D2
Barrow Green . . . 51 C6
Barrow Gurney . . 43 C4
Barrow Haven . . .142 A2
Barrow-in-
Furness 153 D3
Barrow Island . . .153 D2
Barrow Nook . . .136 C3
Barrows Green
Ches E 128 D1
Cumb 154 C4
Barrow's Green .127 A5
Barrow Street. . . 30 B2
Barrow upon
Humber 142 A2
Barrow upon
Soar 114 D3
Barrow upon
Trent. 114 C1
Barry = Y Barri . . 41 E6
Barry Island 41 E6
Barsby. 115 D4
Barsham 105 C4
Barston. 97 D5
Barthestree 78 C3
Barthol Chapel . .256 C3
Barthomley 128 D2
Bartley 32 D2
Bartley Green . . . 96 C3
Bartlow. 86 C1
Barton Cambs. . . 85 B6
Ches W 127 D4
Glos 64 A2
Lancs. 136 C2
Lancs. 145 D5
N Yorks. 157 A6
Oxon. 65 C6
Torbay 8 A3
Warks. 80 B4
Barton Bendish. .102 A3
Barton Hartshorn 82 D3
Barton in Fabis . .114 B3
Barton in the
Beans 97 A6
Barton-le-Clay. . . 84 D2
Barton-le-
Street 159 D6
Barton-le-
Willows 149 A6
Barton Mills. 102 D3
Barton on Sea. . . 17 B6

Barnstone 115 B5
Barnt Green. 96 D3
Barnton Ches W. .127 B6
Edin 209 C4
Barnwell All
Saints. 100 C2
Barton on the
Heath 81 D5
Barton St David . 29 B5
Barton Seagrave . 99 D5
Barton Stacey. . . 32 A3
Barton Turf 121 C5
Barton-under-
Needwood. 113 D5
Barton-upon-
Humber 142 A2
Barton
Waterside. 142 A2
Barugh 139 C6
Barway 102 D1
Barwell. 98 B1
Barwick Herts . . . 68 B3
Som 29 D5
Barwick in
Elmet 148 D2
Baschurch 110 C3
Bascote. 81 A7
Basford Green . .129 D4
Bashall Eaves . . .145 C6
Bashley. 17 B6
Basildon. 51 A4
Basingstoke. 47 D4
Baslow 130 B2
Bason Bridge . . . 28 A3
Bassaleg. 42 A1
Bassenthwaite . .163 A5
Bassett 32 D3
Bassingbourn. . . 85 C5
Bassingfield 115 B4
Bassingham 133 C4
Bassingthorpe . .116 C2
Basta. 284 D7
Baston. 116 D4
Bastwick. 121 D6
Baswick Steer. . .150 C3
Batchworth
Heath 67 D5
Batcombe Dorset. 15 A6
Som 29 B6
Bate Heath 128 B1
Batford 67 B6
Bath. 43 C6
Bathampton 44 C1
Bathealton 27 C5
Batheaston 44 C1
Bathford. 44 C1
Bathgate. 208 D2
Bathley 132 D2
Bathpool Corn . . 10 D3
Som 28 C2
Bathville 208 D2
Batley 139 A5
Batsford 81 D4
Battersby 159 A4
Battersea 49 B5
Battisborough
Cross 7 C4
Battisford 87 B6
Battisford Tye. . . 87 B6
Battle E Sus. 23 A5
Powys 76 D4
Battledown 63 A5
Battlefield 111 D4
Battlesbridge . . . 70 D1
Battlesden 67 A4
Battlesea Green 104 D3
Battleton 27 C4
Battram 98 A1
Battramsley. 18 B2
Baughton 80 C1
Baughurst 46 D3
Baulking 64 D4
Baumber 134 B2
Baunton 63 C6
Baverstock. 31 B4
Bawburgh 104 A2
Bawdeswell 120 C2
Bawdrip 28 B3
Bawdsey 88 C4
Bawtry 141 D4
Baxenden 137 A6
Baxterley 97 B5
Baybridge 17 B6
Baycliff 154 D1
Baydon 45 B6
Bayford Herts. . . 68 C3
Som 30 C1
Bayles 165 A5

Baylham 88 B2
Baynard's Green . 65 A6
Bayston Hill. 94 A2
Baythorn End . . . 86 C3
Bayton. 95 D4
Beach 236 D1
Beachampton . . . 83 D4
Beachamwell . . .102 A3
Beachans 253 B6
Beacharr 202 D1
Beachborough . . 38 B3
Beachley 62 D1
Beacon 14 A1
Beacon End 70 A3
Beacon Hill 34 C1
Beacon's Bottom 66 D2
Beaconsfield 67 E4
Beacrabhaic 288 H2
Beadlam 159 C5
Beadlow 84 D3
Beadnell 189 A5
Beaford. 25 D6
Beal Northumb . .199 B4
N Yorks. 140 A3
Beamhurst. 113 B4
Beaminster 15 A4
Beamish 179 D4
Beamsley 147 B4
Bean 50 B2
Beanacre 44 C3
Beanley. 188 B3
Beaquoy 282 E4
Bear Cross 17 B4
Beardwood 137 A5
Beare Green 35 B4
Bearley. 81 A4
Bearnus 224 B2
Bearpark 167 A5
Bearsbridge. 177 D5
Bearsden 205 A5
Bearsted. 37 A5
Bearstone 111 B6
Bearwood BCP. . . 17 B4
Hereford 78 B1
W Mid. 96 C3
Beattock 184 B3
Beauchamp
Roding 69 B5
Beauchief 130 A3
Beaufort. 60 B3
Beaufort Castle .251 B7
Beaulieu. 18 A2
Beauly. 252 B1
Beaumaris 123 C6
Beaumont Cumb .175 C6
Essex 71 A5
Beaumont Hill. . .167 D5
Beausale 97 D5
Beauworth. 33 C4
Beaworthy 11 B5
Beazley End. 70 A1
Bebington 126 A3
Bebside 179 A4
Beccles 105 B5
Becconsall 136 A3
Beckbury 95 A5
Beckenham 49 C6
Beckermet 162 D3
Beckfoot Cumb. .163 D4
Cumb 174 D3
Beck Foot 155 B5
Beckford 80 D2
Beckhampton . . . 45 C4
Beck Hole 159 A7
Beckingham
Lincs. 132 D3
Notts 141 E5
Beckington. 44 D2
Beckley E Sus . . . 37 D6
Hants 17 B6
Oxon. 65 B6
Beck Row 102 D2
Beck Side. 153 B3
Beckton 50 A1
Beckwithshaw . .147 B6
Becontree 50 A1
Bedale. 157 C6
Bedburn 166 B4
Bedchester 30 D2
Beddau 41 C5
Beddgelert 107 B5
Beddingham 22 B2

Beddington 49 C6
Bedfield 88 A3
Bedford 84 B2
Bedham 34 D3
Bedhampton 19 A6
Bedingfield 88 A2
Bedlam 147 A6
Bedlington. 179 A4
Bedlington
Station 179 A4
Bedlinog. 41 A5
Bedminster 43 B4
Bedmond 67 C5
Bednall 112 D3
Bedrule. 187 B5
Bedstone 94 D1
Bedwas 41 C6
Bedworth 97 C6
Bedworth Heath . 97 C6
Bed-y-coedwr . .108 C2
Beeby 98 A3
Beech Hants 33 B5
Staffs 112 B2
Beech Hill
Gtr Man 137 C4
W Berks 47 C4
Beechingstoke . . 45 D4
Beedon 46 B2
Beeford 151 B4
Beeley. 130 C2
Beelsby 143 C4
Beenham 46 C3
Beeny 10 B2
Beer 14 C2
Beercrocombe . . 28 C3
Beer Hackett. . . . 29 D6
Beesands 8 C2
Beesby 135 A4
Beeson 8 C2
Beeston C Beds. . 84 C3
Ches W. 127 D5
Norf 119 D6
Notts 114 B3
W Yorks 148 D1
Beeston Regis. . .120 A3
Beeswing 173 B6
Beetham. 154 D3
Beetley 119 D6
Begbroke 65 B5
Begelly 55 D7
Beggar's Bush . . 77 A6
Beguildy 93 D5
Beighton Norf . .105 A4
S Yorks 131 A4
Beighton Hill. . . .130 D2
Beith 204 C3
Bekesbourne. . . . 52 D3
Belaugh 121 D4
Belbroughton . . . 96 D2
Belchamp Otten. 87 C4
Belchamp St Paul 86 C3
Belchamp Walter 87 C4
Belchford. 134 B2
Belford 199 C5
Belhaven 210 C3
Belhelvie 245 A6
Belhinnie 255 D5
Bellabeg 243 A6
Bellamore 181 C4
Bellanoch. 213 C5
Bellaty. 231 C6
Bell Bar 68 C2
Bell Busk 146 B3
Belleau 135 B4
Bellehiglash 254 C2
Bell End 96 D2
Bellerby 157 B5
Bellever 12 D1
Belliehill 232 B3
Bellingdon 67 C4
Bellingham 177 A6
Belloch 190 B2
Bellochantuy. . . .190 C2
Bellsbank 182 B2
Bellshill
N Lanark. 207 D5
Northumb 199 C5
Bellspool 195 C6

Bellsquarry 208 D3
Bells Yew Green . . 36 C4
Belmaduthy 252 A2
Belmesthorpe . . . 116 D3
Belmont
  Blackburn 137 B5
  London 49 C5
  S Ayrs 192 C3
  Shetland 284 C7
Belnacraig 243 A6
Belowda 5 A4
Belper 114 A1
Belper Lane End 114 A1
Belsay 178 B3
Belses 187 A4
Belsford 7 B6
Belstead 88 C2
Belston 192 C3
Belstone 11 B7
Belthorn 137 A6
Beltinge 52 C3
Beltoft 141 C6
Belton Leics . . . 114 C2
  Lincs 116 B2
  N Lincs 141 C5
  Norf 105 A5
Belton in Rutland 99 A5
Beltring 37 B4
Belts of
  Collonach 244 C3
Belvedere 50 B1
Belvoir 115 B6
Bembridge 19 C5
Bemersyde 197 C4
Bemerton 31 B5
Bempton 161 D5
Benacre 105 C6
Ben Alder
  Lodge 229 A4
Ben Armine
  Lodge 273 C5
Benbuie 183 C5
Ben Casgro 288 E5
Benderloch 226 C4
Bendronaig
  Lodge 250 C2
Benenden 37 C6
Benfield 171 A5
Bengate 121 C5
Bengeworth 80 C3
Benhall Green . . 89 A4
Benhall Street . . 89 A4
Benholm 233 B6
Beningbrough . . 148 B4
Benington Herts . 68 A2
  Lincs 117 A6
Benllech 123 B5
Benmore Argyll . 215 D4
  Stirling 216 B4
Benmore Lodge . 271 C6
Bennacott 10 B3
Bennan 191 C5
Benniworth 134 A2
Benover 37 B5
Bensham 179 C4
Benslie 204 D3
Benson 65 D7
Bent 233 A4
Bent Gate 137 A6
Benthall
  Northumb 189 A5
  Shrops 95 A4
Bentham 63 B5
Benthoul 245 B5
Bentlawnt 94 A1
Bentley E Yorks . 150 D3
  Hants 33 A6
  Suff 88 D2
  S Yorks 140 C3
  Warks 97 B5
  Worcs 80 A2
Bentley Heath . . 97 D4
Benton 26 B1
Bentpath 185 C6
Bents 208 D2
Bentworth 33 A6
Benvie 220 A3
Benwick 101 B5
Beoley 80 A3

Beoraidbeg 235 A5
Bepton 20 A1
Berden 69 A4
Bere Alston 6 A3
Bere Ferrers 6 A3
Berepper 3 C4
Bere Regis 16 B2
Bergh Apton . . . 104 A4
Berinsfield 65 D6
Berkeley 62 D2
Berkhamsted . . . 67 C4
Berkley 30 A2
Berkswell 97 D5
Bermondsey 49 B6
Bernera 249 D5
Bernice 215 C4
Bernisdale 259 C4
Berrick Salome . . 65 D7
Berriedale 275 B5
Berrier 164 C1
Berriew 93 A5
Berrington
  Northumb 198 B4
  Shrops 94 A3
Berrow 42 D2
Berrow Green . . . 79 B5
Berry Down
  Cross 25 A6
Berry Hill Glos . . 62 B1
  Pembs 72 B3
Berryhillock 267 C6
Berrynarbor 25 A6
Berry Pomeroy . . . 8 A2
Bersham 110 A2
Berstane 282 F5
Berwick 22 B3
Berwick Bassett . 45 B4
Berwick Hill . . . 178 B3
Berwick St James 31 B4
Berwick St John . 30 C3
Berwick
  St Leonard 30 B3
Berwick-upon-
  Tweed 198 A3
Bescar 136 B2
Besford 80 C2
Bessacarr 140 C4
Bessels Leigh . . . 65 C5
Bessingby 151 A4
Bessingham 120 B3
Bestbeech Hill . . 36 C4
Besthorpe Norf . 103 B6
  Notts 132 C3
Bestwood 114 A3
Bestwood
  Village 114 A3
Beswick IoW 18 D4
  W Yorks 147 D5
Betchworth 35 B5
Bethania Ceredig . 75 B4
  Gwyn 107 A6
  Gwyn 108 A2
Bethel Anglesey . 122 C3
  Gwyn 109 B4
  Gwyn 123 D5
Bethersden 38 A1
Bethesda Gwyn . 123 D6
  Pembs 55 C6
Bethlehem 58 C3
Bethnal Green . . 49 A6
Betley 111 A6
Betsham 50 B3
Betteshanger . . . 53 D5
Bettiscombe 14 B3
Bettisfield 110 B3
Betton Shrops . . . 93 A7
  Shrops 111 B5
Bettws Bridgend . 40 C4
  Mon 61 B4
  Newport 61 D4
Bettws Cedewain 93 B5
Bettws Gwerfil
  Goch 109 A5
Bettws Ifan 73 B6
Bettws Newydd . 61 C5
Bettws-y-crwyn . 93 C6
Bettyhill 278 B3
Betws 57 A6
Betws Bledrws . . 75 C4
Betws-Garmon . 107 A5
Betws-y-Coed . . 124 D2
Betws-yn-Rhos . 125 B4
Beulah Ceredig . . 73 B5

Beulah continued
  Powys 76 B3
Bevendean 21 B6
Bevercotes 132 B1
Beverley 150 D3
Beverston 63 D4
Bevington 62 D2
Bewaldeth 163 A5
Bewcastle 176 B3
Bewdley 95 D5
Bewerley 147 A5
Bewholme 151 B4
Bexhill 23 B5
Bexley 50 B1
Bexleyheath 50 B1
Bexwell 102 A2
Beyton 87 A5
Bhaltos 287 A5
Bhatarsaigh 286 G2
Bibury 64 C2
Bicester 65 A6
Bickenhall 28 D2
Bickenhill 97 C4
Bicker 117 B5
Bickershaw 137 C5
Bickerstaffe 136 C3
Bickerton Ches E 127 D5
  N Yorks 148 B3
Bickington Devon . 12 D2
  Devon 25 B6
Bickleigh Devon . . 7 A4
  Devon 13 A4
Bickleton 25 B6
Bickley 49 C7
Bickley Moss . . . 111 A4
Bicknacre 70 C1
Bicknoller 27 B6
Bicknor 37 A6
Bickton 31 D5
Bicton Shrops . . . 93 C6
  Shrops 110 D3
Bidborough 36 B3
Biddenden 37 C6
Biddenham 84 C2
Biddestone 44 B2
Biddisham 42 D2
Biddlesden 82 C3
Biddlestone 188 C2
Biddulph 128 D3
Biddulph Moor . 129 D4
Bideford 25 C5
Bidford-on-Avon . 80 B4
Bidston 136 D1
Bielby 149 C6
Bieldside 245 B5
Bierley IoW 18 D4
  W Yorks 147 D5
Bierton 66 B3
Bigbury 7 C5
Bigbury on Sea . . . 7 C5
Bigby 142 C2
Biggar Cumb . . . 153 D2
  S Lanark 195 C5
Biggin Derbys . . 113 A6
  Derbys 129 D6
  N Yorks 148 D4
Biggings 285 G3
Biggin Hill 36 A2
Biggleswade 84 C3
Bighouse 279 B4
Bighton 33 B5
Bignor 20 A2
Big Sand 261 C4
Bigton 285 L5
Bilberry 5 A5
Bilborough 114 A3
Bilbrook 27 A5
Bilbrough 148 C4
Bilbster 281 C4
Bildershaw 167 C5
Bildeston 87 C5
Billericay 69 D6
Billesdon 99 A4
Billesley 80 B4
Billingborough . . 116 B4
Billinge 136 C4
Billingford 120 C2
Billingham 168 C2
Billinghay 133 D6
Billingley 140 C2
Billingshurst 34 D3
Billingsley 95 C5

Billington C Beds . 67 A4
  Lancs 145 D7
Billockby 121 D6
Billy Row 167 B4
Bilsborrow 145 D5
Bilsby 135 B4
Bilsham 20 B2
Bilsington 38 B2
Bilson Green . . . 62 B2
Bilsthorpe 131 C6
Bilsthorpe Moor 131 D6
Bilston Midloth . 209 D5
  W Mid 96 B2
Bilstone 97 A6
Bilting 38 A2
Bilton E Yorks . . 151 D4
  Northumb 189 B5
  Warks 98 D1
Bilton in Ainsty . 148 C3
Bimbister 282 F4
Binbrook 143 D4
Binchester
  Blocks 167 B5
Bincombe 15 C6
Bindal 265 B5
Binegar 29 A6
Binfield 47 B6
Binfield Heath . . 47 B5
Bingfield 178 B1
Bingham 115 B5
Bingley 147 D5
Bings Heath . . . 111 D4
Binham 120 B1
Binley Hants . . . 46 D2
  W Mid 97 D6
Binley Woods . . . 97 D6
Binniehill 207 C6
Binsoe 157 D6
Binstead 19 B4
Binsted 33 A6
Binton 80 B4
Bintree 120 C2
Binweston 93 A7
Birch Essex 70 B3
  Gtr Man 138 C1
Bircham Newton 119 B4
Bircham Tofts . . 119 B4
Birchanger 69 A5
Birchencliffe . . . 139 B4
Bircher 78 A2
Birch Green 70 B3
Birchgrove Cardiff 41 C6
  Swansea 40 B2
Birch Heath 127 C5
Birch Hill 127 B5
Birchington 53 C4
Birchmoor 97 A5
Birch Vale 129 A5
Birchwood Lincs . 133 C4
  Warr 137 D5
Bircotes 140 D4
Birdbrook 86 C3
Birdforth 158 D3
Birdham 20 C1
Birdholme 130 C3
Birdingbury 82 A1
Birdlip 63 B5
Birds Edge 139 C5
Birdsgreen 95 C5
Birdsmoor Gate . 14 A3
Birdston 205 A6
Birdwell 139 C6
Birdwood 62 B3
Birgham 198 C1
Birkby 158 A2
Birkdale 136 B2
Birkenhead 126 A3
Birkenhills 256 B2
Birkenshaw
  N Lanark 207 D4
  W Yorks 139 A5
Birkhall 243 C6
Birkhill Angus . . 220 A3
  Borders 185 A5
Birkholme 116 C2
Birkin 140 A3
Birley 78 B2
Birling Kent 50 C3
  Northumb 189 C5
Birling Gap 22 C3

Birlingham 80 C2
Birmingham 96 C3
Birnam 230 D4
Birse 244 C2
Birsemore 244 C2
Birstall Leics . . . 98 A2
Birstwith 147 B6
Birthorpe 116 B4
Birtley Hereford . 78 A1
  Northumb 177 B6
  T&W 179 D4
Birts Street 79 D5
Bisbrooke 99 B5
Biscathorpe 134 A2
Biscot 67 A5
Bisham 47 A6
Bishampton 80 B2
Bish Mill 26 C2
Bishop
  Auckland 167 C5
Bishopbridge . . . 142 D2
Bishopbriggs . . . 205 B6
Bishop Burton . . 150 D2
Bishop
  Middleham . . . 167 B6
Bishopmill 266 C3
Bishop Monkton 148 A2
Bishop Norton . . 142 D1
Bishopsbourne . . 52 D3
Bishops Cannings 44 C4
Bishop's Castle . . 93 C7
Bishop's Cleeve . 63 A5
Bishops Frome . . 79 C4
Bishop's Green . . 69 B6
Bishop's Hull . . . 28 C2
Bishop's
  Itchington 81 B6
Bishops Lydeard . 27 C6
Bishops Nympton 26 C2
Bishop's Offley . 112 C1
Bishop's
  Stortford 69 A4
Bishop's Sutton . 33 B5
Bishop's
  Tachbrook 81 A6
Bishops Tawton . 25 B6
Bishopsteignton . 13 D4
Bishopstoke 32 D3
Bishopston 57 D5
Bishopstone Bucks 66 B3
  E Sus 22 B2
  Hereford 78 C2
  Swindon 45 A6
  Wilts 31 C4
Bishopstrow 30 A2
Bishop Sutton . . 43 D4
Bishopswood . . . 28 D2
Bishop's Wood . . 95 A6
Bishopsworth . . . 43 C4
Bishop
  Thornton 147 A6
Bishopthorpe . . . 149 C4
Bishopton Darl . 167 C6
  Dumfries 171 C6
  N Yorks 157 D7
  Renfs 205 A4
Bishop Wilton . . 149 B6
Bishton 42 A2
Bisley Glos 63 C5
  Sur 34 A2
Bispham 144 C3
Bispham Green . 136 B3
Bissoe 4 C2
Bisterne Close . . 17 A6
Bitchfield 116 C2
Bittadon 25 A6
Bittaford 7 B5
Bittering 119 D6
Bitterley 94 D3
Bitterne 32 D3
Bitteswell 98 C2
Bitton 43 C5
Bix 47 A5
Bixter 285 H5
Blaby 98 B2
Blackacre 184 C3
Blackadder
  West 198 A2

Blackawton 8 B2
Blackborough . . . 13 A5
Blackborough
  End 118 D3
Black Bourton . . 64 C3
Blackboys 36 D3
Blackbrook
  Derbys 114 A1
  Mers 136 D4
  Staffs 111 B6
Blackburn
  Aberds 245 A5
  Aberds 255 C6
  Blackburn 137 A5
  W Loth 208 D2
Black Callerton . 178 C3
Black Clauchrie 181 C4
Black Corries
  Lodge 228 C1
Blackcraig 183 D5
Black Crofts . . . 226 C4
Blackden Heath . 128 B2
Blackdog 245 A6
Black Dog 12 A3
Blackfell 179 D4
Blackfield 18 A3
Blackford Cumb . 175 B6
  Perth 218 D3
  Som 28 A4
  Som 29 C6
Blackfordby 114 D1
Blackgang 18 D3
Blackhall
  Colliery 168 B2
Blackhall Mill . . 178 D3
Blackhall Rocks . 168 B2
Blackham 36 C2
Blackhaugh 196 C3
Blackheath Essex . 71 A4
  Suff 105 D5
  Sur 34 B3
  W Mid 96 C2
Black Heddon . . 178 B2
Blackhill Aberds . 257 B5
  Aberds 269 D5
  Highld 258 C3
Blackhills Highld 253 A5
  Moray 266 D3
Blackhorse 43 B5
Blackland 44 C4
Black Lane 137 C6
Blacklaw 268 D1
Blackley 138 C1
Blacklunans 231 B5
Black Marsh 94 B1
Blackmill 40 C4
Blackmoor 33 B6
Blackmoor Gate . 26 A1
Blackmore 69 C6
Blackmore End
  Essex 86 D3
  Herts 67 B6
Black Mount . . . 228 D1
Blackness 208 C3
Blacknest 33 A6
Black Notley . . . 70 A1
Blacko 146 C2
Black Pill 57 C6
Blackpool
  Blackpool 144 D3
  Devon 8 C2
  Pembs 55 C6
Blackpool Gate . 176 B3
Blackridge 208 D1
Blackrock Argyll . 200 B3
  Mon 60 B4
Blackrod 137 B5
Blackshaw 174 B3
Blackshaw Head 138 A2
Blacksmith's
  Green 88 A2
Blackstone 21 A5
Black Tar 55 D5
Blackthorn 65 B7
Blackthorpe 87 A5
Blacktoft 141 A6
Blacktop 245 B5
Black Torrington . 11 A5
Blacktown 42 A1
Blackwall Tunnel 49 A6
Blackwater Corn . 4 C2
  Hants 34 A1

Blackwater continued
IoW 18 C4
Blackwaterfoot . .191 C4
Blackwell Darl . .167 D5
Derbys 129 B6
Derbys 131 D4
Warks. 81 C5
Worcs. 96 D2
W Sus. 36 C1
Blackwood. 194 B2
Blackwood
=Coed Duon 41 B6
Blackwood Hill . .129 D4
Blacon. 126 C3
Bladnoch 171 B6
Bladon 65 B5
Blaenannerch . . .73 B5
Blaenau
Ffestiniog 108 A2
Blaenavon 61 C4
Blaencelyn. 73 A6
Blaendyryn 59 B6
Blaenffos 73 C4
Blaengarw 40 B4
Blaengwrach 59 E5
Blaen-gwynfi 40 B3
Blaenpennal 75 B5
Blaenplwyf 75 A4
Blaenporth 73 B5
Blaenrhondda . . .40 A4
Blaen-waun 73 D5
Blaen-y-coed 73 D6
Blaenycwm 92 D2
Blaen-y-Cwm
Denb. 109 B5
Gwyn 108 C2
Powys 109 C5
Blagdon N Som. . .43 D4
Torbay 8 C2
Blagdon Hill 28 D2
Blagill 165 A5
Blaguegate 136 C3
Blaich 237 B4
Blain 235 D5
Blaina 60 C4
Blair Atholl 230 B2
Blairbeg 191 B6
Blairdaff 244 A3
Blair Drummond 207 A5
Blairglas. 206 B1
Blairgowrie 231 D5
Blairhall 208 B3
Blairingone 208 A2
Blairland 204 D3
Blairlogie 207 A6
Blairlomond 215 C4
Blairmore. 215 D4
Blairnamarrow. .243 A5
Blairquhosh. . . .206 B3
Blair's Ferry. . . .203 B4
Blairskaith 205 A5
Blaisdon 62 B3
Blakebrook 95 D6
Blakedown. 96 D1
Blakelaw 197 C6
Blakeley 95 B6
Blakeley Lane . .112 A3
Blakemere. 78 C1
Blakeney Glos . . .62 C2
Norf 120 A2
Blakenhall
Ches F 111 A6
W Mid. 96 B2
Blakeshall 95 C6
Blakesley 82 B3
Blanchland 178 D1
Blandford Forum 16 A2
Blandford
St Mary 16 A2
Bland Hill 147 B6
Blanefield 205 A5
Blankney 133 C5
Blantyre 194 A1
Blar a'Chaorainn 237 C5
Blaran 214 A1
Blarghour. 214 A2
Blarmachfoldach
. . . . .237 C4
Blarnalearoch. .262 A3
Blashford 17 A5
Blaston 99 B5
Blatherwycke 99 B6

Blawith 154 C1
Blaxhall. 89 B4
Blaxton 141 C4
Blaydon 178 C3
Bleadon 42 D2
Bleak Hey Nook .138 C3
Blean. 52 C3
Bleasby Lincs . . .133 A6
Notts 115 A5
Bleasdale. 145 C5
Bleatarn 165 D5
Blebocraigs 220 C4
Bleddfa. 77 A6
Bledington 64 A3
Bledlow 66 C2
Bledlow Ridge . .66 D2
Blegbie 210 D1
Blencarn 165 B4
Blencogo 175 D4
Blendworth 33 D6
Blenheim Park . .119 B5
Blennerhasset. .175 D4
Blervie Castle . .253 A6
Bletchingdon . . .65 B6
Bletchingley 35 A6
Bletchley
M Keynes 83 D5
Shrops 111 B5
Bletherston 55 B6
Bletsoe 84 B2
Blewbury 46 A3
Blickling 120 C3
Blidworth 131 D5
Blindburn 188 B1
Blindcrake 163 A4
Blindley Heath . .35 B6
Blisland 10 D2
Blissford. 31 D5
Bliss Gate. 95 D5
Blisworth 83 B4
Blithbury 113 C4
Blitterlees 174 C4
Blockley 81 D4
Blofield. 104 A4
Blofield Heath . .121 D5
Blo' Norton 103 D6
Bloomfield. 187 A4
Blore 113 A5
Blount's Green . .113 B4
Blowick. 136 B2
Bloxham. 82 D1
Bloxholm 133 D5
Bloxwich 96 A2
Bloxworth 16 B2
Blubberhouses . .147 B5
Blue Anchor Som . .27 A5
Swansea 57 C5
Blue Row 71 B4
Blundeston 105 B6
Blunham. 84 B3
Blunsdon
St Andrew 45 A5
Bluntington 96 D1
Bluntisham 101 D5
Blunts 6 A2
Blyborough 142 D1
Blyford 105 D5
Blymhill 112 D2
Blyth Northumb. .179 A5
Notts 131 A6
Blyth Bridge 195 B6
Blythburgh 105 D5
Blythe 197 B4
Blythe Bridge . .112 A3
Blyton 141 D6
Boarhills. 221 C5
Boarhunt 19 A5
Boarshead 36 C3
Boars Head 137 C4
Boars Hill 65 C5
Boarstall 66 B1
Boasley Cross . . .11 B5
Boath. 264 C1
Boat of Garten . .242 A2
Bobbing 51 C5
Bobbington 95 B6
Bobbingworth. . .69 C5
Bocaddon 5 B6
Bochastle. 217 D6
Bocking
Churchstreet . .70 A1

Boddam Aberds . .257 B6
Shetland. 285 M5
Boddington. 63 A4
Bodedern 122 B3
Bodelwyddan . .125 B5
Bodenham
Hereford 78 B3
Wilts. 31 C5
Bodenham Moor .78 B3
Bodermid 106 D1
Bodewryd. 122 A3
Bodfari 125 B5
Bodffordd 123 C4
Bodham 120 A3
Bodiam 37 D5
Bodicote. 82 D1
Bodieve 9 D5
Bodinnick 5 B6
Bodle Street
Green 23 A4
Bodmin 5 A5
Bodney 103 B4
Bodorgan 122 D3
Bodsham 38 A3
Boduan 106 C3
Bodymoor Heath .97 B4
Bogallan 252 A2
Bogbrae 257 C5
Bogend Borders . .198 B1
S Ayrs 192 B3
Boghall 208 D2
Boghead. 194 B2
Bogmoor 267 C4
Bogniebrae 255 B6
Bognor Regis 20 C2
Bograxie. 256 E2
Bogside 194 A3
Bogton 268 D1
Bogue 182 D4
Bohenie 239 D6
Bohortha 4 D3
Bohuntine 239 D6
Boirseam 287 F5
Bojewyan 2 B1
Bolam Durham . .167 C4
Northumb. 178 A2
Bolberry 7 D5
Bold Heath. 127 A5
Boldon 179 C5
Boldon Colliery. .179 C5
Boldre 18 B2
Boldron 166 D3
Bole 132 A2
Bolehill 130 D2
Boleside 196 C3
Bolham 27 D4
Bolham Water. . . .27 D6
Bolingey 4 B2
Bollington 129 B4
Bollington Cross 129 B4
Bolney. 35 D5
Bolnhurst 84 B2
Bolshan 233 C4
Bolsover. 131 B4
Bolsterstone . . .139 D5
Bolstone. 78 D3
Boltby 158 C3
Bolter End 66 D2
Bolton Cumb 165 C4
E Loth 210 C2
Boltonfellend . .176 C2
Boltongate. 175 D5
Bolton-le-
Sands 145 A4
Bolton Low
Houses 175 D5
Bolton-on-
Swale 157 B6
Bolton Percy . . .148 C4
Bolton Town
End 145 A4
Bolton upon
Dearne 140 C2
Bolventor 10 D2
Bomere Heath . .110 D3

Bonar Bridge. . .264 A2
Bonawe 227 C5
Bonby 142 B2
Boncath 73 C5
Bonchester
Bridge 187 B4
Bonchurch. 19 D4
Bondleigh 12 A1
Bonehill Devon. . .12 D2
Staffs 97 A4
Bo'ness. 208 B2
Bonhill 206 C1
Boningale 95 A6
Bonjedward. . . .187 A5
Bonkle 194 A3
Bonnavoulin . . .225 A4
Bonnington Edin .208 D4
Kent 38 B2
Bonnybank. 220 D3
Bonnybridge. . .207 B6
Bonnykelly. 268 D3
Bonnyrigg and
Lasswade 209 D6
Bonnyton Aberds 256 C1
Angus. 220 A3
Angus. 233 C4
Bonsall 130 D2
Bonskeid House 230 B2
Bont. 61 B5
Bontddu 91 A4
Bont-Dolgadfan . .91 B6
Bont-goch 91 D4
Bonthorpe 135 B4
Bontnewydd
Ceredig 75 B5
Gwyn 107 A4
Bont-newydd . .125 B5
Bont Newydd
Gwyn 108 A2
Oxon. 108 C2
Bontuchel 125 D5
Bonvilston 41 D5
Bon-y-maen 57 C6
Booker 66 D3
Boon 197 B4
Boosbeck 169 D4
Boot. 163 D4
Booth 138 A3
Boothby Graffoe 133 D4
Boothby Pagnell 116 B2
Boothen 112 A2
Boothferry. 141 A5
Boothville 83 A4
Booth Wood 138 B3
Bootle Cumb 153 B2
Mers. 136 D2
Booton 120 C3
Boquhan 206 B3
Boraston. 95 D4
Borden Kent 51 C5
W Sus. 34 D1
Bordley 146 A3
Bordon 33 B7
Bordon Camp . . .33 B6
Boreham Essex . .70 C1
Wilts. 30 A2
Boreham Street . .23 A4
Borehamwood . .68 D1
Boreland
Dumfries 185 C4
Stirling 217 A5
Borgh W Isles. . .286 F2
W Isles. 287 H4
Borghastan 288 C3
Borgie. 278 C2
Borgue Dumfries .172 D4
Highld. 275 B5
Borley 87 C4
Bornais. 286 D3
Bornesketaig. . .258 A3
Borness 172 D4
Boroughbridge . .148 A2
Borough Green. . .36 A4
Borras Head 126 D3
Borreraig 258 C1
Borrobol Lodge . 274 B2
Borrowash 114 B2
Borrowby 158 C3
Borrowdale 163 C5
Borrowfield 245 C5
Borth. 90 C4

Borthwickbrae . .186 B3
Borthwickshiels 186 B3
Borth-y-Gest . . .107 C5
Borve. 259 D4
Borve Lodge . . .287 E5
Borwick 154 D4
Bosavern 2 B1
Bosbury 79 C4
Boscastle 10 B2
Boscombe BCP . .17 B5
Wilts. 31 B6
Boscoppa. 5 B5
Bosham 19 A7
Bosherston 55 E5
Boskenna 2 C2
Bosley 129 C4
Bossall 149 A6
Bossiney 9 C6
Bossingham. 38 A3
Bossington. 26 A3
Bostock Green . .127 C6
Boston 117 A6
Boston Long
Hedges. 117 A6
Boston Spa 148 C3
Boston West 117 A5
Boswinger 5 C4
Botallack 2 B1
Botany Bay. 68 D2
Botcherby 175 C7
Botcheston 98 A1
Botesdale. 103 D6
Bothal 179 A4
Bothamsall 131 B6
Bothel 163 A4
Bothenhampton. .15 B4
Bothwell. 194 A2
Botley Bucks. 67 C4
Hants 32 D4
Oxon. 65 C5
Botolph Claydon .66 A2
Botolphs 21 B4
Bottacks 263 D6
Bottesford Leics .115 B6
N Lincs 141 C6
Bottisham 86 A1
Bottlesford 45 D5
Bottom Boat . . .139 A6
Bottomcraig. . . .220 B3
Bottom House. .129 D5
Bottom of
Hutton 136 A3
Bottom o' th'
Moor. 137 B5
Botusfleming 6 A3
Botwnnog 106 C2
Bough Beech. . . .36 B2
Boughrood 77 D5
Boughspring. . . .62 D1
Boughton Norf. . .102 A2
Notts 131 C6
W Nhants 83 A4
Boughton Aluph. .38 A2
Boughton Lees. . .38 A2
Boughton
Malherbe. 37 B6
Boughton
Monchelsea . . .37 A5
Boughton Street .52 D2
Boulby 169 D5
Boulden 94 C3
Boulmer 189 B5
Boulston. 55 C5
Boultenstone . . .243 A7
Boultham 133 C4
Bourn 85 B5
Bourne 116 C3
Bourne End
Bucks 48 A1
C Beds 83 C6
Herts 67 C5
Bournemouth . . .17 B4
Bournes Green
Glos 63 C5
Southend 51 A6
Bournheath 96 D2
Bournmoor 179 D5
Bournville 96 C3
Bourton Dorset . .30 B1
N Som. 42 C2
Oxon. 45 A6
Shrops 94 B3

Bourton on
Dunsmore 98 D1
Bourton on the
Hill 81 D4
Bourton-on-the-
Water 64 A2
Bousd 223 A5
Boustead Hill . . .175 C5
Bouth 154 C2
Bouthwaite 157 D5
Boveney 48 B2
Boverton 41 E4
Bovey Tracey. . . .12 D3
Bovingdon 67 C5
Bovingdon Green
Bucks 47 A6
Herts 67 C5
Bovinger. 69 C5
Bovington Camp .16 C2
Bow Borders . . .196 B3
Devon. 12 A2
Orkney 283 H4
Bowbank. 166 C2
Bow Brickhill 83 D6
Bowburn. 167 B6
Bowcombe. 18 C3
Bowd. 13 B6
Bowden Borders .197 C4
Devon. 8 C2
Bowden Hill. 44 C3
Bowderdale. 155 A5
Bowdon 128 A2
Bower 177 A5
Bowerchalke. . . .31 C4
Bowerhill 44 C3
Bower Hinton . . .29 D4
Bowermadden . .280 B4
Bowers Gifford. .51 A4
Bowershall. 208 A3
Bowertower 280 B4
Bowes. 166 D2
Bowgreave. 145 C4
Bowgreen 128 A2
Bowhill 186 A3
Bowhouse 174 B3
Bowland Bridge .154 C3
Bowley 78 B3
Bowlhead Green .34 C2
Bowling W Dunb. .205 A4
W Yorks 147 D5
Bowling Bank . .110 A2
Bowling Green . .79 B6
Bowmanstead . .154 B2
Bowmore 200 C3
Bowness-on-
Solway 175 B5
Bowness-on-
Windermere . .154 B3
Bow of Fife 220 C3
Bowsden 198 B3
Bowside Lodge. .279 B4
Bowston. 154 B3
Bow Street. 90 D4
Bowthorpe. 104 A2
Box Glos 63 C4
Wilts. 44 C2
Boxbush 62 B3
Box End 84 C2
Boxford Suff. 87 C5
W Berks 46 B2
Boxgrove 20 B2
Boxley. 37 A5
Boxmoor. 67 C5
Boxted Essex 87 D6
Suff 87 B4
Boxted Cross. . . .87 D6
Boxted Heath . . .87 D6
Boxworth 85 A5
Boxworth End. . .85 A5
Boyden Gate 53 C4
Boylestone 113 B5
Boyndie 268 C1
Boynton 151 A4
Boysack 233 D4
Boyton Corn 10 B4
Suff 89 C4
Wilts. 30 B3
Boyton Cross. . . .69 C6
Boyton End 86 C3

Bozeat 83 B6
Braaid 152 D3
Braal Castle . . . 280 B3
Brabling Green . . 88 A3
Brabourne 38 A2
Brabourne Lees . 38 A2
Brabster 281 B5
Bracadale 246 A2
Bracara 235 A6
Braceborough . . 116 D3
Bracebridge . . . 133 C4
Bracebridge
Heath 133 C4
Bracebridge Low
Fields 133 C4
Braceby 116 B3
Bracewell 146 C2
Brackenfield . . . 130 D3
Brackenthwaite
Cumb 175 D5
N Yorks 148 B1
Bracklesham . . . 19 B7
Brackletter 239 C6
Brackley Argyll . . 202 D2
W Nhants 82 D2
Brackloch 270 B4
Bracknell 47 C6
Braco 218 D3
Bracobrae 267 D6
Bracon Ash 104 B2
Bracorina 235 A6
Bradbourne 130 D2
Bradbury 167 C6
Bradda 152 E1
Bradden 82 C2
Braddock 5 A6
Bradeley 128 D3
Bradenham Bucks 66 D3
Norf 103 A5
Bradenstoke . . . 44 B4
Bradfield Essex . 88 D2
Norf 121 B4
W Berks 47 B4
Bradfield
Combust 87 B4
Bradfield Green . 128 D1
Bradfield Heath . 71 A5
Bradfield St Clare 87 B5
Bradfield
St George 87 A5
Bradford Corn . . 10 D2
Derbys 130 C2
Devon 11 A5
Northumb 199 C5
W Yorks 147 D5
Bradford Abbas . 29 D5
Bradford Leigh . 44 C2
Bradford-on-
Avon 44 C2
Bradford-on-
Tone 28 C1
Bradford Peverell 15 B6
Brading 19 C5
Bradley Derbys . . 113 A6
Hants 33 A5
NE Lincs 143 C4
Staffs 112 D2
W Mid 96 B2
W Yorks 139 A4
Bradley Green . . 80 A2
Bradley in the
Moors 113 A4
Bradley Stoke . . 43 A5
Bradlow 79 D5
Bradmore Notts . . 114 B3
W Mid 96 B1
Bradninch 13 A5
Bradnop 129 D5
Bradpole 15 B4
Bradshaw
Gtr Man 137 B6
W Yorks 138 B3
Bradstone 11 C4
Bradwall Green . 128 C2
Bradway 130 A3
Bradwell Derbys . 129 A6
Essex 70 A2
M Keynes 83 D5
Norf 105 A6

Bradwell continued
Staffs 112 A2
Bradwell Grove . . 64 C3
Bradwell on Sea . 71 C4
Bradwell
Waterside 70 C3
Bradworthy 24 D4
Bradworthy
Cross 24 D4
Brae Dumfries . . 173 A6
Highld 261 B5
Highld 272 D2
Shetland 284 G5
Braeantra 264 C1
Braedownie 231 A6
Braefield 251 C6
Braegrum 219 B5
Braehead
Dumfries 171 B6
Orkney 282 C5
Orkney 283 G6
S Lanark 194 C3
S Lanark 195 A4
Braehead of
Lunan 233 C4
Braehoulland . . . 284 F4
Braehungie 275 A5
Braelangwell
Lodge 263 A7
Braemar 243 C4
Braemore Highld 262 C3
Highld 275 A4
Brae of
Achnahaird . . . 270 C3
Brae Roy Lodge . 240 C1
Braeside 204 A2
Braes of Enzie . . 267 D4
Braeswick 282 D7
Braewick 285 H5
Brafferton Darl . . 167 C5
N Yorks 158 D3
Brafield-on-the-
Green 83 B5
Bragar 288 C3
Bragbury End . . . 68 A2
Bragleenmore . . 226 D4
Braichmelyn . . . 123 D6
Braid 209 D5
Braides 144 B4
Braidley 156 C4
Braidwood 194 B3
Braigo 200 B2
Brailsford 113 A6
Brainshaugh . . . 189 C5
Braintree 70 A1
Braiseworth 104 D2
Braishfield 32 C2
Braithwaite
Cumb 163 B5
S Yorks 140 B4
W Yorks 147 C4
Braithwell 140 D3
Bramber 21 A4
Bramcote Notts . . 114 B3
Warks 97 C7
Bramdean 33 C5
Bramerton 104 A3
Bramfield Herts . . 68 B2
Suff 105 D4
Bramford 88 C2
Bramhall 128 A3
Bramham 148 C3
Bramhope 147 C6
Bramley Hants . . 47 D4
Sur 34 B3
S Yorks 140 D2
W Yorks 147 D6
Bramling 53 D4
Brampford Speke 13 B4
Brampton Cambs 100 D4
Cumb 165 C4
Cumb 176 C3
Derbys 130 B3
Hereford 78 D2
Lincs 132 B3
Norf 120 C4
Suff 105 C5
S Yorks 140 C2
Brampton
Abbotts 62 A2
Brampton Ash . . 99 C4
Brampton Bryan . 94 D1

Brampton en le
Morthen 131 A4
Bramshall 113 B4
Bramshaw 31 D6
Bramshill 47 C5
Bramshott 34 C1
Branault 235 D4
Brancaster 119 A4
Brancaster
Staithe 119 A4
Brancepeth 167 B5
Branch End 178 C2
Branchill 266 D1
Branderburgh . . . 266 B3
Brandesburton . 151 C4
Brandeston 88 A3
Brand Green 62 A3
Brandhill 94 D2
Brandis Corner . . 11 A5
Brandiston 120 C3
Brandon Durham 167 B5
Lincs 116 A2
Northumb 188 B3
Suff 102 C3
Warks 97 D7
Brandon Bank . . 102 C2
Brandon Creek . 102 B3
Brandon Parva . . 104 A3
Brandsby 159 D4
Brandy Wharf . . 142 D2
Brane 2 C2
Bran End 69 A6
Branksome 17 B4
Branksome Park . 17 B4
Bransby 132 B3
Branscombe 14 C1
Bransford 79 B5
Bransgore 17 B5
Branshill 208 A1
Bransholme 151 D4
Branson's Cross . 96 D3
Branston Leics . . 115 C6
Lincs 133 C5
Staffs 113 C6
Branston Booths 133 C5
Branstone 19 C4
Bransty 162 C2
Brant
Broughton . . . 133 D4
Brantham 88 D2
Branthwaite
Cumb 162 B3
Cumb 163 A5
Brantingham . . . 142 A1
Branton
Northumb 188 B3
S Yorks 140 C4
Branxholme 186 B3
Branxholm Park 186 B3
Branxton 198 C2
Brassey Green . 127 C5
Brassington . . . 130 D2
Brasted 36 A2
Brasted Chart . . . 36 A2
Brathens 244 C3
Bratoft 135 C4
Brattleby 133 A4
Bratton Telford . . 111 D5
Wilts 44 D3
Bratton Clovelly . 11 B5
Bratton Fleming . 26 B1
Bratton Seymour 29 C6
Braughing 68 A3
Braunston 82 A2
Braunston Town 98 A2
Braunston-in-
Rutland 99 A5
Braunton 25 B5
Brawby 159 D6
Brawl 279 B4
Brawlbin 279 C6
Bray 48 B2
Braybrooke 99 C4
Braye Ald 7
Brayford 26 B1
Bray Shop 10 D4
Braystones 162 D3
Braythorn 147 C6
Brayton 149 D5
Bray Wick 48 B1
Brazacott 10 B3
Breach 51 C5

Brampton en le
Breachacha
Castle 223 B4
Breachwood
Green 67 A6
Breacleit 288 D2
Breaden Heath . 110 B3
Breadsall 114 B1
Breadstone 62 C3
Breage 3 C4
Breakachy 251 B6
Bream 62 C2
Breamore 31 D5
Brean 42 D1
Breanais 287 B4
Brearton 148 A2
Breascleit 288 D3
Breaston 114 B2
Brechfa 58 B2
Brechin 232 B3
Breckan 283 G3
Breck of Cruan . 282 F4
Breckrey 259 B5
Brecon
= Aberhonddu . 60 A2
Bredbury 138 D2
Brede 23 A6
Bredenbury 79 B4
Bredfield 88 B3
Bredgar 51 C5
Bredhurst 51 C4
Bredicot 80 B2
Bredon 80 D2
Bredon's Norton . 80 D2
Bredwardine . . . 78 C1
Breedon on the
Hill 114 C2
Breibhig W Isles . 286 G2
W Isles 288 D5
Breich 208 D2
Breightmet 137 C6
Breighton 149 D6
Breinton 78 D2
Breinton
Common 78 C2
Breiwick 285 J6
Bremhill 44 B3
Bremirehoull . . 285 L6
Brenchley 37 B4
Brendon 26 A2
Brenkley 179 B4
Brent Eleigh . . . 87 C5
Brentford 49 B4
Brentingby 115 D5
Brent Knoll 42 D2
Brent Pelham . . 85 D6
Brentwood 69 D5
Brenzett 38 C2
Brereton 113 D4
Brereton Green . 128 C2
Brereton Heath . 128 C3
Bressingham . . 104 C1
Bretby 113 C6
Bretford 98 D1
Bretforton 80 C3
Bretherdale
Head 155 A4
Bretherton 136 A3
Brettabister . . . 285 H6
Brettenham Norf 103 C5
Suff 87 B5
Bretton Derbys . . 130 B2
Flint 126 C3
Brewer Street . . 35 A6
Brewlands
Bridge 231 B5
Brewood 96 A1
Briach 266 D1
Briants Puddle . . 16 B2
Brick End 69 A5
Brickendon 68 C3
Bricket Wood . . . 67 C6
Bricklehampton . 80 C2
Bride 152 A4
Bridekirk 163 A4
Bridell 73 B4
Bridestowe 11 C6
Brideswell 255 C6
Bridford 12 C3
Bridfordmills . . . 12 C3
Bridge 52 D3
Bridge End 116 B4
Bridgefoot Angus 220 A3

Bridgefoot continued
Cumb 162 B3
Bridge Green . . . 85 D6
Bridgehampton . 29 C5
Bridge Hewick . . 158 D2
Bridgehill 178 D2
Bridgemary 19 A4
Bridgemont . . . 129 A5
Bridgend Aberds 244 A2
Aberds 255 C6
Angus 232 B3
Argyll 190 B3
Argyll 200 B3
Argyll 214 C1
Cumb 164 D1
Fife 220 C3
Moray 255 C4
N Lanark 207 C4
Pembs 73 B4
W Loth 208 C3
Bridgend = Pen-y-
bont ar Ogwr . . 40 D4
Bridgend of
Lintrathen . . . 231 C6
Bridge of Alford 244 A2
Bridge of Allan . 207 A5
Bridge of Avon . 254 C2
Bridge of Awe . . 227 D5
Bridge of Balgie 229 D4
Bridge of Cally . 231 C5
Bridge of Canny 244 C3
Bridge of
Craigisla 231 C6
Bridge of Dee . . 173 C5
Bridge of Don . . 245 A6
Bridge of Dun . . 233 C4
Bridge of Dye . . 244 D3
Bridge of Earn . 219 C6
Bridge of Ericht 229 C4
Bridge of Feugh 245 C4
Bridge of Forss . 279 B6
Bridge of Gairn . 243 C6
Bridge of Gaur . 229 C4
Bridge of
Muchalls 245 C5
Bridge of Oich . 240 B1
Bridge of Orchy 216 A2
Bridge of Waith 282 F3
Bridge of Walls . 285 H4
Bridge of Weir . 204 B3
Bridgerule 10 A3
Bridges 94 B1
Bridge Sollers . . 78 C2
Bridge Street . . 87 C4
Bridgeton 205 B6
Bridgetown Corn . 10 C4
Som 27 B4
Bridge Trafford 127 B4
Bridge Yate 43 B5
Bridgham 103 C5
Bridgnorth 95 B5
Bridgtown 96 A2
Bridgwater 28 B3
Bridlington 151 A4
Bridport 15 B4
Bridstow 62 A1
Brierfield 146 D2
Brierley Glos . . . 62 B2
Hereford 78 B2
S Yorks 140 B2
Brierley Hill 96 C2
Briery Hill 60 C3
Brigg 142 C2
Briggswath 160 A2
Brigham Cumb . . 162 A3
E Yorks 150 B3
Brighouse 139 A4
Brighstone 18 C3
Brightgate 130 D2
Brighthampton . 65 C4
Brightling 37 D4
Brightlingsea . . 71 B4
Brighton Brighton 21 B6
Corn 4 B4
Brighton Hill . . . 33 A5
Brightons 208 C2
Brightwalton . . . 46 B2
Brightwell 88 C3
Brightwell
Baldwin 66 D1
Brightwell cum
Sotwell 65 D6

Brignall 166 D3
Brig o'Turk 217 D5
Brigsley 143 C4
Brigsteer 154 C3
Brigstock 99 C6
Brill 66 B1
Brilley 77 C6
Brimaston 55 B5
Brimfield 78 A3
Brimington . . . 131 B4
Brimley 12 D2
Brimpsfield 63 B5
Brimpton 46 C3
Brims 283 J3
Brimscombe . . . 63 C4
Brimstage 126 A3
Brinacory 235 A6
Brind 149 D6
Brindister
Shetland 285 H4
Shetland 285 K6
Brindle 137 A5
Brindley Ford . . 128 D3
Brineton 112 D2
Bringhurst 99 B5
Brington 100 D2
Brinian 282 E5
Briningham . . . 120 B2
Brinkhill 134 B3
Brinkley 86 B2
Brinklow 98 D1
Brinkworth 44 A4
Brinmore 252 D2
Brinscall 137 A5
Brinsea 42 C3
Brinsley 114 A2
Brinsop 78 C2
Brinsworth 131 A4
Brinton 120 B2
Brisco 175 C7
Brisley 119 C6
Brislington 43 B5
Bristol 43 B4
Briston 120 B2
Britannia 138 A1
Britford 31 C5
Brithdir 91 A5
British Legion
Village 37 A5
Briton Ferry 40 B2
Britwell Salome . 66 D1
Brixham 8 B3
Brixton Devon . . 7 B4
London 49 B6
Brixton Deverill . 30 B2
Brixworth 99 D4
Brize Norton . . . 64 C4
Broad Blunsdon . 64 D2
Broadbottom . . . 138 D2
Broadbridge . . . 19 A7
Broadbridge
Heath 35 C4
Broad Campden . 81 D4
Broad Chalke . . . 31 C4
Broadclyst 13 B4
Broadfield
Gtr Man 138 B1
Lancs 136 A4
Pembs 56 B1
W Sus 35 C5
Broadford 247 B5
Broadford Bridge 34 D3
Broad Green
C Beds 83 C6
Essex 70 A2
Worcs 79 B5
Broadhaugh . . . 186 C4
Broadhaven . . . 281 C5
Broad Haven . . . 55 C4
Broadheath . . . 128 A2
Broad Heath . . . 79 A4
Broadhembury . 13 A6
Broadhempston . 8 A2
Broad Hill 102 D1
Broad Hinton . . 45 B5
Broadholme
Derbys 114 A1
Lincs 132 B3
Broadland Row . 23 A6
Broadlay 56 B3
Broad Laying . . . 46 C2
Broadley Lancs . 138 B1

Broadley continued
Moray. 267 C4
Broadley
Common 68 C4
Broad Marston . .80 C4
Broadmayne 16 C1
Broadmeadows .196 C3
Broadmere 33 A5
Broadmoor 55 D6
Broadoak 57 C3
Broad Oak Carms. .58 C2
Cumb 153 A2
Dorset 14 B4
Dorset 30 D1
E Sus 23 A6
E Sus 36 C4
Hereford 61 A6
Mers. 136 C4
Broadrashes . . .267 D5
Broadsea 269 C4
Broadstairs 53 C5
Broadstone BCP . .17 B4
Shrops 94 C3
Broad Street 37 A6
Broad Street
Green 70 C2
Broad Town 45 B4
Broadtown Lane. .45 B4
Broadwas. 79 B5
Broadwater Herts 68 A2
W Sus. 21 B4
Broadway Carms . .56 B2
Pembs 55 C4
Som 28 D3
Suff 105 D4
Worcs. 80 D3
Broadwell Glos . .62 B1
Glos 64 A3
Oxon. 64 C3
Warks. 82 A1
Broadwell
House. 177 D7
Broadwey. 15 C6
Broadwindsor . . .14 A4
Broadwood Kelly .11 A7
Broadwoodwidger
. . . . .11 C5
Brobury 78 C1
Brochel. 248 B2
Brochloch 182 C3
Brochroy 227 C5
Brockamin 79 B5
Brockbridge 33 D5
Brockdam 189 A4
Brockdish 104 D3
Brocketsbrae . . .194 C2
Brockford Street .88 A2
Brockhall 82 A3
Brockham 35 B4
Brockhampton
Glos 63 A6
Hereford 78 D3
Brockholes 139 B4
Brockhurst
Derbys 130 C3
Hants 19 A5
Brocklebank . . .175 D6
Brocklesby 142 B3
Brockley 42 C3
Brockley Green. . .87 B4
Brockleymoor . .164 B2
Brockton Shrops .93 A7
Shrops 94 B3
Shrops 94 C1
Shrops 95 A5
Telford 111 D6
Brockweir 62 C1
Brockwood 33 C5
Brockworth 63 B4
Brocton 112 D3
Brodick 191 B6
Brodsworth 140 C3
Brogaig 259 B4
Brogborough 83 D6
Brokenborough . .44 A3
Broken Cross
Ches E 128 B3
Ches W 128 B1
Bromborough . .126 A3
Brome. 104 D2
Brome Street . . .104 D2

Bromeswell 88 B4
Bromfield Cumb. .175 D4
Shrops 94 B2
Bromham Bedford .84 B2
Wilts. 44 C3
Bromley London. . .49 C7
W Mid. 96 C2
Bromley
Common 49 C7
Bromley Green. . .38 B1
Brompton Medway 51 C4
E Yorks. 158 B2
N Yorks. 160 C3
Brompton-on-
Swale 157 B6
Brompton Ralph. .27 B5
Brompton Regis. .27 B4
Bromsash. 62 A2
Bromsberrow
Heath 79 D5
Bromsgrove. 96 D2
Bromyard. 79 B4
Bromyard Downs .79 B4
Bronaber 108 B2
Brongest 73 B6
Bronington 110 B3
Bronllys 77 D5
Bronnant 75 B5
Bronwydd Arms . .73 D7
Bronydd 77 C6
Bronygarth 110 B1
Brook Carms. 56 B2
Hants 32 C2
Hants 32 D1
IoW 18 C2
Kent 38 A2
Sur 34 B3
Sur 34 C2
Brooke Norf 104 B3
Rutland. 99 A5
Brookenby 143 D4
Brookend 62 D1
Brook End 84 A2
Brookfield 205 B4
Brook Hill. 31 D6
Brookhouse 145 A5
Brookhouse
Green. 128 C3
Brookland 38 C1
Brooklands
Dumfries 173 A6
Gtr Man 137 D6
Shrops 111 A4
Brookmans Park .68 C2
Brooks 93 B5
Brooks Green . . .35 D4
Brook Street Kent .36 B3
Kent 38 B1
W Sus. 35 D6
Brookthorpe 63 B4
Brookville 102 B3
Brookwood 34 A2
Broom C Beds. . . .84 C3
S Yorks 140 D2
Warks. 80 B3
Worcs. 96 C2
Broome Norf . . .105 B4
Shrops 94 C2
Broomedge 128 A2
Broome Park . . .189 B4
Broomer's Corner 35 D4
Broomfield
Aberds 257 C4
Essex 69 B7
Kent 37 A6
Kent 52 C3
Som 28 B2
Broomfleet 141 A6
Broom Green . . .120 C1
Broomhall Ches E 111 A5
Windsor 48 C2
Broomhaugh. . . .178 C2
Broomhill Norf. .102 A2
Northumb. 189 C5
S Yorks. 140 C2
Broom Hill. 17 A4
Broomholm 121 B5
Broomley 178 C2
Broom's Green . .79 D5
Broomy Lodge . . .31 D6
Brora. 274 D3

Broseley 95 A4
Brotherhouse
Bar 117 D5
Brotherstone. . . .197 C5
Brothertoft 117 A5
Brotherton 140 A2
Brotton 169 D4
Broubster. 279 B6
Brough Cumb . . .165 D5
Derbys 130 A1
E Yorks. 142 A1
Highld. 280 A4
Notts 132 D3
Orkney 282 F4
Shetland. 284 F6
Shetland. 284 F7
Shetland. 284 G7
Shetland. 285 H6
Shetland. 285 J7
Broughall 111 A4
Brough Lodge. . .284 D7
Brough
Sowerby 165 D5
Broughton
Borders 195 C6
Cambs 101 D4
Flint 126 C3
Hants 32 B2
Lancs 145 D5
M Keynes 83 C5
N Lincs 142 C1
N Nhants 99 D5
N Yorks. 146 B3
N Yorks. 159 D6
Orkney 282 C5
Oxon. 81 D7
V Glam 40 D4
Broughton Astley. 98 B2
Broughton Beck 154 C1
Broughton
Common 44 C2
Broughton
Gifford 44 C2
Broughton
Hackett 80 B2
Broughton in
Furness 153 B3
Broughton Mills 153 A3
Broughton Moor 162 A3
Broughton Park .138 C1
Broughton Poggs 64 C3
Broughtown 282 C7
Brownhouses . . .175 B5
Browland 285 H4
Brown Candover .33 B4
Brown Edge
Lancs 136 B2
Staffs 129 D4
Brown Heath. . . .127 C4
Brownhill Aberds 256 B1
Aberds 256 B3
Blackburn. 145 D6
Shrops 110 C3
Brownhills Fife .221 C5
W Mid. 96 A3
Brownlow. 128 C3
Brownlow Heath 128 C3
Brownmuir 233 A5
Brown's End 79 D5
Brownshill. 63 C4
Brownston 7 B6
Brownyside 189 A4
Broxa. 160 B3
Broxbourne 68 C3
Broxburn E Loth .210 C3
W Loth 208 C3
Broxholme. 133 B4
Broxted. 69 A5
Broxton. 127 D4
Broxwood. 78 B1
Broyle Side 22 A2
Brù. 288 C4
Bruairnis 286 F3
Bruan 275 A7
Bruar Lodge 230 A2
Brucehill 206 C1
Bruera. 127 C4
Bruern Abbey . . .64 A3
Bruichladdich . .200 B2
Bruisyard 88 A4
Brumby. 141 C6

Brund 129 C6
Brundall 104 A4
Brundish. 88 A3
Brundish Street .104 D3
Brunery. 235 C6
Brunshaw. 146 D2
Brunswick
Village 179 B4
Bruntcliffe 139 A5
Bruntingthorpe . .98 B3
Brunton Fife. . . .220 B3
Northumb. 189 A5
Wilts. 45 D6
Brushford Devon .12 A1
Som 27 C4
Bruton 29 B6
Bryanston. 16 A2
Brydekirk 175 A4
Bryher Scilly 2 E3
Brymbo. 126 D2
Brympton. 29 D5
Bryn Carms 57 B5
Gtr Man 137 C4
Neath. 40 B3
Shrops 93 C6
Brynammam. 59 D4
Brynberian. 72 C4
Brynbryddan. . . .40 B2
Brynbuga = Usk. .61 C5
Bryncae 41 C4
Bryncethin. 40 C4
Bryncir 107 B4
Bryn-coch. 40 B2
Bryncroes 106 C2
Bryncrug. 90 B4
Bryn Du. 122 C3
Bryneglwys 109 A6
Brynford. 126 B1
Bryn Gates 137 C4
Bryn-glas 124 C3
Bryn Golau. 41 C4
Bryngwran. 122 C3
Bryngwyn Ceredig. 73 B5
Mon 61 C5
Powys 77 C5
Brynhenllan. 72 C3
Brynhoffnant. . . .73 A6
Brynithel. 41 A7
Bryn-Iwan 73 C6
Brynmawr 60 B3
Bryn-mawr 106 C2
Brynmenyn 40 C4
Brynmill 57 C6
Brynna 41 C4
Bryn-nantllech. .125 C4
Bryn-penarth . . .93 A5
Brynrefail
Anglesey 123 B4
Gwyn 123 D5
Bryn Rhyd-yr-
Arian. 125 C4
Brynsadler. 41 C5
Bryn Saith
Marchog 125 D5
Brynsiencyn. . . .123 D4
Bryn Sion 91 A6
Brynteg Anglesey 123 B4
Ceredig. 58 A1
Bryn-y-gwenin. . .61 B5
Bryn-y-maen . . .124 B3
Bryn-yr-eryr . . .106 B3
Buaile nam
Bodach. 286 F3
Bualintur 246 B3
Buarthmeini . . .108 B3
Bubbenhall 97 D6
Bubwith 149 D6
Buccleuch 185 A6
Buchanhaven. . .257 B6
Buchanty 218 B4
Buchlyvie 206 A3
Buckabank. 164 A1
Buckden Cambs. .84 A3
N Yorks 156 D3
Buckenham 105 A4
Buckerell 13 A6
Buckfast. 7 A6
Buckfastleigh 7 A6
Buckhaven. 209 A6
Buckholm. 196 C3
Buckholt. 61 B7
Buckhorn Weston 30 C1

Buckhurst Hill. . . .68 D4
Buckie. 267 C5
Buckies. 280 B3
Buckingham 82 D3
Buckland Bucks. . .66 B3
Devon. 7 C5
Glos 80 D3
Hants 18 B2
Herts 85 D5
Kent 39 A5
Oxon. 64 U4
Sur 35 A5
Buckland Brewer 25 C5
Buckland
Common 67 C4
Buckland Dinham 43 D6
Buckland Filleigh 11 A5
Buckland in the
Moor. 12 D2
Buckland
Monachorum . . .6 A3
Buckland Newton 15 A6
Buckland
St Mary 28 D2
Bucklebury 46 B3
Bucklegate 117 B6
Bucklerheads . .221 A4
Bucklers Hard. . .18 B3
Bucklesham. 88 C3
Buckley = Bwcle. 126 C2
Bucklow Hill . . .128 A2
Buckminster . . .116 C1
Bucknall Lincs . .133 C6
Stoke 112 A3
Bucknell Oxon . . .65 A6
Shrops 94 D1
Buckpool 267 C5
Bucksburn 245 B5
Buck's Cross 24 C4
Bucks Green 34 C3
Buckshaw
Village 137 A4
Bucks Horn Oak. .33 A7
Buckskin 47 D4
Buck's Mills. 25 C4
Buckton E Yorks .161 D5
Hereford 94 D1
Northumb. 199 C4
Buckworth. 100 D3
Budbrooke. 81 A5
Budby 131 C6
Budd's Titson . . .10 A3
Bude 10 A3
Budlake 13 B4
Budle. 199 C5
Budleigh
Salterton 13 C5
Budock Water. . . .4 D2
Buerton 111 A5
Buffler's Holt . . .82 D3
Bugbrooke. 82 B3
Buglawton. 128 C3
Bugle. 5 B5
Bugley. 30 A2
Bugthorpe. 149 B6
Buildwas 95 A4
Builth Road 76 B4
Builth Wells =
Llanfair-ym-Muallt . 76 B4
Buirgh. 287 E5
Bulby 116 C3
Bulcote. 115 A4
Buldoo 279 B5
Bulford. 31 A5
Bulford Camp . . .31 A5
Bulkeley. 127 D5
Bulkington Warks 97 C6
Wilts. 44 D3
Bulkworthy 25 D4
Bullamoor 158 B2
Bullbridge 130 D3
Bullbrook. 47 C6
Bulley 62 B3
Bullgill. 162 A3
Bull Hill. 18 B2
Bullington Hants .32 A3
Lincs. 133 B5
Bull's Green. 68 B2
Bullwood 203 A6
Bulmer Essex. . . .87 C4
N Yorks 149 A5
Bulmer Tye 87 D4

Bulphan 50 A3
Bulverhythe. 23 B5
Bulwark 257 B4
Bulwell 114 A3
Bulwick. 99 B6
Bumble's Green . .68 C4
Bun Abhainn
Eadarra. 288 G2
Bunacaimb 235 B5
Bun a'Mhuillin . .286 E3
Bunarkaig 239 D5
Bunbury. 127 D5
Bunbury Heath .127 D5
Bunchrew 252 B2
Bundalloch 249 D5
Buness. 284 C8
Bunessan 224 D2
Bungay 104 C4
Bunkers Hill. . . .65 B5
Bunker's Hill
Lincs. 133 B4
Lincs. 134 D2
Bunloit 251 D7
Bun Loyne 239 B6
Bunnahabhain .201 A4
Bunny 114 C3
Buntait 251 C5
Buntingford. 68 A3
Bunwell. 104 B2
Burbage Derbys. .129 B5
Leics. 98 B1
Wilts. 45 C6
Burchett's Green 47 A6
Burcombe 31 B4
Burcot. 65 D6
Burcott. 66 A3
Burdon 179 D5
Bures. 87 D5
Bures Green 87 D5
Burford Ches E. .127 D6
Oxon. 64 B3
Shrops 78 A3
Burg 224 B2
Burgar. 282 E4
Burgate Hants . . .31 D5
Suff 104 D1
Burgess Hill 21 A6
Burgh. 88 B3
Burgh by Sands .175 C6
Burgh Castle . . .105 A5
Burghclere 46 C2
Burghead 266 C2
Burghfield 47 C4
Burghfield
Common 47 C4
Burghfield Hill . .47 C4
Burgh Heath 35 A5
Burghill 78 C2
Burgh le Marsh .135 C5
Burgh Muir 256 D2
Burgh next
Aylsham. 120 C4
Burgh on Bain. .134 A2
Burgh
St Margaret . . .121 D6
Burgh St Peter .105 B5
Burghwallis 140 B3
Burham. 51 C4
Buriton 33 C6
Burland. 127 D6
Burlawn 9 D5
Burleigh 48 C1
Burlescombe. . . .27 D5
Burleston 16 B1
Burley Hants 17 A6
Rutland. 116 D1
W Yorks 148 D1
Burleydam. 111 A5
Burley Gate 78 C3
Burley in
Wharfedale. . . .147 C5
Burley Lodge. . . .17 A6
Burley Street. . . .17 A6
Burlingjobb 77 B6
Burlow 22 A3
Burlton 110 C3
Burmarsh. 38 B2
Burmington. 81 D5
Burn 140 A3

Burnaston 113 B6
Burnbank 194 A2
Burnby 150 C1
Burncross 139 D6
Burneside 154 B4
Burness 282 C7
Burneston 157 C7
Burnett 43 C5
Burnfoot Borders 186 B3
　Borders 186 B4
　E Ayrs 182 B2
　Perth 219 D4
Burnham Bucks . . 48 A2
　N Lincs 142 B2
Burnham
　Deepdale 119 A5
Burnham Green . . 68 B2
Burnham
　Market 119 A5
Burnham
　Norton 119 A5
Burnham-on-
　Crouch 70 D3
Burnham-on-Sea 28 A3
Burnham Overy
　Staithe 119 A5
Burnham Overy
　Town 119 A5
Burnham
　Thorpe 119 A5
Burnhead
　Dumfries 183 C6
　S Ayrs 181 A4
Burnhervie 245 A4
Burnhill Green . . . 95 A5
Burnhope 167 A4
Burnhouse 204 C3
Burniston 160 B4
Burnlee 139 C4
Burnley 146 D2
Burnley Lane 146 D2
Burn of Cambus 218 D2
Burnopfield 178 D3
Burnsall 147 A4
Burnside Angus . 232 C3
　E Ayrs 182 A3
　Fife. 219 D6
　Shetland. 284 F4
　S Lanark 205 B6
　W Loth 208 C3
Burnside of
　Duntrune. 220 A4
Burnswark 175 A4
Burntcommon. . . 34 A3
Burnt Heath. . . . 130 B2
Burnthouse 4 D2
Burnt Houses . . . 166 C4
Burntisland 209 B5
Burnton 182 B2
Burntwood. 96 A3
Burnt Yates 147 A6
Burnwynd. 208 D4
Burpham Sur 34 A3
　W Sus. 20 B3
Burradon
　Northumb. 188 C2
　T&W. 179 B4
Burrafirth. 284 B8
Burraland
　Shetland. 284 F5
　Shetland. 285 J4
Burras 3 B4
Burravoe
　Shetland. 284 F7
　Shetland. 284 G6
Burray Village. . 283 H5
Burrells. 165 D4
Burrelton 220 A2
Burridge Devon . . 25 B6
　Hants 32 D4
Burrill 157 C6
Burringham 141 C6
Burrington Devon 26 D1
　Hereford 94 D2
　N Som. 42 D3
Burrough Green . 86 B2
Burrough on the
　Hill 115 D5

Burrow-bridge . . 28 C3
Burrowhill 48 C2
Burry 57 C4
Burry Green. 57 C4
Burry Port
　=Porth Tywyn . . 57 B2
Burscough 136 B3
Burscough
　Bridge 136 B3
Bursea 149 D7
Burshill 150 C3
Bursledon 18 A3
Burslem 112 A2
Burstall. 88 C1
Burstock 14 A4
Burston Norf.. . . . 104 C2
　Staffs 112 B3
Burstow 35 B6
Burstwick 143 A4
Burtersett 156 C2
Burtle 28 A3
Burton BCP. 17 B5
　Ches W.. . . . . . . 126 B3
　Ches W.. . . . . . . 127 C5
　Lincs. 133 B4
　Northumb. 199 C5
　Pembs 55 D5
　Som 28 A1
　Wilts. 44 B2
Burton Agnes . . . 151 A4
Burton Bradstock 15 C4
Burton Dassett . . 81 B6
Burton Fleming .161 D4
Burton Green
　W Mid.. . . . . 97 D5
　Wrex 126 D3
Burton Hastings . 97 B7
Burton-in-
　Kendal 154 D4
Burton in
　Lonsdale 155 D5
Burton Joyce.. . . 115 A4
Burton Latimer . . 99 D5
Burton Lazars . . 115 D5
Burton-le-
　Coggles 116 C2
Burton Leonard .148 A2
Burton on the
　Wolds. 114 C3
Burton Overy. . . . 98 B3
Burton
　Pedwardine . . .116 A4
Burton Pidsea. . . 151 D5
Burton Salmon .140 A2
Burton Stather .141 B6
Burton upon
　Stather. 141 B6
Burton upon
　Trent. 113 C6
Burtonwood . . . 137 D4
Burwardsley . . . 127 D5
Burwarton 95 C4
Burwash. 37 D4
Burwash
　Common 36 D4
Burwash Weald . 36 D4
Burwell Cambs.. . 86 A1
　Lincs. 134 B3
Burwen 123 A4
Burwick 283 J5
Bury Cambs. 101 C4
　Gtr Man. 137 B7
　Som 27 C4
Bury Green 20 A3
Bury St Edmunds 87 A4
Burythorpe 149 A6
Busby 205 C5
Buscot. 64 D3
Bush Bank 78 B2
Bushbury 96 A2
Bushby 98 A3
Bush Crathie . . . 243 C5
Bushey 67 D6
Bushey Heath . . . 67 D6
Bush Green 104 C3
Bushley. 80 D1
Bushton 45 B4
Buslingthorpe.. 133 A5
Busta. 284 G5
Butcher's Cross . 36 D3
Butcombe 43 C4

Butetown 41 D6
Butleigh 29 B5
Butleigh Wootton 29 B5
Butler's Cross . . . 66 C3
Butler's End. 97 C5
Butlers Marston . 81 C6
Butley 89 B4
Butley High
　Corner 89 C4
Butterburn. 177 B4
Buttercrambe . . 149 B6
Butterknowle . . 166 C4
Butterleigh 13 A4
Buttermere
　Cumb 163 C4
　Wilts. 46 C1
Buttershaw 139 A4
Butterstone 231 D4
Butterton 129 D5
Butterwick
　Durham 167 C6
　Lincs. 117 A6
　N Yorks 159 D6
　N Yorks 160 D3
Butt Green 127 D6
Buttington 93 A6
Buttonoak 95 D5
Buttsash. 18 A3
Butt's Green 32 C2
Buxhall 87 B6
Buxhall Fen
　Street. 87 B6
Buxley. 198 A2
Buxted 36 D2
Buxton Derbys . . 129 B5
　Norf 120 C4
Buxworth 129 A5
Bwcle = Buckley . 126 C2
Bwlch 60 A3
Bwlchgwyn 126 D2
Bwlch-Llan 75 C4
Bwlchnewydd . . . 73 D6
Bwlchtocyn 106 D3
Bwlch-y-cibau . 109 D6
Bwlchyddar 109 C6
Bwlch-y-fadfa . . 74 D3
Bwlch-y-ffridd . . 93 B4
Bwlchygroes 73 C5
Bwlch-y-sarnau . 92 D4
Byermoor. 178 D3
Byers Green. 167 B5
Byfield 82 B2
Byfleet 48 C3
Byford. 78 C1
Bygrave 85 D4
Byker 179 C4
Bylchau 125 C4
Byley 128 C2
Bynea 57 C5
Byrness 187 C6
Bythorn 100 D2
Byton 78 A1
Byworth 34 D2

C

Cabharstadh . . . 288 E4
Cablea. 218 A4
Cabourne 142 C3
Cabrach Argyll . . 201 B4
　Moray.. . . . . . . .255 D4
Cabrich. 252 B1
Cabus 145 C4
Cackle Street . . . 36 D2
Cadbury 13 A4
Cadbury Barton . 26 D1
Cadder 205 A6
Caddington 67 B5
Caddonfoot 196 C3
Cadeby Leics 97 A7
　S Yorks 140 C3
Cadeleigh 13 A4
Cade Street 36 D4
Cadgwith 3 D5
Cadham 220 D2
Cadishead 137 D6
Cadle. 57 C6
Cadley Lancs. . . . 145 D5
　Wilts. 45 C6
　Wilts. 45 D6
Cadmore End . . . 66 D2

Cadnam 32 D1
Cadney 142 C2
Cadole 126 C2
Cadoxton 41 E6
Cadoxton-Juxta-
　Neath 40 B2
Cadshaw. 137 B6
Cadzow. 194 A2
Caeathro 123 D4
Caehopkin 59 D5
Caenby 133 A5
Caenby Corner . . 133 A4
Caerau Bridgend.. 40 B3
　Cardiff. 41 D6
Caér-bryn 57 A5
Caerdeon 90 A4
Caerdydd
　=Cardiff. 41 D6
Caerfarchell 54 B3
Caerffili
　=Caerphilly 41 C6
Caerfyrddin
　=Carmarthen. . . 73 D7
Caergeiliog 122 C3
Caergwrle 126 D3
Caergybi
　=Holyhead. . . . 122 B2
Caerleon . . . .
　=Caerllion 61 D5
Caer Llan 61 C6
Caerllion
　=Caerleon 61 D5
Caernarfon 123 D4
Caerphilly
　=Caerffili. 41 C6
Caersws 92 B4
Caerwedros 73 A6
Caerwent 61 D6
Caerwych 107 C6
Caerwys 125 B6
Caethle 90 C4
Caim 123 B6
Caio 58 B3
Cairinis 287 H3
Cairisiadar. 287 A5
Cairminis 287 F5
Cairnbaan 213 C6
Cairnbanno
　House 256 B3
Cairnborrow . . . 255 B5
Cairnbrogie 256 D3
Cairnbulg Castle 269 C5
Cairncross Angus 232 A4
　Borders 211 D5
Cairndow 215 A4
Cairness 269 C5
Cairneyhill 208 B3
Cairnfield
　House 267 C5
Cairngaan 170 D3
Cairngarroch. . . 170 C2
Cairnhill 256 C1
Cairnie Aberds . . 245 B5
　Aberds 255 B5
Cairnorrie 256 B3
Cairnpark 245 A5
Cairnryan 170 A2
Cairnton 283 G4
Caister-on-Sea .121 D7
Caistor 142 C3
Caistor
　St Edmund . . . 104 A3
Caistron 188 C2
Caitha Bowland . 196 B3
Calais Street 87 D5
Calanais 288 D3
Calbost 288 F5
Calbourne 18 C3
Calceby 134 B3
Calcot Row 47 B4
Calcott 52 C3
Caldback 284 C8
Caldbeck 163 A6
Caldbergh 157 C4
Caldecote Cambs.. 85 B5
　Cambs 100 C3
　Herts 84 D4
　W Nhants 82 B3
Caldecott
　N Nhants 84 A1
　Oxon. 65 D5
　Rutland. 99 B5

Calderbank 207 D5
Calder Bridge . . 162 D3
Calderbrook . . . 138 B2
Caldercruix 207 D6
Calder Hall. 162 D3
Calder Mains. . . 280 C2
Caldermill 205 D6
Calder Vale 145 C5
Calderwood. . . . 205 C6
Caldhame. 232 D2
Caldicot 42 A3
Caldwell Derbys .113 D6
　N Yorks 167 D4
Caldy 126 A2
Caledrhydiau. . . . 74 C3
Calfsound. 282 D6
Calgary 224 A2
Califer. 266 D1
California Falk. . . 208 C2
　Norf 121 D7
Calke 114 C1
Callakille 248 A3
Callaly. 188 C3
Callander 217 D6
Callaughton. 95 B4
Callestick 4 B2
Calligarry 247 D5
Callington 6 A2
Callow. 78 D2
Callow End 79 C6
Callow Hill Wilts . . 44 A4
　Worcs. 95 D5
Callows Grave. . . 78 A3
Calmore 32 D2
Calmsden 63 C6
Calne 44 B4
Calow 131 B4
Calshot 18 A3
Calstock 6 A3
Calstone
　Wellington 44 C4
Calthorpe 120 B3
Calthwaite 164 A2
Calton N Yorks . . 146 B3
　Staffs 129 D6
Calveley 127 D5
Calver 130 B2
Calverhall 111 B5
Calver Hill 78 C1
Calverleigh 27 D4
Calverley 147 D6
Calvert 66 A1
Calverton
　M Keynes 83 D4
　Notts 115 A4
Calvine 230 B2
Calvo 174 C4
Cam. 62 D3
Camas-luinie . . . 249 D6
Camasnacroise. 236 D2
Camastianavaig. 247 A4
Camasunary . . . 247 C4
Camault Muir . . 251 B7
Camb. 284 D7
Camber. 38 D1
Camberley 47 C6
Camberwell. 49 B6
Camblesforth . . 141 A4
Cambo 178 A2
Cambois 179 A5
Camborne 3 A4
Cambourne 85 B5
Cambridge Cambs. 85 B6
　Glos 62 C3
Cambridge Town 51 A6
Cambus 207 A6
Cambusavie
　Farm. 264 A3
Cambusbarron . 207 A5
Cambuskenneth 207 A6
Cambuslang . . . 205 B6
Cambusmore
　Lodge 264 A3
Camden 49 A5
Camelford 10 C2
Camelsdale 34 C1
Camerory 253 C6
Camer's Green . . 79 D5
Camerton Bath. . 43 D5
　Cumb 162 A3
　E Yorks 143 A4
Camghouran . . . 229 C4

Cammachmore. .245 C6
Cammeringham 133 A4
Camore. 264 A3
Campbeltown . . . 190 C3
Camperdown . . . 179 B4
Camp Hill 97 B6
Campmuir 220 A2
Campsall 140 B3
Campsey Ash. . . . 88 B4
Campton. 84 D3
Camptown 187 B5
Camrose. 55 B5
Camserney. 230 D2
Camster 281 D4
Camuschoirk. . . 235 D6
Camuscross. . . . 247 C5
Camusnagaul
　Highld.. . . . . . . 237 B4
　Highld.. . . . . . . 262 B2
Camusrory 238 C2
Camusteel 249 B4
Camusterrach. . 249 B4
Camusvrachan . 229 D5
Canada 32 D1
Canadia 23 A5
Canal Side 141 B4
Candacraig
　House. 243 A6
Candlesby 135 C4
Candy Mill 195 B5
Cane End 47 B4
Canewdon 70 D2
Canford Bottom . 17 A4
Canford Cliffs . . . 17 C4
Canford Magna . . 17 B4
Canham's Green . 87 A6
Canholes 129 B5
Canisbay. 281 A5
Cann 30 C2
Cannard's Grave . 29 A6
Cann Common . . 30 C2
Cannich 251 C5
Cannington 28 B2
Cannock 96 A2
Cannock Wood . .112 D4
Canonbie 175 A6
Canon Bridge . . . 78 C2
Canon Frome . . . 79 C4
Canon Pyon 78 C2
Canons Ashby . . 82 B2
Canonstown 2 B3
Canterbury. 52 D3
Cantley Norf. . . . 105 A4
　S Yorks 140 C4
Cantlop. 94 A3
Canton 41 D6
Cantraybruich. . 252 B3
Cantraydoune . . 252 B3
Cantraywood. . . 252 B3
Cantsfield 155 D5
Canvey Island . . . 51 A4
Canwick 133 C4
Canworthy Water. 10 B3
Caol 237 B5
Caolas 222 C3
Caolas
　Scalpaigh 288 H3
Caolas Stocinis. .288 H2
Cool Ila 201 A4
Capel 35 B4
Capel Bangor . . . 91 D4
Capel Betws
　Lleucu 75 C5
Capel Carmel . . 106 D1
Capel Coch 123 B4
Capel Curig 124 D2
Capel Cynon 73 B6
Capel Dewi Carms 58 C1
　Ceredig 58 A1
　Ceredig 90 D4
Capel Garmon . 124 D3
Capel-gwyn. . . . 122 C3
Capel Gwyn 58 C1
Capel Gwynfe . . 59 C4
Capel Hendre . . . 57 A5
Capel Hermon . . 108 C2
Capel Isaac 58 C2
Capel Iwan. 73 C5
Capel le Ferne . . 39 B4
Capel Llanilltern . 41 C5
Capel Mawr 123 C4
Capel St Andrew . 89 C4

Capel St Mary 88 D1
Capel Seion 75 A5
Capel Tygwydd . . . 73 B5
Capel Uchaf 107 B4
Capelulo 124 B2
Capel-y-graig 123 D5
Capenhurst 126 B3
Capernwray 154 D4
Capheaton 178 A2
Cappercleuch 196 D1
Capplegill 185 B4
Capton 8 B2
Caputh 219 A5
Carbis Bay 2 B3
Carbost Highld . . . 246 A2
  Highld 259 D4
Carbrook 130 A3
Carbrooke 103 A5
Carburton 131 B6
Carcant 196 A2
Carclaze 5 B5
Car Colston 115 A5
Carcroft 140 B3
Cardenden 209 A5
Cardeston 110 D2
Cardiff = Caerdydd 41 D6
Cardigan = Aberteifi 73 B4
Cardington
  Bedford 84 C2
  Shrops 94 B3
Cardinham 5 A6
Cardonald 205 B5
Cardow 254 B2
Cardrona 196 C2
Cardross 206 C1
Cardurnock 175 C4
Careby 116 D3
Careston Castle . 232 C3
Carew 55 D6
Carew Cheriton . . 55 D6
Carew Newton . . . 55 D6
Carey 78 D3
Carfrae 210 D2
Cargenbridge . . 174 A2
Cargill 219 A6
Cargo 175 C6
Cargreen 6 A3
Carham 198 C2
Carhampton 27 A5
Carharrack 4 C2
Carie Perth 217 A6
  Perth 229 C5
Carines 4 B2
Carisbrooke 18 C3
Cark 154 D2
Carlabhagh 288 C3
Carland Cross . . . 4 B3
Carlby 116 D3
Carlecotes 139 C4
Carlesmoor 157 D5
Carleton Cumb . . 164 C3
  Cumb 176 D2
  Lancs 144 D3
  N Yorks 146 C3
Carleton
  Forehoe 104 A4
Carleton Rode . . 104 B2
Carlingcott 43 D5
Carlin How 169 D5
Carlisle 175 C7
Carlops 195 A6
Carlton Bedford . . 83 B6
  Cambs 86 B2
  Leics 97 A6
  Notts 115 A4
  N Yorks 140 A4
  N Yorks 157 C4
  N Yorks 159 C5
  N Yorks 167 D4
  Stockton 167 C6
  Suff 89 A4
  S Yorks 139 B6
  W Yorks 139 A6
Carlton Colville . 105 C6
Carlton Curlieu . . 98 B3
Carlton
  Husthwaite . . . 158 D3
Carlton in
  Cleveland . . . 158 A4
Carlton in
  Lindrick 131 A5

Carlton le
  Moorland 133 D4
Carlton Miniott . . 158 C2
Carlton on Trent 132 C2
Carlton Scroop . . 116 A2
Carluke 194 A3
Carmarthen
  =Caerfyrddin . . . 73 D7
Carmel
  Anglesey 122 B3
  Carms 57 A5
  Flint 125 B6
  Guern 6
  Gwyn 107 A4
Carmont 245 D5
Carmunnock . . . 205 B6
Carmyle 205 B6
Carmyllie 232 D3
Carnaby 151 A4
Carnach Highld . . 250 D2
  Highld 262 A2
  W Isles 288 H3
Carnachy 278 C3
Càrnais 287 A5
Carnbee 221 D5
Carnbo 219 D5
Carnbrea 3 A4
Carnduff 205 D6
Carnduncan . . . 200 B2
Carne 4 D4
Carnforth 154 D3
Carn-gorm 249 D6
Carnhedryn 54 B4
Carnhell Green . . 3 B4
Carnkie Corn . . . 3 B4
  Corn 4 D2
Carno 92 B3
Carnoch Highld . 251 A4
  Highld 251 C5
Carnock 208 B3
Carnon Downs . . 4 C2
Carnousie 268 D1
Carnoustie 221 A5
Carnwath 195 B4
Carnyorth 2 B1
Carperby 156 C4
Carpley Green . . 156 C3
Carr 140 D3
Carradale 190 B4
Carragraich . . . 288 H2
Carrbridge 253 D5
Carrefour
  Selous Jersey . . . 6
Carreglefn 122 B3
Carreg-wen 73 B5
Carr Hill 179 C4
Carrick Argyll . . 214 D2
  Fife 220 B4
Carrick Castle . . 215 C4
Carrick House . . 282 D5
Carriden 208 B3
Carrington
  Gtr Man 137 D6
  Lincs 134 D3
  Midloth 209 D6
Carrog Conwy . . 108 A2
  Denb 109 A6
Carron Falk . . . 208 B1
  Moray 254 B3
Carronbridge . . 183 C6
Carron Bridge . . 207 B5
Carronshore . . 208 B1
Carrshield 165 A6
Carrutherstown 174 A4
Carrville 167 A6
Carsaig Argyll . . 213 D5
  Argyll 225 D4
Carscreugh . . . 171 B4
Carsegowan . . . 171 B6
Carse Gray 232 C2
Carse House . . . 202 B2
Carseriggan . . . 171 A5
Carsethorn . . . 174 C2
Carshalton 49 C5
Carsington . . . 130 D2
Carskiey 190 E2
Carsluith 171 B6
Carsphairn . . . 182 C3
Carstairs 194 B4
Carstairs
  Junction . . . 195 B4
Carswell Marsh . 64 D4

Carter's Clay . . . 32 C2
Carterton 64 C3
Carterway
  Heads 178 D2
Carthew 5 B5
Carthorpe 157 C7
Cartington 188 C3
Cartland 194 B3
Cartmel 154 D2
Cartmel Fell . . . 154 C3
Carway 57 B4
Cary Fitzpaine . . 29 C5
Cascob 77 A6
Cas-gwent
  =Chepstow . . . 62 D1
Cashlie 228 D3
Cashmoor 30 D3
Casnewydd
  =Newport 42 A2
Cassey Compton . 63 B6
Cassington 65 B5
Cassop 167 B6
Castell 125 C6
Castellau 41 C5
Castell-Howell . . 73 D3
Castell-Nedd
  =Neath 40 B2
Castell Newydd Emlyn
  =Newcastle Emlyn. 73 B6
Castell-y-bwch . . 61 D4
Casterton 155 D5
Castle Acre . . . 119 D5
Castle Ashby . . . 83 B5
Castlebay = Bagh a
  Chaisteil 286 G2
Castle Bolton . . 156 B4
Castle Bromwich . 96 C4
Castle Bytham . . 116 D2
Castlebythe . . . 55 B6
Castle Caereinion 93 A5
Castle Camps . . 86 C2
Castle Carrock . 176 D3
Castlecary 207 C5
Castle Combe . . 44 B2
Castlecraig . . . 265 D4
Castle
  Donington . . . 114 C2
Castle Douglas . 173 B5
Castle Eaton . . . 64 D2
Castle Eden . . . 168 B2
Castlefairn . . . 183 D5
Castle Forbes . . 244 A3
Castleford 140 A2
Castle Frome . . . 79 C4
Castle Green . . . 48 C2
Castle Gresley . 113 D6
Castle Heaton . . 198 B3
Castle
  Hedingham . . . 86 D3
Castlehill
  Borders 195 C7
  Highld 280 B3
  W Dunb 206 C1
Castle Hill 37 B4
Castle Huntly . . 220 B3
Castle Kennedy . 170 B3
Castlemaddy . . 182 D3
Castlemartin . . 55 E5
Castlemilk
  Dumfries . . . 174 A4
  Glasgow 205 C6
Castlemorris . . 55 A5
Castlemorton . . 79 D5
Castle O'er . . . 185 C5
Castle
  Pulverbatch . . 94 A2
Castle Rising . . 118 C3
Castleside . . . 166 A3
Castle Stuart . . 252 B3
Castlethorpe . . 83 C5
Castleton Angus . 232 D1
  Argyll 214 D1
  Derbys 129 A6
  Gtr Man 138 B1
  Newport 42 A1
  N Yorks 159 A5
Castletown
  Ches W 127 D4
  Highld 252 B3
  Highld 280 B3
  IoM 152 E2

Castletown continued
  T&W 179 D5
Castleweary . . 186 C3
Castley 147 C6
Caston 103 B5
Castor 100 B3
Catacol 203 D4
Catbrain 43 A4
Catbrook 61 C7
Catchall 2 C2
Catchems Corner 97 D5
Catchgate 178 D3
Catcleugh 187 C6
Catcliffe 131 A4
Catcott 28 B3
Caterham 35 A6
Catfield 121 C5
Catfirth 285 H6
Catford 49 B6
Catforth 145 D4
Cathays 41 D6
Cathcart 205 B5
Cathedine 60 A3
Catherington . . 33 D5
Catherton 95 D4
Catlodge 241 C4
Catlowdy 176 B2
Catmore 46 A2
Caton 145 A5
Caton Green . . 145 A5
Catrine 193 C5
Cat's Ash 61 D5
Catsfield 23 A5
Catshill 96 D2
Cattal 148 B3
Cattawade 88 D2
Catterall 145 C4
Catterick 157 B6
Catterick Bridge 157 B6
Catterick
  Garrison . . . 157 B5
Catterlen 164 B2
Catterline . . . 233 A6
Catterton 148 C4
Catthorpe 98 D2
Cattistock 15 B5
Catton Northumb 177 D6
  N Yorks 158 D2
Catwick 151 C4
Catworth 100 D2
Caudlesprings . 103 A5
Caulcott 65 A6
Cauldcots 233 D4
Cauldhame . . . 207 A4
Cauldmill 186 B4
Cauldon 113 A4
Caulkerbush . . 174 C2
Caulside 176 A2
Caunsall 95 C6
Caunton 132 D2
Causewayend . . 195 C5
Causeway End . 171 A6
Causeway Foot . 147 D4
Causewayhead
  Cumb 174 C4
  Stirling 207 A5
Causeyend . . . 245 A6
Causey Park
  Bridge 189 D4
Cautley 155 B5
Cavendish 87 C4
Cavendish
  Bridge 114 C2
Cavenham 86 A3
Caversfield . . . 65 A6
Caversham 47 B5
Caverswall . . . 112 A3
Cavil 149 D6
Cawdor 253 B4
Cawkwell 134 B2
Cawood 149 D4
Cawsand 6 B3
Cawston 120 C3
Cawthorne . . . 139 C5
Cawthorpe . . . 116 C3
Cawton 159 D5
Caxton 85 B5
Caynham 94 D3
Caythorpe Lincs . 116 A2
  Notts 115 A4
Cayton 161 C4
Ceann a Bhaigh . 287 H2

Ceannacroc
  Lodge 239 A6
Ceann a Deas Loch
  Baghasdail . . 286 E3
Ceann Shiphoirt 288 F3
Ceann
  Tarabhaigh . . 288 F3
Cearsiadair . . 288 F4
Cefn Berain . . 125 C4
Cefn-brith . . . 125 D4
Cefn Canol . . . 110 B1
Cefn-coch 124 C3
Cefn Coch 109 C6
Cefn-coed-y-
  cymmer 60 C2
Cefn Cribbwr . . 40 C3
Cefn Cross . . . 40 C3
Cefn-ddwysarn . 109 B4
Cefn Einion . . . 93 C6
Cefneithin . . . 57 A5
Cefn-gorwydd . . 76 C3
Cefn-mawr . . . 110 A1
Cefn-y-bedd . . 126 D3
Cefn-y-pant . . . 73 D4
Cei-bach 73 A7
Ceinewydd
  =New Quay . . . 73 A6
Ceint 123 C4
Cellan 75 D5
Cellarhead . . . 112 A3
Cemaes 122 A3
Cemaes 91 B6
Cemaes Road . . 91 B6
Cenarth 73 B5
Cenin 107 B4
Central 204 A2
Ceos 288 E4
Ceres 220 C4
Cerne Abbas . . 15 A6
Cerney Wick . . 63 D6
Cerrigceinwen . 123 C4
Cerrigydrudion . 109 A4
Cessford 187 A6
Ceunant 123 D5
Chaceley 79 D6
Chacewater . . . 4 C2
Chackmore . . . 82 D3
Chacombe 82 C1
Chadderton . . 138 C2
Chadderton
  Fold 138 C1
Chaddesden . . 114 B1
Chaddesley
  Corbett 96 D1
Chaddleworth . . 46 B2
Chadlington . . 64 A4
Chadshunt . . . 81 B6
Chad Valley . . 96 C3
Chadwell 115 C5
Chadwell St Mary. 50 B3
Chadwick End . . 97 D5
Chadwick Green 136 D4
Chaffcombe . . . 28 D3
Chagford 12 C2
Chailey 22 A1
Chainbridge . . 101 A6
Chain Bridge . . 117 A4
Chainhurst . . . 37 B5
Chalbury 17 A4
Chalbury
  Common 17 A4
Chaldon 35 A6
Chaldon Herring
  or 16 C1
Chale 18 D3
Chale Green . . 18 D3
Chalfont
  Common 67 D5
Chalfont St Giles . 67 D4
Chalfont St Peter . 67 D5
Chalford 63 C4
Chalgrove 66 D1
Chalk 50 B3
Challacombe . . 26 A1
Challoch 171 A5
Challock 52 D2
Chalton C Beds . . 67 A5
  Hants 33 D6
Chalvington . . 22 B3
Chancery 75 A4
Chandler's Ford . 32 C3
Channel Tunnel . 38 B3

Channerwick . . 285 L6
Chantry Som . . 29 A7
  Suff 88 C2
Chapel 289 A5
Chapel Allerton
  Som 42 D3
  W Yorks 148 D2
Chapel Amble . . 9 D5
Chapel Brampton 83 A4
Chapel Chorlton 112 B2
Chapel End . . . 97 B6
Chapel-en-le-
  Frith 129 A5
Chapelgate . . . 117 C7
Chapel Green
  Warks 82 A1
  Warks 97 C5
Chapel
  Haddlesey . . 140 A3
Chapelhall . . . 207 D5
Chapel Head . . 101 C6
Chapelhill
  Dumfries . . . 184 C3
  Highld 265 C4
  N Ayrs 204 D2
  Perth 219 A5
  Perth 220 B2
Chapel Hill
  Aberds 257 C5
  Lincs 134 D2
  Mon 62 D1
  N Yorks 148 C2
Chapelknowe . . 175 A6
Chapel Lawn . . 93 D7
Chapel-le-Dale 155 D6
Chapel Milton . 129 A5
Chapel of
  Garioch 256 D2
Chapel Row . . . 46 C3
Chapel
  St Leonards 135 B5
Chapel Stile . . 154 A2
Chapelton Angus 233 D4
  Devon 25 C6
  Highld 242 A2
  S Lanark . . . 194 B1
Chapeltown
  Blackburn . . 137 B6
  Moray 254 D3
  S Yorks 139 D6
Chapmanslade . 30 A2
Chapmans Well . 11 B4
Chapmore End . 68 B3
Chappel 70 A2
Chard 14 A3
Chardstock . . . 14 A3
Charfield 62 D3
Charford 80 A2
Charing 38 A1
Charing Cross . 31 D5
Charing Heath . 38 A1
Charingworth . 81 D5
Charlbury 65 B4
Charlcombe . . . 43 C6
Charlecote . . . 81 B5
Charles 26 B1
Charlesfield . 175 B4
Charleston
  Angus 232 D1
  Renfs 205 B4
Charlestown
  Aberdeen . . . 245 B6
  Corn 5 B5
  Derbys 138 D3
  Dorset 15 D6
  Fife 208 B3
  Gtr Man 137 C7
  Highld 252 D2
  Highld 261 C5
  W Yorks 138 A2
Charlestown of
  Aberlour . . . 254 B3
Charles Tye . . . 87 B6
Charlesworth . 138 D3
Charleton 7 C6
Charlton Hants . 32 A2
  Herts 68 A1
  London 49 B7
  Northumb . . . 177 A6

Charlton continued
Som 43 D5
Telford 111 D4
Wilts. 30 C3
Wilts. 44 A3
Wilts. 45 D5
W Nhants 82 D2
Worcs. 80 C3
W Sus. 20 A1
Charlton Abbots . 63 A6
Charlton Adam . . 29 C5
Charlton-All-
Saints 31 C5
Charlton Down . . 15 B6
Charlton
Horethorne. . . . 29 C6
Charlton Kings . . 63 A5
Charlton
Mackerell 29 C5
Charlton
Marshall 16 A2
Charlton
Musgrove 29 C7
Charlton on
Otmoor 65 B6
Charltons 168 D4
Charlwood 35 B5
Charlynch 28 B2
Charminster . . . 15 B6
Charmouth . . . 14 B3
Charndon 66 A1
Charney Bassett . 65 D4
Charnock
Richard 137 B4
Charsfield 88 B3
Chart Corner . . 37 A5
Charter Alley . . 46 D3
Charterhouse . . 42 D3
Charterville
Allotments . . . 64 B4
Chartham 52 D3
Chartham Hatch . 52 D3
Chartridge 67 C4
Chart Sutton . . 37 B6
Charvil 47 B5
Charwelton . . 82 B2
Chasetown . . . 96 A3
Chastleton . . . 64 A3
Chasty 10 A4
Chatburn . . . 146 C1
Chatcull 112 B1
Chatham. 51 C4
Chathill 189 A4
Chattenden . . . 51 B4
Chatteris . . . 101 C5
Chattisham . . . 88 C1
Chatto 187 B6
Chatton 188 A3
Chawleigh . . . 26 D2
Chawley 65 C5
Chawston . . . 84 B3
Chawton 33 B6
Cheadle Gtr Man. 128 A3
Staffs 112 A4
Cheadle Heath . 128 A3
Cheadle Hulme . 128 A3
Cheam 49 C5
Cheapside . . . 34 A3
Chearsley. . . . 66 B2
Chebsey . . . 112 C2
Checkendon . . 47 A4
Checkley Ches E.. 111 A4
Hereford 78 D3
Staffs 112 B4
Chedburgh. . . 86 B3
Cheddar 42 D3
Cheddington . . 67 B4
Cheddleton . . 129 D4
Cheddon
Fitzpaine . . . 28 C2
Chedglow . . . 63 D5
Chedgrave . . 105 B4
Chedington . . 15 A4
Chediston . . 105 D4
Chedworth . . . 63 B6
Chedzoy 28 B3
Cheeklaw . . . 198 A1
Cheeseman's
Green 38 B2

Cheglinch. . . . 25 A6
Cheldon 26 D2
Chelford . . . 128 B3
Chellaston . . 114 B1
Chell Heath . . 128 D3
Chellington . . 83 B6
Chelmarsh . . . 95 C5
Chelmer Village. . 70 C1
Chelmondiston. . 88 D3
Chelmorton . . 129 C6
Chelmsford . . 69 C7
Chelsea. 49 B5
Chelsfield. . . . 50 C1
Chelsworth . . 87 C5
Cheltenham. . . 63 A5
Chelveston. . . 84 A1
Chelvey 42 C3
Chelwood . . . 43 C5
Chelwood
Common . . . 36 D2
Chelwood Gate. . 36 D2
Chelworth . . . 63 D5
Chelworth Green 64 D1
Chemistry . . . 111 A4
Chenies 67 D5
Cheny Longville . 94 C2
Chepstow
= Cas-gwent. . . 61 D4
Chequerfield . 140 A2
Cherhill. 44 B4
Cherington Glos . 63 D5
Warks. 81 D5
Cheriton Devon . 26 A2
Hants 33 C4
Kent 38 B3
Swansea . . . 57 C4
Cheriton
Fitzpaine . . . 12 A3
Cheriton or Stackpole
Elidor 55 E5
Cherrington. . 111 C5
Cherrybank . . 219 B6
Cherry Burton. . 150 C2
Cherry Hinton. . 85 B6
Cherry Orchard . 79 B6
Cherry
Willingham. . 133 B5
Chertsey. . . . 48 C3
Cheselbourne . . 16 B1
Chesham . . . 67 D4
Chesham Bois. . 67 D4
Cheshunt . . . 68 C3
Cheslyn Hay. . . 96 A2
Chessington . . 49 C4
Chester. . . . 127 C4
Chesterblade . . 29 A6
Chesterfield . . 130 B3
Chester-le-
Street. . . . 179 D4
Chester Moor . . 167 A5
Chesters Borders 187 A5
Borders . . . 187 B5
Chesterton Cambs 85 A6
Cambs 100 B3
Glos 63 C6
Oxon. 65 A6
Shrops 95 B5
Staffs 112 A2
Warks. 81 B6
Chesterwood . . 177 C6
Chestfield . . . 52 C3
Cheston 7 B5
Cheswardine . . 111 C6
Cheswick . . . 198 B4
Chetnole . . . 15 A6
Chettiscombe . . 27 D4
Chettisham . . 102 C1
Chettle 30 D3
Chetton 95 B4
Chetwode . . . 66 A1
Chetwynd Aston 111 D6
Cheveley. . . . 86 A2
Chevening . . . 36 A2
Chevington . . 86 B3
Chevithorne . . 27 D4
Chew Magna . . 43 C4
Chew Stoke . . 43 C4
Chewton
Keynsham . . 43 C5
Chewton Mendip 43 D4
Chicheley. . . . 83 C6

Chichester . . . 20 B1
Chickerell . . . 15 C6
Chicklade. . . . 30 B3
Chicksgrove . . 30 B3
Chidden 33 D5
Chiddingfold . . 34 C2
Chiddingly . . . 22 A3
Chiddingstone . 36 B2
Chiddingstone
Causeway . . 36 B3
Chiddingstone
Hoath 36 B2
Chideock . . . 14 B4
Chidham. . . . 19 A6
Chidswell . . 139 A5
Chieveley . . . 46 B2
Chignall
St James . . . 69 C6
Chignall Smealy. 69 B6
Chigwell . . . 68 D4
Chigwell Row . . 69 D4
Chilbolton . . . 32 B2
Chilcomb . . . 32 C4
Chilcombe . . . 15 B5
Chilcompton . . 43 D5
Chilcote . . . 113 D6
Childer
Thornton. . 126 B3
Child Okeford . . 30 D2
Childrey . . . 46 A1
Child's Ercall. . 111 C5
Childswickham. . 80 D3
Childwall . . . 127 A4
Childwick Green . 67 B6
Chilfrome. . . . 15 B5
Chilgrove . . . 20 A1
Chilham 52 D2
Chilhampton . . 31 B4
Chilla. 11 A5
Chillaton . . . 11 C5
Chillenden . . . 53 D4
Chillerton . . . 18 C3
Chillesford . . 89 B4
Chillingham. . 188 A3
Chillington Devon . 8 C1
Som 28 D3
Chilmark . . . 30 B3
Chilson 64 B4
Chilsworthy Corn.. 11 A5
Devon. 10 A4
Chilthorne
Domer 29 D5
Chiltington . . 22 A1
Chilton Bucks . . 66 B1
Durham . . . 167 C5
Oxon. 46 A2
Chilton Cantelo . 29 C5
Chilton Foliat . . 45 B7
Chilton Lane . . 167 B6
Chilton Polden . 28 B3
Chilton Street . . 86 C3
Chilton Trinity. . 28 B2
Chilvers Coton . 97 B6
Chilwell . . . 114 B3
Chilworth Hants. . 32 D3
Sur 34 B3
Chimney . . . 65 C4
Chineham . . . 47 D4
Chingford. . . 68 D3
Chinley . . . 129 A5
Chinley Head. . 129 A5
Chinnor . . . 66 C2
Chipnall . . . 111 B6
Chippenhall
Green . . . 104 D3
Chippenham
Cambs 86 A2
Wilts. 44 B3
Chipperfield . . 67 C5
Chipping Herts. . 85 D5
Lancs 145 C6
Chipping
Campden. . 81 D4
Chipping Hill. . 70 B2
Chipping Norton . 64 A4
Chipping Ongar . 69 C5
Chipping
Sodbury. . . 43 A6
Chipping Warden 82 C1
Chipstable . . 27 C5
Chipstead Kent . 36 A2
Sur 35 A5

Chirbury 93 B6
Chirk = Y Waun.. 110 B1
Chirk Bank. . 110 B1
Chirmorrie. . . 181 D4
Chirnside . . 198 A2
Chirnsidebridge 198 A2
Chirton 45 D4
Chisbury. . . . 45 C6
Chiselborough . 29 D4
Chiseldon. . . 45 B5
Chiserley . . 138 A3
Chislehampton. . 65 D6
Chislehurst . . 50 B1
Chislet. . . . 53 C4
Chiswell Green . 67 C6
Chiswick . . . 49 B5
Chiswick End . . 85 C5
Chisworth . . 138 D2
Chithurst . . . 34 D1
Chittering . . 101 D6
Chitterne . . . 30 A3
Chittlehamholt . 26 C1
Chittlehampton . 26 C1
Chittoe 44 C3
Chivenor. . . . 25 B6
Chobham . . . 48 C2
Choicelee. . . 197 A6
Cholderton . . 31 A6
Cholesbury . . 67 C4
Chollerford . . 177 B7
Chollerton . . 178 B1
Cholmondeston. 127 C6
Cholsey. . . . 46 A3
Cholstrey . . . 78 B2
Chop Gate . . 159 B4
Choppington . 179 A4
Chopwell . . 178 D3
Chorley Ches E.. 127 D5
Lancs 137 B4
Shrops 95 C4
Staffs 113 D4
Chorleywood. . 67 D5
Chorlton cum
Hardy . . . 137 D7
Chorlton Lane. . 110 A3
Choulton . . . 94 C1
Chowdene . . 179 D4
Chowley . . . 127 D4
Chrishall. . . . 85 D6
Christchurch BCP. 17 B5
Cambs 101 B6
Glos 62 B1
Newport . . . 42 A2
Christian Malford. 44 B3
Christleton . . 127 C4
Christmas
Common . . 66 D2
Christon . . . 42 D2
Christon Bank. . 189 A5
Christow. . . . 12 C3
Chryston. . . 207 C4
Chudleigh . . . 12 D3
Chudleigh
Knighton . . 12 D3
Chulmleigh . . 26 D1
Chunal 138 D3
Church 137 A6
Churcham . . . 62 B3
Church Aston . 111 D6
Churchbank. . . 93 D7
Church Brampton 83 A4
Churchbridge. . 96 A2
Church
Broughton. . 113 B6
Church
Crookham . . 47 D6
Churchdown . . 63 B4
Church Eaton . 112 D2
Churchend Essex. 69 A6
Essex 71 D4
S Glos 62 D3
Church End
Cambs 100 C4
Cambs 101 A5
C Beds 67 A4
C Beds 84 D1
C Beds 84 D3
Essex 69 A7
Essex 86 C1
E Yorks . . . 150 B3
Hants 47 D4
Lincs 117 B5

Church End continued
Warks. 97 B5
Warks. 97 B5
Wilts. 44 B4
Church Enstone . 65 A4
Church Fenton . 148 C2
Churchfield . . 96 B3
Churchgate
Street. . . . 69 B4
Church Green
Devon. 14 B1
Norf 103 B6
Church
Hanborough. . 65 B5
Church Hill . . 127 C6
Church Houses . 159 B5
Church
Laneham . . 132 B3
Church Langton . 99 B4
Church Lawford . 98 D1
Church Lawton. . 128 D3
Church Leigh . . 112 B4
Church Lench . . 80 B3
Church Mayfield 113 A5
Church Minshull 127 C6
Church Norton . 20 C1
Churchover . . 98 C2
Church Preen . 94 B3
Church
Pulverbatch . . 94 A2
Churchstanton . 28 D1
Church Stoke . 93 B6
Churchstow . . 7 C6
Church Stowe . 82 B3
Church Street . . 51 B4
Church Stretton . 94 B2
Churchtown
Derbys . . . 130 C2
IoM 152 B4
Lancs 145 C4
Mers. 136 B2
Church Town
N Lincs . . . 141 C5
Sur 35 A6
Church Village . 41 C5
Church Warsop 131 C5
Churnsike
Lodge . . . 177 B4
Churston Ferrers. . 8 B3
Churt. 34 C1
Churton . . . 127 D4
Churwell. . . . 139 A5
Chute Standen . 45 D7
Chwilog . . . 107 C4
Chyandour . . . 2 B2
Cilan Uchaf . . 106 D2
Cilcain. . . . 126 C1
Cilcennin . . . 75 B4
Cilcewydd . . . 93 A6
Cilfor 107 C6
Cilfrew 40 A2
Cilfynydd . . . 41 B5
Cilgerran . . . 73 B4
Cilgwyn Carms. . 59 C4
Pembs 72 C2
Ciliau Aeron . . 74 C3
Cill Donnain . . 286 D3
Cille Bhrighde. . 286 E3
Cille Pheadair. . 286 E3
Cilmery . . . 76 B4
Cilsan 58 C2
Ciltalgarth . . 108 A3
Cilwendeg . . 73 C5
Cilybebyll . . . 40 A2
Cilycwm . . . 59 B4
Cimla 40 B2
Cinderford . . 62 B2
Cippyn 72 B4
Circebost . . 288 D2
Cirencester . . 63 C6
Ciribhig . . 288 C2
City London . . 49 A6
Powys 93 C6

City Dulas . . 123 B4
Clachaig . . . 215 C1
Clachan Argyll . 202 C2
Argyll 213 A5
Argyll 215 A4
Argyll 226 B3
Highld. . . . 248 C2
W Isles . . . 286 B3
Clachaneasy . . 181 D5
Clachanmore . 170 C2
Clachan na Luib 287 H2
Clachan of
Campsie. . . 205 A6
Clachan of
Glendaruel . 214 D2
Clachan-Seil . 213 A5
Clachan
Strachur . . 214 B3
Clachbreck . . 202 A2
Clachnabrain . . 232 B1
Clachtoll . . 270 B3
Clackmannan . 208 A2
Clacton-on-Sea. . 71 B5
Cladach . . 288 D2
Chireboist . . 287 H2
Claddach-
knockline . . 287 H2
Cladich . . . 227 D5
Claggan Highld. . 225 B5
Highld. . . . 237 B5
Claigan . . . 258 C2
Claines . . . 79 B6
Clandown . . . 43 D5
Clanfield Hants. . 33 D5
Oxon. 64 C3
Clanville . . . 32 A2
Claonaig . . 202 C3
Claonel . . . 272 D3
Clapgate Dorset. . 17 A4
Herts 68 A4
Clapham Bedford. 84 B2
London . . . 49 B5
N Yorks . . . 146 A1
W Sus. . . . 20 B3
Clap Hill . . . 38 B2
Clappers . . 198 A3
Clappersgate . . 154 A2
Clapton . . . 29 A6
Clapton-in-
Gordano . . 42 B3
Clapton-on-the-
Hill 64 B2
Clapworthy . . 26 C1
Clarach . . . 90 D4
Clara Vale . . 178 C3
Clarbeston . . 55 B6
Clarbeston Road. 55 B6
Clarborough . 132 A2
Clardon . . . 280 B3
Clare 86 C3
Clarebrand . 173 B5
Clarencefield . 174 B3
Clarilaw . . . 186 B4
Clark's Green . . 35 C4
Clarkston . . 205 C5
Clashandorran . 251 B7
Clashcoig . . 264 A2
Clashindarroch. 255 C5
Clashmore Highld 264 B3
Highld. . . . 270 A3
Clashnessie . 270 A3
Clashnoir . . 254 D3
Clate 285 G7
Clathy 219 C4
Clatt 255 D6
Clatter 92 B3
Clatterford . . 18 C3
Clatterin Bridge 233 A4
Clatworthy . . 27 B5
Claughton Lancs. 145 A5
Lancs 145 C5
Mers. 126 A3
Claverdon . . 81 A4
Claverham . . 42 C3
Clavering . . . 85 D6
Claverley . . . 95 B5
Claverton . . 44 C1
Clawdd-newydd 125 D5
Clawthorpe . . 154 D4
Clawton . . . 11 B4
Claxby Lincs . 135 B4
Lincs. 142 D3

Claxton Norf 104 A4
N Yorks 149 A5
Claybokie 242 D3
Claybrooke
Magna 98 C1
Claybrooke Parva 98 C1
Clay Coton 98 D2
Clay Common . . . 105 C5
Clay Cross 130 C3
Claydon Oxon 82 B1
Suff 88 B2
Claygate
Dumfries 175 A6
Kent 37 B5
Sur 49 C4
Claygate Cross . . 36 A4
W Mid 96 A3
Clayhanger Devon 27 C5
Clayhidon 27 D6
Clayhill E Sus 37 D6
Hants 18 A2
Clay Hill 46 B3
Clay Lake 117 C5
Claypole 115 A6
Clayton Staffs . . . 112 A2
S Yorks 140 C2
W Sus 21 A5
W Yorks 147 D5
Clayton Green . . 137 A4
Clayton-le-
Moors 146 D1
Clayton-le-
Woods 137 A4
Clayton West . . . 139 B5
Clayworth 132 A2
Cleadale 234 B3
Cleadon 179 C5
Clearbrook 7 A4
Clearwell 62 C1
Cleasby 167 D5
Cleat 283 J5
Cleatlam 166 D4
Cleator 162 C3
Cleator Moor . . . 162 C3
Clebrig 272 A3
Cleckheaton 139 A4
Cleedownton 94 C3
Cleehill 94 D3
Clee St Margaret . 94 C3
Cleethorpes 143 C5
Cleeton St Mary . . 95 D4
Cleeve 42 C3
Cleeve Hill 63 A5
Cleeve Prior 80 C3
Clegyrnant 91 B7
Clehonger 78 D2
Cleish 208 A3
Cleland 194 A3
Clench Common . . 45 C5
Clenchwarton . . . 118 C2
Clent 96 D2
Cleobury
Mortimer 95 D4
Cleobury North . . 95 C4
Cleongart 190 B2
Clephanton 253 A4
Clerklands 186 A4
Clestrain 283 G4
Cleuch Head . . . 187 B4
Cleughbrae 174 A3
Clevancy 45 B4
Clevedon 42 B3
Cleveley 65 A4
Cleveleys 144 C3
Cleverton 44 A3
Clevis 40 D3
Clewer 42 D3
Cley next the
Sea 120 A2
Cliaid 286 F2
Cliasmol 287 D5
Cliburn 164 C3
Click Mill 282 E4
Cliddesden 33 A5
Cliffburn 233 D4
Cliffe Medway . . . 51 B4
N Yorks 149 D5
Cliff End 23 A6
Cliffe Woods 51 B4
Clifford Hereford . 77 C6
W Yorks 148 C3

Clifford
Chambers 81 B4
Clifford's Mesne . 62 A3
Cliffsend 53 C5
Clifton Bristol . . . 43 B4
C Beds 84 D3
Cumb 164 C3
Derbys 113 A5
Lancs 145 D4
Nottingham . . . 114 B3
N Yorks 147 C5
Oxon. 82 D1
Stirling 216 A3
S Yorks 140 D3
Worcs. 79 C6
York 149 B4
Clifton
Campville 113 D6
Cliftoncote 187 A4
Clifton Green . . 137 C6
Clifton Hampden . 65 D6
Clifton Reynes . . 83 B6
Clifton upon
Dunsmore 98 D2
Clifton upon
Teme 79 A5
Cliftonville 53 B5
Climaen gwyn . . . 59 E4
Climping 20 B3
Climpy 194 A4
Clink 30 A1
Clint 147 B6
Clint Green 120 D2
Clintmains 197 C5
Cliobh 287 A5
Clippesby 121 D6
Clipsham 116 D2
Clipston 99 C4
Clipstone 131 C5
Clitheroe 146 C1
Cliuthar 288 H2
Clive 111 C4
Clivocast 284 C8
Clixby 142 C3
Clocaenog 125 D5
Clochan 267 C5
Clock Face 136 D4
Cloddiau 93 A6
Clodock 61 A5
Clola 257 B5
Clophill 84 D2
Clopton
N Nhants 100 C2
Suff 88 B3
Clopton Corner . . 88 B3
Clopton Green . . 86 B3
Closeburn 183 C6
Close Clark 152 D2
Closworth 29 D5
Clothall 85 D4
Clotton 127 C5
Clough Foot 138 A2
Cloughton 160 B4
Cloughton
Newlands 160 B4
Clousta 285 H5
Clouston 282 F3
Clova Aberds. . . 255 D5
Angus 232 A1
Clovelly 24 C4
Clove Lodge . . . 166 D2
Clovenfords. . . . 196 C3
Clovenstone . . . 245 A4
Clovullin 237 C4
Clow Bridge. . . . 137 A7
Clowne 131 B4
Clows Top 95 D5
Cloy 110 A2
Cluanie Inn 239 A4
Cluanie Lodge . . 239 A4
Clun 93 C7
Clunbury 94 C1
Clunderwen 55 C7
Clune. 252 D3
Clunes 239 D6
Clungunford 94 D1
Clunie Aberds . . . 268 D1
Perth 231 D5
Clunton 94 C1
Cluny 209 A5

Cluny Castle . . . 241 C4
Clutton Bath 43 D5
Ches W 127 D4
Clwt-grugoer . . . 125 C4
Clwt-y-bont 123 D5
Clydach Mon 60 B4
Swansea 40 A1
Clydach Vale 41 B4
Clydebank 205 A4
Clydey 73 C5
Clyffe Pypard . . . 45 B6
Clynder 215 D5
Clyne 40 A3
Clynelish 274 D2
Clynnog-fawr . . . 107 A4
Clyro 77 C6
Clyst Honiton 13 B4
Clyst Hydon 13 A5
Clyst St George . . 13 C4
Clyst St Lawrence 13 A5
Clyst St Mary 13 B4
Cnoc Amhlaigh . 288 D6
Cnwch-coch 75 A5
Coachford 255 B5
Coad's Green 10 D3
Coal Aston 130 B3
Coalbrookdale . . . 95 A4
Coalbrookvale . . . 60 C3
Coalburn 194 C3
Coalburns 178 C3
Coalcleugh 165 A6
Coaley 62 C3
Coalhall 182 A2
Coalhill 70 D1
Coalpit Heath . . . 43 A5
Coalport 95 A4
Coalsnaughton . . 208 A2
Coaltown of
Balgonie 209 A5
Coaltown of
Wemyss 209 A6
Coalville 114 D2
Coalway 62 B1
Coat 29 C4
Coatbridge 207 D5
Coatdyke 207 D5
Coate Swindon . . 45 A5
Wilts. 44 C4
Coates Cambs . . 101 B5
Glos 63 C5
Lancs 146 C2
Notts 132 A3
W Sus 20 A2
Coatham 168 C3
Coatham
Mundeville . . . 167 C5
Coatsgate. 184 B3
Cobbaton 25 C7
Cobbler's Green 104 B3
Coberley 63 B5
Cobham Kent 50 C3
Sur 48 C4
Cobholm Island . 105 A6
Cobleland 206 A3
Cobnash 78 A2
Coburty 269 C4
Cockayne 159 B5
Cockayne Hatley . 85 C4
Cock Bank 110 A2
Cock Bridge. . . . 243 B5
Cockburnspath . 211 C4
Cock Clarks 70 C2
Cockenzie and Port
Seton 209 C7
Cockerham 145 B4
Cockermouth . . . 163 A4
Cockernhof
Green 67 A6
Cockfield
Durham 166 C4
Suff 87 B5
Cockfosters 68 D2
Cocking 20 A1
Cockington 8 A2
Cocklake 28 A4
Cockley Beck . . . 163 D5
Cockley Cley . . . 102 A3
Cockshutt 110 C3
Cockthorpe 120 A1
Cockwood 13 C4
Cockyard 78 D2
Codda 10 D2

Coddenham 88 B2
Coddington
Ches W 127 D4
Hereford 79 C5
Notts 132 D3
Codford St Mary . 30 B3
Codford St Peter . 30 B3
Codicote. 68 B2
Codmore Hill 34 D3
Codnor 114 A2
Codrington 43 B6
Codsall 95 A6
Codsall Wood . . . 95 A6
Coed Duon
=Blackwood . . 41 B6
Coedely 41 C5
Coedkernew 42 A1
Coed Mawr 123 C5
Coed Morgan . . . 61 B5
Coedpoeth. 126 D2
Coed-Talon 126 D2
Coedway. 110 D2
Coed-y-bryn 73 B6
Coed-y-paen 61 D5
Coed-yr-ynys . . . 60 A3
Coed
Ystumgwern. . . 107 D5
Coelbren 59 D5
Coffinswell 8 A2
Cofton Hackett . . 96 D3
Cogan 41 D6
Cogenhoe 83 A5
Cogges 65 C4
Coggeshall 70 A2
Coggeshall
Hamlet 70 A2
Coggins Mill 36 D3
Coignafearn
Lodge. 241 A4
Coig
Peighinnean. . . 288 A6
Coig Peighinnean
Bhuirgh 288 B5
Coilacriech 243 C6
Coilantogle 217 D5
Coilleag. 286 E3
Coillore 246 A2
Coity 40 C4
Col 288 C5
Colaboll 272 C3
Colan 4 A3
Colaton Raleigh . 13 C5
Colbost 258 D2
Colburn 157 B5
Colby Cumb. . . . 165 C4
IoM 152 D2
Norf 120 B4
Colchester 71 A4
Colcot 41 E6
Cold Ash 46 C3
Cold Ashby 98 D3
Cold Ashton 43 B6
Cold Aston 64 B2
Coldbackie 277 C7
Coldbeck 155 A6
Coldblow 50 B2
Cold Blow 55 C7
Cold Brayfield . . . 83 B6
Coldean 21 B6
Coldeast 12 D3
Colden 138 A2
Colden Common . 32 C3
Coldfair Green . . 89 A5
Coldham. 101 A6
Cold Hanworth . 133 A5
Coldharbour
Glos 62 C1
Kent 36 A3
Sur 35 B4
Cold Harbour . . 116 B2
Cold Hatton . . . 111 C5
Cold Hesleden . 168 A2
Cold Higham 82 B3
Coldingham . . . 211 D6
Cold Kirby 158 C5
Cold Newton . . . 99 A4
Cold Northcott . . 10 C3
Cold Norton 70 C2
Cold Overton . . . 115 D6
Coldrain 219 D5
Coldred 39 A4
Coldridge 12 A1

Coldstream
Angus 220 A3
Borders 198 C2
Coldwaltham. . . . 20 A3
Coldwells 257 B6
Coldwells Croft . 255 D6
Coldyeld 94 B1
Cole 29 B6
Colebatch 93 C7
Colebrook 13 A5
Colebrooke 12 B2
Coleby Lincs . . . 133 C4
N Lincs 141 B6
Coleford Devon . . 12 A2
Glos 62 B1
Som 29 A6
Cole Green. 68 B2
Cole Henley 46 D2
Colehill 17 A4
Coleman's Hatch . 36 B2
Colemere 110 B3
Colemore 33 B6
Coleorton 114 D2
Colerne 44 B2
Colesbourne 63 B5
Colesden 84 B3
Cole's Green . . . 88 C1
Cole's Green . . . 88 A3
Coleshill Bucks . . 67 D4
Oxon. 64 D3
Warks. 97 C5
Colestocks 13 A5
Colgate. 35 C5
Colgrain 206 B1
Colinsburgh. . . . 221 D4
Colinton 209 D5
Colintraive 203 A5
Colkirk 119 C6
Collace 220 A2
Collafirth 284 G6
Collaton St Mary . . 8 B2
College Milton . . 205 C6
Collessie 220 C2
Collier Row 69 D5
Collier's End 68 A3
Collier's Green . . 37 C5
Collier Street . . . 37 B5
Colliery Row . . . 167 A6
Collieston 257 D5
Collin. 174 A3
Collingbourne
Ducis 45 D6
Collingbourne
Kingston 45 D6
Collingham Notts 132 C3
W Yorks 148 C2
Collington 79 A4
Collingtree 83 B4
Collins Green . . . 137 D4
Colliston 233 D4
Collycroft 97 C6
Collynie 256 C3
Collyweston . . . 100 A1
Colmonell 180 C3
Colmworth. 84 B3
Colnabaichin . . . 243 B5
Colnbrook 48 B3
Colne Cambs . . . 101 D5
Lancs 146 C2
Colne Edge 146 C2
Colne Engaine . . . 87 D4
Colney. 104 A2
Colney Heath . . . 68 C2
Colney Street . . . 67 C6
Coln Rogers. . . . 64 C1
Coln St Aldwyn's 64 C2
Coln St Dennis . . 64 B1
Colpy. 256 C1
Colquhar 196 B2
Colsterdale 157 C5
Colsterworth . . . 116 C2
Colston Bassett . 115 B4
Coltfield 266 C2
Colthouse 154 B2
Coltishall 121 D4
Coltness 194 A3
Colton Cumb . . . 154 C2
Norf 104 A2
N Yorks 148 C4
Staffs 113 C4
W Yorks 148 D2
Col Uarach 288 D5

Cla–Con 301

Colva 77 B6
Colvend 173 C6
Colvister 284 D7
Colwall Green . . . 79 C5
Colwall Stone . . . 79 C5
Colwell 178 B1
Colwich 112 C4
Colwick 115 A4
Colwinston 40 D4
Colworth 20 B2
Colwyn Bay
=Bae Colwyn . 124 B3
Colyford 14 B2
Colyton 14 B2
Combe Hereford . 78 A1
Oxon. 65 B5
W Berks 46 C1
Combe Common . 34 C2
Combe Down . . . 43 C6
Combe Florey . . . 27 B6
Combe Hay 43 D6
Combeinteignhead
. . . . 13 D4
Combe Martin. . . 25 A6
Combe Moor . . . 78 A1
Combe Raleigh . . 13 A6
Comberbach . . . 127 B6
Comberton Cambs. 85 B5
Hereford 78 A2
Combe
St Nicholas . . . 28 D3
Combpyne 14 B2
Combridge. 113 B4
Combrook 81 B6
Combs Derbys . . 129 B5
Suff 87 B6
Combs Ford. 87 B6
Combwich 28 A2
Comers 244 B3
Comins Coch. . . . 90 D4
Commercial End . 86 A1
Commins Capel
Betws 75 C5
Commins Coch . . 91 B6
Commondale . . . 169 D4
Common Edge . . 144 D3
Commonmoor . . . 6 A1
Commonside. . . . 127 B5
Common Side . . 130 B3
Compstall. 138 D2
Compton Devon . . 8 A2
Hants 32 C3
Sur 34 B1
Sur 34 B2
W Berks 46 B3
Wilts. 45 D5
W Sus 33 D6
Compton Abbas . 30 D2
Compton Abdale . 44 B4
Compton
Beauchamp . . . 45 A6
Compton Bishop . 42 D2
Compton
Chamberlayne . 31 C4
Compton Dando . 43 C5
Compton Dundon 29 B4
Compton Martin . 43 D4
Compton
Pauncefoot . . . 29 C6
Compton Valence 15 B5
Comrie Fife. . . . 208 B3
Perth 218 B2
Conaglen House 237 C4
Conchra 214 D3
Concraigie 231 D5
Conder Green . . 145 B4
Conderton 80 D2
Condicote 64 A2
Condorrat 207 C5
Condover 94 A2
Coneyhurst 35 D4
Coneysthorpe . . 159 D6
Coneythorpe . . . 148 B2
Coney Weston . . 103 D5
Conford 33 B7
Congash 253 D6
Congdon's Shop . 10 D3
Congerstone 97 A6

Congham.....119 C4
Congleton.....128 C3
Congl-y-wal....108 A2
Congresbury.....42 C3
Congreve.....112 D3
Conicavel.....253 A5
Coningsby.....134 D2
Conington Cambs 85 A5
 Cambs.....100 C3
Conisbrough.....140 D3
Conisby.....200 B2
Conisholme.....143 D6
Coniston Cumb.....154 B2
 E Yorks.....151 D4
Coniston Cold.....146 B3
Conistone.....146 A3
Connah's Quay.126 C2
Connel.....226 C4
Connel Park.....182 A4
Connor Downs..2 B3
Conon Bridge..252 A1
Conon House...252 A1
Cononley.....146 C3
Conordan.....247 A4
Consall.....112 A3
Consett.....178 D3
Constable
 Burton.....157 B5
Constantine.....3 C5
Constantine Bay..9 D4
Contin.....251 A6
Contlaw.....245 B5
Conwy.....124 B2
Conyer.....51 C6
Conyers Green..87 A4
Cooden.....23 B5
Cooil.....152 D3
Cookbury.....11 A5
Cookham.....48 A1
Cookham Dean..47 A6
Cookham Rise...48 A1
Cookhill.....80 B3
Cookley Suff.....104 D4
 Worcs.....95 C6
Cookley Green..66 D1
Cookney.....245 C5
Cookridge.....147 C6
Cooksbridge.....22 A2
Cooksmill Green.69 C6
Coolham.....35 D4
Cooling.....51 B4
Coombe Corn...4 B4
 Corn.....24 D3
 Hants.....33 C5
 Wilts.....45 D5
Coombe Bissett.31 C5
Coombe Hill.....63 A4
Coombe Keynes.16 C2
Coombes.....21 B4
Coopersale
 Common.....69 C4
Cootham.....20 A3
Copdock.....88 C2
Copford Green..70 A3
Copgrove.....148 A2
Copister.....284 F6
Cople.....84 C3
Copley.....166 B3
Coplow Dale.....129 B6
Copmanthorpe..149 C4
Coppathorne.....10 A3
Coppenhall.....112 D3
Coppenhall
 Moss.....128 D2
Copperhouse...2 B3
Coppingford.....100 C3
Copplestone.....12 A2
Coppull.....137 B4
Coppull Moor...137 B4
Copsale.....35 D4
Copster Green..145 D6
Copston Magna..98 C1
Copt Heath.....97 D4
Copt Hewick.....158 D2
Copthorne
 Shrops.....110 D3
 Sur.....35 C6
Copt Oak.....114 D2
Copy's Green...119 B6

Copythorne.....32 D2
Corbets Tey.....50 A2
Corbridge.....178 C1
Corby.....99 C5
Corby Glen.....116 C2
Cordon.....191 B6
Coreley.....95 D4
Cores End.....48 A2
Corfe.....28 D2
Corfe Castle.....16 C3
Corfe Mullen....16 B3
Corfton.....94 C2
Corgarff.....243 B5
Corhampton.....33 C5
Corlae.....183 C4
Corley.....97 C6
Corley Ash.....97 C5
Corley Moor.....97 C5
Cornaa.....152 C4
Cornabus.....200 D3
Cornel.....124 C2
Corner Row.....144 D4
Corney.....153 A2
Cornforth.....167 B6
Cornhill.....267 D6
Cornhill-on-
 Tweed.....198 C2
Cornholme.....138 C2
Cornish Hall End..86 D2
Cornquoy.....283 H6
Cornsay.....166 A4
Cornsay Colliery.167 A4
Corntown Highld.252 A1
 V Glam.....40 D4
Cornwell.....64 A3
Cornwood.....7 B5
Cornworthy.....8 B2
Corpach.....237 B4
Corpusty.....120 B3
Corran Highld.....237 C4
 Highld.....238 B2
Corranbuie.....202 B3
Corrany.....152 C4
Corrie.....203 D5
Corrie Common.185 D5
Corriecravie.....191 C5
Corriemoillie.....263 D5
Corriemulzie
 Lodge.....263 A5
Corrievarkie
 Lodge.....229 A4
Corrievorrie.....252 D3
Corrimony.....251 C5
Corringham
 Lincs.....141 D6
 Thurrock.....51 A4
Corris.....91 B5
Corris Uchaf.....91 B5
Corrour Shooting
 Lodge.....228 B3
Corrow.....215 B4
Corry.....247 B5
Corrykinloch.....271 B6
Corrymuckloch..218 A4
Corrynachenchy 225 B5
Corry of
 Ardnagrask..251 B7
Corsback.....280 A4
Corscombe.....15 A5
Corse Aberds.....255 B7
 Glos.....62 A3
Corse Lawn.....79 D6
Corse of Kinnoir 255 B6
Corsewall.....170 A2
Corsham.....44 B2
Corsindae.....244 B3
Corsley.....30 A2
Corsley Heath...30 A2
Corsock.....173 A5
Corston Bath.....43 C5
 Wilts.....44 A3
Corstorphine.....209 C4
Cors-y-Gedol...107 D5
Cortachy.....232 C1
Corton Suff.....105 B6
 Wilts.....30 A3
Corton Denham..29 C6
Coruanan Lodge 237 C4
Corunna.....287 H3
Corwen.....109 A5
Coryton Devon...11 C5
 Thurrock.....51 A4

Cosby.....98 B2
Coseley.....96 B2
Cosgrove.....83 C4
Cosham.....19 A5
Cosheston.....55 D6
Cossall.....114 A2
Cossington Leics 115 D4
 Som.....28 A3
Costa.....282 E4
Costessey.....120 D3
Costock.....114 C3
Coston.....115 C6
Cote.....64 C4
Cotebrook.....127 C5
Cotehill.....176 D2
Cotes Cumb.....154 C3
 Leics.....114 C3
 Staffs.....112 B2
Cotesbach.....98 C2
Cotgrave.....115 B4
Cothall.....245 A5
Cotham.....115 A5
Cothelstone.....28 B1
Cotherstone.....166 D3
Cothill.....65 D5
Cotleigh.....14 A2
Cotmanhay.....114 A2
Cotmaton.....13 C6
Coton Cambs.....85 B6
 Staffs.....112 B3
 Staffs.....112 C2
 W Nhants.....98 D3
Coton Clanford..112 C2
Coton Hill Shrops 110 C3
 Staffs.....112 B3
Coton in the
 Elms.....113 D6
Cott.....8 A1
Cottam E Yorks...150 A2
 Lancs.....145 D5
 Notts.....132 B3
Cottartown.....253 C6
Cottenham.....85 A6
Cotterdale.....156 B2
Cottered.....68 A3
Cotteridge.....96 D3
Cotterstock.....100 B2
Cottesbrooke...99 D4
Cottesmore.....116 D2
Cotteylands.....27 D4
Cottingham
 E Yorks.....150 D3
 N Nhants.....99 B5
Cottingley.....147 D5
Cottisford.....82 D2
Cotton Staffs.....113 A4
 Suff.....87 A6
Cotton End.....84 C2
Cottown Aberds..245 A4
 Aberds.....255 D6
 Aberds.....256 B3
Cotwalton.....112 B3
Couch's Mill.....5 B6
Coughton Hereford 62 A1
 Warks.....80 A3
Coulaghailtro...202 B2
Coulags.....249 B6
Coulby Newham 168 D3
Coulderton.....162 D2
Coulin.....250 A2
Coull Aberds.....244 B2
 Argyll.....200 B2
Coulport.....215 D5
Coulsdon.....35 A5
Coulston.....44 D3
Coulter.....195 C5
Coulton.....159 D5
Cound.....94 A3
Coundon Durham 167 C5
 W Mid.....97 C6
Coundon
 Grange.....167 C5
Countersett.....156 C3
Countess.....31 A5
Countess Wear..13 C4
Countesthorpe..98 B2
Countisbury.....26 A2
County Oak.....35 C5
Coupar Angus..231 D6
Coup Green.....137 A4
Coupland.....198 C3
Cour.....202 D3

Courance.....184 C3
Court-at-Street..38 B2
Courteenhall.....83 B4
Court Henry.....58 C2
Courtsend.....71 D4
Courtway.....28 B2
Cousland.....209 D6
Cousley Wood...37 C4
Cove Argyll.....215 D5
 Borders.....211 C4
 Devon.....27 D4
 Hants.....34 A1
 Highld.....261 A5
Cove Bay.....245 B6
Cove Bottom....105 D5
Covehithe.....105 C6
Coven.....96 A2
Coveney.....101 C6
Covenham St
 Bartholomew..143 D5
Covenham
 St Mary.....143 D5
Coventry.....97 D6
Coverack.....3 D5
Coverham.....157 C5
Covington Cambs 100 D2
 S Lanark.....195 C4
Cowan Bridge...155 D5
Cow Ark.....145 C6
Cowbeech.....22 A4
Cowbit.....117 D5
Cowbridge Lincs.117 A6
 Som.....27 A4
Cowbridge
 = Y Bont-Faen..41 D4
Cowdale.....129 B5
Cowden.....36 B2
Cowdenbeath....209 A4
Cowdenburn.....195 A7
Cowers Lane.....113 A7
Cowes.....18 B3
Cowesby.....158 C3
Cowfold.....35 D5
Cowgill.....155 C6
Cowie Aberds.....245 D5
 Stirling.....207 B6
Cowley Devon....13 B4
 Glos.....63 B5
 London.....48 A3
 Oxon.....65 C6
Cowleymoor.....27 D4
Cowling Lancs...137 B4
 N Yorks.....146 C3
 N Yorks.....157 C6
Cowlinge.....86 B3
Cowpe.....138 A1
Cowpen.....179 A4
Cowpen Bewley.168 C2
Cowplain.....33 D5
Cowshill.....165 A6
Cowslip Green...42 C3
Cowstrandburn.208 A3
Cowthorpe.....148 B3
Coxbank.....111 A5
Coxbench.....114 A1
Cox Common....105 C4
Coxford Norf.....119 C5
 Soton.....32 D2
Cox Green.....48 B1
Coxheath.....37 A5
Coxhill.....39 A4
Coxhoe.....167 B6
Coxley.....29 A5
Cox Moor.....131 D5
Coxwold.....158 D4
Coychurch.....40 D4
Coylton.....193 C4
Coylumbridge...242 A2
Coynach.....244 B1
Coynachie.....255 C5
Coytrahen.....40 C3
Crabadon.....7 B6
Crabbs Cross....80 A3
Crabtree.....35 D5
Crackenthorpe..165 C4
Crackington
 Haven.....10 B2
Crackley.....97 D5
Cracklybank.....111 D6
Crackpot.....156 B3
Cracoe.....146 A3

Craddock.....27 D5
Cradhlastadh...287 A5
Cradley.....79 C5
Cradley Heath...96 C2
Crafthole.....6 B2
Craggan.....253 D6
Craggie Highld...252 C3
 Highld.....274 C2
Cragg Vale.....138 A3
Craghead.....179 D4
Crai.....59 C5
Craibstone.....267 D5
Craichie.....232 D3
Craig Dumfries..173 A4
 Dumfries.....173 B4
 Highld.....250 B2
Craiganor
 Lodge.....229 C5
Craig Castle.....255 D5
Craig-cefn-parc.40 A1
Craigdam.....256 C3
Craigdarroch
 Dumfries.....183 C5
 Highld.....251 A6
Craigdhu.....251 B6
Craigearn.....245 A4
Craigellachie...254 B3
Craigencross....170 A2
Craigend Perth...219 B6
 Stirling.....207 B5
Craigendive.....214 D3
Craigendoran...215 D6
Craigends.....205 B4
Craigens Argyll...200 B2
 E Ayrs.....182 A3
Craighat.....206 B2
Craighead.....221 D6
Craighlaw.....171 A5
Craighouse.....201 B5
Craigie Aberds...245 A6
 Dundee.....220 A4
 Perth.....219 B6
 Perth.....231 D5
 S Ayrs.....193 B4
Craigiefield.....282 F5
Craigielaw.....210 C1
Craiglockhart....209 C5
Craigmalloch...182 C2
Craigmaud.....268 D3
Craigmillar.....209 C5
Craigmore.....203 B6
Craignant.....110 B1
Craigneuk
 N Lanark.....194 A2
 N Lanark.....207 D5
Craignure.....225 C6
Craigo.....233 B4
Craigow.....219 D5
Craig Penllyn...41 D4
Craigrothie.....220 C3
Craigroy.....266 D2
Craigruie.....217 B4
Craigston Castle 268 D2
Craigton
 Aberdeen.....245 B5
 Angus.....221 A5
 Angus.....232 C1
 Highld.....264 A2
Craigtown.....279 C4
Craig-y-don.....124 A2
Craig-y-nos.....59 D5
Craik.....185 B6
Crail.....221 D6
Crailing.....187 A5
Crailinghall.....187 A5
Craiselound.....141 D5
Crakehill.....158 D3
Crakemarsh.....113 B4
Crambe.....149 A6
Cramlington.....179 B4
Cramond.....209 C4
Cramond Bridge 209 C4
Cranage.....128 C2
Cranberry.....112 B2
Cranborne.....31 D4
Cranbourne.....48 B2
Cranbrook Devon.13 B5
 Kent.....37 C5
Cranbrook
 Common.....37 C5
Crane Moor.....139 C6

Crane's Corner..119 D6
Cranfield.....83 C6
Cranford.....48 B4
Cranford
 St Andrew.....99 D6
Cranford St John 99 D6
Cranham Glos...63 B4
 London.....50 A2
Crank.....136 D4
Crank Wood....137 C5
Cranleigh.....34 C3
Cranley.....104 D2
Cranmer Green..103 D6
Cranmore.....18 C2
Cranna.....268 D1
Crannich.....225 B4
Crannoch.....267 D5
Cranoe.....99 B4
Cransford.....88 A4
Cranshaws.....210 D3
Cranstal.....152 A4
Crantock.....4 A2
Cranwell.....116 A3
Cranwich.....102 B3
Cranworth.....103 A5
Craobh Haven...213 B5
Crapstone.....7 A4
Crarae.....214 C2
Crask Inn.....272 B3
Craskins.....244 B2
Crask of Aigas..251 B6
Craster.....189 B5
Craswall.....77 D6
Cratfield.....104 D4
Crathes.....245 C4
Crathie Aberds...243 C5
 Highld.....240 C3
Crathorne.....158 A3
Craven Arms....94 C2
Crawcrook.....178 C3
Crawford Lancs..136 C3
 S Lanark.....195 D4
Crawfordjohn...194 D3
Crawick.....183 A5
Crawley Hants...32 B3
 Oxon.....64 B4
 W Sus.....35 C5
Crawley Down...35 C5
Crawleyside.....166 A2
Crawshawbooth 137 A7
Crawton.....233 A6
Cray N Yorks.....156 D3
Crayford.....50 B2
Crayke.....159 D4
Crays Hill.....69 D7
Cray's Pond.....47 A4
Creacombe.....26 D3
Creagan.....227 B4
Creag Ghoraidh.286 B3
Creaguaineach
 Lodge.....228 B2
Creaksea.....70 D3
Creaton.....99 D4
Creca.....175 A5
Credenhill.....78 C2
Crediton.....12 A3
Creebridge.....171 A6
Creech
 Heathfield.....28 C2
Creech
 St Michael.....28 C2
Creed.....4 C4
Creekmouth.....50 A1
Creeting Bottoms 88 B2
Creeting St Mary.88 B1
Creeton.....116 C3
Creetown.....171 B6
Creggans.....214 B3
Cregneash.....152 E1
Creg-ny-Baa....152 C3
Cregrina.....77 B5
Creich.....220 B3
Creigiau.....41 C5
Cremyll.....6 B3
Creslow.....66 A3
Cressage.....94 A3
Cressbrook.....129 B6
Cresselly.....55 D6
Cressing.....70 A1
Cresswell
 Northumb.....189 D5

Cresswell continued
Staffs 112 B3
Cresswell Quay . . 55 D6
Cresswell 131 B5
Cretingham 88 A3
Cretshengan . . . 202 B2
Crewe Ches E . . . 128 D2
　Ches W. 127 D4
Crewgreen 110 D2
Crewkerne 14 A4
Crianlarich 216 B3
Cribyn 75 C4
Criccieth 107 C4
Crich 130 D3
Crichie 257 B4
Crichton 209 D6
Crick Mon 61 D6
　W Nhants 98 D2
Crickadarn 77 C4
Cricket
　Malherbie 28 D3
Cricket
　St Thomas 14 A3
Crickheath 110 C1
Crickhowell 60 B4
Cricklade 64 D2
Cricklewood 49 A5
Cridling Stubbs . 140 A4
Crieff 218 B3
Criggion 110 D1
Crigglestone . . . 139 B6
Crimond 269 D5
Crimonmogate . . 269 D5
Crimplesham . . . 102 A2
Crinan 213 C5
Cringleford 104 A2
Cringles 147 C4
Crinow 56 A1
Cripplesease 2 B3
Cripplestyle 31 D4
Cripp's Corner . . . 37 D5
Croasdale 162 C3
Crockenhill 50 C2
Crockernwell . . . 12 B2
Crockerton 30 A2
Crocketford or
　Ninemile Bar . . 173 A6
Crockey Hill. . . . 149 C5
Crockham Hill. . . 36 A2
Crockleford
　Heath 71 A4
Crockness 283 H4
Crock Street . . . 28 D3
Croeserw 40 B3
Croes-goch 54 A4
Croes-lan 73 B6
Croesor 107 B6
Croesyceiliog
　Carms 57 A4
　Torf 61 D5
Croes-y-
　mwyalch 61 D5
Croesywaun . . . 107 A5
Croft
　Leics. 98 B2
　Lincs. 135 C5
　Pembs 73 B4
　Warr. 137 D5
Croftamie 206 B2
Croftmalloch . . . 208 D2
Crofton Wilts . . . 45 C6
　W Yorks 140 B1
Croft-on-Tees . . 157 A6
Crofts of
　Benachielt 275 A5
Crofts of Haddo 256 C3
Crofts of
　Inverthernie . . 256 B2
Crofts of Meikle
　Ardo 256 B3
Crofty 57 C5
Croggan 225 D6
Croglin 164 A3
Croich 263 A6
Crois Dughaill. . 286 D3
Cromarty 264 D3
Cromblet 256 C2
Cromdale 253 D6
Cromer Herts . . . 68 A2
　Norf 120 A4
Cromford 130 D2
Cromhall 62 D2

Cromhall
　Common 43 A5
Cromor 288 E5
Cromra 240 C3
Cromwell 132 C2
Cronberry 193 C6
Crondall 33 A6
Cronk-y-Voddy . 152 C3
Cronton 127 A4
Crook Cumb . . . 154 B3
　Durham 167 B4
Crookedholm . . 193 B4
Crookes 130 A3
Crookham
　Northumb. 198 C3
　W Berks 46 C3
Crookham
　Village 47 D5
Crookhaugh . . . 195 D6
Crookhouse . . . 187 A6
Crooklands 154 C4
Crook of Devon 219 D5
Cropredy 82 C1
Cropston 114 D3
Cropthorne 80 C2
Cropton 159 C6
Cropwell Bishop 115 B4
Cropwell Butler . 115 B4
Cros 288 A6
Crosbost 288 E4
Crosby Cumb. . . 162 A3
　IoM 152 D3
　N Lincs 141 B6
Crosby Garrett . 155 A6
Crosby
　Ravensworth . 165 D4
Crosby Villa . . . 162 A3
Croscombe 29 A5
Cross 42 D3
Crossaig 202 C3
Crossal 246 A3
Crossapol 222 C2
Cross Ash 61 B6
Cross-at-Hand . . 37 B5
Crossburn 207 C6
Crossbush 20 B3
Crosscanonby . . 162 A3
Crossdale Street 120 B4
Crossens 136 B2
Crossflatts 147 C5
Crossford Fife . . 208 B3
　S Lanark 194 B3
Crossgate 117 C5
Crossgatehall . . 209 D6
Crossgates Fife . 208 B4
　Powys 77 A4
Crossgill 145 A5
Cross Green
　Devon 11 C4
　Suff 87 B4
　Suff 87 B5
　Warks. 81 B6
Cross Hands . . . 57 A5
Cross-hands . . . 73 D4
Cross Hands . . . 55 C6
Crosshill
　E Ayrs 193 C5
　Fife 209 A4
　S Ayrs 192 E3
Cross Hill 114 A2
Crosshouse . . . 192 B3
Cross Houses . . . 94 A3
Crossings 176 B3
Cross in Hand
　E Sus 36 D3
　Leics. 98 C2
Cross Inn Ceredig. 73 A6
　Ceredig 75 B4
　Rhondda. 41 C5
Crosskeys 41 B7
Crosskirk 279 A6
Cross Lane Head . 95 B5
Crosslanes 110 C2
Cross Lanes Corn . 3 A4
　N Yorks 148 A4
　Wrex 110 A2
Crosslee Borders 185 A6
　Renfs 205 B4
Crossmichael . . 173 B5
Crossmoor 144 D4
Cross Oak 60 A3

Cross of
　Jackston 256 C2
Cross o' th'
　hands 113 A6
Crossroads
　Aberds 245 C4
　E Ayrs 193 B4
Cross Street . . . 104 D2
Cross Trickett's . . 17 A4
Crossway Hereford 79 D4
　Mon 61 B6
　Powys 77 B4
Crossway Green . 79 A6
Crossways 16 C1
Crosswell 72 C4
Crosswood 75 A5
Crosthwaite. . . . 154 B3
Croston 136 B3
Crostwick 121 D4
Crostwight 121 C5
Crothair 288 D2
Crouch 36 A4
Croucheston . . . 31 C4
Crouch Hill 29 D7
Crouch House
　Green. 36 B2
Croughton 82 D2
Crovie 268 C3
Crowan 3 B4
Crowborough . . . 36 C3
Crowcombe 27 B6
Crowdecote . . . 129 C6
Crowden 138 D3
Crow Edge 139 C4
Crowell 66 D2
Crowfield Suff . . 88 B2
　W Nhants 82 C3
Crow Hill 62 A2
Crowhurst E Sus. 23 A5
　Sur 36 B1
Crowhurst Lane
　End 36 B1
Crowland 117 D5
Crowlas 2 B3
Crowle N Lincs . . 141 B5
　Worcs. 80 B2
Crowmarsh
　Gifford 47 A4
Crown Corner . . 104 D3
Crownhill 6 B3
Crownland 103 E6
Crownthorpe . . . 104 A1
Crowntown 3 B4
Crows-an-wra . . . 2 C1
Crowshill 103 A5
Crowsnest 94 A1
Crowthorne 47 C6
Crowton 127 B5
Croxall 113 D5
Croxby 142 D3
Croxdale 167 B5
Croxden 113 B4
Croxley Green. . . 67 D5
Croxton Cambs . . 84 A4
　N Lincs 142 B2
　Norf 103 C4
　Staffs 112 B1
Croxtonbank . . . 112 B1
Croxton Kerrial . 115 C6
Croy Highld . . . 252 B3
　N Lanark 207 C5
Croyde 25 B5
Croydon Cambs . 85 C5
　London 49 C6
Crubenmore
　Lodge 241 C4
Cruckmeole 94 A2
Cruckton 110 D3
Cruden Bay . . . 257 C5
Crudgington . . . 111 D5
Crudwell 63 D5
Crug 93 D5
Crugmeer 9 D5
Crugybar 58 B3
Crulabhig 288 D2
Crumlin
　=Crymlyn 41 B7
Crumpsall 138 C1
Crundale Kent . . 38 A2
　Pembs 55 C5
Cruwys Morchard 26 D3
Crux Easton 46 D2

Crwbin 57 A4
Crya 283 G4
Cryers Hill 66 D3
Crymlyn 123 C6
Crymlyn
　=Crumlin 41 B7
Crymych 73 C4
Crynant 40 A2
Crynfryn 75 B4
Cuaig 249 A4
Cuan 213 A5
Cubbington 81 A6
Cubeck 156 C3
Cubert 4 B2
Cubley 139 C5
Cubley Common 113 B5
Cublington Bucks. 66 B3
　Hereford 78 D2
Cuckfield 35 D6
Cucklington 30 C1
Cuckney 131 B5
Cuckoo Hill . . . 141 D5
Cuddesdon 65 C7
Cuddington Bucks. 66 B2
　Ches W. 127 B6
Cuddington
　Heath 110 A3
Cuddy Hill 145 D4
Cudham 36 A2
Cudliptown 11 D6
Cudworth Som. . . 28 D3
　S Yorks 140 C1
Cuffley 68 C3
Cuiashader 288 B6
Cuidhir 286 F2
Cuidhtinis 287 F5
Culbo. 264 C2
Culbokie 252 A2
Culburnie 251 B6
Culcabock 252 B2
Culcairn 264 D2
Culcharry 253 A4
Culcheth 137 D5
Culdrain 255 C6
Culduie 249 B4
Culford 103 D4
Culgaith 165 C4
Culham 65 D6
Culkein 270 A4
Culkein
　Drumbeg. 270 A4
Culkerton. 63 D5
Cullachie 253 D5
Cullen 267 C6
Cullercoats . . . 179 B5
Cullicudden . . . 264 D2
Cullingworth. . . 147 D4
Cullipool. 213 A5
Cullivoe 284 C7
Culloch 218 C2
Culloden. 252 B3
Cullompton 13 A5
Culmaily 265 A4
Culmazie 171 B5
Culmington 94 C2
Culmstock 27 D6
Culnacraig 270 D3
Culnaknock . . . 259 B5
Culpho 88 C3
Culrain 264 A1
Culross 208 B2
Culroy 192 D3
Culsh Aberds . . . 243 C6
　Aberds 256 B3
Culshabbin 171 B5
Culswick. 285 J4
Cultercullen . . . 257 D4
Cults Aberdeen . 245 B5
　Aberds 255 C6
　Dumfries 171 C6
Culverstone
　Green. 50 C3
Culverthorpe . . . 116 A3
Culworth 82 C2
Culzie Lodge . . 263 C7
Cumbernauld
　Village 207 C5
Cumberworth . . 135 B5
Cuminestown . . 268 D3
Cumlewick 285 L6
Cummersdale . . 175 C6

Cummertrees . . 174 B4
Cummingston . . 266 C2
Cumnock 193 C5
Cumnor 65 C5
Cumrew 176 D3
Cumwhinton . . . 176 D2
Cumwhitton . . . 176 D3
Cundall 158 D3
Cunninghamhead
　 . . . . 204 D3
Cunnister 284 D7
Cupar 220 C3
Cupar Muir 220 C3
Cupernham 32 C2
Curbar. 130 B2
Curbridge Hants . 32 D4
　Oxon. 64 C4
Curdridge. 32 D4
Curdworth 97 B4
Curland. 28 D2
Curlew Green . . . 89 A4
Currarie 180 B3
Curridge 46 B2
Currie 209 D4
Curry Mallet 28 C3
Curry Rivel. 28 C3
Curtisden Green. 37 B5
Curtisknowle. . . . 7 B6
Cury 3 C4
Cushnie 268 C2
Cushuish 28 B1
Cusop 77 C6
Cutcloy 171 D6
Cutcombe 27 B4
Cutgate 138 B1
Cutiau 90 A4
Cutlers Green. . . 86 D1
Cutnall Green . . 80 A1
Cutsdean 80 D3
Cutthorpe 130 B3
Cutts 285 K6
Cuxham 66 D1
Cuxton 51 C4
Cuxwold 142 C3
Cwm Bl Gwent. . 60 C3
　Denb 125 B5
　Swansea 40 B1
Cwmafan 40 B2
Cwmaman 41 B5
Cwmann 75 D4
Cwmavon 61 C4
Cwmbach Carms . 57 B4
　Carms 73 D5
　Powys 76 B4
　Powys 77 D5
Cwmbâch. 41 A5
Cwmbelan 92 C3
Cwmbran
　=Cwmbrân 61 D4
Cwmbrân
　=Cwmbran 61 D4
Cwmbrwyno 91 D5
Cwm-byr 58 B3
Cwmcarn 41 B7
Cwmcarvan 61 C6
Cwm-Cewydd . . . 91 A6
Cwm-cou 73 B5
Cwmcych 73 C5
Cwmdare 41 A4
Cwmderwen 92 A3
Cwmdu Carms . . 58 C3
　Powys 60 A3
　Swansea 57 C6
Cwmduad. 73 C6
Cwm-Dulais 57 B6
Cwmdwr. 59 B4
Cwmfelin Bridgend 40 C3
　M Tydf. 41 A5
Cwmfelin Boeth . 56 A1
Cwm-felin-fach . 41 B6
Cwmfelin
　Mynach 73 D5
Cwmffrwd 57 A4
Cwm Ffrwd-oer . 61 C4
Cwmgiedd 59 D4
Cwmgors 59 D4
Cwmgwili 57 A5
Cwmgwrach 40 A3
Cwm-hesgen . . 108 C2
Cwmhiraeth 73 C6
Cwm-hwnt. 59 E6
Cwmifor 58 C3

Cwm Irfon 76 C2
Cwmisfael 57 A4
Cwm-Llinau 91 B6
Cwmllynfell 59 D4
Cwm-mawr 57 A5
Cwmorgan 73 C5
Cwm-parc 40 B4
Cwmpengraig . . 73 C6
Cwm
　Penmachno . . 108 A2
Cwmrhos 60 A3
Cwmsychpant . . 74 D3
Cwmtillery 60 C4
Cwm-twrch Isaf . 59 D4
Cwm-twrch
　Uchaf 59 D4
Cwmwysg. 59 C5
Cwm-y-glo Carms 57 A5
　Gwyn 123 D5
Cwmyoy 61 A4
Cwmystwyth . . . 92 D1
Cwrt. 91 B4
Cwrt-newydd . . . 74 D3
Cwrt-y-cadno . . . 58 A3
Cwrt-y-gollen . . . 60 B4
Cydweli
　=Kidwelly 57 B4
Cyffordd Llandudno =
　Llandudno
　Junction 124 B2
Cyffylliog 125 D5
Cyfronydd 93 A5
Cymer 40 B3
Cyncoed 41 C6
Cynghordy 59 A5
Cynheidre 57 B4
Cynwyd 109 A5
Cynwyl Elfed . . . 73 D6
Cywarch 91 A6

D

Dacre Cumb . . . 164 C2
　N Yorks 147 A5
Dacre Banks . . . 147 A5
Daddry Shield. . 166 B1
Dadford 82 D3
Dadlington. 97 B7
Dafarn Faig . . . 107 A5
Dafen 57 B5
Daffy Green . . . 103 A5
Dagenham 50 A1
Daglingworth . . . 63 C5
Dagnall 67 B4
Dail Beag. 288 C3
Dail bho Dheas . 288 A5
Dail bho Thuath 288 A5
Daill. 200 B3
Dailly 181 A4
Dail Mor 288 C3
Dairsie or
　Osnaburgh . . . 220 C4
Daisy Hill 137 C5
Dalabrog 286 D3
Dalavich 214 A2
Dalbeattie. 173 B6
Dalblair. 182 A4
Dalbog 232 A3
Dalbury 113 B6
Dalby IoM 152 D2
　N Yorks 159 D5
Dalchalloch . . . 229 B6
Dalchalm 274 C2
Dalchenna 214 B3
Dalchirach 254 C2
Dalchork 272 C3
Dalchreichart . . 239 A6
Dalchruin 218 C2
Dalderby 134 C2
Dale 54 D4
Dale Abbey . . . 114 B2
Dale Head 164 C2
Dalelia 235 D6
Dale of Walls . . 285 H3
Daless 253 C4
Dalfaber 242 A2
Dalgarven 204 D2
Dalgety Bay . . . 209 B4

304 Dal–Dow

Dalginross....218 A6
Dalguise....230 D3
Dalhalvaig....279 C4
Dalham....86 A3
Dalinlongart....215 D4
Dalkeith....209 D6
Dallam....137 D4
Dallas....266 D2
Dalleagles....182 A3
Dallinghoo....88 B3
Dallington E Sus..23 A4
  W Nhants....83 A4
Dallow....157 D5
Dalmadilly....245 A4
Dalmally....227 D6
Dalmarnock....205 B6
Dalmary....206 A3
Dalmellington..182 A2
Dalmeny....208 C4
Dalmigavie....241 A5
Dalmigavie
  Lodge....252 D3
Dalmore....264 D2
Dalmuir....205 A4
Dalnabreck....235 D5
Dalnacardoch
  Lodge....229 A6
Dalnacroich....251 A5
Dalnaglar Castle 231 B5
Dalnahaitnach..253 D4
Dalnaspidal
  Lodge....229 A5
Dalnavaid....230 B4
Dalnavie....264 C2
Dalnawillan
  Lodge....279 D6
Dalness....237 D5
Dalnessie....273 C4
Dalqueich....219 D5
Dalreavoch....273 D5
Dalry....204 D2
Dalrymple....192 D3
Dalserf....194 A3
Dalston....175 C6
Dalswinton....184 D2
Dalton Dumfries 174 A4
  Lancs....136 C3
  Northumb....177 D2
  Northumb....178 B3
  N Yorks....157 A5
  N Yorks....158 D3
  S Yorks....140 D2
Dalton-in-
  Furness....153 C3
Dalton-le-Dale.168 A2
Dalton Piercy..168 B2
Dalveich....217 B6
Dalvina Lodge..278 D2
Dalwood....14 A2
Dalwyne....181 B5
Damerham....31 D5
Damgate....105 A5
Dam Green....103 C6
Damnaglaur....170 D3
Damside....195 B6
Dam Side....144 C4
Danbury....70 C1
Danby....159 A6
Danby Wiske..158 B2
Dandaleith....254 B3
Danderhall....209 D6
Danebridge....129 C4
Dane End....68 A3
Danehill....36 D2
Danemoor
  Green....103 A6
Danesford....95 B5
Daneshill....47 D4
Dangerous
  Corner....136 B4
Danskine....210 D2
Darcy Lever....137 C6
Darenth....50 B2
Daresbury....127 A5
Darfield....140 C2
Darfoulds....131 B5
Dargate....52 C2

Darite....6 A1
Darlaston....96 B2
Darley....147 B6
Darley Bridge..130 C2
Darley Head...147 B5
Darlingscott....81 C5
Darlington....167 D5
Darliston....111 B4
Darlton....132 B2
Darnall....130 A3
Darnick....197 C4
Darowen....91 B6
Darra....256 B2
Darracott....25 B5
Darras Hall....178 B3
Darrington....140 A2
Darsham....89 A5
Dartford....50 B2
Dartford Crossing 50 B2
Dartington....8 A1
Dartmeet....12 D1
Dartmouth....8 B2
Darton....139 C6
Darvel....193 B5
Darwell Hole....23 A4
Darwen....137 A5
Datchet....48 B2
Datchworth....68 B2
Datchworth
  Green....68 B2
Daubhill....137 C6
Daugh of
  Kinnermony...254 B3
Dauntsey....44 A3
Dava....253 C6
Davenham....127 B6
Davenport
  Green....128 B3
Daventry....82 A2
Davidson's
  Mains....209 C5
Davidstow....10 C2
David's Well....93 D4
Davington....185 B4
Daviot Aberds...256 D2
  Highld....252 C3
Davoch of
  Grange....267 D5
Davyhulme....137 D6
Dawley....95 A4
Dawlish....13 D4
Dawlish Warren..13 D4
Dawn....124 B3
Daws Heath....51 A5
Daw's House....10 C4
Dawsmere....118 B1
Dayhills....112 B3
Daylesford....64 A3
Ddôl-Cownwy..109 D5
Ddrydwy....122 C3
Deadwater....187 D5
Deaf Hill....167 B6
Deal....53 D6
Deal Hall....71 D4
Dean Cumb....162 B3
  Devon....7 A6
  Devon....25 A6
  Dorset....30 D3
  Hants....33 D4
  Som....29 A6
Deanburnhaugh 186 B2
Deane Gtr Man..137 C5
  Hants....46 D3
Deanich Lodge..263 B5
Deanland....30 D3
Dean Prior....7 A6
Dean Row....128 A3
Deans....208 D3
Deanscales....162 B3
Deanshanger...83 D4
Deanston....218 D2
Dearham....162 A3
Debach....88 B3
Debden Essex...68 D4
  Essex....86 D1
Debden Cross...86 D1
Debenham....88 A2
Dechmont....208 C3
Deddington....82 D1
Dedham....87 D6
Dedham Heath..87 D6
Deebank....244 C3

Deene....99 B6
Deenethorpe....99 B6
Deepcar....139 D5
Deepcut....34 A2
Deepdale....155 C6
Deeping Gate...100 A3
Deeping
  St James....100 A3
Deeping
  St Nicholas...117 D5
Deerhill....267 D5
Deerhurst....63 A4
Deerness....283 G6
Defford....80 C2
Defynnog....59 C6
Deganwy....124 B2
Deighton
  N Yorks....158 A2
  W Yorks....139 B4
  York....149 C5
Deiniolen....123 D5
Delabole....9 C6
Delamere....127 C5
Delfrigs....257 D4
Delliefure....254 C1
Dell Lodge....242 A3
Delnabo....243 A4
Delnadamph....243 B5
Delph....138 C2
Delves....166 A4
Delvine....231 D5
Dembleby....116 B3
Denaby Main...140 D2
Denbigh
  =Dinbych....125 C5
Denbury....8 A2
Denby....114 A1
Denby Dale....139 C5
Denchworth....65 D4
Dendron....153 C3
Denel End....84 D2
Denend....255 C7
Denford....100 D1
Dengie....70 C3
Denham Bucks..48 A3
  Suff....86 A3
  Suff....104 D2
Denham Street..104 D2
Denhead Aberds 269 D4
  Fife....221 C4
Denhead of
  Arbilot....232 D3
Denhead of
  Gray....220 A3
Denholm....187 B4
Denholme....147 D4
Denholme
  Clough....147 D4
Denio....106 C3
Denmead....33 D5
Denmore....245 A6
Denmoss....256 B1
Dennington....88 A3
Denny....207 B6
Dennyloanhead 207 B6
Denny Lodge....18 A2
Denshaw....138 B2
Denside....245 C5
Densole....39 A4
Denston....86 B3
Denstone....113 A5
Dent....155 C6
Denton Cambs..100 C3
  Darl....167 D5
  E Sus....22 B2
  Gtr Man....138 D2
  Kent....39 A4
  Lincs....115 B6
  Norf....104 C3
  N Yorks....147 C5
  Oxon....65 C6
  W Nhants....83 B5
Denton's Green 136 D3
Denver....102 A2
Denwick....189 B5
Deopham....103 A6
Deopham Green 103 B6
Depden....86 B3
Depden Green...86 B3
Deptford London..49 B6
  Wilts....31 B4
Derby....114 B1

Derbyhaven....152 E2
Dereham....120 D1
Deri....41 A6
Derril....10 A4
Derringstone....39 A4
Derrington....112 C2
Derriton....10 A4
Derryguaig....224 C3
Derry Hill....44 B3
Derrythorpe....141 C6
Dersingham....118 B3
Dervaig....224 A3
Derwen....125 D5
Derwenlas....91 C5
Desborough....99 C5
Desford....98 A1
Detchant....199 C4
Detling....37 A5
Deuddwr....110 D1
Devauden....61 D6
Devil's Bridge....75 A6
Devizes....44 C4
Devol....204 A3
Devonport....6 B3
Devonside....208 A2
Devoran....4 D2
Dewar....196 B2
Dewlish....16 B1
Dewsbury....139 A5
Dewsbury Moor.139 A5
Dewshall Court..78 D2
Dhoon....152 C4
Dhoor....152 B4
Dhowin....152 A4
Dial Post....21 A4
Dibden....18 A3
Dibden Purlieu..18 A3
Dickleburgh....104 C2
Didbrook....80 D3
Didcot....46 A3
Diddington....84 A3
Diddlebury....94 C3
Didley....78 D2
Didling....20 A1
Didmarton....44 A2
Didsbury....138 D1
Didworthy....7 A5
Digby....133 D5
Digg....259 B4
Diggle....138 C3
Digmoor....136 C3
Digswell Park....68 B2
Dihewyd....74 C3
Dilham....121 C5
Dilhorne....112 A3
Dillarburn....194 B3
Dillington....84 A3
Dilston....178 C1
Dilton Marsh....30 A2
Dilwyn....78 B2
Dinas Carms....73 C5
  Gwyn....106 C2
Dinas Cross....72 C3
Dinas Dinlle....107 A4
Dinas-Mawddwy.91 A6
Dinas Powys....41 D6
Dinbych
  =Denbigh....125 C5
Dinbych-y-Pysgod
  =Tenby....56 B1
Dinder....29 A5
Dinedor....78 D3
Dingestow....61 B6
Dingle....126 A3
Dingleden....37 C6
Dingley....99 C4
Dingwall....252 A1
Dinlabyre....186 D4
Dinmael....109 A5
Dinnet....244 C1
Dinnington Som...28 D4
  S Yorks....131 A5
  T&W....179 B4
Dinorwic....123 D5
Dinton Bucks....66 B2
  Wilts....31 B4
Dinwoodie
  Mains....185 C4
Dinworthy....24 D4
Dippen....191 C6
Dippenhall....33 A7
Dipple Moray...266 D4

Dipple continued
  S Ayrs....181 A4
Diptford....7 B6
Dipton....178 D3
Dirdhu....254 D1
Dirleton....210 B2
Dirt Pot....165 A6
Discoed....77 A6
Diseworth....114 C2
Dishes....282 E7
Dishforth....158 D2
Disley....129 A4
Diss....104 D2
Disserth....76 B4
Distington....162 B3
Ditchampton....31 B4
Ditcheat....29 B6
Ditchingham....104 B4
Ditchling....21 A6
Ditherington....111 D4
Dittisham....8 B2
Ditton Halton...127 A4
  Kent....37 A5
Ditton Green....86 B2
Ditton Priors....95 C4
Divach....251 D6
Divlyn....59 B4
Dixton Glos....80 D2
  Mon....61 B7
Dobcross....138 C2
Dobwalls....5 A7
Doccombe....12 C2
Dochfour House 252 C2
Dochgarroch...252 B2
Docking....119 B4
Docklow....78 B3
Dockray....164 C1
Dockroyd....147 D4
Doc Penfro
  =Pembroke Dock..55 D5
Dodburn....186 C3
Doddinghurst...69 D5
Doddington
  Cambs....101 B5
  Kent....51 D6
  Lincs....133 B4
  Northumb....198 C3
  Shrops....95 D4
Doddiscombsleigh
  ....12 C3
Dodford
  W Nhants....82 A3
  Worcs....96 D2
Dodington....43 A6
Dodleston....126 C3
Dods Leigh....112 B4
Dodworth....139 C6
Doe Green....127 A5
Doe Lea....131 C4
Dogdyke....134 D2
Dogmersfield....47 D5
Dogridge....45 A4
Dogsthorpe....100 A3
Dog Village....13 B4
Dolanog....109 D5
Dolau Powys....77 A5
  Rhondda....41 C4
Dolbenmaen....107 B5
Dolfach....91 B7
Dolfor....93 C5
Dol-för....91 A6
Dolgarrog....124 C2
Dolgellau....91 A5
Dolgran....58 B1
Dolhendre....108 B3
Doll....274 D2
Dollar....208 A2
Dolley Green....77 A6
Dollwen....91 D4
Dolphin....126 B1
Dolphinholme..145 B5
Dolphinton....195 B6
Dolton....25 D6
Dolwen Conwy..124 B3
  Powys....92 A3
Dolwyd....124 B3
Dolwyddelan....124 D2
Dôl-y-Bont....90 D4
Dol-y-cannau...77 C6
Dolyhir....77 B6
Doncaster....140 C3
Dones Green....127 B6

Donhead
  St Andrew....30 C3
Donhead St Mary 30 C3
Donibristle....209 B4
Donington....117 B5
Donington on
  Bain....134 A2
Donington South
  Ing....117 B5
Donisthorpe....113 D7
Donkey Town....48 C2
Donnington Glos..64 A2
  Hereford....79 D5
  Shrops....94 A3
  Telford....111 D6
  W Berks....46 C2
  W Sus....20 B1
Donnington
  Wood....111 D6
Donyatt....28 D3
Doonfoot....192 D3
Dorback Lodge..242 A3
Dorchester Dorset.15 B6
  Oxon....65 D6
Dordon....97 A5
Dore....130 A3
Dores....252 C1
Dorking....35 B4
Dormansland....36 B2
Dormanstown...168 C3
Dormington....78 C3
Dormston....80 B2
Dornal....181 D4
Dorney....48 B2
Dornie....249 D5
Dornoch....264 B3
Dornock....175 B5
Dorrery....279 C6
Dorridge....97 D4
Dorrington Lincs 133 D5
  Shrops....94 A2
Dorsington....80 C4
Dorstone....77 C7
Dorton....66 B1
Dorusduain....250 D1
Dosthill....97 B5
Dottery....15 B4
Doublebois....5 A6
Dougarie....191 B4
Doughton....63 D4
Douglas IoM....152 D3
  S Lanark....194 C3
Douglas &
  Angus....220 A4
Douglastown....232 D2
Douglas Water..194 C3
Douglas West...194 C3
Doulting....29 A6
Dounby....282 E3
Doune Highld....272 D2
  Stirling....218 D2
Doune Park....268 C2
Douneside....244 B1
Dounie....264 A1
Dounreay....279 B5
Dousland....7 A4
Dovaston....110 C2
Dove Holes....129 B5
Dovenby....162 A3
Dover....39 A5
Dovercourt....88 D3
Doverdale....79 A6
Doveridge....113 B5
Doversgreen....35 B5
Dowally....230 D4
Dowbridge....144 D4
Dowdeswell....63 B5
Dowlais....60 C2
Dowlish Wake....28 D3
Down Ampney...64 D2
Downcraig
  Ferry....204 C1
Downderry....6 B2
Downe....50 C1
Downend IoW....18 C4
  S Glos....43 B5
  W Berks....46 B2
Downfield....220 A3
Downgate....11 D4
Downham Essex..70 D1
  Lancs....146 C1

Downham continued
Northumb.......198 C2
Downham
Market.......102 A2
Down Hatherley..63 A4
Downhead......29 A6
Downhill Perth..219 A5
T&W.........179 D5
Downholland
Cross........136 C2
Downholme....157 B5
Downies......245 C6
Downley.......66 D3
Down St Mary..12 A2
Downside Som...29 A6
Sur..........35 A4
Down Thomas....7 B4
Downton Hants..17 B6
Wilts.........31 C5
Downton on the
Rock.........94 D2
Dowsby......116 C4
Dowsdale.....117 D5
Dowthwaitehead
............163 B6
Doxey.......112 C3
Doxford......189 A4
Doxford Park...179 D5
Doynton......43 B6
Draffan......194 B2
Dragonby.....141 B7
Drakeland Corner.7 B4
Drakemyre....204 C2
Drake's
Broughton....80 C2
Drakes Cross...96 D3
Drakewalls....11 D5
Draughton
N Yorks......147 B4
W Nhants......99 D4
Drax........141 A4
Draycote......98 D1
Draycott Derbys..114 B2
Glos.........81 D4
Som..........42 D3
Draycott in the
Clay.........113 C5
Draycott in the
Moors........112 A3
Drayford......26 D2
Drayton Leics...99 B5
Lincs........117 B5
Norf.........120 D3
Oxon.........65 D5
Oxon.........82 C1
Ptsmth.......19 A5
Som..........28 C4
Worcs........96 D2
Drayton Bassett..97 A4
Drayton
Beauchamp....67 B4
Drayton Parslow..66 A3
Drayton
St Leonard....65 D6
Drebley......147 B4
Dreemskerry...152 B4
Dreenhill.....55 C5
Drefach Carms..57 A5
Carms........73 C6
Dre-fach Carms..57 A4
Ceredig.......75 D4
Drefelin......73 C6
Dreghorn.....192 B3
Drellingore....39 A4
Drem........210 C2
Dresden......112 A3
Dreumasdal...286 C3
Drewsteignton..12 B2
Driby........134 B3
Driffield E Yorks..150 B3
Glos.........63 D6
Drigg.......153 A1
Drighlington...139 A5
Drimnin......225 A4
Drimpton......14 A4
Drimsynie....215 B4
Drinisiadar...288 H2
Drinkstone......7 B4
Drinkstone Green 87 A5
Drishaig.....215 A4
Drissaig.....214 A2
Drochil......195 B6

Drointon......112 C4
Droitwich Spa...80 A1
Droman.......276 C2
Dron........219 C6
Dronfield.....130 B3
Dronfield
Woodhouse..130 B3
Drongan.....182 A2
Dronley......220 A3
Droxford......33 D5
Droylsden....138 D2
Druid........109 A5
Druidston.....55 C4
Druimarbin...237 B4
Druimavuic...227 B5
Druimdrishaig..202 A2
Druimindarroch 235 B5
Druimyeon
More........202 C1
Drum Argyll....203 A4
Perth........219 D5
Drumbeg.....270 A4
Drumblade....255 B6
Drumblair....256 B1
Drumbuie
Dumfries....182 D3
Highld.......249 C4
Drumburgh...175 C5
Drumburn....174 B2
Drumchapel..205 A5
Drumchardine..252 B1
Drumchork....261 B5
Drumclog....193 B6
Drumderfit...252 A2
Drumeldrie...220 D4
Drumelzier...195 C6
Drumfearn...247 C5
Drumgask....241 C4
Drumgley....232 C2
Drumguish....241 C5
Drumin......254 C2
Drumlasie....244 B3
Drumlemble...190 D2
Drumligair...245 A6
Drumlithie....245 D4
Drummoddie..171 C5
Drummond....264 D2
Drummore....170 D3
Drummuir....255 B4
Drummuir
Castle......255 B4
Drumnadrochit..251 D7
Drumnagorrach 267 D6
Drumoak.....245 C4
Drumpark....183 D6
Drumphail....171 A4
Drumrash....173 A4
Drumrunie....271 D4
Drums.......257 D4
Drumsallie....236 B3
Drumstinchall..173 C6
Drumsturdy...221 A4
Drumtochty
Castle.......244 D1
Drumtroddan..171 C5
Drumuie......259 D4
Drumuillie....253 D5
Drumvaich....217 D6
Drumwhindle..257 C4
Drunkendub..233 D4
Drury........126 C2
Drury Square..119 D6
Dry Doddington 115 A6
Dry Drayton....85 A5
Dryhope......196 D1
Drylaw......209 C5
Drym..........3 B4
Drymen......206 B2
Drymuir......257 B4
Drynoch.....246 A3
Dryslwyn.....58 C2
Dryton........94 A3
Dubford......268 C3
Dubton......232 C3
Duchally.....271 C6
Duchlage.....206 B1
Duck Corner...89 C4

Duckington...127 D4
Ducklington...65 C4
Duckmanton..131 B4
Duck's Cross...84 B3
Duddenhoe End..85 D6
Duddingston..209 C5
Duddington...100 A1
Duddleswell...36 D2
Duddo.......198 B3
Duddon......127 C5
Duddon Bridge.153 B3
Dudleston....110 B2
Dudleston
Heath.......110 B2
Dudley T&W...179 B4
W Mid.........96 B2
Dudley Port....96 B2
Duffield.....114 A1
Duffryn Neath...40 B3
Newport.......42 A1
Dufftown.....254 C4
Duffus.......266 C2
Dufton......165 C4
Duggleby.....150 A1
Duirinish....249 C4
Duisdalemore..247 C6
Duisky.......237 B4
Dukestown....60 B3
Dukinfield....138 D2
Dulas.......123 B4
Dulcote.......29 A5
Dulford.......13 A5
Dull.........230 D2
Dullatur......207 C5
Dullingham....86 B2
Dulnain Bridge.253 D5
Duloe Bedford...84 A3
Corn..........6 B1
Dulsie.......253 B5
Dulverton.....27 C4
Dulwich.......49 B6
Dumbarton...205 A3
Dumbleton....80 D3
Dumcrieff....185 B4
Dumfries.....174 A2
Dumgoyne...206 B3
Dummer......33 A4
Dumpford.....34 D1
Dumpton......53 C5
Dun.........233 C4
Dunain House..252 B2
Dunalastair...229 C6
Dunan.......247 B4
Dunans......214 C3
Dunball.......28 A3
Dunbar......210 C3
Dunbeath....275 B5
Dunbeg......226 C3
Dunblane....218 D2
Dunbog......220 C2
Duncanston...252 A1
Duncanstone..255 D6
Dun
Charlabhaigh.288 C2
Dunchurch....98 D1
Duncote......82 B3
Duncow......184 D2
Duncraggan..217 D5
Duncrievie...219 D6
Duncton......20 A2
Dundas House..283 A5
Dundee......220 A4
Dundeugh....182 D3
Dundon.......29 B4
Dundonald...192 B3
Dundonnell..262 B2
Dundonnell
Hotel.......262 B2
Dundonnell
House.......262 B3
Dundraw.....175 D5
Dundreggan..239 A7
Dundreggan
Lodge.......240 A1
Dundrennan..173 D5
Dundry........43 C4
Dunecht.....245 B4
Dunfermline..208 B3
Dunfield......64 D2
Dunford Bridge.139 C4
Dungworth...130 A2
Dunham......132 B3

Dunham-on-the-
Hill.........127 B4
Dunhampton...79 A6
Dunham Town..128 A2
Dunholme....133 B5
Dunino......221 C5
Dunipace....207 B6
Dunira.......218 B2
Dunkeld......230 D4
Dunkerton....43 D6
Dunkeswell....13 A6
Dunkeswick..148 C2
Dunkirk Kent...52 D2
Norf.........120 C4
Dunk's Green...36 A4
Dunlappie....232 B3
Dunley Hants...46 D2
Worcs........79 A5
Dunlichity
Lodge.......252 C2
Dunlop......205 D4
Dunmaglass
Lodge.......252 D1
Dunmore Argyll..202 B2
Falk........208 B1
Dunnet......280 A4
Dunnichen...232 D3
Dunninald...233 C5
Dunning.....219 C5
Dunnington
E Yorks......151 B4
Warks........80 B3
York........149 B5
Dunnockshaw.137 A7
Dunollie.....226 C3
Dunoon......203 A6
Dunragit.....170 B3
Dunrostan...213 D5
Duns........198 A1
Dunsby......116 C4
Dunscore....183 D6
Dunscroft....141 C4
Dunsdale....168 D4
Dunsden Green..47 B5
Dunsfold......34 C3
Dunsford......12 C3
Dunshalt.....220 C2
Dunshillock..257 B4
Dunskey House.170 B2
Dunsley......169 D6
Dunsmore......66 C3
Dunsop Bridge.145 B6
Dunstable.....67 A5
Dunstall......113 C5
Dunstall Common 80 C1
Dunstall Green..86 A3
Dunstan.....189 B5
Dunstan Steads.189 A5
Dunster......27 A4
Duns Tew......65 A5
Dunston Lincs..133 C5
Norf.........104 A3
Staffs.......112 D3
T&W........179 C4
Dunsville....140 C4
Dunswell.....150 D3
Dunsyre.....195 B5
Dunterton....11 D4
Duntisbourne
Abbots......63 C5
Duntisbourne
Leer........63 C5
Duntisbourne
Rouse.......63 C5
Duntish......15 A6
Duntocher...205 A4
Dunton Bucks...66 A3
C Beds.......84 C4
Norf.........119 B5
Dunton Bassett..98 B2
Dunton Green..36 A3
Dunton Wayletts.69 D6
Duntulm.....259 A4
Dunure......192 D2
Dunvant......57 C5
Dunvegan....258 D2
Dunwich.....105 D5
Dunwood....129 D6
Dupplin Castle.219 C5
Durdar......175 C7
Durgates......36 C4
Durham......167 A5

Durisdeer....183 B6
Durisdeermill.183 B6
Durkar.......139 B6
Durleigh......28 B2
Durley Hants...32 D4
Wilts.........45 C6
Durnamuck...262 A2
Durness.....277 B5
Durno.......256 D2
Duror.......236 D3
Durran Argyll..214 B2
Highld.......280 B3
Durrington Wilts..31 A5
W Sus.........21 B4
Dursley.......62 D3
Durston.......28 C2
Durweston....16 A2
Dury.........285 G6
Duston.......83 A4
Duthil.......253 D5
Dutlas........93 D6
Duton Hill.....69 A6
Dutson........10 C4
Dutton......127 B5
Duxford Cambs...85 C6
Oxon.........65 D4
Dwygyfylchi..124 B2
Dwyran......123 D4
Dyce........245 A5
Dye House....178 D1
Dyffryn Bridgend..40 B3
Carms........73 D6
Pembs........72 C2
Dyffryn
Ardudwy....107 D5
Dyffryn Castell..91 D5
Dyffryn Ceidrych.59 C4
Dyffryn Cellwen..59 E5
Dyke Lincs....116 C4
Moray.......253 A5
Dykehead Angus 232 B1
N Lanark.....207 E6
Stirling.....206 A3
Dykelands....233 B5
Dykends.....231 C6
Dykeside.....256 B2
Dykesmains..204 D2
Dylife.........91 C6
Dymchurch....38 C2
Dymock.......79 D5
Dyrham.......43 B6
Dysart......209 A6
Dyserth......125 B5

E

Eachwick....178 B3
Eadar Dha
Fhadhail....287 A5
Eagland Hill..144 C4
Eagle........132 C3
Eagle Barnsdale 132 C3
Eagle Moor...132 C3
Eaglescliffe...168 D2
Eaglesfield Cumb 162 B3
Dumfries....175 A5
Eaglesham...205 C5
Eaglethorpe..100 B2
Eairy........152 D2
Eakley Lanes...83 B5
Eakring......132 C1
Ealand......141 B5
Ealing.......49 A4
Eals........177 D4
Eamont Bridge.164 C3
Earby.......146 C3
Earcroft.....137 A5
Eardington....95 B5
Eardisland....78 B2
Eardisley.....77 C7
Eardiston Shrops 110 C2
Worcs........79 A4
Earith......101 D5
Earle........188 A2
Earley.......47 B5
Earlham.....104 A3
Earlish......258 B3
Earls Barton...83 A5
Earls Colne....70 A2
Earl's Croome..79 C6
Earlsdon......97 D6

Earlsferry....221 E4
Earlsfield....116 B2
Earlsford.....256 C3
Earl's Green...87 A6
Earlsheaton...139 A5
Earl Shilton....98 B1
Earlsmill.....253 A5
Earl Soham....88 A3
Earl Sterndale.129 C5
Earlston Borders.197 C4
E Ayrs.......193 B4
Earl Stonham...88 B2
Earlswood Mon..61 D6
Sur..........35 B5
Warks........96 D4
Earnley.......19 B7
Earsairidh...286 G3
Earsdon.....179 B5
Earsham.....104 C4
Earswick.....149 B5
Eartham......20 B2
Easby N Yorks..157 A5
N Yorks.....159 A4
Easdale......213 A5
Easebourne....34 D1
Easenhall.....98 D1
Eashing.......34 B2
Easington Bucks..66 B1
Durham......168 A2
E Yorks......143 B5
Northumb....199 C5
Oxon.........66 D1
Oxon.........82 D1
Redcar.......169 D5
Easington
Colliery.....168 A2
Easington Lane.167 A6
Easingwold..148 A4
Easole Street...53 D4
Eassie.......232 D1
East Aberthaw..41 E5
East Adderbury..82 D1
East Allington....7 C6
East Anstey....26 C3
East Appleton.157 B6
East Ardsley..139 A6
East Ashling....19 A7
East Auchronie 245 B5
East Ayton...160 C3
East Bank......60 C4
East Barkwith..133 A6
East Barming...37 A5
East Barnby...169 D6
East Barnet....68 D2
East Barns....211 C4
East Barsham..119 B6
East Beckham.120 B3
East Bedfont...48 B3
East Bergholt...87 D6
East Bilney....119 D6
East Blatchington 22 B2
East Boldre....18 A2
Eastbourne....22 C4
East Brent.....42 D2
Eastbridge.....89 A5
East Bridgford.115 A4
East Buckland..26 B1
East Budleigh..13 C5
Eastburn......147 C4
East Burrafirth.285 H5
East Burton....16 C2
Eastbury London..67 D5
W Berks.......46 B1
East Butsfield.166 A4
East Butterwick 141 C6
Eastby.......147 B4
East Cairnbeg..233 A5
East Calder..208 D3
East Carleton.104 A3
East Carlton
N Nhants......99 C5
W Yorks......147 C6
East Chaldon...16 C1
East Challow....46 A1
East Chiltington 21 A6
East Chinnock..29 D4
East Chisenbury..45 D5
Eastchurch....52 B1
East Clandon...34 A3

East Claydon....66 A2
East Clyne....274 D2
East Coker....29 D5
Eastcombe....63 C4
East Combe....27 B6
East Common....149 D5
East Compton....29 A6
Eastcote London....48 A4
W Mid....97 D4
W Hants....82 B3
Eastcott Corn....24 C3
Wilts....44 D4
East Cottingwith 149 C6
Eastcourt Wilts....45 C6
Wilts....63 D5
East Cowes....18 B4
East Cowick....141 A4
East Cowton....157 A7
East Cramlington....179 B4
East Cranmore....29 A6
East Creech....16 C3
East Croachy....252 D2
East Croftmore....242 A2
East Curthwaite....164 A1
East Dean E Sus....22 C3
Hants....31 C6
W Sus....20 A2
East Down....25 A7
East Drayton....132 B2
East Ella....142 A2
East End Dorset....16 B3
E Yorks....143 A4
Hants....18 B2
Hants....33 C5
Hants....46 C2
Herts....69 A4
Kent....37 C6
N Som....42 B3
Oxon....65 B4
Easter Ardross....264 C2
Easter Balmoral 243 C5
Easter Boleskine....251 D7
Easter Compton....43 A4
Easter Cringate 207 B5
Easter Davoch....244 B1
Easter Earshaig....184 B3
Easter Fearn....264 B2
Easter Galcantray....253 B4
Eastergate....20 B2
Easterhouse....207 D4
Easter Ilowgate....209 D5
Easter Howlaws 197 B6
Easter Kinkell....252 A1
Easter Lednathie....232 B1
Easter Milton....253 A5
Easter Moniack....252 B1
Eastern Green....97 C5
Easter Ord....245 B5
Easter Quarff....285 K6
Easter Rhynd....245 B2
Easter Row....207 A5
Easter Silverford....268 C2
Easter Skeld....285 J5
Easterton....44 D4
Eastertown....42 D2
Eastertown of Auchleuchries.257 C5
Easter Whyntie....267 C7
East Farleigh....37 A5
East Farndon....99 C4
East Ferry....141 D6
Eastfield N Lanark....208 D1
N Yorks....160 C4
Eastfield Hall....189 C5
East Fortune....210 C2
East Garston....46 B1
Eastgate Durham 166 B2
Norf....120 C3
East Ginge....46 A2
East Goscote....115 D4
East Grafton....45 C6
East Grimstead....31 C6
East Grinstead....36 C1

East Guldeford....38 C1
East Haddon....82 A3
East Hagbourne....46 A3
East Halton....142 B3
Eastham....126 A4
East Ham....50 A1
Eastham Ferry....126 A4
Easthampstead....47 C6
East Hanney....65 D5
East Hanningfield 70 C1
East Hardwick....140 B2
East Harling....103 C5
East Harlsey....158 B3
East Harnham....31 C5
East Harptree....43 D4
East Harting....33 D6
East Hatley....85 B4
East Hauxwell....157 B5
East Haven....221 A5
Eastheath....47 C6
East Heckington 117 A4
East Hedleyhope....167 A4
East Hendred....46 A2
East Herrington....179 D5
East Heslerton....160 D2
East Hoathly....22 A3
Easthope....94 B3
Easthorpe Essex....70 A3
Leics....115 B6
Notts....132 D2
East Horrington....29 A5
East Horsley....34 A3
East Horton....198 C4
Easthouses....209 D6
East Huntspill....28 A3
East Hyde....67 B6
East Ilkerton....21 E4
East Ilsley....46 A2
Eastington Devon.12 A2
Glos....62 C3
Glos....64 B2
East Keal....134 C3
East Kennett....45 C5
East Keswick....148 C2
East Kilbride....205 C6
East Kirkby....134 C3
East Knapton....160 D2
East Knighton....16 C2
East Knoyle....30 B2
East Kyloe....199 C4
East Lambrook....28 D4
East Lamington....264 C3
East Langdon....39 A5
East Langton....99 B4
East Langwell....273 D5
East Lavant....20 B1
East Lavington....46 D2
East Layton....157 A5
Eastleach Martin.64 C3
Eastleach Turville 64 C2
East Leake....114 C3
East Learmouth 198 C2
Eastleigh Devon....25 C5
Hants....32 D3
East Leigh....12 A1
East Lexham....119 D5
East Lilburn....188 A3
Eastling....51 D6
East Linton....210 C2
East Liss....33 C6
East Looe....6 B1
East Lound....141 D5
East Lulworth....16 C2
East Lutton....150 A2
East Lydford....29 A5
East Mains....244 C3
East Malling....37 A5
East March....220 A4
East Marden....33 D7
East Markham....132 B2
East Marton....146 B3
East Meon....33 C5
East Mere....27 D4
East Mersea....71 B4
East Mey....281 A5
East Molesey....49 C4
Eastmoor Derbys 130 B3
Norf....102 A3
East Morden....16 B3
East Morton....147 C4

East Ness....159 D5
East Newton....151 D5
Eastney....19 B5
Eastnor....79 D5
East Norton....99 A4
East Nynehead....27 C6
East Oakley....46 D3
Eastoft....141 B6
East Ogwell....12 D3
Eastoke....19 B6
Easton Cambs....100 D3
Cumb....175 C5
Cumb....176 B2
Devon....12 C2
Dorset....15 D6
Hants....32 B4
Lincs....116 C2
Norf....120 D3
Som....29 A5
Suff....88 B3
Wilts....44 B2
Easton Grey....44 A2
Easton-in-Gordano....43 B4
Easton Maudit....83 B5
Easton on the Hill....100 A2
Easton Royal....45 C6
East Orchard....30 D2
East Ord....198 A3
East Panson....11 B4
Eastpark....174 B3
East Peckham....37 B4
East Pennard....29 B5
East Perry....84 A3
East Portlemouth....7 D6
East Prawle....8 D1
East Preston....20 B3
East Putford....25 D4
East Quantoxhead....27 A6
East Rainton....167 A6
East Ravendale....143 D4
East Raynham....119 C5
Eastrea....101 B4
East Rhidorroch Lodge....262 A4
Eastriggs....175 B5
East Rigton....148 C2
Eastrington....141 A5
East Rounton....158 A3
East Row....169 D6
East Rudham....119 C5
East Runton....120 A3
East Ruston....121 C5
Eastry....53 D5
East Saltoun....210 D1
East Sleekburn....179 A4
East Somerton....121 D6
East Stockwith....141 D5
East Stoke Dorset.16 C2
Notts....115 A5
East Stour....30 C2
East Stourmouth.53 C4
East Stowford....26 C1
East Stratton....32 B4
East Studdal....39 A5
East Suisnish....248 C2
East Taphouse....5 A6
East Thirston....189 D4
East Tilbury....50 B3
East Tisted....33 B6
East Torrington 133 A6
East Tuddenham....120 D2
East Tytherley....32 C1
East Tytherton....44 B3
East Village....12 A3
Eastville Bristol....43 B5
Lincs....135 D4
East Wall....94 B3
East Walton....119 D4
Eastwell....115 C5
East Wellow....32 C2
East Wemyss....209 A6
East Whitburn....208 D2
Eastwick Herts....68 B4
Shetland....284 F5
East Williamston 55 D6
East Winch....118 D3
East Winterslow..31 B6

East Wittering....19 B6
East Witton....157 C5
Eastwood Notts..114 A2
Southend....51 A5
W Yorks....138 A2
East Woodburn..177 A7
East Woodhay....46 C2
East Worldham....33 B6
East Worlington..26 D2
East Worthing....21 B4
Eatharpe....81 A6
Eaton Ches E....128 C3
Ches W....127 C5
Leics....115 C5
Norf....104 A3
Notts....132 B2
Oxon....65 C5
Shrops....94 C1
Shrops....94 C3
Eaton Bishop....78 D2
Eaton Bray....67 A4
Eaton Constantine....94 A3
Eaton Green....67 A4
Eaton Hastings....64 D3
Eaton on Tern....111 C5
Eaton Socon....84 B3
Eavestone....147 A6
Ebberston....160 C2
Ebbesbourne Wake....30 C3
Ebbw Vale =Glyn Ebwy....60 C3
Ebchester....178 D3
Ebford....13 C4
Ebley....63 C4
Ebnal....110 A3
Ebrington....81 D4
Ecchinswell....46 D2
Ecclaw....211 D4
Ecclefechan....175 A4
Eccles Borders....197 B6
Gtr Man....137 D6
Kent....51 C4
Ecclesall....130 A3
Ecclesfield....139 D6
Ecclesgreig....233 B5
Eccleshall....112 C2
Eccleshill....147 D5
Ecclesmachan....208 C3
Eccles on Sea....121 C6
Eccles Road....103 B6
Eccleston Ches W....127 C4
Lancs....136 B4
Mers....136 D3
Eccleston Park...136 D3
Eccup....148 C1
Echt....245 B4
Eckford....187 A6
Eckington Derbys 131 B4
Worcs....80 C2
Ecton....83 A5
Edale....129 A6
Edburton....21 A5
Edderside....174 D3
Edderton....264 B3
Eddistone....24 C3
Eddleston....196 B1
Edenbridge....36 B2
Edenfield....137 B6
Edenhall....164 B3
Edenham....116 C3
Eden Park....49 C6
Edensor....130 C2
Edentaggart....215 C6
Edenthorpe....140 C4
Edentown....175 C6
Ederline....214 B1
Edern....106 C2
Edgarley....29 B5
Edgbaston....96 C3
Edgcott Bucks....66 A1
Som....26 B3
Edge....94 A1
Edgebolton....111 C4
Edge End....62 B1
Edgefield....120 B2
Edgefield Street 120 B2
Edge Green....127 D4
Edge Hill....136 D2
Edgeside....138 A1

Edgeworth....63 C5
Edgmond....111 D6
Edgmond Marsh 111 C6
Edgton....94 C1
Edgware....68 D1
Edgworth....137 B6
Edinample....217 B5
Edinbane....258 C3
Edinburgh....209 C5
Edingale....113 D6
Edingight House 267 D6
Edingley....131 D6
Edingthorpe....121 B5
Edingthorpe Green....121 B5
Edington Som....28 B3
Wilts....44 D3
Edintore....255 B5
Edithmead....28 A3
Edith Weston....99 A6
Edlesborough....67 B4
Edlingham....189 C4
Edlington....134 B2
Edmondsham....31 D4
Edmondsley....167 A5
Edmondthorpe....115 D6
Edmonstone....282 E6
Edmonton....68 D3
Edmundbyers....178 D2
Ednam....197 C6
Ednaston....113 A6
Edradynate....230 C2
Edrom....198 A2
Edstaston....111 B4
Edstone....81 A4
Edvin Loach....79 B4
Edwalton....114 B3
Edwardstone....87 C5
Edwinsford....58 B3
Edwinstowe....131 C6
Edworth....84 C4
Edwyn Ralph....79 B4
Edzell....232 B3
Efail Isaf....41 C5
Efailnewydd....106 C3
Efailwen....72 D4
Effingham....35 A4
Effirth....285 H5
Efford....12 A3
Egdon....80 B2
Egerton Gtr Man..137 B6
Kent....37 B7
Egerton Forstal..37 B6
Eggborough....140 A3
Eggbuckland....7 B4
Egginton....113 C6
Egglescliffe....168 D2
Eggleston....166 C2
Egham....48 B3
Egleton....99 A5
Eglingham....189 B4
Egloshayle....9 D5
Egloskerry....10 C3
Eglwys-Brewis....41 E5
Eglwys Cross....110 A3
Eglwys Fach....91 C4
Eglwyswen....73 C4
Eglwyswrw....72 C4
Egmanton....132 C2
Egremont Cumb..162 C3
Mers....136 D2
Egton....159 A7
Egton Bridge....159 A7
Eight Ash Green..70 A3
Eignaig....226 B2
Eil....241 A6
Eilanreach....238 A2
Eileanach Lodge 264 D1
Eilean Darach....262 B3
Einacleite....288 E2
Eisgean....288 F4
Eisingrug....107 C6
Elan Village....76 A3
Elberton....43 A5
Elburton....7 B4
Elcho....219 B6
Elcombe....45 A5
Eldernell....101 B5
Eldersfield....79 D6

Elderslie....205 B4
Eldon....167 C5
Eldrick....181 C5
Eldroth....146 A1
Eldwick....147 C5
Elfhowe....154 B3
Elford Northumb..199 C5
Staffs....113 D5
Elgin....266 C3
Elgol....247 C4
Elham....38 A3
Elie....221 D4
Elim....122 B3
Eling....32 D2
Elishader....259 B5
Elishaw....188 D1
Elkesley....132 B1
Elkstone....63 B5
Ellan....253 D4
Elland....139 A4
Ellary....202 A2
Ellastone....113 A5
Ellemford....211 D4
Ellenbrook....152 D3
Ellenhall....112 C2
Ellen's Green....34 C3
Ellerbeck....158 B3
Ellerburn....160 C2
Ellerby....169 D5
Ellerdine Heath .111 C5
Ellerhayes....13 A4
Elleric....227 B5
Ellerker....141 A7
Ellerton E Yorks .149 D6
Shrops....111 C6
Ellesborough....66 C3
Ellesmere....110 B3
Ellesmere Port..127 B4
Ellingham Norf....105 B4
Northumb....189 A4
Ellingstring....157 C5
Ellington Cambs..100 D3
Northumb....189 D5
Elliot....221 A6
Ellisfield....33 A5
Ellistown....114 D2
Ellon....257 C4
Ellonby....164 B2
Ellough....105 C5
Elloughton....142 A1
Ellwood....62 C1
Elm....101 A6
Elmbridge....80 A2
Elmdon Essex....85 D6
W Mid....97 C4
Elmdon Heath....97 C4
Elmers End....49 C6
Elmesthorpe....98 B1
Elmfield....19 B5
Elm Hill....30 C2
Elmhurst....113 D5
Elmley Castle....80 D2
Elmley Lovett....79 A6
Elmore....62 B3
Elmore Back....62 B3
Elm Park....50 A2
Elmscott....24 C3
Elmsett....87 C6
Elmstead Market..71 A4
Elmsted....38 A3
Elmstone....53 C4
Elmstone Hardwicke....63 A5
Elmswell E Yorks 150 B2
Suff....87 A5
Elmton....131 B5
Elphin....271 C5
Elphinstone....209 C6
Elrick....245 B5
Elrig....171 C5
Elsdon....188 D2
Elsecar....140 C1
Elsenham....69 A5
Elsfield....65 B6
Elsham....142 B2
Elsing....120 D2
Elslack....146 C3
Elson....110 B2
Elsrickle....195 B5
Elstead....34 B2
Elsted....33 D7
Elsthorpe....116 C3

Elstob 167 C6
Elston Notts . . . 115 A5
  Wilts. 31 A4
Elstone 26 D1
Elstow 84 C2
Elstree 68 D1
Elstronwick . . . 151 D5
Elswick 144 D4
Elsworth 85 A5
Elterwater 154 A2
Eltham 50 B1
Eltisley 85 B4
Elton Cambs . . . 100 B2
  Ches W. 127 B4
  Derbys. 130 C2
  Glos. 62 B3
  Hereford 94 D2
  Notts. 115 B5
  Stockton. 168 D2
Elton Green . . . 127 B4
Elvanfoot 184 A2
Elvaston 114 B2
Elveden 103 D4
Elvingston . . . 210 C1
Elvington Kent . . . 53 D4
  York 149 C5
Elwick Hrtlpl . . . 168 B2
  Northumb. . . 199 C5
Elworth 128 C2
Elworthy 27 B5
Ely Cambs 102 C1
  Cardiff 41 D6
Emberton 83 C5
Embleton Cumb . . 163 A4
  Northumb. . . . 189 A5
Embo 265 A4
Emborough 43 D5
Embo Street . . . 265 A4
Embsay 147 B4
Emersons Green . 43 B5
Emery Down . . . 18 A1
Emley 139 B5
Emmbrook 47 C5
Emmer Green . . . 47 B5
Emmington 66 C2
Emneth 101 A6
Emneth
  Hungate . . . 101 A7
Empingham . . . 99 A6
Empshott 33 B6
Emstrey 111 D4
Emsworth 19 A6
Enborne 46 C2
Enchmarsh 94 B3
Enderby 98 B2
Endmoor 154 C4
Endon 129 D4
Endon Bank . . . 129 D4
Enfield 68 D3
Enfield Wash. . . 68 D3
Enford 45 D5
Engamoor . . . 285 H4
Engine Common . 43 A5
Englefield 47 B4
Englefield Green . 48 B2
Englesea-brook 128 D2
English Bicknor . 62 B1
Englishcombe . . . 43 C6
English
  Frankton . . . 110 C3
Enham Alamein . 32 A2
Enmore 28 B2
Ennerdale
  Bridge 162 C3
Enoch 183 B6
Enochdhu 231 B4
Ensay 224 B2
Ensbury 17 B4
Ensdon 110 D3
Ensis 25 C6
Enstone 65 A4
Enterkinfoot . . 183 B6
Enterpen 158 A3
Enville 95 C6
Eolaigearraidh . 286 F3
Eorabus 224 D2
Eòropaidh . . . 288 A6
Epperstone . . . 115 A4
Epping 69 C4
Epping Green
  Essex 68 C4
  Herts 68 C2

Epping Upland . . . 68 C4
Eppleby 167 D4
Eppleworth . . . 150 D3
Epsom 49 C5
Epwell 81 C6
Epworth 141 C5
Epworth
  Turbary . . . 141 C5
Erbistock . . . 110 A2
Erbusaig . . . 249 D4
Erchless Castle. . 251 B6
Erdington . . . 96 B4
Eredine 214 B2
Ericstane . . . 184 A3
Eridge Green . . . 36 C3
Erines 202 A3
Eriswell 102 D3
Erith 50 B2
Erlestoke 44 D3
Ermine 133 B4
Ermington . . . 7 B5
Erpingham . . 120 B3
Errogie 252 D1
Errol 220 B2
Erskine 205 A4
Erskine Bridge . 205 A4
Ervie 170 A2
Erwarton . . . 88 D3
Erwood 77 C4
Eryholme . . . 157 A7
Eryrys 126 D2
Escomb 167 C4
Escrick 149 C5
Esgairdawe . . 58 A3
Esgairgeiliog . 91 B5
Esh 167 A4
Esher 48 C4
Esholt 147 C5
Eshott 189 D5
Eshton 146 B3
Esh Winning . 167 A4
Eskadale . . . 251 C6
Eskbank . . . 209 D6
Eskdale Green . 163 D4
Eskdalemuir . 185 C5
Eske 150 C3
Esknish . . . 143 D5
Esk Valley . . 159 A4
Esprick . . . 144 D4
Essendine . . 116 D3
Essendon . . 68 C2
Essich 252 C2
Essington . . 96 A2
Esslemont . . 257 D4
Eston 168 D3
Eswick . . . 285 H6
Etal 198 C3
Etchilhampton . 44 C4
Etchingham . 37 D5
Etchinghill Kent . 38 B3
  Staffs. . . . 112 D4
Ethie Castle . 233 D4
Ethie Mains . 233 D4
Etling Green . 120 D2
Eton 48 B2
Eton Wick . . 48 B2
Etteridge . . 241 C4
Ettersgill . . 166 C1
Ettingshall . 96 B2
Ettington . . 81 C5
Etton E Yorks . 150 C2
  Pboro. . . . 100 A3
Ettrick 185 A5
Ettrickbridge . 186 A2
Ettrickhill . . 185 A5
Etwall 113 B6
Euston 103 D4
Euximoor Drove 101 B6
Euxton 137 B4
Evanstown . . 41 C4
Evanton . . . 264 D2
Evedon . . . 116 A3
Evelix 264 A3
Evenjobb . . . 77 A6
Evenley . . . 82 D2
Evenlode . . . 64 A3
Evenwood . . 167 C4
Evenwood Gate . 167 C4
Everbay . . . 282 E7
Evercreech . . 29 B6
Everdon . . . 82 B2

Everingham . . . 149 C7
Everleigh 45 D6
Everley 160 C3
Eversholt 84 D1
Evershot 15 A5
Eversley 47 C5
Eversley Cross . . 47 C5
Everthorpe . . . 150 D2
Everton C Beds . . 84 B4
  Hants . . . 18 B1
  Mers. . . . 136 D2
  Notts . . . 141 D4
Evertown . . . 175 A6
Evesbatch . . . 79 C4
Evesham 80 C3
Evington 98 A3
Ewden Village . 139 D5
Ewell 49 C5
Ewell Minnis . . 39 A4
Ewelme 66 D1
Ewen 63 D6
Ewenny 40 D4
Ewerby . . . 116 A4
Ewerby Thorpe . 116 A4
Ewes 185 C6
Ewesley . . . 188 D3
Ewhurst . . . 34 B3
Ewhurst Green
  E Sus . . . 37 D5
  Sur 34 C3
Ewloe 126 C3
Ewloe Green . 126 C2
Ewood 137 A5
Eworthy . . . 11 B5
Ewshot 33 A7
Ewyas Harold . 61 A5
Exbourne . . . 11 A7
Exbury 18 B3
Exebridge . . 27 C4
Exelby 157 C6
Exeter 13 B4
Exford 26 B3
Exhall 80 B4
Exley Head . 147 C4
Exminster . . 13 C4
Exmouth . . . 13 C5
Exnaboe . . 285 M5
Exning 86 A2
Exton Devon . 13 C4
  Hants . . . 33 C5
  Rutland. . 116 D2
  Som 27 B4
Exwick 13 B4
Eyam 130 B2
Eydon 82 B2
Eye Hereford . 78 A2
  Pboro. . . 100 A4
  Suff 104 D2
Eye Green . . 100 A4
Eyemouth . . 211 D6
Eyeworth . . . 85 C4
Eyhorne Street . 37 A6
Eyke 88 B4
Eynesbury . . 84 B3
Eynort 246 B2
Eynsford . . . 50 C2
Eynsham . . . 65 C5
Eype 14 B4
Eyre Highld . . 248 C2
  Highld. . . 259 C4
Eythorne . . . 39 A4
Eyton Hereford . 78 A2
  Shrops. . . 94 C1
  Wrex. . . . 110 A2
Eyton upon the Weald
  Moors. . . 111 D5

F

Faccombe 46 D1
Faceby 158 A3
Facit 138 B1
Faddiley 127 D5
Fadmoor 159 C5
Faerdre 40 A1
Failand 43 B4
Failford 193 C4
Failsworth . . . 138 C1
Fain 262 C3
Fairbourne . . . 90 A4
Fairburn 140 A2

Fairfield Derbys . . . 129 B5
  Stockton. . . . 168 D2
  Worcs. 80 C3
  Worcs. 96 D2
Fairford 64 C2
Fair Green . . . 118 D3
Fairhaven . . . 136 A2
Fair Hill 164 B3
Fairlie 204 C2
Fairlight 23 A6
Fairlight Cove . . 23 A6
Fairmile 13 B5
Fairmilehead . . 209 D5
Fairoak 111 B6
Fair Oak 32 D3
Fair Oak Green . 47 C4
Fairseat 50 C3
Fairstead Essex . . 70 B1
  Norf . . . 118 D3
Fairwarp 36 D2
Fairy Cottage . 152 C4
Fairy Cross . . . 25 C5
Fakenham . . . 119 C6
Fakenham
  Magna . . . 103 D5
Fala 210 D1
Fala Dam . . . 210 D1
Falahill 196 A2
Falcon 79 D4
Faldingworth . . 133 A5
Falfield 62 D2
Falkenham . . . 88 D3
Falkirk 208 C1
Falkland . . . 220 D2
Falla 187 B6
Fallgate . . . 130 C3
Fallin 207 A6
Fallowfield . . 138 D1
Fallsidehill . . 197 B5
Falmer 21 B6
Falmouth 4 D3
Falsgrave . . . 160 C4
Falstone . . . 177 A5
Fanagmore . . 276 D2
Fangdale Beck . 159 B4
Fangfoss . . . 149 B6
Fankerton . . 207 B5
Fanmore . . . 224 B3
Fannich Lodge . 262 D4
Fans 197 B5
Far Bank . . . 140 B4
Far Bletchley . 83 D5
Far Cotton . . 83 B4
Farcet 100 B4
Farden 94 D3
Fareham . . . 19 A4
Farewell . . . 113 D4
Far Forest . . 95 D5
Farforth . . . 134 B3
Faringdon . . . 64 D3
Farington . . 136 A4
Farlam 176 D3
Farlary 273 D5
Far Laund . . 114 A1
Farleigh N Som . 42 C3
  Sur 49 C6
Farleigh
  Hungerford . 44 D2
Farleigh Wallop . 33 A5
Farlesthorpe . 135 B4
Farleton Cumb . 154 C4
  Lancs. . . . 145 A5
Farley Shrops . 94 A1
  Staffs. . . 113 A4
  Wilts. . . . 31 C6
Farley Green . 34 B3
Farley Hill Luton . 67 A5
  Wokingham. 47 C5
Farleys End . . 62 B3
Farlington . . 149 A5
Farlow 95 C4
Farmborough . 43 C5
Farmcote Glos . 63 A6
  Shrops. . . 95 B5
Farmington . . 64 B2
Farmoor . . . 65 C5
Farmtown . . 267 D6
Farnborough
  Hants . . . 34 A1
  London. . . 50 C1
  Warks. . . 82 C1
  W Berks. . 46 A2

Farnborough
  Green. . . . 34 A1
Farncombe . . 34 B2
Farndish . . . 83 A6
Farndon Ches W . 127 D4
  Notts. . . 132 D2
Farnell . . . 233 C4
Farnham Dorset . 30 D3
  Essex. . . . 69 A4
  N Yorks. . 148 A2
  Suff 89 A4
  Sur. 34 B1
Farnham
  Common. . 48 A2
Farnham Green . 69 A4
Farnham Royal . 48 A2
Farnhill . . . 147 C4
Farningham . 50 C2
Farnley N Yorks . 147 C6
  W Yorks. . 147 D6
Farnley Tyas . 139 B4
Farnsfield . 131 D6
Farnworth
  Gtr Man . . 137 C6
  Halton. . . 127 A5
Farr Highld . 241 B6
  Highld. . . 252 C2
  Highld. . . 278 B3
Farr House . . 252 C2
Farringdon . . 13 B5
Farrington
  Gurney. . . 43 D5
Far Sawrey . 154 B2
Farsley . . . 147 D6
Farthinghoe . 82 D2
Farthinglee . 39 A4
Farthingstone . 82 B3
Fartown . . . 139 B4
Farway 14 B1
Fasag 249 A5
Fascadale . . 235 C4
Faslane Port . 215 D5
Fasnacloich . 227 B5
Fasnakyle Ho . 251 D5
Fassfern . . . 237 B4
Fatfield . . . 179 D5
Fattahead . . 268 D1
Faugh 176 D3
Fauldhouse . 208 D2
Faulkbourne . 70 B1
Faulkland . . 43 D6
Fauls 111 B4
Faversham . . 52 C2
Favillar . . . 254 C3
Fawdington . 158 D3
Fawfieldhead . 129 C5
Fawkham Green . 50 C2
Fawler 65 B4
Fawley Bucks . 47 A5
  Hants . . . 18 A3
  W Berks. . 46 A1
Fawley Chapel . 62 A1
Faxfleet . . . 141 A6
Faygate . . . 35 C5
Fazakerley . 136 D2
Fazeley . . . 97 A5
Fearby 157 C5
Fearn 265 C4
Fearnan . . . 229 D6
Fearnbeg . . 249 A4
Fearnhead . 137 D5
Fearn Lodge . 264 B2
Fearnmore . 261 D4
Fearn Station . 265 C4
Featherstone
  Staffs. . . 96 A2
  W Yorks. . 140 A2
Featherwood . 187 C7
Feckenham . . 80 A3
Feering . . . 70 A2
Feetham . . . 156 B3
Feizor 146 A1
Felbridge . . 35 C6
Felbrigg . . . 120 B4
Felcourt . . . 36 B1
Felden 67 C5
Felin-Crai . . 59 C5
Felindre Carms . 58 B3

Felindre continued
  Powys 93 C5
  Swansea. . . 57 B6
Felindre Farchog 72 C4
Felinfach Ceredig . 75 C4
  Powys. . . . 77 D4
Felinfoel . . . 57 B5
Felingwmisaf . 58 C2
Felingwmuchaf . 58 C2
Felinwynt . . . 73 A5
Felixkirk . . . 158 C3
Felixstowe . . 88 D3
Felixstowe Ferry . 88 D4
Felkington . . 198 B3
Felkirk 140 B1
Felling 179 C4
Fell Side . . . 163 A6
Felmersham . 84 B1
Felmingham . 120 C4
Felpham . . . 20 C2
Felsham . . . 87 B5
Felsted 69 A6
Feltham 48 B4
Felthorpe . . 120 D3
Felton Hereford . 78 C3
  Northumb. . 189 C4
  N Som. . . . 43 C4
Felton Butler . 110 D2
Feltwell . . . 102 B3
Fenay Bridge . 139 B4
Fence 146 D2
Fence Houses . 179 D5
Fen Ditton . . 85 A6
Fen Drayton . 85 A5
Fen End . . . 97 D5
Fengate Norf . 120 C3
  Pboro. . . 100 B4
Fenham . . . 199 B4
Fenhouses . 117 A5
Feniscliffe . 137 A5
Feniscowles . 137 A5
Feniton . . . 13 B6
Fenlake . . . 84 C2
Fenny Bentley . 130 D1
Fenny Bridges . 13 B6
Fenny Compton . 81 B7
Fenny Drayton . 97 B6
Fenny Stratford . 83 D5
Fenrother . . 189 D4
Fen Side . . . 134 D3
Fenstanton . . 85 A5
Fenton Cambs . 101 D5
  Lincs. . . 132 B3
  Lincs. . . 132 D3
  Stoke. . . 112 A6
Fenton Barns . 210 B2
Fenton Town . 198 C3
Fenwick E Ayrs . 205 D4
  Northumb. . 178 B2
  Northumb. . 199 B4
  S Yorks. . 140 B3
Feochaig . . 190 D3
Feock 4 D3
Feolin Ferry . 201 B4
Ferindonald . 247 D5
Feriniquarrie . 258 C1
Ferlochan . . 226 B4
Fern 232 B2
Ferndale . . . 41 B5
Ferndown. . . 17 A4
Ferness . . . 253 B5
Ferney Green . 154 B3
Fernham . . . 64 D3
Fernhill Heath . 79 B6
Fernhurst. . . 34 B1
Fernie 220 C3
Ferniegair . . 194 A2
Fernilea . . . 246 A2
Fernilee . . . 129 B5
Ferrensby . . 148 A2
Ferring 20 B3
Ferrybridge . 140 A2
Ferryden. . . 233 C5
Ferryhill
  Aberdeen . . 245 B6
  Durham. . . 167 B5
Ferry Hill . . 101 C5
Ferryhill Station 167 B6
Ferry Point . . 264 B3

Ferryside ... 56 A3
Fersfield ... 103 C6
Fersit ... 228 A2
Ferwig ... 73 B4
Feshiebridge ... 241 B6
Fetcham ... 35 A4
Fetterangus ... 269 D4
Fettercairn ... 233 A4
Fettes ... 252 A1
Fewcott ... 65 A6
Fewston ... 147 B5
Ffairfach ... 58 C3
Ffair-Rhos ... 75 B6
Ffaldybrenin ... 58 A3
Ffarmers ... 58 A3
Ffawyddog ... 60 B4
Fforest ... 57 B5
Fforest-fâch ... 57 C6
Ffostrasol ... 73 B6
Ffos-y-ffin ... 74 B3
Ffridd-Uchaf ... 107 A5
Ffrith ... 126 D2
Ffrwd ... 107 A4
Ffynnon ddrain ... 73 D7
Ffynnongroyw ... 125 A6
Ffynnon-oer ... 75 C4
Fidden ... 224 D2
Fiddes ... 245 D5
Fiddington Glos. ... 80 D2
Som ... 28 A2
Fiddleford ... 30 D2
Fiddlers Hamlet ... 69 C4
Field ... 112 B4
Field Broughton 154 C2
Field Dalling ... 120 B2
Field Head ... 98 A1
Fifehead
Magdalen ... 30 C1
Fifehead Neville ... 30 D1
Fifield Oxon ... 64 B3
Wilts. ... 45 D5
Windsor ... 48 B2
Fifield Bavant ... 31 C4
Figheldean ... 31 A5
Filands ... 44 A3
Filby ... 121 D6
Filey ... 161 C5
Filgrave ... 83 C5
Filkins ... 64 C3
Filleigh Devon ... 26 C1
Devon. ... 26 D2
Fillingham ... 133 A4
Fillongley ... 97 C5
Filton ... 43 B5
Fimber ... 150 A1
Finavon ... 232 C2
Finchairn ... 214 B2
Fincham ... 102 A2
Finchampstead ... 47 C5
Finchdean ... 33 D6
Finchingfield ... 86 D2
Finchley ... 68 D2
Findern ... 113 B7
Findhorn ... 265 D6
Findhorn Bridge 253 D4
Findochty ... 267 C5
Findo Gask ... 219 B5
Findon Aberds ... 245 C6
W Sus. ... 21 B4
Findon Mains ... 264 D2
Findrack House 244 B3
Finedon ... 99 D6
Fingal Street ... 88 A3
Fingask ... 256 D2
Fingerpost ... 95 D5
Fingest ... 66 D2
Finghall ... 157 C5
Fingland Cumb. ... 175 C5
Dumfries ... 183 A5
Finglesham ... 53 D5
Fingringhoe ... 71 A4
Finlarig ... 217 A5
Finmere ... 82 D3
Finnart ... 229 C4
Finningham ... 87 A6
Finningley ... 141 D4
Finnygaud ... 267 D6
Finsbury ... 49 A6
Finstall ... 80 A2

Finsthwaite ... 154 C2
Finstock ... 65 B4
Finstown ... 282 F4
Fintry Aberds ... 268 D2
Dundee. ... 220 A4
Stirling ... 207 B4
Finzean ... 244 C3
Fionnphort ... 224 D2
Fionnsbhagh ... 287 F5
Firbeck ... 131 A5
Firby N Yorks ... 149 A6
N Yorks. ... 157 C6
Firgrove ... 138 B2
Firsby ... 135 C4
Firsdown ... 31 B6
First Coast ... 261 A6
Fir Tree ... 166 B4
Fishbourne IoW ... 19 B4
W Sus. ... 20 B1
Fishburn ... 167 B6
Fishcross ... 208 A1
Fisherford ... 256 C1
Fisher Place ... 163 C6
Fisher's Pond ... 32 C3
Fisherstreet ... 34 C2
Fisherton Highld ... 252 A3
S Ayrs. ... 192 D2
Fishguard
= Abergwaun ... 72 C2
Fishlake ... 141 B4
Fishleigh Barton ... 25 C6
Fishponds ... 43 B5
Fishpool ... 62 A2
Fishtoft ... 117 A6
Fishtoft Drove ... 117 A6
Fishtown of
Usan ... 233 C5
Fishwick ... 198 A3
Fiskavaig ... 246 A2
Fiskerton Lincs. ... 133 B5
Notts ... 132 D2
Fitling ... 151 D5
Fittleton ... 31 A5
Fittleworth ... 20 A3
Fitton End ... 118 D1
Fitz. ... 110 D3
Fitzhead ... 27 C6
Fitzwilliam ... 140 B2
Fiunary ... 225 B5
Five Acres ... 62 B1
Five Ashes ... 36 D3
Fivecrosses ... 127 B5
Fivehead ... 28 C3
Five Oak Green ... 36 B4
Five Oaks Jersey ... 6
W Sus. ... 34 D3
Five Roads ... 57 B4
Flack's Green ... 70 B1
Flackwell Heath ... 48 A1
Fladbury ... 80 C2
Fladdabister ... 285 K6
Flagg ... 129 C6
Flamborough ... 161 D6
Flamstead ... 67 B5
Flamstead End ... 68 C3
Flansham ... 20 B2
Flanshaw ... 139 A6
Flasby ... 146 B3
Flash ... 129 C5
Flashader ... 258 C3
Flask Inn ... 160 A3
Flaunden ... 67 C5
Flawborough ... 115 A5
Flawith ... 148 A3
Flax Bourton ... 43 C4
Flaxby ... 148 B2
Flaxholme ... 114 A1
Flaxley ... 62 B2
Flaxpool ... 27 B6
Flaxton ... 149 A5
Fleckney ... 98 B3
Flecknoe ... 82 A2
Fledborough ... 132 B3
Fleet Hants ... 19 A6
Hants. ... 47 D6
Lincs. ... 117 C6
Fleetham ... 189 A4
Fleet Hargate ... 117 C6
Fleetlands ... 19 A4
Fleetville ... 67 C6
Fleetwood ... 144 C3
Flemingston ... 41 D5

Flemington ... 205 C6
Flempton ... 87 A4
Fleoideabhagh ... 287 F5
Fletchertown ... 175 D5
Fletching ... 36 D2
Flexbury ... 10 A3
Flexford ... 34 B2
Flimby ... 162 A3
Flimwell ... 37 C5
Flint = Y Fflint ... 126 B2
Flintham ... 115 A5
Flint Mountain ... 126 B2
Flinton ... 151 D5
Flintsham ... 77 B7
Flitcham ... 119 C4
Flitton ... 84 D2
Flitwick ... 84 D2
Flixborough ... 141 B6
Flixborough
Stather ... 141 B6
Flixton Gtr Man ... 137 D6
N Yorks ... 160 D4
Suff ... 104 C4
Flockton ... 139 B5
Flodaigh ... 286 A4
Flodden ... 198 C3
Flodigarry ... 259 A4
Flood's Ferry ... 101 B5
Flookburgh ... 154 D2
Florden ... 104 B2
Flore ... 82 A3
Flotterton ... 188 C2
Flowton ... 88 C1
Flush House ... 139 C4
Flushing Aberds ... 257 B5
Corn ... 4 D3
Flyford Flavell ... 80 B2
Foals Green ... 104 D3
Fobbing ... 51 A4
Fochabers ... 266 D4
Fochriw ... 60 C3
Fockerby ... 141 B6
Fodderletter ... 254 D2
Fodderty ... 251 A7
Foel ... 109 D4
Foel-gastell ... 57 A5
Foffarty ... 232 D2
Foggathorpe ... 149 D6
Fogo ... 197 B6
Fogorig ... 198 B1
Foindle ... 276 D2
Folda ... 231 B5
Fole ... 112 B4
Foleshill ... 97 C6
Folke ... 29 D6
Folkestone ... 39 B4
Folkingham ... 116 B3
Folkington ... 22 B3
Folksworth ... 100 C3
Folkton ... 161 D4
Folla Rule ... 256 C2
Follifoot ... 148 B2
Folly Gate ... 11 B6
Fonthill Bishop ... 30 B3
Fonthill Gifford ... 30 B3
Fontmell Magna ... 30 D2
Fontwell ... 20 B2
Foolow ... 130 B1
Foots Cray ... 50 B1
Forcett ... 167 D4
Ford Argyll ... 214 B1
Bucks ... 66 C2
Devon. ... 25 C5
Glos ... 64 A1
Northumb. ... 198 C3
Shrops ... 110 D3
Staffs ... 129 D5
Wilts. ... 44 B2
W Sus. ... 20 B2
Fordcombe ... 36 B3
Fordell ... 209 B4
Forden ... 93 A6
Ford End ... 69 B6
Forder Green ... 8 A1
Fordham Cambs. ... 102 D2
Essex ... 70 A3
Norf ... 102 B2
Fordhouses ... 96 A2
Fordingbridge ... 31 D5
Fordon ... 160 D4

Fordoun ... 233 A5
Ford's Green ... 87 A6
Fordstreet ... 70 A3
Ford Street ... 27 D6
Fordwells ... 64 B4
Fordwich ... 52 D3
Forebridge ... 112 C3
Forest ... 165 B6
Forest Becks ... 146 B1
Forestburn Gate 188 D3
Foresterseat ... 266 D2
Forest Gate ... 49 A7
Forest Green ... 35 B4
Forest Hall ... 154 A4
Forest Head ... 176 D3
Forest Hill ... 65 C6
Forest Lane
Head ... 148 B2
Forest Lodge
Argyll ... 228 C1
Highld. ... 242 A3
Perth ... 230 A3
Forest Mill ... 208 A2
Forest Row ... 36 C2
Forestside ... 33 D6
Forest Town ... 131 C5
Forfar ... 232 C2
Forgandenny ... 219 C5
Forge ... 91 C5
Forge Side ... 60 C4
Forgewood ... 194 A2
Forgie ... 267 D4
Forglen House ... 268 D1
Formby ... 136 C2
Forncett End ... 104 B2
Forncett
St Mary ... 104 B2
Forncett
St Peter ... 104 B2
Forneth ... 231 D4
Fornham All
Saints ... 87 A4
Fornham
St Martin ... 87 A4
Forres ... 253 A6
Forrestfield ... 207 D6
Forrest Lodge ... 182 D3
Forsbrook ... 112 A3
Forse ... 275 A6
Forse House ... 275 A6
Forsinain ... 279 D5
Forsinard ... 279 D4
Forsinard
Station ... 279 D4
Forston ... 15 B6
Fort Augustus ... 240 B1
Forteviot ... 219 C5
Fort George Guern ... 6
Highld. ... 252 A3
Forth ... 194 A4
Forthampton ... 79 D6
Forth Road
Bridge ... 208 C4
Fortingall ... 229 D6
Forton Hants ... 32 A3
Lancs ... 145 B4
Shrops. ... 110 D3
Som ... 14 A3
Staffs ... 111 C6
Forton Heath ... 110 D3
Fortrie ... 256 B1
Fortrose ... 252 A3
Fortuneswell ... 15 D6
Fort William ... 237 B5
Forty Green ... 67 D4
Forty Hill ... 68 D3
Forward Green ... 88 B1
Fosbury ... 45 D7
Fosdyke ... 117 B6
Foss ... 230 C1
Foss Cross ... 63 C6
Fossebridge ... 64 B1
Fosterhouses ... 141 B4
Foster Street ... 69 C4
Foston Derbys ... 113 B5
Lincs. ... 115 A6
N Yorks. ... 149 A5
Foston on the
Wolds ... 151 B4
Fotherby ... 143 D5
Fotheringhay ... 100 B2

Foubister ... 283 G6
Foulby ... 140 B1
Foulden Borders ... 198 A3
Norf ... 102 B3
Foul Mile ... 22 A4
Foulis Castle ... 264 D1
Foulridge ... 146 C2
Foulsham ... 120 C2
Fountainhall ... 196 B3
Four Ashes Staffs ... 95 C6
Suff ... 103 D6
Four Crosses
Powys ... 93 A4
Powys ... 110 D1
Wrex ... 126 D2
Four Elms ... 36 B2
Four Forks ... 28 B2
Four Gotes ... 118 D1
Fourlane Ends ... 130 D3
Four Lane Ends ... 127 C5
Four Lanes ... 3 B4
Fourlanes End ... 128 D3
Four Marks ... 33 B5
Four Mile
Bridge ... 122 C2
Four Oaks E Sus ... 37 D6
W Mid. ... 96 B4
W Mid. ... 97 C5
Fourpenny ... 265 A4
Four Roads Carms. ... 57 B4
IoM ... 152 E2
Fourstones ... 177 C6
Four Throws ... 37 D5
Fovant ... 31 C4
Foveran ... 257 D4
Fowey ... 5 B6
Fowley
Common ... 137 D5
Fowlis ... 220 A3
Fowlis Wester ... 218 B4
Fowlmere ... 85 C6
Fownhope ... 78 D3
Foxbar ... 205 B4
Foxcombe Hill ... 65 C5
Fox Corner ... 34 A2
Foxdale ... 152 D2
Foxearth ... 87 C4
Foxfield ... 153 B3
Foxham ... 44 B3
Foxhole Corn ... 5 B4
Swansea ... 57 C6
Foxholes ... 160 D4
Foxhunt Green ... 22 A3
Fox Lane ... 34 A1
Foxley Norf ... 120 C2
Wilts. ... 44 A2
Fox Street ... 71 A4
Foxt ... 112 A4
Foxton Cambs. ... 85 C6
Durham ... 167 C6
Leics. ... 99 B4
Foxup ... 156 D2
Foxwist Green ... 127 C6
Foxwood ... 95 D4
Foy ... 62 A1
Foyers ... 251 D6
Fraddam ... 2 B3
Fraddon ... 4 B4
Fradley ... 113 D5
Fradswell ... 112 B3
Fraisthorpe ... 151 A4
Framfield ... 36 D2
Framingham
Earl ... 104 A3
Framingham
Pigot ... 104 A3
Framlingham ... 88 A3
Frampton Dorset ... 15 B6
Lincs. ... 117 B6
Frampton
Cotterell ... 43 A5
Frampton
Mansell ... 63 C5
Frampton on
Severn ... 62 C3
Frampton West
End ... 117 A5
Framsden ... 88 B2
Framwellgate
Moor ... 167 A5
Franche ... 95 D6
Frankby ... 126 A2

Frankley ... 96 C4
Frank's Bridge ... 77 B5
Frankton ... 98 D1
Frant ... 36 C3
Fraserburgh ... 269 C4
Frating Green ... 71 A4
Fratton ... 19 B5
Freathy ... 6 B3
Freckenham ... 102 D2
Freckleton ... 136 A3
Freeby ... 115 C6
Freehay ... 112 A4
Freeland ... 65 B5
Freester ... 285 H6
Freethorpe ... 105 A5
Freiston ... 117 A6
Fremington Devon ... 25 B6
N Yorks. ... 156 B4
Frenchay ... 43 B5
Frenchbeer ... 12 C1
Frenich ... 216 D4
Frensham ... 34 B1
Fresgoe ... 279 B5
Freshfield ... 136 C1
Freshford ... 44 C1
Freshwater ... 18 C2
Freshwater Bay ... 18 C2
Freshwater East ... 55 E6
Fressingfield ... 104 D3
Freston ... 88 D2
Freswick ... 281 B5
Fretherne ... 62 C3
Frettenham ... 120 D4
Freuchie ... 220 D2
Freuchies ... 231 B6
Freystrop ... 55 C5
Friar's Gate ... 36 C2
Friarton ... 219 B6
Friday Bridge ... 101 A6
Friday Street ... 22 B4
Fridaythorpe ... 150 B1
Friern Barnet ... 68 D2
Friesland ... 223 B4
Friesthorpe ... 133 A5
Frieston ... 116 A2
Frieth ... 66 D2
Frilford ... 65 D5
Frilsham ... 46 B3
Frimley ... 34 A1
Frimley Green ... 34 A1
Frindsbury ... 51 B4
Fring ... 119 B4
Fringford ... 65 A7
Frinsted ... 37 A6
Frinton-on-Sea ... 71 A6
Friockheim ... 233 D3
Friog ... 90 A4
Frisby on the
Wreake ... 115 D4
Friskney ... 135 D4
Friskney
Eaudike ... 135 D4
Friskney Tofts ... 135 D4
Friston E Sus ... 22 C3
Suff ... 89 A5
Fritchley ... 130 D3
Fritham ... 31 D6
Frith Bank ... 117 A6
Frith Common ... 79 A4
Frithelstock ... 25 D5
Frithelstock
Stone ... 25 D5
Frithville ... 134 D3
Frittenden ... 37 B6
Frittiscombe ... 8 C2
Fritton Norf. ... 104 B3
Norf ... 105 A5
Fritwell ... 65 A6
Frizinghall ... 147 D5
Frizington ... 162 C3
Frocester ... 62 C3
Frodesley ... 94 A3
Frodingham ... 141 B6
Frodsham ... 127 B5
Frogden ... 187 A6
Froggatt ... 130 B2
Froghall ... 112 A4
Frogmore Devon ... 7 C6
Hants ... 34 A1
Frognall ... 117 D4
Frogshail ... 121 B4
Frolesworth ... 98 B2

Frome 30 A1
Frome St Quintin 15 A5
Fromes Hill 79 C4
Fron Denb 125 C5
Gwyn 106 C3
Gwyn 107 A5
Powys 77 A4
Powys 93 A6
Powys 93 B5
Froncysyllte. 110 A1
Frongoch 108 B4
Frostenden 105 C5
Frosterley 166 B3
Frotoft 282 E5
Froxfield. 45 C6
Froxfield Green . . 33 C6
Froyle 33 A6
Fryerning. 69 C6
Fryton 159 D5
Fulbeck. 133 D4
Fulbourn 85 B7
Fulbrook. 64 B3
Fulford Som 28 C2
Staffs. 112 B3
York 149 C5
Fulham 49 B5
Fulking 21 A5
Fullarton
Glasgow 205 B6
N Ayrs. 192 B3
Fuller's Moor . . 127 D4
Fuller Street 70 B1
Fullerton 32 B2
Fulletby 134 B2
Full Sutton 149 B6
Fullwood 205 C4
Fulmer 48 A2
Fulmodeston. . . 120 B1
Fulnetby 133 B5
Fulstow. 143 D5
Fulwell 179 D5
Fulwood I ancs.. . 145 D5
S Yorks 130 A3
Fundenhall 104 B2
Fundenhall
Street. 104 B2
Funtington 19 A6
Funtley 19 A4
Funtullich 218 B2
Funzie. 284 D8
Furley 14 A2
Furnace Argyll . 214 B3
Carms 57 B5
Furnace End 97 B5
Furneaux Pelham 68 A4
Furness Vale. . . 129 A5
Furzehill 26 A2
Furze Platt. 48 A1
Fyfett 28 D2
Fyfield Essex . . 69 C5
Glos 64 C3
Hants 32 A1
Oxon. 65 D5
Wilts. 45 C5
Fylingthorpe . . . 160 A3
Fyvie 256 C2

G

Gabhsann bho
Dheas. 288 B5
Gabhsann bho
Thuath. 288 B5
Gablon 264 A3
Gabroc Hill 205 C4
Gaddesby 115 D4
Gadebridge 67 C5
Gaer. 60 A3
Gaerllwyd. 61 D6
Gaerwen. 123 C4
Gagingwell 65 A5
Gaick Lodge . . 241 D5
Gailey 112 D3
Gainford. 167 D4
Gainsborough
Lincs. 141 D6
Suff 88 C2
Gainsford End. . 86 D3
Gairloch 261 C5
Gairlochy 239 D5
Gairney Bank . . 208 A4

Gairnshiel
Lodge. 243 B5
Gaisgill 155 A5
Gaitsgill 164 A1
Galashiels 196 C3
Galgate. 145 B4
Galhampton. . . . 29 C6
Gallaberry 184 D2
Gallachoille. . . . 213 D5
Gallanach Argyll .223 A5
Argyll 226 D3
Gallantry Bank . 127 D5
Gallatown. 209 A5
Galley Common . . 97 B6
Galleyend. 69 C7
Galley Hill 85 A5
Galleywood 69 C7
Gallin. 229 D4
Gallowfauld. . . . 232 D2
Gallows Green . 113 A4
Galltair 249 D5
Galmisdale. . . . 234 B3
Galmpton Devon . 7 C5
Torbay 8 B2
Galphay 157 D6
Galston 193 B5
Galtrigill. 258 C1
Gamblesby 165 B4
Gamesley 138 D3
Gamlingay 84 B4
Gammersgill . . . 157 C4
Gamston. 132 B2
Ganarew. 62 B1
Ganavan 226 C3
Gang 6 A2
Ganllwyd 108 C2
Gannochy Angus .232 A3
Perth 219 B6
Gansclet. 281 D5
Ganstead 151 D4
Ganthorpe 159 D5
Ganton 160 D3
Garbat. 263 D6
Garbhallt 214 C3
Garboldisham . . 103 C6
Garden City . . . 126 C3
Gardenstown . . 268 C2
Garden Village
Wrex 126 D3
W Yorks 148 D3
Garderhouse. . . 285 J5
Gardham 150 C2
Gardin. 284 G6
Gare Hill 30 A1
Garelochhead . . 215 C5
Garford. 65 D5
Garforth 148 D3
Gargrave 146 B3
Gargunnock. . . 207 A5
Garlic Street . . 104 C3
Garlieston 171 C6
Garlinge Green. . 52 D3
Garlogie 245 B4
Garmond 268 D3
Garmony. 225 B5
Garmouth. 266 C4
Garnant 58 D3
Garndiffaith. . . . 61 C4
Garndolbenmaen
. . . . 107 B4
Garnedd 124 D2
Garnett Bridge . 154 B4
Garnfadryn 106 C2
Garnkirk. 207 D4
Garnlydan 60 B3
Garnswllt 57 B6
Garn-yr-erw 60 B4
Garrabost. 288 D6
Garraron. 213 B6
Garras 3 C5
Garreg. 107 B6
Garrick 218 C3
Garrigill 165 A5
Garriston 157 B5
Garroch 182 D3
Garrogie Lodge . 240 A3
Garros 259 B4
Garrow 230 D2
Garryhorn 182 C3
Garsdale. 155 C6
Garsdale Head . 155 B6
Garsdon 44 A3

Garshall Green . . 112 B3
Garsington. 65 C6
Garstang. 145 C4
Garston. 127 A4
Garswood. 137 D4
Gartcosh. 207 D4
Garth Bridgend . . 40 B3
Gwyn 123 C5
Powys 76 C3
Shetland. 285 H4
Wrex 110 A1
Garthamlock . . . 205 B6
Garthbrengy . . . 76 D4
Garthdee 245 B6
Gartheli 75 C4
Garthmyl 93 B5
Garthorpe Leics. .115 C6
N Lincs 141 B6
Garth Row 154 B4
Gartly 255 C6
Gartmore 206 A3
Gartnagrenach . . 202 C2
Gartness
N Lanark. 207 D5
Stirling. 206 B3
Gartocharn 206 B2
Garton. 151 D5
Garton-on-the-
Wolds. 150 B2
Gartsherrie 207 D5
Gartymore 274 C4
Garvald. 210 C2
Garvamore. . . . 240 C3
Garvard. 212 C1
Garvault Hotel . 273 A5
Garve. 263 D5
Garvestone . . . 103 A6
Garvock Aberds .233 A5
Invclyd. 204 A2
Garway 61 A6
Garway Hill 61 A6
Gaskan 236 B1
Gastard 44 C2
Gasthorpe 103 C5
Gatcombe 18 C3
Gateacre. 127 A4
Gatebeck 154 C4
Gate Burton. . . 132 A3
Gateford. 131 A5
Gateforth 140 A3
Gatehead 192 B3
Gate Helmsley . 149 B5
Gatehouse 177 A5
Gatehouse of
Fleet 172 C4
Gatelawbridge . 183 C7
Gateley 119 C6
Gatenby 158 C2
Gateshead 179 C4
Gatesheath . . . 127 C4
Gateside Aberds .244 A3
Angus 232 D2
E Renf. 205 C4
Fife. 219 D6
N Ayrs. 204 C3
Gathurst. 136 C4
Gatley 128 A3
Gattonside 197 C4
Gatwick Airport. . 35 B5
Gaufron 76 A3
Gaulby. 98 A3
Gauldry. 220 B3
Gaunt's Common 17 A4
Gautby 134 B1
Gavinton. 197 A6
Gawber. 139 C6
Gawcott 82 D3
Gawsworth 128 C3
Gawthorpe 139 A5
Gawthrop. 155 C5
Gawthwaite . . . 153 B3
Gaydon 81 B6
Gayfield 282 B5
Gayhurst. 83 C5
Gayle. 156 C2
Gayles. 157 A5
Gay Street 34 D3
Gayton Mers. . . 136 D1
Norf 119 D4
Staffs. 112 C3
W Nhants 83 B4
Gayton le Marsh 135 A4

Gayton le Wold. . 134 A2
Gayton Thorpe . 119 D4
Gaywood 118 C3
Gazeley. 86 A3
Geanies House . 265 C4
Gearraidh
Bhailteas. 286 D3
Gearraidh
Rhaird 288 E4
Gearraidh na
h-Aibhne. 288 D3
Gearraidh na
Monadh 286 E3
Geary 258 B2
Geddes House. . 253 A4
Gedding 87 B5
Geddington 99 C5
Gedintailor 247 A4
Gedling 115 A4
Gedney 117 C7
Gedney
Broadgate . . . 117 C7
Gedney Drove
End 118 C1
Gedney Dyke. . . 117 C7
Gedney Hill 117 D6
Gee Cross. 138 D2
Geilston 206 C1
Geirinis. 286 B3
Geise 280 B3
Geisiadar 288 D2
Geldeston 105 B4
Gell 124 C3
Gelli Pembs. . . . 55 C6
Rhondda. 41 B4
Gellideg 60 C2
Gellifor 125 C6
Gelligaer 41 B6
Gellilydan. 107 C6
Gellinudd 40 A2
Gellyburn 219 A5
Gellywen 73 D5
Gelston Dumfries .173 C5
Lincs. 116 A2
Gembling 151 B4
Gentleshaw . . . 113 D4
Geocrab 288 H2
Georgefield. . . . 185 C5
George Green . . 48 A3
Georgeham 25 B5
George Nympton 26 C2
Georgetown . . . 60 C3
Gerlan. 123 D6
Germansweek. . 11 B5
Germoe. 2 C4
Gerrans. 4 D3
Gerrards Cross . 48 A3
Gestingthorpe . 87 D4
Geuffordd 109 D7
Gibbet Hill 98 C2
Gibbshill. 173 A5
Gib Hill 127 B6
Gidea Park. 50 A2
Gidleigh 12 C1
Giffnock 205 C5
Gifford 210 D2
Giffordland 204 D2
Giffordtown. . . 220 C2
Giggleswick. . . 146 A2
Gilberdyke 141 A6
Gilchriston. . . . 210 D1
Gilcrux 163 A4
Gildersome . . . 139 A5
Gildingwells . . . 131 A5
Gileston 41 E5
Gilfach 41 B6
Gilfach Goch . . . 41 C4
Gilfachrheda . . . 73 A7
Gillamoor 159 C5
Gillar's Green . . 136 D3
Gillen 258 C2
Gilling East . . . 159 D5
Gillingham Dorset 30 C2
Medway 51 C4
Norf 105 B5
Gilling West . . . 157 A5
Gillock 280 C4
Gillow Heath . . 128 D3
Gills 281 A5
Gill's Green 37 C5
Gilmanscleuch . 196 D2
Gilmerton Edin. . 209 D5

Gilmerton continued
Perth 218 B3
Gilmonby 166 D2
Gilmorton 98 C2
Gilmourton 205 D6
Gilsland 176 C4
Gilsland Spa . . . 176 C4
Gilston Borders . 196 A3
Herts 68 B4
Gimingham 121 B4
Giosla 288 E2
Gipping. 87 A6
Gipsey Bridge . . 117 A5
Girdle Toll 204 D3
Girlsta 285 H6
Girsby 158 A2
Girtford. 84 B3
Girthon 172 C4
Girton Cambs . . 85 A6
Notts 132 C3
Girvan 180 B3
Gisburn 146 C2
Gisleham 105 C6
Gislingham . . . 104 D1
Gissing 104 C2
Gittisham 13 B6
Gladestry 77 B6
Gladsmuir 210 C1
Glais 40 A2
Glaisdale 159 A6
Glame 248 B2
Glamis 232 D1
Glan Adda 123 C5
Glanaman 57 A6
Glan Conwy . . . 124 B3
Glandford. 120 A2
Glan-Duar 58 A2
Glandwr 73 D4
Glan-Dwyfach . 107 B4
Glandy Cross. . . 72 D4
Glandyfi 91 C4
Glan Gors. 123 C4
Glangrwyney. . . 60 B4
Glanmule 93 B5
Glanrafon. 90 D4
Glanrhyd Gwyn. .106 C2
Pembs 72 B4
Glan-rhyd 107 A4
Glanton 188 B3
Glanton Pike . . 188 B3
Glan-traeth . . . 122 C2
Glanvilles
Wootton 15 A6
Glan-y-don . . . 125 B6
Glan-y-nant . . . 92 C3
Glan-yr-afon
Anglesey 123 B6
Gwyn 108 A4
Gwyn 109 A5
Glan-y-wern . . 107 C6
Glapthorn 100 B2
Glapwell 131 C4
Glas-allt Shiel. . 243 D5
Glasbury. 77 D5
Glaschoil 253 C6
Glascoed Denb. .125 B4
Mon 61 C5
Powys 109 D6
Glascorrie 243 C6
Glascote 97 A5
Glascwm 77 B5
Glasdrum 227 B5
Glasfryn 125 D4
Glasgow 205 B5
Glashvin 259 B4
Glasinfryn 123 D5
Glasnacardoch . 235 A5
Glasnakille. . . . 247 C4
Glasphein 258 D1
Glaspwll 91 C5
Glassburn 251 C5
Glasserton 171 D6
Glassford 194 B2
Glasshouse Hill. . 62 A3
Glasshouses . . 147 A5
Glasslie. 220 D2
Glasson Cumb. .175 B5
Lancs 144 B4
Glassonby 164 B3
Glasterlaw 232 C3
Glaston 99 A5

Glastonbury. 29 B5
Glatton 100 C3
Glazebrook 137 D5
Glazebury. 137 D5
Glazeley 95 C5
Gleadless 130 A3
Gleadsmoss. . . 128 C3
Gleann
Tholàstaidh. . . 288 C6
Gleaston. 153 C3
Gleiston 92 B3
Glemsford 87 C4
Glen Dumfries . . 172 C3
Dumfries 173 A6
Glenamachrie . . 226 D4
Glen Auldyn. . . 152 B4
Glenbarr 190 B2
Glenbeg Highld. .235 D4
Highld. 253 D6
Glen Bernisdale . 259 D4
Glenbervie 245 D4
Glenboig. 207 D5
Glenborrodale . 235 D5
Glenbranter. . . . 215 C4
Glenbreck 195 D5
Glenbrein Lodge 240 A2
Glenbrittle
House. 246 B3
Glenbuchat
Lodge 243 A6
Glenbuck 194 D2
Glenburn 205 B4
Glencalvie
Lodge 263 B6
Glencanisp
Lodge 270 B4
Glencaple. 174 B2
Glencarron
Lodge 250 A2
Glencarse. 219 B6
Glencassley
Castle. 272 C2
Glenceitlein . . . 227 B6
Glencoe 237 D4
Glencraig. 209 A4
Glencripesdale . 225 A5
Glencrosh 183 D5
Glendavan
House. 244 B1
Glendevon 219 D4
Glendoebeg. . . 240 B2
Glendoe Lodge . 240 B2
Glendoick. 220 B2
Glendoll Lodge . 231 A6
Glendoune 180 B3
Glenduckie . . . 220 C2
Glendye Lodge . 244 D3
Gleneagles
Hotel. 218 C4
Gleneagles
House. 218 D4
Glenegedale . . 200 C3
Glenelg 238 A2
Glenernie 253 B6
Glenfarg 219 C6
Glenfarquhar
Lodge 245 D4
Glenferness
House. 253 B5
Glenfeshie
Lodge 241 C6
Glenfield. 98 A2
Glenfinnan 238 D3
Glenfoot 219 C6
Glenfyne Lodge 215 A5
Glengap 173 C4
Glengarnock . . 204 C3
Glengorm
Castle. 224 A3
Glengrasco . . . 259 D4
Glenhead Farm. 231 B6
Glen Ho. 196 C1
Glenholt. 7 B4
Glenhurich. . . . 236 C2
Glenkerry 185 A5
Glenkiln 173 A6
Glenkindie 244 A1
Glenlatterach . . 266 D2
Glenlee 182 D4

Glenlichorn 218 C2
Glenlivet. 254 D2
Glenlochsie 231 A4
Glenloig 191 B5
Glenluce 171 B4
Glenmallan 215 C5
Glenmarksie 251 A5
Glenmassan 215 D4
Glenmavis 207 D5
Glenmaye. 152 D2
Glenmidge. 183 D6
Glen Mona 152 C4
Glenmore Argyll. .213 A6
Highld. 259 D4
Glenmore Lodge 242 B2
Glenmoy. 232 B2
Glen Nevis
House. 237 B5
Glenogil 232 B2
Glen Parva 98 B2
Glenprosen
Lodge. 231 B6
Glenprosen
Village 232 B1
Glenquiech 232 B2
Glenreasdell
Mains 202 C3
Glenree. 191 C5
Glenridding 164 D1
Glenrossal 272 D2
Glenrothes. 220 D2
Glensanda 226 B3
Glensaugh 233 A4
Glenshero
Lodge 240 C3
Glen Sluain 214 C3
Glenstockadale . .170 A2
Glenstriven 203 A5
Glentaggart 194 D3
Glen Tanar
House. 244 C1
Glentham 142 D2
Glentirranmuir. .207 A4
Glenton 256 D1
Glentress 196 C1
Glentromie
Lodge. 241 C5
Glen Trool
Lodge 181 C6
Glentrool
Village 181 D5
Glentruan 152 A4
Glentruim
House. 241 C4
Glentworth 133 A4
Glenuig. 235 C5
Glenurquhart . . .264 D3
Glen Village 208 C1
Glen Vine 152 D3
Glespin 194 D3
Gletness. 285 H6
Glewstone 62 A1
Glinton 100 A3
Glooston. 99 B4
Glororum 199 C5
Glossop. 138 D3
Gloster Hill 189 C5
Gloucester 63 B4
Gloup 284 C7
Glusburn 147 C4
Glutt Lodge 274 A3
Glutton Bridge .129 C5
Glympton 65 A5
Glynarthen 73 B6
Glynbrochan 92 C3
Glyn-Ceiriog . . .109 B7
Glyncoch 41 B5
Glyncorrwg 40 B3
Glyn-cywarch . . .107 C6
Glynde. 22 B2
Glyndebourne . . .22 A2
Glyndyfrdwy . . .109 A6
Glyn Ebwy
=Ebbw Vale. . . .60 C3
Glynedd
=Glyn-neath. . . .59 E5
Glyn-neath
=Glynedd. 59 E5
Glynogwr 41 C4

Glyntaff. 41 C5
Glyntawe 59 D5
Gnosall 112 C2
Gnosall Heath. . .112 C2
Goadby 99 B4
Goadby
Marwood. 115 C5
Goatacre 44 B4
Goathill. 29 D6
Goathland 160 A2
Goathurst 28 B2
Goat Lees 38 A2
Gobernuisgach
Lodge. 277 D5
Gobhaig 287 D5
Gobowen 110 B2
Godalming 34 B2
Godley. 138 D2
Godmanchester .100 D4
Godmanstone . . .15 B6
Godmersham 52 D2
Godney 29 A4
Godolphin Cross . .3 B4
Godre'r-graig 59 E4
Godshill Hants . . .31 D5
IoW 18 C4
Godstone 35 A6
Godwinscroft . . .17 B5
Goetre. 61 C5
Goferydd 122 B2
Goff's Oak 68 C3
Gogar 209 C4
Goginan 91 D4
Golan. 107 B5
Golant 5 B6
Golberdon 10 D4
Golborne 137 D5
Golcar. 139 B4
Goldcliff 42 A2
Golden Cross 22 A3
Golden Green 36 B4
Golden Grove 57 A5
Goldenhill 128 D3
Golden Hill 17 B6
Golden Pot. 33 A6
Golden Valley 63 A5
Golders Green . . .49 A5
Goldhanger 70 C3
Gold Hill 102 B1
Golding 94 A3
Goldington 84 B2
Goldsborough
N Yorks 148 B2
N Yorks 169 D6
Goldsithney. 2 B3
Goldsworthy 25 C4
Goldthorpe 140 C2
Gollanfield 253 A4
Golspie 274 D2
Golval 279 B4
Gomeldon 31 B5
Gomersal 139 A5
Gomshall 34 B3
Gonalston 115 A4
Gonfirth 285 G5
Good Easter. 69 B6
Gooderstone 102 A3
Goodleigh 25 B7
Goodmanham . .150 C1
Goodnestone Kent 52 C2
Kent 53 D4
Goodrich 62 B1
Goodrington. 8 B2
Goodshaw 137 A7
Goodwick = Wdig .72 C2
Goodworth
Clatford 32 A2
Goole 141 A5
Goonbell. 4 C2
Goonhavern. 4 B2
Goose Eye 147 C4
Goose Green
Gtr Man 137 C4
Norf 104 C2
W Sus. 21 A4
Gooseham 24 D3
Goosey 65 D4
Goosnargh 145 D5
Goostrey 128 B2
Gorcott Hill 80 A3
Gord 285 L6
Gordon 197 B5

Gordonbush 274 D2
Gordonsburgh . .267 C5
Gordonstoun . . .266 C2
Gordonstown
Aberds 256 C2
Aberds 267 D6
Gore 53 D5
Gorebridge 209 D6
Gore Cross. 44 D4
Gorefield 117 D7
Gore Pit 70 B2
Gorey Jersey. 6
Gorgie. 209 C5
Goring 47 A4
Goring-by-Sea . . .21 B4
Goring Heath 47 B4
Gorleston-on-
Sea 105 A6
Gornalwood 96 B2
Gorrachie 268 D2
Gorran
Churchtown 5 C4
Gorran Haven 5 C5
Gorrenberry 186 D3
Gors. 75 A5
Gorsedd 125 B6
Gorse Hill. 45 A5
Gorseinon 57 C5
Gorseness 282 F5
Gorsgoch 74 C3
Gorslas 57 A5
Gorsley. 62 A2
Gorstan. 263 D5
Gorstanvorran . . .236 B2
Gorsteyhill 128 D2
Gorsty Hill 113 C5
Gortantaoid. 200 A3
Gorton 138 D1
Gosbeck 88 B2
Gosberton 117 B5
Gosberton
Clough 117 C4
Gosfield 70 A1
Gosford. 78 A3
Gosforth Cumb. .162 D3
T&W. 179 C4
Gosmore. 68 A1
Gosport. 19 B5
Gossabrough 284 E7
Gossington 62 C3
Goswick 199 B4
Gotham 114 B3
Gotherington 63 A5
Gott 285 J6
Goudhurst 37 C5
Goulceby 134 B2
Gourdas 256 B2
Gourdon 233 A6
Gourock 204 A2
Govan 205 B5
Goveton 7 C6
Govilon. 61 B4
Gowanhill. 269 C5
Gowdall 140 A4
Gowerton 57 C5
Gowkhall 208 B3
Gowthorpe. 149 B6
Goxhill E Yorks . .151 C4
N Lincs. 142 A3
Goxhill Haven . .142 A3
Goytre. 40 C2
Grabhair. 288 F4
Graby. 116 C3
Grade 3 D5
Graffham 20 A2
Grafham Cambs . .84 A3
Sur. 34 B3
Grafton Hereford . .78 D2
N Yorks. 148 A3
Oxon. 64 C3
Shrops 110 D3
Worcs. 78 A3
Grafton Flyford. .80 B2
Grafton Regis . . .83 C4
Grafton
Underwood. . . .99 C6
Grafty Green 37 B6
Graianrhyd. 126 D2
Graig Conwy .124 B3
Denb. 125 B5
Graig-fechan . . .125 D6

Grain 51 B5
Grainsby. 143 D4
Grainthorpe. 143 D5
Grampound. 4 C4
Grampound Road. . .4 B4
Gramsdal 286 A4
Granborough 66 A2
Granby 115 B5
Grandborough . . .82 A1
Grandtully 230 C3
Grange Cumb . . .163 C5
Edin 193 B4
Medway. 51 C4
Mers. 126 A3
Perth 220 B2
Grange
Crossroads . . .267 D5
Grange Hall 265 D6
Grange Hill 68 D4
Grangemill. 130 D2
Grange Moor. . . .139 B5
Grangemouth . . .208 B2
Grange of
Lindores 220 C2
Grange-over-
Sands 154 D3
Grangepans. 208 B3
Grangetown
Cardiff 41 D6
Redcar 168 C3
Grange Villa 179 D4
Granish 242 A2
Gransmoor. 151 B4
Granston 55 A4
Grantchester 85 B6
Grantham 116 B2
Grantley. 147 A6
Grantlodge 245 A4
Granton Dumfries 184 B3
Edin 209 C5
Grantown-on-
Spey 253 D6
Grantshouse 211 D5
Grappenhall 127 A6
Grasby 142 C2
Grasmere 154 A2
Grasscroft 138 C2
Grassendale 126 A3
Grassholme 166 C2
Grassington. 147 A4
Grassmoor. 131 C4
Grassthorpe. 132 C2
Grateley 32 A1
Gratwich. 112 B4
Graveley Cambs. .84 A4
Herts 68 A2
Gravelly Hill. 96 B4
Gravels 94 A1
Graven 284 F6
Graveney 52 C2
Gravesend Herts .68 A4
Kent 50 B3
Grayingham 142 D1
Grayrigg 155 B4
Grays. 50 B3
Grayshott 34 C1
Grayswood. 34 C2
Graythorp. 168 C3
Grazeley 47 C4
Greasbrough 140 D2
Greasby 126 A2
Great Abington . .86 C1
Great Addington . .99 D6
Great Alne 80 B4
Great Altcar. . . .136 C2
Great Amwell 68 B3
Great Asby. 165 D4
Great Ashfield. . . .87 A5
Great Ayton. 168 D3
Great Baddow . . .70 C1
Great Bardfield. . .86 D2
Great Barford . . .84 B3
Great Barr 96 B3
Great Barrington .64 B3
Great Barrow. 127 C4
Great Barton 87 A4
Great Barugh . . .159 D6
Great Bavington 178 A1
Great Bealings . . .88 C3
Great Bedwyn . . .45 C6
Great Bentley 71 A5
Great Billing 83 A4

Great Bircham . .119 B4
Great Blakenham. 88 B2
Great Blencow . .164 B2
Great Bolas 111 C5
Great Bookham . .35 A4
Great Bourton . . .82 C1
Great Bowden . . .99 C4
Great Bradley . . .86 B2
Great Braxted . . .70 B2
Great Bricett. 87 B6
Great Brickhill . .83 D6
Great Bridge 96 B2
Great
Bridgeford . . .112 C2
Great Brington . .82 A3
Great Bromley . . .71 A4
Great Broughton
Cumb 162 A3
N Yorks 158 A4
Great Budworth 127 B6
Great Burdon . . .167 D6
Great Burgh. 35 A5
Great Burstead . .69 D6
Great Busby. . . .158 A4
Great Canfield . . .69 B5
Great Carlton . . .135 A4
Great Casterton .100 A2
Great Chart 38 A1
Great Chatwell . .112 D1
Great
Chesterford . . .85 C7
Great
Cheverell 44 D3
Great Chishill . . .85 D6
Great Clacton . . .71 B5
Great Cliff 139 B6
Great Clifton . . .162 B3
Great Coates . . .143 C4
Great Comberton 80 C2
Great Corby 176 D2
Great Cornard. . . .87 C4
Great Cowden. . .151 C5
Great Coxwell . . .64 D3
Great Crakehall .157 B6
Great Cransley . . .99 D5
Great
Cressingham . .103 A4
Great Crosby . . .136 D2
Great Cubley . . .113 B5
Great Dalby 115 D5
Great Denham . . .84 C2
Great
Doddington . . .83 A5
Great Dunham . .119 D5
Great Dunmow . .69 A6
Great Durnford. . .31 B5
Great Easton
Essex 69 A6
Leics. 99 B5
Great Eccleston .144 C4
Great Edstone. . .159 C6
Great Ellingham 103 B6
Great Elm. 30 A1
Greater Doward . .62 B1
Great Eversden. . .85 B5
Great Fencote. . .157 B6
Great Finborough 87 B6
Great Fransham 119 D5
Great Gaddesden. 67 B5
Great Gidding . . .100 C3
Great Givendale 149 B7
Great Glemham . .88 A4
Great Glen 98 B3
Great Gonerby . .116 B1
Great Gransden . .85 B4
Great Green Norf 104 C3
Suff 87 B5
Great Habton . . .159 D6
Great Hale. 116 A4
Great Hallingbury 69 B5
Greatham Hants. .33 B6
Hrtlpl. 168 C2
W Sus. 20 A3
Great Hampden . .66 C3
Great Harrowden 99 D5
Great Harwood. .146 D1
Great Haseley. . . .66 C1
Great Haywood. .112 C3
Great Heath 97 C6
Great Heck. 140 A3

Great Henny 87 D4
Great Hinton 44 D3
Great Hockham .103 B5
Great Holland . . .71 B6
Great Horkesley. .87 D5
Great Hormead. . .68 A3
Great Horton . . .147 D5
Great Horwood. . .83 D4
Great Houghton
S Yorks 140 C2
W Nhants 83 B4
Great Hucklow . .130 B1
Great Kelk 151 B4
Great Kimble. . . .66 C3
Great Kingshill . .66 D3
Great Langton. . .157 B6
Great Leighs 70 B1
Great Lever 137 C6
Great Limber . . .142 C3
Great Linford 83 C5
Great Livermere 103 D4
Great Longstone 130 B2
Great Lumley . . .167 A5
Great Lyth 94 A2
Great Malvern. . . .79 C5
Great Maplestead 87 D4
Great Marton . . .144 D3
Great
Massingham . .119 C4
Great Melton. . . .104 A2
Great Milton 66 C1
Great Missenden .66 C3
Great Mitton . . .145 D7
Great Mongeham 53 D5
Great Moulton . .104 B2
Great Munden. . . .68 A3
Great Musgrave .165 D5
Great Ness. 110 D2
Great Notley 70 A1
Great Oakley
Essex 71 A5
N Nhants 99 C5
Great Offley 67 A6
Great Ormside . .165 D5
Great Orton 175 C6
Great Ouseburn .148 A3
Great Oxendon . .99 C4
Great Oxney
Green 69 C6
Great Palgrave . .119 D5
Great Parndon . . .68 C4
Great Paxton. 84 A4
Great Plumpton .144 D3
Great
Plumstead. . . .121 D5
Great Ponton . . .116 B2
Great Preston . . .140 A2
Great Raveley. . .101 C4
Great Rissington . .64 B2
Great Rollright. . .81 D6
Great Ryburgh . .119 C6
Great Ryle 188 B3
Great Ryton 94 A2
Great Saling 69 A7
Great Salkeld . . .164 B3
Great Sampford . .86 D2
Great Sankey. . . .127 A5
Great Saxham 86 A3
Great Shefford . . .46 B1
Great Shelford . . .85 B6
Great Smeaton . .158 A2
Great Snoring . . .119 B6
Great Somerford. .44 A3
Great Stainton . .167 C6
Great Stambridge 70 D2
Great Staughton. .84 A3
Great Steeping. .135 C4
Great Stonar 53 D5
Greatstone on
Sea 38 C2
Great Strickland 164 C3
Great Stukeley . .100 D4
Great Sturton . . .134 B2
Great Sutton
Ches W. 126 B3
Shrops 94 C3
Great
Swinburne . . .178 B1
Great Tew 65 A4
Great Tey 70 A2
Great Thurkleby 158 D3
Great Thurlow . . .86 B2

Great Torrington . 25 D5
Great Tosson. . . .188 C3
Great Totham
  Essex 70 B2
  Essex 70 B2
Great Tows 143 D4
Great Urswick. . .153 C3
Great Wakering . .51 A6
Great
  Waldingfield. . . .87 C5
Great
  Walsingham . . .119 B6
Great Waltham. . .69 B6
Great Warley. 69 D5
Great
  Washbourne. . . .80 D2
Great Weldon 99 C6
Great Welnetham 87 B4
Great Wenham . . .87 D6
Great
  Whittington . . .178 B2
Great
  Wigborough . . .70 B3
Great Wilbraham. 86 B1
Great Witchford. . 31 B4
Great Witcombe. . 63 B5
Great Witley 79 A5
Great Wolford. . . .81 D5
Greatworth 82 C2
Great Wratting . . .86 C2
Great Wymondley 68 A2
Great Wyrley. 96 A2
Great
  Wytheford. 111 D4
Great Yarmouth 105 A6
Great Yeldham . . .86 D3
Greave 138 A1
Greeba 152 C3
Green 125 C5
Greenbank 284 C7
Greenburn 208 D2
Greendikes 188 A3
Green End 84 B3
Greenfield C Beds .84 D2
  Flint 126 B1
  Gtr Man 138 C2
  Highld. 239 B6
  Oxon. 66 D2
Greenford 48 A4
Greengairs. 207 C5
Greenham 46 C2
Green
  Hammerton . . .148 B3
Greenhaugh 177 A5
Greenhead. 177 C4
Greenhill Falk . .207 C6
  Kent. 52 C3
  Leics. 114 D2
  London. 49 A4
Greenhills 204 C3
Greenhithe 50 B2
Greenholm. 193 B5
Greenholme 155 A4
Greenhouse. 187 A4
Greenhow Hill. . .147 A5
Greenigoe 283 G5
Greenland 280 B4
Greenlands 47 A5
Green Lane 93 B5
Greenlaw Aberds 268 D1
  Borders 197 B6
Greenlea 174 A3
Greenloaning . . .218 D3
Greenmount 137 B6
Greenmow. 285 L6
Greenock. 204 A2
Greenock West. .204 A2
Greenodd. 154 C2
Green Ore 43 D4
Greenrow. 174 C4
Green St Green. . .50 C1
Greenside 178 C3
Greensidehill . . .188 B2
Greens Norton . . .82 C3
Greenstead
  Green. 70 A2
Greensted 69 C5
Green Street 68 D1
Greenwich 49 B6
Greet. 80 D3
Greete. 94 D3
Greetham Lincs .134 B3

Greetham continued
  Rutland. 116 D2
Greetland. 138 A3
Gregg Hall 154 B3
Gregson Lane . . .137 A4
Greinetobht. 287 G3
Greinton. 28 B4
Gremista 285 J6
Grenaby 152 D2
Grendon N Nhants .83 A5
  Warks. 97 A5
Grendon
  Common 97 B5
Grendon Green. . .78 B3
Grendon
  Underwood. 66 A1
Grenofen 11 D5
Grenoside 139 D6
Greosabhagh . . .288 H2
Gresford. 126 D3
Gresham 120 B3
Greshornish. 258 C3
Gressenhall 119 D6
Gressingham . . .145 A5
Gresty Green. . . .128 D2
Greta Bridge 166 D3
Gretna. 175 B6
Gretna Green . . .175 B6
Gretton Glos. 80 D3
  N Nhants 99 B5
  Shrops. 94 B3
Grewelthorpe . . .157 D6
Greygarth. 157 D5
Grey Green 141 C5
Greynor 57 B5
Greysouthen 162 B3
Greystoke. 164 B2
Greystone Angus 232 D3
  Dumfries 174 A2
Greywell. 47 D5
Griais. 288 C5
Grianan 288 D5
Gribthorpe. 149 D6
Gridley Corner . .11 B4
Griff. 97 C6
Griffithstown. . . .61 D4
Grimbister 282 F4
Grimblethorpe . .134 A2
Grimeford
  Village 137 B5
Grimethorpe 140 C2
Griminis. 286 A3
Grimister 284 D6
Grimley 79 A6
Grimness 283 H5
Grimoldby 134 A3
Grimpo 110 C2
Grimsargh 145 D5
Grimsbury 82 C1
Grimsby 143 B4
Grimscote 82 B3
Grimscott. 10 A3
Grimstone 116 C3
Grimston
  E Yorks 151 D5
  Leics. 115 C4
  Norf 119 C4
  York 149 B5
Grimstone 15 B6
Grinacombe
  Moor. 11 B5
Grindale 161 D5
Grindigar 283 G6
Grindiscol 285 K6
Grindle 95 A5
Grindleford 130 B2
Grindleton 146 C1
Grindley 112 C4
Grindley Brook .111 A4
Grindlow 130 B1
Grindon
  Northumb. 198 B3
  Staffs. 129 D5
Grindonmoor
  Gate 129 D5
Gringley on the
  Hill 141 D5
Grinsdale 175 C6
Grinshill 111 C4
Grinton 156 B4
Griomsidar. 288 E4
Grishipoll 223 B4

Grisling Common 36 D2
Gristhorpe 161 C4
Griston 103 B5
Gritley. 283 G6
Grittenham 44 A4
Grittleton 44 A2
Grizebeck 153 B3
Grizedale 154 B2
Grobister 282 E7
Groby 98 A2
Groes Conwy 125 C5
  Neath 40 C2
Groes-faen 41 C5
Groesffordd
  Marli. 125 B5
Groeslon Gwyn. .107 A4
  Gwyn 123 D5
Groes-lwyd 109 D7
Grogport 202 D3
Gromford. 89 B4
Gronant 125 A5
Groombridge 36 C3
Grosmont Mon. . .61 A6
  N Yorks 160 A2
Groton 87 C5
Grougfoot 208 C3
Grouville Jersey. 6
Grove Dorset. 15 D7
  Kent 53 C4
  Notts 132 B2
  Oxon. 65 D5
Grove Park. 49 B7
Grovesend 57 B5
Grove Vale. 96 B3
Grudie 263 D5
Gruids 272 D3
Gruinard House .261 A6
Grula 246 B2
Gruline 225 B4
Grunasound. . . .285 K5
Grundisburgh . . .88 B3
Grunsagill 146 B1
Gruting 285 J4
Grutness 285 N6
Gualachulain . . .227 B6
Gualin House . . .276 C4
Guardbridge . . .221 C4
Guarlford 79 C6
Guay 230 D4
Guestling Green . .23 A6
Guestling Thorn . .23 A6
Guestwick 120 C2
Guestwick
  Green. 120 C2
Guide 137 A6
Guide Post. 179 A4
Guilden Morden. .85 C4
Guilden Sutton . .127 C4
Guildford 34 B2
Guildtown 219 A6
Guilsborough 98 D3
Guilsfield 109 D7
Guilton 53 D4
Guineaford 25 B6
Guisborough . . .168 D4
Guiseley 147 C5
Guist 120 C1
Guith 282 D6
Guiting Power. . . .64 A1
Gulberwick 285 K6
Gullane 210 B1
Gulval 2 B2
Gulworthy 11 D5
Gumfreston 55 D7
Gumley 98 B3
Gummow's Shop . .4 B3
Gunby E Yorks . .149 D6
  Lincs. 116 C2
Gundleton 33 B5
Gun Hill 22 A3
Gunn 26 B1
Gunnerside 156 B3
Gunnerton 177 B7
Gunness 141 B6
Gunnislake. 11 D5
Gunnista 285 J7
Gunthorpe Norf. .120 B2
  Notts 115 A4
  Pboro 100 A3
Gunville 18 C3
Gunwalloe 3 C4
Gurnard 18 B3

Gurnett. 129 B4
Gurney Slade . . .29 A6
Gurnos 59 E4
Gussage All
  Saints. 31 D4
Gussage
  St Michael. 30 D3
Guston 39 A5
Gutcher. 284 D7
Guthrie 232 C3
Guyhirn. 101 A5
Guyhirn Gull . . .101 A5
Guy's Head 118 C1
Guy's Marsh 30 C2
Guyzance 189 C5
Gwaenysgor 125 A5
Gwalchmai. 122 C3
Gwaun-Cae-
  Gurwen 59 D4
Gwaun-Leision. .59 D4
Gwbert 73 B4
Gweek 3 C5
Gwehelog 61 C5
Gwenddwr 77 C4
Gwennap 4 D2
Gwenter 3 D5
Gwernaffield. . . .126 C2
Gwernesney 61 C6
Gwernogle. 58 B2
Gwernymynydd. .126 C2
Gwersyllt 126 D3
Gwespyr 125 A6
Gwithian 2 A3
Gwredog 123 B4
Gwyddelwern . . .109 A5
Gwyddgrug 58 B1
Gwydyr Uchaf . .124 C2
Gwynfryn 126 D2
Gwystre 77 A4
Gwytherin 124 C3
Gyfelia 110 A2
Gyffin 124 B2
Gyre. 283 G4
Gyrn-goch 107 B4

H

Habberley 94 A1
Habergham 146 D2
Habrough 142 B3
Haceby 116 B3
Hacheston 88 B4
Hackbridge 49 C5
Hackenthorpe. . .131 A4
Hackford 103 A6
Hackforth. 157 B6
Hackland 282 E4
Hackleton 83 B5
Hackness
  N Yorks 160 B3
  Orkney 283 H4
Hackney 49 A6
Hackthorn 133 A4
Hackthorpe 164 C3
Haconby 116 C4
Hacton 50 A2
Hadden 198 C1
Haddenham
  Bucks 66 C2
  Cambs 101 D6
Haddington
  E Loth 210 C2
  Lincs. 133 C4
Haddiscoe 105 B5
Haddon Cambs. .100 B3
  Ches E 129 C4
Hade Edge 139 C4
Hademore 97 A4
Hadfield 138 D3
Hadham Cross . .68 B4
Hadham Ford . . .68 A4
Hadleigh Essex . .51 A5
  Suff 87 C6
Hadley 111 D5
Hadley End 113 C5
Hadlow 36 B4
Hadlow Down . . .36 D3
Hadnall 111 D4
Hadstock 86 C1
Hady 130 B3
Hadzor 80 A2

Haffenden
  Quarter 37 B6
Hafod-Dinbych. .124 D3
Hafod-Iom. 124 B3
Haggate 146 D2
Haggbeck. 176 B2
Haggerston 198 B4
Haggrister 284 F5
Hagley Hereford . .78 C3
  Worcs. 96 C2
Hagworthingham
  . . . . .134 C3
Haigh Gtr Man. .137 C5
  S Yorks 139 B5
Haigh Moor 139 A5
Haighton Green .145 D5
Haile 162 D3
Hailes 80 D3
Hailey Herts 68 B3
  Oxon. 65 B4
Hailsham 22 B3
Hail Weston. 84 A3
Haimer 280 B3
Hainault 69 D4
Hainford 120 D4
Hainton 134 A1
Hairmyres 205 C6
Haisthorpe. 151 A4
Hakin. 55 D4
Halam 132 D1
Halbeath. 208 B4
Halberton 27 D5
Halcro. 280 B4
Hale Gtr Man . . .128 A2
  Halton 127 A4
  Hants 31 D5
Hale Bank 127 A4
Halebarns 128 A2
Hales Norf. 105 B4
  Staffs. 111 B6
Halesfield. 95 A5
Halesgate. 117 C6
Halesowen 96 C2
Hales Place 52 D3
Hale Street 37 A4
Halesworth 105 D4
Halewood 127 A4
Halford Shrops. . .94 C2
  Warks. 81 C5
Halfpenny Furze. .56 A2
Halfpenny Green .95 B6
Halfway Carms. . .58 B3
  Carms 59 B5
  W Berks 46 C2
Halfway Bridge . .34 D2
Halfway House . .110 D2
Halfway Houses . .51 B6
Halifax 138 A3
Halket 205 C4
Halkirk 280 C3
Halkyn 126 B2
Halland 22 A2
Hallaton 99 B4
Hallatrow 43 D5
Hallbankgate. . .176 D3
Hall Dunnerdale 153 A3
Hallen 43 A4
Hall Green W Mid. 96 C4
  W Yorks 139 B6
Hall Grove 68 B2
Halliburton 197 B5
Hallin 258 C2
Halling 51 C4
Hallington Lincs .134 A3
  Northumb. 178 B1
Halliwell. 137 B6
Hall of
  Tankerness. . . .283 G6
Hall of the Forest 93 C6
Halloughton . . .132 D1
Hallow. 79 B6
Hallrule 187 B4
Halls 210 C3
Hallsands 8 D2
Hall's Green 68 A2
Hallthwaites . . .153 B2
Hallworthy. 10 C2
Hallyburton
  House. 220 A2
Hallyne 195 B6
Halmer End 112 A1
Halmore 62 C2

Halmyre Mains . .195 B6
Halnaker. 20 B2
Halsall. 136 B2
Halsall . . . .
Halse Som. 27 C6
  W Nhants 82 C2
Halsetown 2 B3
Halsham 143 A4
Halsinger 25 B6
Halstead Essex . .87 D4
  Kent 50 C1
  Leics. 99 A4
Halstock 15 A5
Haltham 134 C2
Haltoft End 117 A6
Halton Bucks. . . .66 B3
  Halton 127 A5
  Lancs 145 A5
  Northumb. 178 C1
  Wrex 110 B2
  W Yorks 148 D2
Halton East 147 B4
Halton Gill 156 D2
Halton Holegate 135 C4
Halton Lea Gate 176 D4
Halton West. . . .146 B2
Haltwhistle 177 C5
Halvergate. 105 A5
Halwell 8 B1
Halwill. 11 B5
Halwill Junction. .11 A5
Ham Devon 14 A2
  Glos 62 D2
  Highld. 280 A4
  Kent 53 D5
  London 49 B4
  Shetland. 285 K1
  Wilts. 46 C1
Hambleden 47 A5
Hambledon Hants 33 D5
  Sur 34 C2
Hamble-le-Rice. .18 A3
Hambleton
  Lancs 144 C3
  N Yorks 149 D4
Hambridge. 28 C3
Hambrook S Glos. .43 B5
  W Sus. 19 A6
Ham Common . . .30 C2
Hameringham. .134 C3
Hamerton 100 D3
Hametoun 285 K1
Ham Green
  Hereford 79 C5
  Kent 37 D6
  Kent 51 C5
  N Som. 43 B4
  Worcs. 80 A3
Hamilton 194 A2
Hammer 34 C1
Hammerpot. 20 B3
Hammersmith. . .49 B5
Hammerwich 96 A3
Hammerwood. . .36 C2
Hammond Street 68 C3
Hammoon 30 D2
Hamnavoe
  Shetland. 284 E4
  Shetland. 284 E6
  Shetland. 284 F6
  Shetland. 285 K5
Hampden Park . .22 B4
Hamperden End. .86 D1
Hampnett. 64 B1
Hampole. 140 B3
Hampreston 17 B4
Hampstead 49 A5
Hampstead
  Norreys 46 B3
Hampsthwaite . .147 B6
Hampton London . .48 C4
  Shrops 95 C5
  Worcs. 80 C3
Hampton Bishop .78 D3
Hampton Heath .110 A3
Hampton in
  Arden 97 C5
Hampton Loade . .95 C5
Hampton Lovett. .80 A1
Hampton Lucy. . .81 B5

Hampton on the Hill 81 A5
Hampton Poyle . . . 65 B6
Hamrow 119 C6
Hamsey 22 A2
Hamsey Green . . 35 A6
Hamstall Ridware 113 D5
Hamstead IoW . . . 18 B3
  W Mid 96 B3
Hamstead Marshall 46 C2
Hamsterley Durham 166 B4
  Durham 178 D3
Hamstreet 38 B2
Ham Street 29 B5
Hamworthy 16 B3
Hanbury Staffs . 113 C5
  Worcs. 80 A2
Hanbury Woodend 113 C5
Hanby 116 B3
Hanchurch 112 A2
Handbridge . . . 127 C4
Handcross 35 D5
Handforth 128 A3
Handley 127 D4
Handsacre 113 D4
Handsworth S Yorks 131 A4
  W Mid 96 B3
Handy Cross 25 C5
Hanford 112 A2
Hanging Langford 31 B4
Hangleton 20 B3
Hanham 43 B5
Hankelow 111 A5
Hankerton 63 D5
Hankham 22 B4
Hanley 112 A2
Hanley Castle . . . 79 C6
Hanley Child . . . 79 A4
Hanley Swan . . . 79 C6
Hanley William . . . 79 A4
Hanlith 146 A3
Hanmer 110 B3
Hannah 135 B5
Hannington Hants 46 D3
  Swindon 64 D2
  W Nhants 99 D5
Hannington Wick 64 D2
Hansel Village . . 192 B3
Hanslope 83 C5
Hanthorpe 116 C3
Hanwell London . . 49 A4
  Oxon. 82 C1
Hanwood 94 A2
Hanworth London . 48 B4
  Norf 120 B3
Happendon . . . 194 C3
Happisburgh . . 121 B5
Happisburgh Common 121 C5
Hapsford 127 B4
Hapton Lancs . . 146 D1
  Norf 104 B2
Harberton 8 B1
Harbertonford . . . 8 B1
Harbledown 52 D3
Harborne 96 C3
Harborough Magna 98 D1
Harbottle 188 C2
Harbury 81 B6
Harby Leics . . . 115 B5
  Notts 132 B3
Harcombe 13 B6
Harden W Mid . . . 96 A3
  W Yorks 147 D4
Hardenhuish . . . 44 B3
Hardgate 245 B4
Hardham 20 A3
Hardingham . . . 103 A6
Hardingstone . . . 83 B4
Hardington 43 D6
Hardington Mandeville 29 D5

Hardington Marsh 15 A5
Hardley 18 A3
Hardley Street . 105 A4
Hardmead 83 C6
Hardrow 156 B2
Hardstoft 131 C4
Hardway Hants . . 19 A5
  Som 29 B7
Hardwick Bucks . . 66 B3
  Cambs 85 B5
  N Nhants 83 A5
  Norf 104 C3
  Norf 118 D3
  Notts 131 B6
  Oxon. 65 A6
  Oxon. 65 C4
  W Mid 96 B3
Hardwicke Glos . . 62 B3
  Glos 63 A5
  Hereford 77 C6
Hardy's Green . . 70 A3
Hareby 134 C3
Hareden 145 B6
Harefield 67 D5
Hare Green 71 A4
Hare Hatch 47 B6
Harehills 148 D2
Harehope 188 A3
Haresceugh . . . 165 A4
Harescombe . . . 63 B4
Haresfield 63 B4
Hareshaw 207 D6
Hareshaw Head . 177 A6
Hare Street 68 A3
Harewood 148 C2
Harewood End . . 62 A1
Harford Carms . . 58 A3
  Devon. 7 B5
Hargate 104 B2
Hargatewall . . . 129 B6
Hargrave Ches W 127 C4
  N Nhants 100 D2
  Suff 86 B3
Harker 175 B6
Harkland 284 E6
Harkstead 88 D2
Harlaston 113 D6
Harlaxton 116 B1
Harlech 107 C5
Harlequin 115 B4
Harlescott 111 D4
Harlesden 49 A5
Harleston Devon . . 8 C1
  Norf 104 C3
  Suff 87 B6
Harlestone 83 A4
Harle Syke 146 D2
Harley Shrops . . . 94 A3
  S Yorks 139 D6
Harleyholm . . . 194 C4
Harlington C Beds . 84 D2
  London 48 B3
  S Yorks 140 C2
Harlosh 258 D2
Harlow 69 B4
Harlow Hill Northumb 178 C2
  N Yorks 148 B1
Harlthorpe . . . 149 D6
Harlton 85 B5
Harman's Cross . 16 C3
Harmby 157 C5
Harmer Green . . 68 B2
Harmer Hill . . . 110 C3
Harmondsworth . 48 B3
Harmston 133 C4
Harnham 178 B2
Harnhill 63 C6
Harold Hill 69 C5
Haroldston West . 54 C4
Haroldswick . . 284 B8
Harold Wood . . . 69 C5
Harome 159 C5
Harpenden 67 B6
Harpford 13 B5
Harpham 150 A3
Harpley Norf . . 119 C4
  Worcs. 79 A4
Harpole 82 A3
Harpsdale 280 C3

Harpsden 47 A5
Harpswell 133 A4
Harpurhey . . . 138 C1
Harpur Hill . . . 129 B5
Harraby 175 C7
Harrapool 247 B5
Harrier 285 J1
Harrietfield . . . 219 B4
Harrietsham . . . 37 A6
Harrington Cumb 134 B3
  Lincs 134 B3
  N Nhants 99 C4
Harringworth . . . 99 B6
Harris 234 A2
Harrogate 148 B2
Harrold 83 B6
Harrow 49 A4
Harrowbarrow . . . 6 A2
Harrowden 84 C2
Harrowgate Hill . 167 D5
Harrow on the Hill 49 A4
Harrow Street . . 87 D5
Harrow Weald . . 67 D6
Harston Cambs . . 85 B6
  Leics 115 B6
Harswell 150 C1
Hart 168 B2
Hartburn Northumb 178 A2
  Stockton 168 D2
Hart Common . 137 C5
Hartest 87 B4
Hartfield 36 C2
Hartford Cambs . 101 D4
  Ches W 127 B6
Hartfordbridge . . 47 D5
Hartford End . . . 69 B6
Hartforth 157 A5
Harthill Ches W . 127 D5
  N Lanark 208 D2
  S Yorks 131 A4
Hart Hill 67 A6
Hartington . . . 129 C6
Hartland 24 C3
Hartlebury 95 D6
Hartlepool . . . 168 B3
Hartley Cumb . 155 A6
  Kent 37 C5
  Kent 50 C3
  Northumb 179 B5
Hartley Westpall . 47 D4
Hartley Wintney . 47 D5
Hartlip 51 C5
Hartoft End . . . 159 B6
Harton N Yorks . 149 A6
  Shrops 94 C2
  T&W 179 C5
Hartpury 62 A3
Hartshead 139 A4
Hartshill 97 B6
Hartshorne . . . 113 C7
Hartsop 164 D2
Hart Station . . 168 B2
Hartwell 83 B4
Hartwood 194 A3
Harvieston . . . 206 B3
Harvington 80 C3
Harvington Cross 80 C3
Harwell 46 A2
Harwich 88 D3
Harwood Durham 165 B6
  Gtr Man 137 B6
Harwood Dale . 160 B3
Harworth 140 D4
Hasbury 96 C2
Hascombe 34 B2
Haselbech 99 D4
Haselbury Plucknett 29 D4
Haseley 81 A5
Haselor 80 B4
Hasfield 63 A4
Hasguard 55 D4
Haskayne 136 C2
Hasketon 88 B3
Hasland 130 C3
Haslemere 34 C2
Haslingden . . . 137 A6
Haslingfield . . . 85 B6
Haslington . . . 128 C2
Hassall 128 C1

Hassall Green . . 128 D2
Hassell Street . . . 38 A2
Hassendean . . . 186 A4
Hassingham . . . 105 A4
Hassocks 21 A5
Hassop 130 B2
Hastigrow 281 B4
Hastingleigh . . . 38 A2
Hastings 23 B6
Hastingwood . . . 69 C4
Hastoe 67 C4
Haswell 167 A6
Haswell Plough . 167 A6
Hatch C Beds . . . 84 C3
  Hants 47 D4
  Wilts. 30 C3
Hatch Beauchamp . . . 28 C3
Hatch End 67 D6
Hatchet Gate . . . 18 A2
Hatch Green . . . 28 D3
Hatching Green . . 67 B6
Hatchmere 127 B5
Hatcliffe 143 C4
Hatfield Hereford . 78 B3
  Herts 68 C2
  S Yorks 141 C4
  Worcs. 80 B1
Hatfield Broad Oak 69 B5
Hatfield Garden Village 68 C2
Hatfield Heath . . 69 B5
Hatfield Hyde . . . 68 C2
Hatfield Peverel . 70 B1
Hatfield Woodhouse . . 141 C4
Hatford 64 D4
Hatherden 46 D1
Hatherleigh 11 A6
Hathern 114 C2
Hatherop 64 C2
Hathersage . . . 130 A2
Hathershaw . . . 138 C2
Hatherton Ches E 111 A5
  Staffs 112 D3
Hatley St George . 85 B4
Hatt 6 A2
Hattingley 33 B5
Hatton Aberds . 257 C5
  Derbys 113 C6
  Lincs 134 B1
  Shrops 94 B2
  Warks. 81 A5
  Warks. 97 A5
Hatton Castle . 256 B2
Hattoncrook . . 256 D3
Hatton Heath . . 127 C4
Hatton of Fintray 245 A5
Haugh E Ayrs . . 193 C4
  Gtr Man 138 B2
  Lincs 135 B4
Haugham 134 A3
Haugh Head . . 188 A3
Haughley 87 A6
Haughley Green . 87 A6
Haugh of Glass . 255 C5
Haugh of Urr . 173 B6
Haughs of Clinterty 245 A5
Haughton Notts . 132 B1
  Shrops 95 A5
  Shrops 95 B4
  Shrops 110 C2
  Shrops 111 D4
  Staffs 112 C2
Haughton Castle 177 B7
Haughton Green 138 D2
Haughton Moss . 127 D5
Haultwick 68 A3
Haunn Argyll . . 224 B2
  W Isles 286 E3
Haunton 113 D6
Hauxley 189 C5
Hauxton 85 B6
Havant 19 A6
Haven 78 B2
Haven Bank . . . 134 D2
Haven Side . . . 142 A3
Havenstreet . . . 19 B4
Havercroft . . . 140 B1

Haverfordwest =Hwlffordd 55 C5
Haverhill 86 C2
Haverigg 153 C2
Havering-atte-Bower 69 D5
Haveringland . . 120 C3
Haversham 83 C5
Haverthwaite . . 154 C2
Haverton Hill . 168 C2
Hawarden =Penarlâg 126 C3
Hawcoat 153 C3
Hawen 73 B6
Hawes 156 C2
Hawes' Green . 104 B3
Hawes Side . . . 144 D3
Hawford 79 A6
Hawick 186 B4
Hawkchurch . . . 14 A3
Hawkedon 86 B3
Hawkenbury Kent 36 C3
  Kent 37 B6
Hawkeridge 44 D2
Hawkerland 13 C5
Hawkesbury S Glos 43 A6
  Warks. 97 C6
Hawkesbury Upton 44 A1
Hawkes End 97 C6
Hawk Green . . 129 A4
Hawkhill 189 B5
Hawkhurst 37 C5
Hawkinge 39 B4
Hawkley 33 C6
Hawkridge 26 B3
Hawkshead . . . 154 B2
Hawkshead Hill 154 B2
Hawksland 194 C3
Hawkswick . . . 156 D3
Hawksworth Notts 115 A5
  W Yorks 147 C5
  W Yorks 147 D6
Hawkwell 70 D2
  Kent 50 B2
Hawley Hants . . 34 A1
  Kent 50 B2
Hawling 63 A6
Hawnby 158 C4
Haworth 147 D4
Hawstead 87 B4
Hawthorn Durham 168 A2
  Rhondda 41 C6
  Wilts. 44 C2
Hawthorn Hill Brack 48 B1
  Lincs 134 D2
Hawthorpe . . . 116 C3
Hawton 132 D2
Haxby 149 B5
Haxey 141 C5
Haydock 137 D4
Haydon 29 C6
Haydon Bridge . 177 C6
Haydon Wick . . . 45 A5
Haye 6 A2
Hayes London . . 48 A4
  London 49 C7
Hayfield Derbys . 129 A5
  Fife 209 A5
Hay Green 118 D2
Hayhill 182 A2
Hayhillock . . . 232 D3
Hayle 2 B3
Haynes 84 C2
Haynes Church End 84 C2
Hay-on-Wye =Y Gelli Gandryll 77 C6
Hayscastle 55 B4
Hayscastle Cross 55 B5
Hayshead 233 D4
Hay Street 68 A3
Hayton Aberdeen 245 B6
  Cumb 174 D4
  Cumb 175 A4
  E Yorks 149 C7
  Notts 132 A2
Hayton's Bent . . 94 C3
Haytor Vale . . . 12 D2

Haywards Heath . 35 A6
Haywood 140 B3
Haywood Oaks . 131 D6
Hazelbank 194 B3
Hazelbury Bryan . 16 A1
Hazeley 47 D5
Hazel Grove . . 129 A4
Hazelhurst . . . 138 C2
Hazelslade . . . 112 D4
Hazel Street . . . 37 C4
Hazelton 64 B1
Hazelton Walls . 220 B3
Hazelwood . . . 114 A1
Hazlemere 66 D3
Hazlerigg 179 B4
Hazlewood . . . 147 B4
Hazon 189 C4
Heacham 118 B3
Headbourne Worthy 32 B3
Headbrook 77 B7
Headcorn 37 B6
Headingley . . . 148 D1
Headington 65 C6
Headlam 167 D4
Headless Cross . . 80 A3
Headley Hants . . 33 B7
  Hants 46 C3
  Sur. 35 A5
Head of Muir . 207 B6
Headon 132 B2
Heads 194 B2
Heads Nook . . 176 D2
Heage 130 D3
Healaugh N Yorks 148 C3
  N Yorks 156 B4
Heald Green . . 128 A3
Heale Devon . . . 26 A1
  Som 29 A6
Healey Gtr Man . 138 B1
  Northumb 178 D2
  N Yorks 157 C5
Healing 143 B4
Heamoor 2 B2
Heanish 222 C3
Heanor 114 A2
Heanton Punchardon . . . 25 B6
Heapham 132 A3
Hearthstone . . 195 D6
Heasley Mill . . . 26 B2
Heast 45 D6
Heath Cardiff . . . 41 D6
  Derbys 131 C4
Heath and Reach 67 A4
Heathcote 129 C6
Heath End Hants . 46 C3
  Sur. 34 B1
  Warks. 81 A5
Heather 114 D1
Heatherfield . . 259 D4
Heathfield Devon . 12 D3
  E Sus 36 D3
  Som 27 C6
Heathhall 174 A2
Heath Hayes . . 112 D4
Heath Hill 111 D6
Heath House . . . 28 A4
Heathrow Airport . 48 B3
Heathstock 14 A2
Heathton 95 B6
Heath Town 96 B2
Heatley 128 A2
Heaton Lancs . . 144 A4
  Staffs 129 C4
  T&W 179 C4
  W Yorks 147 D5
Heaton Moor . . 138 D1
Heaverham 36 A3
Heaviley 129 A3
Heavitree 13 B4
Hebburn 179 C5
Hebden 147 A4
Hebden Bridge . 138 A2
Hebron Anglesey . 123 B4
  Carms 73 D4
  Northumb 178 A3
Heck 184 D3
Heckfield 47 C5
Heckfield Green 104 D2
Heckfordbridge . . 70 A3

Heckington 116 A4
Heckmondwike . .139 A5
Heddington 44 C3
Heddle 282 F4
Heddon-on-the-
Wall 178 C3
Hedenham 104 B4
Hedge End 32 D3
Hedgerley 48 A2
Hedging 28 C3
Hedley on the
Hill 178 D2
Hednesford 112 D3
Hedon 142 A3
Hedsor 48 A2
Hedworth 179 C5
Hegdon Hill 78 B3
Heggerscales 165 D6
Heglibister 285 H5
Heighington Darl 167 C5
Lincs. 133 C5
Heights of Brae .263 D7
Heights of
Kinlochewe 262 D2
Heilam 277 B5
Heiton 197 C6
Hele Devon 13 A4
Devon. 25 A6
Helensburgh 215 D5
Helford 3 C5
Helford Passage. . . .3 C5
Helhoughton 119 C5
Helions
Bumpstead 86 C2
Hellaby 140 D3
Helland. 10 D1
Hellesdon. 120 D4
Hellidon 82 B2
Hellifield 146 B2
Hellingly 22 A3
Hellington 104 A4
Hellister 285 J5
Helm 189 D4
Helmdon 82 C2
Helmingham 88 B2
Helmington Row 167 B4
Helmsdale 274 C4
Helmshore. 137 A6
Helmsley 159 C5
Helperby 148 A3
Helperthorpe 160 D3
Helpringham 116 A4
Helpston. 100 A3
Helsby 127 B4
Helsey 135 B5
Helston 3 C4
Helstone 10 C1
Helton 164 C3
Helwith Bridge .146 A2
Hemblington 121 D5
Hemel
Hempstead 67 C5
Hemingbrough .149 D5
Hemingby 134 B2
Hemingford
Abbots 101 D4
Hemingford
Grey 101 D4
Hemingstone 88 B2
Hemington Leics 114 C2
N Nhants 100 C2
Som 43 D6
Hemley 88 C3
Hemlington 168 D3
Hemp Green 89 A4
Hempholme. 150 B3
Hempnall 104 B3
Hempnall Green 104 B3
Hempriggs
House 281 D5
Hempstead Essex .86 D2
Medway 51 C4
Norf 120 B3
Norf 121 C4
Hempsted 63 B4
Hempton Norf . . .119 C6
Oxon. 82 D1
Hemsby. 121 D6
Hemswell 142 D1
Hemswell Cliff .133 A4
Hemsworth 140 B2
Hemyock 27 D6

Henbury Bristol . . .43 B4
Ches E 128 B3
Hendon London . . .49 A5
T&W. 179 D6
Hendre 126 C1
Hendre-ddu 124 C3
Hendreforgan. 41 C4
Hendy 57 B5
Hcncglwys. 123 C4
Hen-feddau fawr 73 C5
Henfield 21 A5
Henford 11 B4
Henghurst 38 B1
Hengoed Caerph . .41 B6
Powys. 77 B6
Shrops 110 B1
Hengrave 87 A4
Henham 69 A5
Heniarth 93 A5
Henlade 28 C2
Henley Shrops 94 D3
Som 28 B4
Suff 88 B2
W Sus. 34 D1
Henley-in-Arden 81 A4
Henley-on-
Thames 47 A5
Henley's Down . . .23 A5
Henllan Ceredig . .73 B6
Denb. 125 C5
Henllan Amgoed .73 D4
Henllys 61 D4
Henlow 84 D3
Hennock 12 C3
Henny Street. 87 D4
Henry's Moat. 55 B6
Hensall 140 A3
Henshaw 177 C5
Hensingham 162 C2
Henstead 105 C5
Henstridge. 30 D1
Henstridge Ash. . . .29 C7
Henstridge Marsh 30 C1
Henton Oxon. 66 C2
Som 29 A4
Henwood 10 D3
Heogan. 285 J6
Heol-las 40 B1
Heol-y-Cyw 40 C4
Hepburn 188 A3
Hepple 188 C2
Hepscott. 179 A4
Heptonstall 138 A2
Hepworth Suff . . .103 D5
W Yorks 139 C4
Herbrandston 55 D4
Hereford. 78 C3
Heriot 196 A2
Hermiston 209 C4
Hermitage
Borders 186 D4
Dorset 15 A6
W Berks 46 B3
W Sus. 19 A6
Hermon Anglesey 122 D3
Carms 58 C3
Carms 73 C6
Pembs 73 C5
Herne 52 C3
Herne Bay 52 C3
Herner 25 C6
Hernhill 52 C2
Herodsfoot 5 A7
Herongate 69 D6
Heronsford 180 C3
Herriard 33 A5
Herringfleet 105 B5
Herringswell 102 D3
Herrington 53 C4
Hersden. 53 C4
Hersham Corn 10 A3
Sur. 48 C4
Herstmonceux 22 A4
Herston 283 H5
Hertford. 68 B3
Hertford Heath . . .68 B3
Hertingfordbury . .68 B3
Hesketh Bank . .136 A3
Hesketh Lane . . .145 C6
Hesket
Newmarket 163 A6

Heskin Green 136 B4
Hesleden 168 B2
Hesleyside 177 A6
Heslington 149 B5
Hessay 148 B4
Hessenford 6 B2
Hessett 87 A5
Hessle 142 A2
Hest Bank 145 A4
Heston 48 D4
Hestwall 282 F3
Heswall 126 A2
Hethe 65 A6
Hethersett 104 A2
Hethersgill 176 C2
Hethpool 188 A1
Hett 167 B5
Hetton. 146 B3
Hetton-le-Hole . .167 A6
Hetton Steads. . . .198 C4
Heugh 178 B2
Heugh-head 243 A6
Heveningham 104 D4
Hever. 36 B2
Heversham 154 C3
Hevingham 120 C3
Hewas Water. 5 C4
Hewelsfield 62 C1
Hewish N Som. . . .42 C3
Som 14 A4
Heworth 149 B5
Hexham 178 C1
Hextable 50 B2
Hexton 84 D3
Hexworthy 12 D1
Hey 146 C2
Heybridge Essex . .69 C6
Essex 70 C2
Heybridge Basin. 70 C2
Heybrook Bay 7 C4
Heydon Cambs . . .85 C6
Norf 120 C3
Heydour 116 B3
Heylipol 222 C2
Heylor 284 E4
Heysham 144 A4
Heyshott 20 A1
Heyside. 138 C2
Heytesbury 30 A3
Heythrop 64 A4
Heywood
Gtr Man 138 B1
Wilts. 44 D2
Hibaldstow 142 C1
Hickleton 140 C2
Hickling Norf . . .121 C6
Notts 115 C4
Hickling Green . .121 C6
Hickling Heath . .121 C6
Hickstead. 35 D5
Hidcote Boyce 81 C4
High Ackworth . .140 B2
Higham Derbys . .130 D3
Kent 51 B4
Lancs 146 D2
Suff 86 A3
Suff 87 D6
Higham Dykes . . .178 B3
Higham Ferrers . . .83 A6
Higham Gobion . .84 D3
Higham on the
Hill 97 B6
Highampton 11 A5
Higham Wood. 36 B3
High Angerton . .178 A2
High Bankhill . . .164 A3
High Barnes. 179 D5
High Beach 68 D4
High Bentham . . .145 A6
High Bickington. . .25 C7
High Birkwith . . .155 D6
High Blantyre . . .194 A1
High
Bonnybridge . .207 C6
High Bradfield . .139 D5
High Bray 26 B1
Highbridge
Highld. 239 D5
Som 28 A3
Highbrook 35 C6
High Brooms. 36 B3
High Bullen 25 C6

Highburton 139 B4
Highbury 29 A6
High Buston 189 C5
High Callerton . .178 B3
High Catton 149 B6
Highclere. 46 C2
Highcliffe. 17 B6
High Cogges 65 C4
High Coniscliffe 167 D5
High Cross Hants. .33 C6
Herts 68 B3
High Easter 69 B6
High
Eggborough . . .140 A3
High Ellington . . .157 C5
Higher Ashton 12 C3
Higher Ballam . . .144 D3
Higher Bartle 145 D5
Higher Boscaswell. 2 B1
Higher
Burwardsley . .127 D5
High Ercall. 111 D4
Higher Clovelly . . .24 C4
Higher End 136 C4
Higher
Kinnerton 126 C3
Higher
Penwortham. . .136 A4
Higher Town
Scilly P02 E4
Higher
Walreddon 11 D5
Higher Walton
Lancs 137 A4
Warr. 127 A5
Higher
Wheelton 137 A5
Higher Whitley . .127 A6
Higher
Wincham. 128 B1
Higher Wych 110 A3
High Etherley . . .167 C4
Highfield
E Yorks 149 D6
Gtr Man 137 C6
N Ayrs 204 C3
Oxon. 65 A6
S Yorks 130 A3
T&W. 178 D3
Highfields Cambs .85 B5
Northumb. 198 A3
High Garrett 70 A1
Highgate 49 A5
High Grange 167 B4
High Green Norf .104 A2
S Yorks 139 D6
Worcs. 80 C1
High Halden 37 C6
High Halstow 51 B4
High Ham. 28 B4
High Harrington 162 B3
High Hatton 111 C5
High Hawsker . . .160 A3
High Hesket. 164 A2
High Hesleden . . .168 B2
High Hoyland . . .139 B5
High Hunsley . . .150 D2
High Hurstwood. .36 D2
High Hutton. 149 A6
High Ireby 163 A5
High Kelling 120 A3
High Kilburn 158 D4
High Lands. 166 C4
Highlane Ches E .128 C3
Derbys 131 A4
High Lane
Gtr Man 129 A4
Worcs. 79 A4
High Laver 69 C5
Highlaws 174 D4
Highleadon 62 A3
High Legh 128 A2
Highleigh 20 C1
High Leven 168 D2
Highley 95 C5
High Littleton 43 D5
High Lorton 163 B4
High Marishes . .159 D7
High Marnham . .132 C3
High Melton 140 C3
High Mickley . . .178 C2

High Mindork . . .171 B5
Highmoor Cross. .47 A5
Highmoor Hill. . . .42 A3
Highnam. 62 B3
Highnam Green . .62 A3
High Newton 154 C3
High Newton-by-the-
Sea 189 A5
High Nibthwaite 154 C1
High Offley 112 C1
High Ongar 69 C5
High Onn 112 D2
High Roding 69 B6
High Row 163 A6
High Salvington . .21 B4
High Sellafield . .162 D3
High Shaw 156 B2
High Spen 178 D3
High Stoop. 166 A4
High Street Corn . .5 B4
Kent 37 C5
Suff 87 C4
Suff 89 B5
Suff 105 D5
Highstreet Green 86 D3
High Street
Green 87 B6
Hightae. 174 A3
High Throston. . .168 B2
Hightown Ches E 128 C3
Mers. 136 C2
Hightown Green. .87 B5
High Toynton . . .134 C2
High Trewhitt . . .188 C3
High Valleyfield .208 B3
Highway 44 B4
Highweek 12 D3
High Westwood .178 D3
High Wray 154 B2
High Wych 69 B4
High Wycombe. . .66 D3
Hilborough 103 A4
Hilcote 131 D4
Hilcott. 45 D5
Hildenborough . . .36 B3
Hilden Park 36 B3
Hildersham 86 C1
Hilderstone 112 B3
Hilderthorpe 151 A4
Hilfield 15 A6
Hilgay 102 B2
Hill Pembs 55 D7
S Glos 62 D2
W Mid. 96 B4
Hillam 140 A3
Hillbeck 165 D5
Hillborough. 53 C4
Hillbrae Aberds . .255 B7
Aberds 256 D2
Hill Brow 33 C6
Hillbutts 16 A3
Hillclifflane 113 A6
Hillcommon. 27 C6
Hill Dale 136 B3
Hill Dyke. 117 A6
Hillend 208 B4
Hill End Durham. 166 B3
Fife. 208 A3
N Yorks. 147 B4
Hillerton 12 B2
Hillesden 66 A1
Hillesley 43 A6
Hillfarance 27 C6
Hillhead Aberds .255 C6
Devon. 8 B3
S Ayrs 182 A2
Hill Head Hants . .18 A4
Northumb. 178 C1
Hillhead of
Auchentumb. . .269 D4
Hillhead of
Cocklaw. 257 B5
Hillhouse 197 A4
Hilliclay 280 B3
Hillingdon 48 A3
Hillington
Glasgow 205 B5
Norf 119 C4
Hillmorton 98 D2
Hill Mountain 55 D5

Hillockhead
Aberds 243 B6
Aberds 244 A1
Hill of Beath 209 A4
Hill of Fearn 265 C4
Hill of
Mountblairy . .268 D1
Hill Ridware 113 D4
Hillside Aberds. .245 C6
Angus. 233 B5
Mers. 136 B2
Orkney 283 H5
Shetland. 285 G6
Hillswick 284 F4
Hill Top Durham. 166 C2
Hants. 18 A3
W Mid. 96 B2
W Yorks 139 B6
Hill View. 16 B3
Hillway 19 C5
Hillwell 285 M5
Hilmarton. 44 B4
Hilperton 44 D2
Hilsea 19 A5
Hilston 151 D5
Hilton Aberds . . .257 C4
Cambs 85 A4
Cumb 165 C5
Derbys 113 B6
Dorset 16 A1
Durham 167 C4
Highld 264 B3
Shrops 95 B5
Stockton. 168 D2
Hilton of
Cadboll 265 C4
Himbleton 80 B2
Himley 96 B1
Hincaster 154 C4
Hinckley 98 B1
Hinderclay 103 D6
Hinderton 126 B3
Hinderwell 169 D5
Hindford 110 B2
Hindhead 34 C1
Hindley 137 C5
Hindley Green. . .137 C5
Hindlip 80 B1
Hindolveston . . .120 C2
Hindon 30 B3
Hindringham . . .120 B1
Hingham 103 A6
Hinstock 111 C5
Hintlesham 88 C1
Hinton Hants. 17 B6
Hereford 78 D1
S Glos. 43 B6
Shrops 94 A2
W Nhants 82 B2
Hinton
Charterhouse. . .43 D6
Hinton-in-the-
Hedges. 82 D2
Hinton Martell . . .17 A4
Hinton on the
Green 80 C3
Hinton Parva 45 A6
Hinton St George 28 D4
Hinton St Mary . .30 D1
Hinton Waldrist . .65 D4
Hints Shrops 95 D4
Staffs 97 A4
Hinwick 83 A6
Hinxhill 38 A2
Hinxton. 85 C6
Hinxworth 84 C4
Hipperholme. . . .139 A4
Hipswell 157 B5
Hirael 123 C5
Hiraeth 73 D4
Hirn 245 B4
Hirnant 109 C5
Hirst N Lanark . .207 D6
Northumb. 179 A4
Hirst Courtney . .140 A4
Hirwaen 125 C5
Hirwaun 59 E6

Hiscott 25 C6
Histon 85 A6
Hitcham 87 B5
Hitchin 68 A1
Hither Green 49 B6
Hittisleigh 12 B2
Hive 149 D7
Hixon 112 C4
Hoaden 53 D4
Hoaldalbert 61 A5
Hoar Cross 113 C5
Hoarwithy 62 A1
Hoath 53 C4
Hobarris 93 D7
Hobbister 283 G4
Hobkirk 187 B4
Hobson 178 D3
Hoby 115 D4
Hockering 120 D2
Hockerton 132 D2
Hockley 70 D2
Hockley Heath . . . 97 D4
Hockliffe 67 A4
Hockwold cum
  Wilton 102 C3
Hockworthy 27 D5
Hoddesdon 68 C3
Hoddlesden . . . 137 A6
Hoddomcross . . . 175 A4
Hoddom Mains . 175 A4
Hodgeston 55 E6
Hodley 93 B5
Hodnet 111 C5
Hodthorpe 131 B5
Hoe Hants 33 D4
  Norf 120 D1
Hoe Gate 33 D5
Hoff 165 D4
Hoggard's Green . 87 B4
Hoggeston 66 A3
Hogha
  Gearraidh . . . 287 G2
Hoghton 137 A5
Hognaston 130 D2
Hog Patch 34 B1
Hogsthorpe . . . 135 B5
Holbeach 117 C6
Holbeach Bank . 117 C6
Holbeach
  Clough 117 C6
Holbeach Drove 117 D6
Holbeach Hurn . 117 C6
Holbeach
  St Johns 117 D6
Holbeach
  St Marks 117 B6
Holbeach
  St Matthew . . . 117 B7
Holbeck Notts . . 131 B5
  W Yorks 148 D1
Holbeck
  Woodhouse . . 131 B5
Holberrow Green . 80 B3
Holbeton 7 B5
Holborn 49 A6
Holbrook Derbys . 114 A1
  Suff 88 D2
  S Yorks 131 A4
Holburn 198 C4
Holbury 18 A3
Holcombe Devon . 13 D4
  Som 29 A6
Holcombe Rogus 27 D5
Holcot 83 A4
Holden 146 C1
Holdenby 82 A3
Holdenhurst . . . 17 B5
Holdgate 94 C3
Holdingham . . . 116 A3
Holditch 14 A3
Holefield 198 C2
Holehouses . . . 128 B2
Hole-in-the-Wall 62 A2
Holemoor 11 A5
Holestane 183 C6
Holford 27 A6
Holgate 149 B4
Holker 154 D2
Holkham 119 A5

Hollacombe 11 A4
Holland Orkney . . 282 B5
  Orkney . . 282 E7
Holland Fen . . . 117 A5
Holland-on-Sea . . 71 B6
Hollandstoun . . 282 B8
Hollee 175 B5
Hollesley 89 C4
Hollicombe 8 A2
Hollingbourne . . . 37 A6
Hollington
  Derbys 113 B6
  E Sus 23 A5
  Staffs 113 B4
Hollington
  Grove 113 B6
Hollingworth . . 138 D3
Hollins 137 C7
Hollinsclough . 129 C5
Hollins Green . 137 D5
Hollins Lane . . 145 B4
Hollinwood
  Gtr Man 138 C2
  Shrops 111 B4
Hollocombe 26 D1
Holloway 130 D3
Hollowell 98 D3
Hollow
  Meadows . . . 130 A2
Hollybush Caerph . 41 A6
  E Ayrs 182 A1
  Worcs 79 D5
Holly End 101 A6
Holly Green . . . 79 C6
Hollywood 143 A5
Holmbridge . . . 139 C4
Holmbury
  St Mary 35 B4
Holmbush 5 B5
Holmcroft 112 C3
Holme Cambs . . 100 C3
  Cumb 154 D4
  Notts 132 D3
  N Yorks 158 C2
  W Yorks 139 C4
Holme Chapel . . 138 A1
Holme Green . . 149 C4
Holme Hale . . . 103 A4
Holme Lacy 78 D3
Holme Marsh . . 78 B1
Holme next the
  Sea 119 A4
Holme-on-Spalding-
  Moor 149 D7
Holme on the
  Wolds 150 C2
Holme
  Pierrepont . . 115 B4
Holmer 78 C3
Holmer Green . . 67 D4
Holme
  St Cuthbert . . 174 D4
Holmes Chapel . 128 C2
Holmesfield . . 130 B3
Holmeswood . . 136 B3
Holmewood . . . 131 C4
Holme Wood . . 147 D5
Holmfirth 139 C4
Holmhead
  Dumfries 183 D5
  E Ayrs 193 C5
Holmisdale . . . 258 D1
Holmpton 143 A5
Holmrook 153 A1
Holmsgarth . . . 285 J6
Holmwrangle . . 164 A3
Holne 7 A6
Holnest 15 A6
Holsworthy 10 A4
Holsworthy
  Beacon 11 A4
Holt Dorset 17 A4
  Norf 120 B2
  Wilts 44 C2
  Worcs 79 A6
  Wrex 127 D4
Holtby 149 B5
Holt End Hants . . 33 B5
  Worcs 80 A3
Holt Fleet 79 A6
Holt Heath 79 A6

Holton Oxon 65 C7
  Som 29 C6
  Suff 105 D4
Holton cum
  Beckering . . . 133 A6
Holton Heath . . . 16 B3
Holton le Clay . 143 C4
Holton le Moor . 142 D2
Holton St Mary . . 87 D6
Holt Park 147 C6
Holwell Dorset . . 29 D7
  Herts 84 D3
  Leics 115 C5
  Oxon 64 C3
Holwick 166 C2
Holworth 16 C1
Holybourne 33 A6
Holy Cross 96 D2
Holyhead
  =Caergybi . . . 122 B2
Holy Island . . . 199 B5
Holymoorside . . . 19 C3
Holyport 48 B1
Holystone 188 C2
Holytown 207 D5
Holywell Cambs . 101 D5
  Corn 4 B2
  Dorset 15 A5
  E Sus 22 C3
  Northumb 179 B5
Holywell
  =Treffynnon . . 126 B1
Holywell Green . 138 D3
Holywell Lake . . 27 C6
Holywell Row . . 102 D3
Holywood 184 D2
Homer 95 A4
Homersfield . . 104 C4
Hom Green 62 A1
Homington 31 C5
Honeyborough . . . 55 D5
Honeybourne . . . 80 C4
Honeychurch . . . 12 A1
Honey Hill 52 C3
Honey Street . . . 45 C5
Honey Tye 87 D5
Honiley 97 D5
Honing 121 C5
Honingham . . . 120 D3
Honington Lincs . 116 A2
  Suff 103 D5
  Warks 81 C5
Honiton 13 A6
Honley 139 C4
Hood Green . . . 139 C6
Hooe E Sus 23 B4
  Plym 7 B4
Hooe Common . . 23 A4
Hoo Green 128 A2
Hook E Yorks . . 141 A5
  Hants 47 D5
  London 49 C4
  Pembs 55 C5
  Wilts 45 A4
Hooke 15 B5
Hookgate 111 B6
Hook Green Kent . 37 C4
  Kent 50 C3
Hook Norton . . . 81 D6
Hookway 12 B3
Hookwood 35 B5
Hoole 127 C4
Hooley 35 A5
Hoop 61 C7
Hoo St Werburgh . 51 B4
Hooton 126 B3
Hooton Levitt . 140 D3
Hooton Pagnell . 140 C2
Hooton Roberts . 140 D2
Hope Derbys . . . 129 A6
  Devon 7 D5
  Highld 277 C5
  Powys 93 A6
  Shrops 94 A1
  Staffs 129 D5
Hope = Yr Hôb . 126 D3
Hope Bagot 94 D3
Hope Bowdler . . 94 B2
Hope Green . . . 129 A4
Hopeman 266 C2
Hope Mansell . . 62 B2

Hopesay 94 C1
Hope's Green . . . 51 A4
Hope under
  Dinmore 78 B3
Hopley's Green . . 78 B1
Hopperton 148 B3
Hop Pole 117 D4
Hopstone 95 B5
Hopton Shrops . 110 C2
  Shrops 111 C4
  Staffs 112 C3
  Suff 103 D5
Hopton
  Cangeford 94 C3
Hopton Castle . . 94 D1
Hoptonheath . . . 94 D1
Hopton on Sea . . 105 A6
Hopton Wafers . . 95 D4
Hopwas 97 A4
Hopwood
  Worcs 96 D3
  Gtr Man 138 C1
Horam 22 A3
Horbling 116 B4
Horbury 139 B5
Horcott 64 C2
Horden 168 A2
Horderley 94 C2
Hordle 17 B6
Hordley 110 B2
Horeb Carms . . . 57 B4
  Carms 58 C2
  Ceredig 73 B6
Horfield 43 B5
Horham 104 D3
Horkesley Heath . 70 A3
Horkstow 142 B1
Horley Oxon . . . 81 C7
  Sur 35 B5
Hornblotton
  Green 29 B5
Hornby Lancs . . 145 A5
  N Yorks 157 B6
  N Yorks 158 A2
Horncastle . . . 134 C2
Hornchurch 50 A2
Horncliffe . . . 198 B3
Horndean
  Borders 198 B2
  Hants 33 D6
Horndon 11 D6
Horndon on the
  Hill 50 A3
Horne 35 B6
Horniehaugh . . 232 B2
Horning 121 D5
Horninghold . . . 99 B5
Horninglow . . . 113 C6
Horningsea 85 A6
Horningsham . . . 30 A2
Horningtoft . . 119 C6
Hornsby 176 D3
Horns Corner . . 37 D5
Horns Cross
  Devon 25 C4
  E Sus 37 D6
Hornsea 151 C5
Hornsea Bridge . 151 C5
Hornsey 49 A6
Hornton 81 C6
Horrabridge 7 A4
Horringer 87 A4
Horringford . . . 18 C4
Horsebridge
  Devon 11 D5
  Hants 32 B2
Horse Bridge . 129 D4
Horsebrook . . . 112 D2
Horsehay 95 A4
Horseheath 86 C2
Horsehouse . . . 156 C4
Horsell 34 A2
Horseman's
  Green 110 A3
Horseway 101 C6
Horsey 121 C6
Horsford 120 D3
Horsforth 147 D6
Horsham Worcs . . 79 B5
  W Sus 35 C4
Horsham
  St Faith 120 D4

Horsington Lincs 134 C1
  Som 29 C7
Horsley Derbys . . 114 A1
  Glos 63 D4
  Northumb 178 C2
  Northumb 188 D1
Horsley Cross . . 71 A5
Horsleycross
  Street 71 A5
Horsleyhill . . . 186 B4
Horsleyhope . . . 166 A3
Horsley
  Woodhouse . . 114 A1
Horsmonden . . . 37 B4
Horspath 65 C6
Horstead 121 D4
Horsted Keynes . . 36 D1
Horton Bucks . . . 67 B4
  Dorset 17 A4
  Lancs 146 B2
  S Glos 43 A6
  Shrops 110 C3
  Som 28 D3
  Staffs 129 D4
  Swansea 57 D4
  Wilts 45 C4
  Windsor 48 B3
  W Nhants 83 B5
Horton-cum-
  Studley 65 B6
Horton Green . . 110 A3
Horton Heath . . 32 D3
Horton in
  Ribblesdale . . 155 D7
Horton Kirby . . 50 C2
Hortonlane . . . 110 D3
Horwich 137 B5
Horwich End . . 129 A5
Horwood 25 C6
Hose 115 C5
Hoselaw 198 C2
Hoses 153 A3
Hosh 218 B3
Hosta 287 G2
Hoswick 285 L6
Hotham 150 D1
Hothfield 38 A1
Hoton 114 C3
Houbie 284 D8
Houdston 181 B3
Hough Ches E . 128 B3
  Ches E 128 D2
Hougham 116 A1
Hough Green . . 127 A4
Hough-on-the-
  Hill 116 A2
Houghton Cambs 101 D4
  Cumb 175 C7
  Hants 32 B2
  Pembs 55 D5
  W Sus 20 A3
Houghton
  Conquest 84 C2
Houghton Green
  E Sus 37 D7
  Warr 137 D5
Houghton-le-
  Side 167 C5
Houghton-le-
  Spring 167 A6
Houghton on the
  Hill 98 A3
Houghton Regis . 67 A5
Houghton
  St Giles 119 B6
Houlland
  Shetland 284 F7
  Shetland 285 H5
Houlsyke 159 A6
Hound 18 A3
Hound Green . . 47 D5
Houndslow . . . 197 B5
Houndwood . . . 211 D5
Hounslow 48 B4
Hounslow Green . 69 B6
Housay 284 F8
House of Daviot 252 B3
House of
  Glenmuick . . . 243 C6
Housetter 284 E5
Houss 285 K5
Houston 205 B4

Houstry 275 A5
Houton 283 G4
Hove 21 B5
Hoveringham . . 115 A4
Hoveton 121 D5
Hovingham . . . 159 D5
How 176 D3
Howbrook 139 D6
Howden Borders . 187 A5
  E Yorks 141 A5
Howden-le-
  Wear 167 B4
Howe Highld . . 281 B5
  Norf 104 A3
  N Yorks 158 C2
Howe Bridge . . 137 C5
Howe Green . . . 70 C1
Howell 116 A4
How End 84 C2
Howe of
  Teuchar 256 B2
Howe Street Essex 69 B6
  Essex 86 D2
Howey 77 B4
Howgate 196 A1
How Green 36 B2
Howick 189 B5
Howle Durham . 166 C3
  Telford 111 C5
Howlett End . . . 86 D1
Howley 14 A2
Hownam 187 B6
Hownam Mains . 187 A6
Howpasley . . . 185 B6
Howsham
  N Lincs 142 C2
  N Yorks 149 A6
Howslack 184 B3
Howtel 198 C2
Howton 61 A6
Howtown 164 D2
Howwood 204 B3
Hoxne 104 D2
Hoy 283 G3
Hoylake 126 A2
Hoyland 139 C6
Hoylandswaine . 139 C5
Hubberholme . . 156 D3
Hubbert's
  Bridge 117 A5
Huby N Yorks . . 147 C6
  N Yorks 149 A4
Hucclecote 63 B4
Hucking 37 A6
Hucknall 114 A3
Huddersfield . 139 B4
Huddington . . . 80 B2
Hudswell 157 A5
Huggate 150 B1
Hugglescote . . 114 D2
Hughenden
  Valley 66 D3
Hughley 94 B3
Hugh Town Scilly . 2 E1
Huish Devon . . . 25 D6
  Wilts 45 C5
Huish
  Champflower . . 27 C5
Huish Episcopi . 28 C4
Huisinis 287 C4
Hulcott 66 B3
Hulland 113 A6
Hulland Ward . . 113 A6
Hullavington . . 44 A2
Hullbridge 70 D2
Hulme 138 D1
Hulme End . . . 129 D6
Hulme Walfield . 128 C3
Hulverstone . . . 18 C2
Hulver Street . 105 C5
Humber 78 B3
Humber Bridge . 142 A2
Humberston . . 143 C5
Humbie 210 D1
Humbleton
  E Yorks 151 D5
  Northumb 188 A3
Humby 116 B3
Hume 197 B6
Humshaugh . . . 177 B7
Huna 281 A5

Huncoat 146 D1
Huncote 98 B2
Hundalee 187 B5
Hunderthwaite . .166 C2
Hundleby 134 C3
Hundle Houses . .134 D2
Hundleton 55 D5
Hundon. 86 C3
Hundred Acres . . .33 D4
Hundred End. . . .136 A3
Hundred House . . .77 B5
Hungarton 98 A3
Hungerford Hants 31 D5
  W Berks 46 C1
Hungerford
  Newtown 46 B1
Hungerton 116 C1
Hungladder 258 A3
Hunmanby 161 D4
Hunmanby
  Moor. 161 D5
Hunningham 81 A6
Hunny Hill 18 C3
Hunsdon. 68 B4
Hunsingore 148 B3
Hunslet. 148 D2
Hunsonby. 164 B3
Hunspow 280 A4
Hunstanton 118 A3
Hunstanworth. . .166 A2
Hunsterson 111 A5
Hunston Suff 87 A5
  W Sus. 20 B1
Hunstrete. 43 C5
Hunt End 80 A3
Hunter's Quay . .203 A6
Hunthill Lodge . .232 A2
Huntingdon 100 D4
Huntingfield 104 D4
Huntingford. 30 B2
Huntington
  E Loth 210 C1
  Hereford 77 D6
  Staffs 112 D3
  York 149 B5
Huntingtower . . .219 B5
Huntley. 62 B3
Huntly 255 C6
Huntlywood 197 B5
Hunton Kent 37 B5
  N Yorks. 157 B5
Hunt's Corner . . .103 C6
Hunt's Cross 127 A4
Huntsham 27 C5
Huntspill. 28 A3
Huntworth 28 B3
Hunwick. 167 B4
Hunworth. 120 B2
Hurdsfield 129 B4
Hurley Warks 97 B5
  Windsor 47 A6
Hurlford 193 B4
Hurliness 283 J3
Hurn 17 B5
Hurn's End. 118 A1
Hursley 32 C3
Hurst N Yorks 156 A4
  Som 29 D4
  Wokingham 47 B5
Hurstbourne
  Priors. 32 A3
Hurstbourne
  Tarrant. 46 D1
Hurst Green
  E Sus 37 D5
  Lancs 145 D6
Hurstpierpoint . . .21 A5
Hurst Wickham. . .21 A5
Hurstwood. 146 D2
Hurtmore 34 B2
Hurworth Place .157 A6
Hury. 166 D2
Husabost 258 C2
Husbands
  Bosworth. 98 C3
Husborne
  Crawley 83 D6
Husthwaite 158 D4
Hutchwns. 40 D3
Huthwaite 131 D4
Huttoft 135 B5
Hutton Borders. . .198 A3

Hutton continued
  Cumb 164 C2
  Essex 69 D6
  E Yorks 150 B3
  Lancs 136 A3
  N Som. 42 D2
Hutton Buscel . . .160 C3
Hutton Conyers .158 D2
Hutton
  Cranswick. 150 B3
Hutton End 164 B2
Hutton Gate. . . .168 D3
Hutton Henry . . .168 B2
Hutton-le-Hole .159 B6
Hutton Magna. . .166 D4
Hutton Roof
  Cumb 155 D4
  Cumb 163 A6
Hutton Rudby . . .158 A3
Hutton Sessay. . .158 D3
Hutton Village. . .168 D3
Hutton
  Wandesley 148 B4
Huxley. 127 C5
Huxter Shetland . .285 G7
  Shetland. 285 H5
Huxton 211 D5
Huyton 136 D3
Hwlffordd
  =Haverfordwest . . 55 C5
Hycemoor 153 B1
Hyde
  Glos 63 C4
  Gtr Man 138 D2
  Hants 31 D5
Hyde Heath 67 C4
Hyde Park 140 C3
Hydestile 34 B2
Hylton Castle. . . .179 D5
Hyndford Bridge 194 B4
Hynish. 222 D2
Hyssington 93 B7
Hythe Hants 18 A3
  Kent 38 B3
Hythe End 48 B3
Hythie 269 D5

I

Ibberton 16 A1
Ible. 130 D2
Ibsley. 17 A5
Ibstock 114 D2
Ibstone. 66 D2
Ibthorpe 46 D1
Ibworth. 46 D3
Ichrachan 227 C5
Ickburgh. 103 B4
Ickenham 48 A3
Ickford 66 C1
Ickham 53 D4
Ickleford. 84 D3
Icklesham 23 A6
Ickleton 85 C6
Icklingham. 102 D3
Ickwell Green 84 C3
Icomb 64 A3
Idbury 64 B3
Iddesleigh 11 A6
Ide 12 B3
Ideford 12 D3
Ide Hill 36 A2
Iden 37 D7
Iden Green Kent . .37 C5
  Kent 37 C6
Idle. 147 D5
Idlicote 81 C5
Idmiston 31 B5
Idole 57 A4
Idridgehay 113 A6
Idrigill 258 B3
Idstone 45 A6
Idvies 232 D3
Iffley 65 C6
Ifield 35 C5
Ifold. 34 C3
Iford 22 B2
Ifton Heath 110 B2
Ightfield 111 B4
Ightham 36 A3
Iken 89 B5

Ilam 129 D6
Ilchester 29 C5
Ilderton. 188 A3
Ilford 50 A1
Ilfracombe 25 A6
Ilkeston. 114 A2
Ilketshall
  St Andrew 105 C4
Ilketshall
  St Lawrence . . .105 C4
Ilketshall
  St Margaret . . .104 C4
Ilkley 147 C5
Illey 96 C2
Illingworth. 138 A3
Illogan. 3 A4
Illston on the Hill. 99 B4
Ilmer 66 C2
Ilmington 81 C5
Ilminster. 28 D3
Ilsington 12 D2
Ilston. 57 C5
Ilton N Yorks 157 D5
  Som 28 D3
Imachar 202 D3
Imeraval 200 D3
Immingham. 142 B3
Impington 85 A6
Ince 127 B4
Ince Blundell. . . .136 C2
Ince in
  Makerfield 137 C4
Inchbare. 233 B4
Inchberry. 266 D4
Inchbraoch 233 C5
Incheril 262 D2
Inchgrundle. 232 A2
Inchina 261 A6
Inchinnan. 205 B4
Inchkinloch 277 D6
Inchlaggan. 239 B5
Inchlumpie 264 C1
Inchmore 251 B5
Inchnacardoch
  Hotel. 240 A1
Inchnadamph . . .271 B5
Inch of Arnhall . .233 A4
Inchree 237 C4
Inchture 220 B2
Inchyra 219 B6
Indian Queens. 4 B4
Inerval 200 D3
Ingatestone 69 D6
Ingbirchworth. . .139 C5
Ingestre 112 C3
Ingham Lincs 133 A4
  Norf 121 C5
  Suff 103 D4
Ingham Corner . .121 C5
Ingleborough . . .118 D1
Ingleby Derbys . .114 C1
  Lincs. 132 B3
Ingleby Arncliffe 158 A3
Ingleby Barwick 168 D2
Ingleby
  Greenhow 159 A4
Inglemire 150 D3
Inglesbatch 43 C6
Inglesham 64 D3
Ingleton Durham .167 C4
  N Yorks. 155 D5
Inglewhite 145 C5
Ingliston 208 C4
Ingoe. 178 B2
Ingol 145 D5
Ingoldisthorpe . .118 B3
Ingoldmells 135 C5
Ingoldsby 116 B3
Ingon. 81 B5
Ingram 188 B3
Ingrow. 147 D4
Ings 154 B3
Ingst 43 A4
Ingworth. 120 C3
Inham's End 101 B4
Inkberrow 80 B3
Inkpen. 46 C1
Inkstack 281 A4
Inn 154 A3
Innellan 203 A6
Innerleithen 196 C2
Innerleven 220 D3

Innermessan 170 A2
Innerwick E Loth .211 C4
  Perth 229 D4
Innis Chonain . . .227 D6
Insch 256 D1
Insh 241 B6
Inshore 276 B4
Inskip 145 D4
Instoneville 140 B3
Instow . . . . , 25 B5
Intake 140 C3
Inver Aberds 243 C5
  Highld. 265 B4
  Perth 230 D4
Inverailort 235 B6
Inveraldie. 220 A4
Inveralligin 249 A5
Inverallochy. 269 C5
Inveran 264 A1
Inveraray 214 B3
Inverarish. 248 C2
Inverarity 232 D2
Inverarnan 215 A6
Inverasdale 261 B5
Inverbeg. 206 A1
Inverbervie 233 A6
Inverboyndie. . . .268 C1
Inverbroom 262 B3
Invercassley 272 D2
Invercauld
  House. 243 C4
Inverchaolain . . .203 A5
Invercharnan. . . .227 B6
Inverchoran 251 A4
Invercreran 227 B5
Inverdruie 242 A2
Inverebrie 257 C4
Invereck 215 D4
Inverernan
  House. 243 A6
Invereshie
  House. 241 B6
Inveresk 209 C6
Inverey 242 D3
Inverfarigaig 251 D7
Invergarry 239 B7
Invergelder 243 C5
Invergeldie 218 B2
Invergordon 264 D3
Invergowrie. 220 A3
Inverguseran 247 D6
Inverhadden 229 C5
Inverharroch. . . .255 C4
Inverherive 216 B3
Inverie. 247 E6
Inverinan 214 A2
Inverinate 249 D6
Inverkeilor 233 D4
Inverkeithing. . . .208 B4
Inverkeithny 256 B1
Inverkip 204 A2
Inverkirkaig. 270 C3
Inverlael 262 B3
Inverlochlarig . . .216 C4
Inverlochy Argyll .227 D6
  Highld. 237 B5
Inverlussa 213 D4
Inver Mallie 239 D5
Invermark
  Lodge. 244 D1
Invermoidart . . .235 C5
Invermoriston. . .240 A2
Invernaver 278 B3
Inverneill 213 D6
Inverness 252 B2
Invernettie. 257 B6
Invernoaden 215 C4
Inveroran Hotel .228 D1
Inverpolly
  Lodge. 270 C3
Inverquharity . . .232 C2
Inverquhomery . .257 B5
Inverroy 239 D6
Inversanda 236 D3
Invershiel. 238 A3
Invershin 264 A1
Inversnaid Hotel 215 B6
Inveruglas 215 B6
Inveruglass 241 B6
Inverurie. 256 D2
Invervar 229 D5

Inverythan 256 B2
Inwardleigh 11 B6
Inworth. 70 B2
Iochdar. 286 B3
Iping 34 D1
Ipplepen. 8 A2
Ipsden. 47 A4
Ipsley. 80 A3
Ipstones 129 D5
Ipswich 88 C2
Irby 126 A2
Irby in the
  Marsh. 135 C4
Irby upon
  Humber 142 C3
Irchester. 83 A6
Ireby
  Cumb 163 A5
  Lancs 155 D5
Ireland
  Orkney 283 G4
  Shetland. 285 L5
Ireland's Cross . .111 A6
Ireleth 153 C3
Ireshopeburn . . .165 B6
Irlam 137 D6
Irnham 116 C3
Iron Acton 43 A5
Ironbridge 95 A4
Iron Cross 80 B3
Irongray 173 A7
Ironmacannie . . .173 A4
Ironside 268 D3
Ironville 131 D4
Irstead 121 C5
Irthington 176 C2
Irthlingborough . .99 D6
Irton 160 C4
Irvine 192 B3
Isauld 279 B5
Isbister
  Orkney 282 E3
  Orkney 282 F4
  Shetland. 284 D5
  Shetland. 285 G7
Isfield 22 A2
Isham 99 D5
Isle Abbotts 28 C3
Isle Brewers 28 C3
Isleham. 102 D2
Isle of
  Whithorn 171 D6
Isleornsay 247 C6
Islesburgh 284 G5
Islesteps. 174 A2
Isleworth 49 B4
Isley Walton 114 C2
Islibhig 287 B4
Islington 49 A6
Islip N Hhants 100 D1
  Oxon. 65 B6
Istead Rise. 50 C3
Isycoed 127 D4
Itchen 32 D3
Itchen Abbas 32 B4
Itchen Stoke 33 B4
Itchingfield 35 D4
Itchington 43 A5
Itteringham 120 B3
Itton 12 B1
Itton Common. . .61 D6
Ivegill 164 A2
Iver 48 A3
Iver Heath 48 A3
Iveston 178 D3
Ivinghoe. 67 B4
Ivinghoe Aston . .67 B4
Ivington 78 B2
Ivington Green . . .78 B2
Ivybridge 7 B5
Ivy Chimneys. . . .68 C4
Ivychurch 38 C2
Ivy Cross. 30 C2
Ivy Hatch 36 A3
Iwade 51 C6
Iwerne Courtney or
  Shroton 30 D2
Iwerne
  Minster 30 D2
Ixworth 103 D5
Ixworth
  Thorpe 103 D5

J

Jack Hill 147 B6
Jack in the Green 13 B5
Jacksdale. 131 D4
Jackstown 256 C2
Jacobstow 10 B2
Jacobstowe. 11 A6
Jameston 55 E6
Jamestown
  Dumfries 185 C6
  Highld. 251 A6
  W Dunb. 206 B1
Jarrow 179 C5
Jarvis Brook 36 D3
Jasper's Green . . .69 A7
Java 225 C6
Jawcraig 207 C6
Jaywick 71 B5
Jealott's Hill 47 B6
Jedburgh 187 A5
Jeffreyston 55 D6
Jellyhill. 205 A6
Jemimaville. 264 D3
Jersey Farm 67 C6
Jesmond 179 C4
Jevington. 22 B3
Jockey End 67 B5
Johnby 164 B2
John o' Groats . .281 A5
John's Cross 37 D5
Johnshaven 233 B5
Johnston 55 C5
Johnstone 205 B4
Johnstonebridge
  . . . . .184 C3
Johnstown Carms 57 A4
  Wrex 110 A2
Joppa Edin 209 C6
  S Ayrs. 182 A2
Jordans 67 D4
Jordanthorpe . . .130 A3
Jump. 140 C1
Jumpers Green. . .17 B5
Juniper Green. . .209 D4
Jurby East 152 B3
Jurby West 152 B3

K

Kaber 165 D5
Kaimend. 195 B4
Kaimes 209 D5
Kalemouth. 187 A6
Kames Argyll. . . .203 A4
  Argyll 213 A6
  E Ayrs. 194 D1
Kea 4 C3
Keadby 141 B6
Keal Cotes 134 C3
Kearsley 137 C6
Kearstwick. 155 C5
Kearton. 156 B3
Kearvaig 276 A3
Keasden 145 A7
Keckwick 127 A5
Keddington 134 A3
Kedington 86 C3
Kedleston 113 A7
Keelby. 142 B3
Keele 112 A2
Keeley Green 84 C2
Keeston 55 C5
Keevil 44 D3
Kegworth. 114 C2
Kehelland 3 A4
Keig 244 A3
Keighley 147 C4
Keil 236 D3
Keilarsbrae 208 A1
Keilhill 268 D2
Keillmore. 213 D4
Keillor 231 D6
Keillour 219 B4
Keills 201 B4
Keils 201 B5

Keinton
Mandeville 29 B5
Keir Mill 183 C6
Keisby 116 C3
Keiss 281 B5
Keith 267 D5
Keith Inch 257 B6
Keithock 233 B4
Kelbrook 146 C3
Kelby 116 A3
Keld Cumb 164 D3
N Yorks 156 A2
Keldholme 159 C6
Kelfield N Lincs . 141 C6
N Yorks 149 D4
Kelham 132 D2
Kellan 225 B4
Kellas Angus . . . 221 A4
Moray 266 D2
Kellaton 8 D2
Kelleth 155 A5
Kelleythorpe . . . 150 B2
Kelling 120 A2
Kellingley 140 A3
Kellington 140 A3
Kelloe 167 B6
Kelloholm 183 A5
Kelly 11 C4
Kelly Bray 11 D4
Kelmarsh 99 D4
Kelmscot 64 D3
Kelsale 89 A4
Kelsall 127 C5
Kelsall Hill 127 C5
Kelshall 85 D5
Kelsick 175 C4
Kelso 197 C6
Kelstedge 130 C3
Kelstern 143 D4
Kelston 43 C6
Keltneyburn . . . 229 D6
Kelton 174 A2
Kelty 208 A4
Kelvedon 70 B2
Kelvedon Hatch . 69 D5
Kelvin 205 C6
Kelvinside 205 B5
Kelynack 2 B1
Kemback 220 C4
Kemberton 95 A5
Kemble 63 D5
Kemerton 80 D2
Kemeys
Commander . . 61 C5
Kemnay 245 A4
Kempley 62 A2
Kempsey 79 C6
Kempsford 64 D2
Kemps Green . . . 96 D4
Kempshott 47 D4
Kempston 84 C2
Kempston
Hardwick 84 C2
Kempton 94 C1
Kemp Town 21 B6
Kemsing 36 A3
Kemsley 51 C6
Kenardington . . . 38 B1
Kenchester 78 C2
Kencot 64 C3
Kendal 154 B4
Kendoon 182 D4
Kendray 139 C6
Kenfig 40 C3
Kenfig Hill 40 C3
Kenilworth 97 D5
Kenknock 217 A4
Kenley London . . 35 A6
Shrops 94 A3
Kenmore Highld . 249 A4
Perth 230 D1
Kenn Devon 13 C4
N Som 42 C3
Kennacley 288 H2
Kennacraig 202 B3
Kennerleigh 12 A3
Kennet 208 A2
Kennethmont . . 255 D6
Kennett 86 A2

Kennford 13 C4
Kenninghall . . . 103 C6
Kenninghall
Heath 103 C6
Kennington Kent . 38 A2
Oxon 65 C6
Kennoway 220 D3
Kenny Hill 102 D2
Kennythorpe . . . 149 A6
Kenovay 222 C2
Kensaleyre 259 C4
Kensington 49 B5
Kensworth 67 B5
Kensworth
Common 67 B5
Kentallen 237 D4
Kentchurch 61 A6
Kentford 86 A3
Kentisbeare 13 A5
Kentisbury 25 A7
Kentisbury Ford . 25 A7
Kentmere 154 A3
Kenton Devon . . 13 C4
Suff 88 A2
T&W 179 C4
Kenton
Bankfoot . . . 179 C4
Kentra 235 D5
Kents Bank 154 D2
Kent's Green . . . 62 A3
Kent's Oak 32 C2
Kent Street E Sus . 23 A5
Kent 37 A4
W Sus 35 D5
Kenwick 110 B3
Kenwyn 4 C3
Keoldale 277 B4
Keppanach 237 C4
Keppoch 249 D6
Keprigan 190 D2
Kepwick 158 B3
Keresley 97 C6
Kernborough 8 C1
Kerne Bridge . . . 62 B1
Kerris 2 C2
Kerry 93 C5
Kerrycroy 203 B6
Kerrysdale 261 C5
Kerry's Gate 78 D1
Kersall 132 C2
Kersey 87 C6
Kershopefoot . . . 176 A2
Kersoe 80 D2
Kerswell 13 A5
Kerswell Green . . 79 C6
Kesgrave 88 C3
Kessingland . . . 105 C6
Kessingland
Beach 105 C6
Kessington 205 A5
Kestle 5 C4
Kestle Mill 4 B3
Keston 49 C7
Keswick Cumb . . 163 B5
Norf 104 A3
Norf 121 B5
Ketley 111 D5
Ketley Bank 111 D5
Ketsby 134 B3
Kettering 99 D5
Ketteringham . . 104 A2
Kettins 220 A2
Kettlebaston 87 B5
Kettlebridge . . . 220 D3
Kettleburgh 88 A3
Kettlehill 220 D3
Kettleholm 174 A4
Kettleness 169 D6
Kettleshume . . . 129 B4
Kettlesing
Bottom 147 B6
Kettlesing Head . 147 B6
Kettlestone 119 B6
Kettlethorpe . . . 132 B3
Kettletoft 282 D7
Kettlewell 104 D3
Ketton 100 A1
Kew 49 B4
Kew Bridge 49 B4
Kewstoke 42 C2
Kexbrough 139 C6

Kexby Lincs 132 A3
York 149 B6
Key Green 128 C3
Keyham 98 A3
Keyhaven 18 B2
Keyingham 143 A4
Keymer 21 A6
Keynsham 43 C5
Keysoe 84 A2
Keysoe Row 84 A2
Keyston 100 D2
Keyworth 115 B4
Kibblesworth . . . 179 D4
Kibworth
Beauchamp . . 98 B3
Kibworth
Harcourt 98 B3
Kidbrooke 49 B7
Kiddemore Green 95 A6
Kidderminster . . . 95 D6
Kiddington 65 A5
Kidlington 65 B5
Kidmore End . . . 47 B4
Kidsgrove 128 D3
Kidstones 156 C3
Kidwelly
=Cydweli 57 B4
Kiel Crofts 226 C4
Kielder 187 D5
Kierfiold Ho 282 F3
Kilbagie 208 B2
Kilbarchan 205 B4
Kilbeg 247 D5
Kilberry 202 B2
Kilbirnie 204 C3
Kilbride Argyll . . 226 D3
Argyll 226 D4
Highld 247 B4
Kilburn Angus . . 232 B1
Derbys 114 A1
London 49 A5
N Yorks 158 D4
Kilby 98 B3
Kilchamaig 202 B3
Kilchattan 212 C1
Kilchattan Bay . 203 C6
Kilchenzie 190 C2
Kilcheran 226 C3
Kilchiaran 200 B2
Kilchoan Argyll . 213 A5
Highld 234 D3
Kilchoman 200 B2
Kilchrenan 227 D5
Kilconquhar . . . 221 D4
Kilcot 62 A2
Kilcoy 252 A1
Kilcreggan 215 D5
Kildale 159 A5
Kildalloig 190 D3
Kildary 264 C3
Kildermorie
Lodge 263 C7
Kildonan 191 C6
Kildonan Lodge . 274 B3
Kildonnan 234 B3
Kildrummy 244 A1
Kildwick 147 C4
Kilfinan 203 A4
Kilfinnan 239 C6
Kilgetty 56 B1
Kilgwrrwg
Common 61 D6
Kilham E Yorks . . 150 A3
Northumb 198 C4
Kilkenneth 222 C2
Kilkerran 190 D3
Kilkhampton 24 D3
Killamarsh 131 A4
Killay 57 C6
Killbeg 225 B5
Killean 202 D1
Killearn 206 B3
Killen 252 A2
Killerby 167 D4
Killichonan 229 C4
Killiechonate . . . 239 D6
Killiechronan . . . 225 B5
Killiecrankie . . . 230 B3
Killiemor 224 C3
Killiemore
House 224 D3
Killilan 249 C6

Killimster 281 C5
Killin 217 A5
Killinallan 200 A3
Killinghall 148 B1
Killington 155 C5
Killingworth . . . 179 B4
Killin Lodge . . . 240 B3
Killmahumaig . . 213 C5
Killochyett 196 B3
Killocraw 190 B2
Killundine 225 B4
Kilmacolm 204 B3
Kilmaha 214 B2
Kilmahog 217 D6
Kilmalieu 236 D2
Kilmaluag 259 A4
Kilmany 220 B3
Kilmarie 247 C4
Kilmarnock 193 B4
Kilmaron Castle . 220 C3
Kilmartin 213 C6
Kilmaurs 205 D4
Kilmelford 213 A6
Kilmeny 200 B3
Kilmersdon 43 D5
Kilmeston 33 C4
Kilmichael 190 C2
Kilmichael
Glassary . . . 214 C1
Kilmichael of
Inverlussa . . 213 D5
Kilmington Devon . 14 B2
Wilts 30 B1
Kilmonivaig . . . 239 D5
Kilmorack 251 B6
Kilmore Argyll . . 226 D3
Highld 247 D5
Kilmory Argyll . . 202 A2
Highld 235 C4
Highld 246 D2
N Ayrs 191 C5
Kilmuir Highld . . 252 B2
Highld 258 A3
Highld 258 D2
Highld 264 C3
Kilmun Argyll . . 214 A2
Argyll 215 D4
Kilncadzow 194 B3
Kildown 37 C5
Kilnhurst 140 D2
Kilninian 224 B2
Kilninver 226 D3
Kiln Pit Hill 178 D2
Kilnsea 143 B6
Kilnsey 146 A3
Kilnwick 150 C2
Kilnwick Percy . 149 B7
Kiloran 212 C1
Kilpatrick 191 C5
Kilpeck 78 D2
Kilphedir 274 C3
Kilpin 141 A5
Kilpin Pike 141 A5
Kilrenny 221 D5
Kilsby 98 D2
Kilspindie 220 B2
Kilsyth 207 C5
Kiltarlity 251 B7
Kilton Notts 131 B5
Som 27 A6
Kilton Thorpe . . 169 D4
Kilvaxter 258 B3
Kilve 27 A6
Kilvington 115 A5
Kilwinning 204 D3
Kimberley Norf . 103 A6
Notts 114 A3
Kimberworth . . . 140 D2
Kimblesworth . . 167 A5
Kimble Wick 66 C3
Kimbolton Cambs . 84 A2
Hereford 78 A3
Kimcote 98 C2
Kimmeridge 16 D3
Kimmerston . . . 198 C3
Kimpton Hants . . 32 A1
Herts 68 B1
Kinbrace 274 A2
Kinbuck 218 D2
Kincaple 221 C5
Kincardine Fife . 208 B2
Highld 264 B2

Kincardine
Bridge 208 B2
Kincardine
O'Neil 244 C2
Kinclaven 219 A6
Kincorth 245 B6
Kincorth House . 265 D6
Kincraig 241 B6
Kincraigie 230 D3
Kindallachan . . . 230 D3
Kineton Glos 64 A1
Warks 81 B6
Kinfauns 219 B6
Kingairloch 236 D2
Kingarth 203 C5
Kingcoed 61 C6
King Edward . . . 268 D2
Kingerby 142 D2
Kingham 64 A3
Kingholm Quay . 174 A2
Kinghorn 209 B5
Kingie 239 B5
Kinglassie 209 A5
Kingoodie 220 B3
King's Acre 78 C2
Kingsand 6 B3
Kingsbarns 221 C5
Kingsbridge Devon . 7 C6
Som 27 B4
King's Bromley . 113 C5
Kingsburgh 258 C3
Kingsbury London . 49 A5
Warks 97 B5
Kingsbury
Episcopi 28 C4
King's Caple 62 A1
Kingsclere 46 D3
King's Cliffe . . . 100 B2
Kingscote 63 D4
Kingscott 25 D6
King's Coughton . 80 B3
Kingscross 191 C6
Kingsdon 29 C5
Kingsdown 39 A5
Kingseat 208 A4
Kingsey 66 C2
Kingsfold 35 C4
Kingsford E Ayrs . 205 D4
Worcs 95 C6
Kingsforth 142 B2
Kingsgate 53 B5
Kingsheanton . . 25 B6
King's Heath 96 C3
Kings Hedges . . . 85 A6
King's Hill 37 A4
Kingshouse
Hotel 237 D6
Kingside Hill . . . 175 C4
Kingskerswell . . . 8 A2
Kingskettle 220 D3
Kingsland
Anglesey . . . 122 B2
Hereford 78 A2
Kings Langley . . 67 C5
Kingsley Ches W . 127 B5
Hants 33 B6
Staffs 112 A4
Kingsley Green . 34 C1
Kingsley Holt . . 112 A4
Kingsley Park . . . 83 A4
King's Lynn 118 C3
King's Meaburn . 165 C4
King's Mills 110 A2
Kingsmuir Angus . 232 D2
Fife 221 D5
Kings Muir 196 C1
King's Newnham . 98 D1
King's Newton . . 114 C1
Kingsnorth 38 B2
King's Norton
Leics 98 A3
W Mid 96 D3
King's Nympton . 26 D1
King's Pyon 78 B2
King's Ripton . . . 101 D4
King's Somborne . 32 B2
King's Stag 30 D1
King's Stanley . . . 63 C4
King's Sutton . . . 82 D1
Kingstanding . . . 96 B3
Kingsteignton . . 12 D3
King Sterndale . 129 B5

King's Thorn . . . 78 D3
Kingsthorpe 83 A4
Kingston Cambs . 85 B5
Devon 7 C5
Dorset 16 A1
Dorset 16 D3
E Loth 210 B2
Hants 17 A5
IoW 18 C3
Kent 52 D3
Moray 266 C4
Kingston
Bagpuize 65 D5
Kingston Blount . 66 D2
Kingston by Sea . 21 B5
Kingston Deverill . 30 B2
Kingstone
Hereford 78 D2
Som 28 D3
Staffs 113 C4
Kingston Gorse . 20 B3
Kingston Lisle . . 45 A7
Kingston
Maurward . . . 15 B7
Kingston near
Lewes 22 B1
Kingston on
Soar 114 C3
Kingston Russell . 15 B5
Kingston St Mary . 28 C2
Kingston
Seymour 42 C3
Kingston Upon
Hull 142 A2
Kingston upon
Thames 49 C4
Kingston Vale . . 49 B5
Kingstown 175 C6
King's Walden . . 67 A6
Kingswear 8 B2
Kingswells 245 B5
Kingswinford . . . 96 C1
Kingswood Bucks . 66 B1
Glos 62 D3
Hereford 77 B6
Kent 37 A6
Powys 93 A6
S Glos 43 B5
Sur 35 A5
Warks 97 D4
Kings Worthy . . . 32 B3
Kingthorpe 133 B6
Kington Hereford . 77 B6
Worcs 80 B2
Kington Langley . 44 B3
Kington Magna . 30 C1
Kington
St Michael . . 44 B3
Kingussie 241 B5
Kingweston 29 B5
Kininvie House . 254 B4
Kinkell Bridge . . 218 C4
Kinknockie 257 B5
Kinlet 95 C5
Kinloch Fife . . . 220 C2
Highld 234 A2
Highld 247 C5
Highld 271 A4
Perth 231 D5
Perth 231 D6
Kinlochan 236 C2
Kinlochard 217 D4
Kinlochbeoraid . 238 D2
Kinlochbervie . . 276 C3
Kinlocheil 236 B3
Kinlochewe 262 D2
Kinloch Hourn . 238 B3
Kinloch Laggan . 240 D3
Kinlochleven . . . 237 C5
Kinloch Lodge . . 277 C6
Kinlochmoidart . 235 C6
Kinlochmorar . . 238 C2
Kinlochmore . . . 237 C5
Kinloch
Rannoch . . . 229 C5
Kinlochspelve . . 225 D5
Kinloid 235 B5
Kinloss 265 D6
Kinmel Bay 125 A4
Kinmuck 256 E3
Kinmundy 245 A5
Kinnadie 257 B4

Kin–Lan 317

Kinnaird 220 B2
Kinnaird Castle 233 C4
Kinneff 233 A6
Kinnelhead 184 B3
Kinnell 233 C4
Kinnerley 110 C2
Kinnersley
Hereford 78 C1
Worcs 79 C6
Kinnerton 77 A6
Kinnesswood 219 D6
Kinninvie 166 C3
Kinnordy 232 C1
Kinoulton 115 B4
Kinross 219 D6
Kinrossie 219 A6
Kinsbourne Green 67 B6
Kinsey Heath 111 A5
Kinsham Hereford 78 A1
Worcs 80 D2
Kinsley 140 B2
Kinson 17 B4
Kintbury 46 C1
Kintessack 265 D5
Kintillo 219 C6
Kintocher 244 B2
Kinton Hereford 94 D2
Shrops 110 D2
Kintore 245 A4
Kintour 201 C4
Kintra Argyll 200 D3
Argyll 224 D2
Kintraw 213 B6
Kinuachdrachd 213 C5
Kinveachy 242 A2
Kinver 95 C6
Kippax 148 D3
Kippen 207 A4
Kippford or Scaur 173 C6
Kirbister Orkney 282 E7
Orkney 283 G4
Kirbuster 282 E3
Kirby Bedon 104 A3
Kirby Bellars 115 D5
Kirby Cane 105 B4
Kirby Cross 71 A6
Kirby Grindalythe 150 A2
Kirby Hill
N Yorks 148 A2
N Yorks 157 A5
Kirby Knowle 158 C3
Kirby-le-Soken 71 A6
Kirby Misperton 159 D6
Kirby Muxloe 98 A2
Kirby Row 105 B4
Kirby Sigston 158 B3
Kirby Underdale 149 B7
Kirby Wiske 158 C2
Kirdford 34 D3
Kirk 281 C4
Kirkabister 285 K6
Kirkandrews 172 D4
Kirkandrews upon Eden 175 C6
Kirkbampton 175 C6
Kirkbean 174 C2
Kirk Bramwith 140 B4
Kirkbride 175 C5
Kirkbuddo 232 D3
Kirkburn Borders 196 C1
E Yorks 150 B2
Kirkburton 139 B4
Kirkby Lincs 142 D2
Mers 136 D3
N Yorks 158 A4
Kirkby Fleetham 157 B6
Kirkby Green 133 D5
Kirkby In Ashfield 131 D5
Kirkby-in-Furness 153 B3
Kirkby la Thorpe 116 A4
Kirkby Lonsdale 155 D5
Kirkby Malham 146 A2
Kirkby Mallory 98 A1
Kirkby Malzeard 157 D6
Kirkby Mills 159 C6
Kirkbymoorside 159 C5
Kirkby on Bain 134 C2
Kirkby Overflow 148 C2
Kirkby Stephen 155 A6
Kirkby Thore 165 C4
Kirkby Underwood 116 C3
Kirkby Wharfe 148 C4
Kirkcaldy 209 A5
Kirkcambeck 176 C3
Kirkcarswell 173 D5
Kirkcolm 170 A2
Kirkconnel 183 A5
Kirkconnell 174 B2
Kirkcowan 171 A5
Kirkcudbright 173 C4
Kirkdale 136 D2
Kirk Deighton 148 B2
Kirk Ella 142 A2
Kirkfieldbank 194 B3
Kirkgunzeon 173 B6
Kirk Hallam 114 A2
Kirkham Lancs 144 D4
N Yorks 149 A6
Kirkhamgate 139 A5
Kirk Hammerton 148 B3
Kirkharle 178 A2
Kirkheaton
Northumb 178 B2
W Yorks 139 B4
Kirkhill Angus 233 B4
Highld 252 B1
Midloth 209 D5
Moray 254 C3
Kirkhope 186 A2
Kirkhouse 196 C2
Kirkiboll 277 C6
Kirkibost 247 C4
Kirkinch 231 D7
Kirkinner 171 B6
Kirkintilloch 205 A6
Kirk Ireton 130 D2
Kirkland Cumb 162 C3
Cumb 165 B4
Dumfries 183 A5
Dumfries 183 C6
Kirk Langley 113 B6
Kirkleatham 168 C3
Kirklevington 158 A3
Kirkley 105 B6
Kirklington Notts 132 D1
N Yorks 157 C7
Kirklinton 176 C2
Kirkliston 208 C4
Kirkmaiden 170 D3
Kirk Merrington 167 B5
Kirkmichael
Perth 231 C4
S Ayrs 192 E3
Kirk Michael 152 B3
Kirkmuirhill 194 B2
Kirknewton
Northumb 198 C3
W Loth 208 D4
Kirkney 255 C6
Kirk of Shotts 207 D6
Kirkoswald Cumb 164 A3
S Ayrs 192 E2
Kirkpatrick Durham 173 A5
Kirkpatrick-Fleming 175 A5
Kirk Sandall 140 C4
Kirksanton 153 B2
Kirk Smeaton 140 B3
Kirkstall 147 D6
Kirkstead 134 C1
Kirkstile 255 C6
Kirkstyle 281 A5
Kirkton Aberds 256 D1
Aberds 268 E1
Angus 220 A4
Angus 232 D2
Borders 186 B4
Dumfries 184 D2
Fife 220 B3
Highld 249 B6
Highld 249 D5
Highld 252 A3
Highld 265 A3
Perth 219 C4
S Lanark 194 D4
Stirling 217 D5
Kirktonhill 196 A3
Kirkton Manor 195 C7
Kirkton of Airlie 231 C7
Kirkton of Auchterhouse 220 A3
Kirkton of Auchterless 256 B2
Kirkton of Barevan 253 B4
Kirkton of Bourtie 256 D3
Kirkton of Collace 219 A6
Kirkton of Craig 233 C5
Kirkton of Culsalmond 256 C1
Kirkton of Durris 245 C4
Kirkton of Glenbuchat 243 A6
Kirkton of Glenisla 231 B6
Kirkton of Kingoldrum 232 C1
Kirkton of Largo 220 D4
Kirkton of Lethendy 231 D5
Kirkton of Logie Buchan 257 D4
Kirkton of Maryculter 245 C5
Kirkton of Menmuir 232 B3
Kirkton of Monikie 221 A5
Kirkton of Oyne 256 D1
Kirkton of Rayne 256 D1
Kirkton of Skene 245 B5
Kirkton of Tough 244 A3
Kirktown 269 D5
Kirktown of Alvah 268 C1
Kirktown of Deskford 267 C6
Kirktown of Fetteresso 245 D5
Kirktown of Mortlach 254 C4
Kirktown of Slains 257 D5
Kirkurd 195 B6
Kirkwall 282 F5
Kirkwhelpington 178 A1
Kirk Yetholm 188 A1
Kirmington 142 B3
Kirmond le Mire 142 D3
Kirn 203 A6
Kirriemuir 232 C1
Kirstead Green 104 B3
Kirtlebridge 175 A5
Kirtleton 185 D5
Kirtling 86 B2
Kirtling Green 86 B2
Kirtlington 65 B5
Kirtomy 278 B3
Kirton Lincs 117 B6
Notts 132 C1
Suff 88 D3
Kirton End 117 A5
Kirton Holme 117 A5
Kirton in Lindsey 142 D1
Kislingbury 82 B3
Kites Hardwick 82 A1
Kittisford 27 C5
Kittle 57 D5
Kitt's Green 97 C4
Kitt's Moss 128 A3
Kittybrewster 245 B6
Kitwood 33 B5
Kivernoll 78 D2
Kiveton Park 131 A4
Knaith 132 A3
Knaith Park 132 A3
Knap Corner 30 C2
Knaphill 34 A2
Knapp Perth 220 A2
Som 28 C3
Knapthorpe 132 D2
Knapton Norf 121 B5
Knapton *continued*
York 149 B4
Knapton Green 78 B2
Knapwell 85 A5
Knaresborough 148 B2
Knarsdale 177 D4
Knauchland 267 D6
Knaven 256 B3
Knayton 158 C3
Knebworth 68 A2
Knedlington 141 A5
Kneesall 132 C2
Kneesworth 85 C5
Kneeton 115 A5
Knelston 57 D4
Knenhall 112 B3
Knettishall 103 C5
Knightacott 26 B1
Knightcote 81 B6
Knightley Dale 112 C2
Knighton Devon 7 C4
Leicester 98 A2
Staffs 111 A6
Staffs 111 C6
Knighton =Tref-y-Clawdd 93 D6
Knightswood 205 B5
Knightwick 79 B5
Knill 77 A6
Knipton 115 B6
Knitsley 166 A4
Kniveton 130 D2
Knock Argyll 225 C4
Cumb 165 C4
Moray 267 D6
Knockally 275 B5
Knockan 271 C5
Knockandhu 254 D3
Knockando 254 B2
Knockando House 254 B3
Knockbain 252 A2
Knockbreck 258 B2
Knockbrex 172 D3
Knockdee 280 B3
Knockdolian 180 C3
Knockenkelly 191 C6
Knockentiber 192 B3
Knockespock House 255 D6
Knockfarrel 251 A7
Knockglass 170 B2
Knockholt 36 A2
Knockholt Pound 36 A2
Knockie Lodge 240 A2
Knockin 110 C2
Knockinlaw 193 B4
Knocklearn 173 A5
Knocknaha 190 D2
Knocknain 170 A1
Knockrome 201 A5
Knocksharry 152 C2
Knodishall 89 A5
Knolls Green 128 B3
Knolton 110 B2
Knolton Bryn 110 B2
Knook 30 A3
Knossington 99 A5
Knott End-on-Sea 144 C3
Knotting 84 A2
Knotting Green 84 A2
Knottingley 140 A3
Knotts Cumb 164 C2
Lancs 146 B1
Knotty Ash 136 D3
Knotty Green 67 D4
Knowbury 94 D3
Knowe 181 D5
Knowehead 182 C4
Knowesgate 178 A1
Knowes of Elrick 267 D7
Knoweton 194 A2
Knowhead 269 D4
Knowle Bristol 43 B5
Devon 12 A2
Devon 13 C5
Devon 25 B5
Shrops 94 D3
W Mid 97 D4
Knowle Green 145 D6
Knowle Park 147 C4
Knowl Hill 47 B6
Knowlton Dorset 31 D4
Kent 53 D4
Knowsley 136 D3
Knowstone 26 C3
Knox Bridge 37 B5
Knucklas 93 D6
Knuston 83 A6
Knutsford 128 B2
Knutton 112 A2
Knypersley 128 D3
Kuggar 3 D5
Kyleakin 247 B6
Kyle of Lochalsh 249 D4
Kylerhea 247 B6
Kylesknoydart 238 C2
Kylesku 271 A5
Kylesmorar 238 C2
Kylestrome 271 A5
Kyllachy House 252 D3
Kynaston 110 C2
Kynnersley 111 D5
Kyre Magna 79 A4

L

Labost 288 C3
Lacasaidh 288 E4
Lacasdal 288 D5
Laceby 143 C4
Lacey Green 66 D3
Lach Dennis 128 B2
Lackford 102 D3
Lacock 44 C3
Ladbroke 81 B7
Laddingford 37 B4
Lade Bank 134 D3
Ladock 4 B3
Lady 282 C7
Ladybank 220 C3
Ladykirk 198 B2
Ladysford 269 C4
La Fontenelle Guern 6
Laga 235 D5
Lagalochan 214 A1
Lagavulin 201 D4
Lagg Argyll 201 A5
N Ayrs 191 C5
Laggan Argyll 200 C2
Highld 235 C6
Highld 239 C6
Highld 241 C4
S Ayrs 181 C4
Lagganulva 224 B3
Laide 261 A5
Laigh Fenwick 205 D4
Laigh Glengall 192 D3
Laighmuir 205 D4
Laindon 50 A3
Lair 250 B2
Lairg 272 D3
Lairg Lodge 272 D3
Lairgmore 252 C1
Lairg Muir 272 D3
Laisterdyke 147 D5
Laithes 164 B2
Lake IoW 19 C4
Wilts 31 B5
Lakenham 104 A3
Lakenheath 102 C3
Lakesend 101 B7
Lakeside 154 C2
Laleham 48 C3
Laleston 40 D3
Lamarsh 87 D4
Lamas 120 C4
Lambden 197 B6
Lamberhurst 37 C4
Lamberhurst Quarter 37 C4
Lamberton 198 A3
Lambeth 49 B6
Lambhill 205 B5
Lambley
Northumb 177 D4
Notts 115 A4
Lamborough Hill 65 C5
Lambourn 46 B1
Lambourne End 69 D4
Lambs Green 35 C5
Lambston 55 C5
Lambton 179 D4
Lamerton 11 D5
Lamesley 179 D4
Laminess 282 D7
Lamington Highld 264 C3
S Lanark 195 C4
Lamlash 191 B6
Lamloch 182 C3
Lamonby 164 B2
Lamorna 2 C2
Lamorran 4 C3
Lampardbrook 88 A3
Lampeter = Llanbedr Pont Steffan 75 D4
Lampeter Velfrey 56 A1
Lamphey 55 D6
Lamplugh 162 B3
Lamport 99 D4
Lamyatt 29 B6
Lana 10 B4
Lanark 194 B3
Lancaster 145 A4
Lanchester 167 A4
Lancing 21 B4
Landbeach 85 A6
Landcross 25 C5
Landerberry 245 B4
Landford 31 D6
Landford Manor 31 C6
Landimore 57 C4
Landkey 25 B6
Landore 57 C6
Landrake 6 A2
Landscove 8 A1
Landshipping 55 C6
Landshipping Quay 55 C6
Landulph 6 A3
Landwade 86 A2
Lane 4 A3
Laneast 10 C3
Lane End Bucks 66 D3
Cumb 153 A2
Dorset 16 B2
Hants 33 C4
IoW 19 C5
Lancs 146 C2
Lane Ends Lancs 146 B1
Lancs 146 D1
N Yorks 146 C3
Laneham 132 B3
Lanehead
Durham 165 A6
Northumb 177 A5
Lane Head
Derbys 129 B6
Durham 166 D4
Gtr Man 137 D5
W Yorks 139 C4
Lanercost 176 C3
Laneshaw Bridge 146 C3
Lane Side 137 A6
Lanfach 41 B7
Langar 115 B5
Langbank 204 A3
Langbar 147 B4
Langburnshiels 186 C4
Langcliffe 146 A2
Langdale 278 D2
Langdale End 160 B3
Langdon 10 C4
Langdon Beck 165 B6
Langdon Hills 50 A3
Langdyke 220 D3
Langenhoe 71 B4
Langford C Beds 84 C3
Devon 13 A5
Essex 70 C2
Notts 132 D3
Oxon 64 C3
Langford Budville 27 C6
Langham Essex 87 D6
Norf 120 A2
Rutland 115 D6
Suff 103 E5
Langhaugh 195 C7
Langho 145 D7

Langholm......185 D6
Langleeford....188 A2
Langley Ches E...129 B4
Hants.........18 A3
Herts.........68 A2
Kent..........37 A6
Northumb....177 C6
Slough........48 B3
Warks.........81 A4
W Sus........33 C7
Langley Burrell..44 B3
Langley
Common.....113 B6
Langley Heath...37 A6
Langley Lower
Green........85 D6
Langley Marsh..27 C5
Langley Park...167 A5
Langley Street..105 A4
Langley Upper
Green........85 D6
Langney.......22 B4
Langold.......131 A5
Langore.......10 C4
Langport......28 C4
Langrick......117 A5
Langridge.....43 C6
Langridge Ford..25 C6
Langrigg......175 D4
Langrish.......33 C6
Langsett......139 C5
Langshaw......197 C4
Langside......218 C2
Langskaill.....282 C5
Langstone Hants..19 A6
Newport.......61 D5
Langthorne....157 B6
Langthorpe....148 A2
Langthwaite...156 A4
Langtoft E Yorks..150 A3
Lincs.........116 C4
Langton Durham..167 D4
Lincs.........134 B3
Lincs.........134 C2
N Yorks.......149 A6
Langton by
Wragby......133 B6
Langton Green
Kent..........36 C3
Suff..........104 D2
Langton Herring..15 C6
Langton
Matravers....17 D4
Langtree......25 D5
Langwathby....164 B3
Langwell House..275 B5
Langwell Lodge..271 D4
Langwith......131 C5
Langwith
Junction....131 C5
Langworth.....133 B5
Lanivet.......5 A5
Lanlivery......5 B5
Lanner........4 D2
Lanreath.......5 B6
Lansallos.......5 B6
Lansdown......63 A5
Lanteglos Highway 5 B6
Lanton Borders..187 A5
Northumb....198 C3
Lapford........12 A2
Laphroaig.....200 D3
La Planque Guern..6
Lapley.........112 D2
Lapworth.......97 D4
Larachbeg.....225 B5
Larbert........207 B6
Larden Green...127 D5
Largie.........255 C7
Largiemore....214 D2
Largoward.....221 D4
Largs..........204 C2
Largybeg......191 C6
Largymore.....191 C6
Larkfield.....204 A2
Larkhall......194 A2
Larkhill.......31 A5
Larling.......103 C5
Larriston......186 D4

Lartington.....166 D3
Lary..........243 B6
Lasham........33 A5
Lashenden.....37 B6
Lassington.....62 A3
Lassodie.....208 A4
Lastingham....159 B6
Latcham.......29 A4
Latchford Herts..68 A3
Warr..........127 A6
Latchingdon....70 C2
Latchley.......11 D5
Lately Common..137 D5
Lathbury.......83 C5
Latheron.....275 A5
Latheronwheel..275 A5
Latheronwheel
House.......275 A5
Lathones.....221 D4
Latimer........67 D5
Latteridge......43 A5
Lattiford......29 C6
Latton.........64 D1
Latton Bush....69 C4
Lauchintilly..245 A4
Lauder........197 B4
Laugharne......56 A3
Laughterton...132 B3
Laughton E Sus..22 A3
Leics.........98 C3
Lincs.........116 B3
Lincs.........141 D6
Laughton
Common....131 A5
Laughton en le
Morthen.....131 A5
Launcells......10 A3
Launceston.....10 C4
Launton.......65 A7
Laurencekirk..233 A5
Laurieston
Dumfries....173 B4
Falk.........208 C2
Lavendon......83 B6
Lavenham......87 C5
Laverhay.....185 C4
Laversdale....176 C2
Laverstock.....31 B5
Laverstoke.....32 A3
Laverton Glos....80 D3
N Yorks.......157 D6
Som..........44 D1
Lavister......126 D3
Law..........194 A3
Lawers Perth...217 A6
Perth.........218 B2
Lawford.......88 D1
Lawhitton......11 C4
Lawkland.....146 A1
Lawley.........95 A4
Lawnhead.....112 C2
Lawrenny......55 D6
Lawshall.......87 B4
Lawton........78 B2
Laxey.........152 C4
Laxfield......104 D3
Laxfirth Shetland..285 H6
Shetland.....285 J6
Laxford Bridge..276 D3
Laxo..........285 G6
Laxobigging..284 F6
Laxton E Yorks..141 A5
N Nhants......99 B6
Notts.........132 C2
Laycock......147 C4
Layer Breton...70 B3
Layer de la Haye..70 B3
Layer Marney...70 B3
Layham........87 C6
Laylands Green..46 C1
Laytham......149 D6
Layton.......144 D3
Lazenby......168 C3
Lazonby......164 B3
Lea Derbys....130 D3
Hereford......62 A2
Lincs.........132 A3
Shrops........94 A2
Shrops........94 C1
Wilts.........44 A3
Leabrooks....131 D4
Leac a Li.....288 H2

Leachkin......252 B2
Leadburn.....196 A1
Leadenham....133 D4
Leaden Roding..69 B5
Leadgate Cumb..165 A5
Durham......178 D3
T&W.........178 D3
Leadhills.....183 A6
Leafield.......64 B4
Leagrave......67 A5
Leake.........158 B3
Leake
Commonside..134 D3
Lealholm.....159 A6
Lealt Argyll....213 C4
Highld.......259 B5
Lea Marston...97 B5
Leamington
Hastings.....82 A1
Leamonsley....96 A4
Leamside.....167 A6
Leanaig......252 A1
Leargybreck...201 A5
Leasgill.....154 C3
Leasingham....116 A3
Leasingthorne..167 C5
Leasowe......136 D1
Leatherhead....35 A4
Leatherhead
Common.....35 A4
Leathley......147 C6
Leaton........110 D3
Lea Town......145 D4
Leaveland......52 D2
Leavening.....149 A6
Leaves Green...49 C7
Leazes........178 D3
Lebberston....161 C4
Lechlade-on-
Thames......64 D3
Leck.........155 D5
Leckford.......32 B2
Leckfurin.....278 C3
Leckgruinart..200 B2
Leckhampstead
Bucks........83 D4
W Berks......46 B2
Leckhampstead
Thicket......46 B2
Leckhampton...63 B5
Leckie........262 D2
Leckmelm.....262 A3
Leckwith.......41 D6
Leconfield....150 C3
Ledaig.......226 C4
Ledburn.......67 A4
Ledbury.......79 D5
Ledcharrie...217 B5
Ledgemoor.....78 B2
Ledicot.......78 A2
Ledmore.....271 C5
Lednagullin...278 B3
Ledsham Ches W 126 B3
W Yorks......140 A2
Ledston......140 A2
Ledston Luck...148 D3
Ledwell.......65 A5
Lee Argyll.....224 D3
Devon.........25 A5
Hants.........32 D2
Lancs.........145 B5
Shrops.......110 B3
Leeans.......285 J5
Leebotten.....285 L6
Leebotwood....94 B2
Lee Brockhurst..111 C4
Leece.........153 D3
Leechpool.....55 C5
Lee Clump......67 C4
Leeds Kent.....37 A6
W Yorks......148 D1
Leedstown......3 B4
Leek.........129 D4
Leekbrook....129 D4
Lee Mill........7 B5
Leeming......157 C6
Leeming Bar..157 B6
Lee Moor.......7 A4
Lee-on-the-
Solent......19 A4
Lees Derbys...113 B6

Lees continued
Gtr Man......138 C2
W Yorks......147 D4
Leeswood....126 C2
Legbourne....134 A3
Legberwood...197 B4
Legsby.......133 A6
Leicester......98 A2
Leicester Forest
East.........98 A2
Leigh Dorset...15 A6
Glos..........63 A4
Gtr Man......137 C5
Kent..........36 B3
Shrops........94 A1
Sur...........35 B5
Wilts..........63 D6
Worcs........79 B5
Leigh Beck.....51 A5
Leigh Common..30 C1
Leigh Delamere..44 B2
Leigh Green....37 C7
Leigh on Sea...51 A5
Leigh Park.....19 A6
Leigh Sinton...79 B5
Leighswood....96 A3
Leighterton....63 D4
Leighton N Yorks.157 D5
Powys.........93 A6
Shrops........95 A4
Som...........29 A7
Leighton
Bromswold....100 D3
Leighton Buzzard 67 A4
Leigh upon
Mendip......29 A6
Leigh Woods....43 B4
Leinthall Earls..78 A2
Leinthall Starkes.78 A2
Leintwardine...94 D2
Leire..........98 B2
Leirinmore...277 B5
Leiston.......89 A5
Leitfie.......231 D6
Leith.........209 C5
Leitholm.....198 B1
Lelant..........2 B3
Lelley........151 D5
Lem Hill.......95 D5
Lemington
Hall.........189 B4
Lempitlaw....198 C1
Lenchwick.....80 C3
Lendalfoot....180 C3
Lendrick Lodge..217 D5
Lenham.........37 A6
Lenham Heath...37 B7
Lennel.......198 B2
Lennoxtown...205 A6
Lenton Lincs...116 B3
Nottingham...114 B3
Lentran.......252 B1
Lenwade......120 D2
Leny House....217 D6
Lenzie.......205 A6
Leoch........220 A3
Leochel-
Cushnie.....244 A2
Leominster.....78 B2
Leonard Stanley..63 C4
Leorin........200 D3
Lepe...........18 B3
Lephin.......258 D1
Lephinchapel..214 C2
Lephinmore...214 C2
Le Planel Guern..6
Leppington...149 A6
Lepton.......139 B5
Lerryn..........5 B6
Lerwick.......285 J6
Lesbury......189 B5
Le Skerne
Haughton....167 D6
Leslie Aberds..255 D6
Fife.........220 D2
Lesmahagow...194 C3
Lesnewth......10 B2
Lessendrum...255 B6
Lessingham...121 C5
Lessonhall...175 C5
Leswalt......170 A2
Letchmore Heath 67 D6

Letchworth.....84 D4
Letcombe Bassett 46 A1
Letcombe Regis..46 A1
Letham Angus...232 D3
Falk.........208 B1
Fife.........220 C3
Perth........219 B5
Letham Grange..233 D4
Lethenty......256 B3
Letheringham...88 B3
Letheringsett..120 B2
Lettaford......12 C2
Lettan........282 C8
Letterewe....261 C6
Letterfearn...249 D5
Letterfinlay..239 C6
Lettermorar...235 B6
Lettermore....224 B3
Letters.......262 B3
Letterston.....55 B5
Lettoch Highld..242 A3
Highld.......254 C1
Letton Hereford..78 C1
Hereford......94 D1
Letton Green..103 A5
Letty Green....68 B2
Letwell......131 A5
Leuchars.....221 B4
Leuchars House 266 C3
Leumrabhagh..288 F4
Levan.........204 A2
Levaneap.....285 G6
Levedale......112 D2
Leven E Yorks..151 C4
Fife.........220 D3
Levencorroch..191 C6
Levens.......154 C3
Levens Green...68 A3
Levenshulme..138 D1
Levenwick....285 L6
Leverburgh
=An t-Ob....287 F5
Leverington...118 D1
Leverton.....117 A7
Leverton
Highgate....117 A7
Leverton
Outgate.....117 A7
Le Villocq Guern..6
Levington......88 D3
Levisham.....160 B2
Levishie.....240 A2
Lew...........64 C4
Lewannick....10 C3
Lewdown.......11 C5
Lewes.........22 A2
Leweston......55 B5
Lewisham......49 B6
Lewiston.....251 D7
Lewistown.....40 C4
Lewknor.......66 D2
Leworthy Devon..10 A4
Devon.........26 B1
Lewtrenchard..11 C5
Lexden.........70 A3
Ley Aberds...244 A2
Corn...........5 A6
Leybourne......37 A4
Leyburn......157 B5
Leyfields......97 A5
Leyhill........67 C4
Leyland......136 A4
Leylodge.....245 A4
Leymoor.......139 B4
Leys Aberds..269 D5
Perth........220 A2
Leys Castle...252 B2
Leysdown-on-
Sea..........52 B2
Leysmill.....233 D4
Leys of Cossans 232 D1
Leysters Pole..78 A3
Leyton.........49 A6
Leytonstone....49 A6
Lezant........10 D4
Leziate.......118 D3
Lhanbryde....266 C3
Lhuntley......118 C3
Liatrie.......250 C4
Libanus.......60 A1
Libberton....195 B4

Liberton.....209 D5
Liceasto.....288 H2
Lichfield......96 A4
Lickey........96 D2
Lickey End.....96 D2
Lickfold.......34 D2
Liddel.......283 J5
Liddesdale...236 D1
Liddington....45 A6
Lidgate........86 B3
Lidget.......141 C4
Lidget Green..147 D5
Lidgett......131 C6
Lidlington....84 D1
Lidstone......65 A4
Lieurary.....279 B6
Liff..........220 A3
Lifton.........11 C4
Liftondown....11 C4
Lighthorne....81 B6
Lightwater....48 C2
Lightwood....112 A3
Lightwood Green
Ches E......111 A5
Wrex........110 A2
Lilbourne......98 D2
Lilburn Tower..188 A3
Lilleshall....111 D6
Lilley Herts...67 A6
W Berks.......46 B2
Lilliesleaf...186 A4
Lillingstone
Dayrell......83 D4
Lillingstone
Lovell.......83 C4
Lillington Dorset..29 D6
Warks.........81 A6
Lilliput.......17 B4
Lilstock.......27 A6
Lilyhurst....111 D6
Limbury.......67 A5
Limebrook.....78 A1
Limefield....137 B7
Limekilnburn..194 A2
Limekilns....208 B3
Limerigg.....207 C6
Limerstone....18 C3
Limington.....29 C5
Limpenhoe....105 A4
Limpley Stoke..44 C1
Limpsfield....36 A2
Limpsfield
Chart........36 A2
Linby.........131 D5
Linchmere.....34 C1
Lincluden....174 A2
Lincoln......133 B4
Lincomb.......79 A6
Lincombe.......7 B6
Lindale......154 C3
Lindal in
Furness.....153 C3
Lindean......196 C3
Lindfield......35 D6
Lindford.......33 B7
Lindifferon...220 C3
Lindley......139 B4
Lindley Green..147 C6
Lindores.....220 C2
Lindridge.....79 A4
Lindsell.......69 A6
Lindsey.......87 C5
Linford Hants...17 A5
Thurrock......50 B3
Lingague.....152 D2
Lingards Wood..138 B3
Lingbob......147 D4
Lingdale......169 D4
Lingen........78 A1
Lingfield......36 B1
Lingreabhagh..287 F5
Lingwood.....105 A4
Linicro......258 B3
Linkenholt....46 D1
Linkhill.......37 D6
Linkinhorne...10 D4
Linklater....283 J5
Linksness....283 G3
Linktown.....209 A5
Linley.........94 B1
Linley Green...79 B4
Linlithgow...208 C3

Linlithgow
  Bridge 208 C2
Linshiels. 188 C1
Linsiadar 288 D3
Linsidemore 264 A1
Linslade 67 A4
Linstead Parva . . 104 D4
Linstock 176 D2
Linthwaite 139 R4
Lintlaw 198 A2
Lintmill 267 C6
Linton Borders . . 187 A6
  Cambs 86 C1
  Derbys 113 D6
  Hereford 62 A4
  Kent 37 B5
  Northumb. 189 D5
  N Yorks 146 A3
  W Yorks 148 C2
Linton-on-Ouse 148 A3
Linwood Hants. . . 17 A5
  Lincs. 133 A6
  Renfs 205 B4
Lionacleit. 286 B3
Lional 288 A6
Liphook 34 C1
Liscard 136 D2
Liscombe 26 B3
Liskeard 6 A1
L'Islet Guern 6
Liss 33 C6
Lissett 151 B4
Liss Forest 33 C6
Lissington 133 A6
Lisvane 41 C6
Liswerry 42 A2
Litcham 119 D5
Litchborough . . . 82 B3
Litchfield 46 D2
Litherland 136 D2
Litlington Cambs . . 85 C5
  E Sus 22 B3
Little Abington . . 86 C1
Little Addington . 99 D6
Little Alne 80 A4
Little Altcar 136 C2
Little Asby 155 A5
Little Assynt 271 B4
Little Aston 96 A3
Little Atherfield . . 18 C3
Little Ayre 283 H4
Little-ayre 285 D2
Little Ayton 168 D3
Little Baddow . . . 70 C1
Little Badminton . 44 A2
Little Ballinluig . .230 C3
Little Bampton . .175 C5
Little Bardfield . . 86 D2
Little Barford . . . 84 B3
Little
  Barningham . . .120 B3
Little Barrow . . . 64 B3
Little Barrow 127 B4
Little Barugh . . .159 D6
Little Bavington . 178 B2
Little Bealings. . .88 C3
Littlebeck. 160 A2
Little Bedwyn . . . 45 C6
Little Bentley. . . . 71 A5
Little
  Berkhamsted . . 68 C2
Little Billing. 83 A5
Little Birch. 78 D3
Little Blakenham . 88 C2
Little Blencow . .164 B2
Little Bookham . . 35 A4
Littleborough
  Gtr Man 138 B2
  Notts 132 A3
Littlebourne 53 D4
Little Bowden . . . 99 C4
Little Bradley . . . 86 B2
Little Brampton . 94 C1
Little Brechin . . .232 B3
Littlebredy 8 C4
Little Brickhill. . . 83 D6
Little Brington . . 82 A3
Little Bromley. . . 71 A4
Little Broughton 162 A3
Little Budworth . .127 C5
Little Burstead . . 69 D6

Littlebury 85 D7
Littlebury Green. . 85 D6
Little Bytham. . . .116 D3
Little Carlton
  Lincs. 134 A3
  Notts 132 D2
Little Casterton . 100 A3
Little
  Cawthorpe 134 A3
Little Chalfont. . . 67 D4
Little Chart 38 A1
Little Chesterford 85 C7
Little Cheverell . . 44 D3
Little Chishill. . . . 85 D6
Little Clacton . . . 71 B5
Little Clifton . . .162 B3
Little Colp 256 B2
Little Comberton . 80 C2
Little Common . . 23 B5
Little Compton . 81 D5
Little Cornard . . . 87 D4
Little Cowarne . . 79 B4
Little Coxwell . . . 64 D3
Little Crakehall . 157 B6
Little
  Cressingham . .103 B4
Little Crosby . . .136 C2
Little Dalby 115 D5
Little Dawley 95 A4
Littledean 62 B2
Little Dens 257 B5
Little Dewchurch 78 D3
Little Downham . 101 C7
Little Driffield . . .150 B3
Little Dunham . . .119 D5
Little Dunkeld . . 230 D4
Little Dunmow . . . 69 A6
Little Easton 69 A6
Little Eaton 114 A1
Little Eccleston . 144 C4
Little Ellingham . 103 B6
Little End 69 C5
Little Eversden . . 85 B5
Little Faringdon . 64 C3
Little Fencote . . .157 B6
Little Fenton . . .148 D4
Littleferry 265 A4
Little Finborough. 87 B6
Little Fransham .119 D6
Little Gaddesden . 67 B4
Little Gidding . . .100 C3
Little Glemham . . 88 B4
Little Glenshee . .219 A4
Little Gransden. . 85 B4
Little Green 29 A7
Little Grimsby . .143 D5
Little Gruinard . .261 B6
Little Habton . . .159 D6
Little Hadham . . . 68 A4
Little Hale 116 A4
Little Hallingbury. 69 B4
Littleham Devon. . . 13 C5
  Devon 25 C5
Little Hampden . . 66 C3
Littlehampton. . . 20 B3
Little Harrowden . 99 D5
Little Haseley . . . 66 C1
Little Hatfield . . .151 C4
Little Hautbois . .121 C4
Little Haven 55 C4
Little Hay 96 A4
Little Hayfield . . .129 A5
Little Haywood . .112 C4
Little Heath 97 C6
Littlehempston . . .8 A2
Little Hereford . . 78 A3
Little Horkesley . 87 D5
Little Horsted . . . 22 A2
Little Horton 147 D5
Little Horwood . . 83 D4
Littlehoughton . .189 B5
Little Houghton
  S Yorks 140 C2
  W Nhants 83 B5
Little Hucklow . .129 B6
Little Hulton 137 C6
Little Humber . . .142 A3
Little Hungerford. 46 B3
Little Irchester . . 83 A6
Little Kineton . . . 81 B6
Little Kingshill . . 66 D3

Little Langdale . .154 A2
Little Langford . . 31 B4
Little Laver. 69 C5
Little Leigh 127 B6
Little Leighs 69 B7
Little Lever 137 C6
Little London
  Bucks. 66 B1
  E Sus 22 A3
  Hants 32 A2
  Hants 47 D4
  Lincs. 117 C5
  Lincs. 118 C1
  Norf 120 C3
  Powys 92 C4
Little Longstone 130 B1
Little Lynturk . . .244 A2
Little Malvern . . . 79 C5
Little Maplestead 87 D4
Little Marcle 79 D4
Little Marlow . . . 47 A6
Little Marsden . .146 D2
Little
  Massingham . .119 C4
Little Melton . . .104 A2
Littlemill Aberds . 243 C6
  E Ayrs 182 A2
  Highld 253 A5
  Northumb. 189 B5
Little Mill 61 C5
Little Milton 65 C7
Little Missenden . 67 D4
Littlemoor 15 C6
Littlemore 65 C6
Little Musgrave .165 D5
Little Ness 110 D3
Little Neston . . .126 B2
Little Newcastle . 55 B5
Little Newsham .166 D4
Little Oakley Essex 71 A6
  N Nhants 99 C5
Little Orton 175 C6
Little Ouseburn . 148 A3
Littleover 114 B1
Little Paxton . . . 84 A3
Little Petherick . . 9 D5
Little Pitlurg . . . 255 B5
Little Plumpton . 144 D3
Little Plumstead 121 D5
Little Ponton . . .116 B2
Littleport 102 C1
Little Raveley . . .101 D4
Little Reedness . .141 A6
Little Ribston . . .148 B2
Little Rissington . 64 B2
Little Ryburgh . . .119 C6
Little Ryle 188 B3
Little Salkeld . . .164 B3
Little Sampford . . 86 D2
Little Sandhurst . 47 C6
Little Saxham . . . 86 A3
Little Scatwell . .251 A5
Little Sessay 158 D3
Little Shelford . . . 85 B6
Little Singleton . .144 D3
Little
  Skillymarno . .269 D4
Little Smeaton . .140 B3
Little Snoring . . .119 B6
Little Sodbury . . . 43 A6
Little Somborne . 32 B2
Little Somerford . 44 A3
Little Stainforth .146 A2
Little Stainton . .167 C6
Little Stanney . . .127 B4
Little Staughton . 84 A3
Little Steeping . .135 C4
Little Stoke 112 B3
Littlestone on
  Sea 38 C2
Little Stonham . . 88 A2
Little Stretton
  Leics. 98 A3
  Shrops 94 B2
Little Strickland 164 D3
Little Stukeley . .100 D4
Little Sutton . . .126 B3
Little Tew 65 A4
Little Thetford . .102 D1
Littlethorpe Leics .98 B2
  N Yorks 148 A2

Little Thurlow . . 86 B2
Little Thurrock . . 50 B3
Littleton Ches W .127 C4
  Hants 32 B3
  Perth 220 A2
  Som 29 B4
  Sur 34 B2
  Sur 48 C3
Littleton Drew. . . 44 A2
Littleton-on-
  Severn 43 A4
Littleton Pannell . 44 D4
Little Torboll. . . .264 A3
Little Torrington . 25 D5
Little Totham . . . 70 B2
Little Toux 267 D6
Littletown 167 A6
Little Town Cumb 163 C5
  Lancs 145 D6
Little Urswick . . .153 C3
Little Wakering . . 51 A6
Little Walden . . . 86 C1
Little
  Waldingfield. . . 87 C5
Little
  Walsingham . . .119 B6
Little Waltham . . 69 B7
Little Warley . . . 69 D6
Little Weighton . .150 D2
Little Weldon . . . 99 C6
Little Welnetham 87 A4
Little Wenlock . . 95 A4
Little Whittingham
  Green 104 D3
Littlewick Green . 47 B6
Little Wilbraham . 86 B1
Little Wishford . . 31 B4
Little Witley 79 A5
Little Wittenham . 65 D6
Little Wolford . . . 81 D5
Littleworth
  Bedford 84 C2
  Glos 63 C4
  Oxon. 64 D4
  Staffs 112 D4
  Worcs 80 B1
Little Wratting . . 86 C2
Little Wymington 83 A6
Little Wymondley 68 A2
Little Wyrley . . . 96 A3
Little Yeldham . . 86 D3
Litton Derbys . . .129 B6
  N Yorks 156 D3
  Som 43 D4
Litton Cheney . . . 15 B5
Liurbost 288 E4
Liverpool 136 D2
Liverpool
  Airport 127 A4
Liversedge 139 A5
Liverton Devon . . . 12 D3
  Redcar 169 D5
Livingston 208 D3
Livingston
  Village 208 D3
Lixwm 125 B6
Lizard 3 D5
Llaingoch 122 B2
Llaithddu 93 C4
Llan 91 B6
Llanaber. 90 A4
Llanaelhaearn. . .106 B3
Llanafan 75 A5
Llanafan-fawr. . . 76 B3
Llanallgo 123 B4
Llanandras
  =Presteigne 77 A7
Llanarmon 107 C4
Llanarmon Dyffryn
  Ceiriog 109 B6
Llanarmon-yn-
  Ial 126 D1
Llanarth Ceredig . 73 A7
  Mon 61 B5
Llanarthne 58 C2
Llanasa 125 A6
Llanbabo 122 B3
Llanbadarn Fawr .90 D4
Llanbadarn-y-
  Garreg 77 C5

Llanbadoc 61 C5
Llanbadrig 122 A3
Llanbeder. 61 D5
Llanbedr Gwyn. . .107 D5
  Powys 60 A4
  Powys 77 C5
Llanbedr-Dyffryn-
  Clwyd 125 D6
Llanbedrgoch . . .123 B5
Llanbedrog 106 C3
Llanbedr Pont Steffan
  =Lampeter 75 D4
Llanbedr-y-
  cennin 124 C2
Llanberis 123 D5
Llanbethery 41 E5
Llanbister 93 D5
Llanblethian 41 D4
Llanboidy 73 D5
Llanbradach 41 B6
Llanbrynmair . . . 91 B6
Llancarfan 41 D5
Llancayo 61 C5
Llancloudy 61 A6
Llancynfelyn 90 C4
Llandaff 41 D6
Llandanwg 107 D5
Llandarcy 40 B2
Llandawke 56 A2
Llanddaniel Fab 123 C4
Llanddarog 57 A5
Llanddeiniol 75 A4
Llanddeiniolen . .123 D5
Llandderfel 109 B4
Llanddeusant
  Anglesey 122 B3
  Carms 59 C4
Llanddew 77 D4
Llanddewi 57 D4
Llanddewi
  Rhydderch 61 B5
Llanddewi
  Velfrey 56 A1
Llanddoged 124 C3
Llanddona 123 C5
Llanddowror 56 A2
Llanddulas 125 B4
Llanddwywe 107 D5
Llanddyfnan 123 C5
Llandefaelog
  Fach 76 D4
Llandefaelog-tre'r-
  graig 77 E5
Llandefalle 77 D5
Llandegai 123 C5
Llandegfan 123 C5
Llandegla 126 D1
Llandegley. 77 A5
Llandegveth 61 D5
Llandegwning . . .106 C2
Llandeilo 58 C3
Llandeilo Graban 77 C4
Llandeilo'r Fan . . 59 B5
Llandeloy 55 B4
Llandenny 61 C6
Llandevenny 42 A3
Llandewednock . . 3 D5
Llandewi
  Ystradenny 77 A5
Llandinabo 61 A7
Llandinam 92 C4
Llandissilio 55 B7
Llandogo 62 C1
Llandough
  V Glam 41 D4
  V Glam 41 D6
Llandovery
  =Llanymddyfri . . 59 B4
Llandow 40 D4
Llandre Carms . . 58 A3
  Ceredig 90 D4
Llandrillo 109 B5
Llandrillo-yn-
  Rhos 124 A3
Llandrindod
  =Llandrindod Wells 77 A4
Llandrindod Wells
  =Llandrindod. . . 77 A4
Llandrinio 110 D1
Llandudno 124 A2

Llandudno Junction =
  Cyffordd
  Llandudno. 124 B2
Llandwrog 107 A4
Llandybie 57 A4
Llandyfaelog. . . . 57 A4
Llandyfan 57 A6
Llandyfriog 73 B6
Llandyfrydog . . .123 B4
Llandygwydd. . . . 73 B5
Llandynan 109 A6
Llandyrnog 125 C6
Llandysilio 110 D1
Llandyssil 93 B5
Llandysul 73 B7
Llanedeyrn. 41 C7
Llanedi 57 B5
Llaneglwys. 77 D4
Llanegryn 90 B3
Llanegwad 58 C2
Llaneilian 123 A4
Llanelian-yn-
  Rhos 124 B3
Llanelidan 125 D6
Llanelieu 77 D5
Llanellen 61 B5
Llanelli 57 C5
Llanelltyd 91 A5
Llanelly 60 B4
Llanelly Hill 60 B4
Llanelwedd 76 B4
Llanelwy
  =St Asaph 125 B5
Llanenddwyn. . .107 D5
Llanengan 106 D2
Llanerchymedd .123 B4
Llanerfyl 92 A4
Llanfachraeth . .122 B3
Llanfaelog 122 C3
Llanfaelrhys. . . .106 D2
Llanfaenor 61 B6
Llanfaes
  Anglesey 123 C6
  Powys 60 A2
Llanfaethlu 122 B3
Llanfaglan 123 D4
Llanfair 107 D5
Llanfair-ar-y-
  bryn 59 B5
Llanfair
  Caereinion 93 A5
Llanfair Clydogau 75 C5
Llanfair-Dyffryn-
  Clwyd 125 D6
Llanfairfechan . .124 B1
Llanfair
  Kilgheddin 61 C5
Llanfair-Nant-
  Gwyn 73 C4
Llanfairpwll-
  gwyngyll 123 C5
Llanfair
  Talhaiarn. 125 B4
Llanfair
  Waterdine. 93 D6
Llanfair-ym-Muallt
  =Builth Wells. . . . 76 B4
Llanfairyneubwll 122 C3
Llanfairynghornwy
  . . . . .122 A3
Llanfallteg 56 A1
Llanfaredd. 77 B4
Llanfarian 75 A4
Llanfechain 109 C6
Llanfechan. 76 B3
Llanfechell. 122 A3
Llanfendigaid . . . 90 B3
Llanferres 126 C1
Llan Ffestiniog . .108 A2
Llanfflewyn 122 B3
Llanfihangel-ar-
  arth. 58 B1
Llanfihangel-
  Crucorney 61 A5
Llanfihangel Glyn
  Myfyr 109 A4
Llanfihangel Nant
  Bran 59 B6

Llanfihangel-nant-Melan 77 B5
Llanfihangel Rhydithon 77 A5
Llanfihangel Rogiet 42 A3
Llanfihangel Tal-y-llyn 60 A3
Llanfihangel-uwch-Gwili 58 C1
Llanfihangel-y-Creuddyn 75 A5
Llanfihangel-yn-Ngwynfa 109 D5
Llanfihangel yn Nhowyn 122 C3
Llanfihangel-y-pennant
Gwyn 91 B4
Gwyn 107 B5
Llanfihangel-y-traethau 107 C5
Llanfilo 77 D5
Llanfoist 61 B4
Llanfor 108 B4
Llanfrechfa 61 D5
Llanfrothen . . . 107 B6
Llanfrynach 60 A2
Llanfwrog
Anglesey 122 B3
Denb 125 D6
Llanfyllin 109 D6
Llanfynydd Carms . 58 C2
Flint 126 D2
Llanfyrnach . . . 73 C5
Llangadfan . . . 109 D5
Llangadog 59 C4
Llangadwaladr
Anglesey 122 D3
Powys 109 B6
Llangaffo 123 C4
Llangain 56 A3
Llangammarch Wells 76 C3
Llangan 41 D4
Llangarron 62 A1
Llangasty Talyllyn 60 A3
Llangathen . . . 58 C2
Llangattock 60 B4
Llangattock Lingoed 61 A5
Llangattock nigh Usk 61 C5
Llangattock-Vibon-Avel 61 B6
Llangedwyn 109 C6
Llangefni . . . 123 C4
Llangeinor 40 C4
Llangeitho 75 C5
Llangeler 73 C6
Llangelynin . . . 90 B3
Llangendeirne . 57 A4
Llangennech . . . 57 B5
Llangennith . . . 57 C4
Llangenny 60 B4
Llangernyw . . . 124 C3
Llangian 106 D2
Llanglydwen . . . 73 D4
Llangoed 123 C6
Llangoedmor . . 73 B4
Llangollen . . . 109 A7
Llangolman . . . 55 B7
Llangors 60 A3
Llangovan 61 C6
Llangower . . . 108 B4
Llangrannog . . . 73 A6
Llangristiolus . 123 C4
Llangrove 61 A5
Llangua 61 A5
Llangunllo 93 D6
Llangunnor 57 A4
Llangurig 92 B1
Llangwm Conwy . 109 A4
Mon 61 C6
Pembs 55 D5
Llangwnnadl . . 106 C2
Llangwyfan . . . 123 C4
Llangwyfan-isaf 122 D3
Llangwyllog . . . 123 C4

Llangwyryfon . . . 75 A4
Llangybi Ceredig . . . 75 C5
Gwyn 107 B4
Mon 61 D5
Llangyfelach . . . 57 C6
Llangynhafal . . . 125 C6
Llangynidr 60 B3
Llangynin Carms . . 56 A2
Llangynog Carms . 56 A3
Powys 109 C5
Llangynwyd 40 C3
Llanhamlach . . . 60 A2
Llanharan 41 C5
Llanharry 41 C5
Llanhennock . . . 61 D5
Llanhilleth
=Llanhilleth 41 A7
Llanhilleth
=Llanhiledd 41 A7
Llanidloes 92 C3
Llaniestyn . . . 106 C2
Llanifyny 91 B6
Llanigon 77 D6
Llanilar 75 A5
Llanilid 41 C4
Llanilltud Fawr
=Llantwit Major . . 41 E4
Llanishen
Cardiff 41 C6
Mon 61 C6
Llanllawddog . . 58 C1
Llanllechid . . . 123 D6
Llanllowell . . . 61 D5
Llanllugan 93 A4
Llanllwch 56 A3
Llanllwchaiarn . . 93 B5
Llanllwni 58 B1
Llanllyfni . . . 107 A4
Llanmadoc 57 C4
Llanmaes 41 E4
Llanmartin 42 A2
Llanmihangel . . 41 D4
Llanmorlais . . . 57 C5
Llannefydd . . . 125 B4
Llannon 57 B5
Llannor 106 C3
Llanon 75 B4
Llanover 61 C5
Llanpumsaint . . 73 D7
Llanreithan . . . 55 B4
Llanrhaeadr . . . 125 C5
Llanrhaeadr-ym-Mochnant 109 C6
Llanrhian 54 A4
Llanrhidian . . . 57 C4
Llanrhos 124 A2
Llanrhyddlad . . 122 B3
Llanrhystud . . . 75 B4
Llanrosser 77 D6
Llanrothal 61 B6
Llanrug 123 D5
Llanrumney 41 C7
Llanrwst 124 C3
Llansadurnen . . 56 A2
Llansadwrn
Anglesey 123 C5
Carms 58 B3
Llansaint 56 B3
Llansamlet . . . 40 B1
Llansannan . . . 125 C4
Llansannor . . . 41 D4
Llansantffraed
Ceredig 75 B4
Powys 60 A3
Llansantffraed Cwmdeuddwr . . 76 A3
Llansantffraed-in-Elvel 60 A3
Llansantffraid-ym-Mechain 109 C7
Llansawel 58 B3
Llansilin . . . 109 C7
Llansoy 61 C6
Llanspyddid . . . 60 A2
Llanstadwell . . . 55 D5
Llansteffan . . . 56 A3
Llanstephan . . . 77 C5
Llantarnam 61 D5
Llanteg 56 A1
Llanthony 61 A4
Llantilio Crossenny 61 B5

Llantilio Pertholey 61 B5
Llantood 73 B4
Llantrisant
Anglesey 122 B3
Mon 61 D5
Rhondda 41 C5
Llantrithyd . . . 41 D5
Llantwit Fardre . . . 41 C5
Llantwit Major
=Llanilltud Fawr . . 41 E4
Llanuwchllyn . . 108 B3
Llanvaches 61 D6
Llanvair Discoed . 61 D6
Llanvapley . . . 61 B5
Llanvetherine . . 61 B5
Llanveynoe . . . 77 D7
Llanvihangel Gobion 61 C5
Llanvihangel-Ystern-Llewern 61 B6
Llanwarne . . . 61 A7
Llanwddyn . . . 109 D5
Llanwenog . . . 74 D3
Llanwern . . . 42 A2
Llanwinio . . . 73 D5
Llanwnda
Gwyn 107 A4
Pembs 72 C2
Llanwnnen . . . 75 D4
Llanwnog . . . 92 B4
Llanwrda . . . 59 B4
Llanwrin . . . 91 B5
Llanwrtud
=Llanwrtyd Wells . . 76 C2
Llanwrtyd . . . 76 C2
Llanwrtyd Wells
=Llanwrtud . . . 76 C2
Llanwyddelan . . 93 A4
Llanyblodwel . . 110 C1
Llanybri . . . 56 A3
Llanybydder . . . 58 A2
Llanycefn . . . 55 B6
Llanychaer . . . 72 C2
Llanycil . . . 108 B4
Llanycrwys . . . 75 D5
Llanymawddwy . . 91 A7
Llanymddyfri
=Llandovery . . . 59 B4
Llanymynech . . 110 C1
Llanynghenedl . 122 B3
Llanynys . . . 125 C6
Llan-y-pwll . . 126 D3
Llanyre 76 A4
Llanystumdwy . . 107 C4
Llanywern . . . 60 A3
Llawhaden . . . 55 C6
Llawnt 110 B1
Llawr Dref . . 106 D2
Llawryglyn . . . 92 B3
Llay 126 D3
Llechcynfarwy . 122 B3
Llecheiddior . . 107 B4
Llechfaen . . . 60 A2
Llechryd
Caerph 60 C3
Ceredig 73 B5
Llechrydau . . . 110 B1
Lledrod 75 A5
Llenmerewig . . 93 B5
Llethrid . . . 57 C5
Llidiad Nenog . . 58 B2
Llidiardau . . . 108 B3
Llidiart-y-parc . . 109 A6
Llithfaen . . . 106 B3
Llong 126 C2
Llowes 77 C5
Llundain-fach . . 75 C4
Llwydcoed . . . 41 A4
Llwyn 93 C6
Llwyncelyn . . . 74 C3
Llwyndafydd . . 73 A6
Llwynderw . . . 93 A6
Llwyn-du . . . 61 B4
Llwyndyrys . . 106 B3
Llwyngwril . . . 90 B3
Llwyn-hendy . . 57 C5
Llwynmawr . . 110 B1
Llwyn-têg . . . 57 B5
Llwyn-y-brain . . 56 A1
Llwyn-y-groes . . 75 C4

Llwynypia 41 B4
Llynclys 110 C1
Llynfaes . . . 123 C4
Llysfaen . . . 124 B3
Llyswen 77 D5
Llysworney . . . 41 D4
Llys-y-frân . . . 55 B6
Llywel 59 B5
Loan 208 C2
Loanend 198 A3
Loanhead 209 D5
Loans 192 B3
Loans of Tullich 265 C4
Lobb 25 B5
Loch a Charnain 286 B4
Loch a' Ghainmhich . . 288 C3
Lochailort . . . 235 B6
Lochaline . . . 225 B5
Lochanhully . . 253 D5
Lochans 170 B2
Locharbriggs . . 184 D2
Lochassynt Lodge 271 B4
Lochavich Ho . . 214 A2
Lochawe 227 D6
Loch Baghasdail
=Lochbois-dale . . 286 E3
Lochboisdale =
Loch Baghasdail . 286 E3
Lochbuie . . . 225 D5
Lochcarron . . . 249 C5
Loch Choire Lodge 273 A4
Lochdhu 279 D6
Lochdochart House 216 B4
Lochdon . . . 225 C6
Lochdrum . . . 263 C4
Lochead 202 A2
Lochearnhead . . 217 B5
Lochee 220 A3
Lochend
Highld 252 C1
Highld 281 B4
Loch Euphoirt . . 287 H3
Lochfoot . . . 173 A6
Lochgair . . . 214 C2
Lochgarthside . . 240 A3
Lochgelly . . . 209 A4
Lochgilphead . . 214 C1
Lochgoilhead . . 215 B5
Loch Head . . . 171 C5
Lochhill . . . 266 C3
Lochindorb Lodge 253 D5
Lochinver . . . 270 B3
Lochlane . . . 218 B3
Loch Loyal Lodge 277 D7
Lochluichart . . 263 D5
Lochmaben . . . 184 D3
Lochmaddy = Loch nam Madadh . . 287 H4
Lochmore Cottage 280 D2
Lochmore Lodge 271 A6
Loch nam Madadh
=Lochmaddy . . 287 H4
Lochore 209 A4
Lochportain . . 287 G4
Lochranza . . . 203 C4
Lochs Crofts . . 266 C4
Loch Sgioport . . 286 C4
Lochside
Aberds 233 B5
Highld 253 A4
Highld 274 A2
Highld 277 C5
Lochslin . . . 265 B4
Lochstack Lodge 276 D3
Lochton . . . 245 C4
Lochty Angus . . 232 B3
Fife 221 D5
Perth 219 B5
Lochuisge . . . 236 D1
Lochurr . . . 183 D5
Lochwinnoch . . 204 C3
Lochwood . . . 184 C3

Lochyside 237 B5
Lockengate 5 A5
Lockerbie . . . 185 D4
Lockeridge . . . 45 C5
Lockerley . . . 32 C1
Locking 42 D2
Lockinge 46 A2
Lockington
E Yorks 150 C2
Leics 114 C2
Lockleywood . . 111 C5
Locks Heath . . 18 A4
Lockton . . . 160 B2
Lockwood . . . 139 B4
Loddington Leics . 99 A4
N Nhants . . . 99 D5
Loddiswell . . . 7 C6
Loddon 105 B4
Lode 86 A1
Loders 15 B4
Lodsworth . . . 34 D2
Lofthouse
N Yorks . . . 157 D5
W Yorks . . . 139 A6
Loftus 169 D5
Logan 193 C5
Loganlea . . . 208 D2
Logan Mains . . 170 C2
Loggerheads . . 111 B6
Logie Angus . . 233 B4
Fife 220 B4
Moray 253 A6
Logiealmond Lodge 219 A4
Logie Coldstone 244 B1
Logie Hill . . . 264 C3
Logie Newton . . 256 C1
Logie Pert . . . 233 B4
Logierait . . . 230 C3
Login 73 D4
Lolworth . . . 85 A5
Lonbain . . . 248 A3
Londesborough . 150 C1
London Colney . . 68 C1
Londonderry . . 157 C7
Londonthorpe . . 116 B2
Londubh . . . 261 B5
Long Ashton . . 43 B4
Lonemore . . . 264 B3
Long Ashton . . 43 B4
Longbar . . . 204 C3
Long Bennington . . 115 A6
Longbenton . . 179 C4
Longborough . . 64 A2
Long Bredy . . . 15 B5
Longbridge Warks 81 A5
W Mid 96 D3
Longbridge Deverill 30 A2
Longburton . . . 29 D6
Long Clawson . . 115 C5
Longcliffe . . . 130 D2
Long Common . . 32 D4
Long Compton
Staffs 112 C2
Warks 81 D5
Longcot . . . 64 D3
Long Crendon . . 66 C1
Long Crichel . . 30 D3
Longcroft . . . 207 C5
Longden . . . 94 A2
Long Ditton . . 49 C4
Longdon Staffs . . 113 D4
Worcs 79 D6
Longdon Green . . 113 D4
Longdon on Tern 111 D5
Longdown . . . 12 B3
Longdowns . . . 4 D2
Long Drax . . . 141 A4
Long Duckmanton . . 131 B4
Long Eaton . . 114 B2
Longfield Kent . . 50 C3
Longford Derbys 113 B6
Glos 63 A4
London 48 B3
Shrops 111 D5
Telford . . . 111 D6
W Mid 97 C6

Longfordlane . . . 113 B6
Longforgan . . . 220 B3
Longformacus . . 197 A5
Longframlington 189 C4
Long Green . . . 79 D6
Longham Dorset . . 17 B4
Norf 119 D6
Long Hanborough . . 65 B5
Longhaven . . . 257 C6
Longhill . . . 269 D4
Longhirst . . . 179 A4
Longhope Glos . . 62 B2
Orkney 283 H4
Longhorsley . . 189 D4
Longhoughton . . 189 B5
Long Itchington . . 81 A7
Longlane Derbys 113 B6
W Berks . . . 46 B2
Long Lawford . . 98 D1
Longlevens . . . 63 A4
Longley 139 C4
Longley Green . . 79 B5
Long Load . . . 29 C4
Longmanhill . . 268 C2
Long Marston
Herts 66 B3
N Yorks . . . 148 B4
Warks 81 C4
Long Marton . . 165 C4
Long Melford . . 87 C4
Longmoor Camp . 33 B6
Longmorn . . . 266 D3
Long Newnton . . 63 D5
Longnewton
Borders . . . 187 A4
Stockton . . . 167 D6
Long Newton . . 210 D2
Longney . . . 62 B3
Longniddry . . 210 C1
Longnor Shrops . . 94 A2
Staffs 129 C5
Longparish . . . 32 A3
Longport . . . 112 A2
Long Preston . . 146 B2
Longridge Lancs 145 D6
Staffs 112 D3
Longriggend . . 207 C6
Long Riston . . 151 C4
Longsdon . . . 129 D4
Longshaw . . . 136 C4
Longside . . . 257 B5
Long Sight . . 138 C2
Longstanton . . 85 A5
Longstock . . . 32 B2
Longstone . . . 56 B1
Longstowe . . . 85 B5
Long Stratton . . 104 B2
Long Street . . 83 C4
Long Sutton Hants 33 A5
Lincs 118 C1
Som 29 C4
Longthorpe . . 100 B3
Long Thurlow . . 87 A6
Longthwaite . . 164 C2
Longton Lancs . . 136 A3
Stoke 112 A3
Longtown Cumb . . 175 B6
Hereford . . . 61 A5
Longview . . . 136 D3
Longville in the Dale 94 B3
Long Whatton . . 114 C2
Longwick . . . 66 C2
Long Wittenham . 65 D6
Longwitton . . 178 A2
Longwood . . . 95 A4
Longworth . . . 65 D4
Longyester . . 210 D2
Lonmay 269 D5
Lonmore . . . 258 D2
Looe 6 B1
Loose 37 A5
Loosley Row . . 66 C3
Lopcombe Corner 31 B6
Lopen 28 D4
Loppington . . 110 C3
Lopwell 6 A3
Lorbottle . . . 188 C3
Lorbottle Hall . . 188 C3

Lornty 231 D5
Loscoe 114 A2
Losgaintir 287 E5
Lossiemouth . . . 266 B3
Lossit 200 C1
Lostford 111 B5
Lostock Gralam . 128 B1
Lostock Green . . 128 A1
Lostock Hall . . . 136 A4
Lostock
  Junction 137 C5
Lostwithiel 5 B6
Loth 282 D7
Lothbeg 274 C3
Lothersdale 146 C3
Lothmore 274 C3
Loudwater 67 D4
Loughborough . . 114 D3
Loughor 57 C5
Loughton Essex . . 68 D4
  M Keynes 83 D5
  Shrops 95 C4
Lound Lincs. . . . 116 D3
  Notts 132 A1
  Suff 105 B6
Lount 114 D1
Louth 134 A3
Love Clough . . . 137 A7
Lovedean 33 D5
Lover 31 C6
Loversall 140 D3
Loves Green 69 C6
Lovesome Hill . . 158 B2
Loveston 55 D6
Lovington 29 B5
Low Ackworth . . 140 B2
Low Barlings . . . 133 B5
Low Bentham . . 145 A6
Low Bradfield . . 139 D5
Low Bradley . . . 147 C4
Low Braithwaite 164 A2
Lowbridge
  House 154 A4
Low Brunton . . . 177 B7
Low Burnham . . 141 C5
Low Burton 157 C6
Low Buston 189 C5
Lowca 162 B2
Low Catton 149 B6
Low Clanyard . . 170 D3
Low Coniscliffe . 167 D5
Low Crosby 176 D2
Low Dalby 160 C2
Lowdham 115 A4
Low Dinsdale . . 167 D6
Lowe 111 B4
Lowe Hill 129 D4
Low Ellington . . 157 C6
Lower Aisholt . . . 28 B2
Lower Arncott . . 65 B7
Lower Ashton . . . 12 C3
Lower Assendon . 47 A5
Lower Badcall . . 276 D2
Lower Bartle . . . 145 D4
Lower Basildon . . 47 B4
Lower Beeding . . 35 D5
Lower Benefield 100 C1
Lower
  Boddington . . . 82 B1
Lower Brailes . . . 81 D6
Lower Breakish . 247 B5
Lower
  Broadheath . . . 79 B6
Lower
  Bullingham . . . 78 D3
Lower Cam 62 C3
Lower Chapel . . . 76 D4
Lower Chute 45 D7
Lower Cragabus 200 D3
Lower Crossings 129 A5
Lower
  Cumberworth . 139 C5
Lower Darwen . . 137 A5
Lower Dean 84 A2
Lower Diabaig . 261 D4
Lower Dicker . . . 22 A3
Lower Dinchope . 94 C2
Lower Down 94 C1
Lower Drift 2 C2
Lower
  Dunsforth 148 A3
Lower Egleton . . 79 C4

Lower Elkstone. .129 D5
Lower End 67 A4
Lower Everleigh . 45 D5
Lower Farringdon 33 B6
Lower Foxdale . . 152 D2
Lower Frankton . 110 B2
Lower Froyle. 33 A6
Lower Gledfield .264 A1
Lower Green 120 B1
Lower Ilacheston. 88 B4
Lower Halistra . . 258 C2
Lower Halstow . . 51 C5
Lower Hardres . . 52 D3
Lower
  Hawthwaite . . 153 B3
Lower Heath . . . 128 C3
Lower
  Hempriggs . . . 266 C2
Lower Hergest . . 77 B6
Lower Heyford . . 65 A5
Lower Higham . . 51 B4
Lower Holbrook . 88 D2
Lower Hordley . . 110 C2
Lower
  Horsebridge. . . 22 A3
Lower Killeyan . .200 D2
Lower Kingswood 35 A5
Lower
  Kinnerton . . . 126 C3
Lower Langford . . 42 C3
Lower Largo 220 D4
Lower Leigh 112 B4
Lower Lemington 81 D5
Lower Lenie. 251 D7
Lower Lydbrook . 62 B1
Lower Lye 78 A2
Lower Machen . . 42 A1
Lower Maes-
  coed 78 D1
Lower Mayland. . 70 C3
Lower Midway . . 113 C7
Lower Milovaig. .258 C1
Lower Moor. 80 C2
Lower Nazeing . . 68 C3
Lower
  Netchwood . . . 95 B4
Lower Ollach. . . .247 A4
Lower Penarth . . 41 D6
Lower Penn. 95 B6
Lower
  Pennington. . . . 18 B2
Lower Peover . . . 128 B2
Lower Pexhill . . . 128 B3
Lower Place 138 B2
Lower Quinton . . 81 C4
Lower Rochford . 79 A4
Lower Seagry . . . 44 A3
Lower Shelton . . 84 C1
Lower Shiplake . . 47 B5
Lower
  Shuckburgh . . . 82 A1
Lower Slaughter . 64 A2
Lower Stanton
  St Quintin 44 A3
Lower Stoke 51 B5
Lower Stondon. . 84 D3
Lower Stow
  Bedon. 103 B5
Lower Street
  Norf 121 B4
  Norf 121 D5
Lower Strensham 80 C2
Lower Stretton . .127 A6
Lower Sundon . . 67 A5
Lower Swanwick 18 C3
Lower Swell. 64 A2
Lower Tean 112 B4
Lower Thurlton . 105 B5
Lower Tote 259 B5
Lower Town 72 C2
Lower Tysoe 81 C6
Lower Upham . . . 32 D4
Lower Vexford . . 27 B6
Lower Weare. . . . 42 D3
Lower Welson . . . 77 B6
Lower Whitley. . .127 B6
Lower Wield 33 A5
Lower
  Winchendon. . . 66 B2
Lower
  Withington . . .128 C3
Lower Woodend. . 47 A6

Lower Woodford . 31 B5
Lower Wyche . . . 79 C5
Lowesby 99 A4
Lowestoft 105 B6
Loweswater 163 B4
Low Etherley . . . 167 C4
Low Fell 179 D4
Lowford 32 D3
Low Fulney 117 C5
Low Garth 159 A6
Low Gate 177 C7
Lowgill Cumb . . . 155 B5
  Lancs 145 A6
Low Grantley. . . 157 D6
Low Habberley . . 95 D6
Low Ham 28 C4
Low Hesket 164 A2
Low Hesleyhurst 188 D3
Low Hutton 149 A6
Lowick N Nhants . 100 C1
  Northumb. 198 C4
Lowick Bridge. . 154 C1
Lowick Green . . 154 C1
Low Laithe. 147 A5
Lowlands 61 D4
Low Leighton . . 129 A5
Low Lorton 163 B4
Low Marishes . . 159 D7
Low Marnham. . 132 C3
Low Mill 159 B5
Low Moor Lancs. 146 C1
  W Yorks 139 A4
Lowmoor Row. . 165 C4
Low Moorsley . . 167 A6
Low Newton . . . 154 C3
Low Newton-by-the-
  Sea 189 A5
Lownie Moor. . . 232 D2
Low Row Cumb. . 163 A6
  Cumb 176 C3
  N Yorks. 156 B3
Low Salchrie . . . 170 A2
Low Smerby . . . 190 C3
Lowsonford 81 A4
Lowther 164 C3
Lowthorpe 150 A3
Lowton 137 D5
Lowton
  Common 137 D5
Low Torry. 208 B3
Low Worsall . . . 158 A2
Low Wray 154 A2
Loxbeare 27 D4
Loxhill. 34 C3
Loxhore. 25 B7
Loxley 81 B5
Loxton 42 D2
Loxwood. 34 C3
Lubcroy 271 D6
Lubenham 99 C4
Luccombe 27 A4
Luccombe
  Village 19 D4
Lucker. 199 C5
Luckett 11 D4
Luckington 44 A2
Lucklawhill 220 B4
Luckwell Bridge . 27 B4
Lucton. 78 A2
Ludag 286 E3
Ludborough. . . . 143 D4
Ludchurch 56 A1
Luddenden 138 A3
Luddenden Foot 138 A3
Luddesdown . . . 50 C3
Luddington
  N Lincs 141 B6
  Warks. 81 B4
Luddington in the
  Brook 100 C3
Lude House 230 B2
Ludford Lincs . . . 134 A2
  Shrops 94 D3
Ludgershall Bucks. 66 B1
  Wilts. 45 D6
Ludgvan 2 B3
Ludham 121 D5
Ludlow 94 D3
Ludwell. 30 C3
Ludworth 167 A6
Luffincott 10 B4
Lugar. 193 C5

Luggate Burn . . .210 C3
Lugg Green 78 A2
Luggiebank 207 C5
Lugton 205 C4
Lugwardine 78 C3
Luib 247 B4
Lulham 78 C2
Lullenden 36 B2
Lullington
  Derbys 113 D6
  Som 44 D1
Lulsgate Bottom. 43 C4
Lulsley 79 B5
Lumb 138 A3
Lumby 148 D3
Lumloch 205 B6
Lumphanan . . . 244 B2
Lumphinnans . . 209 A4
Lumsdaine 211 D5
Lumsden 255 D5
Lunan 233 C4
Lunanhead. 232 C2
Luncarty 219 B5
Lund E Yorks . . . 150 C2
  N Yorks 149 D5
  Shetland. 284 C7
Lunderton 269 E6
Lundie Angus . . . 220 A2
  Highld. 239 A5
Lundin Links . . . 220 D4
Lunga 213 B5
Lunna 284 F6
Lunning 284 G7
Lunnon 57 D5
Lunsford's Cross . 23 A5
Lunt 136 C2
Luntley 78 B1
Luppitt 13 A6
Lupset 139 B6
Lupton 155 C4
Lurgashall 34 D2
Lusby 134 C3
Luson 7 C5
Luss 206 A1
Lussagiven. 213 D4
Lusta 258 C2
Lustleigh 12 C2
Luston 78 A2
Luthermuir 233 B4
Luthrie 220 C3
Luton Devon 13 D4
  Luton 67 A5
  Medway 51 C4
Lutterworth 98 C2
Lutton Devon 7 B4
  Lincs. 118 C1
  N Nhants 100 C3
Lutworthy. 26 D2
Luxborough. 27 B4
Luxulyan. 5 B5
Lybster 275 A6
Lydbury North. . 94 C1
Lydcott 26 B1
Lydd 38 C2
Lydden 39 A4
Lyddington 99 B5
Lydd on Sea. . . . 38 C2
Lydeard
  St Lawrence . . . 27 B6
Lyde Green 47 D5
Lydford. 11 C6
Lydford-on-
  Fosse 29 B5
Lydgate. 138 A2
Lydham. 94 B1
Lydiard Green. . . 45 A4
Lydiard Millicent . 45 A4
Lydiate 136 C2
Lydlinch 30 D1
Lydney 62 C2
Lydstep 55 E6
Lye 96 C2
Lye Green Bucks . 67 C4
  E Sus 36 C3
Lyford 65 D4
Lymbridge Green 38 A3
Lyme Regis 14 B3
Lyminge 38 A3
Lymington 18 B2
Lyminster 20 B3
Lymm 128 A1
Lymore 18 B1

Lympne. 38 B3
Lympsham 42 D2
Lympstone. 13 C4
Lynch 241 B5
Lyndale House . . 258 C3
Lyndhurst. 18 A2
Lyndon 99 A6
Lyne. 48 C3
Lyneal 110 B3
Lyne Down. 79 D4
Lyneham Oxon . . 64 A3
  Wilts. 44 B4
Lynemore. 253 D6
Lynemouth 189 D5
Lyne of
  Gorthleck 252 D1
Lyne of Skene . . 245 A4
Lyness 283 H4
Lyng Norf. 120 D2
  Som 28 C3
Lynmouth 26 A2
Lynsted 51 C6
Lynton 26 A2
Lyon's Gate 15 A6
Lyonshall 78 B1
Lytchett
  Matravers 16 B3
Lytchett Minster . 16 B3
Lyth 281 B4
Lytham 136 A2
Lytham
  St Anne's. 136 A2
Lythe 169 D6
Lythes 283 J5

M

Mabe Burnthouse . 4 D2
Mabie 174 A2
Mablethorpe . . . 135 A5
Macclesfield . . . 129 B4
Macclesfield
  Forest. 129 B4
Macduff 268 C2
Mace Green. . . . 88 C2
Macharioch 190 E3
Machen. 41 C7
Machrihanish . . 190 C2
Machynlleth . . . 91 B5
Machynys. 57 C5
Mackerel's
  Common 34 D3
Mackworth 113 B7
Macmerry 210 C1
Madderty 219 B4
Maddiston 208 C2
Madehurst 20 A2
Madeley Staffs . . 111 A6
  Telford 95 A4
Madeley Heath . 112 A1
Madeley Park . . 112 A1
Madingley 85 A5
Madley 78 D2
Madresfield 79 C6
Madron 2 B2
Maenaddwyn. . . 123 B4
Maenclochog . . 55 B6
Maendy 41 D5
Maentwrog 107 B6
Maen-y-groes . . 73 A6
Maer 112 B1
Maerdy Conwy . . 109 A5
  Rhondda. 41 B4
Maesbrook 110 C1
Maesbury 110 C2
Maesbury Marsh 110 C2
Maesgwyn-Isaf. .109 D6
Maesgwynne. . . 73 D5
Maeshafn 126 C2
Maesllyn. 73 B6
Maesmynis. 76 C4
Maesteg 40 B3
Maestir 75 D4
Maes-Treylow . . 77 A6
Maesybont. 57 A5
Maesycrugiau . . 58 A1
Maesy cwmmer . 41 B6
Maesymeillion . . 73 B7
Magdalen Laver . 69 C5
Maggieknocater
  . . . . 254 B4

Magham Down . . 22 A4
Maghull 136 C2
Magor. 42 A3
Magpie Green. . 104 D1
Maiden Bradley . 30 B2
Maidencombe. . . . 8 A3
Maidenhall 88 C2
Maidenhead . . . 48 A1
Maiden Law. . . . 167 A4
Maiden Newton . 15 B5
Maidens 192 E2
Maidensgrave. . . 88 C3
Maiden's Green . 48 B1
Maidenwell Corn. 10 D2
  Lincs. 134 B3
Maiden Wells . . 55 E5
Maidford 82 B3
Maids Moreton. . 83 D4
Maidstone 37 A5
Maidwell 99 D4
Mail 285 L6
Main 109 D6
Maindee 42 A2
Mainsforth. 167 B6
Mains of Airies . 170 A1
Mains of
  Allardice 233 A6
Mains of
  Annochie. 257 B4
Mains of
  Ardestie. 221 A5
Mains of Balhall 232 B3
Mains of
  Ballindarg 232 C2
Mains of
  Balnakettle . . . 233 A4
Mains of
  Birness. 257 C4
Mains of Burgie .266 D1
Mains of Clunas 253 B4
Mains of Crichie 257 B4
Mains of Dalvey .254 C2
Mains of
  Dellavaird 245 D4
Mains of Drum . 245 C5
Mains of
  Edingight. 267 D6
Mains of
  Fedderate 268 E3
Mains of
  Inkhorn 257 C4
Mains of Mayen . 255 B6
Mains of
  Melgund 232 C3
Mains of
  Thornton. 233 A4
Mains of Watten 281 C4
Mainsriddle. . . . 174 C2
Mainstone 93 C6
Maisemore 63 A4
Malacleit 287 G2
Malborough. 7 D5
Malcoff. 129 A5
Maldon 70 C2
Malham 146 A3
Maligar. 259 B4
Mallaig 235 A5
Malleny Mills. . . 209 D4
Malling 217 D5
Malltraeth 123 D4
Mallwyd 91 A6
Malmesbury . . . 44 A3
Malmsmead. . . . 26 A2
Malpas Ches W. . 110 A3
  Corn 4 C3
  Newport. 61 D5
Malswick 62 A3
Maltby Stockton . 168 D2
  S Yorks 140 D3
Maltby le Marsh 135 A4
Malting Green. . 70 A3
Maltman's Hill . . 37 B7
Malton 159 D6
Malvern Link . . . 79 C5
Malvern Wells. . . 79 C5
Mamble 95 D4
Manaccan 3 C5
Manafon 93 A5
Manar House. . .256 D2

Manaton.........12 C2
Manby..........134 A3
Mancetter.......97 B6
Manchester.....138 D1
Manchester
 Airport.......128 A3
Mancot........126 C3
Mandally.......239 B6
Manea.........101 C6
Manfield.......167 D5
Mangaster.....284 F5
Mangotsfield.....43 B5
Mangurstadh....287 A5
Mankinholes....138 A2
Manley........127 B5
Manmoel.......41 A6
Mannal........222 C2
Mannerston....208 C3
Manningford
 Bohune......45 D5
Manningford
 Bruce.......45 D5
Manningham....147 D5
Mannings Heath..35 D5
Mannington.....17 A4
Manningtree....88 D1
Mannofield....245 B6
Manor.........50 A1
Manorbier.....55 E6
Manordeilo.....58 C3
Manor Estate...130 A3
Manorhill.....197 C5
Manorowen.....72 C2
Manselfield....57 D5
Mansel Lacy.....78 C2
Mansell Gamage..78 C1
Mansergh......155 C5
Mansfield E Ayrs.182 A4
 Notts........131 C5
Mansfield
 Woodhouse...131 C5
Mansriggs.....154 C1
Manston Dorset...30 D2
 Kent.........53 C5
 W Yorks......148 D2
Manswood......16 A3
Manthorpe Lincs.116 B2
 Lincs........116 D3
Manton N Lincs..142 C1
 Notts........131 B5
 Rutland.......99 A5
 Wilts.........45 C5
Manuden.......69 A4
Maperton......29 C6
Maplebeck.....132 C2
Maple Cross.....37 D1
Mapledurham....47 B4
Mapledurwell...47 D4
Maplehurst.....35 D4
Maplescombe....50 C2
Mapleton......113 A5
Mapperley.....114 A2
Mapperley Park..114 A2
Mapperton.....15 B5
Mappleborough
 Green.......80 A3
Mappleton.....151 C5
Mappowder.....16 A1
Maraig........288 G2
Marazanvose.....4 B3
Marazion.......2 B3
Marbhig.......288 F5
Marbury......111 A4
March Cambs....101 B6
 S Lanark.....184 A2
Marcham......65 D5
Marchamley....111 C4
Marchington...113 B5
Marchington
 Woodlands....113 C5
Marchroes.....106 D3
Marchwiel.....110 A4
Marchwood.....32 D2
Marcross......40 E4
Marden Hereford..78 C3
 Kent.........37 B5
 T&W.........179 B5
 Wilts........45 D4
Marden Beech...37 B5

Marden Thorn....37 B5
Mardy.........61 B5
Marefield.......99 A4
Mareham le Fen 134 C2
Mareham on the
 Hill........134 C2
Marehay......114 A1
Marehill......20 A3
Maresfield.....36 D2
Marfleet......142 A3
Marford......126 D3
Margam.......40 C2
Margaret Marsh..30 D2
Margaret Roding..69 B5
Margaretting....69 C6
Margate........53 B5
Margnaheglish..191 B6
Margrove Park..169 D4
Marham.......119 D4
Marhamchurch...10 A3
Marholm......100 A3
Mariandyrs.....123 B6
Marianglas.....123 B5
Mariansleigh....26 C2
Marionburgh...245 B4
Marishader.....259 B4
Marjoriebanks..184 D3
Mark Dumfries..170 B3
 S Ayrs.......180 D2
Markbeech......36 B2
Markby.......135 B4
Mark Causeway...28 A3
Mark Cross E Sus..22 A2
 E Sus........36 C3
Market Bosworth 97 A7
Market Deeping 116 E4
Market Drayton .111 B5
Market
 Harborough....99 C4
Markethill....220 A2
Market Lavington 44 D4
Market Overton .116 D1
Market Rasen ..133 A6
Market Stainton 134 B2
Market Warsop .131 C5
Market
 Weighton....150 C1
Market Weston .103 D5
Markfield.....114 D2
Markham.......41 A6
Markham Moor..132 B1
Markinch.....220 D2
Markington...148 A1
Marksbury......43 C5
Marks Tey......70 A3
Markyate......67 B5
Marland......138 B1
Marlborough....45 C5
Marlbrook
 Hereford.....78 B3
 Worcs........96 D2
Marlcliff......80 B3
Marldon........8 A2
Marlesford.....88 B4
Marley Green ..111 A4
Marley Hill....179 D4
Marley Mount...17 B6
Marlingford...104 A2
Mar Lodge....242 C3
Marloes......54 D3
Marlow Bucks....47 A6
 Hereford.....94 D2
Marlow Bottom...47 A6
Marlpit Hill....36 B2
Marlpool.....114 A2
Marnhull......30 D1
Marnoch.....267 D6
Marnock.....207 D5
Marple......129 A4
Marple Bridge..129 A4
Marr.........140 C3
Marrel.......274 C4
Marrick......157 B4
Marrister....285 E7
Marros........56 B2
Marsden T&W ..179 C5
 W Yorks.....138 B3
Marsett......156 C3
Marsh Devon....28 D2
 W Yorks.....147 A4
Marshall's Heath .67 B6

Marshalsea......14 A3
Marshalswick....67 C6
Marsham......120 C3
Marshaw......145 B5
Marsh Baldon...65 D6
Marshborough...53 D5
Marshbrook.....94 C2
Marshchapel...143 D5
Marshfield
 Newport......42 A1
 S Glos........44 B1
Marshgate......10 B2
Marsh Gibbon..66 A1
Marsh Green
 Devon........13 B5
 Kent.........36 B2
 Staffs.......128 D3
Marshland
 St James....101 A7
Marsh Lane....131 B4
Marshside.....136 B2
Marsh Street....27 A4
Marshwood.....14 B3
Marske.......157 A5
Marske-by-the-
 Sea.........168 C4
Marston Ches W.127 B6
 Hereford.....78 B1
 Lincs........116 A1
 Oxon.........65 C6
 Staffs.......112 C3
 Staffs.......112 D2
 Warks........97 B5
 Wilts........44 D3
Marston Doles...82 B1
Marston Green...97 C4
Marston Magna...29 C5
Marston Meysey..64 D2
Marston
 Montgomery..113 B5
Marston
 Moretaine....84 C1
Marston on
 Dove........113 C6
Marston
 St Lawrence..82 C2
Marston Stannett 78 B3
Marston Trussell .98 C3
Marstow.......62 B1
Marsworth......67 B4
Marten........45 D6
Marthall.....128 B3
Martham......121 D6
Martin Hants....31 D4
 Kent.........39 A5
 Lincs........133 D6
 Lincs........134 C2
Martin Dales...101 D1
Martin Drove End 31 C4
Martinhoe......26 A1
Martinhoe Cross..26 A1
Martin
 Hussingtree..80 A1
Martin Mill.....39 A5
Martinscroft...127 A6
Martinstown....15 C6
Martlesham.....88 C3
Martlesham
 Heath........88 C3
Martletwy......55 C6
Martley........79 A5
Martock.......29 D4
Marton Ches E ..128 C3
 E Yorks......151 D4
 Lincs........132 A3
 Mbro........168 D3
 N Yorks......148 A3
 N Yorks......159 C6
 Shrops.......93 A6
 Shrops.......110 C3
 Warks........81 A7
Marton-le-
 Moor........158 D2
Martyr's Green...34 A3
Martyr Worthy...32 B4
Marwick......282 E3
Marwood.......25 B6
Marybank.....251 A6
Maryburgh....252 A1
Maryhill......205 B5
Marykirk.....233 B4
Marylebone....137 C4

Marypark......254 C2
Maryport Cumb .162 A3
 Dumfries.....170 D3
Mary Tavy......11 D6
Maryton......233 C4
Marywell Aberds .244 C2
 Aberds.......245 C6
 Angus.......233 D4
Masham......157 C6
Mashbury......69 B6
Masongill.....155 D5
Masonhill.....192 C3
Mastin Moor...131 B4
Mastrick.....245 B5
Matching......69 B5
Matching Green..69 B5
Matching Tye...69 B5
Matfen.......178 B2
Matfield.......37 B4
Mathern.......62 D1
Mathon........79 C5
Mathry........55 A4
Matlaske.....120 B3
Matlock......130 C2
Matlock Bath...130 D2
Matson........63 B4
Matterdale End.164 C1
Mattersey.....132 A1
Mattersey
 Thorpe......132 A1
Mattingley.....47 D5
Mattishall....120 D2
Mattishall
 Burgh.......120 D2
Mauchline....193 C4
Maud.........257 B4
Maugersbury...64 A3
Maughold.....152 B4
Mauld........251 C6
Maulden.......84 D2
Maulds
 Meaburn....165 D4
Maunby......158 C2
Maund Bryan...78 B3
Maundown......27 C5
Mautby......121 D6
Mavis Enderby .134 C3
Mawbray......174 D3
Mawdesley....136 B3
Mawdlam.......40 C3
Mawgan.........3 C5
Maw Green....128 D2
Mawla..........4 C2
Mawnan........3 C5
Mawnan Smith...3 C5
Mawsley.......99 D5
Mawthorpe....135 B4
Maxey........100 A3
Maxstoke......97 C5
Maxton Borders .197 C5
 Kent.........39 A5
Maxwellheugh .197 C6
Maxwelltown..174 A2
Maxworthy.....10 B3
Mayals........57 C6
Maybole.....192 E3
Mayfield E Sus...36 D3
 Midloth.....209 D6
 Staffs.......113 A5
 W Loth......208 D2
Mayford.......34 A2
Mayland.......70 C3
Maynard's Green 22 A3
Maypole Mon....61 B6
 Scilly.........2 E4
Maypole Green
 Essex.......70 A3
 Norf........105 B5
 Suff.........88 A3
Maywick.....285 L5
Meadle........66 C3
Meadowtown....93 A7
Meaford......112 B2
Meal Bank....154 B4
Mealabost
 Bhuirgh....288 B5
Mealsgate....175 D5
Meanwood....148 D1
Mearbeck.....146 A2
Meare.........29 A4
Meare Green...28 C3

Mears Ashby....83 A5
Measham......114 D1
Meath Green....35 B5
Meathop......154 C3
Meaux.......150 D3
Meavy.........7 A4
Medbourne.....99 B4
Medburn......178 B3
Meddon........24 D3
Meden Vale...131 C5
Medlam......134 D3
Medmenham....47 A6
Medomsley....178 D3
Medstead......33 B5
Meerbrook....129 C4
Meer End......97 D5
Meers Bridge ..135 A4
Meesden.......85 D6
Meeth.........11 A6
Meggethead...195 D6
Meidrim.......73 D5
Meifod Denb....125 D5
 Powys.......109 D6
Meigle N Ayrs..204 B1
 Perth.......231 D6
Meikle Earnock .194 A2
Meikle Ferry ..264 B3
Meikle Forter..231 B5
Meikle Gluich ..264 B2
Meikleour....219 A6
Meikle
 Pinkerton...211 C4
Meikle Strath ..233 A4
Meikle Tarty..257 D4
Meikle Wartle..256 C2
Meinciau......57 A4
Meir.........112 A3
Meir Heath....112 A3
Melbost......288 C5
Melbourn......85 C5
Melbourne
 Derbys......114 C1
 E Yorks.....149 C6
 S Lanark....195 B5
Melbury Abbas...30 C2
Melbury Bubb...15 A5
Melbury Osmond 15 A5
Melbury
 Sampford....15 A5
Melby.......285 H3
Melchbourne....84 A2
Melcombe
 Bingham......16 A1
Melcombe Regis 15 C6
Meldon Devon...11 B6
 Northumb....178 A3
Meldreth......85 C5
Meldrum House 256 D3
Melfort......213 A6
Melgarve.....240 C2
Meliden......125 A5
Melinbyrhedyn...91 C6
Melincourt.....40 A3
Melin-y-coed ..124 C3
Melin-y-ddôl...93 A4
Melin-y-grug...93 A4
Melin-y-Wig...109 A5
Melkinthorpe..164 C3
Melkridge....177 C5
Melksham......44 C3
Melldalloch..203 A4
Melling Lancs ..155 D4
 Mers........136 C2
Melling Mount .136 C3
Mellis.......104 D2
Mellon Charles .261 A5
Mellon Udrigle .261 A5
Mellor Gtr Man..129 A4
 Lancs.......145 D6
Mellor Brook..145 D6
Mells.........30 A1
Melmerby Cumb .165 B4
 N Yorks.....157 C4
 N Yorks.....158 D2
Melplash......15 B4
Melrose......197 C4
Melsetter....283 J3
Melsonby.....157 A5
Meltham......138 B4
Melton.......88 B3
Meltonby.....149 B6
Melton
 Constable ..120 B2

Melton
 Mowbray.....115 D5
Melton Ross ..142 B2
Melvaig......261 B4
Melverley.....110 D2
Melverley Green 110 D2
Melvich......279 B4
Membury......14 A2
Memsie......269 C4
Memus.......232 C2
Menabilly......5 B5
Menai Bridge
 =Porthaethwy .123 C5
Mendham.....104 C3
Mendlesham.....88 A2
Mendlesham
 Green.......88 A1
Menheniot......6 A1
Mennock.....183 B6
Menston.....147 C5
Menstrie.....207 A6
Mentmore......67 B4
Meoble......238 D1
Meole Brace...110 D3
Meols........136 D1
Meonstoke.....33 D5
Meopham......50 C3
Meopham Station 50 C3
Mepal.......101 C6
Meppershall....84 D3
Merbach......77 C7
Mere Ches E ..128 A2
 Wilts........30 B2
Mere Brow....136 B3
Mereclough...146 D2
Mere Green....96 B4
Mereside.....144 D3
Mereworth......37 A4
Mergie......245 D4
Meriden.......97 C5
Merkadale....246 A2
Merkland
 Dumfries....173 A5
 S Ayrs......181 B4
Merkland Lodge 271 B7
Merley........17 B4
Merlin's Bridge ..55 C5
Merrington...110 C3
Merrion.......55 E5
Merriott......28 D4
Merrivale.....11 D6
Merrow.......34 A3
Merrymeet......6 A1
Mersham......38 B2
Merstham......35 A5
Merston.......18 C4
Merther........4 C3
Merthyr......73 D6
Merthyr Cynog..76 D3
Merthyr-Dyfan...41 E6
Merthyr Mawr...40 D3
Merthyr Tudful
 =Merthyr Tydfil .60 C2
Merthyr Tydfil
 =Merthyr Tudful .60 C2
Merthyr Vale...41 B5
Merton
 Devon........25 D6
 London.......49 B5
 Norf........103 B5
 Oxon.........65 B6
Mervinslaw...187 B5
Meshaw.......26 D2
Messing........70 B2
Messingham...141 C6
Metfield.....104 C3
Metheringham .133 C5
Methil.......209 A6
Methlem.....106 C1
Methley......140 A1
Methlick.....256 C3
Methven.....219 B5
Methwold....102 B3
Methwold Hythe 102 B3
Mettingham...105 C4
Mevagissey.....5 C5
Mewith Head...145 A7
Mexborough...140 C2
Mey.........281 A4
Meysey Hampton 64 D2

Miabhag W Isles .287 D5
W Isles 288 H2
Miabhig 287 A5
Michaelchurch . . . 61 A7
Michaelchurch
Escley. 77 D7
Michaelchurch on
Arrow. 77 B6
Michaelston-le-
Pit. 41 D6
Michaelston-y-
Fedw. 42 A1
Michaelstow . . .10 D1
Michaelston-super-
Ely 41 D6
Micheldever . . . 32 B4
Michelmersh. . . . 32 C2
Mickfield 88 A2
Micklebring. . . .140 D3
Mickleby. 169 D6
Mickleham. 35 A4
Mickleover. . . .113 B7
Micklethwaite. . .147 C5
Mickleton
Durham 166 C2
Glos 81 C4
Mickletown 140 A1
Mickle Trafford .127 C4
Mickley. 157 D6
Mickley Square .178 C2
Mid Ardlaw . . .269 C4
Mid Auchinlech .204 A3
Midbea 282 C5
Mid Beltie 244 B3
Mid Calder. . . .208 D3
Mid Cloch
Forbie 268 D2
Mid Clyth 275 A6
Middle Assendon 47 A5
Middle Aston. . . .65 A5
Middle Barton. . .65 A5
Middlebie. 175 A5
Middle
Cairncake 256 B3
Middle Claydon . .66 A2
Middle Drums. . .232 C3
Middleforth
Green 136 A4
Middleham 157 C5
Middle Handley .131 B4
Middlehope. 94 C2
Middle Littleton . 80 C3
Middle Maes-
coed 78 D1
Middlemarsh. . . .15 A6
Middle Mill 54 B4
Middlemuir 257 D4
Middle Rasen . .133 A5
Middle Rigg. . . .219 D5
Middlesbrough. .168 C2
Middleshaw
Cumb 155 C4
Dumfries 174 A4
Middlesmoor. . .157 D4
Middlestone . . .167 B5
Middlestone
Moor. 167 B5
Middlestown . . .139 B5
Middlethird 197 B5
Middleton
Aberds 245 A5
Argyll. 222 C2
Cumb 155 C5
Derbys 130 C1
Derbys 130 D2
Essex 87 D4
Gtr Man 138 C1
Hants 32 A3
Hereford 78 A3
Lancs 144 B4
Midloth. 196 A2
N Nhants 99 C5
Norf 118 D3
Northumb 178 A2
Northumb. 199 C5
N Yorks 147 C5
N Yorks 159 C6
Perth 219 D6
Perth 231 D5
Shrops 93 B6
Shrops 94 D3
Shrops 110 C2

Middleton continued
Suff 89 A5
Swansea 57 D4
Warks. 97 B4
W Yorks 139 A5
Middleton
Cheney. 82 C1
Middleton
Green. 112 B1
Middleton Hall . .188 A2
Middleton-in-
Teesdale 166 C2
Middleton Moor. .89 A5
Middleton One
Row. 167 D6
Middleton-on-
Leven. 158 A3
Middleton-on-
Sea 20 B2
Middleton on the
Hill. 78 A3
Middleton-on-the-
Wolds 150 C2
Middleton Priors . 95 B4
Middleton
Quernham. . . .158 D2
Middleton
St George 167 D6
Middleton
Scriven. 95 C4
Middleton Stoney 65 A6
Middleton Tyas. .157 A6
Middletown
Cumb 162 D2
Powys 110 D2
Middle Tysoe . . .81 C6
Middle Wallop . . 32 B1
Middlewich 128 C1
Middle
Winterslow . . . 31 B6
Middle Woodford. 31 B5
Middlewood
Green 88 A1
Middlezoy 28 B3
Middridge 167 C5
Midfield 277 B6
Midge Hall 136 A4
Midgeholme . . .176 D4
Midgham 46 C3
Midgley W Yorks .138 A3
W Yorks 139 B5
Midhopestones. .139 D5
Midhurst. 34 D1
Mid Lavant. . . . 20 B1
Midlem 186 A4
Mid Main 251 C6
Midmar. 244 B3
Midsomer Norton 43 D5
Midton 204 A2
Midtown Highld. .261 B5
Highld. 277 B6
Midtown of
Buchromb. . . .254 B4
Mid Urchany . . .253 B4
Midville. 134 D3
Mid Walls. 285 H4
Midway 129 A4
Mid Yell 284 D7
Migdale 264 A2
Migvie. 244 B1
Milarrochy. . . .206 A2
Milborne Port. . .29 D6
Milborne
St Andrew . . . 16 B2
Milborne Wick . . 29 C6
Milbourne 178 B3
Milburn. 165 C4
Milbury Heath. . .62 D2
Milcombe. 81 D7
Milden. 87 C5
Mildenhall Suff . .102 B3
Wilts. 45 C6
Milebrook 93 D7
Milebush 37 B5
Mile Cross 120 D4
Mile Elm 44 C3
Mile End Essex . .70 A3
Glos 62 B1
Mileham 119 D6
Mile Oak 21 B5
Milesmark 208 B3
Milfield 198 C3

Milford Derbys. . .114 A1
Devon. 24 C3
Powys 93 B4
Staffs 112 C3
Sur 34 B2
Wilts. 31 C5
Milford Haven =
Aberdaugleddau . .55 D5
Milford on Sea . . 18 B1
Milkwall 62 C1
Milkwell 30 C3
Milland 34 D1
Millarston 205 B4
Millbank Aberds. .257 B6
Highld. 280 B3
Mill Bank 138 A3
Millbeck 163 B5
Millbounds 282 D6
Millbreck 257 B5
Millbridge 34 B1
Millbrook C Beds .84 D2
Corn 6 B3
Soton 32 D2
Millburn 193 C4
Millcombe 8 C2
Mill Common . . .105 C5
Millcorner 37 D6
Milldale 129 D6
Millden Lodge . .232 A3
Milldens 232 C3
Mill End Bucks . . .47 A5
Herts 85 D5
Millerhill 209 D6
Miller's Dale . . .129 B6
Miller's Green . .130 D2
Millgreen. 111 C5
Mill Green Essex . 69 C6
Norf 104 C2
Suff 87 C5
Millhalf 77 C6
Millhayes 14 A2
Millhead 154 D3
Millheugh. 194 A2
Mill Hill 68 D2
Millholme 155 B4
Millhouse Argyll. .203 A4
Cumb 163 A6
Millhousebridge 185 D4
Millhouse Green 139 C5
Millhouses 130 A3
Millikenpark . . .205 B4
Millin Cross 55 C5
Millington 150 B1
Mill Lane 47 D5
Millmeece 112 B2
Mill of
Kingoodie . . .256 D3
Mill of Muiresk . .256 B1
Mill of Sterin. . .243 C6
Mill of Uras . . .245 D5
Millom 153 B2
Millook 10 B2
Mill Place. 142 C1
Millpool 10 D2
Millport 204 C1
Millquarter 182 D4
Mill Side. 154 C3
Mill Street 120 D2
Millthorpe 116 B4
Millthrop 155 B5
Milltimber 245 B5
Milltown Corn . . .5 B6
Derbys 130 C3
Devon. 25 B6
Dumfries 175 A6
Milltown of
Aberdalgie . . .219 B5
Milltown of
Auchindoun . .255 B4
Milltown of
Craigston . . .268 D2
Milltown of
Edinvillie 254 B3
Milltown of
Kildrummy . . .244 A1
Milltown of
Rothiemay . . .255 B6
Milltown of
Towie 244 A1
Milnathort 219 D6
Milner's Heath . .127 C4
Milngavie 205 A5

Milnrow 138 B2
Milnshaw 137 A6
Milnthorpe. . . .154 C3
Milo 57 A5
Milson. 95 D4
Milstead 37 A7
Milston 31 A5
Milton Angus . .232 D1
Cambs 85 A6
Cumb 176 C3
Derbys 113 C7
Dumfries 171 B4
Dumfries 173 A6
Dumfries 183 D6
Highld. 251 A5
Highld. 251 C6
Highld. 252 B1
Highld. 264 C3
Highld. 281 C5
Moray. 267 C6
Notts 132 B2
N Som. 42 C2
Oxon. 65 D5
Oxon. 82 D1
Pembs 55 D6
Perth 219 C4
Ptsmth 19 B5
Stirling 217 D5
Stoke 129 D4
W Dunb. 205 A4
Milton Abbas. . . 16 A2
Milton Abbot . . .11 D5
Milton Bridge . .209 D5
Milton Bryan . . .83 D6
Milton Clevedon . 29 B6
Milton
Coldwells 257 C4
Milton Combe . . .6 A3
Milton Damerel . 25 D4
Miltonduff 266 C2
Milton End 64 C2
Milton Ernest . . 84 B2
Milton Green. . .127 D4
Miltonhill 266 C1
Milton Hill 65 D5
Miltonise 180 D3
Milton Keynes . . 83 D5
Milton Keynes
Village 83 D5
Milton Lilbourne .45 C5
Milton Malsor . . 83 B4
Milton Morenish 217 A6
Milton of
Auchinhove. . .244 B2
Milton of
Balgonie 220 D3
Milton of
Buchanan . . .206 A2
Milton of
Campfield . . .244 B3
Milton of
Cushnie. 244 A2
Milton of
Dalcapon . . .230 C3
Milton of
Edradour 230 C3
Milton of
Gollanfield . . .252 A3
Milton of
Lesmore 255 D5
Milton of Logie. .244 B1
Milton of Murtle 245 B5
Milton of Noth . .255 D6
Milton of Tullich 243 C6
Milton on Stour . 30 C1
Milton Regis . . .51 C6
Milton under
Wychwood . . . 64 B3
Milverton Som . . .27 C6
Warks. 81 A6
Milwich. 112 B3
Minard 214 C2
Minchinhampton 63 C4
Mindrum 198 C2
Minehead 27 A4
Minera 126 D2
Minety 63 D6
Minffordd Gwyn. . .91 A5

Minffordd continued
Gwyn 107 C5
Gwyn 123 C5
Miningsby 134 C3
Minions 10 D3
Minishant. 192 D3
Minllyn 91 A6
Minnes 257 D4
Minngearraidh . .286 D3
Minnigaff 171 A6
Minnonie 268 C2
Minskip. 148 A2
Minstead 32 D1
Minsted 34 D1
Minster Kent. . . .51 B6
Kent. 53 C5
Minsterley 94 A1
Minster Lovell . . 64 B4
Minsterworth . . 62 B3
Minterne Magna . 15 A6
Minting 134 B1
Mintlaw 257 B5
Minto. 187 A4
Minton 94 B2
Minwear 55 C6
Minworth 97 B4
Mirbister 282 E4
Mirehouse 162 C2
Mireland. 281 B5
Mirfield 139 B5
Miserden 63 C5
Miskin 41 C5
Misson 141 D4
Misterton Leics . .98 C2
Notts 141 D5
Som 15 A4
Mistley 88 D2
Mitcham 49 C5
Mitcheldean . . . 62 B2
Mitchell 4 B3
Mitchel Troy . . . 61 B6
Mitcheltroy
Common 61 B6
Mitford 178 A3
Mithian 4 D2
Mitton 112 D2
Mixbury 82 D3
Moat 175 A7
Moats Tye 87 B6
Mobberley
Ches E 128 B2
Staffs 112 A4
Moccas 78 C1
Mochdre Conwy. .124 B3
Powys 93 C4
Mochrum 171 C5
Mockbeggar . . . 17 A5
Mockerkin 162 B3
Modbury. 7 B5
Moddershall . . .112 B3
Moelfre Anglesey 123 B5
Powys 109 C6
Moffat. 184 B3
Moggerhanger . . 84 C3
Moira. 113 D7
Molash 52 D2
Mol-chlach 246 C3
Mold
=Yr Wyddgrug. .126 C2
Moldgreen. 139 B4
Molehill Green . . 69 A5
Molescroft. 150 C3
Molesden 178 A3
Molesworth . . .100 D2
Moll 247 A4
Molland 26 C3
Mollington
Ches W. 126 B3
Oxon. 82 C1
Mollinsburn. . . .207 C5
Monachty. 75 B4
Monachylemore 217 C4
Monar Lodge . . .250 B4
Monaughty 77 A6
Monboddo
House 233 A5
Mondynes 233 A5
Monevechadan . .215 B4
Monewden 88 B3
Moneydie 219 B5
Moniaive 183 C5
Monifieth 221 A4

Monikie 221 A4
Monimail 220 C2
Monington 72 B4
Monk Bretton . .139 C6
Monken Hadley . 68 D2
Monk Fryston . .140 A3
Monkhopton . . . 95 B4
Monkland. 78 B2
Monkleigh 25 C5
Monknash 40 D4
Monkokehampton
. . . . .11 A6
Monkseaton . . .179 B5
Monks Eleigh . . 87 C5
Monk's Gate . . . 35 D5
Monks Heath. . .128 B3
Monk Sherborne . 47 D4
Monkshill 256 B2
Monksilver. 27 B5
Monks Kirby . . . 98 C1
Monk Soham. . . 88 A3
Monkspath. 96 D4
Monks
Risborough . . . 66 C3
Monk Street . . . 69 A6
Monkswood. . . . 61 C5
Monkton Devon . 14 A1
Kent. 53 C4
Pembs 55 D5
S Ayrs. 192 C3
Monkton Combe . 44 C1
Monkton Deverill . 30 B2
Monkton
Farleigh. 44 C2
Monkton
Heathfield. . . . 28 C2
Monkton Up
Wimborne. . . .31 D4
Monkwearmouth
. . . . .179 D5
Monkwood 33 B5
Monmouth
=Trefynwy . . . 61 B7
Monmouth Cap. . 61 A5
Monnington on
Wye. 78 C1
Monreith 171 C5
Monreith Mains .171 C5
Montacute 29 D4
Montcoffer
House. 268 C1
Montford Argyll. .203 B6
Shrops 110 D3
Montford
Bridge 110 D3
Montgarrie 244 A2
Montgomery
=Trefaldwyn . .93 B6
Montrave 220 D3
Montrose 233 C5
Mont Saint Guern . 6
Montsale 71 D4
Monxton. 32 A2
Monyash. 129 C6
Monymusk. 244 A3
Monzie 218 B3
Monzie Castle. . .218 B3
Moodiesburn. . .207 C4
Moonzie 220 C3
Moor Allerton . .148 D1
Moorby 134 C2
Moor Crichel . . . 16 A3
Moordown 17 B4
Moore 127 A5
Moorend 62 C3
Moor End
E Yorks 149 D7
York 149 B5
Moorends. 141 B4
Moorgate 140 D2
Moorgreen 114 A2
Moorhall. 130 B3
Moorhampton . . .78 C1
Moorhead 147 D5
Moorhouse Cumb 175 C6
Notts 132 C2
Moorlinch 28 B3
Moor Monkton . .148 B4
Moor of Granary 253 A6

Moor of
Ravenstone....171 C5
Moor Row 162 C3
Moorsholm 169 D4
Moorside 138 C2
Moor Street.....51 C5
Moorthorpe 140 B2
Moortown Hants..17 A5
 IoW 18 C3
 Lincs..........142 D2
Morangie 264 B3
Morar 235 A5
Morborne......100 B3
Morchard Bishop 12 A2
Morcombelake ..14 B4
Morcott 99 A6
Morda 110 C1
Morden Dorset...16 B3
 London 49 C5
Mordiford 78 D3
Mordon........167 C6
More 94 B1
Morebath.......27 C4
Morebattle......187 A6
Morecambe 144 A4
Morefield 262 A3
Moreleigh 7 B6
Morenish 217 A5
Moresby 162 B2
Moresby Parks .162 C2
Morestead......32 C4
Moreton Dorset..16 C2
 Essex..........69 C5
 Mers..........136 D1
 Oxon...........66 C1
 Staffs.........112 D1
Moreton Corbet 111 C4
Moretonhampstead
..............12 C2
Moreton-in-
 Marsh..........81 D5
Moreton Jeffries.79 C4
Moreton Morrell .81 B6
Moreton on Lugg 78 C3
Moreton Pinkney 82 C2
Moreton Say 111 B5
Moreton Valence 62 C3
Morfa Carms....57 A5
 Carms..........57 C5
Morfa Bach 56 A3
Morfa Bychan ..107 C5
Morfa Dinlle ...107 A4
Morfa Glas 59 E5
Morfa Nefyn ...106 B2
Morfydd 109 A6
Morganls Vale ..31 C5
Moriah 75 A5
Morland 164 C3
Morley Derbys ..114 A1
 Durham........166 C4
 W Yorks........139 A5
Morley Green ..128 A3
Morley
 St Botolph.....104 B4
Morningside
 Edin 209 C5
 N Lanark.......194 A3
Morningthorpe..104 B3
Morpeth 179 A4
Morphie 233 B5
Morrey 113 D5
Morris Green...86 D3
Morriston.......57 C6
Morston 120 A2
Mortehoe 25 A5
Mortimer 47 C4
Mortimer's Cross 78 A2
Mortimer West
 End 47 C4
Mortlake.......49 B5
Morton Cumb ..175 C6
 Derbys........131 C4
 Lincs..........116 C3
 Lincs..........132 C3
 Lincs..........141 D6
 Norf 120 D3
 Notts 132 D2
 S Glos.........62 D2
 Shrops........110 C1

Morton Bagot 80 A4
Morton-on-
 Swale 157 B7
Morvah 2 B2
Morval.........6 B1
Morvich Highld..249 D6
 Highld.........273 D5
Morville 95 B4
Morville Heath ..95 B4
Morwenstow ...24 D3
Mosborough ...131 A4
Moscow 205 D4
Mosedale 163 A6
Moseley W Mid..96 B2
 W Mid.........96 C3
 Worcs..........79 B6
Moss Argyll....222 C2
 Highld.........235 D5
 S Yorks........140 B3
 Wrex 126 D3
Mossat 244 A1
Mossbank......284 F6
Moss Bank 136 D4
Mossbay 162 B2
Mossblown 193 C4
Mossbrow 128 A2
Mossburnford..187 B5
Mossdale 173 A4
Moss Edge 144 C4
Mossend 207 D5
Moss End 47 B6
Mosser 163 B4
Mossfield 264 C2
Mossgiel 193 C4
Mosside 232 C2
Mossley Ches E..129 C4
 Gtr Man 138 C2
Mossley Hill...126 A3
Moss of
 Barmuckity...266 C3
Moss Pit 112 C3
Moss-side 253 A4
Moss Side 144 D3
Mosstodloch ..266 D4
Mosston 232 D3
Mossy Lea 136 B4
Moston Gtr Man..138 C1
 Shrops.........111 C4
Moston Green..128 C2
Mostyn 125 A6
Mostyn Quay ..125 A6
Motcombe 30 C2
Mothecombe ...7 C5
Motherby 164 C2
Motherwell 194 A2
Mottingham...49 B7
Mottisfont 32 C9
Mottistone 18 C3
Mottram in
 Longdendale ..138 D2
Mottram
 St Andrew.....128 B3
Mouilpied Guern..6 E1
Mouldsworth...127 B5
Moulin 230 C3
Moulsecoomb...21 B6
Moulsford 46 A3
Moulsoe 83 C6
Moulton Ches W..127 C6
 Lincs..........117 C6
 N Yorks.......157 A6
 Suff 86 A2
 V Glam.........41 D5
 W Nhants......83 A4
Moulton Chapel 117 D5
Moulton
 Eaugate.......117 D6
Moulton
 St Mary 105 A4
Moulton Seas
 End 117 C6
Mounie Castle..256 D2
Mount Corn.....4 B2
 Corn..........5 A6
 Highld.........253 B6
Mountain 110 C1
Mountain Ash
 =Aberpennar...41 B5
Mountain Cross 195 B6
Mountain Water .55 B5
Mountbenger ..196 D2

Mount Bures 87 D5
Mount Canisp ..264 C3
Mountfield 37 D5
Mountgerald ...264 D1
Mount Hawke ...4 C2
Mountjoy 4 A3
Mountnessing ..69 D6
Mounton.......61 D7
Mount Pleasant
 Ches E........128 D3
 Derbys........113 D6
 Derbys........114 A1
 Flint 126 B2
 Hants..........18 B1
 W Yorks.......139 A5
Mountsorrel....114 D3
Mount Sorrel...31 C4
Mount Tabor ..138 A3
Mousehole......2 C2
Mousen 199 C5
Mouswald 174 A3
Mow Cop 128 D3
Mowhaugh.....187 A7
Mowsley 98 C3
Moxley 96 B2
Moy Highld....240 D2
 Highld.........252 C3
Moy Hall 252 C3
Moy House 265 D6
Moyles Court...17 A5
Moylgrove 72 B4
Moy Lodge 240 D2
Muasdale 202 D1
Muchalls 245 C6
Much Birch 78 D3
Much Cowarne..79 C4
Much Dewchurch 78 D2
Muchelney 28 C4
Much Hadham ..68 B4
Much Hoole....136 A3
Muchlarnick ...5 B7
Much Marcle ...79 D4
Muchrachd 251 C4
Much Wenlock..95 A4
Muckernich 252 A1
Mucking 50 A3
Muckleford 15 B6
Mucklestone...111 B6
Muckleton 111 C4
Muckley Corner..96 A3
Muckton 134 A3
Mudale 272 A3
Muddiford 25 B6
Mudeford 17 B5
Mudford 29 D5
Mudgley.......28 A4
Mugdock 205 A5
Mugeary 246 A3
Muggington ...113 A6
Muggleswick...166 A3
Muie 273 D4
Muir 242 D3
Muirden 268 D2
Muirdrum 221 A5
Muirhead Angus.220 A3
 Fife...........220 D2
 N Lanark......207 D4
 S Ayrs.........192 B3
Muirhouselaw..187 A5
Muirhouses ...208 B3
Muirkirk 194 D1
Muirmill 207 B5
Muir of Fairburn 251 A6
Muir of Fowlis..244 A2
Muir of Ord 252 A1
Muirshearlich..239 D5
Muirskie 245 C5
Muirtack.......257 C4
Muirton Highld..264 D3
 Perth 218 C4
 Perth 219 B6
Muirton Mains..251 A6
Muirton of
 Ardblair.......231 D5
Muirton of
 Ballochy......233 B4
Muiryfold 268 D2
Muker 156 B3
Mulbarton 104 A2
Mulben 267 D4

Mulindry.......200 C3
Mullardoch
 House.......250 C4
Mullion 3 D4
Mullion Cove...3 D4
Mumby 135 B5
Munderfield Row.79 B4
Munderfield
 Stocks.......79 B4
Mundesley 121 B5
Mundford......103 B4
Mundham 104 B4
Mundon 70 C2
Munerigie 239 B6
Mungasdale ...261 A6
Mungrisdale ...163 A6
Munlochy......252 A2
Munsley 79 C4
Munslow 94 C3
Murchington ...12 C1
Murcott 65 B6
Murkle 280 B3
Murlaggan
 Highld........238 C4
 Highld.........239 D7
Murra 283 G3
Murrayfield ...209 C5
Murrow........101 A5
Mursley........66 A3
Murthill 232 C2
Murthly 219 A5
Murton Cumb..165 C5
 Durham........167 A6
 Northumb......198 B3
 York 149 B5
Musbury 14 B2
Muscoates 159 C5
Musdale 226 D4
Musselburgh ..209 C6
Muston Leics..115 B6
 N Yorks........161 D4
Mustow Green ..95 D6
Mutehill 173 D4
Mutford 105 C5
Mutterton......13 A5
Muxton 111 D6
Mybster 280 C3
Myddfai 59 C4
Myddle 110 C3
Mydroilyn 74 C3
Myerscough ...145 D4
Mylor Bridge ...4 D3
Mynachlog-ddu 72 C4
Mynddtown 94 C1
Mynydd Bach ..75 A6
Mynydd-bach ..61 D6
Mynydd
 Bodafon......123 B4
Mynydd Isa ...126 C2
Mynyddygarreg..57 B4
Mynytho 106 C3
Myrebird 245 C4
Myrelandhorn..281 C4
Myreside 220 B2
Myrtle Hill 59 B4
Mytchett.......34 A1
Mytholm 138 A2
Mytholmroyd...138 A3
Myton-on-
 Swale 148 A3
Mytton 110 D3

N

Naast 261 B5
Naburn 149 C4
Nackington 52 D3
Nacton 88 C3
Nafferton 150 B3
Na Gearrannan..288 C2
Nailbridge 62 B2
Nailsbourne ...28 C2
Nailsea 42 B3
Nailstone 97 A7
Nailsworth 63 D4
Nairn 253 A4
Nalderswood ..35 B5
Nancegollan ...3 B4

Nancledra 2 B2
Nanhoron 106 C2
Nannau 108 C2
Nannerch 125 C6
Nanpantan.....114 D3
Nanpean........5 B4
Nanstallon 5 A5
Nant-ddu 60 B2
Nanternis 73 A6
Nantgaredig ...58 C1
Nantgarw 41 C6
Nant-glas 76 A3
Nantglyn......125 C5
Nantgwyn 92 D3
Nantlle 107 A5
Nantmawr 110 C1
Nantmel 76 A4
Nantmor.......107 B6
Nant Peris 107 A6
Nant Uchaf....125 D5
Nantwich 127 D6
Nant-y-Bai 59 A4
Nant-y-cafn ...59 E5
Nantycaws 57 A4
Nant-y-derry ..61 C5
Nant-y-ffin 58 B2
Nantyffyllon....40 B3
Nantyglo.......60 B3
Nant-y-moel ...40 B4
Nant-y-pandy..124 B1
Naphill 66 D3
Nappa 146 B2
Napton on the
 Hill 82 A1
Narberth
 =Arberth.....55 C7
Narborough Leics 98 B2
 Norf 119 D4
Nasareth.......107 A4
Naseby 98 D3
Nash Bucks.....83 D4
 Hereford.......77 A7
 Newport.......42 A2
 Shrops.........95 D4
Nash Lee 66 C3
Nassington 100 B2
Nasty 68 A3
Nateby Cumb..155 A6
 Lancs..........145 C4
Natland 154 C4
Naughton 87 C6
Naunton Glos...64 A2
 Worcs..........80 D1
Naunton
 Beauchamp ...80 B2
Navenby 133 D4
Navestock Heath 69 D5
Navestock Side..69 D5
Navidale 274 C4
Nawton 159 C5
Nayland 87 D5
Nazeing 68 C4
Neacroft 17 B5
Neal's Green...97 C6
Neap 285 H7
Near Sawrey ..154 B2
Neasham 167 D6
Neath
 =Castell-Nedd..40 B2
Neath Abbey ...40 B2
Neatishead 121 C5
Nebo Anglesey..123 A4
 Ceredig 75 B4
 Conwy 124 D3
 Gwyn 107 A4
Necton 103 A4
Nedd 270 A4
Nedderton 179 A4
Nedging Tye ...87 C6
Needham 104 C3
Needham Market.88 B1
Needingworth..101 D5
Needwood 113 C5
Neen Savage ...95 D4
Neen Sollars ...95 D4
Neenton 95 C4
Nefyn 106 B3
Neilston 205 C4
Neinthirion 92 A3
Neithrop 82 C1
Nelly Andrews
 Green 93 A6

Nelson Caerph ..41 B6
 Lancs..........146 D2
Nelson Village..179 B4
Nemphlar......194 B3
Nempnett
 Thrubwell.....43 C4
Nene Terrace...101 A4
Nenthall 165 A5
Nenthead 165 A5
Nenthorn 197 C5
Nerabus 200 C2
Nercwys 126 C2
Nerston 205 C6
Nesbit 198 C3
Ness 126 B3
Nesscliffe 110 D2
Neston Ches W..126 B2
 Wilts..........44 C2
Nether Alderley 128 B3
Netheravon 31 A5
Nether Blainslie 197 B4
Nether Booth ..129 A6
Netherbrae 268 C2
Netherbrough..282 F4
Nether
 Broughton.....115 C4
Netherburn 194 B3
Nether Burrow..155 D5
Netherbury 15 B4
Netherby Cumb..175 A6
 N Yorks........148 C2
Nether Cerne ..15 B6
Nether Compton 29 D5
Nethercote 82 A2
Nethercott 25 B5
Nether Crimond 256 D3
Nether
 Dalgliesh.....185 B5
Nether Dallachy 267 C4
Netherend 62 C1
Nether Exe 13 A4
Netherfield 23 A5
Nether Glasslaw 268 D3
Netherhampton..31 C5
Nether
 Handwick.....232 D1
Nether Haugh..140 D2
Nether Heage ..130 D3
Nether Heyford..82 B3
Nether
 Hindhope.....187 B6
Nether
 Howcleuch....184 A3
Nether Kellet...145 A5
Nether
 Kinmundy....257 B5
Nether Langwith 131 B5
Netherlaw 173 D5
Nether Leask ..257 C5
Nether Lenshie..256 B1
Netherley Aberds 245 C5
 Mers..........127 A4
Nethermill 184 D3
Nether Monynt 211 D4
Nethermuir ...257 B4
Nether Padley..130 B2
Nether Park ...269 D5
Netherplace ...205 C5
Nether
 Poppleton....149 B4
Netherseal 113 D6
Nether Silton ..158 B3
Nether Stowey..28 B1
Netherthird ...182 A3
Netherthong...139 C4
Netherthorpe..131 A5
Netherton Angus 232 C3
 Devon.........12 D3
 Hants..........46 D1
 Mers..........136 C2
 Northumb......188 C2
 Oxon...........65 D5
 Perth 231 C5
 Stirling........205 A5
 W Mid.........96 C2
 Worcs..........80 C2
 W Yorks........139 A4
 W Yorks........139 B5
Nethertown
 Cumb........162 D2
 Highld........281 A5
Nether Urquhart 219 D6

Nether Wallop . . . 32 B2
Nether Wasdale 163 D4
Nether Whitacre . 97 B5
Netherwitton. . . .189 D4
Netherwood 193 C6
Nether Worton . . . 82 D1
Nethy Bridge 253 D6
Netley 18 A3
Netley Marsh. 32 D2
Nettlebed. 69 B4
Nettlebed. 47 A5
Nettlebridge 29 A6
Nettlecombe. 15 B5
Nettleden. 67 B5
Nettleham 133 B5
Nettlestead. 37 A4
Nettlestead
  Green. 37 A4
Nettlestone 19 B5
Nettlesworth. . . .167 A5
Nettleton Lincs. . .142 C3
  Wilts. 44 B2
Neuadd. 58 C3
Nevendon. 20 D1
Nevern 72 B3
New Abbey. 174 B2
New Aberdour . . .268 C3
New Addington. . . 49 C6
Newall. 147 C5
New Alresford. . . . 33 B4
New Alyth. 231 D6
Newark Orkney. . .282 C8
  Pboro. 100 A4
Newark-on-
  Trent. 132 D2
New Arley 97 C5
Newarthill. 194 A2
New Ash Green. . . 50 C3
New Barn. 50 C3
New Barnetby . . .142 B2
Newbarns. 153 C3
New Barton 83 A5
Newbattle 209 D6
New Bewick 188 A3
Newbiggin Cumb 153 A1
  Cumb 153 D3
  Cumb 164 A3
  Cumb 164 C2
  Cumb 165 C4
  Durham 166 C2
  N Yorks. 156 B3
  N Yorks. 156 C3
Newbiggin-by-the-
  Sea. 179 A5
Newbigging
  Angus. 220 A4
  Angus. 221 A4
  Angus. 231 D6
  S Lanark. 195 B5
Newbiggin-on-
  Lune. 155 A6
New Bilton. 98 D1
Newbold Derbys. .130 B3
  Leics. 98 B1
Newbold on Avon 98 D1
Newbold on
  Stour. 81 C5
Newbold Pacey. . .81 B5
Newbold Verdon . 98 A1
New
  Bolingbroke . . .134 D3
Newborough
  Anglesey 123 D4
  Pboro. 100 A4
  Staffs. 113 C5
Newbottle T&W. .179 D5
  W Nhants. 82 D2
New Boultham . . .133 B4
Newbourne. 88 C3
New Bradwell 83 C5
New Brancepeth 167 A5
Newbridge Caerph 41 B7
  Ceredig 75 C4
  Corn 2 B2
  Corn 6 A2
  Dumfries 174 A2
  Edin 208 C4
  Hants 32 D1
  IoW 18 C3
  Pembs 55 A5
New Bridge 110 A1
Newbridge Green 79 D6

Newbridge-on-
  Usk 61 D5
Newbridge on
  Wye. 76 B3
New Brighton
  Flint 126 C2
  Mers. 136 D2
New Brinsley. . . .131 D4
Newbrough 177 C6
New Broughton .126 D3
New
  Buckenham . . .104 B1
Newbuildings . . . 12 A2
Newburgh
  Aberds 257 D4
  Aberds 269 D4
  Borders 185 A6
  Fife. 220 C2
  Lancs 136 B3
Newburn 178 C3
Newbury 46 C2
Newbury Park . . . 50 A1
Newby Cumb. . . .164 C3
  Lancs 146 C2
  N Yorks. 155 D6
  N Yorks. 160 B4
  N Yorks. 168 D3
Newby Bridge . . .154 C2
Newby East 176 D2
New Byth 268 D3
Newby West 175 C6
Newby Wiske . . .158 C2
Newcastle Mon . . 61 B6
  Shrops. 93 C6
Newcastle Emlyn
  = Castell Newydd
  Emlyn 73 B6
Newcastleton or
  Copshaw
  Holm. 176 A2
Newcastle-under-
  Lyme. 112 A2
Newcastle Upon
  Tyne 179 C4
New Catton 120 D4
Newchapel Pembs 73 C5
  Powys. 92 C3
  Staffs. 128 D3
  Sur. 35 B6
New Cheriton 33 C4
Newchurch Carms 73 D6
  IoW 19 C4
  Kent 38 B2
  Lancs 146 D2
  Mon 61 D6
  Powys. 77 B6
  Staffs. 113 C5
New Costessey . .120 D3
Newcott 14 A2
New Cowper 174 D4
Newcraighall. . . .209 C6
New Cross Ceredig 75 A5
  London 49 B6
New Cumnock . . .182 A4
New Deer 256 B3
New Delaval 179 B4
Newdigate 35 B4
New Duston 83 A4
New Earswick . . .149 B5
New Edlington . . .140 D3
New Elgin 266 C3
New Ellerby 151 D4
Newell Green . . . 48 B1
New Eltham 50 B1
New End. 80 B3
Newenden 37 D6
Newent 62 A3
Newerne. 62 C2
New Farnley 147 D6
New Ferry 126 A3
Newfield Durham 167 B5
  Highld. 264 C3
Newford Scilly . . . 2 E4
Newfound 46 D3
New Fryston 140 A2
Newgale 54 B4
New Galloway . . .172 A4
Newgate 120 A2
Newgate Street . . 68 C3
New Gilston 220 D4
New Grimsby Scilly . 2 E3
New Hainford . . .120 D4

Newhall Ches E . .111 A5
  Derbys. 113 C6
Newhall House . .264 D2
Newhall Point . . .264 D3
Newham. 189 A4
Newham Hall . . .189 A4
New Hartley. . . .179 B5
Newhaven
  Derbys. 129 D6
  Edin 209 C5
  E Sus 22 B2
New Haw 48 C3
New Hedges 56 B1
New Herrington 179 D5
Newhey. 138 B2
New Hinksey 65 C6
New Holkham . . .119 B5
New Holland 142 A2
Newholm 169 D6
New Houghton
  Derbys. 131 C4
  Norf 119 C4
Newhouse 207 D5
New Houses 155 D7
New
  Humberstone. .98 A3
New Hutton 155 B4
New Hythe. 37 A5
Newick 36 D2
Newingreen. 38 B3
Newington Kent. . 38 B3
  Kent 51 C5
  Kent 53 C5
  Notts 141 D4
  Oxon. 65 D7
  Shrops 94 C2
New Inn Carms. . . 58 B1
  Mon 61 C6
  Pembs 55 A6
  Torf 61 D5
New Invention
  Shrops 93 B6
  W Mid. 96 A2
New Kelso 249 B6
New Kingston . . .114 C3
New Lanark 194 B3
Newland Glos. . . . 62 C1
  Hull 150 D3
  N Yorks. 141 A4
  Worcs. 79 C5
Newlandrig 209 D6
Newlands
  Borders 186 D4
  Highld. 252 B3
  Moray. 266 D4
  Northumb. 178 D2
Newland's Corner 34 B3
Newlandsmuir . .205 C6
Newlands of
  Geise 280 B2
Newlands of
  Tynet 267 C4
Newlands Park . .122 B2
New Lane. 136 B3
New Lane End. . .137 D5
New Leake 135 D4
New Leeds 269 D4
New Longton . . .136 A4
Newlot 282 F6
New Luce 170 A3
Newlyn 2 C2
Newmachar. 245 A5
Newmains 194 A3
New Malden 49 C5
Newmarket Suff . . 86 A2
  W Isles. 288 D5
New Marske 168 C4
New Marton 110 B2
New Micklefield 148 D3
Newmill Borders .186 B3
  Corn 2 B2
  Moray. 267 D5
New Mill Aberds. .245 D4
  Herts 67 B4
  Wilts. 45 C5
  W Yorks 139 C4
Newmill of
  Inshewan. 232 B2
New Mills Ches E 128 A2
  Corn 4 B3
  Derbys. 129 A4
  Powys. 93 A4

Newmills of
  Boyne. 267 D6
Newmiln. 219 A6
Newmilns. 193 B5
New Milton 17 B6
New Moat. 55 B6
Newnham Cambs. . 85 B6
  Glos 62 B2
  Hants 47 D5
  Herts 84 D4
  Kent 51 D6
  W Nhants 82 B2
Newnham Bridge 79 A4
New Ollerton . . .131 C6
New Oscott 96 B3
Newpark. 221 C4
New Park 148 B1
New Pitsligo 268 D3
New Polzeath 9 D5
Newport Devon . . 25 B6
  Essex 85 D7
  E Yorks 150 D1
  Highld. 275 B5
  IoW 18 C4
  Norf 121 D7
  Telford 111 D6
Newport
  = Casnewydd . . .42 A2
Newport
  = Trefdraeth . . . 72 C3
Newport-
  on-Tay. 220 B4
Newport Pagnell . 83 C5
Newpound
  Common 34 D3
Newquay 4 A3
New Quay
  = Ceinewydd . . . 73 A6
New Rackheath . 121 D4
New Radnor 77 A6
New Rent 164 B2
New Ridley. 178 D2
New Road Side. .146 C3
New Romney 38 C2
New Rossington 140 D4
New Row Ceredig. . 75 A6
  Lancs 145 D6
  N Yorks. 168 D4
New Sarum 31 B5
Newsbank 128 C3
Newseat Aberds. .256 C2
  Aberds 257 B5
Newsham
  Northumb. 179 B5
  N Yorks. 158 C2
  N Yorks. 166 D4
Newsholme
  E Yorks 141 A5
  Lancs 146 B2
New Silksworth .179 D5
Newsome. 139 B4
Newstead
  Borders 197 C4
  Northumb. 189 A4
  Notts 131 D5
New Stevenston 194 A2
New Street. 129 D5
New Street Lane 111 B5
New Swanage. . . . 17 C4
Newthorpe. 148 D3
Newton Argyll. . .214 C3
  Borders 187 B2
  Bridgend 40 D3
  Cambs 85 C6
  Cambs 118 D1
  Cardiff. 42 B1
  Ches W. 127 B5
  Ches W. 127 C4
  Ches W. 127 D5
  Cumb 153 C3
  Derbys. 131 D4
  Dorset 30 D1
  Dumfries 175 A5
  Dumfries 185 C4
  Gtr Man 138 D2
  Hereford 78 B3
  Hereford 78 D1
  Highld. 252 B3
  Highld. 264 D3
  Highld. 271 A6
  Highld. 281 D5
  Lancs 144 D4

Newton continued
  Lancs 145 B6
  Lancs 155 D4
  Lincs. 116 B3
  Moray. 266 C2
  N Nhants 99 C5
  Norf 119 D5
  Northumb. 178 C2
  Notts 115 A4
  Perth 218 A3
  S Lanark. 194 C4
  S Lanark 205 B6
  Staffs 112 C4
  Suff 87 C5
  Swansea 57 D6
  S Yorks 140 C3
  Warks. 98 D2
  Wilts. 31 C6
  W Loth 208 C3
Newton Abbot. . . 12 D3
Newtonairds 183 D6
Newton Arlosh . .175 C4
Newton Aycliffe .167 C5
Newton Bewley .168 C2
Newton
  Blossomville. . 83 B6
Newton
  Bromswold 84 A1
Newton
  Burgoland. 97 A6
Newton by Toft. .133 A5
Newton Ferrers . . 7 C4
Newton Flotman 104 B3
Newtongrange . .209 D6
Newton Hall 178 C2
Newton Harcourt 98 B3
Newton Heath. . .138 C1
Newtonhill
  Aberds 245 C6
  Highld. 252 B1
Newton House . .256 D1
Newton Kyme . . .148 C3
Newton-le-Willows
  Mers. 137 D4
  N Yorks. 157 C6
Newton Longville 83 D5
Newton Mearns .205 C5
Newtonmill 233 B4
Newtonmore . . .241 C5
Newton Morrell .157 A6
Newton
  Mulgrave. 169 D5
Newton of
  Ardtoe 235 C5
Newton of
  Balcanquhal . .219 C6
Newton of
  Falkland. 220 D4
Newton on Ayr . .192 C3
Newton on Ouse 148 B3
Newton-on-
  Rawcliffe. 159 B7
Newton-on-the-
  Moor. 189 C4
Newton on
  Trent. 132 B3
Newton Park . . .203 B6
Newton
  Poppleford. . . . 13 C5
Newton Purcell . . 82 D3
Newton Regis . . . 97 A5
Newton Reigny .164 B2
Newton St Cyres. . 12 B3
Newton St Faith 120 D4
Newton St Loe . . 43 C6
Newton
  St Petrock. 25 D5
Newton Solney . .113 C6
Newton Stacey. . . 32 A3
Newton Stewart 171 A6
Newton Tony 31 A6
Newton Tracey . . 25 C6
Newton under
  Roseberry 168 D3
Newton upon
  Derwent. 149 C6
Newton Valence. . 33 B6
New Totley. 130 B3
Newtown Argyll 214 B3
  BCP. 17 B4
  Ches W. 127 B5
  Corn 3 C5

Newtown continued
  Cumb 174 D3
  Cumb 176 C3
  Derbys 129 A4
  Devon. 26 C2
  Glos 62 C2
  Glos 80 D2
  Hants 18 A3
  Hants 31 D6
  Hants 32 C2
  Hants 32 D4
  Hants 33 D5
  Hants 46 C2
  Hereford 79 C4
  Highld. 240 B1
  IoM 152 D3
  IoW 18 B3
  Northumb. 188 A3
  Northumb. 188 C3
  Northumb. 198 C3
  Shrops 110 B3
  Staffs 129 C4
  Staffs 129 C5
  Wilts. 30 C3
New Town 210 C1
Newtown
  = Y Drenewydd. . 93 B5
Newtown Linford 98 A2
Newtown
  St Boswells. . . .197 C4
Newtown
  Unthank. 98 A1
New Tredegar
  = Tredegar Newydd. 41 A6
New Trows. 194 C3
Newtyle 231 D6
New Ulva 213 D5
New Walsoken . .101 A6
New Waltham . . .143 C4
New
  Whittington . . .130 B3
New Wimpole . . . 85 C5
New Winton 210 C1
New Yatt. 65 B4
New York Lincs . .134 D2
  N Yorks. 147 A5
Neyland 55 D5
Niarbyl 152 D2
Nibley 43 A5
Nibley Green 62 D3
Nibon 284 F5
Nicholashayne . . 27 D6
Nicholaston. 57 D5
Nidd. 148 A2
Nigg Aberdeen . .245 B6
  Highld. 265 C4
Nigg Ferry 264 D3
Nightcott 26 C3
Nilig. 125 D5
Nine Ashes. 69 C5
Ninebanks 177 D5
Nine Mile Burn. .195 A6
Nine Wells 54 B3
Ninfield. 23 A5
Ningwood 18 C2
Nisbet 187 A5
Nisthouse
  Orkney 282 F4
  Shetland. 285 G7
Niton 18 D4
Nitshill 205 B5
Noak Hill 69 D5
Noblethorpe. . . .139 C5
Nobottle 82 A3
Nocton 133 C5
Noke 65 B6
Nolton 55 C4
Nolton Haven . . . 55 C4
No Man's Heath
  Ches W. 111 A4
  Warks. 97 A5
Nomansland
  Devon. 26 D3
  Wilts. 31 D6
Noneley 110 C3
Nonikiln 264 C2
Nonington 53 D4
Noonsbrough . . .285 H4
Norbreck 144 C3

Norbridge . . . 79 C5
Norbury Ches E . 111 A4
Derbys . . . 113 A5
Shrops . . . 94 B1
Staffs . . . 112 C1
Nordelph . . . 102 A1
Norden . . . 138 B1
Norden Heath . . 16 C3
Nordley . . . 95 B4
Norham . . . 198 B3
Norley . . . 127 B5
Norleywood . . . 18 B2
Normanby
N Lincs . . . 141 B6
N Yorks . . . 159 C6
Redcar . . . 168 D3
Normanby-by-
Spital . . . 133 A5
Normanby by
Stow . . . 132 A3
Normanby le
Wold . . . 142 D3
Norman Cross . . 100 B3
Normandy . . . 34 A2
Norman's Bay . . 23 B4
Norman's Green . 13 A5
Normanstone . . 105 B6
Normanton
Derby . . . 114 B1
Leics . . . 115 A6
Lincs . . . 116 A2
Notts . . . 132 D2
Rutland . . . 99 A6
W Yorks . . . 140 A1
Normanton le
Heath . . . 114 D1
Normanton on
Soar . . . 114 C3
Normanton-on-the-
Wolds . . . 115 B4
Normanton on
Trent . . . 132 C2
Normoss . . . 144 D3
Norney . . . 34 B2
Norrington
Common . . . 44 C2
Norris Green . . 136 D2
Norris Hill . . . 114 D1
Northacre . . . 103 B5
Northallerton . . 158 B2
Northam Devon . . 25 C5
Soton . . . 32 D3
Northampton . . 83 A4
North Anston . . 131 A5
North Aston . . . 65 A5
Northaw . . . 68 C2
North Baddesley . 32 D2
North
Ballachulish . . 237 C4
North Barrow . . 29 C6
North Barsham . 119 B6
Northbeck . . . 116 A3
North Benfleet . . 51 A4
North Bersted . . 20 B2
North Berwick . . 210 B2
North Boarhunt . 33 D5
Northborough . . 100 A3
Northbourne . . . 53 D5
North Bovey . . . 12 C2
North Bradley . . 44 D2
North Brentor . . 11 C5
North Brewham . 29 B7
Northbridge
Street . . . 37 D5
North Buckland . 25 A5
North
Burlingham . . 121 D5
North Cadbury . . 29 C6
North Cairn . . . 180 D1
North Carlton . . 133 B4
North Carrine . . 190 E2
North Cave . . . 150 D1
North Cerney . . 63 C6
Northchapel . . . 34 D2
North Charford . 31 D5
North Charlton . 189 A4
North Cheriton . 29 C6
Northchurch . . . 67 C4
North Cliff . . . 151 C5

North Cliffe . . . 150 D1
North Clifton . . . 132 B3
North
Cockerington . 143 D5
North Coker . . . 29 D5
North Collafirth . 284 E5
North Common . . 36 D1
North Connel . . 226 C4
North Cornelly . . 40 C3
North Cotes . . . 143 C5
Northcott . . . 10 B4
North Cove . . . 105 C5
North Cowton . . 157 A6
North Crawley . . 83 C6
North Cray . . . 50 B1
North Creake . . 119 B5
North Curry . . . 28 C3
North Dalton . . 150 B2
North Dawn . . . 283 G5
North Deighton . 148 B2
Northdown . . . 53 B5
North Duffield . . 149 D5
North Dyke . . . 282 E3
North Elkington . 143 D4
North Elmham . . 120 C1
North Elmsall . . 140 B2
Northend Bath . . 44 C1
Bucks . . . 66 D2
Warks . . . 81 B6
North End Bucks . 66 A3
Essex . . . 69 B6
E Yorks . . . 151 B5
Hants . . . 46 C2
Lincs . . . 117 A5
N Som . . . 42 C3
Ptsmth . . . 19 A5
Som . . . 28 C2
W Sus . . . 21 B4
Northenden . . . 137 D7
North Erradale . . 261 B4
North Fambridge . 70 D2
North Fearns . . 248 C3
North
Featherstone . 140 A2
North Ferriby . . 142 A1
Northfield
Aberdeen . . . 245 B6
Borders . . . 211 D6
E Yorks . . . 142 A2
W Mid . . . 96 D3
Northfields . . . 100 A4
Northfleet . . . 50 B3
North
Frodingham . . 151 B4
Northgate . . . 117 C4
North Gorley . . . 31 D5
North Green
Norf . . . 104 C3
Suff . . . 89 A4
North Greetwell . 133 B5
North Grimston . 150 A1
North Halley . . 283 G6
North Halling . . 51 C4
North Hayling . . 19 A6
North Hazelrigg . 199 C4
North Heasley . . 26 B2
North Heath . . . 34 D3
North Hill Cambs . 101 D6
Corn . . . 10 D3
North Hinksey . . 65 C5
North Holmwood . 35 B4
Northhouse . . . 186 C3
North Howden . . 149 D6
North Huish . . . 7 B6
North Hykeham . 133 C4
Northiam . . . 37 D6
Northill . . . 84 C3
Northington . . . 33 B4
North Johnston . 55 C5
North Kelsey . . 142 C2
North Kelsey
Moor . . . 142 C2
North Kessock . 252 B2
North
Killingholme . 142 B3
North Kilvington 158 C3
North Kilworth . 98 C3
North Kirkton . . 35 C5
North Kiscadale 191 C6
North Kyme . . . 133 D6
North Lancing . . 21 B4

Northlands . . . 134 D3
Northlea . . . 179 D6
Northleach . . . 64 B2
North Lee . . . 66 C3
Northleigh . . . 14 B1
North Leigh . . . 65 B4
North Leverton with
Habblesthorpe 132 A2
Northlew . . . 11 B6
North Littleton . 80 C3
North Lopham . 103 C6
North Luffenham 99 A6
North Marden . . 33 D7
North Marston . 66 A2
North Middleton
Midloth . . . 196 A2
Northumb . . . 188 A3
North Molton . . 26 C2
Northmoor . . . 65 C5
Northmoor Green or
Moorland . . . 28 B3
North Moreton . 46 A3
Northmuir . . . 232 C1
North Mundham . 20 B1
North Muskham 132 D2
North Newbald . 150 D2
North Newington 81 D7
North Newnton . 45 D5
North Newton . . 28 B2
Northney . . . 19 A6
North Nibley . . 62 D3
North Oakley . . 46 D3
North Ockendon . 50 A2
Northolt . . . 48 A4
Northop . . . 126 C2
Northop Hall . . 126 C2
North Ormesby . 168 C3
North Ormsby . . 143 D4
Northorpe Lincs . 116 C3
Lincs . . . 117 B5
Lincs . . . 141 D6
North
Otterington . . 158 C2
Northover Som . . 29 B4
Som . . . 29 C5
North Owersby . 142 D2
Northowram . . 139 A4
North Perrott . . 15 A4
North Petherton . 28 B2
North Petherwin 10 C3
North
Pickenham . . 103 A4
North Piddle . . 80 B2
North Poorton . 15 B5
Northport . . . 16 C3
North Port . . . 227 D5
Northpunds . . 285 L6
North
Queensferry . 208 B4
North Radworthy 26 B2
North Rauceby . 116 A3
Northrepps . . . 120 B4
North Reston . . 134 A3
North Rigton . . 148 C1
North Rode . . . 128 C3
North Roe . . . 284 E5
North Runcton . 118 D3
North Sandwick 284 D7
North Scale . . . 153 D2
North Scarle . . 132 C3
North Seaton . . 179 A4
North Shian . . . 226 B4
North Shields . . 179 C5
North Shoebury . 51 A6
North Shore . . . 144 D3
North Side Cumb 162 B3
Pboro . . . 101 B4
North Skelton . . 169 D4
North
Somercotes . . 143 D6
North Stainley . 157 D6
North
Stainmore . . 165 D6
North Stifford . . 50 A3
North Stoke Bath . 44 C1
Oxon . . . 47 A4
W Sus . . . 20 A3
North Street
Hants . . . 33 B5
Kent . . . 52 D2
Medway . . . 51 B5
W Berks . . . 47 B4

North
Sunderland . . 199 C6
North Tamerton . 10 B4
North Tawton . . 12 A1
North Thoresby . 143 D4
North Tidworth . 31 A6
North Togston . 189 C5
Northtown . . . 283 H5
North
Tuddenham . . 120 D2
North Walbottle 178 C3
North Walsham . 121 B4
North Waltham . 33 A4
North
Warnborough . 47 D5
North Water
Bridge . . . 233 B4
North Watten . . 280 C4
Northway . . . 80 D2
North Weald
Bassett . . . 69 C4
North Wheatley . 132 A2
North
Whilborough . . 8 A2
Northwich . . . 127 B6
Northwick . . . 43 A4
North Wick . . . 43 C4
North
Willingham . . 133 A6
North Wingfield 131 C4
North Witham . 116 C2
Northwold . . . 102 B3
Northwood
Derbys . . . 130 C2
IoW . . . 18 B3
Kent . . . 53 C5
London . . . 67 D5
Shrops . . . 110 B3
Northwood Green 62 B3
North Woolwich . 50 B1
North Wootton
Dorset . . . 29 D6
Norf . . . 118 C3
Som . . . 29 A5
North Wraxall . . 44 B2
North Wroughton 45 A5
Norton E Sus . . 22 B2
Glos . . . 63 A4
Halton . . . 127 A5
Herts . . . 84 D4
IoW . . . 18 C2
Mon . . . 61 B6
Notts . . . 131 B5
Powys . . . 77 A7
Shrops . . . 93 A4
Shrops . . . 94 C2
Shrops . . . 95 D5
Stockton . . . 168 C2
Suff . . . 87 A5
S Yorks . . . 140 B3
Wilts . . . 44 A2
W Nhants . . . 82 A3
Worcs . . . 80 B1
Worcs . . . 80 C3
W Sus . . . 20 B2
W Sus . . . 20 C1
Norton Bavant . . 30 A3
Norton Bridge . . 112 B2
Norton Canes . . 96 A3
Norton Canon . . 78 C1
Norton Corner . 120 C2
Norton Disney . . 132 D3
Norton East . . . 96 A3
Norton Ferris . . 30 B1
Norton
Fitzwarren . . . 28 C1
Norton Green . . 18 C2
Norton Hawkfield 43 C4
Norton Heath . . 69 C6
Norton in Hales 111 B6
Norton-in-the-
Moors . . . 128 D3
Norton-Juxta-
Twycross . . . 97 A6
Norton-le-Clay . 158 D3
Norton Lindsey . 81 A5
Norton
Malreward . . . 43 C5
Norton
Mandeville . . 69 C5
Norton-on-
Derwent . . . 159 D6

Norton St Philip . 43 D6
Norton sub
Hamdon . . . 29 D4
Norton
Woodseats . . 130 A3
Norwell . . . 132 C2
Norwell
Woodhouse . . 132 C2
Norwich . . . 104 A3
Norwick . . . 284 B8
Norwood . . . 131 A4
Norwood Hill . . 35 B5
Norwoodside . . 101 B6
Noseley . . . 99 B4
Noss . . . 285 M5
Noss Mayo . . . 7 C4
Nosterfield . . . 157 C6
Nostie . . . 249 D5
Notgrove . . . 64 A2
Nottage . . . 40 D3
Nottingham . . 114 B3
Nottington . . . 15 C6
Notton Wilts . . . 44 C3
W Yorks . . . 139 B6
Nounsley . . . 70 B1
Noutard's Green . 79 A5
Novar House . . 264 D2
Nox . . . 110 D3
Nuffield . . . 47 A4
Nunburnholme . 150 C1
Nuncargate . . 131 D5
Nuneaton . . . 97 B6
Nuneham
Courtenay . . . 65 D6
Nun Hills . . . 138 A1
Nun Monkton . 148 B4
Nunney . . . 30 A1
Nunnington . . 159 D5
Nunnykirk . . . 188 D3
Nunsthorpe . . 143 C4
Nunthorpe Mbro 168 D3
York . . . 149 B5
Nunton . . . 31 C5
Nunwick . . . 157 D7
Nupend . . . 62 C3
Nursling . . . 32 D2
Nursted . . . 33 C6
Nutbourne W Sus . 19 A6
W Sus . . . 20 A3
Nutfield . . . 35 A6
Nuthall . . . 114 A3
Nuthampstead . 85 D6
Nuthurst . . . 35 D4
Nutley E Sus . . . 36 D2
Hants . . . 33 A5
Nutwell . . . 140 C4
Nybster . . . 281 B5
Nyetimber . . . 20 C1
Nyewood . . . 33 C7
Nymet Rowland . 12 A2
Nymet Tracey . . 12 A2
Nympsfield . . . 63 C4
Nynehead . . . 27 C6
Nyton . . . 20 B2

O

Oadby . . . 98 A3
Oad Street . . . 51 C5
Oakamoor . . . 113 A4
Oakbank . . . 208 D3
Oak Cross . . . 11 B6
Oakdale . . . 41 B6
Oake . . . 27 C6
Oaken . . . 95 A6
Oakenclough . . 145 C5
Oakengates . . 111 D6
Oakenholt . . . 126 B2
Oakenshaw
Durham . . . 167 B5
W Yorks . . . 139 A4
Oakerthorpe . . 130 D3
Oakes . . . 139 B4
Oakfield . . . 61 D5
Oakford Ceredig . 74 C3
Devon . . . 27 C4
Oakfordbridge . 27 C4
Oakgrove . . . 129 C4
Oakham . . . 99 A5
Oakhanger . . . 33 B6
Oakhill . . . 29 A6

Oakhurst . . . 36 A3
Oakington . . . 85 A6
Oaklands Herts . 68 B2
Powys . . . 76 B4
Oakle Street . . 62 B3
Oakley BCP . . . 17 B4
Bedford . . . 84 B2
Bucks . . . 66 B1
Fife . . . 208 B3
Hants . . . 46 D3
Oxon . . . 66 C2
Suff . . . 104 D2
Oakley Green . . 48 B2
Oakley Park . . 92 C3
Oakmere . . . 127 C5
Oakridge Glos . . 63 C5
Hants . . . 94 A2
Oaks . . . 94 A2
Oaksey . . . 63 D5
Oaks Green . . . 113 B5
Oakthorpe . . . 113 D7
Oakwoodhill . . 35 C4
Oakworth . . . 147 D4
Oape . . . 272 D2
Oare Kent . . . 52 C2
Som . . . 26 A3
W Berks . . . 46 B3
Wilts . . . 45 C5
Oasby . . . 116 B3
Oathlaw . . . 232 C2
Oatlands . . . 148 B2
Oban Argyll . . . 226 D3
Highld . . . 238 D2
Oborne . . . 29 D6
Obthorpe . . . 116 D3
Occlestone
Green . . . 128 C1
Occold . . . 104 D2
Ochiltree . . . 193 C5
Ochtermuthill . 218 C3
Ochtertyre . . . 218 B3
Ockbrook . . . 114 B2
Ockham . . . 34 A3
Ockle . . . 235 C4
Ockley . . . 35 C4
Ocle Pychard . . 78 C3
Octon . . . 150 A3
Octon Cross
Roads . . . 150 A3
Odcombe . . . 29 D5
Odd Down . . . 43 C6
Oddendale . . . 164 D3
Odder . . . 133 B4
Oddingley . . . 80 B2
Oddington Glos . 64 A3
Oxon . . . 65 B6
Odell . . . 83 B6
Odie . . . 282 E7
Odiham . . . 47 D5
Odstock . . . 31 C5
Odstone . . . 97 A6
Offchurch . . . 81 A6
Offenham . . . 80 C3
Offham E Sus . . 22 A1
Kent . . . 37 A4
W Sus . . . 20 B3
Offord Cluny . . 84 A4
Offord Darcy . . 84 A4
Offton . . . 87 C6
Offwell . . . 14 B1
Ogbourne Maizey 45 B5
Ogbourne
St Andrew . . 45 B5
Ogbourne
St George . . 45 B6
Ogil . . . 232 B2
Ogle . . . 178 B3
Ogmore . . . 40 D3
Ogmore-by-Sea . 40 D3
Ogmore Vale . . 40 D4
Okeford
Fitzpaine . . . 30 D2
Okehampton . . 11 B6
Okehampton
Camp . . . 11 B6
Okraquoy . . . 285 K6
Old . . . 99 D4
Old Aberdeen . 245 B6
Old Alresford . . 33 B4
Oldany . . . 270 A4
Old Arley . . . 97 B5
Old Basford . . 114 A4

Old Basing 47 D4
Oldberrow 80 A4
Old Bewick 188 A3
Old Bolingbroke 134 C3
Oldborough 12 A2
Old Bramhope . . 147 C6
Old Brampton . . 130 B3
Old Bridge of
Tilt 230 B2
Old Bridge of
Urr 173 B5
Old Duckenham . 103 B6
Old Burghclere . . 46 D2
Oldbury Shrops . . 95 B5
Warks 97 B6
W Mid 96 C2
Oldbury-on-
Severn 62 D2
Oldbury on the
Hill 44 A2
Old Byland 159 C4
Old Cassop 167 B6
Oldcastle Bridgend 40 D4
Mon 61 A5
Old Castleton . . 186 D4
Old Catton 120 D4
Old Clee 143 C4
Old Cleeve 27 A5
Old Clipstone . . 131 C6
Old Colwyn 124 B3
Oldcotes 131 A5
Old Coulsdon 35 A6
Old Crombie 267 D6
Old Dailly 181 B4
Old Dalby 115 C4
Old Deer 257 B4
Old Denaby 140 D2
Old Edlington . . 140 D3
Old Eldon 167 C5
Old Ellerby 151 D4
Oldfallow 112 D3
Old Felixstowe . . 88 D4
Oldfield 79 A6
Old Fletton 100 B3
Oldford 44 D1
Old Glossop 138 D3
Old Goole 141 A5
Old Hall 91 D7
Oldham 138 C2
Oldhamstocks . . 211 C4
Old Heath 71 A4
Old Heathfield . . 36 D3
Old Hill 96 C2
Old Hunstanton . 118 A3
Old Hurst 101 D4
Old Hutton 155 C4
Old Kea 4 D4
Old Kilpatrick . . 205 A4
Old Kinnernie . . 245 B4
Old Knebworth . . 68 A2
Oldland 43 B5
Old Langho 145 D7
Old Laxey 152 C4
Old Leake 135 D4
Old Malton 159 D6
Oldmeldrum . . . 256 D3
Old Mickefield . 148 D3
Old Milton 17 B6
Old Milverton . . . 81 A5
Old Monkland . . 207 D5
Old Netley 18 A3
Old Philpstoun . 208 C3
Old Quarrington 167 B6
Old Radnor 77 B6
Old Rattray 269 D5
Old Rayne 256 D1
Old Romney 38 C2
Oldshore Beg . . 276 C3
Oldshoremore . . 276 C3
Old Sodbury 43 A6
Old Somerby . . . 116 B2
Oldstead 158 C4
Old Stratford . . . 83 C4
Old Thirsk 158 C3
Oldtown 255 D6
Old Town Cumb . . 155 C4
Cumb 164 A2
Northumb 188 D1
Scilly 2 E4
Oldtown of Ord . 267 D7
Old Trafford . . . 137 D7
Old Tupton 130 C3

Old Warden 84 C3
Oldway 57 D5
Oldways End 26 C3
Old Weston 100 D2
Oldwhat 268 D3
Old Whittington 130 B3
Old Wick 281 C5
Old Windsor 48 B2
Old Wives Lees . . 52 D2
Old Woking 34 A3
Old Woodhall . . 134 C2
Olgrinmore 200 C2
Oliver's Battery . . 32 C3
Ollaberry 284 D5
Ollerton Ches E . 128 B2
Notts 131 C6
Shrops 111 C5
Olmarch 75 C5
Olney 83 B5
Olrig House 280 B3
Olton 96 C4
Olveston 43 A5
Olwen 75 D4
Ombersley 79 A6
Ompton 132 C1
Onchan 152 D3
Onecote 129 D5
Onen 61 B6
Ongar Hill 118 C2
Ongar Street . . . 78 A1
Onibury 94 D2
Onich 237 C4
Onllwyn 59 D5
Onneley 111 A6
Onslow Village . . 34 B2
Onthank 205 D4
Openwoodgate . 114 A1
Opinan Highld . . 261 A5
Highld 261 C4
Orange Lane . . . 198 B1
Orange Row . . . 118 C2
Orasaigh 288 F4
Orbliston 266 D4
Orbost 258 D2
Orby 135 C4
Orchard Hill 25 C5
Orchard Portman 28 C2
Orcheston 31 A4
Orcop 61 A6
Orcop Hill 61 A6
Ord 247 C5
Ordhead 244 A3
Ordie 244 B1
Ordiequish 266 D4
Ordsall 132 A1
Ore 23 A6
Oreton 95 C4
Orford Suff 89 C5
Warr 137 D5
Orgreave 113 D5
Orlestone 38 B1
Orleton Hereford . 78 A2
Worcs 79 A4
Orlingbury 99 D5
Ormesby 168 D3
Ormesby
St Margaret . . 121 D6
Ormesby
St Michael . . . 121 D6
Ormiclate
Castle 286 C3
Ormiscaig 261 A5
Ormiston 209 D7
Ormsaigbeg . . . 234 D3
Ormsaigmore . . 234 D3
Ormsary 202 A2
Ormsgill 153 C2
Ormskirk 136 C3
Orpington 50 C1
Orrell Gtr Man . 136 C4
Mers 136 D2
Orrisdale 152 B3
Orroland 173 D5
Orsett 50 A3
Orslow 112 D2
Orston 115 A5
Orthwaite 163 A5
Ortner 145 B5
Orton Cumb . . . 155 A5
N Hants 99 D5
Orton
Longueville . . 100 B3

Orton-on-the-
Hill 97 A6
Orton Waterville 100 B3
Orwell 85 B5
Osbaldeston . . . 145 D6
Osbaldwick 149 B5
Osbaston 110 C2
Osbournby 116 B3
Oscroft 127 C5
Ose 258 D3
Osgathorpe 114 D2
Osgodby Lincs . . 142 D2
N Yorks 149 D5
N Yorks 161 C4
Oskaig 248 C2
Oskamull 224 B3
Osmaston Derby . 114 B1
Derbys 113 A6
Osmington 16 C1
Osmington Mills . 16 C1
Osmotherley . . . 158 B3
Ospisdale 264 B3
Ospringe 52 C2
Ossett 139 A5
Ossington 132 C2
Ostend 70 D3
Oswaldkirk 159 D5
Oswaldtwistle . . 137 A6
Oswestry 110 C1
Otford 36 A3
Otham 37 A5
Othery 28 B3
Otley Suff 88 B3
W Yorks 147 C6
Otterbourne 32 C3
Otterburn
Northumb 188 D1
N Yorks 146 B2
Otterburn Camp 188 D1
Otter Ferry 214 D2
Otterham 10 B2
Otterhampton . . 28 A2
Ottershaw 48 C3
Otterswick 284 E7
Otterton 13 C5
Ottery St Mary . . 13 B6
Ottinge 38 A3
Ottringham 143 A4
Oughterby 175 C5
Oughtershaw . . 156 C2
Oughterside . . . 174 D4
Oughtibridge . . 139 D6
Oughtrington . . 128 A1
Oulston 158 D4
Oulton Cumb . . 175 C5
Norf 120 C3
Staffs 112 B3
Suff 105 B6
W Yorks 139 A6
Oulton Broad . . 105 B6
Oulton Street . . 120 C3
Oundle 100 C2
Ousby 165 B4
Ousdale 275 B4
Ousden 86 B3
Ousefleet 141 A6
Ouston Durham . 179 D4
Northumb 178 B2
Outertown 282 F3
Outgate 154 B2
Outhgill 155 A6
Outlane 138 B3
Out Newton . . . 143 A5
Out Rawcliffe . . 144 C4
Outwell 101 A7
Outwick 31 D5
Outwood Sur . . . 35 B6
W Yorks 139 A6
Outwoods 112 D1
Ovenden 138 A3
Ovenscloss . . . 196 C3
Over Cambs . . . 101 D5
Ches W 127 C6
S Glos 43 A4
Overbister 282 C7
Overbury 80 D2
Overcombe 15 C6
Over Compton . 29 D5
Overgreen 130 B3
Over Green 97 B4
Over Haddon . . 130 C2
Over Hulton . . . 137 C5

Over Kellet 154 D4
Over Kiddington . 65 A5
Over Knutsford . 128 B2
Overleigh 29 B4
Overley Green . . 80 B3
Over Monnow . . 61 B7
Over Norton 64 A4
Over Peover . . . 128 B2
Overpool 126 B3
Overscaig
Hotel 271 B7
Overseal 113 D6
Over Silton 158 B3
Oversland 52 D2
Overstone 83 A5
Over Stowey 28 B1
Overstrand 120 A4
Over Stratton . . . 28 D4
Over Tabley 128 A2
Overthorpe 82 C1
Overton
Aberdeen 245 A5
Ches W 127 B5
Dumfries 174 B2
Hants 32 A4
Lancs 144 B4
N Yorks 149 B4
Shrops 94 D3
Swansea 57 D4
W Yorks 139 B5
Overton
=Owrtyn 110 A2
Overton Bridge . 110 A2
Overtown 194 A3
Over Wallop 32 B1
Over Whitacre . . 97 B5
Over Worton 65 A5
Oving
Bucks 66 A2
W Sus 20 B2
Ovingdean 21 B6
Ovingham 178 C2
Ovington
Durham 166 D4
Essex 86 C3
Hants 33 B4
Norf 103 A5
Northumb 178 C2
Ower 32 D2
Owermoigne . . . 16 C1
Owlbury 93 B7
Owler Bar 130 B2
Owlerton 130 A3
Owl's Green 88 A3
Owlswick 66 C2
Owmby 142 C2
Owmby-by-
Spital 133 A5
Owrtyn
=Overton 110 A2
Owslebury 32 C4
Owston
Leics 99 A4
S Yorks 140 B3
Owston Ferry . . 141 C6
Owstwick 151 D5
Owthorne 143 A5
Owthorpe 115 B4
Oxborough 102 A3
Oxcombe 134 B3
Oxenholme 154 C4
Oxenhope 147 D4
Oxen Park 154 C2
Oxenton 80 D2
Oxenwood 45 D7
Oxford 65 C6
Oxhey 67 D6
Oxhill 81 C6
Oxley 96 A2
Oxley Green 70 B3
Oxley's Green . . 37 D4
Oxnam 187 B2
Oxshott 48 C4
Oxspring 139 C5
Oxted 36 A1
Oxton
Borders 196 A3
Notts 131 D6
Oxwich 57 D4
Oxwick 119 C6
Oykel Bridge . . 271 D6
Oyne 256 D1

P

Pabail Iarach . . . 288 D6
Pabail Uarach . . 288 D6
Pace Gate 147 B5
Packington 114 D1
Padanaram 232 C2
Padbury 83 D4
Paddington 49 A5
Paddlesworth . . . 38 B3
Paddockhaugh . 266 D3
Paddockhole . . . 185 D5
Paddock Wood . . 37 B4
Padfield 138 D3
Padiham 146 D1
Padog 124 D3
Padside 147 B5
Padstow 9 D5
Padworth 47 C4
Page Bank 167 B5
Pagham 20 C1
Paglesham
Churchend . . . 70 D3
Paglesham
Eastend 70 D3
Paibeil 287 H2
Paible 287 E5
Paignton 8 A2
Pailton 98 C1
Painscastle 77 C5
Painshawfield . . 178 C2
Painsthorpe . . . 149 B7
Painswick 63 C4
Pairc Shiaboist . 288 C3
Paisley 205 B4
Pakefield 105 B6
Pakenham 87 A5
Pale 109 B4
Palestine 31 A6
Paley Street 47 B6
Palfrey 96 B3
Palgowan 181 C5
Palgrave 104 D2
Pallion 179 D5
Palmarsh 38 B3
Palnackie 173 C6
Palnure 171 A6
Palterton 131 C4
Pamber End 47 D4
Pamber Green . . 47 D4
Pamber Heath . . 47 C4
Pamphill 16 A3
Pampisford 85 C6
Pan 283 H4
Panbride 221 A5
Pancrasweek . . . 10 A3
Pandy Gwyn . . . 90 B4
Mon 61 A5
Powys 91 B7
Wrex 109 B6
Pandy Tudur . . 124 C3
Panfield 70 A1
Pangbourne 47 B4
Pannal 148 B2
Panshanger 68 B2
Pant 110 C1
Pant-glas Carms . 58 B2
Gwyn 107 B4
Pant-glâs 91 C5
Pant-glas 110 B1
Pantgwyn Carms . 58 C2
Ceredig 73 B5
Pant-lasau 57 C6
Pant Mawr 91 D6
Panton 134 B1
Pantperthog 91 B5
Pant-teg 58 C1
Pant-y-Caws . . . 73 D4
Pant-y-dwr 92 D3
Pant-y-ffridd . . . 93 A5
Pantyffynnon . . . 57 A6
Pantymwyn . . . 126 C1
Pant-yr-awel . . . 40 C4
Pant-y-Wacco . 125 B6
Panxworth 121 D5
Papcastle 163 A4
Papigoe 281 C5
Papil 285 K5
Papley 283 H5
Papple 210 C2
Papplewick . . . 131 D5

Papworth
Everard 85 A4
Papworth
St Agnes 85 A4
Par 5 B5
Parbold 136 B3
Parbrook Som . . 29 B5
W Sus 34 D3
Parc 108 D3
Parcllyn 73 A5
Parc-Seymour . . 61 D6
Parc-y-rhôs 75 D4
Pardshaw 162 B3
Parham 88 A4
Park 183 C7
Park Corner Oxon 47 A4
Windsor 47 A6
Parkend 62 C2
Park End Mbro . 168 D3
Northumb 177 B6
Parkeston 88 D3
Parkgate Ches W 126 B2
Dumfries 184 D3
Kent 37 C6
Sur 35 B5
Park Gate 18 A4
Parkham 25 C4
Parkham Ash . . . 25 C4
Park Hill Notts . . 132 D1
N Yorks 148 A2
Parkhill House . 245 A5
Parkhouse 61 C6
Parkhouse
Green 131 C4
Parkhurst 18 B3
Parkmill 57 D5
Parkneuk 233 A5
Parkstone 17 B4
Park Street 35 C4
Parley Cross . . . 17 B4
Parracombe 26 A1
Parrog 72 C3
Parsley Hay . . . 129 C6
Parsonage Green 69 C7
Parsonby 163 A4
Parson Cross . . 139 D6
Parson Drove . . 101 A5
Parson's Heath . 71 A4
Partick 205 B5
Partington 137 D6
Partney 135 C4
Parton Cumb . . 162 B2
Dumfries 173 A4
Glos 63 A4
Partridge Green . 21 A4
Parwich 130 D1
Passenham 83 D4
Paston 121 B5
Patchacott 11 B5
Patcham 21 B6
Patching 20 B3
Patchole 25 A7
Pathway 43 A4
Pateley Bridge . 147 A5
Paternoster
Heath 70 B3
Pathe 28 B3
Pathhead Aberds 233 B5
E Ayrs 182 A4
Fife 209 A5
Midloth 209 D6
Path of Condie . 219 C5
Pathstruie 219 C5
Patna 182 A2
Patney 45 D4
Patrick 152 C2
Patrick
Brompton 157 B6
Patrington 143 A5
Patrixbourne . . . 52 D3
Patterdale 164 D1
Pattingham 95 B6
Pattishall 82 B3
Pattiswick Green 70 A2
Patton Bridge . . 155 B4
Paul 2 C2
Paulerspury 83 C4
Paull 142 A3
Paulton 43 D5

Pavenham 84 B1
Pawlett 28 A3
Pawston 198 C2
Paxford 81 D4
Paxton 198 A3
Payhembury . . . 13 A5
Paythorne 146 B2
Peacehaven 22 B2
Peak Dale 129 B5
Peak Forest 129 B6
Peakirk 100 A3
Pearsie 232 C1
Peasedown
 St John 43 D6
Peasemore 46 B2
Peasenhall 89 A4
Pease Pottage . . 35 C5
Peaslake 34 B3
Peasley Cross . . . 136 D4
Peasmarsh 37 D6
Peaston 210 D1
Peastonbank 210 D1
Peathill 269 C4
Peat Inn 221 D4
Peatling Magna . 98 B2
Peatling Parva . . 98 C2
Peaton 94 C3
Peats Corner 88 A2
Pebmarsh 87 D4
Pebworth 80 C4
Pecket Well 138 A2
Peckforton 127 D5
Peckham 49 B6
Peckleton 98 A1
Pedlinge 38 B3
Pedmore 96 C2
Pedwell 28 B4
Peebles 196 B1
Peel 152 C2
Peel Common . . 19 A4
Peel Park 205 C6
Peening Quarter . 37 D6
Pegsdon 84 D3
Pegswood 179 A4
Pegwell 53 C5
Peinchorran 247 A4
Peinlich 259 C4
Pelaw 179 C4
Pelcomb Bridge . 55 C5
Pelcomb Cross . . 55 C5
Peldon 70 B3
Pellon 138 A3
Pelsall 96 A3
Pelton 179 D4
Pelutho 174 D4
Pelynt 5 B7
Pemberton 137 C4
Pembrey 57 B4
Pembridge 78 B1
Pembroke
 =Penfro 55 D5
Pembroke Dock
 =Doc Penfro 55 D5
Pembury 36 B4
Penallt 61 B7
Penally 55 E7
Penalt 62 A1
Penare 5 C4
Penarlâg
 =Hawarden 126 C3
Penarth 41 D6
Pen-bont
 Rhydybeddau . . 91 D4
Penbryn 73 A5
Pencader 58 B1
Pencaenewydd . . 107 B4
Pencaitland 210 D1
Pencarnisiog . . . 122 C3
Pencarreg 75 D4
Pencelli 60 A2
Pen-clawdd 57 C5
Pencoed 41 C4
Pencombe 78 B3
Pencoyd 61 A7
Pencraig Hereford 62 A1
 Powys 109 C5
Pendeen 2 B1
Penderyn 59 E6
Pendine 56 B2

Pendlebury 137 C6
Pendleton 146 D1
Pendock 79 D5
Pendoggett 9 D6
Pendomer 29 D5
Pendoylan 41 D5
Pendre 40 C4
Penegoes 91 B5
Pen-ffordd 55 B6
Penfro
 =Pembroke 55 D5
Pengam 41 B6
Penge 49 B6
Pengenffordd . . . 77 D5
Pengorffwysfa . . 123 A4
Pengover Green . . 6 A1
Pen-groes-oped . 61 C5
Penhale Corn . . . 3 D4
 Corn 4 B4
Penhalvaen 4 D2
Penhill 45 A5
Penhow 61 D6
Penhurst 23 A4
Peniarth 90 B4
Penicuik 209 D5
Peniel Carms . . . 58 C1
 Denb 125 C5
Penifiler 259 D4
Peninver 190 C3
Penisarwaun . . . 123 D5
Penistone 139 C5
Penjerrick 4 D2
Penketh 127 A5
Penkill 181 B4
Penkridge 112 D3
Penley 110 B3
Penllyn 41 D4
Pen-llyn 122 B3
Pen-lon 123 D4
Penmachno 124 D2
Penmaen 57 D5
Penmaenan 124 B2
Penmaenmawr . . 124 B2
Penmaenpool . . . 91 A4
Penmark 41 E5
Penmarth 4 D2
Penmon 123 B6
Penmore Mill . . . 4 B4
Penmorfa Ceredig 73 A6
 Gwyn 107 B5
Penmynydd 123 C5
Penn Bucks 67 D4
 W Mid 96 B1
Pennal 91 B5
Pennan 268 C3
Pennant Ceredig . 75 B4
 Denb 109 B5
 Denb 125 D5
 Powys 91 C6
Pennant
 Melangell 109 C5
Pennar 55 D5
Pennard 57 D5
Pennerley 94 B1
Pennington
 Cumb 153 C3
 Gtr Man 137 D5
 Hants 18 B2
Penn Street 67 D4
Penny Bridge . . . 154 C2
Pennycross 225 D4
Pennygate 121 C5
Pennygown 225 B4
Pennymoor 26 D3
Pennywell 179 D5
Penparc Ceredig . 73 B5
 Pembs 55 A4
Penparcau 90 D3
Penperlleni 61 C5
Penpillick 5 B5
Penpol 4 D3
Penpoll 5 B6
Penpont Dumfries 183 C6
 Powys 59 C6
Penrherber 73 C5
Penrhiwceiber . . 41 B5
Penrhiw goch . . . 57 A5
Penrhiw-llan 73 B6
Penrhiw-pâl 73 B6
Penrhos 106 C3
Penrhôs 61 B6

Penrhos 59 D4
Penrhosfeilw 122 B2
Penrhyn Bay 124 A3
Penrhyn-coch . . . 90 D4
Penrhyndeudraeth
 . . . . 107 C6
Penrhynside 124 A3
Penrice 57 D4
Penrith 164 B3
Penrose 9 D4
Penruddock 164 C2
Penryn 4 D2
Pensarn Carms . . . 57 A4
 Conwy 125 B4
Pen-sarn Gwyn . . 107 B4
 Gwyn 107 D5
Pensax 79 A5
Pensby 126 A2
Penselwood 30 B1
Pensford 43 C5
Penshaw 179 D5
Penshurst 36 B3
Pensilva 6 A1
Penston 210 C1
Pentewan 5 C5
Pentir 123 D5
Pentire 4 A2
Pentlow 87 C4
Pentney 119 D4
Penton Mewsey . 32 A2
Pentraeth 123 C5
Pentre Carms . . . 57 A5
 Powys 93 B6
 Powys 93 C4
 Rhondda 41 B4
 Shrops 110 D2
 Wrex 109 B6
 Wrex 110 A1
Pentrebach
 M Tydf 41 A5
 Swansea 57 B6
Pentre-bach 59 B6
Pentrebeirdd . . . 109 D6
Pentre Berw 123 C4
Pentre-bont 124 D2
Pentrecagal 73 B6
Pentre-celyn
 Denb 125 D6
 Powys 91 B6
Pentre-chwyth . . . 57 C6
Pentre-cwrt 73 C6
Pentre Dolau-
 Honddu 76 C3
Pentredwr 109 A6
Pentre-dwr 40 B1
Pentrefelin Carms 58 C2
 Ceredig 75 D5
 Conwy 124 B3
 Gwyn 107 C5
Pentrefoelas 124 D3
Pentre-galar 73 C4
Pentregat 73 A6
Pentre-Gwenlais . 57 A6
Pentre
 Gwynfryn 107 D5
Pentre Halkyn . . . 126 B2
Pentreheyling . . . 93 B6
Pentre-Isaf 124 C3
Pentre
 Llanrhaeadr . . . 125 C5
Pentre-llwyn-
 llŵyd 76 B3
Pentre-llyn 75 A5
Pentre-llyn
 cymmer 125 D4
Pentre Meyrick . . 41 D4
Pentre-poeth . . . 42 A1
Pentre'r Felin . . . 124 C3
Pentre'r-felin . . . 59 B6
Pentre-rhew . . . 75 C5
Pentre-tafarn-y-
 fedw 124 C3
Pentre-ty-gwyn . 59 B5
Pentrich 130 D3
Pentridge 31 D4
Pen-twyn 61 C7
Pentyrch 41 C6
Penuchadre 40 D3
Penuwch 75 B4
Penwithick 5 B5
Penwyllt 59 D5

Penybanc 57 A6
Pen-y-banc 58 C3
Penybont 77 A5
Pen-y-bont Carms 73 D6
 Gwyn 91 B5
 Gwyn 107 D5
 Powys 109 C7
Pen-y-bont ar
 Ogwr = Bridgend
 Bridgend 40 D4
 Bridgend 40 D4
Penybontfawr . . . 109 C5
Pen-y-bryn Gwyn . 91 A4
 Pembs 73 B4
Penycae 110 A1
Pen-y-cae 59 D5
Pen-y-cae-mawr 61 D6
Pen-y-cefn 125 B6
Pen-y-clawdd . . . 61 C6
Pen-y-coedcae . . 41 C5
Penycwm 54 B4
Pen-y-fai 40 C3
Penyffordd 126 C3
Penyffridd 107 A5
Pen-y-garn Carms 58 B2
 Ceredig 90 D4
Penygarnedd 109 C6
Pen-y-garnedd . 123 C5
Pen-y-gop 108 A4
Penygraig 41 B4
Pen-y-graig 106 C1
Penygroes
 Gwyn 107 A4
 Pembs 73 C4
Pen-y-groes 57 A5
Pen-y-groeslon 106 C2
Pen-y-Gwryd
 Hotel 107 A6
Penyrheol 41 C6
Pen-yr-heol 61 B6
Pen-yr-
 Heolgerrig 60 C2
Penysarn 123 A4
Pen-y-stryt 126 D1
Penywaun 41 A4
Penzance 2 B2
Peopleton 80 B2
Peover Heath . . . 128 B2
Peper Harow 34 B2
Perceton 204 D3
Percie 244 C2
Percyhorner 269 C4
Periton 27 A4
Perivale 49 A4
Perkinsville 179 D4
Perlethorpe 131 B6
Perranarworthal . . 4 D2
Perranporth 4 B2
Perranuthnoe . . . 2 C3
Perranzabuloe . . 4 B2
Perry Barr 96 B3
Perryfoot 129 A6
Perry Green Herts. 68 B4
 Wilts. 44 A3
Perry Street 50 B3
Pershall 112 B2
Pershore 80 C2
Pert 233 B4
Pertenhall 84 A2
Perth 219 B6
Perthy 110 B2
Perton 95 B6
Pertwood 30 B2
Peterborough . . . 100 B3
Peterburn 261 B4
Peterchurch 78 D1
Peterculter 245 B5
Peterhead 257 B6
Peterlee 168 A2
Petersfield 33 C6
Peter's Green . . . 67 B6
Peters Marland . . 25 D5
Peterstone
 Wentlooge 42 A1
Peterston-super-
 Ely 41 D5
Peterstow 62 A1
Petertown 283 G4
Petham 52 D3
Petrockstow . . . 25 D5
Pett 23 A6

Pettaugh 88 B2
Petteridge 37 B4
Pettinain 195 B4
Pettistree 88 B3
Petton Devon . . . 27 C5
 Shrops 110 C3
Petts Wood 50 C1
Petty 256 C2
Pettycur 209 B5
Pettymuick 257 D4
Petworth 34 D2
Pevensey 22 B4
Pevensey Bay . . 23 B4
Pewsey 45 C5
Philham 24 C3
Philiphaugh 186 A3
Phillack 2 B3
Philleigh 4 D3
Philpstoun 208 C3
Phocle Green . . . 62 A2
Phoenix Green . . 47 D5
Pica 162 B3
Piccotts End . . . 67 C5
Pickering 159 C6
Picket Piece 32 A2
Picket Post 17 A5
Pickhill 158 C2
Picklescott 94 B2
Pickletillem 220 B4
Pickmere 128 B1
Pickney 28 C1
Pickstock 111 C6
Pickwell Devon . . 25 A5
 Leics. 115 D5
Pickworth Lincs. . 116 B3
 Rutland 116 D2
Picton Ches W . . 127 B4
 Flint 125 A6
 N Yorks 158 A3
Piddinghoe 22 B2
Piddington Oxon . 66 B1
 W Nhants. 83 B5
Piddlehinton . . . 15 B7
Piddletrenthide . 15 B7
Pidley 101 D5
Piercebridge . . . 167 D5
Pierowall 282 C5
Pigdon 178 A3
Pikehall 130 D1
Pilgrims Hatch . . 69 D5
Pilham 141 D6
Pill 43 B4
Pillaton 6 A2
Pillerton Hersey . 81 C6
Pillerton Priors . . 81 C5
Pilleth 77 A6
Pilley Hants. 18 B2
 S Yorks. 139 C6
Pilling 144 C4
Pilling Lane 144 C3
Pillowell 62 C2
Pillwell 30 D1
Pilning 43 A4
Pilsbury 129 C6
Pilsdon 14 B4
Pilsgate 100 A2
Pilsley Derbys. . . 130 B2
 Derbys 131 C4
Pilton Devon . . . 25 B6
 N Nhants 100 C2
 Rutland 99 A6
 Som 29 A5
Pilton Green . . . 57 D4
Pimperne 16 A3
Pinchbeck 117 C5
Pinchbeck Bars . 117 C4
Pinchbeck West 117 C5
Pincheon Green 141 B4
Pinfold 136 B2
Pinged 57 B4
Pinhoe 13 B4
Pinkneys Green . 47 A6
Pinley 97 D6
Pin Mill 88 D3
Pinminnoch 180 B3
Pinmore 181 B4
Pinmore Mains . . 181 B4
Pinner 48 A4
Pinvin 80 C2
Pinwherry 180 C3
Pinxton 131 D4

Pipe and Lyde . . . 78 C3
Pipe Gate 111 A6
Piperhill 253 A4
Piper's Pool 10 C3
Pipewell 99 C5
Pippacott 25 B6
Pipton 77 D5
Pirbright 34 A2
Pirnmill 202 D3
Pirton Herts 84 D3
 Worcs. 80 C1
Pisgah Ceredig . . 75 A5
 Stirling 218 D2
Pishill 47 A5
Pistyll 106 B3
Pitagowan 230 B2
Pitblae 269 C4
Pitcairngreen . . . 219 B5
Pitcalnie 265 C4
Pitcaple 256 D2
Pitchcombe 63 C4
Pitchcott 66 A2
Pitchford 94 A3
Pitch Green 66 C2
Pitch Place 34 A2
Pitcombe 29 B6
Pitcorthie 221 D5
Pitcox 210 C3
Pitcur 220 A2
Pitfichie 244 A3
Pitforthie 233 A6
Pitgrudy 264 A3
Pitkennedy 232 C3
Pitkevy 220 D2
Pitkierie 221 D5
Pitlessie 220 D3
Pitlochry 230 C3
Pitmachie 256 D1
Pitmain 241 B5
Pitmedden 256 D3
Pitminster 28 D2
Pitmuies 232 D3
Pitmunie 244 A3
Pitney 29 C4
Pitscottie 220 C4
Pitsea 51 A4
Pitsford 83 A4
Pitsmoor 130 A3
Pitstone 67 B4
Pitstone Green . . 67 B4
Pittendreich 266 C2
Pittentrail 273 D5
Pittenweem 221 D5
Pittington 167 A6
Pittodrie 256 D1
Pitton 31 B6
Pittswood 36 B4
Pittulie 269 C4
Pityme 9 D5
Pity Me 167 A5
Pityoulish 242 A2
Pixey Green 104 D3
Pixham 35 A4
Pixley 79 D4
Place Newton . . . 160 D2
Plaidy 268 D2
Plains 207 D5
Plaish 94 B3
Plaistow 34 C3
Plaitford 32 D1
Plank Lane 137 D5
Plas-canol 90 A3
Plas Gogerddan . 90 D4
Plas Llwyngwern . 91 B5
Plas Nantyr 109 B6
Plastow Green . . 46 C3
Plas-yn-Cefn . . . 125 B5
Platt 36 A4
Platt Bridge 137 C5
Platts Common . . 139 C6
Plawsworth 167 A5
Plaxtol 36 A4
Playden 37 D7
Playford 88 C3
Play Hatch 47 B5
Playing Place . . 4 C3
Playley Green . . 79 D5
Plealey 94 A2
Plean 207 B6
Pleasington 137 A5
Pleasley 131 C5
Pleckgate 145 D6

Plenmeller......177 C5
Pleshey..........69 B6
Plockton........249 C5
Plocrapol.......288 H2
Ploughfield.......78 C1
Plowden..........94 C1
Ploxgreen.......94 A1
Pluckley.........38 A1
Pluckley Thorne..37 B7
Plumbland......163 A4
Plumley.........128 B2
Plumpton Cumb..164 B2
  E Sus..........21 A6
Plumpton Green..21 A6
Plumpton Head..164 B3
Plumstead London. 50 B1
  Norf..........120 B3
Plumtree.......115 B4
Plungar........115 B5
Plush...........15 A7
Plwmp..........73 A6
Plymouth.........6 B3
Plympton.........7 B4
Plymstock........7 B4
Plymtree........13 A5
Pockley........159 C5
Pocklington....149 C7
Pode Hole......117 C5
Podimore........29 C5
Podington.......83 A6
Podmore........112 B1
Point Clear......71 B4
Pointon........116 B4
Pokesdown.......17 B5
Pol a Charra....286 E3
Polbae.........181 D4
Polbain........270 C2
Polbathic........6 B2
Polbeth........208 D3
Polchar........242 B1
Polebrook......100 C2
Pole Elm........79 C6
Polegate........22 B3
Poles..........264 A3
Polesworth......97 A5
Polgigga.........2 C1
Polglass.......270 D3
Polgooth........5 B4
Poling..........20 B3
Polkerris........5 B5
Polla..........277 C4
Pollington.....140 B4
Polloch........236 C1
Pollok.........205 B5
Pollokshields..205 B5
Polmassick.......5 C4
Polmont.......208 C2
Polnessan......182 A2
Polnish........235 B6
Polperro........5 B7
Polruan.........5 B5
Polsham........29 A5
Polstead........87 D5
Poltalloch.....213 C6
Poltimore.......13 B4
Polton.........209 D5
Polwarth.......197 A6
Polyphant.......10 C3
Polzeath.........9 D5
Pondersbridge..101 B4
Ponders End.....68 D3
Pondtail........34 A1
Ponsanooth......4 D2
Ponsworthy......12 D2
Pont Aber-......59 C4
Pont Aber-
  Geirw........108 C2
Pontamman......57 A6
Pontantwn.......57 A4
Pontardawe......40 A2
Pontarddulais...57 B5
Pont-ar-gothi...58 C2
Pont ar Hydfer..59 C5
Pont-ar-llechau..59 C4
Pontarsais......58 C1
Pontblyddyn....126 C2
Pontbren Araeth.58 C3
Pontbren Llwyd..59 E6
Pont Cwm
  Pydew.......109 B5
Pont Cyfyng....124 D2
Pont Cysyllte..110 A1

Pont Dolydd
  Prysor.......108 B2
Pontefract......140 A2
Ponteland......178 B3
Ponterwyd......91 D5
Pontesbury......94 A1
Pontfadog......110 B1
Pontfaen........55 A6
Pont-faen.......76 D3
Pont Fronwydd..108 C3
Pont-gareg......72 B4
Pontgarreg......73 A6
Pont-Henri......57 B4
Ponthir.........61 D5
Ponthirwaun.....73 B5
Pontllanfraith..41 B6
Pontlliw........57 B6
Pont-Llogel....109 D5
Pontllyfni.....107 A4
Pontlottyn......60 C3
Pontneddfechan.59 E6
Pontnewydd......61 D4
Pont Pen-y-
  benglog.....123 D6
Pontrhydfendigaid
  ....75 B6
Pont Rhyd-goch 124 C1
Pont-Rhyd-sarn 108 C3
Pont Rhyd-y-cyff 40 C3
Pontrhydyfen....40 B2
Pont-rhyd-y-
  groes........75 A6
Pontrilas.......61 A5
Pontrobert.....109 D6
Pont-rug......123 D5
Pont Senni
  =Sennybridge..59 C6
Ponts Green.....23 A4
Pontshill.......62 A2
Pont-siân.......74 D3
Pontsticill.....60 B2
Pontwgan......124 B2
Pontyates.......57 B4
Pontyberem......57 A5
Pontyclun.......41 C5
Pontycymer......40 B4
Pontyglasier....72 C4
Pont-y-gwaith...41 B5
Pont-y-pant....124 D2
Pont y Pennant..108 C2
Pontypool
  =Pont-Y-Pŵl..61 C4
Pontypridd......41 C5
Pont-Y-Pŵl
  =Pontypool...61 C4
Pont yr Afon-
  Gam.........108 A2
Pont-yr-hafod...55 B5
Pontywaun.......41 B7
Pooksgreen......32 D2
Pool Corn........3 A4
  W Yorks......147 C6
Poole...........17 B4
Poole Keynes....63 D5
Poolend.......129 D4
Poolewe.......261 B5
Pooley Bridge..164 C2
Poolfold......128 D3
Poolhill........62 A3
Pool o'
  Muckhart....219 D5
Pool Quay......110 D1
Poolsbrook....131 B4
Pootings........36 B2
Pope Hill.......55 C5
Popeswood......47 C6
Popham.........33 A4
Poplar.........49 A6
Popley.........47 D4
Porchester....114 A3
Porchfield......18 B3
Porin.........251 A5
Poringland....104 A3
Porkellis........3 B4
Porlock........26 A3
Porlock Weir....26 A3
Portachoillan..202 C2
Port Ann......214 D2
Port Appin....226 B4
Port Arthur...285 K5
Port Askaig...201 B4
Portavadie....203 B4

Port Bannatyne.203 B5
Portbury........43 B4
Port Carlisle..175 B5
Port Charlotte.200 C2
Portchester.....19 A5
Portclair.....240 A2
Port Clarence..168 C2
Port Driseach..203 A4
Port Ellen....200 D3
Port
  Elphinstone..256 E2
Portencalzie...180 D2
Portencross...204 D1
Port Erin.....152 E1
Port Errol....257 C5
Portesham.......15 C6
Portessie.....267 C5
Port e Vullen..152 B4
Port-Eynon......57 D4
Portfield Gate..55 C5
Portgate.......11 C5
Port Gaverne.....9 C6
Port Glasgow..204 A3
Portgordon....267 C4
Portgower.....274 C4
Port Corn.......4 A3
  Rhondda.......41 B5
Porthaethwy
  =Menai Bridge.123 C5
Porthallow Corn..3 C5
  Corn..........6 B1
Porthcawl......40 D3
Porthcothan.....9 D4
Porthcurno......2 C1
Port Henderson.261 C4
Porthgain......54 A4
Porthill......110 D3
Porthkerry......41 E5
Porthleven......3 C4
Porthllechog..123 A4
Porthmadog....107 C5
Porthmeor.......2 B2
Porth Navas.....3 C5
Portholland.....3 C4
Porthoustock....3 C6
Porthpean.......5 B5
Porthtowan......3 A4
Porth Tywyn
  =Burry Port...57 B4
Porthyrhyd Carms 57 A5
  Carms.........59 B4
Porth-y-waen...110 C1
Portincaple...215 C5
Portington....149 D6
Portinnisherrich 214 A2
Portinscale...163 B5
Port Isaac......9 C5
Portishead......42 B3
Portkil.......215 D5
Portknockie...267 C5
Port Lamont...203 A5
Portlethen....245 C6
Portling......173 C6
Port Lion......55 D5
Portloe.........4 D4
Port Logan....170 C2
Portmahomack.265 B5
Portmeirion...107 C5
Portmellon......5 C5
Port Mholair..288 D6
Port Mor......234 C3
Portmore.......18 B2
Port Mulgrave.169 D5
Portnacroish..226 B4
Portnahaven...200 C1
Portnalong....246 A2
Portnaluchaig..235 B5
Portnancon....277 B5
Port Nan Giùran 288 D6
Port nan Long..287 G3
Portnellan....216 B4
Port Nis......288 A6
Portobello....209 C6
Port of
  Menteith....217 D5
Porton.........31 B5
Portpatrick...170 B2
Port Quin.......9 C5
Port Ramsay...226 B3
Portreath.......3 A4
Portree.......259 D4
Port St Mary..152 E2

Portscatho......4 D3
Portsea........19 A5
Portskerra....279 B4
Portskewett....43 A4
Portslade......21 B5
Portslade-by-Sea 21 B5
Portsmouth
  Ptsmth......19 A5
  W Yorks.....138 A2
Portsonachan..227 D5
Portsoy.......267 C6
Port Sunlight..126 A3
Portswood......32 D3
Port Talbot.....40 B2
Porttanachy...267 C4
Port Tennant...57 C6
Portuairk.....234 D3
Portway Hereford. 78 D2
  Worcs.........96 D3
Port Wemyss...200 C1
Port William..171 C5
Portwrinkle.....6 B2
Poslingford.....86 C3
Postbridge.....12 D1
Postcombe......66 D2
Postling........38 B3
Postwick......104 A3
Potholm......185 D6
Potsgrove......67 A4
Potten End.....67 C5
Potter
  Brompton....160 D3
Potterhanworth.133 C5
Potterhanworth
  Booths......133 C5
Potter Heigham 121 D6
Potterne.......44 D3
Potterne Wick...44 D4
Potternewton..148 D2
Potters Bar....68 C2
Potter's Cross..95 C6
Potterspury....83 C4
Potter Street...69 C4
Potterton
  Aberds......245 A6
  W Yorks.....148 D3
Potto.........158 A3
Potton.........84 C4
Pott Row......119 C4
Pott Shrigley.129 B4
Poughill Corn...10 A3
  Devon.........12 A3
Poulshot.......44 D3
Poulton Glos....64 C2
  Mers........136 D2
Poulton-le-
  Fylde.......144 D3
Pound Bank.....95 D5
Poundfield......36 C3
Pound Green
  E Sus.........36 D3
  IoW..........18 C2
  Worcs.........95 D5
Pound Hill.....35 C5
Poundland....180 C3
Poundon........66 A1
Poundsgate.....12 D2
Poundstock.....10 B3
Powburn......188 B3
Powderham......13 C4
Powerstock.....15 B5
Powfoot......174 B4
Powick.........79 B6
Powmill......208 A3
Poxwell........16 C1
Poyle..........48 B3
Poynings.......21 A5
Poyntington....29 C6
Poynton......129 A4
Poynton Green.111 D4
Poystreet Green.87 B5
Praa Sands......2 C3
Pratt's Bottom..50 C1
Praze...........2 B3
Praze-an-Beeble..3 B4
Predannack
  Wollas........3 D4
Prees.........111 B4
Preesall......144 C3
Prees Green...111 B4
Prees Heath...111 B4

Prees Higher
  Heath.......111 B4
Prees Lower
  Heath.......111 B4
Prenderguest..198 A3
Prendwick....188 B3
Prengwyn.......73 B7
Prenteg.......107 B5
Prenton......126 A3
Prescot.......136 D3
Prescott......110 C3
Pressen.......198 C2
Prestatyn....125 A5
Prestbury Ches E 129 B4
  Glos.........63 A5
Presteigne
  =Llanandras...77 A7
Presthope......94 B3
Prestleigh.....29 A6
Preston Borders.198 A1
  Brighton......21 B6
  Devon.........12 D3
  Dorset........15 C7
  E Loth.......210 C2
  E Yorks......151 D4
  Glos.........63 C6
  Glos.........79 D4
  Herts.........68 A1
  Kent..........52 C2
  Kent..........53 C4
  Lancs.......136 A4
  Northumb.....189 A4
  Rutland.......99 A5
  Shrops.......111 D4
  Wilts.........44 B4
  Wilts.........45 B6
Preston Bagot...81 A4
Preston Bissett..66 A1
Preston Bowyer..27 C6
Preston
  Brockhurst..111 C4
Preston Brook..127 A5
Preston
  Candover.....33 A5
Preston Capes..82 B2
Preston
  Crowmarsh....65 D7
Preston Gubbals 110 D3
Prestonmill...174 C2
Preston on Stour 81 C5
Preston on the
  Hill........127 A5
Preston on Wye..78 C1
Prestonpans...209 C6
Preston
  Plucknett....29 D5
Preston St Mary..87 B5
Preston-under-
  Scar........157 B4
Preston upon the
  Weald Moors.111 D5
Preston Wynne..78 C3
Prestwich.....137 C7
Prestwick
  Northumb.....178 B3
  S Ayrs......192 C3
Prestwood......66 C3
Price Town......40 B4
Prickwillow...102 C1
Priddy.........43 D4
Priesthaugh...186 C3
Priest Hutton..154 D4
Priest Weston...93 B6
Primethorpe....98 B2
Primrose Green.120 D2
Primrosehill...67 C5
Primrose Valley.161 D5
Princes Gate....56 A1
Princes
  Risborough...66 C3
Princethorpe...97 D7
Princetown
  Caerph........60 B3
  Devon........11 D6
Prion.........125 C5
Prior Muir....221 C5
Prior Park....198 A3
Priors Frome...78 D3
Priors Hardwick..82 B1
Priorslee.....111 D6
Priors Marston..82 B1
Priory Wood....77 C6

Priston........43 C5
Pristow Green..104 C2
Prittlewell....51 A5
Privett........33 C5
Prixford.......25 B6
Probus..........4 C3
Proncy.......264 A3
Prospect......174 D4
Prudhoe......178 C2
Ptarmigan
  Lodge......215 B6
Pubil.........228 D3
Puckeridge.....68 A3
Puckington.....28 D3
Pucklechurch...43 B5
Pucknall.......32 C2
Puckrup........80 D1
Puddinglake...128 C2
Puddington
  Ches W......126 B3
  Devon.........26 D3
Puddledock....103 B6
Puddletown.....16 B1
Pudleston......78 B3
Pudsey........147 D6
Pulborough.....20 A3
Puleston......111 C6
Pulford......126 D3
Pulham.........15 A7
Pulham Market.104 C2
Pulham St Mary.104 C3
Pulloxhill.....84 D2
Pumpherston..208 D3
Pumsaint......58 A3
Puncheston.....55 B6
Puncknowle.....15 C5
Punnett's Town..36 D4
Purbrook.......19 A5
Purewell.......17 B5
Purfleet.......50 B2
Puriton........28 A3
Purleigh.......70 C2
Purley London...49 C6
  W Berks......47 B4
Purlogue.......93 D6
Purls Bridge..101 C6
Purse Caundle..29 D6
Purslow........94 C1
Purston Jaglin.140 B2
Purton Glos....62 C2
  Glos.........62 C2
  Wilts.........45 A4
Purton Stoke...64 D1
Pury End.......83 C4
Pusey..........65 D4
Putley.........79 D4
Putney.........49 B5
Putsborough...25 A5
Puttenham Herts..66 B3
  Sur..........34 B2
Puxton.........42 C3
Pwll...........57 B4
Pwllcrochan....55 D5
Pwll-glas.....125 D6
Pwllgloyw......76 D4
Pwllheli......106 C3
Pwllmeyric.....61 D7
Pwll-trap......56 A2
Pwll-y-glaw....40 B2
Pyecombe......21 A5
Pye Corner.....42 A2
Pye Green.....112 D3
Pyewipe......143 B4
Pyle...........18 D3
Pyle = Y Pîl....40 C3
Pylle..........29 B5
Pymoor........101 C6
Pyrford........34 A3
Pyrton.........66 D1
Pytchley.......99 D5
Pyworthy.......10 A4

Q

Quabbs.........93 C6
Quadring......117 B5
Quainton.......66 B2
Quarley........31 A6

Quarndon.......114 A1
Quarrier's
　Homes.......204 B3
Quarrington....116 A3
Quarrington Hill 167 B6
Quarry Bank....96 C2
Quarryford....210 D2
Quarryhill....264 B3
Quarrywood....266 C2
Quarter......194 A2
Quatford......95 B5
Quatt......95 C5
Quebec.....167 A4
Quedgeley....63 B4
Queen Adelaide.102 C1
Queenborough...51 B6
Queen Camel...29 C5
Queen Charlton..43 C5
Queen Dart....26 D3
Queenhill......79 D6
Queen Oak......30 B1
Queensbury....147 D5
Queensferry Edin 208 C4
　Flint.......126 C3
Queensferry
　Crossing.....208 C4
Queen's Head....110 C2
Queen's Park
　Bedford........84 C2
　W Nhants.......83 A4
Queenstown....144 D3
Queen Street Kent 37 B4
　Wilts..........44 A4
Queenzieburn..207 C4
Quemerford....44 C4
Quendale......285 M5
Quendon......85 D7
Queniborough..115 D4
Quenington....64 C2
Quernmore....145 B5
Quethiock......6 A2
Quholm......282 F3
Quicks Green...46 B3
Quidenham...103 C6
Quidhampton
　Hants........46 D3
　Wilts........31 B5
Quilquox......257 C4
Quina Brook...111 B4
Quindry......283 H5
Quinton W Mid...96 C2
　W Nhants........83 B4
Quintrell Downs...4 A3
Quixhill......113 A5
Quoditch......11 B5
Quoig......210 D3
Quorndon......114 D3
Quothquan....195 C4
Quoyloo......282 E3
Quoyness......283 G3
Quoys Shetland..284 B8
　Shetland.....285 G6

R

Raasay House...248 C3
Rabbit's Cross...37 B5
Raby......126 B3
Rachan Mill...195 C6
Rachub......123 D6
Rackenford....26 D3
Rackham......20 A3
Rackheath....121 D4
Racks......174 A3
Rackwick Orkney 282 C5
　Orkney.....283 H3
Radbourne....113 B6
Radcliffe
　Gtr Man....137 C6
　Northumb....189 C5
Radcliffe on
　Trent......115 B4
Radclive......82 D3
Radcot......64 D3
Raddery......252 A3
Radernie......221 D4
Radford Semele..81 A6
Radipole......15 C6

Radlett......67 D6
Radley......65 D6
Radmanthwaite .131 C5
Radmoor......111 C5
Radmore Green .127 D5
Radnage......66 D2
Radstock......43 D5
Radstone......82 C2
Radway......81 C6
Radway Green..128 D2
Radwell Bedford..84 B2
　Herts......84 D4
Radwinter......86 D2
Radyr......41 C6
Rafford......253 A6
Ragdale......115 D4
Raglan......61 C6
Ragnall......132 B3
Rahane......215 D5
Rainford......136 C3
Rainford
　Junction.....136 C3
Rainham London..50 A2
　Medway......51 C5
Rainhill......136 D3
Rainhill Stoops..136 D4
Rainow......129 B4
Rainton......158 D2
Rainworth......131 D5
Raisbeck......155 A5
Raise......165 A5
Rait......220 B2
Raithby Lincs...134 A3
　Lincs........134 C3
Rake......33 C7
Rakewood......138 B2
Ram......75 D4
Ramasaig......258 D1
Rame Corn......4 D2
　Corn.........6 C3
Rameldry Mill
　Bank......220 D3
Ram Lane......38 A1
Ramnageo....284 C8
Rampisham.....15 A5
Rampside......153 D3
Rampton Cambs...85 A6
　Notts........132 B2
Ramsbottom...137 B6
Ramsbury......45 B6
Ramscraigs....275 B5
Ramsdean......33 C6
Ramsden......65 B4
Ramsden
　Bellhouse....69 D7
Ramsden Heath..69 D7
Ramsey Cambs..101 C4
　Essex.......88 D3
　IoM........152 B4
Ramseycleuch .185 A5
Ramsey Forty
　Foot......101 C5
Ramsey Heights 101 C4
Ramsey Island..70 C3
Ramsey
　Mereside....101 C4
Ramsey
　St Mary's...101 C4
Ramsgate......53 C5
Ramsgill......157 D5
Ramshorn....113 A4
Ramsnest
　Common......34 C2
Ranais......288 E5
Ranby Lincs...134 B2
　Notts.......131 A6
Rand......133 B6
Randwick......63 C4
Ranfurly......204 B3
Rangag......280 D3
Rangemore....113 C5
Rangeworthy....43 A5
Rankinston....182 A2
Ranmoor......130 A3
Ranmore
　Common......35 A4
Rannerdale....163 C4
Rannoch Station 228 C3
Ranochan......238 D2
Ranskill......131 A6
Ranton......112 C2

Ranworth......121 D5
Raploch......207 A5
Rapness......282 C6
Rascal Moor...149 D7
Rascarrel......173 D5
Rashiereive....257 D4
Raskelf......158 D3
Rassau......60 B3
Rastrick......139 A4
Ratagan......238 A3
Ratby......98 A2
Ratcliffe Culey...97 B6
Ratcliffe on
　Soar......114 C2
Ratcliffe on the
　Wreake.....115 D4
Rathen......269 C5
Rathillet......220 B3
Rathmell......146 B2
Ratho......208 C4
Ratho Station..208 C4
Rathven......267 C5
Ratley......81 C6
Ratlinghope....94 B2
Rattar......281 A4
Ratten Row....144 C4
Rattery......7 A6
Rattlesden......87 B5
Rattray......231 D5
Raughton Head .164 A1
Raunds......100 D1
Ravenfield....140 D2
Ravenglass....153 A1
Raveningham...105 B4
Ravenscar....160 A3
Ravenscraig...204 A2
Ravensdale....152 B3
Ravensden......84 B2
Ravenseat....156 A2
Ravenshead...131 D5
Ravensmoor...127 D6
Ravensthorpe
　W Nhants......98 D3
　W Yorks......139 A5
Ravenstone Leics 114 D2
　M Keynes......83 B5
Ravenstonedale 155 A6
Ravenstown...154 D2
Ravenstruther..194 B4
Ravensworth...157 A5
Raw......160 A3
Rawcliffe
　E Yorks......141 A4
　York.......149 B4
Rawcliffe
　Bridge.....141 A4
Rawdon......147 D6
Rawmarsh....140 D2
Rawreth......70 D1
Rawridge......14 A2
Rawtenstall...137 A7
Raxton......256 C3
Raydon......87 D6
Raylees......188 D2
Rayleigh......70 D2
Rayne......70 A1
Rayners Lane...48 A4
Raynes Park...49 C5
Reach......86 A1
Read......146 D1
Reading......47 B5
Reading Street...37 C7
Reagill......165 D4
Rearquhar....264 A3
Rearsby......115 D4
Reaster......281 B4
Reawick......285 J5
Reay......279 B5
Rechullin......249 A5
Reculver......53 C4
Redberth......55 D6
Redbourn......67 B6
Redbourne....142 D1
Redbrook Mon...62 B1
　Wrex.......111 A4
Redburn Highld..253 B5
　Highld......264 D1
　Northumb....177 C5
Redcar......168 C4
Redcastle Angus 233 C4
　Highld......252 B1
Redcliff Bay....42 B3

Red Dial......175 D5
Redding......208 C2
Reddingmuirhead
　　......208 C2
Reddish......138 D1
Redditch......80 A3
Rede......87 B4
Redenhall....104 C3
Redesdale
　Camp......187 D7
Redesmouth...177 A6
Redford Aberds..233 A5
　Angus......232 D3
　Durham.....166 B3
Redfordgreen..185 A6
Redgorton....219 B5
Redgrave......103 D6
Redhill Aberds..245 B4
　Aberds.....256 C1
　N Som......42 C3
　Sur........35 A5
Red Hill......79 B6
Redhouse....202 B3
Redhouses....200 B3
Red Houses Jersey..6
Redisham....105 C5
Redland Bristol..43 B4
　Orkney.....282 E4
Redlingfield...104 D2
Red Lodge....102 D2
Redlynch Som...29 B7
　Wilts......31 C6
Redmarley
　D'Abitot.....79 D5
Redmarshall...167 C6
Redmile......115 B5
Redmire......156 B4
Redmoor......5 A5
Rednal......110 C2
Redpath......197 C4
Redpoint....261 D4
Red Rail......62 A1
Red Rock....137 C4
Red Roses......56 A2
Red Row......189 D5
Redruth......3 A4
Redvales......137 C7
Red Wharf Bay..123 B5
Redwick Newport..42 A3
　S Glos......43 A4
Redworth....167 C5
Reed......85 D5
Reedham....105 A5
Reedness......141 A5
Reeds Beck...134 C2
Reepham Lincs..133 B5
　Norf.......120 C2
Reeth......156 B4
Regaby......152 B4
Regoul......253 A4
Reiff......270 C2
Reigate......35 A5
Reighton....161 D5
Reighton Gap..161 D5
Reinigeadal...288 G3
Reiss......281 C5
Rejerrah......4 B2
Releath......3 B4
Relubbus......2 B3
Relugas......253 B5
Remenham....47 A5
Remenham Hill...47 A5
Remony......229 D6
Rempstone....114 C3
Rendcomb......63 C6
Rendham......88 A4
Rendlesham....88 B4
Renfrew......205 B5
Renhold......84 B2
Renishaw......131 B4
Rennington....189 B5
Renton......206 C1
Renwick......164 A3
Repps......121 D6
Repton......113 C7
Reraig......249 D5
Rescobie......232 C3
Resipole......235 D6
Resolis......264 D2
Resolven......40 A3
Reston......211 D5

Reswallie......232 C3
Retew......4 B4
Retford......132 A2
Rettendon......70 D1
Rettendon Place .70 D1
Revesby......134 C2
Revesby Bridge .134 C3
Rewe......20 B3
Rew Street......18 B3
Reydon......105 D5
Reydon Smear ..105 D5
Reymerston....103 A6
Reynalton......55 D6
Reynoldston....57 C4
Rezare......11 D4
Rhaeadr Gwy
　=Rhayader....76 A3
Rhandirmwyn...59 A4
Rhayader
　=Rhaeadr Gwy ..76 A3
Rhedyn......106 C2
Rhemore....225 A4
Rhencullen....152 B3
Rhes-y-cae....126 B1
Rhewl Denb....109 A6
　Denb.......125 C6
Rhian......272 C3
Rhicarn......270 B3
Rhiconich....276 C3
Rhicullen....264 C2
Rhidorroch
　House......262 A3
Rhifail......278 C3
Rhigos......59 E6
Rhilochan....273 D5
Rhiroy......262 B3
Rhisga = Risca...60 D4
Rhiw......106 D2
Rhiwabon
　=Ruabon.....110 A2
Rhiwbina......41 C6
Rhiwbryfdir...107 B6
Rhiwderin......42 A1
Rhiwlas Gwyn...108 B4
　Gwyn.......123 D5
　Powys......109 B6
Rhodes......138 C1
Rhodesia......131 B5
Rhodes Minnis...38 A3
Rhodiad......54 B3
Rhondda......41 B4
Rhonehouse or
　Kelton Hill..173 C5
Rhoose = Y Rhws..41 E5
Rhôs Carms....73 C6
　Neath......40 A2
Rhosaman......59 D4
Rhosbeirio....122 A3
Rhoscefnhir...123 C5
Rhoscolyn....122 C2
Rhoscrowther...55 D5
Rhosesmor....126 C2
Rhos-fawr....106 C3
Rhosgadfan...107 A5
Rhosgoch......123 B4
Rhos-goch......77 C5
Rhos-hill......73 B4
Rhoshirwaun...106 D1
Rhoslan......107 B4
Rhoslefain......90 B3
Rhosllanerchrugog
　　......110 A1
Rhosmaen......58 C3
Rhosmeirch....123 C4
Rhosneigr......122 C3
Rhosnesni....124 A3
Rhos-on-Sea..124 A3
Rhosrobin....126 D3
Rhossili......57 D4
Rhosson......54 B3
Rhostryfan....107 A4
Rhostyllen....110 A2
Rhosybol......123 B4
Rhos-y-brithdir 109 C6
Rhos-y-garth...75 A5
Rhos-y-gwaliau 108 B4
Rhos-y-llan....106 C2
Rhos-y-Madoc..110 A2
Rhos-y-meirch..77 A6
Rhu Argyll....202 B3
　Argyll......215 D5

Rhuallt......125 B5
Rhuddall Heath .127 C5
Rhuddlan Ceredig 73 B6
　Denb.......125 B5
Rhue......262 A2
Rhulen......77 B5
Rhunahaorine..202 D2
Rhuthun
　=Ruthin....125 D6
Rhyd Gwyn....107 B6
　Powys......92 A3
Rhydaman
　=Ammanford...57 A6
Rhydargaeau....58 C1
Rhydcymerau....58 B3
Rhydd......79 C6
Rhyd-Ddu....107 A5
Rhydding......40 B2
Rhydfudr......75 B4
Rhydlewis......73 B6
Rhydlios......106 C1
Rhydlydan....124 D3
Rhyd-moel-ddu ..93 D4
Rhydness......77 C5
Rhydowen......74 D3
Rhyd-Rosser...75 B4
Rhydspence....77 C6
Rhydtalog....126 D2
Rhyd-uchaf...108 B4
Rhyd-wen......91 A5
Rhydwyn......122 B3
Rhyd-y-clafdy..106 C3
Rhydycroesau..110 B1
Rhydyfelin Ceredig 75 A4
　Rhondda.....41 C5
Rhyd-y-fro......59 E4
Rhyd-y-gwin...57 B6
Rhydymain....108 C3
Rhyd-y-meirch..61 C5
Rhyd-y-
　meudwy.....125 D6
Rhydymwyn..126 C2
Rhyd-y-pandy...57 B6
Rhyd-yr-onen...90 B4
Rhyd-y-sarn..107 B6
Rhyl = Y Rhyl...125 A5
Rhymney
　=Rhymni.....60 C3
Rhymni
　=Rhymney....60 C3
Rhynd Fife....221 B4
　Perth......219 B6
Rhynie Aberds..255 D5
　Highld......265 C4
Ribbesford......95 D5
Ribblehead....155 D6
Ribbleton....145 D5
Ribchester....145 D6
Ribigill......277 C6
Riby......142 C3
Riby Cross
　Roads......142 C3
Riccall......149 D5
Riccarton....193 B4
Richards Castle..78 A2
Richings Park...48 B3
Richmond London..49 B4
　N Yorks.....157 A5
Rickarton....245 D5
Rickinghall....103 D6
Rickleton......179 D4
Rickling......85 D6
Rickmansworth...67 D5
Riddings Cumb..175 A7
　Derbys.....131 D4
Riddlecombe...25 D7
Riddlesden....147 C4
Riddrie......205 B6
Ridge Dorset....16 C3
　Hants......32 D2
　Wilts......30 B3
Ridgebourne....77 A4
Ridge Green....35 B6
Ridgehill......43 C4
Ridge Lane......97 B5
Ridgeway Cross .79 C5
Ridgewell......86 C3
Ridgewood....22 A2
Ridgmont......84 D1
Riding Mill...178 C2
Ridleywood....127 D4
Ridlington Norf .121 B5

Ridlington continued
Rutland 99 A5
Ridsdale 177 A7
Riechip 231 D4
Riemore 230 D4
Rienachait 270 A3
Rievaulx 159 C4
Rift House 168 B2
Rigg 175 B5
Riggend 207 C5
Rigsby 135 B4
Rigside 194 C3
Riley Green 137 A5
Rileyhill 113 D5
Rilla Mill 10 D3
Rillington 160 D2
Rimington 146 C2
Rimpton 29 C6
Rimswell 143 A5
Rinaston 55 B5
Ringasta 285 M5
Ringford 173 C4
Ringinglow 130 A2
Ringland 120 D3
Ringles Cross 36 D2
Ringmer 22 A2
Ringmore 7 C5
Ringorm 254 B3
Ring's End 101 A5
Ringsfield 105 C5
Ringsfield
Corner 105 C5
Ringshall Herts . . 67 B4
Suff 87 B6
Ringshall Stocks . 87 B6
Ringstead
N Nhants 100 D1
Norf 119 A4
Ringwood 17 A5
Ringwould 39 A5
Rinmore 243 A7
Rinnigill 283 H4
Rinsey 2 C3
Riof 288 D2
Ripe 22 A3
Ripley Derbys 130 D3
Hants 17 B5
N Yorks 148 A1
Sur 34 A3
Riplingham 150 D2
Ripon 157 D7
Rippingale 116 C3
Ripple Kent 39 A5
Worcs 79 D6
Ripponden 138 B3
Rireavach 262 A2
Risabus 200 D3
Risbury 78 B3
Risby 86 A3
Risca = Rhisga . . . 60 D4
Rise 151 C4
Riseden 36 C4
Risegate 117 C5
Riseholme 133 B4
Riseley Bedford . . 84 A2
Wokingham 47 C5
Rishangles 88 A2
Rishton 146 D1
Rishworth 138 B3
Rising Bridge 137 A6
Risley Derbys 114 B2
Warr 137 D5
Risplith 147 A6
Rispond 277 B5
Rivar 45 C7
Rivenhall End 70 B2
River Bank 86 A1
Riverhead 36 A3
Rivington 137 B5
Roachill 26 C3
Roade 83 B4
Road Green 104 B3
Roadhead 176 B3
Roadmeetings . . . 194 B3
Roadside 280 B3
Roadside of
Catterline 233 A6
Roadside of
Kinneff 233 A6
Roadwater 27 B5
Roag 258 D2
Roa Island 153 D3

Roath 41 D6
Roberton Borders 186 B3
S Lanark 194 D4
Robertsbridge 37 D5
Roberttown 139 A4
Robeston Cross . . 55 D4
Robeston Wathen 55 C6
Robin Hood 139 A6
Robin Hood's
Bay 160 A3
Roborough Devon . 7 A4
Dcvon 25 D6
Roby 136 D3
Roby Mill 136 C4
Rocester 113 B5
Roch 55 B4
Rochdale 138 B1
Roche 5 A4
Rochester Medway 51 C4
Northumb 188 D1
Rochford 70 D2
Roch Gate 55 B4
Rock Corn 9 D5
Northumb 189 A5
Worcs 95 D5
W Sus 21 A4
Rockbeare 13 B5
Rockbourne 31 D5
Rockcliffe Cumb 175 B6
Dumfries 173 C6
Rock Ferry 126 A3
Rockfield Highld . 265 B5
Mon 61 B6
Rockford 17 A5
Rockhampton 62 D2
Rockingham 99 B5
Rockland All
Saints 103 B5
Rockland
St Mary 104 A4
Rockland
St Peter 103 B5
Rockley 45 B5
Rockwell End 47 A5
Rockwell Green . . 27 C6
Rodborough 63 C4
Rodbourne
Swindon 45 A5
Wilts 44 A3
Rodbourne
Cheney 45 A5
Rodd 77 A7
Roddam 188 A3
Rodden 15 C6
Rode 44 D2
Rodeheath 128 C3
Rode Heath 128 D3
Roden 111 D4
Rodhuish 27 B5
Rodington 111 D4
Rodley Glos 62 B3
N Yorks 147 D6
Rodmarton 63 D5
Rodmell 22 B2
Rodmersham 51 C6
Rodney Stoke 42 D3
Rodsley 113 A6
Rodway 28 B2
Rodwell 15 D6
Roecliffe 148 A2
Roe Green 85 D5
Roehampton 49 B5
Roesound 284 G5
Roffey 35 C4
Rogart 273 D5
Rogart Station . . . 273 D5
Rogate 33 C7
Rogerstone 42 A1
Roghadal 287 F5
Rogiet 42 A3
Rogue's Alley 101 A5
Roke 66 D1
Roker 179 D6
Rollesby 121 D6
Rolleston Leics . . . 99 A4
Notts 132 D2
Rolleston-on-
Dove 113 C6
Rolston 151 C5
Rolvenden 37 C6
Rolvenden Layne 37 C6
Romaldkirk 166 C2

Romanby 158 B2
Romannobridge 195 B6
Romansleigh 26 C2
Romford 50 A2
Romiley 138 D2
Romsey 32 C2
Romsey Town 85 B6
Romsley Shrops . . . 95 C5
Worcs 96 D2
Ronague 152 D2
Rookhope 166 A2
Rooklcy 18 C4
Rooks Bridge 42 D2
Roos 151 D5
Roosebeck 153 D3
Rootham's Green . 84 B3
Rootpark 195 A4
Ropley 33 B5
Ropley Dean 33 B5
Ropsley 116 B2
Rora 269 D5
Rorandle 244 A3
Rorrington 93 A7
Roscroggan 3 A4
Rose 4 B2
Roseacre Kent 37 A5
Lancs 144 D4
Rose Ash 26 C2
Rosebank 194 B3
Rosebrough 189 A4
Rosebush 55 B6
Rosecare 10 B2
Rosedale Abbey 159 B6
Roseden 188 A3
Rosefield 253 A4
Rose Green 20 C2
Rose Grove 146 D2
Rosehall 272 D2
Rosehaugh
Mains 252 A2
Rosehearty 269 C4
Rosehill 111 B5
Rose Hill E Sus . . . 22 A2
Lancs 146 D2
Suff 88 C2
Roseisle 266 C2
Roselands 22 B4
Rosemarket 55 D5
Rosemarkie 252 A3
Rosemary Lane . . . 27 D6
Rosemount 231 D5
Rosenannon 5 A4
Rosewell 209 D5
Roseworth 168 C2
Roseworthy 3 B4
Rosgill 164 D3
Roshven 235 C6
Roskhill 258 D2
Roskill House 252 A2
Rosley 175 D6
Roslin 209 D5
Rosliston 113 D6
Rosneath 215 D5
Ross Dumfries 172 D4
Northumb 199 C5
Perth 218 B2
Rossett 126 D3
Rossett Green . . . 148 B2
Rossie Ochill 219 C5
Rossie Priory 220 A2
Rossington 140 D4
Rosskeen 264 D2
Rossland 205 A4
Ross-on-Wye 62 A2
Roster 281 E4
Rostherne 128 A2
Rosthwaite 163 C5
Roston 113 A5
Rosyth 208 B4
Rothbury 188 C3
Rotherby 115 D4
Rotherfield 36 D3
Rotherfield Greys 47 A5
Rotherfield
Peppard 47 A5
Rotherham 140 D2
Rothersthorpe . . . 83 B4
Rotherwick 47 D5
Rothes 254 B3
Rothesay 203 B5
Rothiebrisbane . . . 256 C2
Rothienorman . . . 256 C2

Rothiesholm 282 E7
Rothley Leics 114 D3
Northumb 178 A2
Rothley Shield
East 188 D3
Rothmaise 256 C1
Rothwell Lincs . . . 142 D3
N Nhants 99 C5
W Yorks 139 A6
Rothwell Haigh . 139 A6
Rotsea 150 B3
Rottal 232 B1
Rotten End 89 A4
Rottingdean 21 B6
Rottington 162 C2
Roud 18 C4
Rougham Norf . . . 119 C5
Suff 87 A5
Rougham Green . . 87 A5
Roughburn 240 D1
Rough Close 112 B3
Rough Common . . 52 D3
Roughlee 146 C2
Roughley 96 B4
Roughsike 176 B3
Roughton Lincs . . . 134 C2
Norf 120 B4
Shrops 95 B5
Roughton Moor 134 C2
Roundhay 148 D2
Roundstonefoot 185 B4
Roundstreet
Common 34 D3
Roundway 44 C4
Rousdon 14 B2
Rous Lench 80 B3
Routenburn 204 B1
Routh 150 C3
Row Corn 10 D1
Cumb 154 C3
Rowanburn 175 A7
Rowardennan 206 A1
Rowde 44 C3
Rowen 124 B2
Rowfoot 177 C4
Row Heath 71 B5
Rowhedge 71 A4
Rowhook 35 C4
Rowington 81 A5
Rowland 130 B2
Rowlands Castle . . 33 D6
Rowlands Gill 178 D3
Rowledge 33 A7
Rowlestone 61 A5
Rowley E Yorks . . . 150 D2
Shrops 93 A7
Rowley Hill 139 B4
Rowley Regis 96 C2
Rowly 34 B3
Rowney Green . . . 96 D3
Rownhams 32 D2
Rowrah 162 C3
Rowsham 66 B3
Rowsley 130 C2
Rowstock 46 A2
Rowston 133 D5
Rowton Ches W . . 127 C4
Shrops 110 D2
Telford 111 D5
Roxburgh 197 C6
Roxby N Lincs 141 B7
N Yorks 169 D5
Roxton 84 B3
Roxwell 69 C6
Royal Leamington
Spa 81 A6
Royal Oak Darl . . . 167 C5
Lancs 136 C3
Royal Tunbridge
Wells 36 C3
Royal Wootton
Bassett 45 A4
Roybridge 239 D6
Roydhouse 139 B5
Roydon Essex 68 C4
Norf 104 C1
Norf 119 C4
Roydon Hamlet . . 68 C4
Royston Herts 85 C5
S Yorks 139 B6
Royton 138 C2
Rozel Jersey 6

Ruabon
= Rhiwabon 110 A2
Ruaig 222 C3
Ruan Lanihorne . . 4 C3
Ruan Minor 3 D5
Ruarach 249 D6
Ruardean 62 B2
Ruardean
Woodside 62 B2
Rubery 96 D2
Ruckcroft 164 A3
Ruckhall 78 D2
Ruckinge 38 B2
Ruckland 134 B3
Ruckley 94 A3
Rudbaxton 55 B5
Rudby 158 A3
Ruddington 114 B3
Rudford 62 A3
Rudge Shrops 95 B6
Som 44 D2
Rudgeway 43 A5
Rudgwick 34 C3
Rudhall 62 A2
Rudheath 128 B1
Rudley Green 70 C2
Rudry 41 C6
Rudston 150 A3
Rudyard 129 D4
Rufford 136 B3
Rufforth 148 B4
Rugby 98 D2
Rugeley 112 D4
Ruglen 181 A4
Ruilick 251 B7
Ruishton 28 C2
Ruisigearraidh . . . 287 F4
Ruislip 48 A3
Ruislip Common . 48 A3
Rumbling
Bridge 208 A3
Rumburgh 104 C4
Rumford 9 D4
Rumney 41 D7
Runcorn 127 A5
Runcton 20 B1
Runcton Holme . 102 A2
Rundlestone 11 D6
Runfold 34 B1
Runhall 103 A6
Runham Norf 105 A6
Norf 121 D6
Runnington 27 C6
Runsell Green . . . 70 C1
Runswick Bay . . . 169 D6
Runwell 70 D1
Ruscombe 47 B5
Rush Green 50 A2
Rushall Hereford . . 79 D4
Norf 104 C2
Wilts 45 D5
W Mid 96 A3
Rushbrooke 87 A4
Rushbury 94 B3
Rushden Herts 85 D5
N Nhants 83 A6
Rushenden 51 B6
Rushford 103 C5
Rush Green 50 A2
Rushlake Green . . 22 A4
Rushmere 105 C5
Rushmere
St Andrew 88 C3
Rushmoor 34 B1
Rushock 96 D1
Rusholme 138 D1
Rushton Ches W . . 127 C5
N Nhants 99 C5
Shrops 95 A4
Rushton
Spencer 129 C4
Rushwick 79 B6
Rushyford 167 C5
Ruskie 217 D6
Ruskington 133 D5
Rusland 154 C2
Rusper 35 C5
Ruspidge 62 B2
Russell's Water . . 47 A5
Russel's Green . . . 104 D3
Rusthall 36 C3
Rustington 20 B3

Ruston 160 C3
Ruston Parva 150 A3
Ruswarp 160 A2
Rutherford 197 C5
Rutherglen 205 B6
Ruthernbridge . . . 5 A5
Ruthin
= Rhuthun 125 D6
Ruthrieston 245 B6
Ruthven Aberds . . 255 B6
Angus 231 D6
Highld 241 C5
Ruthven House . 231 D7
Ruthvoes 4 A4
Ruthwell 174 B3
Ruyton-XI-
Towns 110 C2
Ryal 178 B2
Ryal Fold 137 A5
Ryall 14 B4
Ryarsh 37 A4
Rydal 154 A2
Ryde 19 B4
Rye 37 D7
Ryecroft Gate . . . 129 C4
Rye Foreign 37 D6
Rye Harbour 38 D1
Ryehill 143 A4
Rye Park 68 B3
Rye Street 79 D5
Ryhall 116 D3
Ryhill 140 B1
Ryhope 179 D6
Rylstone 146 B3
Ryme Intrinseca . 29 D5
Ryther 149 D4
Ryton Glos 79 D5
N Yorks 159 D6
Shrops 95 A5
T&W 178 C3
Ryton-on-
Dunsmore 97 D6

S

Sabden 146 D1
Sacombe 68 B3
Sacriston 167 A5
Sadberge 167 D6
Saddell 190 B3
Saddington 98 B3
Saddle Bow 118 D3
Saddlescombe . . . 21 A5
Sadgill 154 A3
Saffron Walden . . 86 D1
Sageston 55 D6
Saham Hills 103 A5
Saham Toney 103 A5
Saighdinis 287 H3
Saighton 127 C4
St Abbs 211 D6
St Abb's Haven . . 211 D6
St Agnes Corn . . . 4 B2
Scilly 2 F3
St Albans 67 C6
St Allen 4 B3
St Andrews 221 C5
St Andrew's
Major 41 D6
St Anne Ald 7
St Annes 136 A2
St Ann's 184 C3
St Ann's Chapel
Corn 11 D5
Devon 7 C5
St Anthony-in-
Meneage 3 C5
St Anthony's Hill . 22 B4
St Arvans 61 D7
St Asaph
= Llanelwy 125 B5
St Athan 41 E5
St Aubin Jersey . . 6
St Austell 5 B5
St Bees 162 C2
St Blazey 5 B5
St Boswells 197 C4

St Brelade Jersey 6
St Breock.........9 D5
St Breward.......10 D1
St Briavels.......62 C1
St Bride's.......54 C4
St Brides Major ..40 D3
St Bride's
  Netherwent.....42 A3
St Brides-
  super-Ely.....41 D5
St Brides
  Wentlooge.....42 A1
St Budeaux........6 B3
Saintbury........80 D4
St Buryan.........2 C2
St Catherine....44 B1
St Catherine's..215 B4
St Clears
  =Sanclêr.....56 A2
St Cleer..........6 A1
St Clement........4 C3
St Clements Jersey....6
St Clether.......10 C3
St Colmac.......203 B5
St Columb Major ..4 A4
St Columb Minor ..4 A3
St Columb Road...4 B4
St Combs.......269 C5
St Cross South
  Elmham......104 C3
St Cyrus.......233 B4
St David's......218 B4
St David's
  =Tyddewi.....54 B3
St Day............4 C2
St Dennis.........4 B4
St Devereux.....78 D2
St Dogmaels....73 B4
St Dogwells....55 B5
St Dominick......6 A3
St Donat's......40 E4
St Edith's......44 C3
St Endellion....9 D5
St Enoder........4 B3
St Erme..........4 B3
St Erney.........6 B2
St Erth..........2 B3
St Ervan.........9 D4
St Eval..........4 A3
St Ewe...........5 C4
St Fagans......41 D6
St Fergus......269 C6
St Fillans......217 B6
St Florence.....55 D6
St Genny's......10 B2
St George......125 B4
St George's....41 D5
St Germans.......6 B2
St Giles.......133 B4
St Giles in the
  Wood.......25 D6
St Giles on the
  Heath......11 B4
St Harmon......92 D3
St Helena.......97 A5
St Helen
  Auckland....167 C4
St Helens IoW....19 C5
  Mers.......136 D4
St Helen's......23 A6
St Helier Jersey....6
  London......49 C5
St Hilary Corn....2 B3
  V Glam......41 D5
Saint Hill......36 C1
St Illtyd.......41 A7
St Ippollytts....68 A1
St Ishmael's....54 D4
St Issey.........9 D5
St Ive...........6 A2
St Ives Cambs...101 D5
  Corn.........2 A3
  Dorset......17 A5
St James South
  Elmham......104 C4
St Jidgey.......9 E5
St John..........6 B3
St John's IoM...152 C2
  Jersey.........6

St John's continued
  Sur..........34 A2
  Worcs........79 B6
St John's Chapel 166 B1
St John's Fen
  End.......118 D2
St John's
  Highway....118 D2
St John's Town of
  Dalry......182 D4
St Judes.......152 B3
St Just..........2 B1
St Just in
  Roseland......2 C3
St Katherine's..256 C2
St Keverne.......3 C5
St Kew...........9 D5
St Kew Highway...9 D6
St Keyne.........6 A1
St Lawrence Corn...5 A5
  Essex.......70 C3
  IoW..........18 D4
St Leonards
  Dorset......17 A5
  E Sus.......23 B5
St Leonard's.....4 C3
Saint Leonards..205 C6
St Levan.........2 C1
St Lythans.......41 D6
St Mabyn.........9 D6
St Madoes......219 B6
St Margarets.....68 B3
St Margaret's....78 D1
St Margaret's at
  Cliffe.......39 A4
St Margaret's
  Hope.......283 H5
St Margaret South
  Elmham......104 C4
St Mark's.......152 D2
St Martin........6 B1
St Martins Corn...3 C4
  Perth......219 A6
St Martin's Jersey....6
  Shrops.....110 B2
St Mary Bourne..46 D2
St Mary Church..41 D5
St Mary Cray....50 C1
St Mary Hill....41 D4
St Mary Hoo....51 B5
St Mary in the
  Marsh......38 C2
St Mary's Jersey....6
  Orkney.....283 G5
St Mary's Bay...38 C2
St Maughans....61 B6
St Mawes.........4 D3
St Mawgan........4 A3
St Mellion.......6 A2
St Mellons......42 A1
St Merryn........9 D4
St Mewan.........5 B4
St Michael
  Caerhays.....5 C4
St Michael
  Penkevil.....4 C3
St Michaels......78 A3
St Michael's....37 C6
St Michael's on
  Wyre......145 C4
St Michael South
  Elmham......104 C4
St Minver........9 D5
St Monans.....221 D5
St Neot..........5 A6
St Neots........84 A3
St Newlyn East...4 B3
St Nicholas Pembs 72 C1
  V Glam......41 D5
St Nicholas at
  Wade.......53 C4
St Ninians.....207 A5
St Osyth........71 B5
St Osyth Heath..71 B5
St Ouens Jersey....6
St Owens Cross..62 A1
St Paul's Cray...50 C1
St Paul's Walden..68 A1
St Peter Port Guern...6
St Peter's Jersey....6
  Kent.........53 C5
St Petrox.......55 E5

St Pinnock.......5 A7
St Quivox.......192 C3
St Ruan..........3 D5
St Sampson Guern....6
St Stephen.......4 B4
St Stephens Corn ..6 B3
  Herts......67 C6
St Stephen's....10 C4
St Teath.........9 C6
St Thomas......13 B4
St Tudy..........9 D6
St Twynnells....55 E5
St Veep..........5 B6
St Vigeans.....233 D4
St Wenn..........5 A4
St Weonards....61 A6
Salcombe.........7 D6
Salcombe Regis..13 C6
Salcott........70 B3
Sale..........137 D6
Saleby........135 B4
Sale Green......80 B2
Salehurst......37 D5
Salem Carms.....58 C3
  Ceredig.....91 D4
Salen Argyll...225 B4
  Highld......235 D5
Salesbury.....145 D6
Salford C Beds...83 D6
  Gtr Man....137 D7
  Oxon........64 A3
Salford Priors...80 B3
Salfords.......35 B5
Salhouse......121 D5
Saline........208 A3
Salisbury......31 C5
Sallachan.....236 C3
Sallachy Highld..249 C6
  Highld.....272 D3
Salle.........120 C3
Salmonby......134 B3
Salmond's Muir..221 A5
Salperton......64 A1
Salph End......84 B2
Salsburgh.....207 D6
Salt..........112 C3
Saltaire......147 D5
Saltash..........6 B3
Saltburn......264 D3
Saltburn-by-the-
  Sea.......169 C4
Saltby........115 C6
Saltcoats Cumb..153 A1
  N Ayrs.....204 D2
Saltdean.......22 B1
Salt End......142 A3
Salter........145 A6
Salterforth....146 C2
Saltfleet......143 D6
Saltfleetby All
  Saints.....143 D6
Saltfleetby
  St Clements..143 D6
Saltfleetby
  St Peter....135 A4
Saltford.......43 C5
Salthouse.....120 A2
Saltmarshe....141 A5
Saltney.......126 C3
Salton........159 D6
Saltwick......178 B3
Saltwood.......38 B3
Salum........222 C3
Salvington.....21 B4
Salwarpe.......80 A1
Salwayash......15 B4
Sambourne.....80 A3
Sambrook.....111 C6
Samhla.......287 H2
Samlesbury....145 D5
Samlesbury
  Bottoms....137 A5
Sampford
  Arundel.....27 D4
Sampford Brett ..27 A5
Sampford
  Courtenay...12 A1
Sampford
  Peverell....27 D5
Sampford Spiney 11 D6
Sampool Bridge 154 C3

Samuelston....210 C1
Sanachan......249 B5
Sanaigmore....200 A2
Sanclêr
  =St Clears....56 A2
Sancreed........2 C2
Sancton.......150 D2
Sand Highld....261 A6
  Shetland....285 J5
Sandaig.......247 D6
Sandale.......175 D5
Sandal Magna..139 B6
Sandbach......128 C2
Sandbank......215 D4
Sandbanks......17 C4
Sandend.......267 C6
Sanderstead....49 C6
Sandfields.....63 A5
Sandford Cumb..165 D5
  Devon........12 A3
  Dorset......16 C3
  IoW..........18 C4
  N Som.......42 D3
  Shrops.....111 B4
  S Lanark...194 B2
Sandfordhill..257 B6
Sandford on
  Thames.....65 C6
Sandford Orcas ..29 C6
Sandford
  St Martin....65 A5
Sandgate.......38 B3
Sandgreen.....172 C3
Sandhaven....269 C4
Sandhead.....170 C2
Sandhills......34 C2
Sandhoe.......178 C1
Sand Hole.....149 D7
Sandholme
  E Yorks.....150 D1
  Lincs......117 B6
Sandhurst Brack ..47 C6
  Glos........63 A4
  Kent........37 D5
Sandhurst Cross..37 D5
Sandhutton...158 C2
Sand Hutton...149 B5
Sandiacre.....114 B2
Sandilands Lincs.135 A5
  S Lanark...194 C3
Sandiway......127 B6
Sandleheath....31 D5
Sandling.......37 A5
Sandlow Green..128 C2
Sandness.....285 H3
Sandon Essex...70 C1
  Herts.......85 D5
  Staffs.....112 B3
Sandown........18 C4
Sandplace......6 B1
Sandridge Herts..67 B6
  Wilts.......44 C3
Sandringham...118 C3
Sandsend.....169 D6
Sandside House 279 B5
Sandsound....285 L6
Sandtoft.......141 C5
Sandway........37 A6
Sandwell.......96 C3
Sandwich.......53 D5
Sandwick Cumb..164 D2
  Orkney.....283 J5
  Shetland....285 L6
Sandwith......162 C2
Sandy Carms....57 B4
  C Beds......84 C3
Sandy Bank....134 D2
Sandycroft....126 C3
Sandyford
  Dumfries....185 C5
  Stoke......128 D3
Sandygate.....152 B3
Sandy Haven....55 D4
Sandyhills....173 C6
Sandylands....144 A4
Sandy Lane Wilts..44 C3
Sandypark......12 C2
Sandysike....141 D4
Sangobeg......277 B5
Sangomore....277 B5
Sanna........234 D3

Sanndabhaig
  W Isles.....286 B4
  W Isles.....288 D5
Sannox.......203 D5
Sanquhar.....183 B5
Santon........142 B1
Santon Bridge..163 D4
Santon
  Downham....103 C4
Sapcote........98 B1
Sapey Common...79 A5
Sapiston......103 D5
Sapley........100 D4
Sapperton Glos...63 C5
  Lincs......116 B3
Saracen's Head .117 C6
Sarclet.......281 D5
Sardis.........57 B5
Sarn Bridgend...40 C4
  Powys.......93 B6
Sarnau Carms....56 A3
  Ceredig.....73 A6
  Gwyn......109 B4
  Powys.......76 D4
  Powys......110 D1
Sarn Bach.....106 D3
Sarnesfield....78 B1
Sarn Meyllteyrn.106 C2
Saron Carms....57 A6
  Carms.......73 C6
  Denb.......125 C5
  Gwyn......107 A4
  Gwyn......123 D5
Sarratt........67 D5
Sarre..........53 C4
Sarsden........64 A3
Sarsgrum.....277 B4
Satley........166 A4
Satron........156 B3
Satterleigh....26 C1
Satterthwaite..154 B2
Satwell........47 A5
Sauchen......244 A3
Saucher......219 A6
Sauchie.......208 A1
Sauchieburn...233 B4
Saughall.....126 B3
Saughtree....187 D4
Saul...........62 C3
Saundby......132 A2
Saunderfoot....56 B1
Saunderton....66 C2
Saunton.......25 B5
Sausthorpe....134 C3
Saval.........272 D2
Savary........225 B4
Savile Park...138 A3
Sawbridge......82 A2
Sawbridgeworth .69 C4
Sawdon.......160 C3
Sawley Derbys..114 B2
  Lancs......146 C1
  N Yorks....147 A6
Sawston........85 C6
Sawtry........100 C2
Saxby Leics....115 D6
  Lincs......133 A5
Saxby All Saints 142 B1
Saxelbye......115 C5
Saxham Street..88 A1
Saxilby.......132 B3
Saxlingham
  Green......104 B3
Saxlingham
  Nethergate..104 B3
Saxlingham
  Thorpe.....104 B3
Saxmundham....89 A4
Saxondale....115 B4
Saxon Street...86 B2
Saxtead.......88 A3
Saxtead Green..88 A3
Saxthorpe....120 B2
Saxton........148 D3
Sayers Common..21 A5
Scackleton....159 D5
Scadabhagh...288 H2
Scaftworth....141 D4
Scagglethorpe.160 D2
Scaitcliffe...137 A6
Scalasaig.....212 C1

Scalby E Yorks...141 A6
  N Yorks.....160 B4
Scaldwell......99 D4
Scaleby.......176 C2
Scaleby Hill...176 C2
Scale Houses..164 A3
Scales Cumb....153 C3
  Cumb.......163 B6
  Lancs......145 D4
Scalford......115 C5
Scaling.......169 D5
Scallastle....225 C5
Scalloway....285 K6
Scalpay......288 H3
Scalpay House..247 B5
Scalpsie......203 C5
Scamadale....235 A6
Scamblesby...134 B2
Scamodale....236 B2
Scampston....160 D2
Scampton.....133 B4
Scapa.........283 G5
Scapegoat Hill.138 B3
Scar..........282 C7
Scarborough...160 C4
Scarcliffe....131 C4
Scarcroft....148 C2
Scarcroft Hill.148 C2
Scardroy.....250 A4
Scarff........284 E4
Scarfskerry...281 A4
Scargill......166 D3
Scarinish.....222 C3
Scarisbrick...136 B2
Scarning......119 D6
Scarrington...115 A5
Scartho.......143 C4
Scarwell......282 E3
Scatness.....285 M5
Scatraig......252 C3
Scawby.......142 C1
Scawsby......140 C3
Scawton......158 C4
Scayne's Hill...35 D6
Scethrog......60 A3
Scholar Green.128 D3
Scholes W Yorks..139 A4
  W Yorks....139 C4
  W Yorks....148 D2
School Green..127 C6
Scleddau.......55 A5
Scofton......131 A6
Scole.........104 D2
Scolpaig.....287 G2
Scone.........219 B6
Sconser......247 A4
Scoonie......220 D3
Scoor........224 E3
Scopwick.....133 D5
Scoraig......262 A2
Scorborough..150 C3
Scorrier........4 C2
Scorton Lancs...145 C5
  N Yorks....157 A6
Sco Ruston...121 C4
Scotbheinn...286 A4
Scotby.......176 D2
Scotch Corner..157 A6
Scotforth....145 B4
Scothern.....133 B5
Scotland Gate..179 A4
Scotlandwell..219 D6
Scotsburn....264 C3
Scotscalder
  Station....280 C2
Scotscraig....220 B4
Scots' Gap....178 A2
Scotston Aberds..233 A5
  Perth......230 D3
Scotstown....205 B5
Scotstown....236 C2
Scotswood....178 C3
Scottas......247 D6
Scotter......141 C6
Scotterthorpe.141 C6
Scottlethorpe.116 C3
Scotton Lincs...141 D6
  N Yorks....148 B2
  N Yorks....157 B5
Scottow......121 C4
Scoughall....210 B3
Scoulag......203 C6

Scoulton....103 A5
Scourie....276 D2
Scourie More....276 D2
Scousburgh....285 M5
Scrabster....280 B2
Scrafield....134 C3
Scrainwood....188 C2
Scrane End....117 A6
Scraptoft....98 A3
Scratby....121 D7
Scrayingham....149 A6
Scredington....116 A3
Scremby....135 C4
Scremerston....198 B4
Screveton....115 A5
Scrivelsby....134 C2
Scriven....148 B2
Scrooby....141 D4
Scropton....113 B5
Scrub Hill....134 D2
Scruton....157 B6
Sculcoates....150 D3
Sculthorpe....119 B5
Scunthorpe....141 B6
Scurlage....57 D4
Seaborough....14 A4
Seacombe....136 D2
Seacroft Lincs....135 C5
  W Yorks....148 D2
Seadyke....117 B6
Seafield S Ayrs....192 C3
  W Loth....208 D3
Seaford....22 C2
Seaforth....136 D2
Seagrave....115 D4
Seaham....168 A2
Seahouses....199 C6
Seal....36 A3
Sealand....126 C3
Seale....34 B1
Seamer N Yorks....160 C4
  N Yorks....168 D2
Seamill....204 D2
Sea Palling....121 C6
Searby....142 C2
Seasalter....52 C2
Seascale....162 D3
Seathorne....135 C5
Seathwaite Cumb 153 A4
  Cumb....163 C5
Seatoller....163 C5
Seaton Corn....6 B2
  Cumb....162 A3
  Devon....14 B2
  Durham....179 D5
  E Yorks....151 C4
  Northumb....179 B5
  Rutland....99 B6
Seaton Burn....179 B4
Seaton Carew....168 C3
Seaton Delaval....179 B5
Seaton Ross....149 C6
Seaton Sluice....179 B5
Seatown Aberds....267 C6
  Dorset....14 B4
Seave Green....159 A4
Seaview....19 B5
Seaville....175 C4
Seavington
  St Mary....28 D3
Seavington
  St Michael....28 D4
Sebergham....164 A1
Seckington....97 A5
Second Coast....261 A6
Sedbergh....155 B5
Sedbury....62 D1
Sedbusk....156 B2
Sedgeberrow....80 D3
Sedgebrook....115 B6
Sedgefield....167 C6
Sedgeford....119 B4
Sedgehill....30 C2
Sedgley....96 B2
Sedgwick....154 C4
Sedlescombe
  Street....23 A5
Seend....44 C3
Seend Cleeve....44 C3
Seer Green....67 D4
Seething....104 B4

Sefton....136 C2
Seghill....179 B4
Seifton....94 C2
Seighford....112 C2
Seilebost....287 E5
Seion....123 D5
Seisdon....95 B6
Seisiadar....288 D6
Selattyn....110 B1
Selborne....33 B6
Selby....149 D5
Selham....34 D2
Selhurst....49 C6
Selkirk....186 A3
Sellack....62 A1
Sellafirth....284 D7
Sellarston
Sellindge....38 B2
Sellindge Lees....38 B3
Selling....52 D2
Sells Green....44 C3
Selly Oak....96 C3
Selmeston....22 B3
Selsdon....49 C6
Selsey....20 C1
Selsfield
  Common....35 C6
Selsted....39 A4
Selston....131 D4
Selworthy....27 A4
Sembister....285 H5
Semer....87 C5
Semington....44 C2
Semley....30 C2
Send....34 A3
Send Marsh....34 A3
Senghenydd....41 B6
Sennen....2 C1
Sennen Cove....2 C1
Sennybridge
  =Pont Senni....59 C6
Serlby....131 A6
Sessay....158 D3
Setchey....118 D3
Setley....18 A2
Setter Shetland....284 E6
  Shetland....285 H5
  Shetland....285 J7
Settiscarth....282 F4
Settle....146 A2
Settrington....160 D2
Sevenhampton....63 A6
Seven Kings....50 A1
Sevenoaks....36 A3
Sevenoaks Weald 36 A3
Seven Sisters....59 E5
Severn Beach....43 A4
Severnhampton....64 D3
Severn Stoke....79 C6
Sevington....38 A2
Sewards End....86 D1
Sewardstone....68 D3
Sewardstonebury 68 D3
Sewerby....151 A4
Seworgan....4 D2
Sewstern....116 C1
Sezincote....81 D4
Sgarasta Mhor....287 E5
Sgiogarstaigh....288 A6
Shabbington....66 C1
Shackerstone....97 A6
Shackleford....34 B2
Shade....138 A2
Shadforth....167 A6
Shadingfield....105 C5
Shadoxhurst....38 B1
Shadsworth....137 A6
Shadwell Norf....103 C5
  W Yorks....148 D2
Shaftesbury....30 C2
Shafton....140 B1
Shalbourne....45 C7
Shalcombe....18 C2
Shalden....33 A5
Shaldon....13 D4
Shalfleet....18 C3
Shalford Essex....69 A7
  Sur....34 B3
Shalford Green....69 A7
Shallowford....26 A2
Shalmsford
  Street....52 D2

Shalstone....82 D2
Shamley Green....34 B3
Shandon....215 D5
Shandwick....265 C4
Shangton....99 B4
Shankhouse....179 B4
Shanklin....19 C4
Shanquhar....255 C6
Shanzie....231 C6
Shap....164 D3
Shapwick Dorset....16 A3
  Som....28 B4
Shardlow....114 B2
Shareshill....96 A2
Sharlston....140 B1
Sharlston
  Common....140 B1
Sharnbrook....84 B1
Sharnford....98 B1
Sharoe Green....145 D5
Sharow....158 D2
Sharpenhoe....84 D2
Sharperton....188 C2
Sharpness....62 C2
Sharp Street....121 C5
Sharpthorne....35 C6
Sharrington....120 B2
Shatterford....95 C5
Shaugh Prior....7 A4
Shavington....128 D2
Shaw Gtr Man....138 C2
  W Berks....46 C2
  Wilts....44 C2
Shawbury....111 C4
Shawdon Hall....188 B3
Shawell....98 C2
Shawford....32 C3
Shawforth....138 A1
Shaw Green....136 B4
Shawhead....173 A6
Shawhill....175 B5
Shaw Mills....147 A6
Shawton....194 B1
Shawtonhill....194 B1
Shear Cross....30 A2
Shearington....174 B3
Shearsby....98 B3
Shebbear....11 A5
Shebdon....111 C6
Shebster....279 B6
Sheddens....205 C5
Shedfield....33 D4
Sheen....129 C6
Sheepscar....148 D2
Sheepscombe....63 B4
Sheepstor....7 A4
Sheepwash....11 A5
Sheepway....42 B3
Sheepy Magna....97 A6
Sheepy Parva....97 A6
Sheering....69 B5
Sheerness....51 B6
Sheet....33 C6
Sheffield....130 A3
Sheffield Bottom....47 C4
Sheffield Green....36 D2
Shefford....84 D3
Shefford
  Woodlands....46 B1
Sheigra....276 B3
Sheinton....95 A4
Shelderton....94 D2
Sheldon Derbys....129 C6
  Devon....13 A6
  W Mid....97 C4
Sheldwich....52 D2
Shelf....139 A4
Shelfanger....104 C2
Shelfield Warks....80 A4
  W Mid....96 A3
Shelford....115 A4
Shellacres....198 B2
Shelley Essex....69 C5
  Suff....87 D6
  W Yorks....139 B5
Shellingford....64 D4
Shellow Bowells....69 C6
Shelsley
  Beauchamp....79 A5
Shelsley Walsh....79 A5
Shelthorpe....114 D3
Shelton Bedford....84 A1

Shelton continued
  Norf....104 B3
  Notts....115 A5
  Shrops....110 D3
Shelton Green....104 B3
Shelve....94 B1
Shelwick....78 C3
Shenfield....69 D6
Shenington....81 C6
Shenley....68 C1
Shenley Brook
  End....83 D5
Shenleybury....68 C1
Shenley Church
  End....83 D5
Shenmore....78 D1
Shennanton....171 A5
Shenstone Staffs....96 A4
  Worcs....95 D6
Shenton....97 A6
Shenval Highld....251 D6
  Moray....254 D3
Shepeau Stow....117 D6
Shephall....68 A2
Shepherd's Green 47 A5
Shepherd's Port 118 B3
Shepherdswell....39 A4
Shepley....139 C4
Shepperdine....62 D2
Shepperton....48 C3
Shepreth....85 C5
Shepshed....114 D2
Shepton
  Beauchamp....28 D4
Shepton Mallet....29 A6
Shepton
  Montague....29 B6
Shepway....37 A5
Sheraton....168 B2
Sherborne Dorset....29 D6
  Glos....64 B2
Sherborne
  St John....47 D4
Sherbourne....81 A5
Sherburn Durham 167 A6
  N Yorks....160 D3
Sherburn Hill....167 A6
Sherburn in
  Elmet....148 D3
Shere....34 B3
Shereford....119 C5
Sherfield English 32 C1
Sherfield on
  Loddon....47 D4
Sherford....8 C1
Sheriffhales....111 D6
Sheriff Hutton....149 A5
Sheringham....120 A3
Sherington....83 C5
Shernal Green....80 A2
Shernborne....119 B4
Sherrington....30 B3
Sherston....44 A2
Sherwood Green....25 C6
Shettleston....205 B6
Shevington....136 C4
Shevington
  Moor....136 B4
Shevington Vale 136 C4
Sheviock....6 B2
Shide....18 C3
Shiel Bridge....238 A3
Shieldaig Highld....261 A5
  Highld....261 D5
Shieldhill
  Dumfries....184 D3
  Falk....208 C1
  S Lanark....195 B5
Shielfoot....235 D5
Shielhill Angus....232 C2
  Invclyd....204 A2
Shifford....65 C4
Shifnal....95 A5
Shilbottle....189 C4
Shildon....167 C5
Shillingford Devon 27 C4
  Oxon....65 D6
Shillingford
  St George....13 C4
Shillingstone....30 D2
Shillington....84 D3
Shillmoor....188 C1

Shilton Oxon....64 C3
  Warks....97 C7
Shilvington....178 A3
Shimpling Norf....104 C2
  Suff....87 B4
Shimpling Street....87 B4
Shincliffe....167 A5
Shiney Row....179 D5
Shinfield....47 C5
Shingham....102 A3
Shingle Street....89 C4
Shinner's Bridge....8 A1
Shinness....272 C3
Shipbourne....36 A3
Shipdham....103 A5
Shipham....42 D3
Shiphay....8 A2
Shiplake....47 B5
Shipley Derbys....114 A2
  Northumb....189 B4
  Shrops....95 B6
  W Sus....35 D4
  W Yorks....147 D5
Shipley Shiels....187 D6
Shipmeadow....105 C4
Shippea Hill
  Station....102 C2
Shippon....65 D5
Shipston-on-
  Stour....81 C5
Shipton Glos....63 B6
  N Yorks....149 B4
  Shrops....94 B3
Shipton Bellinger 31 A6
Shipton Gorge....15 B4
Shipton Green....19 A7
Shipton Moyne....44 A2
Shipton on
  Cherwell....65 B5
Shipton Solers....63 B6
Shiptonthorpe....150 C1
Shipton-under-
  Wychwood....64 B3
Shirburn....66 D1
Shirdley Hill....136 B2
Shirebrook....131 C5
Shiregreen....139 D6
Shirehampton....43 B4
Shiremoor....179 B5
Shirenewton....61 D6
Shireoaks....131 A5
Shirland....130 D3
Shirley Derbys....113 A6
  London....49 C6
  Soton....32 D3
  W Mid....96 D4
Shirl Heath....78 B2
Shirrell Heath....33 D4
Shirwell....25 B6
Shirwell Cross....25 B6
Shiskine....191 C5
Shobdon....78 A2
Shobnall....113 C6
Shobrooke....12 A3
Shoby....115 D4
Shocklach....110 A3
Shoeburyness....51 A6
Sholden....53 D5
Sholing....32 D3
Shoot Hill....110 D3
Shop Corn....9 D4
  Corn....24 D3
Shop Corner....88 D3
Shoreditch....49 A6
Shoreham....50 C2
Shoreham-by-
  Sea....21 B5
Shore Mill....264 D3
Shoresdean....198 B3
Shoreswood....198 B3
Shoreton....264 D2
Shorncote....63 D6
Shorne....50 B3
Shortacombe....11 C6
Shortgate....22 A2
Short Heath....96 A2
Shortlanesend....4 C3
Shortlees....193 B4
Shortstown....84 C2
Shorwell....18 C3
Shoscombe....43 D6

Shotatton....110 C2
Shotesham....104 B3
Shotgate....70 D1
Shotley....88 D3
Shotley Bridge....178 D2
Shotleyfield....178 D2
Shotley Gate....88 D3
Shottenden....52 D2
Shottermill....34 C1
Shottery....81 B4
Shotteswell....81 C7
Shottisham....88 C4
Shottle....113 A7
Shottlegate....113 A7
Shotton Durham....168 B2
  Flint....126 C3
  Northumb....198 C2
Shotton Colliery 167 A6
Shotts....207 D6
Shotwick....126 B3
Shouldham....102 A2
Shouldham
  Thorpe....102 A2
Shoulton....79 B6
Shover's Green....37 C4
Shrawardine....110 D3
Shrawley....79 A6
Shrewley
  Common....81 A5
Shrewsbury....110 D3
Shrewton....31 A4
Shripney....20 B2
Shrivenham....45 A6
Shropham....103 B5
Shrub End....70 A3
Shucknall....78 C3
Shudy Camps....86 C2
Shulishadermor 259 D4
Shurdington....63 B5
Shurlock Row....47 B6
Shurrery....279 C6
Shurrery Lodge 279 C6
Shurton....28 A2
Shustoke....97 B5
Shute Devon....12 A3
  Devon....14 B2
Shutford....81 C6
Shuthonger....80 D1
Shutlanger....83 B4
Shuttington....97 A5
Shuttlewood....131 B4
Siabost bho
  Dheas....288 C3
Siabost bho
  Thuath....288 C3
Siadar....288 B4
Siadar Iarach....288 B4
Siadar Uarach....288 B4
Sibbaldbie....185 D4
Sibbertoft....98 C3
Sibdon Carwood....94 C2
Sibford Ferris....81 D6
Sibford Gower....81 D6
Sible Hedingham 86 D3
Sibsey....134 D3
Sibson Cambs....100 B2
  Leics....97 A6
Sibthorpe....115 A5
Sibton....89 A4
Sibton Green....105 D4
Sicklesmere....87 A4
Sicklinghall....148 C2
Sid....13 C6
Sidbury Devon....13 B6
  Shrops....95 C4
Sidcot....42 D3
Sidcup....50 B1
Siddick....162 A3
Siddington
  Ches E....128 B3
  Glos....63 D6
Sidemoor....96 D2
Sidestrand....121 B4
Sidford....13 B6
Sidlesham....20 C1
Sidley....23 B5
Sidlow....35 B5
Sidmouth....13 C6
Sigford....12 D2

Sigglesthorne...151 C4
Sighthill........209 C4
Sigingstone......41 D4
Signet..........64 B3
Silchester.......47 C4
Sildinis........288 F3
Sileby.........114 D3
Silecroft.......153 B2
Silfield.......104 B2
Silian.........75 C4
Silkstone......139 C5
Silkstone
  Common......139 C5
Silk Willoughby .116 A3
Silloth.......174 C4
Sills..........188 C1
Sillyearn......267 D6
Siloh..........59 B4
Silpho.........160 B3
Silsden........147 C4
Silsoe..........84 D2
Silverburn.....209 C5
Silverdale Lancs..154 D3
  Staffs.......112 A2
Silver End.......70 B2
Silvergate.....120 C3
Silverhill......23 A5
Silverley's
  Green........104 D3
Silverstone......82 C3
Silverton.......13 A4
Silvington......95 D4
Silwick.......285 J4
Simmondley.....138 D3
Simonburn......177 B6
Simonsbath......26 B2
Simonstone.....146 D1
Simprim.......198 B2
Simpson.........83 D5
Simpson Cross ...55 C4
Sinclair's Hill ...198 A2
Sinclairston.....182 A2
Sinderby.......158 C2
Sinderhope.....177 D6
Sindlesham......47 C5
Singdean.......187 C4
Singleborough....83 D4
Singleton Lancs ..144 D3
  W Sus.........20 A1
Singlewell......50 B3
Sinkhurst Green ..37 B6
Sinnahard.....244 A1
Sinnington....159 C6
Sinton Green 79 A6
Sipson.........48 B3
Sirhowy........60 B3
Sisland.......104 B4
Sissinghurst 37 C5
Sisterpath.....197 B6
Siston.........43 B5
Sithney..........3 C4
Sittingbourne 51 C5
Six Ashes......95 C5
Sixhills.......133 A6
Six Hills......115 C4
Six Mile Bottom ..86 B1
Sixpenny Handley 30 D3
Sizewell.......89 A5
Skail..........278 D3
Skaill Orkney....282 D5
  Orkney.......283 G6
Skares.......182 A3
Skateraw......211 C4
Skaw.........284 D2
Skeabost......259 D4
Skeabrae......282 E3
Skeeby........157 A6
Skeffington.....99 A4
Skeffling......143 B5
Skegby........131 C4
Skegness......135 C5
Skelberry.....285 M5
Skelbo........264 A3
Skelbrooke....140 B3
Skeldyke......117 B6
Skellingthorpe .133 B4
Skellister....285 H6
Skellow.......140 B3

Skelmanthorpe..139 B5
Skelmersdale...136 C3
Skelmonae.....256 C3
  W Sus........20 B2
Skelpick......278 C3
Skelton Cumb...164 B2
  E Yorks......141 A5
  N Yorks......157 A4
  Redcar......169 D4
  York........149 B4
Skelton-on-Ure 148 A2
Skelwick......282 C5
Skelwith Bridge 154 A2
Skendleby.....135 C4
Skene House...245 B4
Skenfrith......61 A6
Skerne........150 B3
Skeroblingarry .190 C3
Skerray......278 B2
Skerton......145 A4
Sketchley......98 B1
Sketty.........57 C6
Skewen.........40 B2
Skewsby......159 D5
Skeyton......120 C4
Skiag Bridge...271 B5
Skibo Castle...264 B3
Skidbrooke....143 D6
Skidbrooke North
  End.........143 D6
Skidby........150 D3
Skilgate.......27 C4
Skillington....116 C1
Skinburness...174 C4
Skinflats.....208 B2
Skinidin......258 D2
Skinnet.......277 B6
Skinningrove..169 C5
Skipness......202 C3
Skippool......144 C3
Skipsea.......151 B4
Skipsea Brough .151 B4
Skipton......146 B3
Skipton-on-
  Swale.......158 D2
Skipwith......149 D5
Skirbeck.......117 A6
Skirbeck
  Quarter.....117 A6
Skirlaugh.....151 D4
Skirling......195 C5
Skirmett.......47 A5
Skirpenbeck ...149 B6
Skirwith......165 B4
Skirza.......281 B5
Skulamus.....247 B5
Skullomie.....277 B7
Skyborry Green ..93 D6
Skye of Curr...253 D5
Skyreholme....147 A4
Slackhall.....129 A5
Slackhead.....267 C5
Slad...........63 C4
Slade Devon....25 A6
  Pembs........55 C5
Slade Green....50 B2
Slaggyford....177 D4
Slaidburn.....145 B7
Slaithwaite...138 B3
Slaley.......178 D1
Slamannan....207 C6
Slapton Bucks....67 A4
  Devon..........8 C2
W Nhants......82 C3
Slatepit Dale...130 C3
Slattocks.....138 C1
Slaugham......35 D5
Slaughterford ...44 B2
Slawston.......99 B4
Sleaford Hants...33 B7
  Lincs.......116 A3
Sleagill......164 D3
Sleapford.....111 D5
Sledge Green....79 D6
Sledmere......150 A2
Sleightholme...152 A2
Sleights......160 A2
Slepe..........16 B3
Slickly......281 B4
Sliddery.....191 C5
Sligachan Hotel .246 B3

Slimbridge......62 C3
Slindon Staffs...112 B2
  W Sus........20 B2
Slinfold.......35 C4
Sling.........123 D6
Slingsby......159 D5
Slioch.......255 C6
Slip End C Beds ..67 B5
  Herts........85 D4
Slipton.........99 D6
Slitting Mill...112 D4
Slochd.......253 D4
Slockavullin..213 C6
Sloley.......121 C4
Sloothby......135 B4
Slough.........48 B2
Slough Green....35 D5
Sluggan......253 D4
Slumbay......249 C5
Slyfield.......34 A2
Slyne.........145 A4
Smailholm....197 C5
Smallbridge...138 B2
Smallburgh....121 C5
Smallburn
  Aberds......257 B5
  E Ayrs......194 D1
Small Dole.....21 A5
Smalley.......114 A2
Smallfield.....35 B6
Small Hythe....37 C6
Smallridge.....14 A3
Smannell.......32 A2
Smardale.....155 A6
Smarden.......37 B6
Smarden Bell ...37 B6
Smeatharpe....28 D1
Smeeth.........38 B2
Smeeton
  Westerby.....98 B3
Smercleit....286 E3
Smerral.......275 A5
Smethwick......96 C3
Smirisary.....235 C5
Smisby.......114 D1
Smithfield....176 C2
Smith Green...145 B4
Smithincott....27 D5
Smith's Green ...69 A5
Smithstown...261 C4
Smithton.....252 B3
Smithy Green ..128 B2
Smockington....98 C1
Smoogro......283 G4
Smythe's Green ..70 B3
Snaigow House .231 D4
Snailbeach.....94 A1
Snailwell......86 A2
Snainton......160 C3
Snaith.......140 A4
Snape N Yorks...157 C6
  Suff.........89 B4
Snape Green...136 B2
Snarestone.....97 A6
Snarford.....133 A5
Snargate.......38 C1
Snave.........38 C2
Snead.........93 B7
Sneath Common 104 C2
Sneaton......160 A2
Sneatonthorpe .160 A3
Snelland.....133 A5
Snelston.....113 A5
Snettisham....118 B3
Sniseabhal...286 C3
Snitter......188 C3
Snitterby.....142 D1
Snitterfield ...81 B5
Snitton........94 D3
Snodhill.......77 C7
Snodland......51 C3
Snowden Hill...139 C5
Snowdon.......53 D4
Snowshill......80 D3
Snydale......140 B2
Soar Anglesey..122 C3
  Carms.......58 C3
  Devon..........7 D6
Soar-y-Mynydd ..76 B1
Soberton.......33 D5
Soberton Heath ..33 D5
Sockbridge....164 C3

Sockburn......158 A2
Soham........102 D1
Soham Cotes...102 D1
Solas.........287 G3
Soldon Cross...24 D4
Soldridge......33 B5
Sole Street Kent..38 A2
  Kent.........50 C3
Solihull........97 D4
Sollers Dilwyn...78 B2
Sollers Hope....79 D4
Sollom.......136 B3
Solva..........54 B3
Somerby Leics..115 D5
  Lincs........142 C2
Somercotes...131 D4
Somerford......17 B5
Somerford
  Keynes.......63 D6
Somerley.......19 B7
Somerleyton...105 B5
Somersal
  Herbert......113 B5
Somersby.....134 B3
Somersham
  Cambs.......101 D5
  Suff.........88 C1
Somerton Oxon...65 A5
  Som..........29 C4
Sompting.......21 B4
Sonning........47 B5
Sonning Common 47 A5
Sonning Eye....47 B5
Sontley.......110 A2
Sopley.........17 B5
Sopwell........67 C6
Sopworth.......44 A2
Sorbie.......171 C6
Sordale......280 B3
Sorisdale....223 A5
Sorn.........193 C5
Sornhill.....193 B5
Sortat.......281 B4
Sotby.........134 B2
Sots Hole.....133 C6
Sotterley....105 C5
Soudley......111 C6
Soughton.....126 C2
Soulbury.......66 A3
Souldern.......82 D2
Souldrop......84 A1
Sound Ches E...111 A5
  Shetland....285 H5
  Shetland....285 J6
Sound Heath...111 A5
Soundwell......43 B5
Sourhope.....188 A1
Sourin.......282 D5
Sourton........11 B6
Soutergate....153 B3
South Acre....119 D5
Southall.......48 A4
South Allington ..8 D1
South Alloa...208 A1
Southam Glos...63 A5
  Warks........81 A7
South
  Ambersham....34 D2
Southampton....32 D3
South Anston..131 A5
South Ascot....48 C2
South
  Ballachulish .237 D4
South Balloch..181 B5
South Bank....168 C3
South Barrow...29 C6
South Beach...106 C3
South Benfleet..51 A4
South Bersted...20 B2
Southborough....36 B3
Southbourne BCP.17 B5
  W Sus........19 A6
South Brent.....7 A5
South Brewham ..29 B7
South Broomhill 189 D5
Southburgh....103 A5
South
  Burlingham...105 A4
South Cadbury...29 C6
South Cairn...170 A1

South Carlton .133 B4
South Cave....150 D2
South Cerney....63 D6
South Chard....14 A3
South Charlton .189 A4
South Cheriton ..29 C6
Southchurch....51 A6
South Cliffe...150 D1
South Clifton..132 B3
South
  Cockerington .134 A3
South Cornelly ..40 C3
South Cove....105 C5
South Creagan .227 B4
South Creake...119 B5
South Croxton..115 D4
South Croydon...49 C6
South Dalton..150 C2
South Darenth...50 C2
Southdean....187 C5
Southdene....136 D3
South Duffield .149 D5
Southease......22 B2
South Elkington 134 A2
South Elmsall..140 B2
South End Bucks..66 A3
  Cumb.......153 D3
  N Lincs.....142 A3
Southend-on-
  Sea..........51 A5
Southerndown...40 D3
Southerness...174 C2
South Erradale .261 C4
Southery.....102 B2
South Fambridge 70 D2
South Fawley...46 A1
South Ferriby..142 A1
Southfield...179 B4
Southfleet.....50 B3
South Garth...284 D7
South Garvan...236 B3
Southgate Ceredig 75 A4
  London.......68 D2
  Norf........120 C3
  Swansea......57 D5
South Glendale .286 E3
South Godstone ..35 B6
South Gorley....31 D5
South Green
  Essex........69 D6
  Kent.........51 C5
South-haa....284 E5
South Ham.....47 D4
South
  Hanningfield ..70 D1
South Harting...33 D6
South Hatfield..68 C2
South Hayling...19 B6
South Hazelrigg 199 C4
South Heath....67 C4
South Heighton ..22 B2
South Hetton..167 A6
South Hiendley .140 B1
South Hill.....10 D4
South Hinksey...65 C6
South Hole.....24 C3
South Holme...159 D5
South Holmwood..35 B4
South
  Hornchurch ...50 A2
South Hykeham .133 C4
South Hylton..179 D5
Southill.......84 C3
South Kelsey..142 D2
South Kessock .252 B2
South
  Killingholme .142 B3
South
  Kilvington...158 C3
South Kilworth..98 C3
South Kirkby...140 B2
South Kirkton .245 B4
South Kiscadale 191 C6
South Kyme....117 A4
South Lancing...21 B4
Southleigh......14 B2

South Leigh.....65 C4
South Leverton .132 A2
South Littleton ..80 C3
South Lopham .103 C6
South Luffenham 99 A6
South Malling...22 A2
South Marston...45 A5
South
  Middleton....188 A2
South Milford..148 D3
South Millbrex .256 B3
South Milton....7 C6
South Mimms...68 C2
Southminster...70 D3
South Molton...26 C2
South Moreton...46 A3
South Mundham .20 B1
South Muskham 132 D2
South Newbald..150 D2
South Newington 81 D7
South Newton...31 B4
South
  Normanton...131 D4
South Norwood...49 C6
South Nutfield ..35 B6
South Ockendon .50 A2
Southoe........84 A3
Southolt.......88 A2
South Ormsby..134 B3
Southorpe.....100 A2
South
  Otterington..158 C2
South Owersby .142 D2
Southowram...139 A4
South Oxhey....67 D6
South Perrott ...15 A4
South Petherton .28 D4
South Petherwin .10 C4
South
  Pickenham...103 A4
South Pool.....7 C6
Southport....136 B2
South Port....227 D5
Southpunds....285 L6
South Radworthy 26 B2
South Rauceby..116 A3
South Raynham .119 C5
Southrepps....121 B4
South Reston..135 A4
Southrey......133 C6
Southrop.......64 C2
Southrope......33 A5
South Runcton .102 A2
South Scarle..132 C3
Southsea......19 B5
South Shian...226 B4
South Shields .179 C5
South Shore..144 D3
South
  Somercotes ..143 D6
South Stainley .148 A2
South
  Stainmore...165 D6
South Stifford...50 B3
Southstoke.....43 C6
South Stoke Oxon 46 A3
  W Sus........20 B3
South Tawton...12 B1
South Thoresby .135 B4
South Tidworth ..31 A6
Southtown Norf..105 A6
  Orkney......283 H5
South Town....33 B5
South View.....47 D4
Southwaite....164 A2
South Walsham .121 D5
Southwark......49 B6
South
  Warnborough...33 A6
Southwater.....35 D4
Southwater
  Street.......35 D4
Southway......29 A5
South Weald....69 D5
Southwell Dorset..15 D6
  Notts.......132 D1

South Weston....66 D2
South Wheatley
  Corn...........10 B3
  Notts.........132 A2
South
  Whiteness....285 J5
Southwick Hants. 19 A5
  N Nhants.......100 B2
  T&W...........179 D5
  Wilts...........44 D2
  W Sus...........21 B5
South
  Widcombe....43 D4
South Wigston...98 B2
South
  Willingham...134 A1
South Wingfield 130 D3
South Witham...116 D2
Southwold......105 D6
South Wonston.. 32 B3
Southwood Norf 105 A4
  Som...........29 B5
South Woodham
  Ferrers.......70 D2
South Wootton. 118 C3
South Wraxall.. 44 C2
South Zeal.....12 B1
Soval Lodge.. 288 E4
Sowber Gate.. 158 C2
Sowerby N Yorks. 158 C3
  W Yorks.......138 A3
Sowerby Bridge 138 A3
Sowerby Row..164 B1
Sowood........138 B3
Sowton..........13 B4
Soyal..........264 A1
Spacey Houses. 148 B2
Spa Common..121 B4
Spadeadam
  Farm.........176 B3
Spalding......117 C5
Spaldington...149 D6
Spaldwick....100 D3
Spalford......132 C3
Spanby........116 B3
Sparham.......120 D2
Spark Bridge..154 C2
Sparkford......29 C6
Sparkhill......96 C3
Sparkwell.......7 B4
Sparrow Green.119 D6
Sparrowpit....129 A5
Sparsholt Hants.. 32 B3
  Oxon..........46 A1
Spartylea.....165 A6
Spaunton.....159 C6
Spaxton........28 B2
Spean Bridge. 239 D6
Spear Hill......21 A4
Speen Bucks...66 D3
  W Berks........46 C2
Speeton.......161 D5
Speke.........127 A4
Speldhurst.....36 B3
Spellbrook.....69 B4
Spelsbury......64 A4
Spelter........40 B3
Spencers Wood..47 C5
Spennithorne..157 C5
Spennymoor...167 B5
Spetchley......80 B1
Spetisbury.....16 A3
Spexhall......105 C4
Spey Bay......267 C4
Speybridge...253 D6
Speyview.....254 B3
Spilsby.......135 C4
Spindlestone..199 C5
Spinkhill.....131 B4
Spinningdale..264 B2
Spirthill.......44 B3
Spital Hill....140 D4
Spital in the
  Street........133 A4
Spithurst......22 A2
Spittal Dumfries.171 B5
  E Loth........210 C1
  Highld........280 C3
  Northumb.....198 A4
  Pembs.........55 B5
  Stirling......206 B3
Spittalfield...231 D5

Spittal of
  Glenmuick.....243 D6
Spittal of
  Glenshee.....231 A5
Spixworth.....120 D4
Splayne's Green..36 D2
Spofforth.....148 B2
Spon End.......97 D6
Spon Green....126 C2
Spooner Row...104 B1
Sporle.........119 D5
Spott.........210 C3
Spratton.......99 D4
Spreakley......34 B1
Spreyton.......12 B1
Spridlington..133 A5
Springburn...205 B6
Springfield
  Dumfries.....175 B6
  Essex.........69 C7
  Fife..........220 C3
  Moray.........253 A6
  W Mid..........96 C3
Springhill.....96 A2
Springholm...173 B6
Springkell....175 A5
Springside....192 B3
Springthorpe..132 A3
Spring Vale...139 C5
Spring Valley..152 D3
Springwell....179 D4
Sproatley.....151 D4
Sproston Green 128 C2
Sprotbrough..140 C3
Sproughton....88 C2
Sprouston.....197 C6
Sprowston....120 D4
Sproxton Leics..115 C6
  N Yorks.......159 C5
Spurstow.....127 D5
Spynie........266 C3
Squires Gate..144 D3
Srannda.......287 F5
Sronphadruig
  Lodge........229 A6
Stableford Shrops. 95 B5
  Staffs........112 B2
Stacey Bank...139 D5
Stackhouse...146 A2
Stackpole......55 E5
Staddiscombe...7 B4
Staddlethorpe..141 A6
Stadhampton...65 D7
Stadhlaigearraidh
  ....286 C3
Staffield.....164 A3
Staffin.......259 B4
Stafford......112 C3
Stagsden......84 C1
Stainburn Cumb. 162 B3
  N Yorks.......147 C6
Stainby.......116 C2
Staincross....139 B6
Staindrop....166 C4
Staines-upon-
  Thames.......48 B3
Stainfield Lincs..116 C3
  Lincs........133 B6
Stainforth
  N Yorks.......146 A2
  S Yorks.......140 B4
Staining......144 D3
Stainland....138 B3
Stainsacre...160 A3
Stainsby......131 C4
Stainton Cumb..154 C4
  Cumb.........164 C2
  Durham.......166 D3
  Mbro........168 D2
  N Yorks.......157 B5
  S Yorks.......140 D3
Stainton by
  Langworth....133 B5
Staintondale..160 B3
Stainton le Vale.142 D3
Stainton with
  Adgarley.....153 C3
Stair Cumb.....163 B5
  E Ayrs.......193 C4
Stairhaven....171 B4
Staithes......169 D5

Stakeford......179 A4
Stake Pool....144 C4
Stalbridge......30 D1
Stalbridge
  Weston........29 D7
Stalham........121 C5
Stalham Green..121 C5
Stalisfield
  Green..........51 D6
Stallingborough 142 B3
Stalling Busk..156 C3
Stalmine......144 C3
Stalybridge...138 D2
Stambourne....86 D3
Stambourne
  Green.........86 D3
Stamford......100 A2
Stamford Bridge
  Ches W.......127 C4
  E Yorks......149 B6
Stamfordham..178 B2
Stanah........163 C6
Stanborough...68 B2
Stanbridge
  C Beds.........67 A4
  Dorset.........17 A4
Stanbrook......79 C6
Stanbury......147 D4
Stand Gtr Man..137 C6
  N Lanark......207 D5
Standburn....208 C2
Standeford.....96 A2
Standen........37 B6
Standford.....33 B7
Standingstone..162 A3
Standish......137 B4
Standlake......65 C4
Standon Hants..32 C3
  Herts.........68 A3
  Staffs.......112 B2
Stane.........194 A3
Stanfield.....119 C6
Stanford C Beds..84 C3
  Kent..........38 B3
Stanford Bishop..79 B4
Stanford Bridge..79 A5
Stanford Dingley..46 B3
Stanford in the
  Vale..........64 D4
Stanford-le-
  Hope..........50 A3
Stanford on Avon 98 D2
Stanford on
  Soar.........114 C3
Stanford on
  Teme..........79 A5
Stanford Rivers..69 C5
Stanfree.......131 B4
Stanghow......169 D4
Stanground....100 B4
Stanhoe......119 B5
Stanhope
  Borders......195 D6
  Durham.......166 B2
Stanion........99 C6
Stanley Derbys..114 A2
  Durham.......178 D3
  Lancs........136 C3
  Perth........219 A6
  Staffs.......129 D4
  W Yorks......139 A6
Stanley
  Common.....114 A2
Stanley Gate..136 C3
Stanley Hill...79 C4
Stanlow......127 B4
Stanmer........21 B6
Stanmore Hants..32 C3
  London........67 D6
  W Berks.......46 B2
Stannergate..220 A4
Stanningley..147 D6
Stannington
  Northumb....179 B4
  S Yorks......130 A3
Stansbatch....78 A1
Stansfield.....86 B3
Stanstead......87 C4
Stanstead
  Abbotts.......68 B3
Stansted.......50 C3
Stansted Airport..69 A5

Stansted
  Mountfitchet...69 A5
Stanton Glos.....80 D3
  Mon...........61 A5
  Northumb.....178 A3
  Staffs........113 A5
  Suff.........103 D5
Stanton by
  Bridge.......114 C1
Stanton-by-
  Dale.........114 B2
Stanton Drew...43 C4
Stanton
  Fitzwarren....64 D2
Stanton Harcourt 65 C5
Stanton Hill...131 C4
Stanton in Peak.130 C2
Stanton Lacy...94 D2
Stanton Long...94 B3
Stanton-on-the-
  Wolds........115 B4
Stanton Prior...43 C5
Stanton
  St Bernard....45 C4
Stanton St John..65 C6
Stanton
  St Quintin....44 B3
Stanton Street...87 A5
Stanton under
  Bardon.......114 D2
Stanton upon Hine
  Heath........111 C4
Stanton Wick...43 C5
Stanwardine in the
  Fields.......110 C3
Stanwardine in the
  Wood........110 C3
Stanway Essex...70 A3
  Glos...........80 D3
Stanway Green..104 D3
Stanwell.......48 B3
Stanwell Moor..48 B3
Stanwick.....100 D1
Stanwick-St-
  John........167 D4
Stanwix.......175 C7
Stanydale....285 H4
Staoinebrig...286 C3
Stape.........159 B6
Stapehill......17 A4
Stapeley......111 A5
Stapenhill....113 C6
Staple Kent....53 D4
  Som...........28 B1
Staple Cross...37 D5
Staplefield....35 D5
Staple Fitzpaine.28 D2
Stapleford Cambs. 85 B6
  Herts.........68 B3
  Leics........115 D6
  Lincs........132 D3
  Notts........114 B2
  Wilts.........31 B4
Stapleford
  Abbotts.......69 D5
Stapleford
  Tawney........69 D5
Staplegrove....28 C2
Staplehay......28 C2
Staplehurst....37 B5
Staplers.......18 C4
Stapleton Bristol..43 B5
  Cumb........176 B3
  Hereford......78 A1
  Leics..........98 B1
  N Yorks......167 D5
  Shrops........94 A2
  Som...........29 C4
Stapley........28 D1
Staploe........84 A3
Staplow........79 C4
Star Fife......220 D3
  Pembs.........73 C5
  Som...........42 D3
Stara.........282 E3
Starbeck......148 B2
Starbotton....156 D3
Starcross......13 C4
Stareton.......97 D6
Starkholmes..130 D3
Starlings Green..85 D6
Starston......104 C3

Startforth....166 D3
Startley.......44 A3
Stathe.........28 C3
Stathern.....115 B5
Station Town..168 B2
Staughton Green 84 A3
Staughton
  Highway.......84 A3
Staunton Glos...62 A3
  Glos..........62 B1
Staunton in the
  Vale.........115 A6
Staunton on
  Arrow.........78 A1
Staunton on Wye 78 C1
Staveley Cumb..154 B3
  Cumb.........154 C2
  Derbys.......131 B4
  N Yorks......148 A2
Staverton Devon..8 A1
  Glos...........63 A4
  Wilts..........44 C2
  W Nhants......82 A2
Staverton Bridge. 63 A4
Stawell........28 B3
Staxigoe......281 C5
Staxton......160 D4
Staylittle.....91 C6
Staynall......144 C3
Staythorpe...132 D2
Stean.........157 D4
Stearsby......159 D5
Steart.........28 A2
Stebbing.......69 A6
Stebbing Green..69 A6
Stedham.......34 D1
Steele Road...186 D4
Steen's Bridge..78 B3
Steep..........33 C6
Steeple Dorset..16 C3
  Essex.........70 C3
Steeple Ashton..44 D3
Steeple Aston..65 A5
Steeple Barton..65 A5
Steeple
  Bumpstead....86 C2
Steeple Claydon..66 A1
Steeple Gidding 100 C3
Steeple Langford..31 B4
Steeple Morden..85 C4
Steep Marsh....33 C6
Steeton......147 C4
Stein.........258 C2
Steinmanhill..256 B2
Stelling Minnis..38 A3
Stemster.......280 B3
Stemster House..280 B3
Stenalees.......5 B5
Stenhousemuir. 207 B6
Stenigot......134 A2
Stenness.....284 F4
Stenscholl...259 B4
Stenso........282 E4
Stenson......114 C1
Stenton E Loth..210 C3
  Fife.........209 A5
Stenwith.....115 B6
Stepaside......56 B1
Stepping Hill..129 A4
Steppingley....84 D2
Stepps........205 B6
Sternfield......89 A4
Sterridge......25 A6
Stert..........44 D4
Stetchworth....86 B2
Stevenage......68 A2
Stevenston...204 D2
Steventon Hants..32 A4
  Oxon..........65 D5
Stevington.....84 B1
Stewartby......84 C2
Stewarton Argyll.190 D2
  E Ayrs.......205 D4
Stewkley......66 A3
Stewton......134 A3
Steyne Cross...19 C5
Steyning......21 A4
Steynton......55 D5
Stibb..........24 D3
Stibbard......120 C1
Stibb Cross....25 D5

Stibb Green....45 C6
Stibbington..100 B2
Stichill......197 C6
Sticker........5 B4
Stickford.....134 D3
Sticklepath....12 B1
Stickney......134 D3
Stiffkey......119 A6
Stifford's Bridge..79 C5
Stillingfleet..149 C4
Stillington
  N Yorks......149 A4
  Stockton......167 C6
Stilton.......100 C3
Stinchcombe....62 D3
Stinsford......15 B7
Stirchley......95 A5
Stirkoke House..281 C5
Stirling Aberds..257 B6
  Stirling......207 A5
Stisted........70 A1
Stithians.......4 D2
Stittenham...264 C2
Stivichall......97 D6
Stixwould....134 C1
Stoak.........127 B4
Stobieside....193 B6
Stobo.........195 C6
Stoborough....16 C3
Stoborough
  Green.........16 C3
Stobshiel.....210 D1
Stobswood....189 D5
Stock..........69 D6
Stockbridge....32 B2
Stockbury......51 C5
Stockcross.....46 C2
Stockdalewath. 164 A1
Stockerston....99 B5
Stock Green....80 B2
Stockheath.....19 A6
Stockiemuir..206 B3
Stockingford....97 B6
Stocking Pelham 69 A4
Stockland......14 A2
Stockland
  Bristol.......28 A2
Stockleigh
  English.......12 A3
Stockleigh
  Pomeroy......12 A3
Stockley.......44 C4
Stocklinch.....28 D3
Stockport.....138 D1
Stocksbridge..139 D5
Stocksfield...178 C2
Stockton Hereford. 78 A3
  Norf.........105 A4
  Shrops........93 A6
  Shrops........95 B5
  Warks.........82 A1
  Wilts..........30 B3
Stockton Heath. 127 A6
Stockton-on-
  Tees.........168 D2
Stockton on
  Teme..........79 A5
Stockton on the
  Forest.......149 B5
Stock Wood.....80 B3
Stodmarsh......53 C4
Stody.........120 B2
Stoer.........270 B3
Stoford Som....29 D5
  Wilts..........31 B4
Stogumber......27 B5
Stogursey......28 A2
Stoke Devon....24 C3
  Hants.........19 A6
  Hants.........46 D2
  Medway........51 B5
  Suff..........88 C2
Stoke Abbott...15 A4
Stoke Albany...99 C5
Stoke Ash.....104 D2
Stoke Bardolph.115 A4
Stoke Bliss....79 A4
Stoke Bruerne..83 C4
Stoke by Clare..86 C3

Stoke-by-
Nayland........87 D5
Stoke Canon......13 B4
Stoke Charity....32 B3
Stoke Climsland..11 D4
Stoke D'Abernon 35 A4
Stoke Doyle....100 C2
Stoke Dry......99 B5
Stoke Farthing..31 C4
Stoke Ferry....102 B3
Stoke Fleming...8 C2
Stokeford......16 C2
Stoke Gabriel...8 B2
Stoke Gifford...43 B5
Stoke Golding..97 B6
Stoke Goldington 83 C5
Stoke Green....48 A2
Stokeham......132 B2
Stoke Hammond .66 A3
Stoke Heath....111 C5
Stoke Holy
Cross........104 A3
Stokeinteignhead 13 D4
Stoke Lacy.....79 C4
Stoke Lyne.....65 A6
Stoke Mandeville.66 B3
Stokenchurch...66 D2
Stoke Newington 49 A6
Stokenham......8 C2
Stoke on Tern..111 C5
Stoke-on-Trent 112 A2
Stoke Orchard ..63 A5
Stoke Poges....48 A2
Stoke Prior
Hereford......78 B3
Worcs........80 A2
Stoke Rivers...26 B1
Stoke Rochford .116 C2
Stoke Row......47 A4
Stoke St Gregory 28 C3
Stoke St Mary ..28 C2
Stoke St Michael .29 A6
Stoke
St Milborough ..94 C3
Stokesay.......94 C2
Stokesby......121 D6
Stokesley.....158 A4
Stoke sub
Hamdon.......29 D4
Stoke Talmage ..66 D1
Stoke Trister...30 C1
Stoke Wake....16 A1
Stolford.......28 A2
Stondon Massey..69 C5
Stone Bucks....66 B2
Glos.........62 D2
Kent.........38 C1
Kent.........50 B2
Staffs.......112 B3
S Yorks......131 A5
Worcs........95 D6
Stone Allerton ..42 D3
Ston Easton....43 D5
Stone Bridge
Corner.......101 A4
Stonebroom...131 D4
Stone Chair....139 A4
Stone Cross E Sus..22 B4
Kent........53 D5
Stone-edge
Batch........42 B3
Stoneferry....151 D4
Stonefield....194 A1
Stonegate E Sus...37 D4
N Yorks......159 A6
Stonegrave....159 D5
Stonehaugh....177 B5
Stonehaven....245 D5
Stonehouse Glos..63 C4
Northumb....177 D4
S Lanark.....194 B2
Stone House....155 C6
Stoneleigh.....97 D6
Stonely........84 A3
Stoner Hill.....33 C6
Stonesby......115 C6
Stonesfield....65 B4
Stone's Green...71 A5
Stone Street Kent..36 A3

Stone Street continued
Suff...........87 D5
Suff..........105 C4
Stonethwaite...163 C5
Stoneybreck...285 R4
Stoneyburn...208 D2
Stoney Cross...31 D6
Stoneygate
Aberds.......257 C5
Leicester.....98 A3
Stoneyhills.....70 D3
Stoneykirk....170 B2
Stoney
Middleton....130 B2
Stoney Stanton..98 B1
Stoney Stoke...29 B7
Stoney Stratton .29 B6
Stoney Stretton .94 A1
Stoneywood
Aberdeen.....245 A5
Falk.........207 B5
Stonganess....284 C7
Stonham Aspal ..88 B2
Stonnall.......96 A3
Stonor.........47 A5
Stonton Wyville ..98 B1
Stony Cross....79 C5
Stonyfield....264 C2
Stony Stratford .83 C4
Stoodleigh.....27 D4
Stopes........130 A2
Stopham.......20 A3
Stopsley.......67 A6
Stores Corner...89 C4
Storeton......126 A3
Stornoway....288 D5
Storridge.......79 C5
Storrington....20 A3
Storrs........154 B2
Storth........154 C3
Storwood......149 C6
Stotfield......266 B3
Stotfold.......84 D4
Stottesdon.....95 C4
Stoughton Leics..98 A3
Sur..........34 A2
W Sus........33 D7
Stoul.........235 A6
Stoulton.......80 C2
Stourbridge....96 C2
Stourpaine.....16 A2
Stourport on
Severn.......95 D6
Stour Provost ..30 C1
Stour Row.....30 C2
Stourton Staffs...95 C6
Warks........81 D5
Wilts.........30 B1
Stourton Caundle 29 D7
Stove Orkney...282 D7
Shetland.....285 L6
Stoven.......105 C5
Stow Borders ..196 B3
Lincs.......116 B3
Lincs.......132 A3
Stow Bardolph .102 A2
Stow Bedon...103 B5
Stowbridge...102 A2
Stow cum Quy...85 A7
Stowe.........93 D7
Stowe-by-
Chartley.....112 C4
Stowe Green...62 C1
Stowell.......29 C6
Stowford......27 D4
Stowlangtoft...87 A5
Stow Longa...100 D3
Stow Maries...70 D2
Stowmarket....87 B6
Stow-on-the-
Wold........64 A2
Stowting......38 A3
Stowupland....87 B6
Straad.......203 B5
Strachan......244 C3
Stradbroke....104 D3
Stradishall.....86 B3
Stradsett.....102 A2
Stragglethorpe.133 D4
Straid........180 B3
Straith.......183 D6
Straiton Edin ..209 D5

Straiton continued
S Ayrs.......181 A5
Straloch Aberds..256 D3
Perth.......230 B4
Stramshall....113 B4
Strang........152 D3
Stranraer......170 A2
Stratfield
Mortimer......47 C4
Stratfield Saye ..47 C4
Stratfield Turgis..47 D4
Stratford......49 A6
Stratford
St Andrew....89 A4
Stratford St Mary 87 D6
Stratford Sub
Castle........31 B5
Stratford Tony ..31 C4
Stratford-upon-
Avon........81 B4
Strath Highld...261 C4
Highld.......281 C4
Strathan Highld .238 C3
Highld.......270 B3
Highld.......277 B6
Strathaven....194 B2
Strathblane...205 A5
Strathcanaird ..271 D4
Strathcarron...249 B6
Strathcoil....225 C5
Strathdon.....243 A6
Strathellie....269 C5
Strathkinness ..221 C4
Strathmashie
House.......240 C3
Strathmiglo....220 C2
Strathmore
Lodge.......280 D3
Strathpeffer...251 A6
Strathrannoch .263 C5
Strathtay.....230 C3
Strathvaich
Lodge.......263 C5
Strathwhillan .191 B6
Strathy.......279 B4
Strathyre.....217 C5
Stratton Corn...10 A3
Dorset.......15 B6
Glos.........63 C6
Stratton Audley ..65 A7
Stratton on the
Fosse.......43 D5
Stratton
St Margaret ..45 A5
Stratton
St Michael...104 B3
Stratton
Strawless.....120 C4
Stravithie.....221 C5
Streat........21 A6
Streatham......49 B6
Streatley C Beds..67 A5
W Berks......46 A3
Street Lancs...145 B5
N Yorks......159 A6
Som..........29 B4
Street Dinas...110 B2
Street End Kent...52 A6
W Sus........20 C1
Street Gate...179 D4
Streethay.....113 D5
Streetlam.....157 B7
Streetly.......96 B3
Street Lydan ..110 B3
Streetly End...86 C2
Strefford......94 C2
Strelley......114 A3
Strensall....149 A5
Stretcholt....28 A2
Strete.........8 C2
Stretford.....137 D7
Strethall......85 D6
Stretham.....101 D7
Strettington...20 B1
Stretton Ches W..127 D4
Derbys.......130 C3
Rutland.....116 D2
Staffs.......112 D2
Staffs.......113 C6
Warr........127 A5
Stretton
Grandison....79 C4

Stretton-on-
Dunsmore.....97 D7
Stretton-on-
Fosse.........81 D5
Stretton Sugwas .78 C2
Stretton under
Fosse........98 C1
Stretton
Westwood.....94 B3
Strichen......269 D4
Strines......129 A4
Stringston.....28 A1
Strixton.......83 A6
Stroat........62 D1
Stromeferry...249 C5
Stromemore...249 C5
Stromness....283 G3
Stronaba.....239 D6
Stronachlachar .216 C4
Stronchreggan .237 B4
Stronchrubie...271 C5
Strone Argyll...215 D4
Highld.......239 D5
Highld.......252 D1
Invclyd......204 A2
Stronmilchan ..227 D6
Strontian.....236 C2
Strood........51 C4
Strood Green Sur .35 B5
W Sus........34 D3
W Sus........35 C4
Stroud Glos....63 C4
Hants........33 C6
Stroud Green...70 D2
Stroxton......116 B2
Struan Highld ..246 A2
Perth.......230 B2
Strubby......135 A4
Strumpshaw...104 A4
Strutherhill....194 B2
Struy........251 C5
Stryt-issa....110 A1
Stuartfield....257 B4
Stubbington....19 A4
Stubbins......137 B6
Stubbs Cross...38 B1
Stubbs Green ..105 B4
Stubb's Green ..104 B3
Stubhampton...30 D3
Stub Place....153 A1
Stubton......115 A6
Stuckgowan....215 B6
Stuckton......31 D5
Stud Green.....48 B1
Studham......67 B5
Studland......17 C4
Studley Warks...80 A3
Wilts.........44 B3
Studley Roger..157 D6
Stump Cross...85 C7
Stuntney.....102 D1
Sturbridge....112 B2
Sturmer.......86 C2
Sturminster
Marshall......16 A3
Sturminster
Newton.......30 D1
Sturry........52 C3
Sturton......142 C1
Sturton by Stow 132 A3
Sturton le
Steeple......132 A2
Stuston......104 D2
Stutton N Yorks..148 C3
Suff.........88 D2
Styal........128 A3
Styrrup......140 D4
Suainebost...288 A6
Suardail......288 D5
Succoth Aberds..255 C5
Argyll.......215 B5
Suckley.......79 B5
Suckquoy.....283 J5
Sudborough...99 C6
Sudbourne....89 B5
Sudbrook Lincs..116 A2
Mon.........43 A4
Sudbrooke....133 B5
Sudbury Derbys..113 B5
London......49 A4
Suff.........87 C4
Suddie......252 A2

Sudgrove......63 C5
Suffield Norf....120 B4
N Yorks......160 B3
Sugnall......112 B1
Sugwas
Pool........78 C2
Suladale.....258 C3
Sulaisiadar....288 D6
Sulby........152 B3
Sulgrave......82 C2
Sulham........47 B4
Sulhamstead ..47 C4
Sulland......282 C6
Sullington....20 A3
Sullom.......284 F5
Sullom Voe Oil
Terminal.....284 F5
Sully..........41 E6
Sumburgh.....285 N6
Summer Bridge .147 A6
Summercourt....4 B3
Summerfield...119 B4
Summergangs .151 D4
Summer-house .167 D5
Summerleaze...42 A3
Summersdale...20 B1
Summerseat...137 B6
Summertown...65 C6
Summit.......138 C2
Sunbury-on-
Thames......48 C4
Sundaywell....183 D6
Sunderland
Argyll.......200 B2
Cumb.......163 A4
T&W........179 D5
Sunderland
Bridge.......167 B5
Sundhope....196 D2
Sundon Park...67 A5
Sundridge.....36 A2
Sunipol......224 A2
Sunk Island...143 B4
Sunningdale...48 C2
Sunninghill...48 C2
Sunningwell...65 C5
Sunniside
Durham......166 B4
T&W........179 D4
Sunnyhurst...137 A5
Sunnylaw.....207 A5
Sunnyside.....36 C1
Sunton........45 D6
Surbiton......49 C4
Surby........152 D2
Surfleet......117 C5
Surfleet Seas
End........117 C5
Surlingham...104 A4
Sustead......120 B3
Susworth.....141 C6
Sutcombe.....24 D4
Suton........104 B1
Sutors of
Cromarty.....265 D4
Sutterby......134 B3
Sutterton....117 B5
Sutton Cambs..101 D6
C Beds.......84 C4
Kent.........39 A5
London.......49 C5
Mers........136 D4
Norf........121 C5
Notts.......115 B5
Notts.......132 A1
N Yorks......140 A2
Oxon........65 C5
Pboro......100 B2
Shrops......95 C5
Shrops......111 B5
Som..........29 B6
Staffs.......111 C6
Suff.........88 C4
Sur..........34 A4
S Yorks......140 B3
W Sus........20 A2
Sutton at Hone...50 B2
Sutton Bassett ..99 B4
Sutton Benger ..44 B3
Sutton
Bonington....114 C3
Sutton Bridge ..118 C1
Sutton Cheney ..97 A7
Sutton Coldfield .96 B4

Sutton Courtenay 65 D6
Sutton Crosses..118 C1
Sutton Grange .157 D6
Sutton Green...34 A3
Sutton
Howgrave....157 D7
Sutton In
Ashfield.....131 D4
Sutton-in-
Craven.......147 C4
Sutton Ings...151 D4
Sutton in the
Elms........98 B2
Sutton Lane
Ends........129 B4
Sutton Leach...136 D4
Sutton Maddock .95 A5
Sutton Mallet ..28 B3
Sutton
Mandeville....30 C3
Sutton Manor..136 D4
Sutton Montis...29 C6
Sutton on Hull .151 D4
Sutton on Sea .135 A5
Sutton-on-the-
Forest.......149 A4
Sutton on the
Hill.........113 B6
Sutton on Trent .132 C2
Sutton
St Edmund...117 D6
Sutton St James 117 D6
Sutton
St Nicholas...78 C3
Sutton
Scarsdale...131 C4
Sutton Scotney ..32 B3
Sutton under
Brailes.......81 D6
Sutton-under-White-
stonecliffe....158 C3
Sutton upon
Derwent....149 C6
Sutton Valence..37 B5
Sutton Veny....30 A2
Sutton Waldron .30 D2
Sutton Weaver .127 B5
Sutton Wick....43 A4
Swaby........134 B3
Swadlincote...113 D7
Swaffham.....103 A4
Swaffham
Bulbeck......86 A1
Swaffham Prior .86 A1
Swafield......121 B4
Swainby......158 A3
Swainshill....78 C2
Swainsthorpe..104 A3
Swainswick....43 C6
Swalcliffe.....81 D6
Swalecliffe....52 C3
Swallow......142 C3
Swallowcliffe...30 C3
Swallowfield...47 C5
Swallownest...131 A4
Swallows Cross .69 D6
Swanage......17 D4
Swanbister...283 G4
Swanbourne...66 A3
Swan Green
Ches W......128 B2
Suff........104 D3
Swanland....142 A1
Swanley......50 C2
Swanley Village .50 C2
Swanmore.....33 D4
Swannington
Leics.......114 D2
Norf........120 D3
Swanscombe...50 B3
Swansea
=Abertawe ..57 C6
Swanton Abbott 121 C4
Swanton Morley 120 D2
Swanton Novers 120 B2
Swanton Street .37 A6
Swanwick Derbys 131 D4
Hants........18 A4
Swarby.......116 A3
Swardeston...104 A3
Swarister.....284 E7
Swarkestone...114 C1

Swarland 189 C4
Swarland Estate 189 C4
Swarthmoor 153 C3
Swathwick 130 C3
Swaton 116 B4
Swavesey 85 A5
Sway 18 B1
Swayfield 116 C2
Swaythling 32 D3
Sweet Green 79 A4
Sweetham 12 B3
Sweethouse. 5 A5
Sweffling 88 A4
Swepstone 114 D1
Swerford 81 D6
Swettenham 128 C3
Swetton 157 D5
Swffryd. 60 D4
Swiftsden. 37 D5
Swilland 88 B2
Swillington 148 D2
Swimbridge. 25 C7
Swimbridge
  Newland 25 B7
Swinbrook 64 B3
Swinderby 132 C3
Swindon Glos. 63 A5
  Staffs 95 B6
  Swindon 45 A5
Swine 151 D4
Swinefleet 141 A5
Swineshead
  Bedford 84 A2
  Lincs. 117 A5
Swineshead
  Bridge 117 A5
Swiney 275 A6
Swinford Leics 98 D2
  Oxon. 65 C5
Swingate 114 A3
Swingfield
  Minnis 39 A4
Swingfield Street 39 A4
Swinhoe 189 A5
Swinhope 143 D4
Swining 284 G6
Swinithwaite. . . .156 C4
Swinnow Moor . .147 D6
Swinscoe 113 A5
Swinside Hall . . .187 B6
Swinstead 116 C3
Swinton Borders .198 B2
  Gtr Man 137 C6
  N Yorks. 157 D6
  N Yorks. 159 D6
  S Yorks 140 D2
Swintonmill. 198 B2
Swithland 114 D3
Swordale 264 D1
Swordland 238 C1
Sworton Heath . .128 A1
Swydd ffynnon . . .75 B5
Swynnerton 112 B2
Swyre 15 C5
Sychtyn. 92 A3
Syde 63 B5
Sydenham London . 49 B6
  Oxon. 66 C2
Sydenham
  Damerel 11 D5
Syderstone 119 B5
Sydling
  St Nicholas 15 B6
Sydmonton 46 D2
Syerston 115 A5
Syke. 138 B1
Sykehouse 140 B4
Sykes. 145 B6
Syleham 104 D3
Sylen. 57 B5
Symbister. 285 G7
Symington
  S Ayrs 192 B3
  S Lanark. 195 C4
Symondsbury 12 E3
Symonds Yat 62 B1
Synod Inn 73 A7
Syre 278 D2
Syreford 63 A6
Syresham. 82 C3
Syston Leics 115 D4

Syston continued
  Lincs. 116 A2
Sytchampton. 79 A6
Sywell 83 A5

T

Taagan 262 D2
Tàbost. 288 A6
Tabost. 200 Γ4
Tackley 65 A5
Tacleit. 288 D2
Tacolneston 104 B2
Tadcaster 148 C3
Taddington 129 B6
Taddiport 25 D5
Tadley 47 C4
Tadlow 85 C4
Tadmarton. 81 D6
Tadworth 35 A5
Tafarnau-bach 60 B3
Tafarn-y-gelyn. .126 C1
Tafolwern 91 B6
Tai 124 C2
Taibach. 40 C2
Tai-bach 109 C6
Taigh a
  Ghearraidh 287 G2
Tai-mawr. 109 A4
Tain Highld 264 B3
  Highld. 280 B4
Tainant 110 A1
Tainlon 107 A4
Tairbeart
  =Tarbert 288 G2
Tai'r-Bull 60 A1
Tairgwaith 59 D4
Tai-Ucha 125 D5
Takeley 69 A5
Takeley Street . . .69 A5
Talachddu 77 D4
Talacre 125 A6
Talardd 108 C3
Talaton 13 B5
Talbenny 54 C4
Talbot Green. 41 C5
Talbot Village 17 B4
Tale 13 A5
Talerddig 92 A3
Talgarreg 74 C3
Talgarth 77 D5
Talisker 246 A2
Talke 128 D3
Talkin 176 D3
Talladale 261 C6
Talla Linnfoots . .195 D6
Tallarn Green . . .110 A3
Tallentire 163 A4
Talley 58 B3
Tallington 100 A2
Talmine 277 B6
Talog 73 D6
Talsarn 59 C4
Tal-sarn 75 C4
Talsarnau. 107 C6
Talskiddy 4 A4
Talwrn Anglesey .123 C4
  Wrex 110 A1
Tal-y-bont
  Ceredig 91 B4
  Conwy 124 C2
  Gwyn 107 D5
  Gwyn 123 C6
Talybont-on-Usk 60 A3
Tal-y-cafn 124 B2
Talygarn 41 C5
Talyllyn 60 A3
Tal-y-llyn 91 B5
Talysarn 107 A4
Talywain 61 C4
Tal-y-wern 91 B6
Tame Bridge 158 A4
Tamerton Foliot . . .6 A3
Tamworth 97 A5
Tandem 139 B4
Tandridge 35 A6
Tanerdy 73 D7
Tanfield 178 D3
Tanfield Lea 178 D3

Tangasdal 286 G2
Tangiers 55 C5
Tangley 46 D1
Tanglwst 73 C6
Tangmere 20 B2
Tangwick 284 F4
Tan Hinon 91 D6
Tankersley 139 C6
Tankerton 52 C3
Tan-lan Conwy . . .124 C2
  Gwyn 107 B6
Tannach 281 D5
Tannachie 245 D4
Tannadice 232 C2
Tannington 88 A3
Tansley. 130 D3
Tansley Knoll . . .130 C3
Tansor. 100 B2
Tantobie 178 D3
Tanton 168 D3
Tanworth-in-
  Arden 96 D4
Tan-y-bwlch. . . .107 B6
Tan-y-fron 125 C4
Tan-y-graig
  Anglesey 123 C5
  Gwyn 106 C3
Tanygrisiau 107 B6
Tan-y-groes 73 B5
Tan-yr-allt 107 A4
Tanyrhydiau 75 B6
Taobh a
  Chaolais. 286 E3
Taobh a' Ghlinne 288 F4
Taobh a Thuath Loch
  Aineort. 286 D3
Taobh a Tuath Loch
  Baghas-
  dail 286 D3
Taobh Tuath 287 F4
Taplow 48 A2
Tapton 130 B3
Tarbat House . . .264 C3
Tarbert Argyll . . .202 B3
  Argyll 202 C1
  Argyll 213 D4
Tarbert
  =Tairbeart. . . .288 G2
Tarbet Argyll. . . .215 B6
  Highld. 238 C1
  Highld. 276 D2
Tarbock Green . .127 A4
Tarbolton 193 C4
Tarbrax. 195 A5
Tardebigge 80 A3
Tarfside 232 A2
Tarland 244 B1
Tarleton 136 A3
Tarlogie 264 B3
Tarlscough 136 B3
Tarlton 63 D5
Tarnbrook 145 B5
Tarporley 127 C5
Tarr 27 B6
Tarrant Crawford 16 A3
Tarrant Gunville . 30 D3
Tarrant Hinton . . 30 D3
Tarrant
  Keyneston. 16 A3
Tarrant
  Launceston. . . .16 A3
Tarrant Monkton 16 A3
Tarrant Rawston . 16 A3
Tarrant Rushton. . 16 A3
Tarrel 265 B4
Tarring Neville . . 22 B2
Tarrington 79 C4
Tarsappie 219 B6
Tarskavaig 247 D4
Tarves 256 C3
Tarvie Highld. . . .251 A6
  Perth 230 B4
Tarvin 127 C4
Tasburgh 104 B3
Tasley 95 B4
Taston. 65 A4
Ten Mile Bank. . .102 B2
Tenston 282 F3
Tenterden 37 C6
Terling 70 B1
Ternhill 111 B5
Terregles Banks 174 A2

Tatsfield 36 A2
Tattenhall 127 D4
Tattenhoe 83 D5
Tatterford 119 C5
Tattersett. 119 B5
Tattershall 134 D2
Tattershall
  Bridge 134 D1
Tattershall
  Thorpe 134 D2
Tattingstone 88 D2
Tatworth 14 A3
Taunton 28 C2
Taverham. 120 D3
Tavernspite 56 A1
Tavistock 11 D5
Taw Green 12 B1
Tawstock 25 C6
Taxal 129 B5
Tay Bridge 220 B4
Tayinloan 202 D1
Taymouth
  Castle. 230 D1
Taynish 213 D5
Taynton Glos 62 A3
  Oxon. 64 B3
Taynuilt 227 C5
Tayport 221 B4
Tayvallich. 213 D5
Tealby 142 D3
Tealing 220 A4
Teangue 247 D5
Teanna
  Mhachair. 287 H2
Tebay 155 A4
Tebworth 67 A4
Tedburn St Mary . 12 B3
Teddington Glos . . 80 D2
  London 49 B4
Tedstone
  Delamere 79 B4
Tedstone Wafre . . 79 B4
Teeton 98 D3
Teffont Evias 30 B3
Teffont Magna . . . 30 B3
Tegryn 73 C5
Teigh 115 D6
Teigncombe 12 C1
Teigngrace 12 D2
Teignmouth. 13 D4
Telford 95 A4
Telham 23 A5
Tellisford 44 D2
Telscombe 22 B2
Telscombe Cliffs . 22 B1
Templand. 184 D3
Temple Corn. 10 D2
  Glasgow. 205 B5
  Midloth. 196 A2
Temple Balsall . . .97 D5
Temple Bar Carms 57 A5
  Ceredig 75 C4
Temple Cloud 43 D5
Temple Combe . . .29 C7
Temple Ewell 39 A4
Temple Grafton . . 80 B4
Temple Guiting. . . 64 A1
Templehall 209 A5
Temple
  Herdewyke 81 B6
Temple Hirst 140 A4
Temple
  Normanton . . .131 C4
Temple
  Sowerby 165 C4
Templeton Devon . 26 D3
  Pembs 55 C7
Templeton
  Bridge 26 D3
Templetown 178 D3
Tempsford. 84 B3
Tenbury Wells. . . .78 A3
Tenby = Dinbych-y-
  Pysgod. 56 B1
Tendring 71 A5
Tendring Green . . 71 A5

Terrick 66 C3
Terrington 159 D5
Terrington
  St Clement 118 D2
Terrington
  St John 118 D2
Teston 37 A5
Testwood 32 D2
Tetbury 63 D4
Tetbury Upton. . . .63 D4
Tetchill 110 B2
Tetcott 10 B4
Tetford 134 B3
Tetney. 143 C5
Tetney Lock. 143 C5
Tetsworth 66 C1
Tettenhall 96 B1
Teuchan 257 C5
Teversal 131 C4
Teversham. 85 B6
Teviothead. 186 C3
Tewel 245 D5
Tewin 68 B2
Tewkesbury. 80 D1
Teynham 51 C6
Thackthwaite . . .163 B4
Thainston. 233 A4
Thakeham 21 A4
Thame. 66 C2
Thames Ditton . . .49 C4
Thames Haven . . .51 A4
Thamesmead 50 A1
Thanington 52 D3
Thankerton 195 C4
Tharston. 104 B2
Thatcham. 46 C3
Thatto Heath. . . .136 D4
Thaxted 86 D2
The Aird 259 C4
Theakston 157 C7
Thealby 141 B6
Theale Som. 29 A4
  W Berks 47 B4
Thearne 150 D3
The Arms 103 B4
The Bage 77 C6
The Balloch 218 C3
The Barony 282 E3
Theberton 89 A5
The Bog 94 B1
The Bourne 33 A7
The Braes 247 A4
The Broad 78 A2
The Butts 30 A1
The Camp Glos . . .63 C5
  Herts 67 C6
The Chequer 110 A3
The City 66 D2
The Common 31 B6
The Craigs 263 A6
The Cronk 152 B3
Theddingworth. . . 98 C3
Theddlethorpe All
  Saints 135 A4
Theddlethorpe
  St Helen. 135 A4
The Dell 105 B5
The Den 204 C3
The Eals 177 A5
The Eaves. 62 C2
The Flatt. 176 B3
The Four Alls. . . .111 B5
The Garths 284 B8
The Green Cumb .153 B2
  Wilts. 30 B2
The Grove 174 A2
The Hall 284 D8
The Haven 34 A3
The Heath Norf . .120 C3
  Suff. 88 D2
The Hill. 153 B2
The Howe Cumb. .154 C3
  IoM 152 E1
The Hundred 78 A3
Thelbridge
  Barton 26 D2
The Lee. 67 C4
The Lhen 152 A3
Thelnetham. 103 D6
Thelveton. 104 C2
Thelwall 127 A6
The Marsh Powys . 93 B7

The Marsh continued
  Wilts. 45 A4
Themelthorpe. . . .120 C2
The Middles 179 D4
The Moor 37 D5
The Mumbles
  =Y Mwmbwls. . . .57 D6
The Murray 205 C6
The Neuk 245 C4
Thenford 82 C2
The Oval 43 C6
The Pole of
  Itlaw 268 D1
The Quarry 62 D3
Therfield 85 D5
The Rhos 55 C6
The Rock 95 A4
The Ryde 68 C2
The Sands 34 B1
The Stocks 37 D7
Thetford Lincs . .116 D4
  Norf 103 C4
The Throat. 47 C6
The Vauld 78 C3
The Wyke 95 A5
Theydon Bois 68 D4
Thickwood. 44 B2
Thimbleby Lincs. .134 C2
  N Yorks. 158 B3
Thingwall. 126 A2
Thirdpart 204 D1
Thirlby 158 C3
Thirlestane 197 B4
Thirn 157 C6
Thirsk 158 C3
Thirtleby. 151 D4
Thistleton Lancs .144 C4
  Rutland. 116 D2
Thistley Green . . .102 D2
Thixendale. 150 A1
Thockrington . . .178 B1
Tholomas Drove 101 A5
Tholthorpe. 148 A3
Thomas Chapel . .55 D7
Thomas Close . . .164 A2
Thomastown 255 C6
Thompson 103 B5
Thomshill. 266 D3
Thong 50 B3
Thongsbridge . . .139 C4
Thoralby. 156 C4
Thoresway 142 D3
Thorganby Lincs .143 D4
  N Yorks. 149 C5
Thorgill 159 B6
Thorington 105 D5
Thorington
  Street 87 D6
Thorlby 146 B3
Thorley 69 B4
Thorley Street
  Herts 69 B4
  IoW 18 C2
Thormanby 158 D3
Thornaby-on-
  Tees 168 D2
Thornage 120 B2
Thornborough
  Bucks. 83 D4
  N Yorks. 157 D6
Thornbury Devon . 11 A5
  Hereford 79 B4
  S Glos. 62 D2
  W Yorks 147 D5
Thornby 98 D3
Thorncliffe. 129 D5
Thorncombe
  Dorset 14 A3
  Dorset 16 A2
Thorncombe
  Street 34 B3
Thorncote Green . 84 C3
Thorncross 18 C3
Thorndon 88 A2
Thorndon Cross . . 11 B6
Thorne 141 B4
Thorner 148 C2
Thorne
  St Margaret 27 C5

Thorney Notts ...132 B3
Pboro 101 A4
Thorney Crofts .143 A4
Thorney Green ...87 A6
Thorney Hill 17 B5
Thorney Toll 101 A5
Thornfalcon......28 C2
Thornford 29 D6
Thorngumbald ..143 A4
Thornham 119 A4
Thornham
Magna 104 D2
Thornham
Parva 104 D2
Thornhaugh......100 A2
Thornhill Cardiff ..41 C6
Cumb 162 D3
Derbys 130 A1
Dumfries 183 C6
Soton 32 D3
Stirling 207 A4
W Yorks 139 B5
Thornhill Edge .139 B5
Thornhill Lees..139 B5
Thornholme 151 A4
Thornley Durham 166 B4
Durham 167 B6
Thornliebank ..205 C5
Thorns 86 B3
Thornsett......129 A5
Thorns Green ...128 A2
Thornthwaite
Cumb 163 B5
N Yorks 147 B5
Thornton Angus .232 D1
Bucks 83 D4
E Yorks 149 C6
Fife 209 A5
Lancs 144 C3
Leics 98 A1
Lincs 134 C2
Mbro 168 D2
Mers. 136 C2
Northumb. 198 B3
Pembs 55 D5
W Yorks 147 D5
Thornton Curtis .142 B2
Thorntonhall ...205 C6
Thornton Heath ..49 C6
Thornton Hough 126 A3
Thornton in
Craven 146 C3
Thornton-le-
Beans 158 B2
Thornton-le-
Clay..........149 A5
Thornton-le-
Dale 160 C2
Thornton le
Moor..........142 D2
Thornton-le-
Moor..........158 C2
Thornton-le-
Moors.........127 B4
Thornton-le-
Street 158 C3
Thorntonloch ...211 C4
Thorntonpark ..198 B3
Thornton Rust ..156 C3
Thornton
Steward 157 C5
Thornton
Watlass 157 C6
Thornwood
Common 69 C4
Thornydykes ...197 B5
Thoroton 115 A5
Thorp Arch 148 C3
Thorpe Derbys ..129 D6
E Yorks 150 C2
Lincs 135 A4
Norf 105 B5
Notts 115 A5
N Yorks 147 A4
Sur............48 C3
Thorpe Abbotts .104 D2
Thorpe Acre ...114 C3
Thorpe Arnold .115 C5
Thorpe Audlin..140 B2

Thorpe Bassett ..160 D2
Thorpe Bay 51 A6
Thorpe by Water ..99 B5
Thorpe Common ..88 D3
Thorpe
Constantine 97 A5
Thorpe Culvert ..135 C4
Thorpe End 121 D4
Thorpe
Fendykes......135 C4
Thorpe Green
Essex 71 A5
Suff 88 C3
Thorpe Hesley .140 D1
Thorpe in Balne 140 B3
Thorpe in the
Fallows 133 A4
Thorpe Langton ..99 B4
Thorpe Larches .167 C6
Thorpe-le-Soken 71 A5
Thorpe le Street 150 C1
Thorpe Malsor ..99 D5
Thorpe
Mandeville 82 C2
Thorpe Market .120 B4
Thorpe Marriot .120 D3
Thorpe Morieux ..87 B5
Thorpeness 89 B5
Thorpe on the
Hill 133 C4
Thorpe
St Andrew....104 A3
Thorpe St Peter .135 C4
Thorpe Salvin ..131 A5
Thorpe
Satchville 115 D5
Thorpe Thewles 168 C2
Thorpe Tilney ..133 D6
Thorpe
Underwood.....148 B3
Thorpe
Waterville 100 C2
Thorpe
Willoughby ...149 D4
Thorrington......71 A4
Thorverton......13 A4
Thrandeston ...104 D2
Thrapston 100 D1
Thrashbush 207 D5
Threapland
Cumb 163 A4
N Yorks 146 A3
Threapwood
Ches W. 110 A3
Staffs 112 A4
Three Ashes 61 A7
Three Bridges ...35 C5
Three Burrows ...4 C2
Three Chimneys .37 C6
Three Cocks 77 D5
Three Crosses ...57 C5
Three Cups
Corner 36 D4
Threehammer
Common 121 D5
Three Holes 101 A7
Threekingham ..113 A5
Three Leg Cross .37 C4
Three Legged
Cross 17 A4
Three Mile Cross .47 C5
Threemilestone ...4 C2
Threemiletown .208 C3
Three Oaks 23 A6
Threlkeld 163 B6
Threshfield 146 A3
Thrigby.........121 D6
Thringarth 166 C2
Thringstone....114 D2
Thrintoft 157 B7
Thriplow........85 D5
Throckenholt ..101 A5
Throcking 85 D5
Throckley......178 C3
Throckmorton ...80 C2
Throphill......178 A3
Thropton 188 C3
Throsk.........207 A6
Throughgate ...183 D6
Throwleigh 12 B1
Throwley 52 D1
Thrumpton 114 B3
Thrumster 281 D5

Thrunton 188 B3
Thrupp Glos 63 C4
Oxon...........65 B5
Thrushelton.....11 C5
Thrussington ..115 D4
Thruxton Hants ...32 A1
Hereford.......78 D2
Thrybergh 140 D2
Thulston 114 B2
Thundergay 202 D3
Thundersley 51 A4
Thundridge 68 B3
Thurcaston 114 D3
Thurcroft 131 A4
Thurgarton Norf .120 B3
Notts 115 A4
Thurgoland 139 C5
Thurlaston Leics ..98 B2
Warks..........98 D1
Thurlbear.......28 C2
Thurlby Lincs ...116 D4
Lincs 133 C4
Thurleigh 84 B2
Thurlestone......7 C5
Thurloxton......28 B2
Thurlstone 139 C5
Thurlton 105 B5
Thurlwood 128 D3
Thurmaston.....98 A3
Thurnby 98 A3
Thurne 121 D6
Thurnham Kent ..37 A6
Lancs 145 B4
Thurning
N Nhants 100 C2
Norf 120 C2
Thurnscoe 140 C2
Thurnscoe East. .140 C2
Thursby 175 C6
Thursford 120 B1
Thursley 34 C2
Thurso 280 B3
Thurso East ...280 B3
Thurstaston ...126 A2
Thurston 87 A5
Thurstonfield ..175 C6
Thurstonland ..139 B4
Thurton 104 A4
Thurvaston 113 B6
Thuxton 103 A6
Thwaite N Yorks .156 B2
Suff 88 A2
Thwaites.......147 C4
Thwaite St Mary 104 A4
Thwaites Brow .147 C4
Thwing 160 D4
Tibbermore 219 B5
Tibberton Glos. ..62 A3
Telford........111 C5
Worcs..........80 B2
Tibenham 104 C2
Tibshelf 131 C4
Tibthorpe......150 B2
Ticehurst 37 C4
Tichborne 33 B4
Tickencote 100 A1
Tickenham......42 B3
Tickhill 140 D3
Ticklerton......94 B2
Ticknall.......114 C1
Tickton 150 C3
Tidcombe.......45 D6
Tiddington Oxon .66 C1
Warks..........81 B5
Tidebrook 36 D4
Tideford 6 B2
Tideford Cross ...6 A2
Tidenham 62 D1
Tideswell 129 B6
Tidmarsh 47 B4
Tidmington 81 D5
Tidpit 31 D4
Tidworth 31 A6
Tiers Cross 55 C5
Tiffield 82 B3
Tifty 256 B2
Tigerton 232 B3
Tigh-na-Blair ..218 C2
Tighnabruaich .203 A4
Tighnafiline ...261 B5
Tigley 7 A6

Tilbury 50 B3
Tilbury Juxta
Clare.........86 C3
Tile Cross 97 C4
Tile Hill 97 D5
Tilehurst 47 B4
Tilford 34 B1
Tilgate 35 C5
Tilgate Forest
Row...........35 C5
Tillathrowie....255 C5
Tilley 111 C4
Tillicoultry 208 A2
Tillingham 70 C3
Tillington Hereford 78 C2
W Sus..........34 D2
Tillington
Common 78 C2
Tillyarblet 232 B3
Tillybirloch ...244 B3
Tillycorthie ...257 D4
Tillydrine 244 C3
Tillyfour 244 A3
Tillyfourie 244 A3
Tillygarmond...244 C3
Tillygreig 256 D3
Tillykerrie 256 D3
Tilmanstone 53 D5
Tilney All Saints 118 D2
Tilney High End .118 D2
Tilney
St Lawrence ..118 D2
Tilshead 31 A4
Tilstock 111 B4
Tilston 127 D4
Tilstone
Fearnall 127 C5
Tilsworth 67 A4
Tilton on the Hill .99 A4
Timberland 133 D6
Timbersbrook .128 C3
Timberscombe ...27 A4
Timble.........147 B5
Timperley 128 A2
Timsbury Bath ...43 D5
Hants 32 C2
Timsgearraidh .287 A5
Timworth Green. .87 A4
Tincleton 16 B1
Tindale 176 D4
Tingewick 82 D3
Tingley 139 A5
Tingrith 84 D2
Tingwall 282 E4
Tinhay 11 C4
Tinshill 147 D6
Tinsley 140 D2
Tintagel 9 C6
Tintern Parva ...62 C1
Tintinhull 29 D5
Tintwistle 138 D3
Tinwald 184 D3
Tinwell 100 A2
Tipperty 257 D4
Tipps End 101 B7
Tipton 96 B2
Tipton St John ..13 B5
Tiptree 70 B2
Tirabad 59 A5
Tiraghoil 224 D2
Tirley 63 A4
Tirphil 41 A6
Tir-y-dail 57 A6
Tisbury 30 C3
Tisman's
Common 34 C3
Tissington 130 D1
Titchberry 24 C3
Titchfield 18 A4
Titchmarsh 100 D2
Titchwell 119 A4
Tithby 115 B4
Titley 78 A1
Titlington 189 B4
Titsey 36 A2
Tittensor 112 B2
Tittleshall 119 C5
Tiverton Ches W. .127 C5
Devon..........27 D4
Tivetshall
St Margaret ..104 C2

Tivetshall
St Mary 104 C2
Tividale 96 B2
Tivy Dale 139 C5
Tixall 112 C3
Tixover 99 A6
Toab Orkney 283 G6
Shetland 285 M5
Toadmoor 130 D3
Tobermory 225 A4
Toberonochy ...213 B5
Tobha Mor 286 C3
Tobhtarol......288 D2
Tobson 288 D2
Tocher 256 C1
Tockenham......44 B4
Tockenham Wick 44 A4
Tockholes 137 A5
Tockington......43 A5
Tockwith 148 B3
Todber 30 C2
Todding 94 D2
Toddington
C Beds 67 A5
Glos 80 D3
Todenham.......81 D5
Todhills 175 B6
Todlachie 244 A3
Todmorden 138 A2
Todrig 186 B3
Todwick 131 A4
Toft Cambs 85 B5
Lincs 116 D3
Toft Hill Durham. .167 C4
Lincs 134 C2
Toft Monks 105 B5
Toft next
Newton 133 A5
Toftrees 119 C5
Toftwood 120 D1
Togston 189 C5
Tokavaig 247 C5
Tokers Green ...47 B5
Tolastadh a
Chaolais......288 D2
Tolastadh bho
Thuath 288 C6
Toll Bar 140 C3
Tollard Royal ...30 D3
Toll End 96 B2
Toller Fratrum ..15 B5
Toller Porcorum .15 B5
Tollerton Notts .115 B4
N Yorks 148 A4
Tollesbury 70 B3
Tolleshunt D'Arcy 70 B3
Tolleshunt Major .70 B3
Toll of Birness .257 C5
Tolm 288 D5
Tolpuddle 16 B1
Tolvah 241 C6
Tolworth 49 C4
Tomatin 253 D4
Tombreck 252 C2
Tomchrasky....239 A6
Tomdoun 239 B5
Tomich Highld .251 D5
Highld. 264 C2
Tomich House. .252 B1
Tomintoul
Aberds 242 C4
Moray. 243 A4
Tomnaven 255 C5
Tomnavoulin ..254 D3
Tonbridge 36 B3
Tondu 40 C3
Tonfanau 90 B3
Tong Shrops 95 A5
W Yorks 147 D6
Tonge 114 C2
Tongham 34 B1
Tongland 173 C4
Tong Norton 95 A5
Tongue 277 C6
Tongue End ...117 D4
Tongwynlais 41 C6
Tonna 40 B2
Ton-Pentre 41 B4
Tonwell 68 B3

Tonypandy......41 B4
Tonyrefail 41 C5
Toot Baldon 65 C6
Toothill 32 D2
Toot Hill 69 C5
Topcliffe......158 D3
Topcroft 104 B3
Topcroft Street. .104 B3
Top of Hebers. .138 C1
Toppesfield 86 D3
Toppings 137 B6
Topsham 13 C4
Torbay 8 B3
Torbeg 191 C5
Torboll Farm ...264 A3
Torbrex........207 A5
Torcross 8 C2
Tore 252 A2
Torinturk 202 B3
Torksey 132 B3
Torlum 286 A3
Torlundy 237 B5
Tormarton 43 B6
Tormisdale 200 C1
Tormitchell ...181 B4
Tormore 191 B4
Tornagrain....252 B3
Tornahaish 243 B5
Tornaveen 244 B3
Torness 252 D1
Toronto 167 B4
Torpenhow 163 A5
Torphichen 208 C2
Torphins 244 B3
Torpoint 6 B3
Torquay 8 A3
Torquhan 196 B3
Torran Argyll. ..214 B1
Highld. 248 B2
Torrance 205 A6
Torrans 224 D3
Torranyard 204 D3
Torre 8 A3
Torridon 249 A6
Torridon House .249 A5
Torrin 247 B4
Torrisdale 278 B2
Torrisdale-
Square 190 B3
Torrish 274 C3
Torrisholme ...145 A4
Torroble 272 D3
Torry Aberdeen .245 B6
Aberds 255 C5
Torryburn 208 B3
Torterston 257 B5
Torthorwald ...174 A3
Tortington 20 B3
Tortworth 62 D3
Torvaig 259 D4
Torver 154 B1
Torwood 207 B6
Torworth 131 A6
Tosberry 24 C3
Toscaig 249 C4
Toseland 84 A4
Tosside 146 B1
Tostock 87 A5
Totaig Highld ..249 D5
Highld. 258 C2
Tote 259 D4
Totegan 279 B4
Tothill 135 A4
Totland 18 C2
Totnes 8 A2
Toton 114 B3
Totronald 223 B4
Totscore 258 B3
Tottenham 68 C3
Tottenhill 118 D3
Tottenhill Row .118 D3
Totteridge 68 D2
Totternhoe 67 A4
Tottington 137 B6
Totton 32 D2
Touchen End ...48 B1
Tournaig 261 B5
Toux 269 D4
Tovil 37 A5
Toward 203 B6

Towcester 82 C3
Towednack 2 B2
Tower End 118 D3
Towersey 66 C2
Towie Aberds 244 A1
  Aberds 268 C3
Towiemore 255 B4
Tow Law 166 B4
Townend 205 A4
Town End Cambs 101 B6
  Cumb 154 C3
Towngate 116 D4
Townhead Cumb .164 B3
  Dumfries 173 D4
  S Ayrs 181 A4
  S Yorks 139 C4
Townhead of
  Greenlaw. 173 B5
Townhill 208 B4
Town Row 36 C3
Townsend Bucks . 66 C2
  Herts 67 C6
Townshend 2 B3
Town Yetholm . 187 A7
Towthorpe 149 B5
Towton 148 D3
Towyn 125 B4
Toxteth 126 A3
Toynton All
  Saints 134 C3
Toynton Fen
  Side 134 C3
Toynton
  St Peter 135 C4
Toy's Hill 36 A2
Trabboch 193 C4
Traboe 3 C5
Tradespark
  Highld. 253 A4
  Orkney 283 G5
Trafford Park . . 137 D6
Trallong 59 C6
Tranent 209 C7
Tranmere 126 A3
Trantlebeg 279 C4
Trantlemore 279 C4
Tranwell 178 A3
Trapp 57 A6
Traprain 210 C2
Traquair 196 C2
Trawden 146 D3
Trawsfynydd . . . 108 B2
Trealaw 41 B5
Treales 144 D4
Trearddur 122 C2
Treaslane 258 C3
Trebanog 41 B5
Trebanos 40 A2
Trebartha 10 D3
Trebarwith 9 C6
Trebetherick 9 D5
Treborough 27 B5
Trebudannon 4 A3
Trebullett 10 D4
Treburley 10 D4
Trebyan 5 A5
Trecastle 59 C5
Trecenydd 41 C6
Trecwn 55 A5
Trecynon 41 A4
Tredavoe 2 C2
Treddiog 55 B4
Tredegar 60 C3
Tredegar Newydd
  =New Tredegar . 41 A6
Tredington Glos . 63 A5
  Warks. 81 C5
Tredinnick 9 D5
Tredomen 77 D5
Tredunnock 61 D5
Tredustan 77 D5
Treen. 2 C1
Treeton 131 A4
Trefaldwyn
  =Montgomery . . 93 B6
Trefasser 72 C1
Trefdraeth 123 C4
Trefdraeth
  =Newport 72 C3
Trefecca 77 D5
Trefechan 90 D3
Trefeglwys 92 B3

Trefenter 75 B5
Treffgarne 55 B5
Treffynnon 54 B4
Treffynnon
  =Holywell 126 B1
Trefgarn Owen . . 55 B4
Trefil 60 B3
Trefilan. 75 C4
Trefin 54 A4
Treflach 110 C1
Trefnanney 109 D7
Trefnant 125 B5
Trefonen 110 C1
Trefor Anglesey . 122 B3
  Gwyn 106 B3
Treforest 41 C5
Trefriw 124 C2
Tref-y-Clawdd
  =Knighton
  Powys 93 D6
  Powys 93 D6
Trefynwy
  =Monmouth. . . . 61 B7
Tregadillett 10 C3
Tregaian. 123 C4
Tregare 61 B6
Tregaron 75 C5
Tregarth 123 D6
Tregeare 10 C3
Tregeiriog 109 B6
Tregele 122 A3
Tre-Gibbon 60 C1
Tregidden 3 C5
Treglemais 54 B4
Tregole 10 B2
Tregonetha 5 A4
Tregony 4 C4
Tregoss 5 A4
Tregoyd 77 D6
Tregroes 73 B7
Tregurrian 4 A3
Tregynon 93 B4
Trehafod 41 B5
Treharris 41 B5
Treherbert 40 B4
Trekenner 10 D4
Treknow 9 C6
Trelan 3 D5
Trelash 10 B2
Trelassick 4 B3
Trelawnyd 125 B5
Trelech 73 C5
Treleddyd-fawr . 54 B3
Trelewis 41 B6
Treligga 9 C6
Trelights 9 D5
Trelill 9 D6
Trelissick 4 D3
Trelleck 61 C7
Trelleck
  Grange. 61 C6
Trelogan 125 A6
Trelystan 93 A6
Tremadog 107 B5
Tremail 10 C2
Tremain 73 B5
Tremaine 10 C3
Tremar 6 A1
Trematon 6 B3
Tremeirchion . . 125 B5
Trenance 4 A3
Trenarren 5 C5
Trench 111 D5
Treneglos 10 C3
Trenewan 5 B6
Trent 29 D5
Trentham 112 A2
Trentishoe 26 A1
Trent Vale 112 A2
Treoes 40 D4
Treorchy
  =Treorci 41 B4
Treorci
  =Treorchy 41 B4
Tre'r-ddôl 91 C4
Trerulefoot 6 B2
Tresaith 73 A5
Tresawle 4 C3
Trescott 95 B6
Trescowe 2 B3
Tresham 62 D3
Tresillian 4 C3

Tresinwen 72 B1
Treskinnick Cross 10 B3
Tresmeer 10 C3
Tresparrett 10 B2
Tresparrett Posts. 10 B2
Tressait. 230 B2
Tresta Shetland. . 284 D8
  Shetland. 285 H5
Treswell 132 B2
Tre-Taliesin 91 C4
Trethosa. 4 B4
Trethurgy 5 B5
Tretio 54 B3
Tretire. 62 A1
Tretower 60 A3
Treuddyn 126 D2
Trevalga 10 C1
Trevalyn 126 D3
Trevanson 9 D5
Trevarren. 4 A4
Trevarrian 4 A3
Trevarrick 5 C4
Trevaughan 56 A1
Tre-vaughan 73 D7
Treveighan 9 D6
Trevellas 4 B2
Treverva 4 D2
Trevethin 61 C4
Trevigro 6 A2
Treviscoe 4 B4
Trevone 9 D4
Trewarmett 9 C6
Trewassa 10 C2
Trewellard 2 B1
Trewen 10 C3
Trewennack 3 C4
Trewern 110 D1
Trewethern 9 D6
Trewidland 6 B1
Trewint Corn . . . 10 B2
  Corn 10 C3
Trewithian 4 D3
Trewoofe 2 C2
Trewoon. 5 B4
Treworga 4 C3
Treworlas 4 D3
Tre-wyn 61 A5
Treyarnon 9 D4
Treyford W Sus. . . 20 A1
  W Sus. 33 D7
Trezaise 5 B4
Ty'r-felin-isaf. . 124 C3
Triangle 138 A3
Triffleton 55 B5
Trimdon 167 B6
Trimdon
  Colliery 167 B6
Trimdon Grange 167 B6
Trimingham. . . . 121 B4
Trimley Lower
  Street. 88 D3
Trimley St Martin 88 D3
Trimley St Mary . 88 D3
Trimpley. 95 D5
Trimsaran 57 B4
Trimstone 25 A5
Trinafour 229 B6
Trinant 41 A7
Tring 67 B4
Tring Wharf. 67 B4
Trinity Angus . . 233 B4
  Jersey 6
Trisant 75 A6
Trislaig 237 B4
Trispen 4 B3
Tritlington 189 D5
Trochry. 230 D3
Trodigal 190 C2
Troed-rhiwdalar . 76 B3
Troedyraur 73 B6
Troedyrhiw 41 A5
Tromode 152 D3
Trondavoe 284 F5
Troon Corn 3 B4
  S Ayrs 192 B3
Trosaraidh 286 E3
Trossachs Hotel 217 D5
Troston 103 D4
Trottiscliffe 50 C3
Trotton 34 D1
Troutbeck Cumb .154 A3
  Cumb 164 C1

Troutbeck
  Bridge 154 A3
Trowbridge 44 D2
Trowell 114 B2
Trow Green 62 C1
Trowle Common . 44 D2
Trowley Bottom . 67 B5
Trows 197 C5
Trowse Newton .104 A3
Trudoxhill 30 A1
Trull. 28 C2
Trumaisgearraidh 287 G3
Trumpan. 258 B2
Trumpet 79 D4
Trumpington. . . . 85 B6
Trunch 121 B4
Trunnah 144 C3
Truro 4 C3
Trusham. 12 C3
Trusley 113 B6
Trusthorpe 135 A5
Trysull. 95 B6
Tubney 65 D5
Tuckenhay 8 B2
Tuckhill 95 C5
Tuckingmill 3 A4
Tuddenham
  St Martin 88 C2
Tudeley 36 B4
Tudhoe 167 B5
Tudorville 62 A1
Tudweiliog. 106 C2
Tuesley 34 B2
Tuffley 63 B4
Tufton Hants. . . . 32 A3
  Pembs 55 B6
Tugby 99 A4
Tugford 94 C3
Tullibardine 218 C4
Tullibody 207 A6
Tullich Argyll . . . 214 A3
  Highld. 252 D2
Tullich Muir. . . . 264 C3
Tulliemet 230 C3
Tulloch Aberds . . 233 A5
  Aberds 256 C3
  Perth 219 B5
Tulloch Castle. . 264 D1
Tullochgorm. . . . 214 C2
Tulloes 232 D3
Tullybannocher . 218 B2
Tullybelton 219 A5
Tullyfergus 231 D6
Tullymurdoch . . 231 C5
Tullynessle 244 A2
Tumble 57 A5
Tumby
  Woodside 134 D2
Tummel Bridge .229 C6
Tunga 288 D5
Tunstall E Yorks . 151 D6
  Kent 51 C5
  Lancs 155 D5
  Norf 105 A5
  N Yorks 157 B6
  Stoke 128 D3
  Suff 89 B4
  T&W 179 D5
Tunstead Derbys 129 B6
  Gtr Man 138 C3
  Norf 121 C4
Tunworth 33 A5
Tupsley 78 C3
Tupton 130 C3
Turgis Green. . . . 47 D4
Turin 232 C3
Turkdean 64 B2
Tur Langton. 99 B4
Turleigh 44 C2
Turn. 137 B7
Turnastone 78 D1
Turnberry 192 E2
Turnditch 113 A6
Turners Hill 35 C6
Turners Puddle . 16 B2
Turnford. 68 C3
Turnhouse 209 C4
Turnworth 16 A2
Turriff 268 D2
Turton Bottoms . 137 B6

Turves 101 B5
Turvey 83 B6
Turville 66 D2
Turville Heath. . . 66 D2
Turweston 82 D3
Tushielaw 185 A6
Tutbury 113 C6
Tutnall 96 D2
Tutshill 62 D1
Tuttington 120 C4
Tutts Clump. 46 B3
Tuxford. 132 B2
Twatt Orkney. . . . 282 E3
  Shetland. 285 H5
Twechar 207 C4
Tweedmouth. . . . 198 A3
Tweedsmuir 195 D5
Twelve Heads 4 C2
Twemlow Green 128 C2
Twenty 117 C4
Twerton 43 C6
Twickenham 49 B4
Twigworth 63 A4
Twineham 21 A5
Twinhoe 43 D6
Twinstead 87 D4
Twinstead Green 87 D4
Twiss Green . . . 137 D5
Twiston. 146 C2
Twitchen Devon . . 26 B2
  Shrops 94 D1
Two Bridges 11 D7
Two Dales 130 C2
Two Mills 126 B3
Twycross 97 A6
Twyford Bucks . . 66 A1
  Derbys 114 C1
  Hants 32 C3
  Leics. 115 D5
  Lincs. 116 C2
  Norf 120 C2
  Wokingham 47 B5
Twyford Common 78 D3
Twynholm 173 C4
Twyning 80 D2
Twyning Green . . 80 D2
Twynllanan 59 C4
Twynmynydd. . . . 57 A6
Twyn-y-Sheriff . 61 C6
Twywell 99 D6
Tyberton 78 D1
Tyburn 96 B4
Tycrwyn 109 D6
Tyddewi
  =St David's 54 B3
Tydd Gote 118 D1
Tydd St Giles . . 118 D1
Tydd St Mary. . . 118 D1
Tyddyn-mawr . . 107 B5
Ty-draw 124 D3
Tye Green Essex . 69 C4
  Essex 70 A1
  Essex 86 D1
Ty-hen Carms. . . 73 D6
  Gwyn 106 C1
Tyldesley 137 C5
Tyler Hill. 52 C3
Tylers Green 67 D4
Tylorstown. 41 B5
Tylwch 92 C3
Ty-mawr 123 B4
Ty Mawr 58 A2
Ty Mawr Cwm. . 108 A4
Ty-nant Conwy. . 109 A4
  Gwyn 108 C4
Tyncelyn. 75 B5
Tyndrum. 216 A3
Tyneham 16 C2
Tynehead 196 A2
Tynemouth 179 C5
Tyne Tunnel . . . 179 C5
Tynewydd. 40 B4
Tyninghame . . . 210 C3
Tynron 183 C6
Tyn-y-celyn. . . . 109 B6
Tyn-y-coed. 110 C1
Tyn-y-fedwen. . 109 B6
Tyn-y-ffridd . . . 109 B6
Tynygongl 123 B5
Tynygraig 75 B5
Tyn-y-graig. 76 B4

Ty'n-y-groes. . . . 124 B2
Ty'n-y-maes. . . . 123 D6
Tyn-y-pwll. 123 B4
Ty'n-yr-eithin. . . 75 B5
Tyrie 269 C4
Tyringham 83 C5
Tythecott 25 D5
Tythegston. 40 D3
Tytherington
  Ches E 129 B4
  S Glos. 43 A5
  Som 30 A1
  Wilts. 30 A3
Tytherleigh 14 A3
Ty-uchaf 109 C5
Tywardreath 5 B5
Tywyn Conwy . . 124 B2
  Gwyn 90 B3

U

Uachdar 286 A3
Uags 249 C4
Ubbeston Green 104 D4
Ubley. 43 D4
Uckerby 157 A6
Uckfield 36 D2
Uckington 63 A5
Uddingston 207 D4
Uddington 194 C3
Udimore 23 A6
Udny Green 256 D3
Udny Station . . . 257 D4
Udston 194 A1
Udstonhead 194 B2
Uffcott 45 B5
Uffculme 27 D5
Uffington Lincs . 100 A2
  Oxon. 45 A7
  Shrops 111 D4
Ufford Pboro. . . 100 A2
  Suff 88 B3
Ufton 81 A6
Ufton Nervet . . . 47 C4
Ugadale 190 C3
Ugborough 7 B5
Uggeshall. 105 C5
Ugglebarnby . . . 160 A2
Ughill 139 D5
Ugley. 69 A5
Ugley Green 69 A5
Ugthorpe 169 D5
Uidh. 286 G2
Uig Argyll. 215 D4
  Highld. 258 B3
  Highld. 258 C1
Uigen 287 A5
Uigshader 259 D4
Uisken 224 E2
Ulbster 281 D5
Ulceby Lincs . . . 135 B4
  N Lincs 142 B3
Ulceby Skitter. . 142 B3
Ulcombe. 37 B6
Uldale 163 A5
Uley 62 D3
Ulgham 189 D5
Ullapool 262 A3
Ullenhall. 80 A4
Ullenwood 63 B5
Ulleskelf. 148 C4
Ullesthorpe 98 C2
Ulley 131 A4
Ullingswick 78 C3
Ullinish 246 A2
Ullock 162 B3
Ulnes Walton . . 136 B4
Ulpha. 153 A2
Ulrome 151 B4
Ulsta 284 E6
Ulva House 224 C3
Ulverston 154 D1
Ulwell 17 C4
Umberleigh 25 C7
Unapool 271 A5
Unasary 286 D3
Underbarrow . . . 154 B3
Undercliffe 147 D5

Underhoull 284 C7
Underriver 36 A3
Underwood 131 D4
Undy 42 A3
Unifirth 285 H4
Union Cottage . . 245 C5
Union Mills 152 D3
Union Street 37 C5
Unstone 130 B3
Unstone Green . 130 B3
Unthank Cumb . . 164 B2
Cumb 165 A4
Unthank End . . . 164 B2
Upavon 45 D5
Up Cerne 15 A6
Upchurch 51 C5
Upcott 78 B1
Upend 86 B2
Up Exe 13 A4
Upgate 120 D3
Uphall 208 C3
Uphall Station . 208 C3
Upham Devon . . 12 A3
Hants 32 C4
Uphampton 79 A6
Up Hatherley . . . 63 A5
Uphill 42 D2
Up Holland 136 C4
Uplawmoor 205 C4
Upleadon 62 A3
Upleatham 168 D4
Uplees 52 C1
Uploders 15 B5
Uplowman 27 C5
Uplyme 14 B3
Up Marden 33 D6
Upminster 50 A2
Up Nately 47 D4
Upnor 51 B4
Upottery 14 A2
Upper Affcot . . . 94 C2
Upper
 Ardchronie . . 264 D2
Upper Arley 95 C5
Upper Arncott . . 65 B7
Upper Astrop . . . 82 D2
Upper Badcall . . 276 D2
Upper Basildon . . 46 B3
Upper Beeding . . 21 A4
Upper Benefield 100 C1
Upper
 Boddington . . . 82 B1
Upper Borth 90 D4
Upper Boyndlie . 269 C4
Upper Brailes . . . 81 D6
Upper Breakish . 247 B5
Upper Breinton . 78 C2
Upper
 Broadheath. . . 79 B6
Upper
 Broughton. . . 115 C4
Upper
 Bucklebury . . . 46 C3
Upper
 Burnhaugh . . . 245 C5
Upperby 175 C7
Upper Caldecote . 84 C3
Upper Catesby . . 82 B2
Upper Chapel . . . 76 C4
Upper Church
 Village 41 C5
Upper Chute . . . 45 D6
Upper Clatford . . 32 A2
Upper Clynnog . 107 B4
Upper
 Cumberworth . 139 C5
Upper Cwmbran . 61 D4
Upper Dallachy . 267 C4
Upper Dean 84 A2
Upper Denby . . . 139 C5
Upper Denton . . 176 C4
Upper Derraid . . 253 C6
Upper Dicker . . . 22 B3
Upper
 Dovercourt . . . 88 D3
Upper Druimfin . 225 A4
Upper
 Dunsforth . . . 148 A3

Upper Eathie . . . 264 D3
Upper Elkstone . 129 D5
Upper End 129 B5
Upper Farringdon 33 B6
Upper Framilode . 62 B3
Upper
 Glenfintaig . . 239 D6
Upper Gornal . . . 96 B2
Upper
 Gravenhurst . . 84 D3
Upper Green Mon . 61 B5
W Berks 46 C1
Upper Grove
 Common 62 A1
Upper Hackney . 130 C2
Upper Hale 34 B1
Upper Halistra . 258 C2
Upper Halling . . 50 C3
Upper Hambleton 99 A5
Upper Hardres
 Court 52 D3
Upper Hartfield . 36 C2
Upper Haugh . . . 140 D2
Upper Heath . . . 94 C3
Upper
 Hellesdon . . . 120 D4
Upper Helmsley 149 B5
Upper Hergest . . 77 B6
Upper Heyford
 Oxon 65 A5
W Nhants 82 B3
Upper Hill 78 B2
Upper Hopton . 139 B4
Upper
 Horsebridge . . 22 A3
Upper Hulme . . . 129 C5
Upper Inglesham 64 D3
Upper
 Inverbrough . 253 C4
Upper Killay . . . 57 C5
Upper
 Knockando . . . 254 B2
Upper Lambourn . 45 A7
Upper Leigh 112 B4
Upper Lenie . . . 251 D7
Upper Lochton . 244 C3
Upper Longdon . 113 D4
Upper Lybster . . 275 A6
Upper Lydbrook . 62 B2
Upper Maes-
 coed 78 D1
Upper Midway . . 113 C6
Uppermill 138 C2
Upper Milovaig . 258 D1
Upper Minety . . . 63 D6
Upper Mitton . . . 95 D6
Upper North
 Dean. 66 D3
Upper Obney . . . 219 A5
Upper Ollach . . . 247 A4
Upper Padley . . 130 B2
Upper Pollicott . 66 B2
Upper
 Poppleton . . . 149 B4
Upper Quinton . . 81 C4
Upper Ratley . . . 32 C2
Upper Rissington 64 B3
Upper Rochford . 79 A4
Upper
 Sandaig 238 A1
Upper Sanday . 283 G6
Upper Sapey . . . 79 A4
Upper
 Saxondale . . . 115 B4
Upper Seagry . . . 44 A3
Upper Shelton . . 84 C1
Upper
 Sheringham . 120 A3
Upper
 Skelmorlie . . . 204 B2
Upper Slaughter . 64 A2
Upper Soudley . . 62 B2
Uppersound . . . 285 J4
Upper Stondon . . 84 D3
Upper Stowe . . . 82 B3
Upper Stratton . . 45 A5
Upper Street
 Hants 31 D5
Norf 121 D5
Norf 121 D5
Suff 88 D2
Upper Strensham 80 D2
Upper Sundon . . 67 A5

Upper Swell 64 A2
Upper Tean 112 B4
Upperthong 139 C4
Upperthorpe 141 C5
Upper Tillyrie . . 219 D6
Upperton 34 D2
Upper Tooting . . . 49 B5
Upper Tote 259 C5
Uppertown
 Derbys 130 C3
Highld 281 A5
Orkney 283 H5
Upper Town 43 C4
Upper
 Treverward . . . 93 D6
Upper Tysoe 81 C6
Upper Upham . . 45 B6
Upper
 Wardington . . 82 C1
Upper Weald 83 D4
Upper Weedon . . 82 B3
Upper Wield . . . 33 B5
Upper
 Winchendon . 66 B2
Upper Witton . . . 96 B3
Upper Woodend 244 A3
Upper Woodford 31 B5
Upper Wootton . 46 D3
Upper Wyche . . 79 C5
Uppingham 99 B5
Uppington 95 A4
Upsall 158 C3
Upshire 68 C4
Up Somborne . . 32 B2
Upstreet 53 C4
Up Sydling 15 A6
Upthorpe 103 D5
Upton Cambs . . 100 D3
Ches W 127 C4
Corn 10 A3
Dorset 16 B3
Dorset 16 C1
Hants 32 D2
Hants 46 D1
Leics 97 B6
Lincs 132 A3
Mers 126 A2
Norf 121 D5
Notts 132 B2
Oxon 46 A3
Pboro 100 A3
Slough 48 B2
Som 27 C4
W Nhants 83 A4
W Yorks 140 B2
Upton Bishop . . 62 A2
Upton Cheyney . 43 C5
Upton Cressett . 95 B4
Upton Cross . . . 10 D3
Upton Grey 33 A5
Upton Hellions . 12 A3
Upton Lovell . . . 30 A3
Upton Magna . . 111 D4
Upton Noble . . . 29 B7
Upton Pyne . . . 13 B4
Upton
 St Leonard's . . 63 B4
Upton
 Scudamore . . 30 A2
Upton Snodsbury. 80 B2
Upton upon
 Severn 79 C6
Upton Warren . . 80 A2
Upwaltham 20 A2
Upware 102 D1
Upwell 101 A6
Upwey 15 C6
Upwood 101 C4
Uradale 285 K6
Urafirth 284 F5
Urchfont 44 D4
Urdimarsh 78 C3
Ure 284 F4
Ure Bank 157 D7
Urgha 288 H2
Urishay Common 77 D7
Urlay Nook . . . 167 D6
Urmston 137 D6
Urpeth 179 D4
Urquhart Highld . 252 A1
Moray 266 D3

Urra 159 A4
Urray 251 A7
Ushaw Moor . . . 167 A5
Usk = Brynbuga . . 61 C5
Usselby 142 D2
Usworth 179 D5
Utkinton 127 C5
Utley 147 C4
Uton 12 B3
Utterby 143 D5
Uttoxeter 113 B4
Uwchmynydd . . 106 D1
Uxbridge 48 A3
Uyeasound 284 C7
Uzmaston 55 C5

V

Valley 122 C2
Valleyfield 173 C4
Valley Truckle . . 10 C1
Valsgarth 284 B8
Valtos 259 B5
Van 92 C3
Vange 51 A4
Varteg 61 C4
Vatten 258 D2
Vaul 222 C3
Vaynor 60 B2
Veensgarth . . . 285 J6
Velindre 77 D5
Vellow 27 B5
Veness 282 E6
Vennington 94 A1
Venn Green 25 D4
Venny Tedburn . 12 A3
Ventnor 19 D4
Vernham Dean . 46 D1
Vernham Street . 46 D1
Vernolds
 Common 94 C2
Verwood 17 A4
Veryan 4 D4
Vicarage 14 C2
Vickerstown . . . 153 D2
Victoria Corn . . . 5 A4
S Yorks 139 C4
Vidlin 284 G6
Viewpark 207 D5
Vigo Village . . . 50 C3
Vinehall Street . 37 D5
Vine's Cross . . . 22 A3
Viney Hill 62 C2
Virginia Water . 48 C2
Virginstow 11 B4
Vobster 29 A7
Voe
 Shetland 284 E5
 Shetland 285 G6
Vowchurch 78 D1
Voxter 284 F5
Voy 282 F3

W

Wackerfield 167 C4
Wacton 104 B2
Wadbister 285 J6
Wadborough . . . 80 C2
Waddesdon 66 B2
Waddingham . . . 142 D1
Waddington
 Lancs 146 C1
 Lincs 133 C4
Wadebridge . . . 9 D5
Wadeford 28 D3
Wadenhoe 100 C2
Wadesmill 68 B3
Wadhurst 36 C4
Wadshelf 130 B3
Wadworth 140 D3
Waen Denb 125 C4
Denb 125 C6
Waen Fach 109 D7
Waen
 Goleugoed . . . 125 B5
Wag 274 B2

Wainfleet All
 Saints 135 D4
Wainfleet Bank. 135 D4
Wainfleet
 St Mary 135 D5
Wainfleet Tofts. 135 D4
Wainhouse
 Corner 10 B2
Wainscott 51 B4
Wainstalls 138 A3
Waitby 155 A6
Waithe 143 C4
Wakefield 139 A6
Wake Lady
 Green 159 B5
Wakerley 99 B6
Wakes Colne . . . 70 A2
Walberswick . . 105 C5
Walberton 20 B2
Walbottle 178 C3
Walcot Lincs . . 116 B3
N Lincs 141 A6
Shrops 94 C1
Swindon 45 A5
Telford 111 D4
Walcote Leics . . 98 C2
Warks 80 B4
Walcot Green . 104 C2
Walcott Lincs . . 133 D6
Norf 121 B5
Walden 156 C4
Walden Head . . 156 C3
Walden Stubbs . 140 B3
Waldersey 101 A6
Walderslade . . . 51 C4
Walderton 33 D6
Waldingfield . . . 15 A4
Waldley 113 B5
Waldridge 179 D4
Waldringfield . . 88 C3
Waldringfield
 Heath 88 C3
Waldron 22 A3
Wales 131 A4
Walesby Lincs . . 142 D3
Notts 132 B1
Walford Hereford . 62 A1
Hereford 94 D1
Shrops 110 C3
Walford Heath . 110 D3
Walgherton . . . 111 A4
Walgrave 99 D5
Walhampton . . . 18 B2
Walkden 137 C6
Walker 179 C4
Walker Barn . . . 129 B4
Walkerburn 196 C2
Walker Fold . . . 145 C6
Walkeringham . 141 D5
Walkerith 141 D5
Walkern 68 A2
Walker's Green . 78 C3
Walkerville 157 B6
Walkford 17 B6
Walkhampton . . 7 A4
Walkington 150 D2
Walkley 130 A3
Walk Mill 146 D2
Wall Northumb . 177 C7
Staffs 96 A4
Wallaceton . . . 183 D6
Wallacetown
 S Ayrs 181 A4
 S Ayrs 192 C3
Wallands Park . 22 A2
Wallasey 136 D2
Wall Bank 94 B3
Wallcrouch . . . 37 C4
Wall Heath 96 C1
Wallingford . . . 47 A4
Wallington Hants . 19 A4
Herts 85 D4
London 49 C5
Wallis 55 B6
Walliswood . . . 35 C4
Walls 285 J4
Wallsend 179 C4
Wall under
 Heywood 94 B3
Wallyford 209 C6
Walmer 53 D5

Walmer Bridge . . 136 A3
Walmersley 137 B7
Walmley 96 B4
Walpole 105 D4
Walpole Cross
 Keys 118 D2
Walpole
 Highway 118 D2
Walpole Marsh . 118 D1
Walpole
 St Andrew . . . 118 D2
Walpole
 St Peter 118 D2
Walsall 96 B3
Walsall Wood . . 96 A3
Walsden 138 A2
Walsgrave on
 Sowe 97 C6
Walsham le
 Willows 103 D5
Walshaw 137 B6
Walshford 148 B3
Walsoken 118 D1
Walston 195 B5
Walsworth 84 D4
Walters Ash . . . 66 D3
Walterston 41 D5
Walterstone . . . 61 A5
Waltham Kent . . 38 A3
NE Lincs 143 C4
Waltham Abbey . 68 C3
Waltham Chase . 33 D4
Waltham Cross . 68 C3
Waltham on the
 Wolds 115 C6
Waltham
 St Lawrence . . 47 B6
Walthamstow . . 49 A6
Walton Cumb . . 176 C3
Derbys 130 C3
Leics 98 C2
Mers 136 D2
M Keynes 83 D5
Pboro 100 A3
Powys 77 B6
Som 29 B4
Staffs 112 B2
Suff 88 D3
Telford 111 D4
Warks 81 B5
W Yorks 139 B6
W Yorks 148 C3
Walton Cardiff . . 80 C2
Walton East . . . 55 B6
Walton-in-
 Gordano 42 B3
Walton-le-Dale . 137 A4
Walton-on-
 Thames 48 C4
Walton on the Hill
 Staffs 112 C3
 Sur 35 A5
Walton-on-the-
 Naze 71 A6
Walton on the
 Wolds 114 D3
Walton-on-
 Trent 113 D6
Walton West . . . 55 C4
Walwen 126 B2
Walwick 177 B7
Walworth 167 D5
Walworth Gate . 167 C5
Walwyn's Castle . 55 C4
Wambrook 14 A2
Wanborough Sur . 34 B2
Swindon 45 A6
Wandsworth . . . 49 B5
Wangford 105 D5
Wanlockhead . . 183 A6
Wansford
 E Yorks 150 B3
 Pboro 100 B2
Wanstead 49 A7
Wanstrow 29 A7
Wanswell 62 C2
Wantage 46 A1
Wapley 43 B6
Wappenbury . . . 81 A6
Wappenham . . . 82 C2
Warbleton 22 A4
Warblington . . . 19 A6

Warborough 65 D6
Warboys 101 C5
Warbreck 144 D3
Warbstow. 10 B3
Warburton 128 A2
Warcop. 165 D5
Warden Kent 52 B2
  Northumb. 177 C7
Ward End 96 C4
Ward Green. 87 A6
Wardhill 282 E7
Wardington. 82 C1
Wardlaw. 185 A5
Wardle Ches E . . .127 D6
  Gtr Man 138 B2
Wardley 99 A5
Wardlow. 130 B1
Wardy Hill 101 C6
Ware Herts 68 B3
  Kent 53 C4
Wareham 16 C3
Warehorne 38 B1
Warenford 189 A4
Waren Mill. 199 C5
Warenton 199 C5
Wareside 68 B3
Waresley Cambs . . 84 B4
  Worcs. 95 D6
Warfield 48 B1
Warfleet 8 B2
Wargrave 47 B5
Warham 119 A6
Warhill 138 D2
Wark Northumb. . .177 B6
  Northumb. 198 C2
Warkleigh 26 C1
Warkton 99 D5
Warkworth
  Northumb. 189 C5
  W Nhants 82 C1
Warlaby 158 B2
Warland 138 A2
Warleggan 5 A6
Warlingham . . . 35 A6
Warmfield 140 A1
Warmingham . . .128 C2
Warmington
  N Nhants 100 B2
  Warks. 81 C7
Warminster 30 A2
Warmlake 37 A6
Warmley. 43 B5
Warmley Tower . . 43 B5
Warmonds Hill . . 83 A6
Warmsworth. . . .140 C3
Warmwell 16 C1
Warndon 80 B1
Warnford 33 C5
Warnham 35 C4
Warninglid. 35 D5
Warren Ches E . . .128 B3
  Pembs 55 C5
Warren Heath . . .88 C3
Warren Row 47 A6
Warren Street. . . .51 D6
Warrington
  M Keynes 83 B5
  Warr. 127 A6
Warsash 18 A3
Warslow 129 D5
Warter 150 B1
Warthermarske .157 D6
Warthill 149 B5
Wartling 23 B4
Wartnaby 115 C5
Warton Lancs . . .128 B3
  Lancs 154 D3
  Northumb. 188 C3
  Warks. 97 A5
Warwick 81 A5
Warwick Bridge 176 D2
Warwick on
  Eden 176 D2
Wasbister 282 D4
Wasdale Head. . .163 D4
Washaway 5 A5
Washbourne . . . 8 B1
Wash Common . . 46 C2
Washfield. 27 D4
Washfold 157 A4
Washford 27 A5
Washford Pyne. . 26 D3

Washingborough
  . . . . .133 B5
Washington
  T&W. 179 D5
  W Sus. 21 A4
Wasing 46 C3
Waskerley 166 A3
Wasperton. 81 B5
Wasps Nest 133 C5
Wass 159 D4
Watchet 27 A5
Watchfield Oxon . . 64 D3
  Som 28 A3
Watchgate 154 B4
Watchhill 175 D4
Watcombe 8 A3
Watendlath 163 C5
Water Devon 12 C2
  Lancs 138 A1
Waterbeach. . . . 85 A6
Waterbeck 175 A5
Waterden 119 B5
Water End
  E Yorks 149 D6
  Herts 67 B5
  Herts 68 C2
Waterfall 129 D5
Waterfoot
  E Renf 205 C5
  Lancs 138 A1
Waterford Hants . 18 B2
  Herts 68 B3
Waterhead Cumb 154 A2
  Dumfries 185 C4
Waterheads 196 A1
Waterhouses
  Durham 167 A4
  Staffs 129 D5
Wateringbury . . . 37 A4
Waterloo BCP. . . . 17 B4
  Gtr Man 138 C2
  Highld. 247 B5
  Mers. 136 D2
  N Lanark. 194 A3
  Norf 120 D4
  Perth 219 A5
  Shrops 111 B4
Waterloo Port . . .123 D4
Waterlooville . . . 19 A5
Watermeetings .184 A2
Watermillock . . .164 C2
Water Newton . . 100 B3
Water Orton . . . 97 B4
Waterperry 66 C1
Waterrow 27 C5
Watersfield 20 A3
Waterside
  Aberds 257 D5
  Blackburn. 137 A6
  Cumb 175 D5
  E Ayrs 182 B2
  E Ayrs 205 D4
  E Dunb 207 C4
  E Renf. 205 C5
Water's Nook . . .137 C5
Waterstock 66 C1
Waterston 55 D5
Water Stratford . 82 D3
Waters Upton . . .111 D5
Water Yeat. 154 C1
Watford Herts . . . 67 D6
  W Nhants 82 A3
Watford Gap . . . 96 A4
Wath N Yorks. . . .147 A5
  N Yorks 157 D7
  N Yorks 159 D5
Wath Brow 162 C3
Wath upon
  Dearne 140 C2
Watley's End 43 A5
Watlington Norf. .118 D3
  Oxon. 66 D1
Watnall 114 A3
Watten 280 C4
Wattisfield. 103 D6
Wattisham 87 B6
Wattlesborough
  Heath 110 D2
Watton E Yorks . .150 B3
  Norf 103 A5
Watton at Stone . 68 B3
Wattston. 207 C5

Wattstown 41 B5
Wauchan 238 D3
Waulkmill
  Lodge 283 G4
Waun 91 B6
Waunarlwydd . . .57 C6
Waunclunda . . . 58 B3
Waunfawr 107 A5
Waungron 57 B5
Waunlwyd 60 C3
Waun-y-clyn. . . . 57 B4
Wavendon 83 D6
Waverbridge 175 D5
Waverton Ches W 127 C4
  Cumb 175 D5
Wavertree 126 A3
Wawne 150 D3
Waxham 121 C6
Waxholme 143 A5
Way 53 C5
Wayfield 51 C4
Wayford 14 A4
Waymills 111 A4
Wayne Green . . . 61 B6
Way Village 26 D3
Wdig = Goodwick . 72 C2
Weachyburn . . .268 D1
Weald 64 C4
Wealdstone 49 A4
Weardley 148 C1
Weare 42 D3
Weare Giffard. . . 25 C5
Wearhead 165 B6
Weasdale. 155 A5
Weasenham All
  Saints. 119 C5
Weasenham
  St Peter 119 C5
Weatherhill 35 B6
Weaverham 127 B6
Weaverthorpe . .160 D3
Webheath 80 A3
Wedderlairs. . . .256 C3
Wedderlie 197 A5
Weddington . . . 97 B6
Wedhampton . . 45 D4
Wedmore 28 A4
Wednesbury . . . 96 B2
Wednesfield . . . 96 A2
Weedon 66 B3
Weedon Bec . . . 82 B3
Weedon Lois . . . 82 C3
Weeford 96 A4
Week 26 D2
Weeke. 32 B3
Weekley 99 C5
Week St Mary . . . 10 B3
Weel 150 D3
Weeley 71 A5
Weeley Heath . . .71 A5
Weem 230 D2
Weeping Cross . .112 C3
Weethley Gate . . 80 B3
Weeting 102 C3
Weeton E Yorks . .143 A5
  Lancs 144 D3
  N Yorks 148 C1
Weetwood Hall. .188 A3
Weir. 138 A1
Weir Quay 6 A3
Welborne 120 E2
Welbourn 133 D4
Welburn N Yorks .149 A6
  N Yorks 159 C5
Welbury 158 A2
Welby 116 B2
Welches Dam . . .101 C6
Welcombe 24 D3
Weld Bank 137 B4
Weldon 189 D4
Welford W Berks . .46 B2
  W Nhants 98 C3
Welford-on-Avon 81 B4
Welham Leics. . . .99 B4
  Notts 132 A2
Welham Green . . 68 C2
Well Hants. 33 A6
  Lincs. 135 B4
  N Yorks 157 C6
Welland 79 C5
Wellbank 221 A4
Welldale. 175 B4

Well End. 48 A1
Wellesbourne . . . 81 B5
Well Heads 147 D4
Well Hill 50 C1
Welling 50 B1
Wellingborough. .83 A5
Wellingham 119 C5
Wellingore. 133 D4
Wellington Cumb 162 D3
  Hereford 78 C2
  Som 27 C6
  Telford. 111 D5
Wellington Heath 79 C5
Wellington Hill . .148 D2
Wellow Bath. . . . 43 D6
  IoW 18 C2
  Notts 131 C6
Wellpond Green. .68 A4
Wells 29 A5
Wellsborough . . . 97 A6
Wells Green. . . .128 D1
Wells-next-
  the-Sea 119 A6
Wellswood. 8 A3
Well Town 13 A4
Wellwood. 208 B3
Welney 102 B1
Welshampton . . .110 B3
Welsh Bicknor . . 62 B1
Welsh End 111 B4
Welsh Frankton . 110 B2
Welsh Hook 55 B5
Welsh Newton . . 61 B6
Welshpool
  =Y Trallwng. . . .93 A6
Welsh St Donats . 41 D5
Welton Cumb . . .164 A1
  E Yorks 142 A1
  Lincs. 133 B5
  W Nhants 82 A2
Welton Hill 133 A5
Welton le Marsh 135 C4
Welton le Wold. .134 A2
Welwick 143 A5
Welwyn. 68 B2
Welwyn Garden
  City 68 B2
Wem 111 C4
Wembdon 28 B2
Wembley 49 A4
Wembury 7 C4
Wembworthy . . . 12 A1
Wemyss Bay . . .204 B1
Wenallt Ceredig . .75 A5
  Gwyn 109 A4
Wendens Ambo . 85 D7
Wendlebury 65 B6
Wendling 119 D6
Wendover 66 C3
Wendron 3 B4
Wendy. 85 C5
Wenfordbridge. . 10 D1
Wenhaston 105 D5
Wennington
  Cambs 100 D4
  Lancs 155 D5
  London 50 A2
Wensley Derbys . .130 C2
  N Yorks 157 C4
Wentbridge 140 B2
Wentnor 94 B1
Wentworth
  Cambs 101 D6
  S Yorks 140 D1
Wenvoe 41 D6
Weobley 78 B2
Weobley Marsh . . 78 B2
Wereham 102 A2
Wergs 95 A6
Wern Powys 109 D4
  Powys 110 D1
Wernffrwd 57 C5
Wernyrheolydd. .61 B5
Werrington Corn. .10 C4
  Pboro 100 A3
  Staffs 112 A3
Wervin 127 B4
Wesham 144 D4
Wessington 130 D3
West Acre 119 D4
West Adderbury . .82 D1

West Allerdean . .198 B3
West Alvington . . 7 C6
West Amesbury . . 31 A5
West Anstey 26 C3
West Ashby 134 B2
West Ashling . . . 19 A7
West Ashton . . . 44 D2
West Auckland . .167 C4
West Ayton 160 C3
West Bagborough 27 B6
West Barkwith . .133 A6
West Barnby 169 D6
West Barns 210 C3
West Barsham . . .119 B6
West Bay 15 B4
West Beckham . .120 B3
West Bedfont . . . 48 B3
West Benhar . . .208 D1
Westbere 52 C3
West Bergholt . . . 70 A3
West Bexington . . 15 C5
West Bilney 119 D4
West
  Blatchington . . 21 B5
Westborough. . .115 A6
Westbourne BCP. . .17 B4
  Suff 88 C2
  W Sus. 19 A6
West Bowling . . .147 D5
West Bradford . .146 C1
West Bradley. . . . 29 B5
West Bretton . . .139 B5
West Bridgford . .114 B3
West Bromwich . . 96 B3
Westbrook 46 B2
West Buckland
  Devon. 26 B1
  Som 28 C1
West Burrafirth .285 H4
West Burton
  N Yorks 156 C4
  W Sus. 20 A2
Westbury Bucks. . .82 D3
  Shrops 94 A1
  Wilts. 44 D2
Westbury Leigh . . 44 D2
Westbury-on-
  Severn 62 B3
Westbury on
  Trym 43 B4
Westbury-sub-
  Mendip 29 A5
West Butterwick 141 C6
Westby 144 D3
West Byfleet . . . 48 C3
West Caister . . .121 D7
West Calder. . . .208 D3
West Camel 29 C5
West Challow . . . 46 A1
West
  Chelborough . . 15 A5
West
  Chevington. . .189 D5
West Chiltington 20 A3
West Chiltington
  Common 20 A3
West Chinnock . . 29 D4
West Chisenbury 45 D5
West Clandon . . 34 A3
West Cliffe 39 A5
Westcliff-on-Sea 51 A5
West Clyne. 274 D2
West Clyth 275 A6
West Coker 29 D5
Westcombe 29 B6
West Compton
  Dorset 15 B5
  Som 29 A5
Westcote 64 A3
Westcott Bucks . . 66 B2
  Devon. 13 A5
  Sur 35 B4
Westcott Barton . 65 A5
West Cowick . . .140 A4
West Cranmore . . 29 A6
West Cross. 57 D6
West Cullerry . . .245 B4
West Curry 10 B3
West
  Curthwaite . . .175 D6

West Dean Wilts . . 31 C6
  W Sus. 20 A1
West Deeping . . .100 A3
Westdene 21 B5
West Derby 136 D2
West Dereham . .102 A2
West Didsbury . .138 D1
West Ditchburn .189 A4
West Down 25 A6
West Drayton
  London 48 B3
  Notts 132 B2
West Ella 142 A2
West End Bedford . 84 B1
  E Yorks 150 D3
  E Yorks 151 D4
  Hants 32 D3
  Lancs 137 A6
  Norf 103 A5
  Norf 121 D7
  N Som. 42 C3
  N Yorks 147 B5
  Oxon. 65 C5
  S Lanark. 195 B4
  Suff 105 C5
  Sur 48 C2
  S Yorks 141 C4
  Wilts. 30 C3
  Wilts. 44 B3
  W Sus. 21 A6
West End Green . . 47 C4
Wester
  Aberchalder . . .252 C1
Wester Balgedie 219 D6
Wester
  Culbeuchly . . .268 C1
Westerdale
  Highld. 280 C3
  N Yorks 159 A5
Wester
  Dechmont . . .208 D3
Wester Denoon . 232 D1
Westerfield
  Shetland. 285 H5
  Suff 88 C2
Wester Fintray . .245 A5
Westergate. . . . 20 B2
Wester
  Gruinards 263 A7
Westerham 36 A2
Westerhope. . . .178 C3
Wester Lealty . .264 C2
Westerleigh. . . . 43 B6
Wester Milton . .253 A5
Wester
  Newburn 220 D4
Wester Quarff . .285 K6
Wester Skeld. . .285 J4
Westerton Angus 233 C4
  Durham 167 B5
  W Sus. 20 B1
Westerwick 285 J4
West Farleigh . . . 37 A5
West Felton 110 C2
West Fenton . . .210 B1
West Ferry 221 A4
Westfield Cumb . 162 B2
  E Sus 23 A6
  Hereford 79 C5
  Highld. 279 B6
  N Lanark. 207 C5
  Norf 103 A5
  W Loth 208 C2
Westfields of
  Rattray 231 D5
West Firle 22 B2
Westgate Durham 166 B2
  N Lincs 141 C5
  Norf 119 A5
  Norf 119 A6
Westgate on Sea 53 B5
West Ginge 46 A2
West Grafton. . . 45 C6
West Green 47 D5
West
  Greenskares . .268 C2
West Grimstead . 31 C6
West Grinstead . .35 D4

West Haddlesey 140 A3
West Haddon 98 D3
West Hagbourne .46 A3
West Hagley 96 C2
Westhall Aberds .256 D1
Suff 105 C5
West Hall 176 C3
West Hallam 114 A2
West Halton. 141 A7
Westham Dorset . 15 D6
E Sus 22 B4
Som 23 B4
West Ham 49 A7
Westhampnett . . . 20 B1
West Handley . . .130 B3
West Hanney 65 D5
West
  Hanningfield . . .70 D1
West Hardwick . .140 B2
West Harnham . . 31 C5
West Harptree . . .43 D4
West Hatch 28 C2
Westhay 28 B4
Westhead. 136 C3
West Head. 102 A1
West Heath
  Ches E 128 C3
  Hants 34 A1
  Hants 46 D3
West Helmsdale 274 C4
West Hendred. . .46 A2
West Heslerton. .160 D3
Westhide 78 C3
Westhill Aberds .245 B5
  Highld. 252 B3
West Hill Devon . 13 B5
  E Yorks 151 A4
  N Som. 42 B3
West Hoathly . . .35 C6
West Holme 16 C2
Westhope
  Hereford 78 B2
  Shrops 94 C2
West Horndon . . .50 A3
Westhorpe Lincs .117 B5
  Suff 87 A6
West Horrington .29 A5
West Horsley. . . .34 A3
West Horton 198 C4
West Hougham . .39 A4
Westhoughton . .137 C5
West Houlland .285 H4
Westhouse. 155 D5
Westhouses 131 D4
Westhumble 35 A4
West
  Huntington 149 B5
West Hythe 38 B3
West Ilsley 46 A2
Westing 284 C7
West Itchenor . . .19 A6
West Keal. 134 C3
West Kennett 45 C5
West Kilbride . . .204 D2
West Kingsdown .50 C2
West Kington . . .44 B2
West
  Kinharrachie .257 C4
West Kirby 126 A2
West Knapton . . .160 D2
West Knighton . .16 C1
West Knoyle 30 B2
West Kyloe. 199 B4
Westlake 7 B5
West Lambrook . .28 D4
West Langdon. . . .39 A5
West Langwell . .273 D4
West Lavington
  Wilts. 44 D4
  W Sus. 34 D1
West Layton 157 A5
West Lea 168 A2
West Leake 114 C3
West Learmouth 198 C2
  Devon. 27 D5
  Gtr Man 137 C5
West Leigh. 12 A1
Westleton 89 A5

West Lexham 119 D5
Westley Shrops . .94 A1
  Suff 87 A4
Westley
  Waterless 86 B2
West Lilling 149 A5
Westlington. 66 B2
Westlinton. 175 B6
West Linton 195 A6
West Liss 33 C6
West Littleton . . .43 B6
West Looe 6 B1
West Luccombe . .26 A3
West Lulworth . . .16 C2
West Lutton 150 A2
West Lydford 29 B5
West Lyng 28 C3
West Lynn 118 C3
West Malling 37 A4
West Malvern 79 C5
West Marden 33 D6
West Marina 23 B5
West Markham . .132 B2
Westmarsh 53 C4
West Marsh 143 B4
West Marton 146 B2
West Meon 33 C5
West Mersea 71 B4
Westmeston 21 A6
Westmill 68 A3
West Milton. 15 B5
Westminster 49 B6
West Minster. . . .51 B6
West Molesey . . .48 C4
West Monkton . . .28 C2
West Moors 17 A4
West Morriston .197 B5
Westmuir 232 C1
West Muir 232 B3
Westness 282 E4
West Ness 159 D5
West Newham . .178 B2
Westnewton
  Cumb 174 D4
  Northumb. 198 C3
West Newton
  E Yorks 151 D4
  Norf 118 C3
West Norwood . .49 B6
Westoe 179 C5
West Ogwell 12 D3
Weston Bath. 43 C6
  Ches E 128 D2
  Devon. 13 C6
  Dorset 15 D6
  Halton. 127 A5
  Hants 33 C6
  Herts 85 D4
  Lincs. 117 C5
  Notts 132 C2
  N Yorks 147 C5
  Shrops 94 B3
  Shrops 111 C4
  Staffs 112 C3
  W Berks 46 B1
  W Nhants 82 C2
Weston Beggard .78 C3
Westonbirt. 44 A2
Weston by
  Welland 99 B4
Weston Colville . .86 B2
Westoncommon 110 C3
Weston Coyney. .112 A3
Weston Favell . . .83 A4
Weston Green
  Cambs 86 B2
  Norf 120 D3
Weston Heath. . .112 D1
Weston Hills 117 C5
Westoning 84 D2
Weston-in-
  Gordano 42 B3
Weston Jones . . .111 C6
Weston
  Longville 120 D3
Weston
  Lullingfields . . .110 C3
Weston-on-the-
  Green 65 B6
Weston-on-
  Trent 114 C2
Weston Patrick . .33 A5

Weston Rhyn. . . .110 B1
Weston-Sub-
  Edge 80 C4
Weston-super-
  Mare. 42 C2
Weston Turville . .66 B3
Weston under
  Lizard 112 D2
Weston under
  Penyard 62 A2
Weston under
  Wetherley 81 A6
Weston Underwood
  Derbys 113 A6
  M Keynes 83 B5
Westonzoyland. . .28 B3
West Orchard . . .30 D2
West Overton . . .45 C5
Westow. 149 A6
West Park 168 B2
West Parley 17 B4
West Peckham . . .36 A4
West Pelton. 179 D4
West Pennard. . . .29 B5
West Pentire 4 A2
West Perry. 84 A3
Westport Argyll . .190 C2
  Som 28 D3
West Putford. 25 D4
West
  Quantoxhead . . .27 A6
West Rainton . . .167 A6
West Rasen 133 A5
West Raynham . .119 C5
West Retford. . . .132 A1
Westrigg 208 D2
West Rounton . . .158 A3
West Row. 102 D2
West Rudham . . .119 C5
West Runton 120 A3
Westruther 197 B5
Westry 101 B5
West Saltoun. . . .210 D1
West Sandwick . .284 E6
West Scrafton . . .157 C4
West Sleekburn .179 A4
West Somerton .121 D6
West Stafford . . .16 C1
West Stockwith .141 D5
West Stoke 20 B1
West
  Stonesdale 156 A2
West Stoughton . .28 A4
West Stour. 30 C1
West Stourmouth 53 C4
West Stow 103 D4
West Stowell. 45 C5
West Strathan . . .277 B6
West Stratton . . .32 A4
West Street 37 A7
West Tanfield. . . .157 D6
West Taphouse. . . .5 A6
West Tarbert. . . .202 B3
West Thirston . . .189 D4
West Thorney . . .19 A6
West Thurrock . . .50 B2
West Tilbury 50 B3
West Tisted 33 C5
West Tofts Norf . .103 B4
  Perth 219 A6
West Torrington 133 A6
West Town Hants . 19 B6
  N Som. 42 C3
West Tytherley . .32 C1
West Tytherton. . .44 B3
Westville 114 A3
West Walton 118 D1
West Walton
  Highway. 118 D1
Westward. 175 D5
Westward Ho!. . . .25 C5
Westwell Kent . . .38 A1
  Oxon. 64 C3
Westwell Leacon 38 A1
West Wellow. 32 D1
West Wemyss . . .209 A6
Westwick Cambs . .85 A6
  Durham 166 D3
  Norf 121 C4
West Wick 42 C2
West Wickham
  Cambs 86 C2

West Wickham
  continued
  London 49 C6
West Williamston 55 D6
West
  Willoughby 116 A2
West Winch. 118 D3
West Winterslow . 31 B6
West Wittering . . . 19 B6
West Witton 157 C4
Westwood Devon. . 13 B5
  Wilts. 44 D2
West Woodburn 177 A6
West Woodhay . .46 C1
West Woodlands .30 A1
West Worldham . .33 B6
Westwoodside . .141 D5
West Worlington .26 D2
West Worthing . . .21 B4
West Wratting . . .86 B2
West Wycombe . .66 D3
West Wylam 178 C3
Wetheral 176 D2
Wetherby 148 C3
Wetherden. 87 A6
Wetheringsett. . . .88 A2
Wethersfield 86 D3
Wethersta 284 G5
West
  Wetherup Street . 88 A2
Wetley Rocks . . .112 A3
Wettenhall 127 C6
Wetton 129 D6
Wetwang 150 B2
Wetwood 111 B6
Wexcombe. 45 D6
Wexham Street. . .48 A2
Weybourne 120 A3
Weybread 104 C3
Weybridge. 48 C3
Weycroft 14 B3
Weydale 280 B3
Weyhill 32 A2
Weymouth 15 D6
Whaddon Bucks . .83 D5
  Cambs 85 C5
  Glos 63 B4
  Wilts. 31 C5
Whale 164 C3
Whaley 131 B5
Whaley Bridge . .129 A5
Whaley Thorns .131 B5
Whaligoe 281 D5
Whalley 146 D1
Whalton 178 A3
Wham 146 A1
Whaplode 117 C6
Whaplode
  Drove 117 D6
Whaplode
  St Catherine . . .117 C6
Wharfe 146 A1
Wharles 144 D4
Wharncliffe
  Side 139 D5
Wharram le
  Street 150 A1
Wharton 127 C6
Wharton Green. .127 C6
Whashton 157 A5
Whatcombe. 16 A2
Whatcote 81 C6
Whatfield 87 C6
Whatley Som 14 A3
  Som 30 A1
Whatlington 23 A5
Whatstandwell . .130 D3
Whatton 115 B5
Whauphill 171 C6
Whaw 156 A3
Wheatacre 105 B5
Wheatcroft 130 D3
Wheathampstead. 68 B1
Wheathill 95 C4
Wheatley Devon. . 13 B4
  Hants 33 A6
  Oxon. 65 C6
  S Yorks 140 C3
  W Yorks 138 A3
Wheatley Hill . . .167 B6
Wheaton Aston. .112 D2
Wheddon Cross . 27 B4

Wheedlemont . . .255 D5
Wheelerstreet. . . .34 B2
Wheelock. 128 D2
Wheelock Heath 128 D2
Wheelton. 137 A5
Wheen 232 A1
Wheldrake 149 C5
Whelford 64 D2
Whelpley Hill 67 C4
Whempstead. 68 A3
Whenby 149 A5
Whepstead 87 B4
Wherstead 88 C2
Wherwell 32 A2
Wheston. 129 B6
Whetsted 37 B4
Whetstone 98 B2
Whicham 153 B2
Whichford 81 D6
Whickham 179 C4
Whiddon Down . . 12 B1
Whigstreet. 232 D2
Whilton 82 A3
Whimble 11 A4
Whim Farm 195 A7
Whimple 13 B5
Whimpwell
  Green 121 C5
Whinburgh 103 A6
Whinnieliggate. .173 C5
Whinnyfold 257 C5
Whippingham 18 B4
Whipsnade. 67 B5
Whipton 13 B4
Whirlow 130 A3
Whisby 133 C4
Whissendine . . .115 D6
Whissonsett 119 C6
Whistlefield
  Argyll 215 C4
  Argyll 215 C5
Whistley Green. . .47 B5
Whiston Mers. . .136 D3
  Staffs 112 A4
  Staffs 112 D2
  S Yorks 131 A4
  W Nhants 83 A5
Whitbeck 153 B2
Whitbourne 79 B5
Whitburn T&W . .179 C6
  W Loth 208 D2
Whitby Ches W . .126 B3
  N Yorks 169 D6
Whitbyheath . . .126 B3
Whitchurch Bath. .43 C5
  Bucks 66 A2
  Cardiff 41 C6
  Devon. 11 D5
  Hants 32 A3
  Hereford 62 B1
  Oxon. 47 B4
  Pembs 54 B3
  Shrops 111 A4
Whitchurch
  Canonicorum . . 14 B3
Whitchurch Hill . .47 B4
Whitcombe 15 C7
Whitcott Keysett . 93 C6
Whiteacen 254 B3
Whiteacre Heath . 97 B5
Whitebridge 240 A2
Whitebrook 62 C1
Whiteburn 197 B4
Whitecairn 171 B4
Whitecairns 245 A6
Whitecastle 195 B5
Whitechapel 145 C5
Whitecleat 283 G6
White Coppice . .137 B5
Whitecraig. 209 C6
Whitecroft 62 C2
Whitecross Corn . .9 D5
  Falk 208 C2
  Staffs 112 C4
Whiteface 264 B3
Whitefarland . . .202 D3
Whitefaulds 192 E2
Whitefield
  Gtr Man 137 C7
  Perth 219 A6

Whiteford. 256 D2
Whitegate 127 C6
Whitehall
  Blackburn. 137 A5
  W Sus. 35 D4
Whitehall
  Village 282 E7
Whitehaven. 162 C2
Whitehill 33 B6
Whitehills Aberds .245 A4
  S Lanark 205 C6
Whitehough 129 A5
Whitehouse
  Aberds 244 A3
  Argyll 202 B3
Whiteinch 205 B5
Whitekirk. 210 B2
White Lackington 15 B7
White Ladies
  Aston 80 B2
Whitelaw 205 D6
Whiteleas. 179 C5
Whiteley Bank . . .19 C4
Whiteley Green .129 B4
Whiteley Village. .48 C3
White Lund 144 A4
Whitemans
  Green 35 D6
White Mill 58 C1
Whitemire 253 A5
Whitemoor 5 B4
Whitemore. 128 C3
Whitenap 32 C2
White Ness 285 J5
White Notley 70 B1
Whiteoak Green. .64 B4
Whiteparish. 31 C6
White Pit 134 B3
White Post 131 D6
Whiterashes . . .256 D3
White Rocks 61 A6
White Roding . . .69 B5
Whiterow 281 D5
Whiteshill 63 C4
Whiteside
  Northumb. 177 C5
  W Loth 208 D2
Whitesmith 22 A3
Whitestaunton . . .28 D2
Whitestone Devon. 12 B3
  Devon. 25 A5
  Warks. 97 C6
Whitestones 268 D3
Whitestreet
  Green 87 D5
Whitewall
  Corner 159 D6
White Waltham . . 47 B6
Whiteway Glos. . .63 B5
  Glos 63 D4
Whitewell Aberds 269 C4
  Lancs 145 C6
Whitewell
  Bottom. 138 A1
Whiteworks. 11 D7
Whitfield Kent . . .39 A5
  Northumb. 177 D5
  S Glos. 62 D2
  W Nhants 82 D3
Whitford Devon . . 14 B2
  Flint 125 B6
Whitgift 141 A6
Whitgreave 112 C2
Whithorn 171 C6
Whiting Bay 191 C6
Whitkirk 148 D2
Whitland 56 A1
Whitletts 192 C3
Whitley N Yorks . .140 A3
  Reading 47 B5
  Wilts. 44 C2
Whitley Bay 179 B5
Whitley Chapel. .178 D1
Whitley Lower . .139 B5
Whitley Row 36 A2
Whitlock's End . .96 D4
Whitminster 62 C2
Whitmore 112 A2
Whitnage 27 D5
Whitnash 81 A6
Whitney-on-Wye 77 C6
Whitrigg Cumb. . .163 A4

Whitrigg continued
Cumb **175** C5
Whitsbury **31** D5
Whitsome **198** A2
Whitson **42** A2
Whitstable **52** C3
Whitstone **10** B3
Whittingham . . . **188** B3
Whittingslow **94** C2
Whittington Glos . . . .
Lancs **155** D5
Norf **102** D3
Shrops **110** B2
Staffs **95** C6
Staffs **97** A4
Worcs **80** B1
Whittlebury **82** C3
Whittle-le-
Woods **137** A4
Whittlesey **101** B4
Whittlesford **85** C6
Whittlestone
Head **137** B6
Whitton Borders . . **187** A6
N Lincs **141** A7
Northumb **188** C3
Powys **77** A6
Shrops **94** D3
Stockton **167** C6
Suff **88** C2
Whittonditch **45** B6
Whittonstall **178** D2
Whitway **46** D2
Whitwell Derbys . . **131** B5
Herts **68** A1
IoW **18** D4
N Yorks **157** B6
Rutland **99** A6
Whitwell-on-the-
Hill **149** A6
Whitwell Street . . **120** C3
Whitwick **114** D2
Whitwood **140** A2
Whitworth **138** B1
Whixall **111** B4
Whixley **148** B3
Whoberley **97** D6
Whorlton
Durham **166** D4
N Yorks **158** A3
Whygate **177** B5
Whyle **78** A3
Whyteleafe **35** A6
Wibdon **62** D1
Wibsey **147** D5
Wibtoft **98** C1
Wichenford **79** A5
Wichling **37** A7
Wick BCP **17** B5
Devon **13** A6
Highld **281** C5
S Glos **43** B6
Shetland **285** K6
V Glam **40** D4
Wilts **31** C5
Worcs **80** C2
W Sus **20** B3
Wicken Cambs . . **102** D1
N Nhants **83** D4
Wicken Bonhunt . **85** D6
Wickenby **133** A5
Wicken Green
Village **119** B5
Wickersley **140** D2
Wickford **70** D1
Wickham Hants . . **33** D4
W Berks **46** B1
Wickham
Bishops **70** B2
Wickhambreux . . **53** D4
Wickhambrook . . **86** B3
Wickhamford . . **80** C3
Wickham Market . **88** B4
Wickhampton . . **105** A5
Wickham St Paul . **87** D6
Wickham Skeith . **88** A1
Wickham Street
Suff **86** B3
Suff **88** A1
Wick Hill **47** C5
Wicklewood **104** A1
Wickmere **120** B3

Wick
St Lawrence **42** C2
Wickwar **43** A6
Widdington **86** D1
Widdrington **189** D5
Widdrington
Station **189** D5
Widecombe in the
Moor **12** D2
Widegates **6** B1
Widemouth Bay . **10** A3
Wide Open **179** D4
Widewall **283** H5
Widford Essex . . **69** C6
Herts **68** B4
Widham **45** A4
Widmer End **66** D3
Widmerpool **115** C4
Widnes **127** A5
Wigan **137** C4
Wiggaton **13** B6
Wiggenhall
St Germans **118** D2
Wiggenhall St Mary
Magdalen **118** D2
Wiggenhall St Mary
the Virgin **118** D2
Wigginton Herts . . **67** B4
Oxon **81** D6
Staffs **97** A5
York **149** B4
Wigglesworth . . **146** B2
Wiggonby **175** C5
Wiggonholt **20** A3
Wighill **148** C3
Wighton **119** B6
Wigley **32** D2
Wigmore Hereford . **78** A2
Medway **51** C5
Wigsley **132** B3
Wigsthorpe **100** C2
Wigston **98** B3
Wigthorpe **131** A5
Wigtoft **117** B5
Wigton **175** D5
Wigtown **171** B6
Wigtwizzle **139** D5
Wike **148** C2
Wike Well End . . **141** B4
Wilbarston **99** C5
Wilberfoss **149** B6
Wilberlee **138** B3
Wilburton **101** C6
Wilby N Nhants . . **83** A5
Norf **103** C6
Suff **104** D3
Wilcot **45** C5
Wilcott **110** D2
Wilcrick **42** A3
Wilday Green . . **130** B3
Wildboarclough **129** C4
Wilden Bedford . . . **84** B2
Worcs **95** D6
Wildhern **46** D1
Wildhill **68** C2
Wildmoor **96** D2
Wildsworth **141** D6
Wilford **114** B3
Wilkesley **111** A5
Wilkhaven **265** B5
Wilkieston **208** D4
Willand **27** D5
Willaston Ches E . **128** D1
Ches W **126** B3
Willen **83** C5
Willenhall W Mid . **96** B2
W Mid **97** D6
Willerby E Yorks . . **160** D4
N Yorks **160** D4
Willersey **80** D4
Willersley **77** C7
Willesborough . . **38** A2
Willesborough
Lees **38** A2
Willesden **49** A5
Willett **27** B6
Willey Shrops . . **95** B4
Warks **98** C1
Willey Green **34** A2
Williamscott **82** C1
Willian **84** D4
Willingale **69** C5

Willingdon **22** B3
Willingham **101** D6
Willingham by
Stow **132** A3
Willington Bedford **84** C3
Derbys **113** C6
Durham **167** B4
T&W **179** C5
Warks **81** D5
Willington
Corner **127** C5
Willisham Tye . . **87** B6
Willitoft **149** D6
Williton **27** A5
Willoughbridge . **111** A6
Willoughby Lincs **135** B4
Warks **82** A2
Willoughby-on-the-
Wolds **115** C4
Willoughton **142** D1
Willows Green . . **69** B7
Willsbridge **43** B5
Willsworthy **11** C6
Wilmcote **81** B4
Wilmington Devon **14** B2
E Sus **22** B3
Kent **50** B2
Wilminstone **11** D5
Wilmslow **128** A3
Wilnecote **97** A5
Wilpshire **145** D6
Wilsden **147** D4
Wilsford Lincs . . **116** A3
Wilts **31** B5
Wilts **45** D5
Wilsill **147** A5
Wilsley Pound . . **37** C5
Wilsom **33** B6
Wilson **114** C2
Wilsontown **195** A4
Wilstead **84** C2
Wilsthorpe **116** D3
Wilstone **67** B4
Wilton Borders . . **186** B3
Cumb **162** C3
N Yorks **160** C2
Redcar **168** D3
Wilts **31** B4
Wilts **45** C4
Wimbish **86** D1
Wimbish Green . **86** D2
Wimblebury **112** D4
Wimbledon **49** B5
Wimblington **101** B6
Wimborne
Minster **17** B4
Wimborne
St Giles **31** D4
Wimbotsham . . **102** A2
Wimpson **32** D2
Wimpstone **81** C5
Wincanton **29** C7
Wincham **128** B1
Winchburgh **208** C3
Winchcombe **63** A6
Winchelsea **23** A7
Winchelsea
Beach **23** A7
Winchester **32** C3
Winchet Hill **37** B5
Winchfield **47** D5
Winchmore Hill
Bucks **67** D4
London **68** D3
Wincle **129** C4
Wincobank **140** D1
Windermere **154** B3
Winderton **81** C6
Windhill **252** B1
Windhouse **284** D6
Windlehurst **129** A4
Windlesham **48** C2
Windley **113** A7
Windmill Hill
E Sus **22** A4
Som **28** D3
Windrush **64** B2
Windsor N Lincs . . **141** B5
Windsor **48** B2
Windsoredge **63** C4

Windygates **220** D3
Windyknowe **208** D2
Windywalls **197** C6
Wineham **35** D5
Winestead **143** A4
Winewall **146** C3
Winfarthing **104** C2
Winford IoW **19** C4
N Som **43** C4
Winforton **77** C6
Winfrith
Ncwburgh **16** C2
Wing Bucks **66** A3
Rutland **99** A5
Wingate **168** B2
Wingates
Gtr Man **137** C5
Northumb **189** D4
Wingerworth **130** C3
Wingfield C Beds . . **67** A4
Suff **104** D3
Wilts **44** D2
Wingham **53** D4
Wingmore **38** A3
Wingrave **66** B3
Winkburn **132** D2
Winkfield **48** B2
Winkfield Row . . **48** B1
Winkhill **129** D5
Winklebury **47** D4
Winkleigh **12** A1
Winksley **157** D6
Winkton **17** B5
Winlaton **178** C3
Winless **281** C5
Winmarleigh **145** C4
Winnal **78** D2
Winnall **32** C3
Winnersh **47** B5
Winscales **162** B3
Winscombe **42** D3
Winsford Ches W **127** C6
Som **27** B4
Winsham **14** A3
Winshill **113** C6
Winskill **164** B3
Winslade **33** A5
Winsley **44** C2
Winslow **66** A2
Winson **64** C1
Winson Green . . **96** C3
Winsor **32** D2
Winster Cumb . . **154** B3
Derbys **130** C2
Winston Durham **166** D4
Suff **88** A2
Winstone **63** C5
Winston Green . . **88** A2
Winswell **25** D5
Winterborne
Clenston **16** A2
Winterborne
Herringston . . **15** C6
Winterborne
Houghton **16** A2
Winterborne
Kingston **16** B2
Winterborne
Monkton **15** C6
Winterborne
Stickland **16** A2
Winterborne
Whitechurch . . **16** A2
Winterborne
Zelston **16** B2
Winterbourne
S Glos **43** A5
W Berks **46** B2
Winterbourne
Abbas **15** B6
Winterbourne
Bassett **45** B5
Winterbourne
Dauntsey **31** B5
Winterbourne
Down **43** B5
Winterbourne
Earls **31** B5
Winterbourne
Gunner **31** B5
Winterbourne
Monkton **45** B5

Winterbourne
Steepleton **15** C6
Winterbourne
Stoke **31** A4
Winterburn **146** B3
Winter Gardens . **51** A4
Winterley **128** D2
Wintersett **140** B1
Wintershill **32** D4
Winterton **142** B1
Winterton-on-
Sea **121** D6
Winthorpe Lincs . **135** C5
Notts **132** D3
Winton BCP **17** B4
Cumb **165** D5
N Yorks **158** B3
Wintringham **160** D2
Winwick Cambs . . **100** C3
Warr **137** D5
N Nhants **98** D3
Wirksworth **130** D2
Wirksworth
Moor **130** D3
Wirswall **111** A4
Wisbech **101** A6
Wisbech
St Mary **101** A6
Wisborough
Green **34** D3
Wiseton **132** A2
Wishaw N Lanark **194** A2
Warks **97** B4
Wisley **34** A3
Wispington **134** B2
Wissenden **37** B7
Wissett **105** D4
Wistanstow **94** C2
Wistanswick **111** C6
Wistaston **128** D1
Wistaston
Green **128** D1
Wiston Pembs . . **55** C6
S Lanark **195** C4
W Sus **21** A4
Wistow Cambs . . **101** C4
N Yorks **149** D4
Wiswell **146** D1
Witcham **101** C6
Witchampton **16** A3
Witchford **101** D7
Witham **70** B2
Witham Friary . . **30** A1
Witham on the
Hill **116** D3
Withcall **134** A2
Witheridge **26** D3
Witherley **95** B6
Withern **135** A4
Withernsea **143** A5
Withernwick **151** C4
Withersdale
Street **104** C3
Withersfield **86** C2
Witherslack **154** C3
Withiel **5** A4
Withiel Florey . . **27** B4
Withington Glos . . **63** B6
Gtr Man **138** D1
Hereford **78** C3
Shrops **111** D4
Staffs **112** B4
Withington
Green **128** B3
Withleigh **27** D4
Withnell **137** A5
Withybrook **98** C1
Withycombe **27** A5
Withycombe
Raleigh **13** C5
Withyham **36** C2
Withypool **26** B3
Witley **34** C2
Witnesham **88** B2
Witney **65** B4
Wittering **100** A2
Wittersham **37** D6
Witton Angus . . **232** A3
Witton **80** A1

Witton Bridge . . **121** B5
Witton Gilbert . . **167** A5
Witton-le-Wear **166** B4
Witton Park **167** B4
Wiveliscombe . . **27** C5
Wivelrod **33** B5
Wivelsfield **35** D6
Wivelsfield Green **35** D6
Wivenhoc **71** A1
Wivenhoe Cross . **71** A4
Wiveton **120** A2
Wix **71** A5
Wixford **80** B3
Wixhill **111** C4
Wixoe **86** C3
Woburn **83** D6
Woburn Sands . . **83** D6
Wokefield Park . . **47** C4
Woking **34** A3
Wokingham **47** C6
Wolborough **12** D3
Woldingham **35** A6
Wold Newton
E Yorks **160** D4
NE Lincs **143** D4
Wolfclyde **195** C5
Wolferton **118** C3
Wolfhill **219** A6
Wolf's Castle . . **55** B5
Wolfsdale **55** B5
Woll **186** A3
Wollaston
N Nhants **83** A6
Shrops **110** D2
Wollaton **114** B3
Wollerton **111** B5
Wollescote **96** C2
Wolsingham **166** B3
Wolstanton **112** A2
Wolston **97** D7
Wolvercote **65** C5
Wolverhampton . **96** B2
Wolverley Shrops **110** B3
Worcs **95** D6
Wolverton Hants . **46** D3
M Keynes **83** C5
Warks **81** A5
Wolverton
Common **46** D3
Wolvesnewton . . **61** D6
Wolvey **98** C1
Wolviston **168** C2
Wombleton **159** C5
Wombourne **95** B6
Wombwell **140** C1
Womenswold . . **53** D4
Womersley **140** B3
Wonastow **61** B6
Wonersh **34** B3
Wonson **12** C1
Wonston **32** B3
Wooburn **48** A2
Wooburn Green . **48** A2
Woodacott **11** A4
Woodale **156** D4
Woodbank **190** D2
Woodbastwick . **121** D5
Woodbeck **132** A2
Woodborough
Notts **115** A4
Wilts **45** D5
Woodbridge
Dorset **29** D7
Suff **88** C3
Woodbury **13** C5
Woodbury
Salterton **13** C5
Woodchester **63** C4
Woodchurch Kent **38** B1
Mers **126** A2
Woodcombe **27** A4
Woodcote **47** A4
Woodcott **46** D2
Woodcroft **67** C1
Woodcutts **30** D3
Wood Dalling . . **120** C2
Woodditton **86** B2
Woodeaton **65** B6
Woodend Cumb . **153** A2

Woodend *continued*
W Nhants 82 C3
W Sus. 19 A7
Wood End Herts . . 68 A3
Warks. 96 D4
Warks. 97 B5
Wood Enderby . . 134 C2
Woodend Green . . 82 C3
Woodfalls. 31 C5
Woodfield Oxon . . 65 A6
S Ayrs. 192 C3
Wood Field 35 A4
Woodford Corn . . 24 D3
Devon. 8 B1
Glos 62 D2
Gtr Man 128 A3
London 68 D4
N Nhants 99 D6
Woodford Bridge 68 D4
Woodford Halse . . 82 B2
Woodgate Norf . . 120 D2
W Mid. 96 C2
Worcs. 80 A2
W Sus. 20 B2
Woodgreen 31 D5
Wood Green 68 D3
Woodhall Herts . . 68 B2
Invclyd. 204 A3
N Yorks 156 B3
Woodhall Spa . . 134 C1
Woodham 48 C3
Woodham
  Ferrers 70 D1
Woodham
  Mortimer. 70 C2
Woodham Walter 70 C2
Woodhaven 220 B4
Wood Hayes 96 A2
Woodhead 256 C2
Woodhey 137 B6
Woodhill. 95 C5
Woodhorn 179 A4
Woodhouse
  Leics. 114 D3
  N Lincs 141 C5
  S Yorks 131 A4
  W Yorks 140 A1
  W Yorks 148 D1
Woodhouse
  Eaves 114 D3
Woodhouselee . 209 D5
Woodhouselees 175 A6
Woodhouse
  Park 128 A3
Woodhouses . . . 113 D5
Woodhurst 101 D5
Woodingdean . . 21 B6
Woodkirk 139 A5
Woodland Devon . . 8 A1
  Durham 166 C3
Woodlands
  Aberds 245 C4
  Dorset 17 A4
  Hants 32 D2
  Highld. 264 D1
  N Yorks 148 B2
  S Yorks 140 C3
Woodlands Park . 47 B6
Woodlands
  St Mary 46 B1
Woodlane 113 C5
Wood Lanes. . . 129 A4
Woodleigh 7 C6
Woodlesford . . 139 A6
Woodley
  Gtr Man 138 D2
  Wokingham . . 47 B5
Woodmancote
  Glos 62 D3
  Glos 63 A5
  Glos 63 C6
  W Sus. 19 A6
  W Sus. 21 A5
Woodmancott. . 33 A4
Woodmansey . . 150 D3
Woodmansterne . 35 A5
Woodminton . . 31 C4
Woodnesborough
  . . . . 53 D5

Woodnewton . . . 100 B2
Wood Norton . . . 120 C2
Woodplumpton . 145 D5
Woodrising 103 A5
Woodseaves
  Shrops. 111 B5
  Staffs 112 C1
Woodsend 45 B6
Woodsetts 131 A5
Woodsford. 16 B1
Wood's Green . . 36 C4
Woodside
  Aberdeen 245 B6
  Aberds 257 B5
  Brack 48 B2
  Fife. 220 D4
  Hants 18 B2
  Herts 68 C2
  Perth 220 A2
Woodside of
  Arbeadie 245 C4
Woodstock Oxon . 65 B5
  Pembs 55 B6
Wood Street
  Norf 121 C5
  Sur 34 A2
Woodthorpe
  Derbys 131 B4
  Leics. 114 D3
  Lincs. 135 A4
  York 149 C4
Woodton 104 B3
Woodtown Devon . 25 C5
  Devon. 25 C5
Woodvale 136 B2
Woodville. 113 D7
Wood Walton . . 100 C4
Woodyates. . . . 31 D4
Woofferton . . . 78 A3
Wookey 29 A5
Wookey Hole. . . 29 A5
Wool 16 C2
Woolacombe . . 25 A5
Woolage Green . 39 A4
Woolaston 62 D1
Woolavington . . 28 A3
Woolbeding. . . . 34 D1
Wooldale 139 C4
Wooler 188 A2
Woolfardis-
  worthy
  Devon. 12 A3
  Devon. 24 C4
Woolfords
  Cottages 195 A5
Woolhampton . . 46 C3
Woolhope 79 D4
Woolhope
  Cockshoot. . . . 79 D4
Woolland 16 A1
Woollaton 25 D5
Woolley Bath . . 43 C6
  Cambs 100 D3
  Corn 24 D3
  Derbys 130 C3
  W Yorks 139 B6
Woolmere Green 80 A2
Woolmer Green . 68 B2
Woolpit. 87 A5
Woolscott 82 A1
Woolsington . . 178 C3
Woolstanwood. 128 D1
Woolstaston . . 94 B2
Woolsthorpe
  Lincs. 115 B6
  Lincs. 116 C2
Woolston Devon. . 7 C6
  Shrops. 94 C2
  Shrops. 110 C2
  Soton 32 D3
  Warr. 127 A6
Woolstone
  M Keynes 83 D5
  Oxon. 45 A6
Woolton 127 A4
Woolton Hill . . 46 C2
Woolverstone . . 88 D2
Woolverton . . . 44 D1
Woolwich. 50 B1
Woolwich Ferry . 50 B1
Woonton 78 B1

Woore. 111 A6
Wootten Green. 104 D3
Wootton Bedford . . 84 C2
  Hants 17 B6
  Hereford 78 B1
  Kent 39 A4
  N Lincs 142 B2
  Oxon. 65 B5
  Oxon. 65 C5
  Shrops 94 D2
  Shrops 110 C2
  Staffs 112 C2
  Staffs 113 A5
  W Nhants 83 B4
Wootton Bridge . 18 B4
Wootton
  Common 18 B4
Wootton
  Courtenay . . . 27 A4
Wootton
  Fitzpaine 14 B3
Wootton Rivers . 45 C5
Wootton
  St Lawrence . . 46 D3
Wootton Wawen . 81 A4
Worcester 79 B6
Worcester Park . 49 C5
Wordsley 96 C1
Worfield 95 B5
Work 282 F5
Workington . . . 162 B2
Worksop 131 B5
Worlaby 142 B2
World's End . . . 46 B2
Worle 42 C2
Worleston 127 D6
Worlingham . . . 105 C5
Worlington . . . 102 D2
Worlingworth . . 88 A3
Wormald Green 148 A2
Wormbridge . . . 78 D2
Wormegay 118 D3
Wormelow Tump 78 D2
Wormhill 129 B6
Wormingford . . 87 D5
Worminghall. . . 66 C1
Wormington . . . 80 D3
Worminster . . . 29 A5
Wormit 220 B3
Wormleighton . . 82 B1
Wormley Herts . . 68 C3
  Sur 34 C2
Wormley West
  End 68 C3
Wormshill 37 A6
Wormsley 78 C2
Worplesdon . . . 34 A2
Worrall 139 D6
Worsbrough . . . 139 C6
Worsbrough
  Common 139 C6
Worsley 137 C6
Worstead 121 C5
Worsthorne . . . 146 D2
Worston 146 C1
Worswell 7 C4
Worth Kent 53 D5
  W Sus. 35 C6
Wortham 104 D1
Worthen 94 A1
Worthenbury . . 110 A3
Worthing Norf . . 120 D1
  W Sus. 21 B4
Worthington . . 114 C2
Worth Matravers 15 D6
Worting 47 D4
Wortley S Yorks . 139 D6
  W Yorks 147 D6
Worton N Yorks . 156 B3
  Wilts. 44 D3
Wotherton 93 A6
Wotter. 7 A4
Wotton 35 B4
Wotton-under-
  Edge 62 D2
Wotton
  Underwood . . 66 B1
Woughton on the
  Green. 83 D5
Wouldham 51 C4
Wrabness. 88 D2

Wrafton 25 B5
Wragby Lincs . . 133 B6
  W Yorks 140 B2
Wragholme . . . 143 D5
Wramplingham . 104 A2
Wrangbrook . . . 140 B2
Wrangham . . . 256 C1
Wrangle 135 D4
Wrangle Bank . 135 D4
Wrangle
  Lowgate. 135 D4
Wrangway 27 D6
Wrantage 28 C3
Wrawby 142 C2
Wraxall Dorset . 15 A5
  N Som. 42 B3
  Som 29 B6
Wray 145 A6
Wraysbury 48 B3
Wrayton 155 D5
Wrea Green. . . 144 D3
Wreay Cumb . . 164 A2
  Cumb 164 C2
Wrecclesham . . 34 B1
Wrecsam
  =Wrexham . . 126 D3
Wrekenton . . . 179 D4
Wrelton 159 C6
Wrenbury 111 A4
Wrench Green . 160 C3
Wreningham . . 104 B2
Wrentham 105 C5
Wrenthorpe. . . 139 A6
Wrentnall 94 A2
Wressle E Yorks . 149 D6
  N Lincs 142 C1
Wrestlingworth . 85 C4
Wretham 103 C5
Wretton 102 B2
Wrexham
  =Wrecsam . . 126 D3
Wrexham Industrial
  Estate. 110 A2
Wribbenhall . . . 95 D5
Wrightington
  Bar 136 B4
Wrinehill 111 A6
Wrington 42 C3
Writhlington . . . 43 D6
Writtle 69 C6
Wrockwardine . 111 D5
Wroot 141 C5
Wrotham 36 A4
Wrotham Heath . 36 A4
Wroughton 45 A5
Wroxall IoW . . . 19 D4
  Warks. 97 D5
Wroxeter 94 A3
Wroxham 121 D5
Wroxton 81 C7
Wyaston 113 A5
Wyberton 117 A6
Wyboston 84 B3
Wybunbury . . . 111 A6
Wychbold. 80 A2
Wych Cross . . . 36 C2
Wyck 33 B6
Wyck Rissington 64 A2
Wycoller 146 D3
Wycomb 115 C5
Wycombe Marsh 66 D3
Wyddial 85 D5
Wye 38 A2
Wyesham 61 B7
Wyfordby 115 D5
Wyke Dorset . . . 30 C1
  Shrops 95 A4
  Sur 34 A2
  W Yorks 139 A4
Wykeham
  N Yorks 159 D7
  N Yorks 160 C3
Wyken 97 C6
Wyke Regis . . . 15 D6
Wykey 110 C2
Wylam 178 C3
Wylde Green . . 96 B4
Wyllie 41 B6
Wylye 31 B4
Wymering 19 A5
Wymeswold. . . 115 C4
Wymington . . . 83 A6

Wymondham
  Leics. 115 D6
  Norf 104 A2
Wyndham 40 B4
Wynford Eagle . 15 B5
Wyng 283 H4
Wynyard Village 168 C2
Wyre Piddle. . . 80 C2
Wysall 115 C4
Wythall 96 D3
Wytham 65 C5
Wythburn . . . 163 C6
Wythenshawe. . 128 A3
Wythop Mill. . . 163 B4
Wyton 101 D4
Wyverstone . . . 87 A6
Wyverstone
  Street 87 A6
Wyville 116 C1
Wyvis Lodge . . 263 C6

Y

Yaddlethorpe . . 141 C6
Yafford 18 C3
Yafforth 158 B2
Yalding 37 A4
Yanworth 63 B6
Yapham 149 B6
Yapton 20 B2
Yarburgh 143 D5
Yarcombe 14 A2
Yard. 27 B5
Yardley 96 C4
Yardley Gobion. 83 C4
Yardley Hastings 83 B5
Yardro. 77 B6
Yarkhill. 79 C4
Yarlet 112 C3
Yarlington 29 C6
Yarlside 153 D3
Yarm 168 D2
Yarmouth. 18 C2
Yarnbrook 44 D2
Yarnfield 112 B2
Yarnscombe . . . 25 C6
Yarnton 65 B5
Yarpole 78 A2
Yarrow 196 D2
Yarrow Feus . . 196 D2
Yarsop 78 C2
Yarwell 100 B2
Yate 43 A6
Yateley 47 C6
Yatesbury. . . . 45 B4
Yattendon 46 B3
Yatton Hereford . 78 A2
  N Som. 42 C3
Yatton Keynell . 44 B2
Yaverland. 19 C5
Yaxham. 120 D2
Yaxley Cambs . . 100 B3
  Suff 104 D2
Yazor 78 C2
Y Bala 108 B4
Y Barri = Barry . 41 E6
Y Bont-Faen
  =Cowbridge . . 41 D4
Y Drenewydd
  =Newtown . . . 93 B5
Yeading 48 A4
Yeadon 147 C6
Yealand
  Conyers 154 D4
Yealand
  Redmayne . . 154 D4
Yealmpton 7 B4
Yearby 168 C4
Yearsley 159 D4
Yeaton 110 D3
Yeaveley. 113 A5
Yedingham . . . 160 D2
Yeldon 84 A2
Yelford 65 C4
Yelland 25 B5
Yelling 85 A4
Yelvertoft 98 D2
Yelverton Devon . 7 A4
  Norf 104 A3
Yenston 29 C7
Yeoford 12 B2

Yeolmbridge. . . 10 C4
Yeo Mill 26 C3
Yeovil 29 D5
Yeovil Marsh. . . 29 D5
Yeovilton 29 C5
Yerbeston 55 D6
Yesnaby 282 F3
Yetlington . . . 188 C3
Yetminster. . . . 29 D5
Yettington 13 C5
Yetts o'
  Muckhart. . . 219 D5
Y Felinheli . . . 123 D5
Y Fenni
  =Abergavenny . . 61 B4
Y Fflint = Flint. 126 B2
Y Ffôr. 106 C3
Y-Ffrith 125 A5
Y Gelli Gandryll
  =Hay-on-Wye . 77 C6
Yieldshields. . . 194 A3
Yiewsley. 48 A3
Y Mwmbwls
  =The Mumbles . 57 D6
Ynysboeth . . . 41 B5
Ynysddu 41 B6
Ynysgyfflog . . . 90 A4
Ynyshir 41 B5
Ynyslas 90 C4
Ynys-meudwy. . 59 E4
Ynystawe 40 A1
Ynysybwl 41 B5
Yockenthwaite . 156 D3
Yockleton. . . . 110 D2
Yokefleet . . . 141 A6
Yoker 205 B5
Yonder Bognie . 255 B6
York. 149 B4
Yorkletts 52 C2
Yorkley 62 C2
York Town 47 C6
Yorton. 111 C4
Youlgreave . . . 130 C2
Youlstone 24 D3
Youlthorpe . . . 149 B6
Youlton. 148 A3
Young's End . . . 70 B1
Young Wood . . 133 B6
Yoxall 113 D5
Yoxford. 89 A4
Y Pîl = Pyle . . . 40 C3
Yr Hôb = Hope . 126 D3
Y Rhws =Rhoose . . 41 E5
Y Rhyl = Rhyl. . 125 A5
Yr Wyddgrug
  =Mold 126 C2
Ysbyty-Cynfyn . 75 A6
Ysbyty Ifan . . 108 A3
Ysbyty Ystwyth . 75 A6
Ysceifiog 125 B6
Yspitty 57 C5
Ystalyfera. . . . 59 E4
Ystrad 41 B4
Ystrad Aeron. . . 75 C4
Ystradfellte . . . 59 D6
Ystradffin. . . . 76 C1
Ystradgynlais . . 59 D4
Ystradmeurig . . 75 B6
Ystrad-mynach . 41 B6
Ystradowen
  Carms 59 D4
  V Glam 41 D5
Ystumtuen . . . 75 A6
Ythanbank. . . . 257 C4
Ythanwells . . . 256 C1
Ythsie 256 C3

Z

Zeal
  Monachorum . 12 A2
Zeals 30 B1
Zelah 4 B3
Zennor 2 B1